Philip Cowley • Dennis Kavanagh

The British General Election of 2017

palgrave
macmillan

Philip Cowley
Queen Mary University of London
London, UK

Dennis Kavanagh
University of Liverpool
Liverpool, UK

ISBN 978-3-319-95935-1   ISBN 978-3-319-95936-8   (eBook)
https://doi.org/10.1007/978-3-319-95936-8

Library of Congress Control Number: 2018952784

Front cover credit: Bloomberg / Contributor
Back cover credit: Ian Forsyth / Stringer

This Palgrave Macmillan imprint is published by the registered company Springer Nature Switzerland AG
The registered company address is: Gewerbestrasse 11, 6330 Cham, Switzerland

Praise for previous editions

'The Bible of General Elections' —David Dimbleby, BBC

'It's popular academic writing at its best, combining a clear narrative (using anecdotes and quotes garnered from more than 300 background interviews) with lots of solid, meaty number-crunching' —*The Guardian*

'Dennis Kavanagh and Philip Cowley have penned a political thriller … The book is distinguished by the quality of its sources: the ministers, aides and strategists who open up to these academics in a way they might not to journalists' —*The Observer*

'Indispensable' —Matthew d'Ancona, *Daily Telegraph*

'If you want real insight into the last election, Kavanagh and Cowley look like they're on the money' —*London Evening Standard*

'The quality of the analysis is as sharp as ever' —*Fabian Review*

'… a riveting read … this is easily the best political book of the year' —*PoliticalBetting.com*

'The studies have become by now almost part of our democratic fabric' —*The Listener*

'The best series anywhere on national elections' —*Annals of American Academy of Political and Social Science*

PREFACE

This volume is the twentieth in a series of books which originated in 1945 in Nuffield College, Oxford. The first volume in the series was the result of Ronald McCallum's frustration with what he saw as the constant misinterpretation of the 1918 election; he wanted to place on record the events of the 1945 contest before similar myths took root. It began what is now the longest-running national election series in the world. This is the third volume in the series where neither of the authors is based at Nuffield, but our aim remains the same: to create an accurate and, as far as possible, impartial account and explanation of the general election.

In the introduction to the 1945 volume, McCallum and his co-author Alison Readman began with the Duke of Wellington's observation that you could no more describe a battle than you could describe a ballroom. 'Still less', they remarked, 'can you describe a general election.' The only thing they said that was certain about a general election was: 'It is not simple.' Their comments certainly apply to the 2017 contest, which was a particularly difficult election to write about. Once an election is over and it is possible to talk openly with the participants, it is usually the case that for all the complexity in any election, there is a broad consensus about what happened. For the most part, Labour staffers and politicians agree with their rival counterparts about why one campaign struggled and why the other succeeded. There are nuances and differences—sometimes genuine, and a result of the different perspectives of participants, sometimes driven by self-interest or partisanship—but these are often quite marginal. When it comes to the fundamentals, there is normally little disagreement.

This was not true this time. Once we move beyond the merely descriptive—that is, the Conservatives had a huge opinion poll lead, which they proceeded to lose—there is little consensus about what happened in the 2017 general election or, at least, why it happened. Perhaps most striking of all, there is no intra-party consensus on these questions. There are at least two versions of the Labour campaign, both passionately believed, along with a similar number of views of the Conservative campaign. During interviews, the phrases used by insiders about supposed comrades or colleagues were often much cruder, and more industrial, than those about their supposed opponents.

Much remains contested. For example, below, we report the claim that at various points during his leadership, Jeremy Corbyn 'wobbled'. Any wobbles would have been understandable. Leadership was not a position he had ever expected to hold. He had faced repeated—and often brutal—criticism. (Which of us, under similar conditions, would not have wondered whether this was the game for us?) Some of these accounts have Corbyn in tears, with members of his family telling him that it is not worth it, while some of his aides tell him that he must hang on for the good of the left. Yet members of his key team vehemently deny that any of this ever happened. Something similar applies to Theresa May on the night of the election, once the result of the election became clear. Did she wobble? Again, it would be understandable. She had called an election, run on a hugely personalised campaign, in which she had been front and centre, and squandered an enormous opinion poll lead. (Which of us, under similar conditions, would not have considered throwing in the towel?) There are multiple claims that she came close to resigning on the night of the election—although these claims vary hugely depending on who is recounting them—but again the official line remains that she did not do so. Similar differences, more trivial perhaps but just as frustrating for those attempting to chronicle the contest, attach to many key moments in the campaign.

As will become clear, in what follows, the snap nature of the contest presented problems for all of the parties (ironically, perhaps, the Conservatives most of all) but it also made life harder for us as authors. Normally with a book like this, much of the preparation—drafting, data collection, background interviews and so on—is carried out in the run-up to the election. After the Prime Minister's shock announcement on 18 April 2017, we started with a blank page. The same goes for our contributors, all of whom did not expect to be spending much of 2017 writing about a general election. We owe them a huge debt for meeting demanding deadlines and repeated editorial requests. In addition to writing Appendix 1, John Curtice, Stephen Fisher, Robert Ford and Patrick English also supplied the data from which Appendix 2 has been compiled.

Yet despite all the hard work, it was a fascinating election to write about. Both the decision to call the 2017 election and the eventual outcome can fairly be described as surprises, but then they were merely the latest surprises to hit British politics. Since the 2015 contest (the result of which was itself a surprise), Jeremy Corbyn became Labour leader, Britain voted to leave the European Union, the Prime Minister resigned after a year in office as head of a majority government, and a year later his successor—having repeatedly declared she would not do so—called another general election in search of a bigger majority of seats, which she then failed to achieve, despite seemingly being on course for a landslide.

The dramatis personae of the 2017 election were very different from those of 2015. In our last volume, Jeremy Corbyn did not feature—other than, at the end of the book, to note his election as Labour leader. John McDonnell did not feature at all. The pair might, perhaps, have been worth a mention for their promise to make life difficult for an incoming Miliband government from the backbenches. But this all seemed too trivial, the pair too far removed from power. Yet within months, they were transforming the Labour Party. Even Theresa May received only a handful of passing mentions in the 2015 volume; she may have been Home Secretary, but when it came to the election, she was a bit player at most.

Corbyn's elevation to the Labour leadership tested many well-established assumptions about British political parties. Could a party in Parliament have a leader who had so little support among his MPs? Could a party thrive when there was such a gap between the views of the mass membership and its MPs? Could a leader survive a decisive vote of no confidence by his colleagues? And, when the election was called, could a party do well in a general election fighting on a left-of-centre manifesto? The answers were more positive than many would have thought.

In writing this book, we were helped, as always, by the very generous support of many of the participants. We spoke to hundreds of people from the different parties and we are very grateful for the time they gave us. We deliberately do not list them here, as many spoke to us on the condition of strict confidentiality, but we hope they will recognise the picture we paint—although we know that not all will agree with our conclusions. Unsourced information or quotations in the following text are taken from these interviews, unless otherwise indicated. Many also agreed to look at draft chapters, helping to suggest improvements and challenging our judgements, and again we are very grateful, as we are to the many friends and colleagues who also read early drafts of the book or helped with queries. These include Caitlin Milazzo, Chris Prosser, Jon Mellon, Paula Surridge, Ross Hawkins, David Cowling, Monica Poletti, Ben Worthy, Jane Green, Peter Kellner, Colin Rallings, Richard McKay, Alia Middleton, Peter Geoghegan, Matthew Shaddick, Richard Kelly, Justin Fisher, Will Jennings, Mark Pickup, Matthew Bailey, Mark Byrne, Roger Scully, Mark Stuart, Tim Bale, Jon Tonge, Joe Twyman, Paul Webb and Roger Mortimore. We are especially indebted to Wes Ball, who worked as a researcher, as well as co-writing Chapter 8. Lizzy Adam and Mercy Muroki also provided research assistance. The British Academy generously provided funding (BA Special Project 2017/1).

We were aided by the excellent volumes already published on, or which covered, the election. These included Tim Shipman's *Fall Out*, Tim Ross and Tom McTague's *Betting the House* and Jon Tonge et al.'s edited collection *Britain Votes 2017*. We differ from them in interpretation in some places and very occasionally in matters of fact. Responsibility for any remaining errors rests with us alone.

We are indebted to all those who supplied or allowed us to reproduce material. The political parties all generously allowed us to reproduce campaign posters or images. Martin Rowson, Steve Bell, Ben Jennings and the Telegraph Media Group (for Adams, Matt and Bob) and News UK (for Peter Brookes, Morten Morland and Steve Bright) granted us permission to print their excellent cartoons. The majority of photos in the plates come courtesy of either Getty or Alamy, although other pictures, some of them thanks to the now-ubiquitous camera phone, come from Bruce Cutts/ The After Alice Project, Ned Simons, Iain McNicol, Richard Cracknell, Tori Cowley and Freida Moore. The picture of the Lib Debate rehearsal on p. 210 comes from someone who would prefer to remain anonymous. The Polling Observatory team allowed us to reproduce the graphs in chapters 1 and 16. We are grateful to all of them.

This book follows the broad structure of the previous volumes in the series, but each election is different, so we have included separate chapters specifically on Brexit and the decision to call the election. The long campaign—the longest and most consequential of modern British politics— has resulted in three chapters. Like most of its predecessors, our story ends with the announcement of the result, and only briefly covers the process of formation of the government.

The team at Palgrave Macmillan have been supportive and encouraging, and have allowed us to tell what we think is a fascinating story.

London, UK   Philip Cowley
Liverpool, UK   Dennis Kavanagh
May 2018

CONTENTS

LIST OF FIGURES AND BOX

List of Tables

LISTS OF ILLUSTRATIONS

Photographs

Party Advertisements

Cartoons

Theresa May announces the election outside Number 10, 18 April. © Xinhua/ Alamy Stock Photo

Jeremy Corbyn campaigning in Cardiff. © Andrew Bartlett/Alamy Stock Photo

Tim Farron and the Lib Dem campaign bus. © Bettina Strenske/Alamy Stock Photo

Nicola Sturgeon launching the SNP's manifesto. © Steven Scott Taylor/Alamy Stock Photo

Paul Nutall launching UKIP's immigration policy. © Vickie Flores/ Alamy Stock Photo

Caroline Lucas launching the Green Party's environment manifesto. © Mark Kerrison/Alamy Stock Photo

Leanne Wood campaigning for Plaid Cymru in Rhondda Cynon Taf. © Matthew Horwood/Alamy Stock Photo

Ruth Davidson speaking at the launch of the Scottish Conservative manifesto. © Steven Scott Taylor/Alamy Stock Photo

Jeremy Corbyn arriving at the ITV studios, flanked by Seumas Milne (l) and James Schneider (r). © Tommy London/Alamy Stock Photo

Nick Timothy and Fiona Hill outside Conservative Campaign Headquarters. © Chris J Ratcliffe/Stringer

Jim Messina (l), Lynton Crosby (c), and Mark Textor (r). © Barcroft Media/ Contributor

Andrew Gwynne (l) and Ian Lavery (r). © Stephen Chung/Alamy Stock Photo

John McDonnell speaking at the Museum of London. © Matthew Chattle/Alamy Stock Photo

Theresa May speaking in Edinburgh, at a removals company. © Steven Scott Taylor/Alamy Stock Photo

A Corbyn crowd, in Hebden Bridge. © Bruce Cutts/The After Alice Project

The Shadow Cabinet watch on as Jeremy Corbyn launches the Labour manifesto.
© Leon Neal/Getty Images

Corbyn support in Norwich. © John Birdsall/Alamy Stock Photo

#satire. © Tori Cowley

The leaders debate, with one notable absentee. © WPA Pool/Pool

The Maidenhead declaration. © Mark Kerrison/Alamy Stock Photo

Iain McNicol (l) and Karie Murphy (r), with Jeremy Corbyn at Labour HQ, the day after the election. © amer ghazzal/Alamy Stock Photo

Arlene Foster and Nigel Dodds visit Number 10 for talks, 13 June. © WENN Ltd/Alamy Stock Photo

Anti-DUP protest. © Matthew Chattle/Alamy Stock Photo

Signing of the DUP-Conservative deal, 26 June. Seated: Jeffrey Donaldson (l) and Gavin Williamson (r). Standing, from left to right: Nigel Dodds, Arlene Foster, Theresa May, Damian Green. © WPA Pool/Getty

Not Going According to Plan

There was not supposed to be a general election in 2017. In May 2015, David Cameron had formed the first Conservative majority government for 23 years, having won what he called 'the sweetest victory of all'. Committed to hold a referendum on Britain's membership of the EU, his plan was to negotiate a reformed relationship with the EU, which he would then put before the country, where a campaign focusing heavily on the economic risks of leaving the EU would secure a relatively easy victory. The Conservatives would then govern for the rest of the Parliament, before he handed over to his successor, widely assumed to be the Chancellor, George Osborne. Instead, at 7 am on 24 June 2016 and with Britain having voted by 52% to 48% to leave the EU, Cameron remarked dryly to his advisors: 'Well, that didn't go according to plan.'[1] In his first party conference speech as leader back in 2006, he had said he wanted the Conservatives to stop 'banging on' about Europe, 'while parents worried about childcare, getting the kids to school, balancing work and family life'. There was therefore an irony in a referendum over Europe resulting in him announcing his resignation as Prime Minister at 8.23 am, when many parents were getting their kids to school.[2] The third successive Conservative Prime Minister to have been fatally damaged by his party's European divide, he had been Prime Minister of a majority Conservative administration for just over a year.

Six days later, on 30 June, launching her bid to be Cameron's successor, Theresa May explicitly ruled out holding an early general election if she were to become Prime Minister. 'There should be no general election until

© The Author(s) 2018

P. Cowley, D. Kavanagh, *The British General Election of 2017*,

https://doi.org/10.1007/978-3-319-95936-8_1

2020', she declared, to a chorus of approval from the MPs present. It was a pledge she made repeatedly in private during the leadership contest to any Conservative MP who, however well they saw their party polling nationally, worried about the prospects in their own seat.[3] Indeed, such was the scepticism about an early election among Conservative MPs that the May camp deliberately started a rumour that Boris Johnson, one of her rivals for the leadership, was planning an early election if he became Prime Minister. Yet May's opposition to an early election was not solely the product of internal Conservative Party politics. Given the uncertainty generated by the referendum result and Cameron's resignation, she believed it was important for a new administration to promise stability. Therefore, not only did she promise no early election, but also that there would be no emergency budget—something George Osborne had threatened in the event of a Leave vote—and a normal Autumn Statement 'held in the normal way at the normal time'. In September 2016, in her first major broadcast interview after becoming Prime Minister, she told the BBC's Andrew Marr: 'I'm not going to be calling a snap election.' She made the same point in an interview with the *Sunday Times* the next month: 'I think it's right that the next general election is in 2020 … I think an early general election would introduce a note of instability for people.'

The press reaction, 19 April. Credit: Lenscap/Alamy Stock Photo

Behind the scenes, however, there was growing pressure on the Prime Minister to renege on her pledge. David Davis, the Secretary of State responsible for Britain's exit from the EU ('Brexit'), argued forcefully in private that the timing of a Brexit in 2019 and the preparations for a 2020 election would clash awkwardly. Davis was one of the most gung-ho of all those calling for an early election, even to the point of being relaxed about the possibility of being defeated over the legislation to trigger Brexit—the European Union (Notification of Withdrawal) Bill—since he argued that this would give a perfect excuse to go to the country. He also privately contacted Sir Lynton Crosby, who had run the Conservative campaign in 2015, hoping to recruit Crosby to his cause.[4] The Chancellor, Philip Hammond, had similarly been arguing for an early election since the summer of 2016, both because the 2015 manifesto severely limited his fiscal room for manoeuvre and on the grounds that there would need to be a transitional period after Britain's exit from the EU, and it was better for an election to be held before then in order to remove any risk of the government not having been seen to have fulfilled its promise to implement the referendum decision.[5] Many of May's Downing Street advisors were also in favour of an early election.

As the Conservative lead in the opinion polls grew throughout late 2016 and early 2017, so did the calls for an early poll. In February 2017, the Conservatives won the Copeland by-election, taking the seat from Labour, the first time a governing party had gained a seat in a by-election since 1982 and increasing the pressure on May to call an early election yet further. In March 2017, after a newspaper column by the former party leader William Hague in which he argued that an early election would give May a mandate to pursue her own policy agenda, Number 10 were swift to close the story down.[6] It was not something she 'plans to do or wishes to do', they said. Following further rumours later in the month, they briefed: 'It's not going to happen ... We have been clear that there's not going to be an early general election and the Prime Minister is getting on with delivering the will of the British people.' Off-the-record briefings were even stronger; journalists and MPs were all firmly told that there was absolutely no chance of an early election.

It is not clear precisely when Theresa May first began, privately, to entertain the idea of an early election. Earlier attempts to float the idea with her had always been firmly knocked back—to the point where most of her team had stopped even trying to raise the topic—but by early March, one of those close to her dared to mention the idea again and was surprised when 'she didn't slap it down'. Later that month, she was willing to have a formal meeting with four of her key advisors—Nick Timothy, Fiona Hill, Joanna Penn and Chris Wilkins—to discuss the idea. The four met with the Prime Minister and her husband for drinks in her flat in Number 10. All of her aides were backers of an early poll and had been privately discussing the idea between themselves for several months. Both the Prime Minister and her husband were cautious, being especially concerned about how the decision would be viewed by the public, but she did not rule the idea out and promised to consider it further.

In early April, some of the party's private polling found its way into the *New Statesman*.[7] It was reported as finding that the Liberal Democrats could make gains from the Conservatives in the South West and London, retaking almost all of the seats they had lost in 2015.[8] This was widely interpreted as yet more evidence that there would be no early election—although by then the Prime Minister was actively considering going to the polls. At a further meeting in Downing Street in the first week of April, her aides stressed that a window of opportunity would exist between the formal triggering of Brexit (known as Article 50 after the relevant clause in the Lisbon Treaty) and negotiations with the EU commencing in June. In the words of one of her advisors, this was 'the only time such a period of calm existed in the Brexit process until 2020'.

The Prime Minister then departed for a five-day walking holiday in Wales. She claimed not to discuss politics with her husband whilst walking because, reported *Wales Online*, 'she says you have to concentrate too hard on where you're treading in the hills or you may slip'.[9] The walking holiday was later to be presented as the scene of a Damascene conversion by the Prime Minister, but the momentum for an early election was already well under way before she departed for Wales. Before going, she spoke to Lord (Stephen) Gilbert, a former Number 10 advisor who had been a key figure in the 2015 campaign. Separately, she spoke to the Brexit Secretary and the Chief Whip to tell them of her thinking. Gilbert in turn briefed Crosby. The latter, at that point on holiday in Fiji, initiated some private polling and focus groups on the subject. Until this point—and despite a separate polling operation being run from Number 10 since May had become Prime Minister—the party had conducted no polling to discover how the public might react to an early election.

On 12 April, a small meeting convened at Theresa May's house in Sonning, outside of Maidenhead. The party Chairman, Sir Patrick McLoughlin, arrived first, and had a one-to-one meeting with the Prime

Minister. Of those close to May, McLoughlin was the most sceptical, worried about the state of the Conservative campaign machine, but even he had to concede that it would be difficult to find a better time to call an election. Also in attendance were May's key Number 10 aides, along with Gilbert and Darren Mott, the party's director of campaigning; Crosby, out of the country, contributed via speaker phone. The meeting ended without any formal decision having been taken, but by the end of the meeting, most of these attending were in little doubt there would be an early election. 'I came away convinced there was going to be an election', said one of those present.

We also do not know the exact point over the next couple of days at which the Prime Minister finally made the decision to call the election, but over the long Easter weekend, phone calls began to go out from Downing Street to the key members of the campaign team. On 17 April, the Prime Minister phoned the Queen to tell her of her plans. That evening, she invited both the Chancellor and the Brexit Secretary to her Downing Street flat to brief them. Well aware of what had happened to Gordon Brown soon after taking office in 2007, when he had allowed Westminster speculation about an early election to build to fever pitch—only then to get cold feet at the last minute, with ruinous consequences for his reputation—the team around May had stressed utmost secrecy.[10] '"Don't do a Brown" was a phrase used repeatedly', one of her aides said. One reason those responsible for briefing the media on the Prime Minister's behalf had been so firm in their rebuttal of any talk of an election was because they were kept completely out of the loop. Both May's Director of Communications, Katie Perrior, and her press secretary, Lizzie Loudon, knew nothing of the ongoing discussions and continued to brief accordingly. (Both Loudon and Perrior left Number 10 within days of the election being called.) There could be no briefings or leaks that in any way indicated even the possibility of an early election—nor could there be any preparations for the election that might give the game away. The self-discipline involved was impressive. Such was the secrecy with which it was discussed, and the strength of previous briefings ruling out an election, that even when it was announced early on 18 April 2017 that there was going to be a Prime Ministerial statement in Downing Street, it was still not obvious that its subject would be a general election. It was not until a podium was brought out into Downing Street lacking the prime ministerial crest, giving away that this was to be party political rather than governmental business, that the penny dropped for many observers.

We need a General Election now to secure the *strong* and *stable leadership* the country needs to see us through Brexit and beyond.

Conservatives

Just after 11 am on 18 April, less than a year after becoming Prime Minister, Theresa May emerged from the front door at Number 10 and announced: 'I have just chaired a meeting of Cabinet, where we agreed that the government should call a general election to be held on 8 June.' In addition to those who had been told previously, immediately prior to the Cabinet meeting she informed the Home Secretary and the Foreign Secretary of her plans. Other members of the Cabinet had no inkling before the meeting began. Standing around in the anteroom prior to the meeting, one Cabinet minister remarked that the day's agenda looked rather sparse; one of those in the know replied: 'I'm sure we'll manage to fill the time.' Most of the Cabinet meeting discussed the election. No one dissented from the decision to call it.[11] Several ministers urged fighting on a policy platform that was relatively light and producing a short manifesto.[12] After the Prime Minister departed for her announcement, the rest of the Cabinet stayed behind in the Cabinet room to watch it on TV.

The research that Crosby's company, CTF Partners, had produced for the Conservatives had found the public were not keen on an election—although contrary to some immediate post-election briefing, Crosby never formally advised the Prime Minister not to call the election.[13] CTF's report to the party leadership summing up both focus group and opinion polling noted 'there is clearly a lot of risk involved with holding an early election'. It went on: 'there is a real need to nail down the 'why' for doing so now ... Therefore, Theresa May must be able to show that by holding an election *now* she is minimising *future* uncertainty and instability' (emphasis in original). In one email to Number 10 aides, Crosby wrote that 'winning the fight over the context of an election is the single most important thing—ahead of any policy or message'. The report ended with five key action points ('WHAT THE CONSERVATIVES MUST DO') which would go on to be central to the Conservative campaign. First, the party needed to be 'clear why this election is needed *now*—to prevent *future* uncertainty that would hamper Britain's ability to make a success of Brexit, maintain economic competitiveness, and improve voters' standard of living'. Second, they needed to 'frame the election as a choice between continuity and stability, or chaos and uncertainty'. Third, it was important to show that 'the only way to secure a better future is through strong leadership, backed up by a stable and united party, that voters can trust to make the right decisions', as well as, fourth, that 'the only way to secure strong leadership (and Theresa May as Prime Minister) with the stable government needed to secure a good deal for the UK and a better future is by voting Conservative'. The fifth point was to focus on May herself: 'Use Theresa May as the campaign's main communication vehicle—and take every opportunity to contrast her with Jeremy Corbyn.'[14]

The Prime Minister's speech in Downing Street lasted just under seven minutes and ticked off all five of these pieces of advice. She began by admitting that she had said there should be no election until 2020, but that she had now 'concluded that the only way to guarantee certainty and stability for the years ahead is to hold this election and seek your support for the decisions I must take'. She added that she had 'only recently and reluctantly' come to the conclusion that an election was necessary—although as Michael Deacon wrote in the *Daily Telegraph*, she 'looked about as reluctant as a pitbull sniffing a pork chop'.[15]

Despite previously claiming that an election would be a cause of instability, the Prime Minister now claimed that she needed the election in order to avoid it. The country, she argued, had come together after the EU referendum, but at Westminster there was division, with opposition politicians and the 'unelected Lords' trying to delay or block Brexit. 'Every vote for the Conservatives will make it harder for opposition politicians who want to stop me from getting the job done', she said:

> Every vote for the Conservatives will make me stronger when I negotiate for Britain with the prime ministers, presidents and chancellors of the EU. Every vote for the Conservatives will mean we can stick to our plan for a stronger Britain and take the right long-term decisions for a more secure future.

'We have to stop
meeting like this'

Matt, *Daily Telegraph*, 19 April 2017 © Matt/Telegraph Media Group Ltd

In a speech of under 1,000 words, the word 'strong' (or 'stronger') featured eight times and the phrase 'strong and stable leadership' appeared three times—the first of hundreds of occasions on which it would be heard over the coming weeks—and, following Crosby's advice, the Prime Minister explicitly framed the election as a choice between her and the Labour leader, Jeremy Corbyn:

> [T]he decision facing the country will be all about leadership. It will be a choice between strong and stable leadership in the national interest, with me as your prime minister, or weak and unstable coalition government led by Jeremy Corbyn, propped up by the Liberal Democrats, who want to reopen the divisions of the referendum, and Nicola Sturgeon and the SNP.

There was another speech, one which was drafted but never delivered. Written by Chris Wilkins, it repeated many of the themes Theresa May had expressed on the steps of Number 10 in her first day as Prime Minister, when she had spoken of the 'burning injustices' facing many in Britain, and it was one that several of her Downing Street team would have preferred her to have given. Their plan had always been for a very different campaign. This alternate speech began by arguing that with the triggering of Article 50, the Prime Minister had fulfilled the mandate she had been given when the Queen asked her to form a government; indeed, one idea which some of her aides had initially discussed was for the Prime Minister to announce the election on the day that Article 50 was triggered—quite possibly, in the Commons, as she finished her statement—but prevarication over its calling had scuppered that plan. The Prime Minister would then fight the election not on Brexit, but to seek a mandate for the next stage of her government.

Brexit was to be avoided as the defining feature of any election strategy because it was considered too divisive.[16] The draft speech did still open with a section on Brexit and the threats to its successful delivery posed by the opposition parties:

> The plain fact is that my party has only a small majority in the House of Commons and no majority at all in the House of Lords. And despite months of discussion and debate, the Government's strategy for the negotiations ahead continues to be disputed, in many cases opposed, in Parliament and by other political parties.

But rather than use Brexit to justify the election, it then moved quickly to link Brexit to a series of wider changes that the Prime Minister wanted to see delivered:

> [T]hese same forces have also pledged to stand in the way of the Government's wider agenda of economic and social reform designed to rebalance Britain in the interests of ordinary working class people.

> Yet that agenda is essential. For as I have often said, the referendum was not just a vote to leave the EU, but an instruction to change the way the country works—and the people for whom it works—forever.

> It was a call from all those who have been let down, ignored and left behind for too long, to change Britain into a country that works for everyone, not just the privileged few.

> And to respond to that cry for change, we need an ambitious programme of economic and social reform on a par with the great eras of progress our country has experienced before.

The explicit aim of this alternate strategy was to present May as the 'change candidate' in the forthcoming election. This draft, never-delivered, speech then sketched out what the government wanted to deliver: education reforms, pledges on affordable housing, immigration reform, economic reform, a new modern industrial strategy, a crackdown on corporate irresponsibility and investment in the country's infrastructure, including the NHS. The phrase 'strong and stable' featured not once, because this would not have been a strategy for stability, but for change. Moreover, instead of using Theresa May as the campaign's 'main communication vehicle', as Crosby wanted, this strategy would have used her sparingly in the campaign. As one private Number 10 briefing note setting out the principles for this sort of campaign argued:

> *We will seek to find 'leadership moments' throughout the campaign.* The Prime Minister will continue to govern the country—and be seen to be doing so—throughout the period

> *The Prime Minister will be a unifying figure.* Throughout the campaign, the Prime Minister should stay out of 'politics as usual' and be the candidate that can bring people together. That means finding ways to talk directly to people as often as possible

> *We will run a positive, forward looking campaign.* The campaign will focus on our 'plan', on the issues that really matter to people and on the solutions we offer

> *We will not shy away from big issues and decisions.* As part of the rationale for this election is the need to confront big challenges, raising those issues—and offering solutions to them—will be an essential part of our message

> *We will campaign to win in all parts of the country.* That means being aggressive and ambitious in our approach and visibly targeting areas that we have not targeted for some time.

This was the strategy that the team around May had been working on ever since she entered Number 10, and it was on the basis of a campaign broadly along these lines which they had been arguing for an early election. Yet it was not Lynton Crosby's preferred strategy, and it was Crosby who had been chosen to run the 2017 campaign. This distinction—between the Prime Minister representing change or stability—was fundamental, yet it remained largely unresolved and was to run like a fault line throughout the entire Conservative campaign.

The rules contained in the Fixed-term Parliaments Act set the date of the next election at 2020, save in two circumstances. The first was if two-thirds of the House of Commons voted for an early election. The second was if there was a vote of no confidence in the government, and no alternate government could then be formed within two weeks. May ended her speech by challenging the opposition parties to vote for the former: 'Let us tomorrow vote for an election, let us put forward our plans for Brexit and our alternative programmes for government and then let the people decide.'

Trailing in the opinion polls by as much as 20 percentage points, most in the Labour Party had no desire to face a general election, but the party leadership had already repeatedly said that they would agree to any motion calling for one. The Labour leadership formally welcomed the announcement of the election—if questioning its motives—and the following day, after a debate lasting a mere 90 minutes, the Commons approved the motion for an early general election by 522 to 13, easily more than the 434 MPs required.[17] Almost all the political parties voted for the measure,

Peter Brookes, *The Times*, 20 April 2017 © News UK/News Licensing

with just a handful of dissidents opposing and the SNP abstaining.[18] The overwhelming Commons majority and the fairly desultory nature of the debate understated the unease that existed among some MPs. Although the Prime Minister was greeted enthusiastically when she spoke to the 1922 Committee that night, with much banging of tables, some Conservative MPs had misgivings in private. Some worried about the government reneging on its repeated promises not to call an election, while some were angry that the Prime Minister had promised them, to their face, that she would not do so. Nor, despite their national poll lead, were all Conservative MPs entirely confident about their own seats.

There were also some Labour MPs who felt that their party was wrong to vote for the motion triggering the early election; without Labour support, they argued, the Conservatives would be forced to utilise the alternate route to an early election, with the symbolic value of the government moving a motion of no confidence in itself. These, though, were minority opinions. Most Conservative MPs thought victory—and probably a significant victory—was on the cards, whilst the Labour leadership believed that anything other than support for an early election would be seen as political game-playing and felt they had no alternative but to support the motion triggering an early election. As one of those involved in the discussions put it: 'What would the public hear? People would think we didn't want a general election, and we're frit. We're just going to come off worse. It was a great political wheeze, but it would just look terrible.' Corbyn himself had been consistent in all private discussions on the subject within the party; Labour could not, in his view, be seen to be doing anything that propped up a Conservative government—which meant that Labour had no choice but to vote for the early election.

In the event that Labour had decided not to back the motion calling for an early election—an outcome several of May's closest advisors thought was possible—the Conservatives in any case had no intention of following the route of voting no confidence in their own government. Their fallback plan, devised over the weekend before May announced the election, was to introduce a short bill specifically setting the date of the next parliamentary election (see Box 1.1). The bill's passage would merely require simple majorities in Parliament rather than the two-thirds required to trigger the Fixed-term Parliaments Act. The Conservatives were prepared to gamble that the House of Lords, which theoretically could delay the bill, would acquiesce quickly in front of a government trying to go to the country. In the event, Labour's support meant that the Fixed-term Parliaments Act 2017 was never needed, but its possible introduction had one important consequence: in order to allow for the bill's introduction and debate—and for any difficulties with its passage—it was agreed to leave around a fortnight between the announcement of the election and the dissolution of Parliament.[19]

Box 1.1   Plan B

<u>The Fixed-Term Parliaments Act 2017</u>

1. Polling day for the next parliamentary general election
(1) Notwithstanding anything in the Fixed-term Parliaments Act 2011 ('the 2011 Act'), the polling day for the next parliamentary general election shall be X.
(2) The 2011 Act is amended by substituting, for section 1 (2):

'1 (2). The polling day for the next parliamentary general election is to be X' and the rest of the 2011 Act shall apply accordingly

2. Final provisions
(1) This Act may be cited as the Fixed-term Parliaments Act 2017.
(2) This Act comes into force on the day it is passed.

The campaign's extended duration was also the result of a series of other factors. The Electoral Registration and Administration Act 2013 had extended the length of the timetable for the formal election campaign from 17 to 25 working days, making a very short four-week campaign impossible. When they had first begun to consider an early election, May's team had all assumed it would be a short campaign, and it was later a source of regret to many that they had not managed this. Yet current election law prevents very short campaigns, and the timing envisaged by many of her team—at one point the aim was to have the general election coincide with the local elections in May—included three bank holidays. At a minimum, this would have resulted in a campaign of almost six weeks.[20] In addition, although the Commons returned for business on 18 April, the Lords were still on recess until 24 April, making it difficult to make progress with the so-called 'wash-up' of legislation, and holding the election one week earlier would have clashed with half-term holidays. The combination of all these factors was a lengthy election campaign, of more than seven weeks from announcement to polling day, significantly longer than any in recent years.[21] The 2017 election was routinely described as a 'snap' election, but it was not quick.

Coverage of the announcement was dominated by two themes: widespread surprise ('May's Bolt from the Blue'—*Daily Telegraph*; 'May's Election Bombshell'—*The Sun*; 'Theresa May Shocks Brexit Britain with Snap Election She Said She'd Never Call for'—*The Independent*)—and by the expectation that the election would result in a clear Conservative victory ('May Heads for Election Landslide'—*The Times*; 'Blue Murder'—*The Sun*). The *Daily Mail* saw the election as 'a stunning move' in which the Prime Minister had 'called the bluff of the "game-playing" Remoaners', and in which she would 'Crush the Saboteurs'. Only the *Morning Star*, the Labour leader's paper of choice, saw much hope for Labour: '50 Days to Show May the Door' was its headline.

Despite so few people seeing it coming, in retrospect the calling of the general election in 2017 seemed more obvious. As Figure 1.1 shows, the Conservatives had run ahead of Labour in the polls throughout the Parliament, but those leads had increased dramatically after the Brexit vote and May's becoming Prime Minister in 2016.[22] The Conservative poll lead ran at between 13 and 19 percentage points throughout March 2017, and even extended in some polls to 21 points in early April. Yet in the Commons, the Conservatives had only a slim majority, and whilst she had been able to get the legislation through Parliament to initiate Britain's exit from the EU, the Prime Minister was much less secure on more run-of-the-mill legislation. The Conservative whips had also calculated that they would struggle to pass the detailed legislation required to implement Brexit. The legislation to trigger Article 50 had been a simple two-clause bill, but even it had taken an enormous amount of effort by the whips to keep dissent to a minimum, and its eventual passage, with barely a dissenting vote, masked the effort that had been involved, as well as making it clear to the whips the problems that lay ahead. As one said: 'We kept spotting all these groups that were forming—"second referendum",

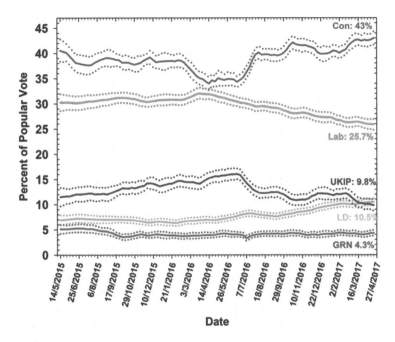

Figure 1.1   Estimated party vote intention, May 2015–April 2017.
Source: Polling Observatory

"process", "meaningful parliamentary vote"—all put forward by erudite and articulate people. And we knew we couldn't ever satisfy them. They'd demand breakfast and you'd give them breakfast, and then they'd want dinner...'

In addition, the Crown Prosecution Service was shortly due to report on the cases of more than a dozen Conservative MPs' election expenses from 2015, with at least the potential to reduce the government's majority yet further. At the time, much was made of this as a reason why the Conservatives wanted an early election. In reality, the Conservatives were relatively confident that they would not face many court cases—a confidence which proved well-founded, when the charging decisions were eventually announced during the campaign. Even if there were court cases, for these to result in reducing the government's majority would have required MPs to have been found guilty *and* for opposition parties to have won any subsequent by-election. The likelihood that this would have reduced the government's majority by much was in reality always relatively small and the issue was trivial in the Conservatives' pre-election discussions.

More significant, at least to those in Number 10, was that the Prime Minister lacked her own mandate; she was bound by manifesto pledges made by the Conservatives in 2015, some of which had been intended merely as bargaining chips to be dispensed with in the event of any post-election negotiations with other parties. As one of May's team put it: 'We had governed up until that point on the exhaust fumes of David and George's agenda, much of which was both tonally and materially different from Theresa's conservatism.' This argument had particular resonance with the Prime Minister. At one point in the discussions, she asked what would happen if she called the election only to end up with roughly the same majority; she did not dissent when her aides replied that this was not necessarily about increasing her majority, but rather was about getting her own majority—her own mandate—because it was the lack of a mandate that was such a problem.[23] The Chancellor in particular was hamstrung by the 2015 pledge not to increase income tax, VAT or National Insurance—and the combination of a small majority and a lack of any mandate had coalesced in March, when the government had been forced to do a U-turn on a rise in National Insurance for the self-employed following backbench opposition. For some of May's advisors, it was more personal: they hated implementing Cameron's programme. This was said to apply especially to Nick Timothy—'he wanted to be king of his own castle', as one of May's other aides put it.[24] Plus, the Conservatives led in almost all key political indicators and May herself comprehensively trumped the Labour leader Jeremy Corbyn on most polling measures of leadership, and there were repeated rumours that Corbyn might step down after the forthcoming local elections, potentially being replaced by someone who the Conservatives feared would be more electorally appealing.

Against this, the Conservative leadership—and in particular May her-self—worried about the political costs involved in being seen to perform a U-turn. An early election would also occur before the proposed boundary changes which were expected to yield the Conservatives a net gain of around 20 seats (but what were 20 extra seats when set against poll leads of over 20%?) and without the ability to judge how the party was perform-ing in local elections, something Margaret Thatcher had found valuable. Crosby's research warned that there was the risk that the Conservatives would end up with a vote share similar to that secured in 2015, and the potential for a 'significant number of seats won from the Liberal

Democrats in 2015 to return to Tim Farron's party'. It is, in retrospect, striking that neither of Crosby's concerns turned out to be problems, yet many of actual pitfalls of the campaign—the volatility of the electorate, the Prime Minister under-performing on the campaign trail, Jeremy Corbyn's rising popularity, Labour uniting and advancing a popular policy programme, an unpopular Conservative manifesto and Labour squeezing the other minor parties' votes—were hardly considered.

After the election had been announced, the media made much of a vox pop with a woman called Brenda from Bristol, whose reaction when interviewed by the BBC was: 'You're joking. Not another one! Oh for God's sake. Honestly, I can't stand this. There's too much politics going on at the moment' The preceding three years had seen a Scottish referendum in 2014, a general election in 2015 and the Brexit referendum in 2016; there had been devolved elections in Scotland, Wales and Northern Ireland (twice in the case of the last), as well as Mayoral and Assembly elections in London. In addition to May's replacement of Cameron in 2016, there had been Labour leadership elections in both 2015 and 2016—with the party in turmoil for much of the period—along with leadership changes in the Liberal Democrats, UKIP (multiple occasions), all of the major parties in Northern Ireland and the Greens. Some commentators wondered if there was the potential for voter fatigue. The *Scottish Sun*'s front-page story began 'Weary Scots will trudge to the polls for a seventh time in three years...', below the headline 'What a Load of Ballots'.

Yet opinion polls showed a majority approval for May's decision, together with no sign of the decision hurting the Conservatives. Brenda's vox pop finished with a plaintive: 'Why does she need to do it?' One poll found 62% believed that she was 'exploiting the weakness of the Labour Party'.[25] As Nick Robinson, the former BBC political editor, put in, when interviewing the Prime Minister early in the campaign: 'What is it about the recent 20% opinion poll [lead] that first attracted you to the idea of a general election?' Yet this did not seem to hurt her. A snap ICM poll on the day the election was called found support for the election on 55%, with only 15% opposed. A ComRes poll a few days later also found 55% support, with just 21% disagreement. The ICM poll taken on the day showed a 21-point Conservative lead and a private internal Conservative poll showed an immediate four-point rise in party support. A YouGov poll published shortly after the election was called found that 63% of respondents expected a Conservative majority (including 47% of Labour voters) and 21% expected it to be a landslide. Just 4% predicted a Labour majority, 1% expected a Labour landslide. Only 8% expected the election to result in a hung parliament.

Few of that 8% worked in, or for, political parties. On the night that the election was called, one of Labour's election coordinators, Andrew Gwynne, was shown details of Labour's own polling, which showed the party on course to win just 157 seats. The last of Labour's casualties would be Gwynne himself, set to lose his seat of Denton & Reddish, where Labour had a majority of over 10,000. A senior figure in the Parliamentary Labour Party summed up their feelings: 'We were fucking toast.' A member of the Labour whips' office described the mood in the Parliamentary Labour Party as akin to a wake for much of the two weeks before dissolution: 'we had MPs in tears, they knew it was all over for them'. Theresa May's first campaign stop, after her Downing Street statement, was a visit by helicopter to Bolton North East, forty-eighth on the Conservative target list. The visit was indicative of where almost everyone expected the election battleground to be: Labour held-seats, in which the majority had voted for Brexit, and with the potential to create a landslide Conservative majority on a par with that of 1983 or 1987.

That, too, did not go entirely to plan.

NOTES

1. Craig Oliver, *Unleashing Demons*. Hodder & Stoughton, 2016, p. 367.
2. His 2013 speech proposing a referendum on the EU was also given at exactly the same time as other people would have been taking their children to school.
3. In particular, there was resistance to the idea from some newly elected Conservative MPs, who had not yet had the chance to establish themselves in their constituencies—especially those who had taken seats from Liberal Democrats, those in Wales or those in London. It turned out that many were right to be concerned.
4. Tim Ross and Tom McTague, *Betting the House*. Biteback, 2017, pp. 87–88.
5. Hammond was also said to be concerned about the state of the economy, with the possibility of both consumer and business confidence declining. See Francis Elliot, 'Poll to Clear the Air Has Added to the Fog', in *The Times Guide to the House of Commons 2017*. Times Books, 2017, p. 9.
6. See William Hague, 'The Case for an Early General Election: Theresa May Should be Free to Put Her Brexit Plans to the People', *Daily Telegraph*, 6

March 2017. Speculation that this article had been encouraged by Number 10 as an exercise in kite-flying, testing how the idea of an early election was received, is denied by those close to May.

7. George Eaton, 'Exclusive: Conservative Poll Showed Party Would "Lose Seats" to the Liberal Democrats', *New Statesman*, 5 April 2017, https://www.newstatesman.com/politics/uk/2017/04/exclusive-conservative-poll-showed-party-would-lose-seats-liberal-democrats.

8. The polling was somewhat more nuanced than this, as discussed below (p. 61).

9. Abbie Wightwick, 'Theresa May on Her Love of Walking in Snowdonia, Reviving the Tory Vote in Wales and Why She Can't Eat Welsh Cakes', *Wales Online*, 19 March 2017, https://www.walesonline.co.uk/news/wales-news/theresa-love-walking-snowdonia-reviving-12760499.

10. See Dennis Kavanagh and Philip Cowley, *The British General Election of 2010*. Palgrave Macmillan, 2010, Chapter 1.

11. There is a claim that although he did not dissent in the meeting, the Foreign Secretary had privately tried to persuade the Prime Minister to change her mind, which resulted in the start of the Cabinet meeting being delayed (Tim Shipman, *Fall Out*. William Collins, 2017, p. 194). This account is disputed.

12. However, as discussed in Chapter 8, there were very good arguments for putting forward a more substantial manifesto.

13. For this claim, see 'Revealed: How Theresa May's Two Aides Seized Control of the Tory Election Campaign to Calamitous Effect', *Evening Standard*, 16 June 2017.

14. This was, at least in part, informed by some of the polling CTF had undertaken, which revealed that only two Conservative front-rank politicians polled well—May and the Scottish Conservative leader, Ruth Davidson. As one of those involved noted: 'everyone else had terrible numbers, even Boris (which surprised me for a CTF poll...)'.

15. Michael Deacon, 'Vote Tory, or Brexit is at Risk: Theresa May's Startling Warning to Voters', *Daily Telegraph*, 18 April 2017.

16. In addition, some of May's aides felt that using Brexit as a justification for the election was counterproductive. As one said: 'The simple fact is that if you ask people if they think there should be an election, they will say no ... No one likes elections. But it still doesn't follow that you then have to spend ages justifying why you have called it.' He continued: 'we concocted a false reason—the need for stability and to "strengthen my hand" in the negotiations—which everyone knew to be complete disingenuous nonsense, and which meant we just talked about Brexit for seven weeks'.

17. HC Debs, 19 April 2017, cc. 681–712.

18. Given the rules required a two-thirds majority of the whole House, rather merely than of those voting, the SNP abstention de facto had the same

effect as voting against the motion; it was also noticeable that of the handful of MPs to vote against, two were former SNP MPs, now sitting as independents.

19. The Conservative approach had one further apparent advantage: assuming that the legislation could be passed in time, it still allowed for an election on 8 June. Had the government gone down the route of voting no confidence in itself, the two-week delay required by section 2(3) of the Fixed term-Parliaments Act would have delayed the date of the election beyond that scheduled.

20. This, moreover, is without allowing any time for the wash-up of legislation. The claim made by some of May's team that she should have called the election on the day that Article 50 was triggered and then hold the election simultaneously with the local elections would only have been possible if Article 50 had been triggered on a different day, as there were insufficient working days between the two events.

21. There is also a claim in Mark Wallace's excellent account of the Conservative campaign ('Our CCHQ Election Audit: The Rusty Machine, Part One. Why the Operation That Succeeded in 2015 Failed in 2017', *ConservativeHome*, 5 September 2017, https://www.conservativehome.com/majority_conservatism/2017/09/our-cchq-election-audit-the-rusty-machine-part-one-why-the-operation-that-succeeded-in-2015-failed-in-2017.html) that the delay was partly due to advice from Sue Gray, the Cabinet Office's Director General of Propriety and Ethics, that under the Fixed-term Parliaments Act, an election should last seven weeks 'at minimum'. It is not clear on what basis such a claim would be made, and one senior member of May's team has denied to us that any such advice was given.

22. Using data from the Polling Observatory team (Rob Ford, William Jennings, Mark Pickup and Christopher Wlezien), Figure 1.1 shows the pooled estimates of every poll from the beginning of the Parliament until the election was called. This method controls for companies' varying methodologies ('house effects'). The methodology employed is explained Mark Pickup and Richard Johnston. 'Campaign Trial Heats as Election Forecasts: Measurement Error and Bias in 2004 Presidential Campaign Polls', *International Journal of Forecasting*, 24(2) (2008): 270–82.

23. As one of her aides later remarked, 'That did mean we had to carefully control the narrative so that people didn't get carried away—and I accept that that was something we utterly failed to do. From day one, all the talk was of a landslide—which was never our expectation nor motivation'.

24. See also the comments reported in Ross and McTague, *Betting the House*, p. 93.

25. See also the comments of focus groups reported in Lord Ashcroft's *The Lost Majority*. Biteback, 2017, p. 18.

CHAPTER 2

Brexit

Jack Glynn and Anand Menon

On 23 January 2013, in the London offices of Bloomberg, David Cameron announced that, if re-elected in the general election, he would negotiate a 'new settlement' for Britain inside the European Union before holding a referendum on EU membership. The political momentum for such a vote had been building within the Prime Minister's party for some time. In October 2011, 81 Conservatives had defied a three-line whip to vote in favour of a referendum on EU membership.[1] This followed the creation of nascent campaign group the People's Pledge—openly backed by 86 sitting MPs, including those backbenchers who had forced the vote in the House of Commons—as well as a string of polling figures revealing support for a referendum. This parliamentary pressure was persistent and cumulative. In October 2012 the government suffered a Commons defeat over EU policy. In May 2014, even after Cameron had promised a referendum, more than 100 Conservative MPs backed an amendment regretting the absence of a referendum bill from the Queen's Speech.

Political pressure was not confined to the Conservative benches. By November 2012, UKIP was finishing second in by-elections in Rotherham and Middlesbrough, and the pressure on the Prime Minister was increasing. In the month before David Cameron announced the referendum, 11 of 27 published polls had UKIP ahead of the Liberal Democrats; six of them had the Conservatives at less than 30%.[2] By this time many believed that, should he fail to publicly call for a referendum, Cameron could face a leadership challenge.

© The Author(s) 2018
P. Cowley, D. Kavanagh, *The British General Election of 2017*,
https://doi.org/10.1007/978-3-319-95936-8_2

The strategic case for promising a referendum was driven by these electoral and parliamentary considerations. Yet at the top of the Conservative Party, opinion was divided on the wisdom of Cameron's Bloomberg speech. Some senior members of the Cabinet, such as the Justice Secretary Kenneth Clarke, claimed not to be consulted and to have first found out about the decision in the newspapers.[3] George Osborne was opposed, sensing it was an avoidable gamble.[4] Michael Gove argued it was a tactical mistake.[5] But the balance of opinion among Cameron's inner circle was that a referendum pledge was politically unavoidable. This was the view of both Cameron and William Hague, whose voice carried significant weight as both the Foreign Secretary and a former leader of the party.[6]

The referendum pledge did little to deflate UKIP's polling. However, the promise was credited by senior Conservatives as being a key element in helping the party secure a slim and largely unexpected majority in the 2015 election. A small, though potentially electorally significant, number of voters prioritised Cameron's referendum pledge when voting in 2015: just 1.3% of respondents in the British Election Study (BES) named the referendum as their most important issue in March 2015, rising to 3% in their first post-election survey.[7] What was key was that this pledge was tied to David Cameron deploying strong language on controlling immigration with increasing force and regularity (the issue, strikingly, had not figured at all in his Bloomberg speech). However, Cameron was then faced with the task of securing the renegotiation of the terms of British EU membership that he had promised. In many respects, he fared better in this undertaking than many had predicted. He obtained concessions when it came to excluding the UK from future Eurozone bailouts and from steps towards 'ever closer union,' as well as winning the ability to restrict payments of child support and in-work benefits to EU migrants.[8] Polling showed most voters were supportive of the reforms Cameron gained in isolation, but were unconvinced that the package as a whole went far enough. This was particularly true on the key issue of immigration. Internal Downing Street polling showed that if Cameron had produced a deal that could have united senior figures in his party, particularly Boris Johnson, he would have received a polling dividend. Instead, following the renegotiation, polling recorded a swing to the Leave campaign.[9]

The Prime Minister himself was partly responsible for this. It was he who had declared to the Conservative conference in 2014: 'Britain, I know you want this sorted so I will go to Brussels, I will not take no for an answer and—when it comes to free movement—I will get what Britain needs.' Set against these ambitious words, limiting benefit payments to EU migrants fell short of an ability to limit the numbers of those coming. Cameron banked on being able to frame the negotiation as a success. Instead, the reaction of the Eurosceptic press was predictably critical: *The Sun* mocked up the Prime Minister as Captain Mainwaring from Dad's Army, next to a headline that asked: 'Who Do EU Think You are Kidding, Mr Cameron?' Perhaps just as worrying was the reaction of those publications Cameron needed to enthusiastically rally behind the negotiation. *The Times* was critical of Cameron's deal as 'thin gruel' and a 'fudge', while *The Economist* described it as 'more of a throat-clearing exercise than a roar of reinvention'.[10] All this suggested that the renegotiation as a useful campaigning device was dead in the water.

Some pushback from the press, albeit not at the level Cameron experienced, was expected. What was not factored into Downing Street's calculations was the bleeding of support to Leave within the Parliamentary Conservative Party. One-third of Conservative MPs who had waited until the renegotiation was complete before deciding how to campaign opted to defy their leader and support the Leave camp.[11] Downing Street calculated that up to 70 Conservative MPs would be publicly pro-Brexit, but by the final tally the eventual number was over double that.[12] Six Cabinet members came out for Leave, including so-called big beasts such as Michael Gove and Boris Johnson. Gove and Johnson were to prove critical to the impact of the Leave campaign, and Cameron, in part based on private assurances, had originally assumed both would fall into line and support Remain.[13]

For the Leave campaign, a tussle over the official designation defined the pre-campaign period. This boiled down to two camps: those who advocated a less 'Westminster-based' approach, similar to that which Nigel Farage and UKIP had successfully adopted to force a referendum; and those who felt the image of credibility and moderation needed to attract a broad-based coalition of voters meant distancing the official campaign from UKIP. On the former side was Grassroots Out, led by the veteran Eurosceptic Conservative Peter Bone and backed by the Labour donor John Mills. The group was primarily associated with UKIP's key figures. Following its launch, it was swiftly jumped on as a tactical vehicle that could create a broader base of support than could be provided by Leave.EU, which had been founded by the UKIP donor Aaron Banks immediately after the general election. On the other side was Vote Leave, which held the support of all six Cabinet ministers and Boris Johnson, as well as deeper support from across the political parties. In truth, given the Electoral Commission's criteria, it always looked highly unlikely that Grassroots Out would win the designation. But this internecine warfare within the Leave camp delighted Remain campaigners and appeared to confirm their suspicions of their opposition: a mixture of passionate political eccentrics without the organisational capacity, or message discipline, to sustain a successful and coherent campaign.[14]

Vote Leave planned a visceral campaign focused on the theme of sovereignty. This was brilliantly encapsulated in the campaign's key phrase 'taking back control'. The ownership over the campaign's key slogan is uncontested. Dominic Cummings, Vote Leave's Campaign Director, is credited with the slogan, drawn from experience of focus group research—a 19-page unpublished report Cummings drew together in 2014 from this research mentioned 'control' 37 times and 'take back control' five times.[15] The Leave campaign's Chief Executive was Matthew Elliott. His experience included acting as Campaign Director of the NotoAV campaign in the referendum on the Alternative Vote in 2011, which had successfully moulded a message harnessing distrust of political elites with claims centred on the financial cost of the referendum.

In contrast, the equivalent key strategists within the Remain campaign had relatively less experience of success in British politics. Will Straw was an energetic and organisationally capable Campaign Director, but his track record did not extend far beyond the think-tank world; Ryan Coetzee acted as Britain Stronger in Europe's Head of Strategy, as he had been for the Liberal Democrats during the 2015 general election campaign, in which the party lost 86% of their seats and 66% of their vote share. They were joined, however, by political strategists whose CVs had been boosted by the Conservatives' surprise majority in 2015. Jim Messina—Barack Obama's campaign manager in 2012—joined as a senior strategic advisor, after winning plaudits for his success in a similar role for Cameron in 2015. Craig Elder and Tom Edmonds, who had been recognised as the Tories' 'secret weapon' due to their sophisticated digital campaigns, were also brought on board. The Remain campaign, Britain Stronger in Europe, appeared to have a coherent economic-based strategy and a more settled organisation: from the summer of 2015, backed financially from the start principally by the Labour peer Lord Sainsbury, the cross-party group was formed. But this was without cooperation with Cameron and his team. This created a strategic rift within the Remain campaign between 10

Downing Street and the Britain Stronger in Europe camp, which widened as the campaign gathered pace.

Despite this, Remain appeared to have the early momentum in the pre-campaign 'purdah' period. The Treasury weighed in, with a series of reports and dramatic headlines on its website stressing the economic dangers inherent in leaving the EU: each household would be £2,600 worse off each year, 500,000 jobs would disappear from the economy and GDP would be 3.6% lower if the UK voted to leave.[16] A government-produced leaflet was sent to 27 million households, firmly backing a vote to remain. The campaign also profited from the support of FTSE 100 CEOs as well as a plethora of domestic and international institutions. At first, the view across Westminster was that these warnings were working. Cameron had an earned reputation as a political winner—drawn from a leadership election, two general elections from which he had emerged as Prime Minister, and successful referendum campaigns on the electoral system and the Scottish independence referendum in 2014. Downing Street was also willing to use the weight of the machinery of government to hammer home its core economic message.

Yet, as the campaign progressed, the Remain side provided little in the way of a positive vision of the future. Macro-economic claims about the effect of a Leave win failed to resonate, due to their unremitting negativity and their lack of real-life emotional resonance. The door was left open for their opponents to brandish the Remain camp as scaremongers peddling 'Project Fear'—a phrase borrowed from the No campaign in the Scottish referendum, on which it was clearly based. Cameron, who had been a mild but persistent Eurosceptic, was not well-placed to provide an optimistic case for the Remain campaign.[17] Not for nothing did Boris Johnson brand his opponents as the 'Gerald Ratners of modern politics'—insisting the EU was 'crap', but maintaining there was no alternative to it.

Vote Leave initially focused on the issues of sovereignty and the money sent to the EU. However, the gradual intertwining of this clear message on democratic control with concerns about immigration was key to the Leave campaign. This strategy was bolstered by foreseeable political events. Towards the end of May, figures released by the Office for National Statistics revealed that net migration was at 330,000 in 2015, its second-highest level ever, with 184,000 and 188,000 new immigrants from within and without the EU, respectively.[18] Vote Leave insisted that the EU could not prevent Turkey joining the EU, which would generate a new wave of immigration into the EU. These startling figures were grist to the mill for those arguing that Brexit was needed in order for Britain to be able to 'take back control of its borders'.

At the same time, the Leave camp skilfully crafted a populist appeal designed to tap into the suspicions about politics and politicians in general. Johnson attacked the 'vast clerisy of lobbyists and corporate affairs gurus—all the thousands of Davos men and women who have their jaws firmly clamped around the euro-teat'.[19] He went on to argue not only that it was not the rich who were exposed to the practical pressures caused by large scale immigration, but that they used EU regulation to maintain their oligarchic position. The Leave campaign bus—emblazoned with "We send the EU £350 million a week" and "Let's fund our NHS instead"—was one of the most memorable sights of the campaign. Such claims were at best misleading (although the UK's net contribution to the EU was hardly negligible) and were supplemented by blatant untruths (such as the claim that the UK could not stop Turkey joining the EU). But they had cut through and were widely believed: polling in early June suggested that 78% of people had heard the £350 million claim and that 47% believed the figure. A week before the referendum, more people believed that Turkey would join the EU than that the UK would fall into recession if it left the Union.[20]

Divisions in the Conservative Party over Europe—along with Cameron's suspension of Cabinet responsibility—meant that prominent figures were always going to feature in both camps. While Cameron was reluctant to be seen to be engaging in attacks on Conservative colleagues, the Leave side exploited the 'blue on blue' dynamic assiduously. They took every opportunity to criticise the government and its record, making for a particularly ruinous experience for Cameron as former allies—most notably Michael Gove and Steve Hilton—publicly and repeatedly attacked him. The tactic proved effective for Leave, earning them extensive media coverage and contributing to the gradual erosion of trust in Cameron and Osborne. Tensions within the Conservative Party reached a peak as Osborne declared on 15 June that he would, in the event of a Brexit vote, have to announce an emergency budget to plug a £30 billion black hole in public finances. In response, 57 Tory MPs, including former Cabinet ministers, issued a statement pledging to vote any such budget down, declaring it absurd to make a political promise to punish voters—and break Conservative manifesto promises into the bargain. Cameron's reluctance to attack senior Leave figures such as Gove and Johnson, in the hope of reuniting his party following the referendum, frustrated the Britain Stronger in Europe campaign. When polled in May, by a two-to-one margin, voters felt that Johnson was 'more likely to tell the truth about the EU' than Cameron.[21] Not incidentally, this fascination of the media with Conservative in-fighting also had the effect of turning off supporters of other parties.

If what the Tories stood for in the referendum was not clear, this was all the more the case when it came to the Labour Party. The party had been badly scarred by events around the Scottish referendum, when the decision to campaign against Scottish independence alongside the Conservatives had led many voters to conclude there was nothing to choose between the parties. Consequently, Labour opted not to join the official Remain campaign. Instead, it set up a separate movement, Labour in for Britain, led by former Home Secretary Alan Johnson.

Remain desperately needed to attract Labour voters inherently suspicious of a Conservative Prime Minister. Yet the new party leadership under Jeremy Corbyn was, to put it mildly, far from convinced of the benefits of EU membership. Corbyn himself was soon accused of sabotaging the Remain campaign. He refused to focus on—or even plan for—the referendum until after the local elections in May. His team cut pro-EU lines from his speeches (the phrase 'that's why I'm campaigning to remain in the EU' was reportedly a frequent victim of such editing) and he avoided events organised by Labour in for Britain. Corbyn's office even signed off on a visit to Turkey to talk about the value of open borders, though opposition from within the party meant that this did not go ahead.[22]

The Labour Party in Parliament and, indeed, in the country at large were comparatively united on the referendum compared to the deep divide in the Conservative Party. But they were split over the key issue of the political management of immigration. While Corbyn and the Shadow Foreign Secretary Hilary Benn expounded on the benefits of migration without controls, other senior Labour figures such as Deputy Leader Tom Watson or former Shadow Home Secretary Yvette Cooper argued in favour of a revision of EU rules on free movement. As the campaign unfolded, Labour MPs detected strong public discontent about immigration, but were unable to point to a single, clear party position on the issue. One staffer from Britain Stronger in Europe was quoted as saying that we 'understand that Labour needs to sort out its immigration policy. But the time to do it is not a week before polling day on live fucking television'.[23]

Meanwhile, Corbyn frequently attacked what was nominally his own side, arguing that Treasury forecasts about the consequences of a vote to leave were 'histrionic'. Following a speech at the start of June (in which he accused both sides of 'myth making'), the top Google search for Corbyn was: 'Does he want in or out?' Leaked focus groups for Britain Stronger in

Europe found voters 'uniformly confused' on Labour's position, and YouGov found that just 42% of all voters (and 55% of Labour voters) were aware of the party's official support for Remain: the rest were unsure, thought Labour were split down the middle or thought they were supporting Brexit.[24]

While the parties squabbled amongst themselves, the referendum also generated unexpected cross-party alliances. Labour MP Gisela Stuart was a prominent figure in the campaign, chairing Vote Leave. And her colleague Kate Hoey proved willing to share platforms with UKIP leader Nigel Farage. Perhaps more importantly, however, the Remain campaign brought together what one insider referred to as the 'pluralist, liberal, centrist force in British politics'. *The Guardian* journalist Rafael Behr labelled these people, who hailed from the Conservatives, Labour and the Liberal Democrats, the ruling class of 'Remainia'. As he pointed out, prior to the rise of UKIP and Jeremy Corbyn, these people conducted political debate in terms of 'shades of difference within a broad consensus'.[25] It was their defeat that heralded the profound shifts in British politics that were to follow.

Morten Morland, *The Times*, 15 June 2016 © News UK/News Licensing

The UK voted to leave the EU by a margin of 51.9% (17.4 million votes) to 48.1% (16.1 million votes). Significant geographical divisions were revealed by the vote. England and Wales had both voted to leave (by 53.3% and 52.5%, respectively). Northern Ireland and Scotland in fact voted to remain by wider margins (55.8% and 62%, respectively). Not a single voting area in Scotland voted to leave. Within England, London was the only voting region *not* to vote to leave (though given its demographic, social and ethnic makeup, its Remain vote was actually less than would be expected).[26]

It came as no surprise that areas where UKIP had long been fostering support—affluent rural areas and coastal areas with older populations—were strong backers of Leave, nor that inner-city London, with large numbers of young, educated and ethnic-minority voters, was overwhelmingly pro-Remain. However, perhaps the most interesting spatial dimension of the Brexit vote was the sharp contrast between cities and their surrounding towns, especially in the north. For example, the North West region voted to leave by a 7.2% margin. Liverpool and Manchester both supported Remain at levels of around 60%, yet the only neighbouring councils to follow suit were affluent suburban areas such as Trafford, Wirral and Sefton. Most other towns like Oldham, Bury and St Helens all voted for Leave with large majorities. The vote revealed this longstanding tension between major cities at ease with immigration and their peripheries, deindustrialised towns that had suffered most from economic degradation and had seen jobs and prosperity persistently drift outwards to their larger neighbours.

To some extent, the roots of Brexit and the map of results that emerged can be traced back to phenomena present in British politics for many years. This is not to say that the campaign made no difference or that the larger-than-life characters who dominated it played no role, but rather that the foundations of the rebellion they helped foment were laid long beforehand. The referendum provided a unique opportunity for those dissatisfied with the political status quo to voice their discontent. In itself, this was not sufficient to get the Leave vote over 50%, but it provided a rationale for many of those who had effectively opted out of politics to re-engage, and saw the majority of those who turned out ignoring the advice of the vast majority of the political establishment.

An increasing elite consensus around market economics and socially liberal positions had left those opposed to these policies with no mainstream political options. Declining political engagement was more marked among some sectors of society than others. Turnout was relatively consistent amongst social classes and those with different levels of educational attainment before the 1990s. In 1987, the poorest quintile of the population had a turnout rate only 4% lower than that of the richest quintile. By 2010, this gap was 25% and in 2015, only 48% of those with low levels of education and a working-class occupation turned out to vote.[27] The lower levels of party allegiance that resulted in part helps explain the steady increase in the UKIP vote, the direct result of which was the referendum vote.[28]

These longer-term changes were exacerbated by the political responses to events. As a result of austerity measures, in 2014 almost twice as many people felt financially worse off than when the Coalition government entered office. And, of course, these problems were not hitting everyone equally. The Institute for Fiscal Studies (IFS) concluded that middle-class and upper-class households were left 'unscathed' by government cuts. By 2016, 43% of men without qualifications were out of the workforce, at a time of positive employment statistics.[29] British voters have always had a healthy distrust of political elites. But the British Social Attitudes survey, tracking across three decades, found that those who believed that politicians would act in the national interest to be at an all-time low, and concluded that the British were 'on the verge of being straightforwardly cynical towards government and politicians'.[30] The Audit of Political Engagement reported a 'disturbing' trend towards indifference to politics in 2012.[31] Low levels of faith in the political system created fertile ground for a party or movement which sold itself as the anti-establishment alternative.

As the referendum approached, a combination of long- and short-term factors had conspired to negatively impact on public attitudes towards politics. Growing detachment from politics and distrust of politicians made such a rebellion not only conceivable but even desirable, not least as the impact of the financial crisis made many voters suspicious of claims that the status quo was worth defending.

Yet, at first glance, the Leave campaign appears to have had only a limited impact. Indeed, there is little to suggest that either campaign managed to change many minds. Panel studies performed by the BES asked Leave and Remain voters both before and during the campaign what they thought Brexit would mean with regard to a variety of matters, including unemployment, trade and British influence. What was striking was how little opinions changed over time.[32] A post-referendum analysis of 121 polls, carried out in the six months prior to the vote, found that Leave had led throughout the campaign, and indeed the Remain campaign picked up more votes from 'Don't knows' as the Referendum grew closer.[33]

Nevertheless, nearly all academic experts and commentators continued to argue that the political 'fundamentals' favoured Remain up until polling day. Those who study referendums tend to think that, when confronted with a choice, voters have a strong disposition to opt for the status quo rather than risking the unknown.[34] Coupled with this bias for the status quo was the fact that the core demographics of the Leave vote—the less well-off, the elderly and the less educated—tend to be the most risk-averse. Persuading them otherwise was no mean feat. The impact of the Leave campaign can be gleaned from the striking levels of turnout achieved among its supporters. The 'participation gap' between the university-educated and those in manual jobs—largely Remain and Leave voters, respectively—was reduced from 39% in the previous general election to 20%.[35] Young people were also notably less likely to vote than older voters. This age difference in turnout was not, in itself, decisive: to have overturned the result, the under-45s would have had to make it to the ballot box at a rate of 97%, rather than the 65% who actually voted.[36]

A notable feature of the campaign was the decline of party allegiance or loyalty as a cue or driver for voters. The referendum did not divide people along traditional left-right party lines, but rather along a cleavage centred on values.[37] This battle between social liberals and social conservatives, in which education represents a key dividing line, cut across party lines. How a voter related to the EU relied on deep-rooted beliefs on questions to do with authority, identity and freedom, issues not properly reflected by the traditional left-right spectrum. NatCen found a crystal-clear link between values and attitudes towards the EU: 66% of social traditionalists voted to leave, while 18% of liberals did so.[38] Leave/Remain became somewhat synonymous with traditional/liberal, exposing a cleavage of political competition which had not been effectively expressed in the prior decades.

The divide in values was complemented by divisions in the social makeup of the vote. Class has long dominated political competition in the UK and once again had a role to play in the referendum. The working class represented the group most likely to disengage from politics and who were hit worst by the financial crisis. Perhaps predictably, then, they tended to vote against the political establishment. Holding for other social identifiers, the gap between working-class Leave voters and their middle-class counterparts was 10 percentage points.[39] Geographically, 'white British working class' areas had the strongest Leave support.[40] The rift is even more startling if we consider education: the gap between those voting Leave with no qualifications and those doing so with a university degree was 30 percentage points.[41]

'Let's never ask the public
for their views ever again'

Matt, *Daily Telegraph*, 26 June 2016 © Matt/Telegraph Media Group Ltd

However, to argue that those who voted Brexit represented merely the economically 'left behind' is a major over-simplification. The declining size of the working class in the UK meant that a substantial number of middle-class voters had to have voted Leave in order for it to win. Indeed, according to the BES, only 21% of Leave votes came from those with routine or semi-routine jobs—the same proportion as were provided from lower and intermediate professionals. However, it was the middle classes whose support was most important for Brexit—they made up 59% of the Leave voters.

Overall, then, the Leave vote was a much broader social coalition than can be explained simply by a class-based argument. Indeed, factors such as age hold much more explanatory power than class. NatCen viewed such a coalition as comprising three main groups: the older working class, affluent Eurosceptics and a smaller group of economically worse-off, anti-immigration voters.[42] In many ways, we should be talking less about the 'left behind' and more about the 'left out'—a coalition of those working classes left behind, but also those who are economically affluent, yet whose social values were in discordance with the predominant liberal consensus.

And so, prefiguring the political shifts to come in 2017, education and age proved to be crucial determinants of the outcome of the referendum. Britain's post-referendum society, then, is one which is profoundly divided; divided by generation, by culture, by class, and by town and city. The resultant shifts in British politics reflect, and to an extent reinforce, these divisions.

It soon became evident that it was far from clear what the British people had voted for. The Leave vote offered to the electorate encompassed at least three distinct options: the 'Norway model' of ending EU membership while remaining within the Single Market; the 'Canada option' of leaving both the Single Market and the Customs Union, but signing a bilateral trade agreement with the EU; and departure from the EU without an agreement, operating on WTO rules of trade. The shorthand adopted to cover these choices was that between 'hard' and 'soft' Brexit. A hard Brexit implied the latter two options: a clean break from the EU and the country's departure from both the Single Market and the Customs Union. Those advocating a 'soft' Brexit, either implicitly or explicitly, endorsed something as close as possible to the 'Norway model' and the continued membership—or as close to it as possible—of the frameworks that underpinned UK–EU trade and cooperation.

A hard Brexit option holds obvious merits, not least as leaving the European Economic Area is the only feasible way of obtaining the key demands set out by many Leave voters: to regain control of immigration and to free Britain from the jurisdiction of the Court of Justice of the European Union. Equally, a country within the EU's Customs Union cannot negotiate independent trade deals, viewed by many as a necessary capacity of the newly independent UK. However, the economic implications of a 'hard Brexit' could be significant. It would result in the imposition of tariffs as well as increased checks on British goods entering the EU. As such, 'soft' Brexit advocates—including many if not most previous Remain voters—argued in favour of respecting the four freedoms of the EU in return for the maintenance of strong trading relations between the UK and the EU.

Consequently, over the summer of 2016, divisions formed not merely between Leavers and Remainers, but between proponents of 'hard' and 'soft' Brexit. Opinion in Parliament did not mirror that in the country at large. A substantial majority of MPs had voted to remain, though this disconnect was tempered by MPs' understanding that the result needed, unequivocally, to be seen to be enacted. In November, the Supreme Court ruled by 8 to 3 that Parliament must be given the chance to vote on the triggering of Article 50, offering opponents of the hard Brexit course charted by the Prime Minister the chance to challenge her. Ugly and often personal attacks dominated headlines—the *Daily Mail* branded the Supreme Court judges 'Enemies of the People'—as rumours swirled that a Conservative faction led by the likes of Kenneth Clarke and Anna Soubry were willing to defy the government on the vote.

However, Conservative opposition began to evaporate following Theresa May's Lancaster House speech in January 2017 recommitting her government to a position of hard Brexit. In the speech, May stressed that control over borders and laws were paramount to her agenda, killing any hopes of continued Single Market membership. While much less clear regarding the Customs Union, she laid out a clear position on the Single Market that effectively, for the time being at least, silenced her critics on her own backbenches. In the event, the parliamentary vote proved to be an anti-climax. Labour imposed a three-line whip to vote for the bill and on 29 March 2017, following Royal Assent four days earlier, Theresa May wrote to the President of the European Council to trigger Article 50 and begin the process of removing the UK from the EU.

Estimating the potential economic impact of Brexit is far from straight-forward, not least as we are, at the time of writing, wholly unaware of the form that 'Brexit' will take. The Treasury's forecasts regarding the short-term impact of a Leave vote were to some extent subsequently disproved by events. But the UK's relative economic slowdown suggests its longer-term forecasts—which estimated that British GDP outside both the Customs Union and the Single Market would be 4.6–7.8% lower by 2031 than had the UK remained—could be borne out.[43] Whatever the political or social merits, a 'hard' Brexit is likely to have some significant detrimental impacts on trade: studies suggest that the 'Canada option' would trigger a 40% reduction in trade with the EU, while the signing of trade deals with other states would bring comparatively meagre gains—a free trade deal with the US is thought to bring with it around a 0.3% increase in GDP.[44]

The referendum and resultant arguments over the form Brexit should take profoundly divided both major parties. Brexit exacerbated tensions between the hard-left and centrist factions within the Labour Party. Jeremy Corbyn remains committed to leaving the EU, but on the UK's future relationship with the EU, the leadership holds a different position from the Labour Party membership: 87% of the party's membership voted to remain, 66% still think the UK should remain in the Single Market despite the result and only 9% firmly oppose a referendum on the final deal the UK makes with the EU.[45]

In the nine months following the referendum, profound divisions were exposed as leading figures came out with contradictory statements on the party's approach to leaving the EU. Labour's Brexit spokesperson, Keir Starmer, clashed with the party leadership in January 2017 when he emphasised the need for tighter immigration controls only a week after Corbyn had suggested that free movement ought to persist following the UK's departure. Starmer's views were shared by various other prominent Labour figures such as Emma Reynolds, Yvette Cooper and Andy Burnham, while Welsh First Minister Carwyn Jones attacked the Labour leadership's defence of free movement as being 'London-centric'. Divisions within the party were not only deep but also very public. Open defiance of the leadership's position was most obvious over the parliamentary voting to trigger Article 50. Nearly a quarter of Labour MPs—including 11 shadow ministers and three party whips—defied the three-line whip and voted against the Bill. Several ministers left the Shadow Cabinet over the party's support for triggering Article 50, including, crucially, some of Corbyn's key erstwhile allies.

The issue of Europe had divided the Conservative Party since at least the 1980s. Little wonder, then, that the referendum caused the party further problems. Theresa May's attempts to impose unity from above largely failed. Behind a façade of comfort provided by their lead in the polls, divisions within the Conservatives were nonetheless real enough within the Cabinet. The matter dominated May's first party conference as leader, with 'hard' and 'soft' Brexiters using the occasion to try and coax the leadership and membership towards their preferred positions. Significantly, her speech stressed a return to domestic authority over the judiciary, legislation and immigration, suggesting an early leaning towards a 'hard' Brexit and further alienating the 'soft' factions.

As the parties squabbled among themselves, the substance of politics was itself evolving in response. Jeremy Corbyn had long supported a radical platform—his first interview the morning after the vote argued that the vote was a result of political marginalisation and the government's austerity policies. Theresa May was quick to interpret the referendum as a call for change. Her maiden speech as Prime Minister offered support for families who were 'just about managing' in the face of 'burning injustice' (see below, pp. 50–51). The political rationale for this was clear-cut. Labour were struggling to garner support among voters. Polling in August 2016 found that Labour supporters even preferred Theresa May to Corbyn. An internal party report by Jon Cruddas found that the party was losing traditionalist voters to UKIP, a party which was in the apparent process of a slow-burning implosion.[46] Defecting Labour votes were up for grabs and May appeared willing to park herself squarely in Labour heartlands to get them.

The continued impact of Brexit could be seen in the persistence of the divisions which emerged during the referendum. Class politics appeared to have finally been dealt a potentially lethal blow by Brexit, leaving YouGov to conclude that 'class would tell you little more about a person's voting intention than looking at their horoscope or reading their palms'.[47] And as class waned, the 'new' identifiers which emerged from Brexit—age and education—surfaced as its replacements.[48] Perhaps the most profound impact has been the creation of a new electoral cleavage between Leave and Remain supporters. This divide encapsulated much more than views on the EU and served as a cipher for a values divide within the country. The BES found that, 12 months on from the vote, identification with the Leave and Remain campaigns had not declined.[49] This persistence of Remain/Leave identities created dilemmas for all parties heading into the general election.

With the referendum results adding further evidence to diverging inter-ests with the rest of the UK, the SNP hoped that Brexit—and Scotland's clear opposition to it—could engender support and legitimacy for a sec-ond independence referendum. Meanwhile, the Liberal Democrats saw Brexit as an avenue for their renaissance. With Labour in conflict under the leadership of a begrudging Remain supporter, Tim Farron shifted his party to brand itself as the 'true' opposition party to the 'hard' Brexit, in the hope of collecting cosmopolitan Remain voters disillusioned by Labour. And then there was UKIP. The party whose exponential growth helped provoke the referendum feared being the victim of its own success.

For Labour, Brexit revealed a broad disconnect between the parliamen-tary party and many of its voters. Research by Chris Hanretty indicated that 149 (64%) of Labour seats had voted to Leave, but only 10 of these constituencies had pro-Leave MPs.[50] Elections aside, this posed serious questions for the Parliamentary Labour Party as to the role of an MP in representing both constituents and the party's agenda. With the Leave/Remain divide being largely synonymous with traditional/liberal values, Labour found itself increasingly divided between a liberal, cosmopolitan membership and a larger electorate with more traditional views.

More immediately, however, Labour confronted the task of defending a large number of pro-Leave marginals in the North and the Midlands which had become vulnerable to UKIP and the Conservatives. The chal-lenge was that the party also needed to defend heavily pro-Remain London marginals in seats such as Hornsey and Wood Green or Hampstead & Kilburn. Labour somehow needed to appeal to both extremes of the

Leave/Remain divide in order to offer a challenge in the election. The Conservatives, for their part, faced Brexit-related problems of their own. One in four Conservative seats had voted to Remain. While many Labour seats appeared ripe for the taking, hard Brexit rhetoric had the potential to lose them seats in cosmopolitan suburban constituencies.[51]

Neither the Conservatives nor Labour sit comfortably on one side of the Leave/Remain divide. This new cleavage cut through both parties, exposing deep internal divisions. Equally, it created the potential for the political geography of the country to be completely rewritten, opening up the possibility of parties challenging in seats where previously they might have assumed they stood no chance of success.

NOTES

1. P. Cowley and M. Stuart, 'The Cambusters: The Conservative European Union Referendum Rebellion of October 2011', *Political Quarterly*, 83 (2012): 402–6.
2. A. Wells, 'Voting Intention since 2016', *UK Polling Report*, 2016, http://ukpollingreport.co.uk/voting-intention-2.
3. K. Clarke, *Kind of Blue: A Political Memoir*. Pan Macmillan, 2016, p. 472.
4. A. Seldon and P. Snowdon, *Cameron at 10: The Inside Story 2010–15*. William Collins, 2015, p. 258.
5. D. Laws, *Coalition Diaries, 2012–2015*. Biteback, 2015, p. 80; T. Shipman, *All Out War*. William Collins, 2016, p. 10.
6. Shipman, *All Out War*, p. 3.
7. For the political science that raises doubts about the importance of Cameron's referendum pledge, given other key campaign dynamics and the low salience of the EU, see M. Goodwin and C. Milazzo, *UKIP: Inside the Campaign to Redraw the Map of British Politics*. Oxford University Press, 2015; and P. Lynch and R. Whitaker, 'Continuing Fault Lines and New Threats: European Integration and the Rise of UKIP' in G. Peele and J. Francis (eds), *David Cameron and Conservative Renewal: The Limits of Modernisation?* Manchester University Press, 2016, pp. 132–33.
8. G. Evans and A. Menon, *Brexit and British Politics*. Polity, 2017, pp. 46–47.
9. Shipman, *All Out War*, p. 175. For a comprehensive analysis of the immediate polling implications of the renegotiation, see H. Clarke et al., *Brexit: Why Britain Voted to Leave the European Union*. Cambridge University Press, 2017, pp. 25–27.
10. 'The Accidental Europhile', *The Economist*, 4 February 2016; 'Thin Gruel', *The Times*, 20 February 2016; 'Who Do EU Think You are Kidding, Mr Cameron?', *The Sun*, 3 February 2016.

11. 'Profound Divisions among MPs over Brexit, Survey Reveals', *The UK in a Changing Europe*, 1 February 2017, http://ukandeu.ac.uk/profound-divisions-among-mps-over-brexit-survey-reveals.
12. Shipman, *All Out War*, p. 143. The political gossip website *Guido Fawkes* kept a running tally of MPs' referendum positions—at the final count, they counted 140 Conservative MPs who had publicly supported the Leave campaign: https://order-order.com/2016/02/16/introducing-guidos-mp-referendum-list.
13. N. Robinson, 'David Cameron and Michael Gove: A Torn Friendship', *BBC News*, 16 June 2016, www.bbc.co.uk/news/uk-politics-eu-referendum-36548748; T. Bale, *The Conservative Party from Thatcher to Cameron*. Oxford University Press, 2016, p. 438; Shipman, *All Out War*, p. 91.
14. For an entertaining first-hand account of this dispute from the Leave.EU perspective, see A. Banks, *The Bad Boys of Brexit*. Biteback, 2016; key Vote Leave figures heavily involved in this dispute, such as Dominic Cummings and Douglas Carswell, endorse Tim Shipman's account.
15. J. Farrell and P. Goldsmith, *How to Lose a Referendum*. Biteback, 2017, pp. 307–9.
16. HM Treasury, 'HM Treasury Analysis: The Immediate Economic Impact of Leaving the EU', 2016, https://www.gov.uk/government/uploads/system/uploads/attachment_data/file/524967/hm_treasury_analysis_the_immediate_economic_impact_of_leaving_the_eu_web.pdf.
17. T. Bale, *The Conservative Party from Thatcher to Cameron*. Oxford University Press, 2016, pp. 264–360.
18. Office on National Statistics, 'Migration Statistics Quarterly Report: May 2016', 26 May 2016, https://www.ons.gov.uk/peoplepopulationandcommunity/populationandmigration/internationalmigration/bulletins/migrationstatisticsquarterlyreport/may2016#net-migration-to-the-uk.
19. B. Johnson, 'Of Course Our City Fat Cats Love the EU – It's Why They Earn So Much', *The Telegraph*, 15 May, 2016, www.telegraph.co.uk/news/2016/05/15/of-course-our-city-fat-cats-love-the-eu%2D%2Dits-why-they-earn-so-mu.
20. See 'June 2016 Political Monitor', *Ipsos MORI*, 16 June 2016, https://www.ipsos.com/sites/default/files/migrations/en-uk/files/Assets/Docs/Polls/pm-16-june-2016-topline.pdf; T. Mludzinski, 'Leave's Ingredients for Victory', *ComRes*, 1 July 2016, www.comresglobal.com/leaves-ingredients-for-victory.
21. 'Independent/Sunday Mirror: May Poll', *ComRes*, 14 May 2016, www.comresglobal.com/polls/independent-sunday-mirror-may-2016-poll.
22. P. Waugh, 'Jeremy Corbyn Allies "Sabotaged" Labour's in Campaign on the EU Referendum, Critics Claimed', *Huffington Post UK*, 25 June 2016, www.huffingtonpost.co.uk/entry/jeremy-corbyn-allies-sabotaged-labour-in-campaign-and-fuelled-brexit_uk_576eb1b5e4b0d2571149b b1f; K. McCann, 'Jeremy Corbyn Forced to Abandon Speech Calling for

Turkey to Join the EU Amid Fears it Would Push UK to Brexit', *The Telegraph*, 5 May 2016, www.telegraph.co.uk/news/2016/05/05/jeremy-corbyn-forced-to-abandon-speech-calling-for-turkey-to-joi.

23. R. Behr, 'How Remain Failed: The Inside Story of a Doomed Campaign', *The Guardian*, 5 July 2016, https://www.theguardian.com/politics/2016/jul/05/how-remain-failed-inside-story-doomed-campaign.

24. YouGov/Times Survey Results, 23–24 May, https://d25d2506sfb94s.cloudfront.net/cumulus_uploads/document/j84ytv1far/TimesResults_160524_EURef&Parties_W.pdf.

25. Behr, 'How Remain Failed'.

26. R. Harris and M. Charlton, 'Voting out of the European Union: Exploring the Geography of Leave', *Environment and Planning A*, 48(11) (2016): 2116–28.

27. G. Evans and J. Tilley, 'The New Class War: Excluding the Working Class in 21st-Century Britain', *Juncture*, 21(4) (2015): 265–71; Geoffrey Evans and James Tilley, *The New Politics of Class: The Political Exclusion of the British Working Class*. Oxford University Press, 2017, pp. 170–75.

28. R. Ford and M. Goodwin, *Revolt on the Right: Explaining Support for the Radical Right in Britain*. Routledge, 2014.

29. S. Dhingra, 'Salvaging Brexit: The Right Way to Leave the EU', *Foreign Affairs*. November/December 2016, pp. 90–100.

30. A. Park et al. (eds), *British Social Attitudes: The 27th Report. Exploring Labour's Legacy*. Sage Publications, 2010, p. 145.

31. Hansard Society, *Audit of Political Engagement 9. The 2012 Report: Part One*, https://assets.ctfassets.net/rdwvqctnt75b/3N7Lqnn5LqkIMwME8qGqkq/f0193b1541b68fe368a5ad69ce47828b/Audit_of_Political_Engagement_9_-_Part_One__2012_.pdf, p. 1.

32. G. Evans and A. Menon, *Brexit and British Politics*. Polity, 2017, p. 75.

33. H.D. Clarke, M. Goodwin and P. Whiteley, 'Leave was Always in the Lead: Why the Polls Got the Referendum Wrong', *LSE British Politics and Policy Blog*, 5 July 2016, http://blogs.lse.ac.uk/politicsandpolicy/eu-referendum-polls.

34. For a discussion of this attitude within the Remain camp, see P. Kellner, 'Don't Celebrate Too Soon, Brexiters. History Favours Remain.' *New Statesman*, 6 June 2016, www.newstatesman.com/politics/elections/2016/06/dont-celebrate-too-soon-brexiters-history-favours-remain. For an academic assessment of this effect, see L. LeDuc, 'Opinion Change and Voting Behaviour in Referendums', *European Journal of Political Research*, 41 (2002): 711–32.

35. Evans and Tilley, The *New Politics of Class*, pp. 201–7.

36. M. Goodwin and O. Heath, 'The 2016 Referendum, Brexit and the Left Behind: An Aggregate-Level Analysis of the Result', *Political Quarterly*, 87(3) (2016): 323–32; Michael Ashcroft, 'How the United Kingdom Voted on Thursday ... and Why?', *Lord Ashcroft Polls*, 24 June 2016,

http://lordashcroftpolls.com/2016/06/how-the-united-kingdom-voted-and-why.

37. J. Curtice, 'Brexit Reflections – How the Polls Got it Wrong Again', *Centre on Constitutional Change*, 28 June 2016, www.centreonconstitutionalchange.ac.uk/blog/brexit-reflections-how-polls-got-it-wrong-again.

38. K. Swales, 'Understanding the Leave Vote: NatCen Social Research', https://whatukthinks.org/eu/wp-content/uploads/2016/12/NatCen_Brexplanations-report-FINAL-WEB2.pdf.

39. Evans and Tilley, *The New Politics of Class*, p. 202.

40. E. Kaufman, 'It's NOT the Economy, Stupid: Brexit as a Story of Personal Values', *LSE British Politics and Policy Blog*, 7 July 2016, http://blogs.lse.ac.uk/politicsandpolicy/personal-values-brexit-vote.

41. Evans and Tilley, *The New Politics of Class*.

42. Ibid.

43. HM Treasury, 'HM Treasury Analysis: The Long-Term Economic Impact of EU Membership and the Alternatives', 18 April 2016, https://www.gov.uk/government/publications/hm-treasury-analysis-the-long-term-economic-impact-of-eu-membership-and-the-alternatives.

44. Centre for Economic Performance, *Brexit 2016: Policy Analysis from the Centre for Economic Performance*, 2017, http://cep.lse.ac.uk/pubs/download/brexit08_book.pdf; S. Dhingra, 'EU Referendum: One Year on – UK Economic Policy'. *The UK in a Changing Europe*, 28 June 2017, http://ukandeu.ac.uk/eu-referendum-one-year-on-uk-economic-policy.

45. Polling Evidence carried out by YouGov on behalf of the ESRC Party Members Project: https://esrcpartymembersproject.org.

46. J. Cruddas, 'What We Can Learn from Labour's Crushing Election Defeat', *LabourList*, 23 May 2016, http://labourlist.org/2016/05/labours-future-what-we-can-learn-from-the-election-loss.

47. D. Curtis, 'The Demographics Dividing Britain', *YouGov*, 25 April 2017, https://yougov.co.uk/news/2017/04/25/demographics-dividing-britain.

48. In April 2017, YouGov polling indicated that for every ten years older a voter was, the likelihood of them voting Conservative grew by eight percentage points. Ibid.

49. Evans and Menon, *Brexit and British Politics*, pp. 90–116.

50. C. Hanretty, 'Areal Interpolation and the UK's Referendum on EU Membership', *Journal of Elections, Public Opinion and Parties*, 27(4) (2017): 466–83.

51. Ibid.

CHAPTER 3

From Stockbroker's Son to Vicar's Daughter: The Conservatives

When the general election results came through in May 2015, David Cameron and his team were both elated and taken aback. He had been prepared for various outcomes, including defeat, but now found himself leading the first majority Conservative government since John Major in 1992. He was the first Conservative Prime Minister since 1955 to increase the party's vote share in successive general elections, albeit by less than 1%.

Delivering the party's manifesto, however, would present challenges. It had been drawn up with the expectation that proposals would have to be negotiated with other parties, most probably the Liberal Democrats, and some of which had been set as traps for Labour. It contained some expensive commitments, including raising the threshold for paying inheritance tax and for the personal allowance for the standard and higher rates of income tax, and yet somehow it promised to cut the deficit further and balance the books by 2020. Moreover, the government majority in the House of Commons was just 12, whilst a good number of MPs on the right and Eurosceptic wings had form as rebels—what one of Cameron's aides cheerfully described as 'headbangers'. There was the additional possibility of obstruction in the House of Lords. For the last five years, the combined support of the Conservatives and Liberal Democrats had provided a sizeable government majority in the Commons and a de facto majority in the Lords. Cameron now had a tiny majority in the lower House and no majority at all in the upper House; indeed, he was the first Prime Minister of a Conservative government not to enjoy a majority in the Lords. His authority was bound to wane over time because he had

© The Author(s) 2018   41
P. Cowley, D. Kavanagh, *The British General Election of 2017*,
https://doi.org/10.1007/978-3-319-95936-8_3

revealed during the election campaign that he would not fight the 2020 election and, above all, he would have to try to agree a package of reform with EU leaders that he could sell to both his party and the country in a referendum.

Cameron quickly declared that he wanted to reclaim for his government the idea of One Nation Conservatism, usually associated with policies to improve the life chances of the less well-off, but in this case also referring to the geographical divisions that the election had made so obvious.[1] 'I want to bring our country together', he said, 'not least by implementing as fast as we can the devolution that we rightly promised and came together with other parties to agree both for Wales and for Scotland. In short, I want my party, and I hope a government I would like to lead, to reclaim a mantle that we should never have lost—the mantle of One Nation, one United Kingdom.'

In reality, not much progress was made on the policy front in Cameron's year-long second premiership. Negotiations with the EU took up much of his time and energy, and the life of the government was on hold waiting on the referendum—and whatever else the referendum did, it did not bring the country together. Cameron had always been cautious about ministerial reshuffles, believing they often created more problems than they solved.[2] Even freed from the constraints of coalition and with more ministerial posts to offer to Conservative MPs, he kept in post the 'big three' ministers: George Osborne at the Treasury (now with the additional honorific title of First Secretary of State), Philip Hammond at the Foreign Office and Theresa May at the Home Office. Osborne's July 2015 Budget introduced a 'National Living Wage', to start at £7.20, rising to £9.00 an hour, by 2020, but froze benefits for those of working age. Iain Duncan Smith resigned from his Work and Pensions post following Osborne's second Budget in March 2016. He claimed to object to Osborne's targeting of benefit cuts on the disabled while protecting the pensions triple lock and tax cuts for the well-off. His relations with the Chancellor had always been tense as Osborne looked for savings in the welfare budget, and the Chancellor had long viewed Duncan Smith as an ineffectual minister. Duncan Smith's resignation came shortly before the referendum and, given his strong anti-EU views, plenty of those in Number 10 suspected that the real motivation for his departure from government was to undermine the Prime Minister.[3]

For reasons explained in the preceding chapter, the referendum proved to be a bruising experience for the Remain campaign and particularly for Cameron and Osborne—and for the Conservative Party. To Cameron's annoyance, and somewhat stronger reactions among his team, the Home Secretary played little part in the campaign, despite pressure from Number

10 for her to reveal her position and then campaign on justice and home affairs issues for Remain. May had not declared her views even to her special advisers because Cameron had asked Cabinet colleagues not to declare until the campaign started, for fear of dividing the Cabinet publicly. She refused to take part in the official Remain campaign, regarding it as too hyperbolic, according to one ally. When she eventually made a speech on the subject, in April 2016, some Number 10 staff regarded it as too nuanced to be helpful; they were also angered that the speech was briefed to newspapers before it had been agreed with Number 10.[4] This was a deliberate decision by May's team, who did not want Number 10 to control the media narrative around the speech. May argued for Britain remaining in the EU—it made Britain 'more secure … more prosperous … [and] more influential beyond our shores'—but this was very much an 'on balance' judgment, and her statement that she did not believe 'the sky will fall in if we vote to leave' angered some in Number 10. Her low profile in the campaign earned her the nickname 'Submarine'. Her team suspected the term came from Osborne, the irony being that he had been known as the submarine chancellor for some years. Cameron's team suspected that May had been prepared to launch a leadership challenge had the Conservatives lost the 2015 general election and saw her behaviour during the referendum as similar positioning for a possible leadership bid in the event of a Leave victory and/or a leadership vacancy.[5]

Steve Bell, *The Guardian*, 3 February 2016 © Steve Bell

Until the results came through, Cameron and his team believed that Remain would win, although some aides cautioned that a narrow victory would not suffice to gain the consent of the more determined anti-EU faction in the party. A narrow victory would leave the party in Parliament still divided, the membership still hostile, the tabloids still opposed and the Prime Minister's authority compromised. Although always an optimist, Cameron had already sensed that even a victory in the referendum might not settle anything for the party or for the country. In 2015, when sharing a car journey with Craig Oliver, his Director of Communications, the latter asked him if he could see the case against a referendum and Cameron replied: 'You could unleash demons of which ye know not.'[6] The demons had led to a Leave victory, with the potential for a split Conservative Party, economic turmoil, and opportunities for his party critics and for Labour. Throughout the campaign, Cameron had for tactical reasons denied that a Leave vote would trigger his resignation, but within Number 10 the working assumption all along was that were they to lose, he would not be able to remain in office—a decision that Cameron confirmed in private shortly before polling. In the final days of the campaign, he had given a last-ditch speech in Downing Street in which he had used the phrase 'Brits don't quit', yet he had resigned within 24 hours of the vote and by September he had announced he was standing down as an MP as well. He had been an MP for 15 years, most of which he had spent as party leader, and Prime Minister for six, including of a coalition government for five.

The leadership election to succeed Cameron was a saga of unexpected candidates, withdrawals and backstabbing, and ended prematurely. Osborne, whose stock had fallen with the referendum result given his prominent role in the Remain campaign, announced that he would not be a candidate. By contrast, Boris Johnson's stock had risen because of his leading role in the Leave campaign and, according to his cheerleaders in the media, the former London Mayor was the frontrunner. Theresa May was the most senior Cabinet minister to enter and, helped by her soft-spoken endorsement of Remain, enjoyed support across the party. As far as the public was concerned, according to YouGov, the two were neck and neck, with May on 19% and Johnson on 18%, with a plurality of 44% expressing no preference, although among Conservative voters May led by 31% to 24%.[7] Yet, in a separate poll of party members, May led by 36% to 27%.[8] According to the polls, party members regarded May as a stronger leader, prepared to take tough decisions and good in a crisis, as well as more likely to unite the party. They saw Johnson as more in touch with the public, better with the media and more likely to win elections.

The candidacies of Michael Gove and Andrea Leadsom, the Minister of State for Energy, were more unexpected. Gove, a Leave ally of Johnson, developed late doubts about Johnson's suitability for the leadership, withdrew his support and decided to run himself. He announced his decision just hours before nominations were closed. 'I have come, reluctantly', he said, 'to the conclusion that Boris cannot provide the leadership or build a team for the task ahead.' Leadsom, another Leave supporter, had originally decided not to run, but to support Johnson in return for his promise of a top job in the Cabinet. When this assurance did not arrive in time—more a Johnson cock-up than a conspiracy—she entered the race. The other candidates were Stephen Crabb, the Work and Pensions Secretary, and Liam Fox, the former Defence Secretary who had been out of the Cabinet since 2011. Following Gove's late decision to abandon him, a shocked Johnson found his support among MPs melting away and announced his withdrawal from the race. Gove gained a bad press as a double-dealer—a view already held by Cameron—and was attacked by Johnson's allies as untrustworthy.

All five candidates ruled out holding an early general election. Although May had not been in favour of Brexit, her stance that the referendum would be respected and delivered on meant that the contest largely ceased to be a rerun of the issue. The speech launching her candidacy contained what would become a much-discussed tautology: 'Brexit means Brexit.'[9] As she explained:

> The campaign was fought, the vote was held, turnout was high, and the public gave their verdict. There must be no attempts to remain inside the EU, no attempts to rejoin it through the back door, and no second referendum. The country voted to leave the European Union, and it is the duty of the Government and of Parliament to make sure we do just that.

In the first ballot among Conservative MPs on 5 July, May, by now the clear favourite, received 165 votes, more than half the parliamentary party; Leadsom gained 66 and Gove 48. Fox came last with 16 votes and was eliminated, and Crabb, fourth with 34, withdrew. On the second ballot two days later, May's support rose to 199 and Leadsom's to 84, whilst Gove's fell slightly to 46 and he was eliminated. The first two were then to go forward to a ballot of the full membership, with the result to be declared in October. Although Leadsom was the outsider and well behind May among MPs, it was uncertain how the largely pro-Leave grassroots would vote after a summer of campaigning by the two women.[10] The only certainty at this point was that the next Prime Minister would be a woman, for only the second time in British history.[11] 'Who'll Be the New Maggie?' asked the headline on the front cover of the *Daily Mail* on 8 July.

The answer came sooner than most people had expected. Leadsom had already been having doubts about whether she should continue in the contest, given the scale of May's lead amongst MPs. She then gave an interview to *The Times* in which she tactlessly pointed to the advantages that she had over May because she was a mother.[12] The paper splashed its front page on 9 July with: 'Being a Mother Gives Me an Edge on May'. The reaction to the story was so hostile, including from some of her own backers, that Leadsom decided to withdraw two days later. The Conservative Party's Board announced that May had been elected leader unopposed and she visited Buckingham Palace to accept the Queen's invitation to form a government. She was the seventh of 14 Prime Ministers since 1945 to take office without having won a general election. It was the fourth Conservative leadership contest election since the party membership had been given a formal say in the process, but the second in which they had been denied that say in practice.[13] A scheduled nine-week leadership campaign had been completed in 17 days. Some of the candidates had played a part in their own destruction. The coronation meant that the new Prime Minister, like Gordon Brown in 2007, had not had the opportunity—or been forced—to face questions about her plans in government.

Peter Brookes, *The Times*, 12 July 2016 © News UK/News Licensing

It was often said that little was known about Theresa May, a view summed up by the subtitle of Rosa Prince's biography, *The Enigmatic Prime Minister*.[14] The party's pollster Mark Textor later cautioned that in calling an election, she should be aware that while she was popular, she was also largely unknown to the public and it was not certain how they would react to prolonged exposure. Yet she was one of the most experienced members of the Cabinet. She had been a Shadow Cabinet minister between 1999 and 2010, and served four different party leaders, starting with William Hague. Her six-year term as Home Secretary was the longest for 60 years and, although some of her record would later come back to bite her, she was one of the few holders of the post to leave with her reputation enhanced.

May had managed to escape criticism for failing to bring down net immigration figures to the 'tens of thousands' promised for (but not by) her in the party's 2010 election manifesto and which proved to be a hostage to fortune. She could do little about EU immigration because of freedom of movement rules, but tightened the rules on non-EU immigration. Yet in 2014, the net figures for immigration exceeded 300,000 and were a factor behind the surge in support for UKIP. She gained praise among Conservatives for achieving the deportation of the radical preacher Abu Qatada to Jordan in 2013 and ordering an inquiry into police behaviour at the 1989 Hillsborough tragedy in which 96 people lost their lives. She blocked the deportation of the British computer hacker Gary McKinnon to the US in 2012 and she showed her determination in 2014 at the Police Federation Conference, when she addressed the allegations of police corruption and cases of misconduct, and police use of stop and search, which bore so disproportionately on young men from ethnic minorities. She had also campaigned strongly against modern slavery and oversaw the Modern Slavery Act 2015.

As party chair, May had addressed the 2002 party conference after its second comprehensive general election defeat and warned representatives that the party was perceived as 'nasty'. The remarks infuriated some colleagues and right-wing commentators, not least because it was an open goal for political opponents (less often quoted was her caveat: 'I know how unfair that is'). Many reform-minded people agreed with her warnings that the party had to change, be more tolerant of people of different lifestyles and more like the country it claimed to represent. She cofounded Women2Win, encouraging the recruitment of more female candidates for Parliament. Friends said that she was the original party moderniser, the mantle claimed later by Cameron and Osborne. Unlike them, she was not a metropolitan liberal and spent little time with the so-called Notting Hill set. Perhaps the fullest statement of her beliefs came in

March 2013, when she addressed the ConservativeHome conference. Distinctly post-Thatcher, she talked of her belief in active government, the need to tackle vested interests, rising inequality, corporate tax avoidance and rising crime, and to support key industries. The wide-ranging speech was seen as a statement of her leadership credentials and as such was attacked by some of Cameron's Cabinet supporters, most forcefully by Michael Gove in front of colleagues. She made few *tour d'horizon* speeches after that experience, uncomfortable with what she regarded as the over-interpretation of what she said by some colleagues and the media.

May was not an extrovert or glad-handing politician. When launching her leadership bid on 30 June, she had said 'I know I'm not a showy politician. I don't tour the television studios'. One of the few things the public heard and read about her was that she wore colourful shoes. At Westminster, she had a reputation for being somewhat unclubbable, slightly socially awkward, avoiding gossip and was—for journalists—not worth taking for lunch. As one female journalist unkindly put it: 'Theresa May has shoes where other women have personality.' Her closest aides would reject such a characterisation, arguing that in private she could be funny and charming, but they do accept she was not at her best when engaging with journalists. 'She doesn't enjoy dealing with the media, and she doesn't see why it matters', said one of her team. 'And when you try to explain why it does matter, it irritates her that it does. She thinks it shouldn't matter.' Another said that she seemed to regard explaining things to the media as 'an irritating afterthought'. Those working on her media appearances knew that she found the experience unnatural and this could result in her coming across as wooden or hard; as one aide said, 'trying to get her to come out of her shell, and engage better, was a long-term project'—one on which aides admit they had not made much progress when the election was called.

There was, to use the jargon, an interesting 'back story' to May: she was an only child of a Church of England vicar, state-educated, a diabetic, who lost both of her parents when she was relatively young—her father dying in a car accident just months after her mother, who had suffered from multiple sclerosis—and who had been unable to have children herself. Yet she found questions about such personal matters especially difficult and had a tendency to fall back on a handful of 'safe' topics, such as the shoes and her fondness for cookery books. 'They are her coping mechanisms', said one of her advisers, 'like the tricks you teach a shy child so they don't feel awkward.' There is an oft-recounted story of one of her aides attempting to discuss a forthcoming interview in which May was going to be asked about the death of her parents. Initially, the Prime Minister simply refused to engage; when the aide, in desperation, suggested one possible response based on the death of their own father, the Prime Minister still failed to engage, only later to use the aide's version in the interview, almost word-for-word, as if it were her own experience. Few paused to wonder how she might cope with the intense media scrutiny that is a part of modern campaigning.

As Home Secretary, May had difficult relations with some Cabinet colleagues, with Gove (over Islamic extremism) and Osborne (over immigration), and irritated Cameron and many of his aides with what they saw as her obstinacy. Colleagues would complain that she was slow to take decisions, but, having made them, she was remorseless in sticking with them. In his account of the 2017 election, Tim Shipman refers to May as 'a grinder, a determined reader of documents who moved towards her conclusion with all the felicity of a static caravan on a low loader'.[15] *The Times* columnist Daniel Finkelstein, who made the transition from helping Cameron to prepare for PMQs to doing the same for May, said she was not a 'transactional' politician, code for being averse to doing deals. The phrase 'getting on with the job' was one which her closest aides used to employ repeatedly. Later, the former Cabinet Minister Kenneth Clarke was accidentally recorded saying that she was 'a bloody difficult woman'; the soubriquet initially proved as helpful to her as the 'Iron Lady' was to Margaret Thatcher. During one leadership hustings, she was asked about the phrase and replied, to applause, that: 'The next man to find that out will be Jean-Claude Juncker.' Less frequently quoted were the rest of Clarke's remarks—that he regarded the quality as a good thing and that he got on well with her.

May's upbringing had impressed on her the values of hard work, sound finance and personal responsibility. No worshipper of free markets, she believed that government could be a force for good. She was prepared to impose a cap on energy process, complaining that the market was dysfunctional (when Ed Miliband had made a similar proposal in 2013, the Conservatives had ridiculed it). She thought that business should serve a higher purpose than just profit making and had wider obligations. Aware of the negative public reaction to some business activities, notably Sir Philip Green's handling of the pensions for his BHS workforce and Mike Ashley's work practices at Sports Direct, she supposedly favoured corporate governance reforms, the recruitment of workers to boards and action on excessive executive pay. Her interpretation of the referendum vote went further than the narrow issue of the EU. She thought it reflected a growing rift between people and democratic institutions, and that the rise of UKIP, the election of President Trump in the US, the EU referendum vote and the populist surges in Greece and Spain were symptoms of this breakdown of trust. As she was to say in her speech to party's spring conference in Cardiff in March 2017: 'The EU referendum result was an instruction to change the way our country works, and the people for whom it works, forever. It was a call to make Britain a country that works for everyone, not just the privileged few.'

Referring to her awareness of the resentment of 'ordinary working families', an aide said May regarded the referendum vote as 'a cry for change'. She was therefore receptive to the arguments of her closest advisers for frankness about what lay ahead and what needed to be done. The country faced long-term demographic and financial challenges—bearing particularly on the NHS, social care, pensions, educational under-achievement and inter-generational inequality—and it was time for the government to address them. However, her view that Brexit was part of a broader political picture was not necessarily one shared by Brexiteers on the right wing of the party or by all of the Cabinet.

These themes came through in almost all of May's public speeches. On her return from Buckingham Palace after becoming Prime Minister, she set out her vision for her premiership, claiming that she wanted to fight against 'the burning injustice that, if you're born poor, you will die on average nine years earlier than others' or 'if you're black, you're treated more harshly by the criminal justice system than if you're white':

If you're a white, working-class boy, you're less likely than anybody else in Britain to go to university.

If you're at a state school, you're less likely to reach the top professions than if you're educated privately.

If you're a woman, you will earn less than a man. If you suffer from mental health problems, there's not enough help to hand.

If you're young, you'll find it harder than ever before to own your own home.

She made an appeal to those who were 'just managing':

> If you're one of those families, if you're just managing, I want to address you directly. I now you're working around the clock, I know you're doing your best, and I know that sometimes life can be a struggle. The government I lead will be driven not by the interests of the privileged few, but by yours.

She ended by saying that when taking decisions, the government would 'think not of the powerful but you'. She was so committed to this speech (known by her team as the 'burning injustices' speech) that she had a framed copy placed in Number 10.

In her party conference speech in October 2016, May warned her audience that 'change has got to come' and 'I want to set our party and our country on the path towards the new centre ground of British politics … built on the values of fairness and opportunity … where everyone plays by the same rules and where every single person—regardless of their background or that of their parents—is given the chance to be all they want to be'. Her speech also contained the claim that 'if you believe you're a citizen of the world, you're a citizen of nowhere'. That sentence was intended as an attack on employers who did not pay their fair share of tax, yet it was soon widely ascribed more negative meanings—as divisive and nationalistic. It was, ironically, in a section of the speech on citizenship, designed to appeal to young, idealistic voters. 'All of this was designed to appeal to those voters—it was about fairness and Conservatism with a heart—but then one bloody line blew the whole thing apart', said one of those involved.

May made a forceful impression with the choices for her first Cabinet—with a high number of dismissals as well as significant changes to the machinery of government.[16] During the leadership contest, she had pointedly cut off attempts by aides to discuss possible appointments if she won. Her sackings of Gove (she deplored his disloyalty to Johnson and interpreted the reactions among MPs as meaning he was 'not appointable', said an adviser) and Osborne were both carried out woundingly. Gove's dismissal earned him the distinction of being the first Cabinet minister ever to formally contest a party leadership race and then be immediately sacked by the victor.[17] Philip Hammond was appointed Chancellor of the Exchequer and Amber Rudd Home Secretary. Both had been on the Remain side in the referendum. They were balanced by the appointments of Boris Johnson as Foreign Secretary, David Davis as Brexit Secretary and Liam Fox as International Trade Secretary. All had been prominent Leave campaigners and had not been members of Cameron's final Cabinet.[18] Davis and Fox were appointed to departments that May, during the leadership contest, had announced she would create. Fox's remit was to prepare post-Brexit trade deals with non-EU countries, while Davis' was the more ambitious one of negotiating the terms of departure with the EU and the future working relationship with it. (An early draft of the appointments had Davis in charge of international trade and Fox as Brexit Secretary). The various EU appointments were a way of insulating herself from charges of backsliding on withdrawal. The Cabinet as a whole still had a pro-Remain majority, with only marginally more Leavers than Cameron's outgoing ministry, but as well as the three Brexit Cabinet positions being held by pro-Leavers, the key European Union Exit and Trade Committee contained every senior Cabinet member who had voted to Leave. The Cabinet was noticeably less upper crust than her predecessor's; ten ministers had been to state schools, compared to five in Cameron's last Cabinet.[19]

Cameron's Number 10 staff had been dominated by alumni, like himself and Osborne, of Oxbridge and the Conservative Research Department. May's team had a broadly similar background, but the tone was different; nobody called them 'the posh boys'. She imported a number of aides who had worked with her at the Home Office. The key ones were her co-chiefs of staff, Nick Timothy and Fiona Hill. Both had been special advisers at the Home Office, where they had acquired a reputation for ferocious loyalty and assertiveness on her behalf in Whitehall. Both had reason to feel resentment at their treatment under Cameron. Hill had been involved in a briefing war with Gove in 2014, which had resulted in her departure from the Home Office, whilst Timothy had been removed from the list of Conservative candidates in December 2014 because of his refusal to campaign in the Rochester & Strood by-election. After the 2015 general election, Timothy left the Home Office and headed the new Schools Network charity to establish free schools, and had written blogs for the ConservativeHome website in favour of pensions reform, more grammar schools and more rigorous scrutiny of foreign takeovers of British firms. May recalled him and he was expected to shape her plans for promoting social justice and an industrial policy. He was an original and forceful thinker on policy and wanted the party to strike out in a new direction. Timothy's luxurious beard reminded some of the former Tory Prime Minister Lord Salisbury and May would joke to Number 10 visitors that Timothy's portrait was on the staircase wall of past Prime Ministers.

Although Timothy was widely regarded as the policy adviser and Hill as the communications adviser, the division was more blurred, and both were involved in policy and briefing. The two advisers were, to quote one Number 10 aide, 'indivisible' ('almost symbiotic and instinctive' said another) and effectively ran Number 10. Collectively known as 'the Chiefs', they guarded access to May and plenty of Cabinet ministers complained that they were too forceful and abrasive.[20] Especially problematic were relations between Number 10 and Number 11. Briefing wars over the Budget in March 2017 saw Hammond castigating May's staff as 'economically illiterate', with those in Number 10 said to have used much stronger industrial language about the Chancellor. The advisers' strong policy views and interventions on the Prime Minister's behalf undoubtedly cost her some goodwill in other departments.

Other key figures were the Political Secretary Stephen Parkinson, also an ex-Home Office aide, and Chris Wilkins, head of strategy and responsible for the grid and speechwriting; he had worked for May when she was party chair and had drafted the 'nasty party' speech in 2002. Joanna Penn was deputy chief of staff, Lizzie Loudon was press secretary and Katie Perrior was brought in as communications director. The last especially clashed routinely with Hill and Timothy, and resigned on the day that the election was called, having been excluded from its discussion entirely.[21]

Blessed with an extremely good memory, the Prime Minister had the ability to read a full statement and repeat it almost verbatim. As one of her team noted: 'She reads it through once, it's an almost photographic memory. And I mean word-for word, not paraphrasing.' But unlike some Prime Ministers, May did not get closely involved in preparing speeches. She would occasionally cut stuff out, but there was never much back and forth. 'At times', said another aide, 'I found it a bit worrying just how easy it was to get the Prime Minister to say things.' In contrast, her immediate predecessors in Number 10 had often engaged in vigorous discussions with aides and some were skilled writers themselves. May trusted her long-term advisers to write for her. Timothy often provided much of the substance, with Wilkins as the wordsmith. Timothy and Hill were her sounding boards and knew her mind better than anybody else, apart perhaps from her husband, Philip. She was not unusual in this; other Prime Ministers had surrounded themselves with advisers they had known for some years and who could be identified as Blairites, Brownites and Cameronites. Yet there were few Mayites, and the new Prime Minister was to deprecate the term. She also listened carefully to the views of David Davis and Jeremy Heywood, the Cabinet Secretary, but she was self-contained. Such was the coincidence of views between May and her advisers that some wondered how much of the policy direction was truly down to her and how much was her being guided by her advisers. Timothy was sometimes called 'May's brain' (which embarrassed him); another aide said: 'Nick just knows the substance of what she wants to say even if she does not articulate it.' There had been a similar coincidence between Hill's interest in modern-day slavery and it becoming something in which May took an interest. As one Number 10 insider put it: 'Fi told her to be interested in modern day slavery, so she's interested in that. But does she really care about it?'

The key players on the policy front, along with Timothy, were Ben Gummer, the Cabinet Office Minister, sometimes referred to as 'the most important Minister you have never heard of', John Godfrey, head of the Number 10 policy unit, and his deputy Will Tanner. All were aware of the need to move beyond the 2015 manifesto. May's plans for creating more grammar schools had not been mentioned and the Chancellor's Budget proposal to increase the self-employed's National Insurance contributions breached the manifesto promise not to do so. The government soon abandoned the Osborne target of achieving a budget surplus by 2020, postponing it to the end of the following Parliament. The Northern Powerhouse (another Osborne project) was broadened into a national industrial strategy, rather than having its focus on Manchester (Osborne's Tatton constituency was in the Greater Manchester region, while Timothy had been brought up in the Midlands).

The Number 10 Policy Unit worked on a number of May's favoured themes: reforming corporate governance, strengthening workers' rights, setting an energy price cap and reforming social care. Although different types of Conservatives—Gummer was more pro-EU, socially liberal and 'greener' than Timothy—the two worked well together. Timothy's priority was to use the levers of government to help the less well-off, even where this inconvenienced traditional Conservative supporters and interests. Gummer had a wide domestic policy remit. He sat on numerous

Cabinet committees, all of the task forces concerned with implementing policy save that on immigration (which was chaired by May), and would be in a good position to liaise with ministers when it came to writing an election manifesto.

Despite May's bold rhetoric, she had made relatively little progress on her reformist policies by the time the general election was called. Her defenders could fairly point out that she had been in office for less than a year and lacked a mandate. Plans to open more grammar schools faced not just predictable Labour and teaching union opposition but also the reservations expressed by some Conservative backbenchers. Plans to have representatives on boards were put up for consultation, but faced objections from business and doubts expressed by Hammond as well as the Business Secretary, Greg Clark. Had May gone ahead with a radical 'social justice' agenda, it is probable that she would have faced divisions in the Cabinet and among MPs. There were Green Papers on subjects like mental health and corporate governance, and reformers could point to the existence of the National Productivity Fund and the Industrial Strategy. There were also one-off interventions like the assurances provided to the Nissan car company in Sunderland promising to protect it against any adverse consequences of withdrawal from the Single Market. However, it did not amount to much of a record for a self-styled 'change' leader.

The exception was Brexit. The Lancaster House speech in January 2017 had set out a clear set of priorities and the party whips had successfully piloted the bill required to trigger Article 50 of the Lisbon Treaty through Parliament. The European Union (Notification of Withdrawal) Bill received Royal Assent on 16 March and on 29 March the Prime Minister wrote to President Donald Tusk of the European Council to inform him of the UK's intention to leave. But even here, the lack of a sizeable Commons majority was a problem. As noted in Chapter 1, the apparent ease with which the withdrawal bill moved through the Commons masked the effort required by the party whips, which had alerted them to problems they would expect with subsequent Brexit legislation. The government had suffered two defeats on the bill in the Lords, which they had managed to overturn when the bill returned to the Commons, but the whips could see how they would suffer many similar defeats on future legislation which they might lack the strength in the Commons to reverse. Moreover, the Article 50 bill, with the legitimacy of the referendum behind it, was supposed to be the easy bit of the process. 'We were well aware of how thin our majority was', one senior whip said, 'even if the media sometimes forgot.'

Contrary to many Treasury-inspired warnings about the economic damage that leaving the EU would cause, the only short-term downside was the fall in the value of the pound against the dollar and the euro. Britain had the fastest rate of growth in the G7 in 2016 and unemployment continued to decline, indeed falling to a 40-year low. But by the first quarter of 2017, the growth figure of 0.3% put Britain at the bottom of the G7. The pound's depreciation fuelled a rise in inflation; by May 2017, it stood at 2.9%. With wage growth at less than 2% and the public sector pay cap still in place at 1%, there was a continuing squeeze on living standards. In 2016, Mark Carney, Governor of the Bank of England, spoke of a 'lost decade', as average real wages had not reached the pre-crisis levels from a decade earlier, something that had not happened since the 1860s. In normal circumstances, the economic background was hardly the basis for a vote-winning election campaign. These, however, did not seem like normal circumstances.

Previous mid-term changes of Conservative Prime Ministers had often helped the party in the subsequent general elections. This happened with the transition from Churchill to Eden in 1955, Eden to Macmillan in 1957, and Thatcher to Major in 1990. All were followed by general election successes. The exception was the replacement of Macmillan by Home in 1963, although even that nearly brought victory in the 1964 general election. Public and private opinion polls showed a steadily narrowing lead for the Conservatives over Labour while David Cameron was leader. By the time he left Number 10, the pollster Ipsos MORI found that his net favourability score was −38 and he had only a fractional lead over Jeremy Corbyn. But the party's fortunes were transformed immediately after May's election as leader. Her ratings were far higher than Cameron's and her lead over Corbyn on who would make the best Prime Minister regularly exceeded 30% in YouGov polls (although less so in some other polls).

From November 2016, Chris Wilkins commissioned monthly tracker polls and regular focus groups on behalf of the Number 10 team. The polls, run by James Johnson, tracked public opinion on issues, voting intentions, and party and May attributes. They showed that voters were positive about May across the board and that the party had a steady lead in voting intentions, if a slightly smaller one than reported in most of the public polls. Shortly before May announced the election date, the party's lead over Labour had grown from 5.3% in November to 14.3%, with the Conservatives up from 36.3% to 40.3% and Labour down from 31% to 26%.

The Number 10 team used its polling data to segment the electorate into five groups. Conservative core support was found in what they called 'Traditional Conservatives': people who were affluent, often retired, had voted Leave in the referendum and were largely found in the South East. Conservative support among this group had grown from 67% in the 2015 election to 75% by February 2017. But the Conservatives were also doing well among two other key groups, covering 45% of the electorate. 'Working Class Strugglers' encompassed C1 and C2 voters, mostly not educated beyond secondary school level, many of whom voted Leave in the EU referendum. They were found mainly in the Conservative-Labour marginal seats in small cities and suburbs. They were the classic just about managing or, in Number 10 discussions, 'ordinary working families'. The other key group were 'Conservative Leaners', who were younger, better-educated, socially liberal and many of whom had voted Remain in the referendum. Compared to the 2015 general election, the party had made gains among the 'Strugglers', whilst slightly losing ground among the 'Leaners', but were comfortably ahead of any other party amongst both. (Conservative support was much weaker amongst the other two groups of 'Working Class Core'—down to precisely 0%—and 'Internationalists', at just 6%).

Number 10's polling revealed that Labour were being squeezed on multiple fronts. Amongst the Working Class Core group, Labour were down five points from 2015, with that support mainly going to UKIP; amongst Working Class Strugglers, Labour were down six points, almost all going to the Conservatives; and amongst Internationalists, it was the Liberal Democrats who benefited, up seven points on 2015. 'There was', one of May's aides noted, 'a real existential crisis for Labour.'[22]

May's high ratings surprised the team. 'We couldn't really believe it', said one. They kept worrying that the honeymoon would end, that some event would cut through, damaging her standing with the public. They were surprised, for example, when she went to the US to meet the newly elected President Trump—and was photographed holding his hand—to discover it made no difference to her poll ratings. They were concerned about the Budget row over the National Insurance hike, and the government's retreat, only similarly to discover that most voters were unaware of, or not bothered by, it; in one focus group they ran, it took 30 minutes before a single participant brought up the subject.

Wilkins used the polling work as part of a project, in which they would promote the Prime Minister as a leader who would provide 'strong leadership in the national interest'. This would address the need for change and at the same time present her as a unifying figure at a time of division. Pointedly, in view of the later general election slogan, there was no mention of 'stability'—and the aim was to demonstrate these qualities rather than use it as a slogan. As one of those involved said, it 'was not something we were ever supposed to say ... You don't say you are strong, you demonstrate it'. Few appreciated the potential significance of the polling not being carried out by CTF, the party's pollster. Wilkins had deliberately commissioned others to conduct the research. He suspected that Lynton Crosby would have claimed ownership of such work and would have a different view of strategy; the subsequent general election campaign proved that he was correct. Tensions surfaced at an away-day stock-taking conference at Chequers on 16 February 2017, which has since become totemic. The meeting was Hill's initiative and people were surprised when she put it in the dairy; some, including Timothy and Wilkins, attended reluctantly.[23] The ostensible purpose of the meeting was to learn the lessons of the 2015 general election. Presentations by Crosby and Stephen Gilbert explained how the party had won. Most of the Number 10 aides believed that May's premiership should be one of radical social and economic reform. The flavour of the arguments can be conveyed in some extracts from Wilkins' paper (written by Johnson):

- Between now and 2020, we have a unique opportunity to move forward and gain ground, fortifying our existing support and gaining votes in new parts of the electorate
- Brexit also provides an opportunity to address a deep discontent with and mistrust in the political class—much of which played a part in the referendum, which was a vote for a fundamental change to how the country works as well as a vote to leave the EU
- as things stand, we are poised to increase our support from the last election, and we have the potential to make gains in areas and with groups we may not have previously considered and who may not have previously considered us
- But it also means clearly demonstrating that we are the 'change candidate', that we are the government and the Party which will change

Britain and continue to do so, and understanding that we must win the values and identity argument. It means focusing on new groups of voters available to us—not so much Middle England as Working—Class England—more resolutely than before.

That vision was bluntly contradicted by Crosby. Crosby had no truck with the idea of politics as brand. One of his Chequers presentation slides contained the phrase: 'it's not about brand'. He also did not think much of Number 10's message. 'No mate, it won't be about change', he told Wilkins. Crosby thought that Brexit had created so much uncertainty that the public was looking for stability. He was dismissing six months of research by the Number 10 team. He was later to dismiss the Number 10 work as 'classic woolly populist bullshit', to which one of those involved would reply that it was at least 'very effective and strongly researched classic woolly populist bullshit'. The exchange was the first indication of a difference between Crosby and the party machine on one side, and Number 10 aides on the other about political strategy and what the May premiership should be about. That was not the only difference to emerge. The Number 10 team, including Timothy and Hill, wanted May to be used sparingly in any campaign; they believed that this was how she had got to Number 10 and was regarded so highly by voters. As one aide said: 'From the outset, we resolved that the PM would not be a Cameron style "commentator in chief" but would only say something when it was well considered and thought through.' The Wilkins/Johnson paper reinforced the point, advising:

> Harness the strength and popularity of the Prime Minister <u>when it is appropriate</u> ... But one of the things people like about her approach is that it is business-like, and that she is quietly getting on with the job, and <u>not always in the public spotlight</u> ... The very strength of the PM's presence is that <u>she is not always present</u>. (Emphasis in original)

Crosby, however, regarded May as the party's main asset and in any case believed that a leader had to be the main communicator of a party's message in modern campaigns. There were two very different political strategies on offer and there was no move to integrate them after Chequers. Those present were thinking that an election was still over three years away and there seemed no urgency.

It had not at that point been decided that Crosby would direct the strategy at a 2020 general election. When somebody informally raised the topic at the close of the Chequers meeting, May was overheard saying 'but I remember the 2005 election and we don't want that' (Cameron too had hated the 2005 campaign, which Crosby had run for Michael Howard, and it is one of the ironies of British politics that despite this, Crosby had become such an influential figure with both subsequent leaders). May had also not been a fan of the campaign that Crosby's company had run for Zac Goldsmith to be London Mayor in 2016 and which had been criticised for playing the race card against Sadiq Khan.[24] She expressed the need to look around to see who might be available to run a campaign in 2020. 'The PM herself was a CTF sceptic', said one aide.[25] At least one of May's aides departed Chequers expecting that they would soon be searching for a strategist with a 2020 election in mind—but again, with an election three years away, there seemed little urgency.

The Number 10 research led into the *Plan for Britain*, launched by the government in March 2017. Written by Wilkins and Timothy, it was an attempt to keep May's broad coalition of voters together. As one of those involved put it: 'Commentators who argue that we were simply chasing the UKIP vote are misguided. Our strategy was always to lock in the Cameron coalition before extending out. We were not oblivious to the challenge we faced with young, metropolitan liberals and developed a strategy ... that specifically responded to that.' The *Plan* set out the government's objectives for the Brexit negotiations, but also echoed the themes May had mentioned outside Number 10 when she became Prime Minister. It covered four themes: a fairer society, a strong economy, a united nation and a global Britain. It was deliberately framed as a plan for Britain and not solely for Brexit—as Wilkins and those working for him believed that focusing solely on Brexit could be divisive and would put off those they described as 'Conservative Leaners'. Those themes were repeated in the Prime Minister's later speeches at the party conference and at Davos, in January 2017, when she spoke of trying to achieve a 'fairer society' where 'success is defined by work and talent, not birth or circumstance', and which would help 'people with everyday costs and bills by acting to ensure consumer markets work in the way they should'.

Much of this was inspired by May's own beliefs, as well as those of Timothy, but it was also informed by the polling. The feature most often mentioned as a reason for not supporting the party, particularly among Conservative Leaners, was that it and May were thought to 'stand up for the richest'. Cameron's modernisation project had battled to overcome this perception and it lay at the heart of a policy agenda which Wilkins and Timothy were trying to develop. Concerns over the cost of living also came through in the party's polling. In March, without an election in mind, Conservative Campaign Headquarters (CCHQ) commissioned two days of deliberative research (conducted by Populus) exploring different policy ideas and understanding voters' priorities. It again showed the cost of living at the top, followed by housing, skills and public sector pay.

The polling that was leaked to the *New Statesman* in April (see above, p. 4) was often said to be Crosby's presentation to the Chequers meeting. It was, however, a separate piece of work conducted by Crosby's company on behalf of the party. It showed that where the Liberal Democrats had well-established candidates, especially former MPs in the South West, the new Conservative MPs had yet to make much of an impact. 'On any number of measures, things like name recognition, they were behind', said one of those involved. This information had been shared with the vulnerable MPs, with the intention of spurring them on to raise their profile, and had made its way into the press.[26] However, Stephen Gilbert, who had been in charge of field operations in the 2015 election, did not share the pessimism and suspected that the party would be better off fighting an election before the Liberal Democrats could regroup.

More of a concern was Scotland and the threat of a second independence referendum. The party's polling showed that many Scots were wary of another referendum and were concerned about the future. Research by Wilkins and Johnson pointed to voters' dissatisfaction with the SNP's record in office and advised against agreeing to a referendum. CTF reportedly suggested the opposite: that Brexit uncertainty had weakened the SNP and that May should call their bluff and agree to a referendum.[27] That advice was disregarded. More influential was the work done by Populus in January and February, this time for the Scottish Conservatives. It was more upbeat than CCHQ about the party's electoral prospects and suggested that the party could gain at worst six seats in Scotland and, if everything went well, as many as 18; it settled on 12 as a midpoint, given the decline in popularity of the SNP and the Scottish First Minister, Nicola Sturgeon. The latter had made a formal request for a second Scottish independence referendum after the Brexit referendum and again at the beginning of 2017. As May and her advisers were considering how to reply, Populus' Andrew Cooper's note about his focus groups for Ruth Davidson, the Scottish Conservative leader, was passed to Number 10. He suggested: 'Most reject her [Sturgeon's] rationale for another referendum because they see her as so single-mindedly obsessed with having a second referendum, she would have argued for one whatever the result of the Brexit referendum.' He added: 'Most people in these focus groups agreed, however, that "Not now", rather than "No", would be an acceptable and fair response from the Prime Minister, which would not provoke a backlash other than among nationalist diehards—provided that it was delivered and explained respectfully.' In, March 'now is not the time' was the Prime Minister's polite but firm message to the First Minister.

In policy terms, May's team wanted a programme for tackling the triple lock of pensions which guaranteed a 2.5% annual increase regardless of what happened to prices or wages, to means test winter fuel payments, and which dealt with the rising costs of social care. They looked for changes to existing policies which were unaffordable in the long run as well as exacerbating inter-generational inequality. May had often hinted in public interviews and in discussions with aides that the government was working on plans for a social care package and referred to short-, medium- and long-term plans. Ministers were aware of the growing concern about inter-generational inequity, particularly when it came to owning assets, notably housing. Some looked back with regret to Osborne's manifesto pledge to protect many homeowners against inheritance tax. 'That was irresponsible', said one Cabinet minister. 'People think care is free.' The social care package was developed in the Policy Unit in cooperation with the Cabinet Office and Jeremy Hunt, the Health Secretary. May asked the Unit for policy options and in the autumn a working group was set up that reported to John Godfrey. He presented May with a paper setting out the problems facing the sector—financial, inter-generational fairness and demographic, and how they impacted on local government finances and hospitals—and how they would increase in 30 years' time. The problem was to strike a balance between the demands on the state (taxpayers) and asset holders (homeowners). The Cabinet Social Reform Committee discussing the policy accepted that owners of expensive homes (often Tory voters in the South East) should not have their assets shielded while hard-pressed people (often younger and/or of working age) without such assets were paying taxes to fund the care and protect the inheritance of the former.

The proposals by Sir Andrew Dilnot's Commission on Funding of Care and Support made in 2011 had recommended a cap of £35,000 for the lifetime costs for care and an insurance scheme to protect against escalating bills. Before the 2015 general election, the party had suggested a cap of £72,000, to come into effect by 2020. May, however, objected strongly to a cap and the group settled on individuals using their assets to pay for all their domiciliary and residential care. A Cabinet minister said: 'Theresa disagreed fundamentally with the idea of a cap, asking why should poor taxpayers in the North pay, while people in the South were sitting on their huge housing capital?' But there would be sweeteners in the package; anyone seeking residential care or care at home would not be forced to leave their homes during their and their spouse's lifetimes, and the figure of £23,000 which a person in care could retain would be increased to a figure yet to be determined, the so-called 'floor'. The Chancellor made £2 billion available in his March Budget as an interim measure. The policy group was considering schemes to protect against excess costs and providing protection against such early-onset conditions as motor neurone disease and Alzheimer's, where the costs could run into hundreds of thousands. Neither was finalised by the time May called an election.

Little noted during the early election preparations was the reluctance, or lack of enthusiasm, of the most senior and experienced campaign figures to take up arms again in 2017. Gilbert was willing to help, but saw his role initially as an interim one, helping to assemble a team to run the campaign. He had developed a new career as a consultant and was a working peer. He had found the EU referendum gruelling and regarded it as his last main involvement in a campaign. Crosby also wanted to step back, had found his heavy commitment running the 2015 campaign wearying and had told at least one colleague at the time that it would be his last one. May did not doubt Crosby's skills as a campaign director—running a campaign, building a team and instilling discipline—but it is not clear that she or her team expected him to decide the strategy. The Number 10 aides remained unapologetic about their work and strategy, pointing to the opinion polls, by-elections and May's ratings as proof that it was working. 'Why would you change?', said one. But just before May went into the Cabinet on 18 April to tell colleagues of the election date, Hill, Timothy and Wilkins met and quickly agreed that she would have to tell the Cabinet that Crosby would be involved. They were aware that most of the Cabinet expected Crosby to be involved and given the shortage of time, they needed to appoint an experienced team quickly. One senior figure, not a May aide, said: 'She appointed Lynton out of weakness.' 'Nothing more was said', said another, aware of what kind of campaign would follow. May as the candidate of stability had trumped May as the candidate of change almost by default.

CCHQ in the spring of 2017 was hardly on a war footing, although it was preparing for the local and mayoral elections. Staff had accepted the many assurances from Number 10 that there would not be a general election until 2020. Key personnel had moved on since the 2015 victory. Patrick McLoughlin, unlike his predecessor as chairman, Lord Feldman, had a constituency to manage as well as overseeing CCHQ. Since the general election, Stephen Gilbert had been ennobled and replaced as Director of Organisation by Darren Mott, his former deputy. Crosby, Mark Textor, the pollster, and Jim Messina, the US data analyst, all members of the successful 2015 election team, were on retainers to help the party, but all were abroad.

By contrast, in 2015 Crosby had been in charge of preparations for 18 months before the campaign began and had had regular one-to-one meetings with Cameron, and Textor had run a major polling programme for several months. The party had also hammered home its narrative of the 'Long-Term Economic Plan' for target voters over several months. In 2017, there was no prepared narrative. There is little doubt that CCHQ was ill-prepared for an election. One consultant who kept in touch with CCHQ over the months since the 2015 election said that on his return, he 'found it pretty lethargic and certainly not battle-ready'.

Perhaps the lack of preparations would not matter, although only the rigours of an election campaign would demonstrate that. The broader political scene seemed benign. Few governments had gone to the polls with such favourable electoral prospects. The threat posed by UKIP in 2015 had receded, and Labour were divided and led by a leader whose standing in the polls was abysmal. Just before the election was called, Number 10 conducted an analysis of issues that might damage the party, testing their salience amongst the public. In the top-left quadrant of the table were the issues that might damage the party *and* which people cared about: it was blank.

NOTES

1. See A. Seldon and P. Snowdon, *Cameron at 10.* William Collins, 2015, pp. 529–30.
2. Ibid., p. 226.
3. Tim Shipman, *All Out War.* William Collins, 2016, p. 204.
4. Craig Oliver, *Unleashing Demons.* Hodder & Stoughton, 2016, pp. 200–1.

5. Discussing May's apparently unenthusiastic support, Oliver commented at the time: 'It's making life uncomfortable for us and many feel she owes DC more, but in purely selfish terms, this positions her best.' Ibid., pp. 125–26.
6. Ibid., p. 10.
7. Luke Chambers, 'Theresa May Leads Boris Johnson amongst General Public', *YouGov*, 27 June 2016, https://yougov.co.uk/news/2016/06/27/theresa-may-leads-boris-johnson-amongst-general-pu.
8. Freddie Sayers, 'Theresa May Storms Ahead of Boris among Tory Party Membership', *YouGov*, 29 June 2016, https://yougov.co.uk/news/2016/06/29/theresa-may-storms-ahead-boris-among-tory-party-me.
9. The phrase was coined by her aide, Nick Timothy, in a discussion with May right at the beginning of the leadership election; it then took on a life of its own. See Tim Shipman, *Fall Out*. William Collins, 2017, p. 3.
10. The YouGov polling (above, note 8) had tested various pairs of candidates in hypothetical run-offs, but not May versus Leadsom.
11. The fact that May and Leadsom topped the poll meant that in every Conservative leadership contest to feature a woman, no man has (yet) out-polled a woman. Conversely, in every Labour leadership contest to feature a woman, no woman has (yet) outpolled a man.
12. Although Leadsom rejected this interpretation of her words, the transcript did not leave much room for doubt. She said she wanted to approach the issue 'really carefully' and did not want it to become a case of '"Andrea's got children, Theresa hasn't"—do you know what I mean? Because I think that would be really horrible'. But she also said that being a mother 'means you have a very real stake in the future of our country. A tangible stake', and implied that she better understood how policies concerned people as a result: 'When you are thinking about the issues that other people have, you worry about your kids' exam results, what direction their careers are taking, what we are going to eat on Sunday.'
13. In 2003 Michael Howard had been elected unopposed by MPs to succeed Iain Duncan Smith.
14. See Rosa Prince, *Theresa May: The Enigmatic Prime Minister*. Biteback, 2017.
15. Shipman, *Fall Out*, p. xxiv.
16. See Nicholas Allen, 'Brexit, Butchery and Boris: Theresa May and Her First Cabinet', *Parliamentary Affairs*, 70 (2017): 633–44.
17. Ibid., p. 641.
18. Although Cameron had given Johnson the right to attend political Cabinets from May 2015 onwards.
19. Shipman, *All Out War*, p. 575.
20. The behaviour and attitudes of Hill and Timothy are covered in much more detail in Shipman, *Fall Out*, esp. Chapters 10 and 11; and Tim Ross and Tom McTague, *Betting the House*. Biteback, 2017, Chapter 2.

21. After the general election, she wrote a number of articles and was quoted in books complaining at length about the role of Timothy and Hill. See, for example, 'I was Staggered by Their Arrogance', *The Times*, 10 June 2017.

22. See also Jonathan Mellon, Geoffrey Evans, Edward Fieldhouse, Jane Green and Christopher Prosser, 'Brexit or Corbyn? Campaign and Inter-election Vote Switching in the 2017 UK General Election', 17 November 2017, https://ssrn.com/abstract=3073203.

23. The meeting comprised mostly the Number 10 team (in addition to the Prime Minister, there was Hill, Timothy, Penn, Parkinson and Political Director Alex Dawson). They were joined by Mark Fullbrook, Crosby's business partner, and the party chairman Sir Patrick McLoughlin.

24. As detailed in Dave Hill, *Zac versus Sadiq: The Fight to Become London Mayor*. Double Q Books, 2016.

25. Adding that the decision to have another pollster doing research in Number 10 might itself 'be read as a rejection of Lyntonism'.

26. There was an obvious paradox in having previously told many new MPs they were on weak ground and then expecting them to be upbeat about an early election—summed up by one of those involved as: 'You've got shit visibility, and no one knows who the fuck you are, but you'll be fine.'

27. 'Sir Lynton Crosby Told Prime Minister to Call SNP's Bluff on Independence Referendum 2', *The Times*, 26 June 2016.

CHAPTER 4

From Miliband to Corbyn: Labour

There was no shortage of election inquests, both official and unofficial, into Labour's defeat in the 2015 general election. They included the Fabian Society's *The Mountain to Climb*, the party's official Beckett report in January 2016, an independent inquiry, *Labour's Future*, chaired by Labour MP Jon Cruddas, and an internal and private report, '2015: What Happened?' All acknowledged the need for the party to reach out to former Labour voters, but also to win over some Conservative and UKIP voters if it was to have any chance of gaining the seats it needed to win a majority next time.

A common theme of the analyses was that the party had lacked credible leadership under Ed Miliband in 2015 and voters did not trust it to manage the economy. There was little evidence to support Miliband's belief that the financial crash of 2008 had moved public opinion to the left, notably on welfare and immigration and particularly among the white working class. The larger context was also not favourable. Numbers of trade union members, working-class voters and public-sector employees, the staples of Labour's core vote, were all in decline. The only demographic groups in which Labour clearly led were the under-29s (and under half of them bothered to vote) and ethnic minorities. And while globalisation was increasing inequality, it was also undermining the capacity of national governments to act in order to offset these trends. Not one of these reports or analyses recommended that Labour should shift dramatically to the left, elect as leader one of its most rebellious backbench MPs—

© The Author(s) 2018
P. Cowley, D. Kavanagh, *The British General Election of 2017*,
https://doi.org/10.1007/978-3-319-95936-8_4

one who had never held a frontbench position—and embark on a two-year civil war.

The outcome of the election to choose a new leader shaped the history of the party for the next two years and beyond. Following the Collins Review (2014) of the party's relationship with the trade unions, the election took place under a new system. No longer would it be decided by an electoral college with equal thirds for the MPs and MEPs, affiliated organisations, and members of local constituency parties. It would now operate a one-member, one-vote system, with a new category of voter, 'registered supporters', those who were supporters but not members of the party. The party's interim leader Harriet Harman made decisions that, accidentally, made it easier for an outsider to do well in a leadership contest. She wanted as many people as possible to vote in the election, pressed for a lower threshold fee for registered supporters and supported a longer campaign than many in the Parliamentary Labour Party (PLP) and the candidates wanted.

The first formally to enter the race was Liz Kendall, a forthright Blairite from the 2010 intake. She was joined by Andy Burnham and Yvette Cooper, both former Cabinet ministers and the early frontrunners. On 15 June, only minutes before the closing date for entries, Jeremy Corbyn finally attracted the 35 nominations from MPs required to enter the race.

Corbyn had been MP for Islington North for 32 years and a serial rebel, having defied the party whip on 617 occasions—and was the most rebellious of all Labour MPs during the Blair and Brown years. His rebellions were so frequent that a wit described them as almost a part of the constitution. He was described by one of his aides as 'a political activist who happens to be an MP', one who was happier out of the office or Parliament and campaigning. He managed to be nominated only because he was 'lent' nominations by some MPs who had no intention of voting for him as leader, but agreed that a voice from the left should be represented—some doing so as a result of considerable pressure from party members. Corbyn received 36 nominations in the end because Andrew Smith and Gordon Marsden nominated him simultaneously, neither wanting to be the one to push him over the line. Others, including Tom Watson, had agreed to be the thirty-fifth if they were needed.

Margaret Beckett, a former deputy leader, later called herself 'a moron' for nominating Corbyn and later other MPs expressed remorse.[1] His candidacy was not taken seriously within or outside the party. The bookmakers priced his chances at 100-1 and higher. 'I don't know why everyone is panicking', said one of those who nominated him the day after he made the list, 'he isn't going to win.'

Corbyn had never expected to be a candidate, only agreeing to stand when others on the left, including Jon Trickett and Ian Lavery, had been approached and refused. John McDonnell, a fellow serial rebel, was the nominal leader of the Labour left and his attempts to enter leadership contests in 2007 and 2010 had failed because he could not reach the required number of nominations from fellow MPs and MEPs. Initially, McDonnell seemed reluctant to back anybody from the Campaign Group of left-wing Labour MPs to enter the contest, but his hand was forced by the newer members and he backed Corbyn's nomination, although he was not optimistic that Corbyn would get on the ballot. Diane Abbott similarly had been 'lent' nominations to enter the contest in 2010, but finished last on the first ballot.[2] Corbyn was an accidental candidate; it was merely his turn.

A symbolic moment in the leadership contest came when the Shadow Cabinet decided its stance on the government's Welfare Reform and Work Bill. The bill included a household benefit cap and restricted benefits and tax credits for people with three or more children. Harman believed that Labour could not simply oppose the bill as this would cede the ground on economic credibility straight after an election, as she felt they had done in 2010; the frontbench therefore agreed to table a reasoned amendment which set out its objections to the bill. The amendment was defeated and most of the parliamentary party, including the Shadow Cabinet, then abstained on the second reading itself. The Corbyn campaign seized on the vote as an example of how Labour had become indistinguishable from the Conservatives, and 48 Labour MPs, including Corbyn, voted against it on the second reading. Burnham, Cooper and Kendall were torn between appealing to the membership but not wanting to appear 'soft' on welfare, and abstained on the second reading. The idea that Labour had not voted against the bill—despite the reasoned amendment which would have similarly blocked the bill—became one of the great creation myths of the Corbyn leadership, and the vote is frequently seen as key to his victory.[3] Even if this is to place too much significance on one parliamentary vote, one of Corbyn's closest aides described Harman's decision as 'idiotic' and said that it was the moment that their support on social media went stratospheric.

Corbyn's initial team of volunteers, including Jon Lansman, Simon Fletcher and Anneliese Midgley, started from scratch. The first had been an ally of Tony Benn in the 1980s and active in the Campaign for Labour Democracy, and the last two had worked in Ken Livingstone's team when he was Mayor of London. Gavin Sibthorpe organised events and Kat Fletcher organised volunteers and liaised with supporters to gain local party nominations. Andrew Fisher also joined and wrote policy papers, some of which would figure in the party's general election manifesto nearly two years later. One said 'we did not expect to win but we wanted to run a proper campaign, as if we were trying to win', adding 'we wanted to get across our politics and have fun'. For much of August, McDonnell was sailing with his family on the Norfolk Broads, although he would Skype into initial meetings. But when Corbyn's meetings and rallies started to attract large and enthusiastic crowds, particularly of students and the young, he was taken more seriously. The rallies became the centrepiece of the campaign. The Corbyn team were also the first to exploit the potential of the registered supporters, and invested time and resources in making sure they signed people up; a button placed on Corbyn's campaign website allowed users to click through direct to the £3 Labour online registration form. Soon there were over 550,000 members eligible to vote either as members or supporters, and the membership exceeded that of all the other UK parties combined and was the largest in Western Europe.

Many were drawn by Corbyn's brand of left-wing politics, others to the man himself. Often tieless and casually dressed, devoted to his allotment, with a modest lifestyle and seemingly averse to spin, he impressed supporters with his authenticity. They queued to have selfies taken with him and wanted to touch him. Apart from Boris Johnson, he was the only British politician to have something like a rock star quality; one of his aides described the reaction as akin to that which had greeted the Beatles. The younger party members often bypassed the national press (mainstream media, or MSM, as they derogatorily called it), most of which ridiculed and/or attacked Corbyn. One poll found that 60% of the new members used social media as their main source for news, keeping in touch with each other and for rebutting what they saw as the anti-Corbyn coverage in the mass media, particularly in the press.[4]

Corbyn's CV was well known and, for many members, if not most of his parliamentary colleagues, it was to his credit. Aged 66, he had been a prominent activist in various protest groups—for example, Anti-Apartheid, Stop the War and CND—opposed NATO and much American foreign policy, and regularly voting against counterterrorism legislation. The Conservative Research Department had compiled a large file on his links with groups associated with terrorism and with various authoritarian regimes. He had organised visits to Westminster for Sinn Féin and welcomed talks with Hezbollah and Hamas, refusing to label the latter as a terrorist group. He was a member of the Palestine Solidarity Group and the Cuba Solidarity Campaign, and supported the authoritarian rule of Presidents Chavez and Maduro in Venezuela. Labour MPs feared that his record would expose him to right-wing press attacks as being 'soft' on terror and an 'extremist', charges eagerly taken up by sections of the press. His defenders pointed out that he had only engaged in dialogue with Sinn Féin (more than a decade ago) and Hezbollah, and expressed sympathy for the ideas of a united Ireland and an independent Palestine, but not their methods.

Like his close friends and allies on the left of the party like Abbott and McDonnell, much of Corbyn's career as an MP had been spent in the wilderness. He did not approve of much of what New Labour did and looked back to the 1945 Labour government for inspiration. He floated the idea of reviving the famous Clause IV of the party's 1918 constitution, promising widespread public ownership. When Blair overturned it in 1995, it was seen as a symbolic break with old Labour. Corbyn's message was distinctive. He claimed that austerity was not an economic necessity but a political choice and said that if he were to become its leader, Labour would be an anti-austerity party. He would restore democracy in the party and end 'presidential' politics where the policies were handed down from the leader. 'We lose our way when we don't listen to our people, our communities and instead listen to the counsel of the Westminster commentariat' and, he added, 'the press barons and the papers owned by "tax-dodging billionaires"'.[5] It was a bold appeal beyond the PLP and to sympathisers who had not joined or had left the party during the New Labour years.

The other leadership candidates looked colourless in comparison. They were criticised as members of a party establishment. Even before Corbyn entered the contest, there was a marked lack of enthusiasm for them. He stood apart and presented himself—and was seen—as an outsider, offering radical change. At the first BBC leadership debate when the candidates were asked about the importance of clearing the deficit, Corbyn's answer was that his priority was jobs, education and housing; he was met with loud applause. His rivals found he was very difficult to debate against. As one of those involved in the debate preparation noted: 'Most serious politicians try to give answers to questions that indicate they've understood the details of a policy and thought about its costs. Jeremy just goes straight to: do you want to live in a country that doesn't do some nice thing? It instantly makes you the baddie.' His speeches contained what Mark Bennister et al. called 'the rhetoric of hope and ideals, not of governing, compromise and shared solutions'.[6] He announced a series of eye-catching policies, including scrapping tuition fees, expanding free childcare and establishing a National Education Service.

Whether fair or not, the other candidates were being held responsible for the disappointments and alleged 'betrayals' of the Blair, Brown and Miliband years. One MP explained the outcome as 'in effect an accident waiting to happen', a comment on their own failings as gatekeepers or selectors of who the candidates would be. That the writing was on the wall was confirmed on 10 August when a YouGov/*The Times* poll reported that with over 50% of first preference votes, Corbyn was heading for victory on the first ballot. By the time he was elected leader on 12 September, with 59.5% of the vote on the first ballot and winning clearly among all categories of voters, including over 80% of registered supporters, the result was no surprise. As he walked from the room where he had been told the result to prepare for its announcement, he turned to McDonnell, put his arm around him and said: 'It's bigger even than we thought it would be, John. Think what we can do.' The bookmakers had by then narrowed his odds to 1-16, an extraordinary turnaround. It was clear that his campaign had the most momentum and appealed to the members, and he and it became a media story. By the end, his aides reckoned he had addressed over 50,000 people at his rallies.

It did not matter that Corbyn had never held a ministerial or shadow ministerial post. In no way had he been groomed or sponsored for any leadership role, let alone the leadership of the party. A vote for Corbyn was at least an implied criticism of the PLP, given that the new leader was backed by only a handful of Labour MPs. The traditionally valued attributes of leadership candidates include an ability to unite the party and win a general election, yet Corbyn's supporters had very different motivations. Only 5% of party supporters reckoned he would unite the party or stood the best chance of winning the 2020 election, but by large majorities they thought he was a break from New Labour and had the best policies for Britain.[7] Not many, including most Labour MPs and many in the press, thought that this novel situation would play out well.

If Corbyn's election was a shock to most of the PLP, the way he had mobilised thousands of online activists to his cause came as another and was a portent of a different style of political campaigning. Labour MPs had been bombarded with activists' tweets and Facebook messages urging them to support the inclusion of a left-winger on the ballot. Corbyn's style of campaigning and success in firing the enthusiasm of the young resembled the rise of the leftist 'movement' politics of Syriza in Greece, Podemos in Spain and Bernie Sanders in the US, which were challenging established centre-left parties. Corbyn's supporters raised money, volunteered to work at phone banks, used social media to keep in touch and communicate, and attended his rallies and meetings; #JezWeCan copied Obama's successful 'Yes We Can' in the 2008 presidential election. The other candidates had more money and more endorsements from MPs and senior party figures. But they could not compete with the numbers and commitment prompted by Corbyn's new politics.[8] His distaste for the media, most of which had ridiculed his candidacy, was seen in his decision to decline an invitation to appear on TV with Andrew Marr the day after he was elected; instead, he went to a pre-arranged mental health event in his Islington constituency.

The *Financial Times* called Corbyn Britain's 'first digital party leader' as his team disrupted the traditional methods of campaigning. Yet Corbyn had gained more local party nominations than any other candidate and also had strong support among trade union activists. He gained the endorsement of nine trade unions (including the powerful Unite and Unison), while Burnham had the backing of just three and Cooper two. One of his allies with strong union links said: 'The unions have felt for many years the party has moved away from us and been taken for granted. Not just Blair, the same with Brown.' Len McCluskey, the General Secretary of the Unite union, the party's largest financial backer, had been supporting Burnham as the least-worst option; according to a close associate, he remained 'in a state of suspended animation' until Corbyn entered the ballot; the source added that if Kendall had been elected, 'Unite might have split from the party'.

Corbyn's team—known as LOTO, the acronym formally standing for the Leader of the Opposition, but in practice almost always referring to his staff—had no experience of running a political party. Few of them had ever been at the heart of the PLP and its various committees or ways of working. The team now had to meet deadlines, attend meetings, organise media briefings and visits for the leader, and prepare him for interviews, the Shadow Cabinet and Prime Minister's Questions (PMQs). At the outset, he had only a handful of staff and they were overwhelmed by the pressure of work. At times, the operation was 'chaotic', as one of them admitted. One of Corbyn's team complained that the leader's office operated 'like a hippy commune', with meetings randomly occurring just because the leader was interested in a topic, but with no broader sense of strategy or priorities. As one of those inside many of the early meetings noted: 'They are not used to operating at this level. So a lot of the problem is just caused by incompetence and inexperience. But they also don't understand their place in the constitution. He is Leader of Her Majesty's Opposition. You want to say to them sometimes, this is the Shadow Cabinet, not the Islington branch of Stop the War.' Some of the early appointments—often inherited from the team that had won the leadership election—were soon to leave, frequently disenchanted.[9]

It did not help that relations were also often fractious with the experienced members of headquarters staff—based at Southside on Victoria Street—and that Corbyn personally and politically was opposed by most of his Shadow Cabinet and the PLP. Much of the Corbyn team's time and energy was taken up negotiating compromises between them and other sections of the party. The atmosphere in meetings was often unpleasant, leaks were frequent and there was little support, let alone deference, for Corbyn as the legitimately elected leader of the party.

In forming his Shadow Cabinet, Corbyn's first and crucial decision was to appoint McDonnell, his close ally and friend, as Shadow Chancellor. Although the two agreed on policies and strategy, and had been long-standing members of the Campaign Group, they were different personalities. Corbyn was less confrontational, while McDonnell was a more divisive and ideological figure. If Corbyn had previously been humoured in the PLP, McDonnell was widely disliked. Some possible Shadow Cabinet recruits had sought assurances in advance that McDonnell would not hold this key economic post, and the announcement of the appointment was held back. Rosie Winterton, the chief whip, played a crucial role in retaining the services of experienced figures; she used the early acceptance of Hilary Benn, as Shadow Foreign Secretary, and Andy Burnham, with the Home Office brief, to persuade others who had served with Miliband to join. Cooper and Kendall refused and several others signalled in advance that they would not join. Given the combined number of refuseniks, newly elected MPs and outright opponents, Corbyn's room for making appointments was limited. With only a score of his MPs having voted for him as leader, Corbyn's team felt like a besieged minority in the PLP (their own analysis listed just 20 members of the PLP who could be described as 'core' supporters).[10] The reshuffle was chaotic; as Winterton was phoning with offers to MPs, her conversations could be overheard by journalists parked outside her office. Defence proved difficult to fill as possible appointees were quizzed about their views on Trident (Corbyn was opposed) and NATO (Corbyn was critical). There were to be three more reshuffles in the next 18 months and by the end of the parliament, there had been four shadow defence secretaries. Corbyn's initial Shadow Cabinet contained just four who could be described as 'Corbynite' in their politics, and he relied on soft left MPs to fill most of the posts. His aides in retrospect considered the inclusion of so many who opposed his politics to have been a mistake and one which had encouraged divisions. Although more than half of the initial shadow team were women, none shadowed any of the traditionally great offices of state. That was to change with the promotions of Diane Abbott to Shadow Home Secretary and Emily Thornberry as Shadow Foreign Secretary in June 2016.

Corbyn's relationship with Benn, in particular, was always delicate; the latter was pro-NATO, pro-Trident and pro-EU, and the tensions in the Shadow Cabinet were exposed in the Commons as early as November 2015. Corbyn opposed the government's plans to extend RAF bombing against ISIS in Syria, but Benn was in favour. Corbyn claimed that the conditions for British action which had been agreed by party conference two months earlier gave the party room to oppose the plans; Benn responded by saying that the conditions had been met and the party should therefore support action. The Shadow Cabinet meeting soon got out of hand because Corbyn's line was leaked on social media as the discussion was only just beginning, long before anything had been agreed. Trying to remove the decision from the meeting, McDonnell's suggestion that Benn and Corbyn agree a position privately was not accepted. Although the Shadow Cabinet did not vote as a majority against Corbyn's view, the episode illustrated how limited his authority was in the Shadow Cabinet and he had to settle for a free vote. Corbyn opened the debate in the Commons for Labour and Benn closed, articulating different positions. Benn's support for intervention was backed by a third of the PLP and when many Labour MPs applauded his passionate speech, Corbyn sat beside him showing no emotion. Yet whilst Benn spoke for many Labour MPs on this issue, more voted with the party leader.

Other early pratfalls were caused by the novelty of the position and the inexperience of Corbyn's team—such as when he did not sing the national anthem at a Battle of Britain memorial shortly after his election. For his defenders, this was an understandable position (why should an atheist republican sing a song about a god saving a queen?) without appreciating the wider political reality (that whatever the words, it was the national anthem)—and some within his team worried at the time that such unforced errors could irreparably damage his leadership. He also struggled at times with the message discipline required of a frontline politician. In November 2015, after terrorist attacks in Paris killed 130 people, he became embroiled in a row over whether he would support the police in shooting-to-kill in Britain. Behind the scenes, the Shadow Cabinet agreed a position that they could all hold to. 'It wasn't very good', said one of those involved, 'but it was something everyone could agree.' The Labour leader then gave an interview to the BBC's Laura Kuenssberg in which he departed from the line, only to then go off script again later at the meeting of the PLP. 'We'd spent hours agreeing the line', complained one of those involved, 'and he couldn't even hold it for ten minutes ... McDonnell, he can lie for the party for weeks, no problem, but Jeremy has never had to have that discipline.'

Gradually, however, Corbyn began to build his team—and settled into the role. Key figures included his head of strategy and communications, Seumas Milne, initially on leave from *The Guardian*, office manager and from June 2016 chief of staff Karie Murphy, political secretary Katy Clark, a Scottish MP until she lost her seat in 2015, and speechwriter and policy adviser Andrew Fisher, the policy director of the Public and Commercial Services Union. The appointments were frequently controversial. Fisher, for example, had been in trouble for describing Ed Miliband's Shadow Cabinet as 'the most abject collection of absolute shite', as well as being less than complimentary about Tony Blair, Alastair Campbell and Jack Straw—and appearing to back the Class War candidate in Croydon South at the 2015 election. When Milne was introduced to the Shadow Cabinet, Corbyn said: 'You've all read the things Seumas has written in *The Guardian*.' One Shadow Cabinet member thought to himself: 'I've tried very hard not to.'[11]

The cerebral Milne provided much of the strategic and tactical thinking and helped with speeches. Fisher was probably the closest to the leader and was trusted to express Corbyn's ideas in speeches. Murphy had been an aide to the Labour MP Grahame Morris and had helped to organise the left in the Campaign Group and left-wing trade union activists. She brooked no opposition in her determination to advance Corbyn's agenda within the party. The three held a political planning meeting each Monday for Corbyn's schedule and tactics for the week ahead; in cases of disagreement between them, the majority view prevailed. The plans frequently involved working around the headquarters staff and the more recalcitrant members of the Shadow Cabinet and the PLP. Although there were often arguments and rivalry within Corbyn's team, they shared with him a commitment to making Labour into a more left-wing party and empowering the membership. Few would disagree with the claim of a colleague that: 'For them the political agenda overrides everything.'

Some of the staff at the party's Southside headquarters regarded LOTO as a cabal, politically naïve when it came to understanding the electoral mood or electoral realities. They could point to depressing polling and election results; they thought that Corbyn was not up to the job and was leading the party to a heavy electoral defeat. At times, communications between the two sides were fitful, as the staff only found out about LOTO initiatives at the last moment. LOTO in turn would complain of important figures at Southside (some called it 'Darkside') being 'obstructive and categorically defiant'. There were frequently 'epic rows'. The source also complained that the staff, some whom had been first appointed when Blair was leader, were wedded to old methods of management and campaigning, seemingly unwilling to recognise Corbyn's authority and unsympathetic to his political agenda. The dysfunctional relations between the two sides were to be exposed for all to see in the EU referendum.[12]

One Corbyn aide was forthright about the headquarters staff and what LOTO were doing about it: 'I decided to work round them. We built links with outriders like *The Canary*, *Skwawkbox* and Momentum, providing scripts for bloggers, and platforms for friendly journalists and academics who could not publish stuff in right-wing papers. Also we had Jeremy going out every Thursday and Friday to rallies and meetings. We were building a different structure to Southside.'

Many Labour MPs regarded—and some feared—McDonnell as the de facto leader. Corbyn looked to him for advice on strategy and tactics, and in Shadow Cabinet meetings McDonnell's voice, in support of Corbyn, was often decisive. Where Corbyn at times appeared relaxed about insisting on a policy line and disliked confrontation, McDonnell would insist on collective responsibility. Shadow ministers rarely had one-to-one meetings with Corbyn to discuss their policy briefs. 'You know how he works', said one Corbynite shadow minister. 'He'd much rather chew the fat with you and have a cup of tea rather than tell you what you should be doing.' At some of his meetings with shadow ministers, McDonnell would arrive unannounced, perhaps in case Corbyn did not hold a line. His was not always a calming presence.

Another potentially key figure in the party was Tom Watson, who, when easily elected as Deputy Leader in 2015, could claim his own mandate from members. He had good contacts with the unions and had once shared a flat with Len McCluskey prior to the two falling out. A regular visitor to constituencies, he busied himself with efforts to revive the party's grassroots and improve local parties' campaign techniques. His plans to provide bursaries for financially hard-pressed Labour candidates were approved by the NEC, but were not implemented in time for the general election.

Yet Corbyn and all that followed from his election would hardly have been possible without the expansion and drive of the membership which joined from 2015. They became his Praetorian Guard defending him against attempts by the PLP to rein him in or oust him. He was more at ease in the packed rallies of his supporters, buoyed by being among them. Some three-quarters of members were middle class, over half were university graduates, and the average age was 51. But the newer members were decidedly more socially liberal, more attracted by the new leadership and more likely to feel that the leadership respected ordinary members. Some of the post-May 2015 recruits were returnees whose party membership had lapsed during the New Labour years. They supported many of Corbyn's causes; they were pro-immigration, pro-redistribution, pro-environmental safeguards (many had voted Green in the 2015 general election) and hostile to big business, but, unlike the leader, they strongly supported Britain's membership of the EU. They also strongly backed his call for the members to have a greater say in making party policy. They took seriously the party's formal commitment to inner party democracy, which, they claimed, had withered. They did not seem to attend constituency party meetings or canvass, but were likely to attend rallies and sign petitions, and were busier on social media than they were on the doorstep. They appeared at the time to be 'clicktivists'.[13]

Some of the activists gravitated to a new group, Momentum, a network of some 20,000 Corbyn supporters, strong among students and in inner and university cities, and operating separately from local constituency parties. It was founded soon after his election by core members of Corbyn's team and was run by Jon Lansman. Its leaders seized on the surge in membership when Corbyn stood for the leadership. Not expecting him to win the leadership, the original plan had been to utilise the campaign's database of supporters and new members, and encourage grassroots activity to campaign for a new political direction for the party.

Plenty of MPs suspected that Momentum's activities were often more directed at changing the party and its rules (for example, making it easier for local parties to deselect MPs and lower the number of MP nominees a candidate required to stand in a leadership election) than winning over voters and some felt under threat by its activities. Some Momentum members did join other party activists to demand internal party reforms, including mandatory reselection, more local representatives on the National Executive Committee (NEC) and greater conference control over party policy.[14] In this respect, it was redolent of the Bennite surge in the party during the early 1980s and, indeed, some figures (like Lansman) from that campaign were prominent again. In December 2015, Tom Watson called it 'a rabble'. Yet for all the talk of pressure on non-Corbynite MPs, perhaps only in a handful of cases (such as Hove, Wallasey, Leeds Central and Walthamstow) did the sitting MP face a significant challenge from local left-wing activists. It eventually established formal membership rules and structures, and members were required to support the aims and values of the Labour Party (and from January 2017 were required to be members of the party). But suspicion remained—a senior PLP figure acknowledged the constructive work of some Momentum activists, but attacked those he called the 'vanguardists': 'These bastards have been in the Labour Party for five minutes after trying to wipe us off the face of the earth in the 80s and now they're telling us to be loyal.'

The party leadership was also plagued with complaints about anti-Semitism. The Bradford West MP Naz Shah, a PPS for McDonnell, apologised for calling for Israel to be relocated to the US on Facebook. But in a radio interview, Ken Livingstone, the former Mayor of London and co-convenor of the party's defence policy review, defended her and reignited the issue with his claim that Hitler had once supported Zionism. He was suspended in April 2016 for two years by the party's National Constitutional Committee for bringing the party into disrepute, To Corbyn's defenders and supporters, these were trumped-up issues designed to harm the leader. To his critics, they were, at best, one of his blind spots or, worse, a lack of judgement. The party asked Shami Chakrabarti, the former Director of Liberty, to conduct a broader inquiry into anti-Semitism and racism in the party, It started in April 2016, with Chakrabarti joining the party soon after. Her report was delivered in June and cleared the party of the charge of being riddled with anti-Semitism and racism. She was then awarded a peerage in August and joined the Shadow Cabinet as Shadow Attorney-General in October.

Contrary to Corbyn's expressed desire of introducing a kinder, gentler politics, some of his supporters engaged in online abuse of MPs and others who were thought to be his critics. Angela Eagle came under bitter attacks locally and nationally after she had mooted a challenge for the leadership and the NEC suspended her Wallasey constituency party over allegations of bullying. Corbyn condemned such activity, although his critics thought it too little and too late, and it had little effect. His supporters could point to the vile social media attacks on Diane Abbott, with strong undertones of misogyny and racism. The end result was that a good number of MPs and officials complained of an unpleasant and even threatening atmosphere in some local parties.

For all Corbyn's popularity with the membership, there was little evidence this was translating into broader support. For the third successive election, Labour had chosen a leader who trailed both his Conservative opponent and his own party in the polls. Corbyn's approval ratings were, apart from those of Michael Foot in 1983, the lowest of any major party leader since polling records began. Some polls showed him behind Theresa May among every demographic. Surveys showed that Labour voters were divided on whether Corbyn was the right person to lead the party and in some polls less than half thought he was doing a good job as leader.

Election results and opinion polling were depressing for Labour. Optimists could point to Sadiq Khan's election as Mayor of London in May 2016; the capital returned to being a Labour city and there was some evidence of a positive Corbyn effect.[15] And whilst Khan had largely kept his distance from Corbyn during the campaign, the Labour leader had played a larger role in Marvin Rees' successful mayoral campaign in Bristol. But the party's internal report to the NEC on the local elections noted that while its gains were largely in Labour-held areas, its losses were in key battleground areas, and added: 'The results in 2017 and 2018 will need to be vastly better if the Tories are not to win a second overall majority.'[16]

The loss of Copeland (on a pro-Conservative swing of 7%) in Cumbria in February 2017, a seat held in Labour's heartland for over 80 years, was another blow to the party and to Corbyn's defenders. It was only partly compensated by narrowly holding the previously safe Stoke-on-Trent

Central seat on a swing to the Conservatives of 2%. Both seats had been held by youngish anti-Corbyn MPs who were abandoning what had (pre-Corbyn) been promising political careers. In opinion polls, the party regularly trailed the Conservatives by double-digit margins. In Scotland, Labour did not appear to be recovering any ground against the SNP and in some polls even lost second place to the Conservatives, as the two parties battled to be the main pro-Union voice. In the 2016 elections for the Scottish Parliament, the Conservatives for the first time gained more seats than Labour. Ian Warren and James Morris, the party's pollster under Ed Miliband, conducted groups among low-wage workers in Labour strongholds in the Manchester area in October 2016 and reported bleakly: 'There is no floor under the Labour vote anymore.'[17]

Corbyn convinced few of his fellow MPs. His performances in the Commons, particularly at PMQs, were not impressive.[18] His innovation of reading out questions sent in to him by members of the public rarely caused problems for David Cameron or May and was soon largely abandoned. His appearances at the Monday night meetings of the PLP were uncomfortable; his team thought that he was being unfairly criticised and he found excuses to miss some. He deflected dissident MPs' complaints about the poor polling figures by referring to the surge in party membership, the large and enthusiastic crowds at his rallies, and the party's impressive social media presence. All of these points were true, but when he called for patience and said the polls would turn in Labour's favour, MPs struggled to hide their dismay. 'I went in with low expectations', complained one MP after a meeting with Corbyn, 'which were more than met.'

Corbyn's role in the EU referendum in June 2016 set in train multiple attempts to unseat him. His success in overcoming them proved to be a turning point in his leadership. Many already dissatisfied Labour MPs regarded his lukewarm leadership of Labour's campaign for Britain's continued EU membership (p. 27 above) as the final straw. He took a six-day holiday during the campaign and showed little enthusiasm for the EU. A veteran Eurosceptic (once attacking the EU as a 'bankers' Europe'), he had voted against Britain's membership in the 1975 referendum and against the Maastricht Treaty—and, indeed, every attempt to expand the EU's role. He spent much of the campaign pointing out the defects of the EU, although he expressed approval of its Social Chapter and protection of workers' rights. In a television interview on 10 June, he rated his

'Thank you for resigning from the shadow cabinet. Unfortunately you've called at a particularly busy time and you're being held in a queue ...'

Matt, *Daily Telegraph*, 28 June 2016 © Matt/Telegraph Media Group Ltd

approval of the EU between 'seven and seven and a half out of ten'; a member of his core team suggested this was over-generous and it was more like five out of ten at best. Another source (who voted Leave) close to Corbyn explained:

> Jeremy has a singular lack of guile so he could never pretend to be an EU enthusiast; it would make a mockery of his record of criticising pro-capitalist EU policies. The referendum presented a silly binary choice with no room for shading; like many he had a certain ambivalence and was honest about it. But he could have been more vigorous during the campaign in the view of many.

In Corbyn's defence, the EU referendum exposed a problem any leader would have faced. A majority (63%) of the party's voters were Remainers, but majorities in over 60% of Labour-held seats were estimated to have voted Leave. Many Labour voters in coastal areas, the North and the Midlands were Leavers and were often elderly, lacked educational qualifications and were called the 'left-behinds'. Yet other Labour voters, often middle-class and university graduates, in university towns, London and major cities were Remainers; they were also more socially liberal, pro-immigration and cosmopolitan, in contrast to many of their party's Leave voters. Brexit laid bare the tensions in Labour's electoral coalition.

Campaigners emphasised to Corbyn how important it was for the party and for his authority that the Remain side won. But core members of his team did not engage with the party's campaign and often failed to turn up to scheduled meetings. Labour's campaign was split between the 'Labour In' organisation (led by Alan Johnson, appointed by Harriet Harman when she was acting leader), which was stressing the importance of defending jobs and workers' rights, and Corbyn's more nuanced 'Remain and Reform' position. Surveys showed that many Labour voters were unsure about the party's position. Corbyn's team believed that the Labour In campaign shared too many messages with the official Remain campaign and there was only a weak Labour message. With most of the PLP and party members and voters on the side of Remain, the result was a massive blow. Speaking to the media hours after the referendum result, Corbyn accepted the outcome and, to the horror of many of his MPs, appeared to call on the Prime Minister to trigger Article 50.[19] The result and the nature of the campaign—including the murder of one of their colleagues—proved too much for many Labour MPs.[20]

Late in the evening of Saturday 25 June, press reports of Hilary Benn's alleged involvement in organising Shadow Cabinet resignations began to circulate. It was the first step in an attempt to force Corbyn out. Following a tense series of phone calls between the two men, Corbyn dismissed Benn from the Shadow Cabinet shortly after 1 am on the Sunday. He had appointed Benn, despite the known policy differences between them, largely because of his attachment to Benn's father. But his team had long called for Benn's dismissal, regarding him as 'disloyal and obnoxious', in the words of one. Over the next two days following Benn's sacking, 11 members of the Shadow Cabinet resigned, one after the other. In the end, over 20 of the 31 other shadow ministers left ('the phone never stopped ringing' said one of Corbyn's team) and for a time Corbyn was unable to fill all his frontbench posts.

At a PLP meeting on 27 June, a succession of MPs and former Shadow Cabinet members argued that Corbyn should resign or make plans for a departure in the interests of the party. A succession of speakers harangued him, saying that he was incompetent, divisive and an electoral liability. Concern over his unelectability figured more prominently in the charge sheet than his policies. He did not argue or even engage with his critics, but, in the words of an observer, 'zoned out and twiddled with his pen'. At the end of the meeting, two senior MPs, Margaret Hodge and Anne Coffey, proposed a motion of no confidence in the leader, to be voted on the following day. Few doubted that it would be carried with a large majority.

On 28 June, MPs supported the no-confidence motion in the leader by 172 to 42, two-thirds of Labour MEPs declaring their lack of confidence in him. But Corbyn was unmoved and told his critics that he was the legitimate leader of the party; he had been elected by and was accountable to the mass membership. Both Hugh Gaitskell and Neil Kinnock had faced formal leadership challenges, but never before had the leader also lost a vote of confidence among his MPs. A delegation of 'soft left' shadow ministers, including John Healey, Lisa Nandy, Owen Smith and Kate Green, arranged to meet Corbyn and Katy Clark in his office to talk about a resolution to the crisis caused by the PLP's vote of no confidence. When Clark asked if McDonnell could join them, they refused. McDonnell barged in anyway and harangued them. The meeting ended acrimoniously and all resigned from the Shadow Cabinet—something they say they had not initially intended to do.[21]

Some MPs, disappointed with Corbyn, looked to the Deputy Leader Tom Watson to resolve the issue. Relations between the two worsened when Watson told Corbyn it was up the Labour leader to decide whether to continue in the job, but said it would be very difficult for him to lead the party given the depth of opposition in the PLP. Watson hoped to broker a deal with McCluskey in which Corbyn would step down after an interval with a guaranteed place on the leadership ballot for a left-winger—'Corbynism without Corbyn'—but the talks collapsed acrimoniously in July 2016.[22]

With Corbyn standing firm, the next stage in the attack on his leadership came with a formal challenge mounted in July by Owen Smith, the Shadow Work and Pensions Minister until his recent resignation (Angela Eagle, another former Shadow Cabinet member, had launched a bid, but withdrew after losing to Smith in an indicative vote of Labour MPs). It was initially uncertain whether party rules allowed Corbyn automatic entry to the ballot; if not, it was doubtful whether he could gain the necessary number of nominations. On 12 July, the NEC, fairly evenly balanced between pro- and anti-Corbyn members, ruled after a lengthy session by 18 to 14 that as leader he would automatically be on the ballot. Corbyn then left the meeting to receive the acclaim of his supporters outside party headquarters at Southside. He therefore missed a crucial vote of the NEC to bar anyone who had been a member for less than six months from voting in the leadership election. The vote was tied 16-16 and, in accordance with the party's constitution, the proposal carried.

Michael Foster, a party donor, tested the party's rule book when he appealed against the NEC ruling to allow Corbyn on the ballot. On 28 July, a High Court judge backed the NEC. The NEC decision about who could vote was also subject to legal challenge. Some NEC members complained that the use of the £3 fee for registered supporters had allowed too many non- or even anti-Labour people to vote in the 2015 leadership contest. 'Bearing in mind that an aim involved in party membership was to support a Labour Party in Parliament, there was feeling that the £3 scheme delegitimised the first leadership election', said a senior official. The fee was therefore raised from £3 to £25 for registered supporters of less than six months' standing, but they had to apply within a 48-hour window. That decision was ruled illegal by the High Court, but was then reversed by the Court of Appeal. An astonishing figure of over 180,000 paid the increased one-off fee.

Smith's challenge was easily defeated—by 62% to 38%. His campaign was uninspiring and featured too many gaffes. Smith accepted most of Corbyn's policy positions—in one important sense, the contest demonstrated the extent to which Corbyn had already managed to shift the party's tone and language—but based his campaign on what he claimed was his greater appeal to voters. But as in 2015, those who claimed to be the political professionals with the necessary skills and electoral appeal appeared amateurish and failed to enthuse members. There was a huge difference in the reach of the two sides' social media operations. At the time, Corbyn had over 600,000 followers on Twitter and 800,000 on Facebook; Smith had fewer than 3,000 followers.[23] Smith led among members who had joined before 2015, but was overwhelmed by the post-2015 recruits, over 80% of whom voted for Corbyn. Smith's challenge had only strengthened Corbyn, who in private would often mention his new found 'mandate', and Corbyn's critics abandoned plans for further leadership challenges.

Dissident MPs were not all of one mind. Some regarded Corbyn as unelectable and feared they would lose their seats if he led them in a general election, some were critical of his performance as leader (and that of his team) and some disagreed with the leftward thrust of his policies. But they now became reconciled to him leading the party into the next general election and to an inevitable and heavy defeat. The dissidents' hope was that either Corbyn would then resign or that there would be such a reaction to a bad defeat that he would be ousted. It would, said one MP, at best be salvation through catastrophe. Some hoped for an early election so that salvation could begin.

Moran, *Daily Telegraph*, 25 September 2016 © Bob Moran/Telegraph Media Group Ltd

As such, after the defeat of Smith, there ensued a period of relative calm in the PLP and a regrouping in the LOTO team. Further leadership challenges were taken off the table; as far as anti-Corbynite MPs could see, they only strengthened the leader and showed how out of touch they were with the membership. They mostly resolved to let Corbyn fail on his own terms. This was dubbed 'the Sibthorpe Doctrine', after a phrase used by Corbyn's aide Gavin Sibthorpe during a documentary on the leader's office.[24] His critics agreed to bide their time.

The calm, however, was relative. Towards the end of the Parliament, the party's divisions and challenges to Corbyn's authority were again exposed in the Commons votes in February 2017 to implement Article 50 and give effect to the referendum vote to leave the EU. At the Third Reading, nearly a quarter (52) of Labour MPs defied the whips and voted against the bill; at the Second Reading, 47 did so. Dissidents included three whips and 11 shadow ministers. All kept their posts, but four other shadow ministers decided to resign. Even the Corbyn team's unity broke down: Clive Lewis was one of those to resign, while Diane Abbott, the Shadow Home Secretary—whose constituency had voted four to one for Remain—failed to turn up for the second reading vote, pleading illness.

The party offered little or no clarity on what settlement it wanted after Britain's withdrawal and on what terms. Some MPs, particularly from Leave-voting seats, wanted tighter controls on immigration. Although Corbyn agreed that freedom of movement would end, he also defended continued immigration which met the needs of the economy and the rights of immigrant families to be together; he refused to commit to immigration targets. The party wanted access to the Single Market, to protect jobs and the economy, but was silent on how this could be reconciled with ending freedom of movement which EU leaders insisted was a condition of access. It therefore settled on a policy of opposing a 'Tory Brexit' which would harm British jobs and living standards. This so-called 'studied ambiguity' was a means of bridging the divisions in the PLP and the gap between the Remain MPs and their constituencies which had voted Leave.

Corbyn showed remarkable resilience. There were claims that he 'wobbled' a couple of times under the attacks (including once, after the referendum, following a brutal put-down by David Cameron at a session of PMQs) and at times wondered aloud among his aides if he should carry on, but was always sustained by the support of Milne and McDonnell, who urged him to stay for the good of the left in the party. Perhaps no other leader of a major British party would have survived so many Shadow Cabinet resignations—many of them pointedly disagreeing with his leadership—a crushing vote of no confidence by his MPs, damaging opinion polls and by-election reverses. But then other leaders were measuring themselves against different standards; it was a mark of how different Corbyn was from a conventional party leader that he would not stand down because he was widely expected to lose a general election or because he had lost the support of his colleagues. He was still an outsider and operated according to different rules. His supporters, particularly among the mass membership, blamed biased media coverage, divisions in the PLP, resignations and consistent talk of leadership challenges for his problems. It may have been that overcoming so much adversity helped to develop his self-confidence as a leader. He had survived and gradually was building a Shadow Cabinet that had come to terms with his leadership of the party.

Although Corbyn guarded his privacy, he became more tolerant of what he regarded as some of the trivialities of the modern media. For many years, he had spoken at left-wing rallies, but always low down in the pecking order, behind people such as Tony Benn, Ken Livingstone or

Dennis Skinner. Now he was the main attraction and blossoming among his supporters. McDonnell correctly pointed out that many of the policies (such as nationalising the railways, scrapping tuition fees and higher taxes on the rich) were popular with voters. Although Corbyn's supporters disagreed with party critics' claims that he was unelectable, some also objected that the critics were mistaken in thinking that winning elections should be the primary aim of a left-wing party; rather, it was to stand for a set of socialist principles and not to bend them to temporary shifts in public opinion, often shaped by a right-wing media. His defenders claimed that he was providing a clear sense of direction; one aide even compared him to Ronald Reagan in the way in which he combined a lack of policy detail with a bold statement of his values.

Corbyn and most of his second Shadow Cabinet (some of whom were only elected as MPs in 2015) could credibly break with New Labour in a way that Ed Miliband and his senior colleagues could not, given that so many of them had served in Blair's or Brown's Cabinets. Corbyn and McDonnell were untouched by any association with previous Labour governments and their regular defiance of the party whips in parliamentary votes underlined their sense of separation and even opposition. Over the lifetime of the Parliament, resignations and dismissals meant that in the course of four reshuffles, 81 people had served in the Shadow Cabinet; on occasion, shadow ministers were doubling up and posts were left unfilled. Some senior Labour MPs looked to forge careers outside the Shadow Cabinet. Hilary Benn and Yvette Cooper became chairs of heavyweight select committees, Sadiq Khan, Steve Rotheram and Andy Burnham resigned as MPs to become elected mayors, and Tristram Hunt resigned to become Director of the V&A Museum. But the dismissals and resignations gave an opportunity for some of the 2015 intake to make a mark, including Angela Rayner, Rebecca Long-Bailey and Clive Lewis. They were touted as potential successors to Corbyn if the membership wanted another left-winger.

Following the September 2016 annual party conference, Corbyn's team turned their thoughts to preparing for the possibility that May might call an election before 2020. This was one thing that both LOTO and Southside could agree on. Various pollsters made ad hoc presentations to the Shadow Cabinet and gave informal advice. When the pollster Ben Page addressed the Shadow Cabinet, he drew on the public polls to point to the popularity of many party policies as well as the party's bad image and poor ratings on leadership. Some shadow ministers present were taken aback by these depressing findings, even though many of them were in the public domain. 'Some live in a bubble', said one shadow minister who was present.

In October 2016, Jon Trickett, the party's campaigns coordinator, appointed BMG, a Birmingham-based polling company, to conduct surveys and advise on strategy and key seats. He also appointed the communications and branding agency Krow Communications (on a monthly retainer of around £50,000) to handle the party's billboards, adverts, posters and election broadcasts. For the first time since the 1997 general election—and for only the second time since 1983—Labour would not have any input from US opinion pollsters or campaign strategists.

With the exception of Fisher, most of Corbyn's team had little experience of policy work. He was identified with many left-wing causes and policies, and wanted Labour under his leadership to be the anti-austerity party. He and McDonnell were campaigning for a very different economy. They attacked what they called neoliberalism, a set of policies identified with Margaret Thatcher and Reagan, encompassing deregulation, tax cuts, privatisation and flexible labour markets. They argued that these policies had led to under-funded public services, poor pay, and capital collaring the largest share of extra wealth created while workers suffered stagnant living standards. This, they claimed, proved that austerity was not working.

Fisher was initially Corbyn's personal policy adviser, but after a battle on the NEC was made Executive Director of Policy for the whole party with responsibility for drawing up an election manifesto. Until then, he had worked more to the leader than for the party or the Shadow Cabinet as a whole. Under his watch, the policy priorities were clear: extending public ownership, ending or reversing the privatisation of public services, halting austerity and building more local council housing.

There was little policy development in the first year because of the turnover of so many shadow ministers and advisers. This changed with Corbyn's second leadership victory and his new Shadow Cabinet, although the most of the new appointments were very inexperienced and had inexperienced advisers. An important step was the passage of a Ten Point Plan of action for a Labour government at the party's annual conference in September 2016. It included promises for one million new homes, one million new good-quality jobs, a £500 billion infrastructure fund, reductions in inequality in terms of income and wealth, and stronger employment rights.

Corbyn's team believed they now had a mandate for a radical left-wing manifesto. A senior aide commented: 'we wanted to be outwith the party's policy consensus of the past 25 years'.

McDonnell was the key figure in driving policy development, not just on his own brief, but across the board. He recruited his staff from more leftist quarters than previous Labour shadow chancellors and assembled a team of economic advisers from academe who shared his ideas about redistribution and radical reforms of capitalism. It had initially included David Blanchflower, formerly an external member of the Bank of England's monetary policy group, the tax expert Richard Murphy, and Professor Thomas Picketty, author of the best-selling *Capital*. But within a year, all three had left either because they had been disappointed at the party's referendum campaign or were critical of divisions and a lack of direction in the policy-making group. McDonnell supported increased capital spending on infrastructure and housing, but he surprised some colleagues with his emphasis on making the spending promises 'add up'. (Diane Abbott remarked on how he appeared to have transformed himself into 'a friendly bank manager type figure', adding, 'you see him, and you think, who are you, what have you done to John McDonnell?'). He planned to tackle the deficit over a longer period than the government and raise money by a combination of tax increases (raising the top rate of income tax to 50%) and reversing planned Conservative cuts in corporation tax and inheritance tax. He commissioned private polling before the Budget to test a proposal to increase income tax or National Insurance contributions for the highly paid and hypothecating the extra funds to the NHS; he decided against doing so. Even though many of these policies were popular individually, Labour still lagged the government on perceived economic competence.

Many of the New Labour political guidelines, written by Blair, Brown and Peter Mandelson, were set aside by Corbyn and McDonnell. Blair's mantra was that Labour would no longer be the party of tax and spend, nationalisation and welfare. It would attack the inefficiencies and injustices of capitalism while keeping business on side, supporting the market, backing membership of the EU and reforming the public services. But the thrust of the rhetoric of Corbyn and McDonnell about welfare, unfairness, 'rip off' business, public ownership and equality was very different. In words remarkably similar to those of Theresa May, Corbyn said he was campaigning for an economy that worked for all and for all parts of the country, not one that worked just for the City and big business.

The challenge for the policy team was to integrate Corbyn's preferred policies into a coherent policy platform in time for an election, whenever it was called. There was not much pressure from constituency parties and trade unions for policies that he would find unacceptable. Both usually press for leftist policies that the leadership wants to dilute or head off; this time, it was different. Moreover, following the second leadership election, most of the PLP similarly took the view that 'It's our job to give Corbyn the manifesto he wants', however doubtful they were about its likely electoral popularity. Expecting something like the party's 1983 election humiliation, they took the view that Corbyn and his team should bear responsibility for the defeat.

Corbyn entered 2017 in a determined frame of mind. He had been decisively re-elected as leader, had chosen a Shadow Cabinet more to his liking and had won conference backing for his policies. The NEC was broadly onside and agreed that the party should concentrate on preparing for a snap general election. 'We have spent enough time talking to ourselves', said one official.

Milne, who had now terminated his leave of absence from *The Guardian*, informed journalists in late 2016 that the party was on a war footing in case May called a snap election. It was the kind of statement spokesmen are expected to make, but this one had some truth. He was convinced that there would be an election in the next few months. He thought that the Conservative lead in the polls, the difficulties of passing Brexit legislation with a tiny minority and the likelihood of pressures on living standards in the coming months all made an early election a 'no brainer'. Corbyn's aides set about what they informally called a 'relaunch'. This thinking inspired significant changes in campaign personnel and thinking in the first weeks of 2017. As members of the PLP and the Shadow Cabinet complained that the party's campaigning was lacklustre and demanded improvements, Jon Trickett was in the firing line. Critics said that his strategy presentations lacked substance and he appeared unwilling to come up with a list of target seats (which would indicate if he thought the party was looking to campaign for a majority of seats or was prepared for defeat). His list, shown only to a select few, pointed to a clear Labour defeat. Trickett was switched from his post in January, was appointed Shadow Minister for the Cabinet Office and was replaced as campaign coordinator by the MPs Ian Lavery and Andrew Gwynne. The new coordinators were astonished when they eventually learnt of the Trickett list.

But although he was ridiculed in Southside (where he was known as 'Trigger' by some), Trickett was held in high regard in Corbyn's office and he remained involved in broader discussions about electoral strategy. The leadership seized on a paper of Trickett's in January 2017 suggesting how the party could reach 40% of the vote in a general election. He argued that a new Labour voting coalition could be built around a coalition of public-sector workers, squeezing Greens and disillusioned Liberal Democrats, and attracting former Labour voters who had switched to UKIP, non-voters, the young and those who liked Corbyn. But in order to mobilise these groups, the party had to offer a 'transformational manifesto' rather than a transactional one. Corbyn and his team were enthused. Ed Miliband's team had identified a similar set of target voters for the 2015 general election, but had made little progress. Corbyn's team looked back on Miliband's leadership as one that had 'always lacked the courage of his convictions'. Another aide granted that Miliband had taken the party in the right direction—and applauded his cap on energy prices and distinction between producer and predatory capitalism—but thought he had been 'too hesitant and did not command his Shadow Cabinet'.

In February, Milne recruited Steve Howell, the chief executive of Freshwaters UK, a multimedia communications agency, as his deputy. His digital communications skills complemented those of Milne, whose interests lay in handling the mainstream media. He pressed, successfully, for a much bigger budget if the party was to compete with the Conservatives and it was increased from a planned £200,000 to £1.3 million. In the same month, Niall Sookoo joined from Unite as campaigns director. This double banking between LOTO and Southside for policy, communications and strategy led to what Howell said was 'paralysis in decision-making'.[25]

In February, Krow Communications presented a list of attack advertisements for BMG to test among Labour 'considerers' and 'undecideds'. Many of the proposed attack lines tested badly with the audience. Among the slogans tested were:

If you don't have the money, the Tories don't care
Conservative policies have no conscience
The devoted servants of the privileged
When the privileged call, the Tories jump
No money means you're no concern of the Tories
Hopeless government. Heartless policies. Helpless millions

7 Tory years, unlucky for most of us
The Tories have made Britain 7 years poorer

The voters thought these and similar messages were too divisive and, the agency warned, failed partly because many did not understand where Labour stood on key issues; they were more likely to engage with positive messages where Labour had clear suggestions about how it would improve society's problems. BMG added that the weakness meant 'therefore attacking the Conservatives tended only to worsen Labour's position'. Voters at times regarded the attacks on the Conservatives as attacks on their own views and values. The report concluded:

> While a majority of the public remain closed in their views towards the Labour party, softer lines of engagement, through detailed policy and credible alternatives tended to have greater traction with non-supporters. This view is also supported by the polling evidence which suggests the public aren't clear where Labour stands on a number of key policy areas.

BMG's head of polling Michael Turner later commented: 'We needed to build-up, by winning voters' trust, to a position where the public would be open to listening to attack-lines.' A Krow proposal to hire the bus used by the Leave campaign in the EU referendum and have it decorated with the promise of £350 million per week for the NHS impressed McDonnell. He was keen to do it for the local elections, but ultimately backed away when his team could not convincingly make the sums add up.

Milne also recruited two communications advisers, Marc Lopatin and Jem Bendell, to help frame a 'shifting the narrative' project for the party.[26] Their narrative frame, 'A Richer Britain', was tested extensively by BMG in April. The authors wrote that it would help to 'overturn and drown out oft-cited criticisms made about Labour under the current leadership', negative perceptions which had been shaped 'by years of Tory countermessaging on Labour's economic record'. The Labour Party needed what they called 'permission to be heard' before it could make its case as a credible alternative. The research showed that among those who had left Labour since 2015 and the undecideds, the party's divisions and Corbyn's leadership were a handicap, but among Labour supporters there was pride in the party's past achievements and approval for its values and that it stuck up for the working class. The project was conducted in the utmost secrecy—with the intention to reveal it 'like Steve Jobs did the iPhone'—

but the election came too soon for it to be fully developed and it was abandoned. A more successful slogan was 'Being Held Back', which inspired one of the party's election slogans, 'The Tories Have Held Britain Back Long Enough'.

At Southside, Patrick Heneghan, the Executive Director for Elections, Organisation and Campaigns, had also suspected since May's election as leader that she would find a reason to call an early general election. Always pressing LOTO for election planning meetings, not always with success, he made contingency plans for an election in 2017/2018 and one in 2020. Given that Corbyn's team had only been involved in party leadership campaigns, a large burden of the general election preparations would fall on the Southside staff. The nuts and bolts of a national election campaign were beyond LOTO. While waiting on Milne to draw up an authoritative war book, Heneghan prepared his own informal one and took the initiative in drawing up draft lists of key seats. The pollster BMG supplied data for Heneghan's data team to identify types of voters and seats to be targeted. Given the feedback from many MPs and party organisers and the relentlessly negative opinion polls, most in the party organisation agreed that Labour's task was to defend its seats at risk rather than chase unlikely gains.

Corbyn's team, however, were thinking along very different lines and were going to go their own way. Their insistence on following Trickett's target of a 40% share of the vote faced scepticism in Southside. A director rebuffed their call to mobilise non-voters with the claim that: 'They are called non-voters because they don't vote.' During April, and with an eye on the local elections, the party announced a series of policies, including raising the minimum wage and financing an extension of free school meals by imposing VAT on private schools. While May was walking in Wales and her staff were secretly drawing up plans for an election, Labour was already in campaign mode.

So low were the expectations that some of Corbyn's team believed that managing to hold on to its present number of seats and increasing its vote share could be judged a success. Such a result would safeguard Corbyn's position and he would then have ample time to reform the party's institutions and rules to empower the membership and entrench the party's shift to the left.[27] That was no consolation to many MPs, who would refer to the 'Corbyn cushion'—the size of an MP's majority required to survive the election. If Labour lost heavily in 2017, it was almost taken for granted that Corbyn would face a leadership challenge if he refused to resign. Few party leaders survive their party's election defeat. After 2015, the Labour, Liberal Democrat and UKIP leaders all resigned; the last Labour leader to survive a defeat had been Neil Kinnock in 1987 (who had been challenged after his defeat) and the last Conservative had been Edward Heath in February 1974 (and he had gone within a year). It was rumoured that some hopefuls—the names of Yvette Cooper and Chuka Umunna were mentioned—were booking venues and lining up supporters for a leadership challenge the weekend following the expected decisive election defeat. And if the membership voted again for a left-winger with little support in the PLP, there was serious talk that a sufficient number of Labour MPs would break away to set up a new party and be recognised as the Official Opposition. The election might well decide the future of the Labour Party. The former leader Neil Kinnock was quoted as saying that he did not expect to see another Labour government in his lifetime.

NOTES

1. See, for example, J. Cox and N. Coyle, 'We Nominated Jeremy Corbyn for the Leadership. Now We Regret it', *The Guardian*, 6 May 2016.
2. Abbott would point out that in 2010, she polled relatively well amongst the non-parliamentary parts of the election, and well enough to finish in third place had the contest been fought under the same rules as in 2015: 'I knew there was much more left-wing sentiment in the Labour Party than the lobby thought', she said. See Stephen Bush, 'Having the Last Laugh', *New Statesman*, 17 January 2017, https://www.newstatesman.com/politics/uk/2017/01/having-last-laugh.
3. As, for example, in *The Guardian* headline: 'Corbyn Becomes Only Labour Leadership Candidate to Vote against Welfare Bill' (20 July 2017). The reality was that there were two votes, both of which would have blocked the bill: the reasoned amendment saw Corbyn et al. abstain, while the Second Reading saw the Shadow Cabinet et al. abstain. But this was not how the vote was reported at the time or has been seen since.
4. Complaints of media bias were ever-present during the Corbyn leadership. See, for example, the LSE Media Group's 'Journalistic Representations of Jeremy Corbyn in the British Press: From "Watchdog" to "Attack Dog"', www.lse.ac.uk/media-and-communications/research/research-projects/representations-of-jeremy-corbyn. See also Alex Nunns, *The Candidate*. Orb Books, 2017, Chapter 10.
5. Andy Burnham et al., *Leading Labour: The Fabian Essays*. Fabian Society, 2015, pp. 14–16, www.fabians.org.uk/wp-content/uploads/2015/08/Leading-Labour-the-Fabian-essays-Aug-15.pdf.

6. Mark Bennister, Ben Worthy and Dan Keith, 'Jeremy Corbyn and the Limits of Authentic Rhetoric' in Judi Atkins and John Gaffney (eds), *Voices of the UK Left: Rhetoric, Ideology and the Performance of Politics*. Palgrave Macmillan, 2017. Or, as Alan Finlayson observed: 'He is certainly not a great orator but his stumbles and plain style lend credence to his almost exclusively moral arguments.' See his 'Why is Corbyn Doing Better on Social Media?', *openDemocracyUK*, 19 August 2015, https://www.opendemocracy.net/ourkingdom/alan-finlayson/why-is-corbyn-doing-better-on-social-media.

7. See Peter Dorey and Andrew Denham, '"The Longest Suicide Note in History": The Labour Party Leadership Election of 2015', *British Politics*, 11 (2016): 259–82.

8. On Corbyn and Corbynism, see Mark Perryman (ed.), *The Corbyn Effect*. Lawrence & Wishart, 2017; Richard Seymour, *Corbyn: The Strange Rebirth of Radical Politics*, Verso, 2016; and Nunns, *The Candidate*.

9. For example, Neale Coleman, who was head of policy and rebuttal, and had previously worked for both Ken Livingstone and Boris Johnson during their time as Mayor of London, quit in January 2016; Anneliese Midgley, a former Unite staffer who was deputy chief of staff, left in April 2016; Simon Fletcher, who also had experience working for Livingstone as well as Ed Miliband, was Corbyn's first Chief of Staff and then campaigns director, but left in February 2017.

10. Sarah Pine, 'Leaked List Ranks Labour MPs by "Hostility" to Corbyn', *LabourList*, 23 March 2016, https://labourlist.org/2016/03/leaked-list-ranks-labour-mps-by-hostility-to-corbyn.

11. Corbyn added: 'Now you'll be saying the things he writes.' It was, apparently, meant as a joke, but it did not go down well.

12. Tim Shipman, *All Out War*. William Collins, 2016, pp. 342 ff.

13. Monica Poletti, Tim Bale and Paul Webb, 'Explaining the Pro-Corbyn Surge in Labour's Membership', *LSE British Politics and Policy Blogs*, 16 November 2016, http://blogs.lse.ac.uk/politicsandpolicy/explaining-the-pro-corbyn-surge-in-labours-membership; and Tim Bale, 'Jezza's Bezzas: Labour's New Members', *Huffington Post*, 28 June 2016, https://www.huffingtonpost.co.uk/tim-bale/jeremy-corbyn-labour-membership_b_10713634.html.

14. Stephen Bush, 'Labour MPs are Worried about Momentum. Should They Be?', *New Statesman*, 26 October 2015.

15. For example, see Stephen Bush, 'Victory in London was Jeremy Corbyn's, Not Sadiq Khan's', *New Statesman*, 20 May 2016, https://www.newstatesman.com/politics/devolution/2016/05/victory-london-was-jeremy-corbyn-s-not-sadiq-khan-s.

16. Having analysed the 2016 local elections, the psephologist Matt Singh argued that Labour, as the opposition, should have had more than a 1%

lead over the government at that stage of the Parliament and the results would translate to a Conservative lead of 10–12% in a general election.

17. 'Labour's Connection to its Core Vote is Badly Frayed', *The Times*, 27 October 2016.

18. One of those briefing him for PMQs was struck by how, since so much of Corbyn's career had been spent fighting internal Labour battles, he and those around him had little understanding of how the actual opposition—that is, the Conservatives—might respond to his questions. See also Ayesha Hazarika and Tom Hamilton's *Punch and Judy Politics*. Biteback, 2018.

19. It is often said that Corbyn called for Article 50 to be triggered 'immediately'. Yet the actual phrasing, in a live TV interview with David Dimbleby at 7.28 am on the morning after the referendum, was less dramatic. He said: 'We must respect that result and Article 50 has to be invoked now so that we negotiate an exit from the European Union.' As he later explained, although the wording was not as precise as it could have been, by 'now' he did not mean 'immediately', but rather at some point as a consequence of the referendum. What muddied the water further was that when the next question from Dimbleby asked why he wanted to trigger Article 50 quickly rather than wait, he did not challenge the premise of the question. See, for example, 'Reality Check: Has Corbyn Changed His Mind on Article 50?', *BBC News*, 22 July 2016, www.bbc.co.uk/news/uk-politics-uk-leaves-the-eu-36866170.

20. Afterwards, several would admit that they were not thinking rationally at the time. 'I lost the plot', admitted one.

21. As with so many events in the Parliament, those in the Corbyn team have a very different view on what happened from the MPs involved; as one of Corbyn's aides said, 'I don't believe for one second that [they] had not intended to resign before the meeting'.

22. McCluskey's reported objective in the talks had been to appease the critics without Corbyn resigning. See, for example, Nunns, *The Candidate*, pp. 278–79.

23. Shipman, *All Out War*, p. 482.

24. In a 2016 VICE documentary, *The Outsider*, Sibthorpe commented that 'if they want to get rid of him the best thing would be to wait and let Jeremy fail on his own … in his own time'.

25. Steve Howell, *Game Changer: Eight Weeks That Transformed British Politics*. Accent Press, 2018, p. 76.

26. They had written a hard-hitting anti-austerity blog the previous December, 'Democracy Demands a Richer Britain'; see www.huffingtonpost.co.uk/jem-bendell/democracy-demands-a-riche_b_13348586.html.

27. *The Times* in an editorial claimed that this had already been accomplished. 'There is a new party in British politics and it is called the Labour party', it said. *The Times*, 26 September 2016.

CHAPTER 5

The Liberal Democrats and Others

Once considered a hallmark of the British political system, the concept of two-party politics was thought to have been consigned to history. The share of the popular vote captured by the two main parties had been in almost constant decline since the 1970s, falling as low at 65% in 2010. The 2015 contest had seen a very small reversal, with both the main parties seeing their vote share rising, but only very slightly, and with record-breaking performances from UKIP (especially in England and Wales), the SNP and the Greens, the 2015 contest provided plenty of evidence of a highly fragmented party system. It was the first election since 1832 in which different parties had topped the poll in all four parts of the UK. Yet the following two years proved difficult for the 'other' parties. In Scotland, as discussed below in Chapter 6, the SNP found it hard to maintain the dominance they had achieved just two years before, while elsewhere the smaller parties found themselves struggling to respond to a rapidly changing political environment.

© The Author(s) 2018   99
P. Cowley, D. Kavanagh, *The British General Election of 2017*,
https://doi.org/10.1007/978-3-319-95936-8_5

Entering government in 2010 had been a shock to the Liberal Democrats; leaving government in 2015 proved just as great a jolt. The party was reduced to a rump of just eight MPs, the worst result for the Liberal Democrats, or their predecessors, since 1970. The election represented a reversal of a generation's work. Many of the senior figures in the party—Danny Alexander, Vince Cable, Charles Kennedy and Ed Davey—lost their seats (Kennedy died a month after the election, aged just 55). Whether measured in terms of seats or votes, the party had lost its status as Britain's third party. Nick Clegg held on, narrowly, in Sheffield Hallam, but resigned as party leader on 8 May, taking personal responsibility for the defeat.

Two candidates, Tim Farron and Norman Lamb, bid to replace him, with Farron quickly emerging as the frontrunner. The party's president between January 2011 and January 2015, he had not served in government and had voted against the increase in tuition fees in 2010, which had become such a toxic symbol of the Coalition era. His opposition to the fees increase allowed him to present himself as a fresh start, untainted by events that occurred during the Coalition. Lamb, by contrast, had been a minister—earning plaudits as Minister of State for Care and Support—and had voted to increase tuition fees. For the most part, and like most Liberal Democrat leadership contests, the election was low-key and relatively amiable, partly because the outcome was rarely in doubt and because there were few sizeable policy differences between the two (again like most Liberal Democrat leadership contests)—but also because to outsiders it was a fundamentally less consequential matter. There seemed little prospect of the party re-entering government or deciding the outcome of elections any time soon. In a speech in June 2015, Farron set out the conditions under which the Liberal Democrats would be prepared to go into coalition again—demanding electoral reform, without a referendum—only then to note that 'clearly we have a long way to go before we're in any position to demand anything like that'.[1] The immediate priorities for the party ranged from survival to incremental, piecemeal, advance.

The only significant dispute of the contest came when Lamb had to apologise after two of his aides were caught polling party members with leading questions about Farron's beliefs and the candidates' stances on issues such as abortion and gay marriage. Farron disliked being described as a born-again evangelical Christian; 'I don't like labels', he told one interviewer, although as a label it was not inaccurate. He argued that the election would be a good test of whether one could be a Christian and

Peter Brookes, *The Times*, 26 April 2017 © News UK/News Licensing

Liberal politician: 'In the US, everyone has to invent a faith to get elected. Here you're not allowed to have one. But my faith is my faith, and nothing is going to change that.'[2] He did, however, express regret for abstaining on the Third Reading vote on the bill to legalise gay marriage, despite previously voting in favour during the earlier stages of the bill. On 16 July 2015, he was elected leader with 56.5% of the vote—a slightly narrower margin than many had expected—on a turnout of 56%.

The day after Farron's election as leader, the subject of his beliefs resurfaced, when he faced, and avoided answering, questions about whether he believed homosexual sex to be a sin. His responses—which included a defence of liberalism as meaning that his personal views were not important and that the nature of Christianity was that 'we are all sinners'—did not address the fundamental question, posed three times during an interview by Cathy Newman on *Channel 4 News* as to whether he, personally, saw gay sex as sinful. Many party figures privately warned Farron that he needed to deal with this issue before it became a problem and several later came to regret that the issue had not been more openly debated during the leadership contest, where it had become one about the behaviour of Lamb's supporters rather than Farron's beliefs. As one Lib Dem put it: 'I remember thinking, if he was facing someone like Chris Huhne for this, they'd have been hosing Tim down off the walls by now.'

The aftermath of the 2015 defeat resulted in a significant reorganisation of the internal structures of the party. During the Coalition, there had been three de facto centres of power: the Deputy Prime Minister along with his special advisers; the parliamentary party; and the party HQ. The first vanished after 2015, whilst the second was severely reduced in size and influence (with the parliamentary party in the Lords becoming relatively more significant); no longer the third party in Parliament, the Liberal Democrats lost their leader's office suite in the Palace of Westminster to the SNP, along with the automatic right to ask questions at Prime Minister's Questions, and instead moved into the party's headquarters in Great George Street. This led to an effective centralising of the organisation, seen by many of those involved as beneficial. It accompanied a significant shrinkage in the scale of the professional party due to a lack of funds. The field team, for example, fell from around two dozen paid staff, scattered around the country, to just six. A mere two staff were left running the party's entire website and social media operation. The Director of Elections, Hilary Stephenson, stepped down in 2016, being replaced by Shaun Roberts, to a newly created role of Director of Campaigns and Elections. Phil Reilly, who had previously been Nick Clegg's speechwriter, became Head of Communications. The return to opposition allowed the party to regain 'Short money'—the funds given to opposition parties in Parliament—but the party's much-reduced electoral fortunes meant that this stood at just over £550,000 in 2016/2017, less than a third of the level in 2009/2010, the last full year before going into government. The party's Chief Executive, Tim Gordon, was widely regarded as an effective marshal of the party's limited finances. That the party did not go bankrupt was no small achievement.

The Liberal Democrats played a fairly marginal role in the referendum campaign and the result was a blow to a party that was so strongly pro-EU. But it also appeared to present them with a political opportunity. By offering a second referendum on Brexit, the Liberal Democrats could present themselves as the only major UK-wide party in favour of trying to remain in the EU. It gave them a distinct identity—something the party had previously always struggled to achieve—and one which spoke to up to 48% of the population, although in practice, as they would discover, the percentage who wanted to reverse the Brexit vote was noticeably smaller than the percentage who had voted Remain. Having experienced one membership increase following the 2015 defeat, the party then saw a huge increase in members after the referendum, growing by more than 50,000. During his leadership campaign, Farron had pledged to increase the party's membership to 100,000 by the time of the next general election. This is the sort of pledge that leadership candidates often make knowing that it will never particularly matter if they fail to achieve it, yet the Liberal Democrats managed it within two years, with the party membership growing to its largest size ever.[3]

As soon as Theresa May became Prime Minister, the party drew up plans to face a snap election. Based on the assumption that the earliest an election could realistically be held was 13 October, a Manifesto Working Group, headed by Dick Newby, then Chief Whip in the Lords, aimed to finish its work by the meeting of the party's Federal Policy Committee (FPC) in early September. By the time the FPC met to discuss the document on 6 September, it had become clear that there was not going to be an election in 2016 and *Opportunity Britain* (as it was provisionally called) would never see the light of day. The exercise did at least mean that the party had a full draft manifesto, of almost 21,000 words, ready for adaptation a year later. It also revealed areas in which the party lacked up-to-date policy. ('Nothing about badgers' read one internal note.[4]) Although work to address these gaps had begun, relatively little of it had been completed by the time the election was called.

The party also rushed ahead with candidate selection, at least in seats where it felt it had a chance. Priority was given to people who fought seats in 2015 if they were willing to stand again; this included several former MPs, who the party found gained an advantage from high name recognition. Several of these ex-MPs let it be known that they were willing to stand again in the event of a snap election, although they were not intending to do so in the event of a 2019 or 2020 campaign.

Starting in the autumn of 2016, the party began what was, by its standards, a significant polling operation to look at how it was viewed by the public. As one of those involved put it: 'The first question we wanted to look at was: is the brand so badly damaged that it's irretrievable?' An early part of the research generated a word cloud of people's impressions of the party. The two stand-out phrases were 'Nothing' and 'Don't Know'. It was a sign of how bad things were seen to be that those involved in the exercise saw this as a positive. As one party staffer said: 'We were relieved. At least it wasn't "Coalition" and "Tuition Fees".' The research revealed that there was a tiny Lib Dem core vote of just 5% of the public, albeit with a much larger group who were at least amenable to the messages and values of the party. These potential Lib Dem voters were more educated, more middle-class, younger and much more likely to have voted Remain. The aim of this work was to try to work towards an election in 2019 or 2020, building a core vote and thus making the party less reliant on local campaigns.[5] The next stage of the project was intended to investigate how the party could best engage with these potential voters—which messages worked and which did not—although the snap election meant the party never got that far.

There were initial signs that the party's post-Brexit approach was working. The devolved elections of 2016 had seen the party tread water in Scotland and slip further back in Wales, falling to just one Assembly Member in the latter. The London Assembly elections also saw the party reduced to just one seat. A mild uptick in performance in the English local elections—the first time the party's vote share had increased since it had entered Coalition in 2010—had to be balanced against a flatlining performance in Commons by-elections: the four Westminster by-elections prior to the referendum saw the Liberal Democrats' vote share improve by an average of just 0.05 percentage points. After the EU referendum, however, things began to change. In the Witney by-election in October 2016, caused by David Cameron standing down as an MP, the Liberal Democrats increased their share of the vote by 24 percentage points, coming from fourth place to finish second, on their best share of the vote in the seat since 1983. Five days later, on 25 October, the government announced support for a new (third) runway at Heathrow. Zac Goldsmith, the Conservative MP for Richmond Park, who had previously stated that he would resign if the government supported the Heathrow expansion, followed through on his promise and triggered a by-election. Goldsmith stood as an Independent candidate and claimed that the 'by-election must be a referendum on Heathrow expansion'. Farron, however, pledged to make the by-election a 'vote on Brexit'. Goldsmith had voted Leave in the EU referendum, but sat for one of the most pro-Remain constituencies in the country, and one that had been held by the Liberal Democrats until 2010.[6] The Liberal Democrats selected a candidate, Sarah Olney, who had only joined the party in 2015 after the end of the Coalition, but who was both against Heathrow expansion and a pro-EU campaigner. Olney overturned Goldsmith's 2015 majority of 23,015 to win by 1,872 votes, with the Liberal Democrats increasing their share of the vote by just over 30 percentage points. It was the first Liberal Democrat gain in a by-election for a decade.

Both Witney and Richmond Park were Conservative constituencies with pro-Remain majorities; subsequent by-elections during the Parliament were held in much less promising places—all seats with pro-Brexit majorities—although even here the post-referendum Lib Dems still did better than the party had done in any by-election prior to the referendum. To test its strategy fully, what the party needed was a Labour-held Remain-voting constituency. In late February 2017, Sir Gerald Kaufman, the Labour MP for Manchester Gorton and Father of the House of Commons, died aged 86. The by-election was scheduled for 4 May, the same day as the local elections. Kaufman had held the seat in 2015 with a majority of over 24,000, but it was a seat in which over 60% were thought to have voted Remain. As the campaign progressed, the Lib Dems briefed that their polling showed they were on course to take the seat. The party has form in briefing positively, if not always entirely honestly, about its performance as a way of building campaign momentum, although in this case it is a view which its campaign team still holds. For their part, Labour staff responsible for the by-election remain sceptical about such claims, believing they would have held the seat, but everyone involved accepts it would have been a close result either way. For a seat in which the Lib Dems had come fifth in 2015, losing their deposit, even to have come a good second would have been an achievement. It would have vindicated their strategy and destabilised Labour yet further. Theresa May's announcement of an early general election led to the Gorton by-election being cancelled, much to the Liberal Democrats' frustration.[7]

On the day that the general election was called, Tim Farron was flying to the South West to launch the Liberal Democrat local election campaign. Based on performances in council by-elections, they were expecting to do well. They were optimistic that they were at least on the way back.

The 2015 election had been frustrating for UKIP. They had polled almost four million votes, but won just one seat. They achieved an impressive 120 second places, many with little more than paper candidates—although in just two of these seats did the party need a swing of less than 5% to move into first. The election also saw party leader Nigel Farage fail to win the constituency of Thanet South, which he had always said was the minimum requirement for him to remain leader. He duly announced his resignation, albeit holding out the prospect of standing again when the party held a leadership election later in the year, but by 11 May he had in any case withdrawn his resignation after the party's National Executive Committee rejected his offer, if indeed he had ever formally made it.[8] It was not the last time he would stand down as leader during the Parliament, nor the last time he would return.

Although not part of the Vote Leave campaign, which was keen to distance itself from UKIP, Farage was a highly visible presence in the referendum campaign. He took part in a televised debate with the Prime Minister in May 2016, despite protests from the Vote Leave campaign. He was involved in a flotilla of fishing boats—Fishing for Leave—on 15 June, and the following day he unveiled one of the most controversial posters of the referendum, depicting a line of migrants at the Slovenian border with the slogan 'Breaking Point: The EU Has Failed Us All'. Unveiled on the day the Labour MP Jo Cox was murdered, the poster was widely condemned, including by Vote Leave.

UKIP continued to poll well for the first half of the Parliament, averaging around 14% between the 2015 election and the referendum. Whilst showing no signs of a breakthrough, they managed second place in the first three by-elections of the Parliament and gained a record seven seats in the Assembly elections in Wales, despite a campaign that was not without significant internal difficulties.[9] The result of the referendum, however, presented the party with a problem. For one thing, it lost its frontman. On 4 July, Farage resigned as UKIP leader (for the third time), having achieved his long-term political ambition: 'During the referendum I said I wanted my country back', he declared, 'now I want my life back.' More fundamentally, the result of the referendum threatened to remove the party's raison d'être. Once it became clear that the Conservatives were promising to deliver a relatively 'hard' form of Brexit—and with almost all Conservative MPs rallying behind that position—and with Labour pledging to accept the referendum result, albeit with less clarity, it was not obvious why UKIP was needed. The process of extricating Britain from the

EU would present opportunities for a party to push for harder, or faster, change; UKIP could—and did—promise to hold the government's feet to the fire over the issue, and they could continue to exist as a broader anti-establishment party challenging what they saw as out-of-touch political elites, but it was not obvious that this would be sufficient. UKIP had always been an eclectic group, bound together by hostility towards the EU and little else. Even this had not always been enough to prevent the ideological and personal divisions within the party from bubbling over. The potential for discord was even greater without the EU to function as a binding agent, as became clear throughout the rest of the Parliament.

Finance became a significant problem for the party. One of the earliest of many rows during the Parliament between Nigel Farage and the party's one MP, Douglas Carswell, came almost immediately after the election over the issue of Short money. UKIP's impressive vote haul allowed the one-MP party potentially over £600,000 per year. Short money was supposed to facilitate opposition parties in carrying out their parliamentary business. This sum would have allowed Carswell to hire more than a dozen staff, far more than any MP needed for their parliamentary business. Carswell objected, arguing that it would have been 'improper' to have taken the money and that UKIP was supposed to behave differently from other parties when it came to such matters. Others within the party argued that the party still needed money, whatever virtue came from occupying the moral high ground. A compromise was reached and, in March 2016, the Commons introduced a cap on the maximum funds a party with fewer than five MPs could receive, which limited UKIP's Short money to just over £200,000. Donations also fell away, especially after the referendum; the second half of 2016 saw total declared donations to the party amount to less than £80,000. Despite attempts prior to 2015 to professionalise the party's organisation, there had always been a touch of the Marx Brothers about UKIP internally, and operating on a shoestring only made things worse.

The party held two leadership elections in 2016. The first, in September, saw Diane James elected as the party's first female leader with 47% of the vote. She lasted 18 days, before standing down on 4 October, claiming not to have sufficient authority 'nor the full support of all my MEP colleagues and party officers to implement changes I believe necessary and upon which I based my campaign'. She later said: 'One can obviously continue to bang your head against a brick wall, going to bed at night hoping things might change and that you might be able to make a break-through. But when it became clear I couldn't make that breakthrough, I felt it was the right decision for me and the credibility of the party that someone else assume the mantle.' The next month she left the UKIP group in the European Parliament, to sit as an independent. Farage complained that: 'This is yet another act of irrational selfishness from Diane James. This pattern of behaviour says that she is unfit to continue as an MEP. She should do the honourable thing and resign.'

One of the early frontrunners in that leadership contest had been MEP Steven Woolfe, only for him to fail to submit his nomination papers in time. Woolfe then considered defecting to the Conservatives, before announcing that he would instead stand for the leadership following James' resignation. However, the day after his announcement, he was involved in an altercation at the European Parliament building in Strasbourg with another UKIP MEP, Mike Hookem, which resulted in Woolfe being hospitalised with a head injury. Eleven days after being released from hospital, he had not only withdrawn his candidacy but also resigned from the party as well, joining James as an independent MEP and describing UKIP as 'ungovernable'. Serious political parties do not see contenders for the party leadership—let alone winners—depart the party entirely just weeks after announcing an intention to lead it.

The second UKIP leadership election of 2016 saw Paul Nuttall elected, with just over 62% of the vote. Farage's deputy between 2010 and 2016, he was a very different character. In place of the Dulwich College-educated former City trader came someone born in Bootle and educated at a comprehensive. He vowed to replace Labour 'in the next five years and become the patriotic party of the working people'. He was, on paper, the perfect leader for what UKIP had referred to as 'Project 2020'—the idea that UKIP would use the 2015 election to establish themselves in second place in Labour-held seats, to then advance substantially in 2020. As one article noted at the time, Nuttall's election was 'the moment dozens of Labour MPs in the north of England were dreading'. 'He isn't exactly JFK', said one Labour MP, 'but he does represent a clear and present danger to Labour in the north of England, particularly at a time when we are haemorrhaging so many white, working class votes.'[10] At the time, he was seen as a skilled media performer.[11]

Yet Nuttall's leadership was marked by a series of difficult episodes, revealing that he had a complicated relationship with the truth. In December 2016 on the BBC's *The Andrew Marr Show*, he denied being responsible for claims that he had completed a PhD and been a professional footballer for Tranmere Rovers. Both claims were significant exaggerations: he had played for Tranmere's youth squad and he had begun but not completed a PhD analysing the fate of the Conservatives in Liverpool.

The party's poll rating began to decline slowly but steadily after Brexit, although the Stoke-on-Trent Central by-election in February 2017 appeared to offer a way back to relevance. Labour nationally were deeply divided and the constituency had voted overwhelmingly for Brexit whilst Labour's local candidate had voted Remain. It might not have been quite the perfect constituency for UKIP to test their ability to take seats from Labour, but it was not far off.[12] Nuttall was selected as the UKIP candidate and his campaign explicitly targeted Labour's working-class and pro-Brexit voters. Farage claimed that the by-election was 'fundamental … for the futures of both the Labour Party and indeed UKIP', which turned out to be broadly accurate, if not quite in the way he intended. Nuttall almost immediately became embroiled in a police investigation for electoral fraud when journalist Michael Crick tweeted a

'The party is divided. The loonies may split from the fruitcakes'

Matt, *Daily Telegraph*, 17 September 2016 © Matt/Telegraph Media Group Ltd

picture of a property which Nuttall had declared as his current home address on his nomination papers, but which appeared to be entirely empty. There was also a disputed claim that he had been at Hillsborough in 1989 when 96 Liverpool football fans were killed. During the by-election, following questioning about Nuttall's claim that he had survived the disaster, *The Guardian* was provided with two statements on behalf of Nuttall, one from his father and another from a UKIP employee, saying that they and Nuttall had been at Hillsborough on the day of the disaster, although his father's statement gave an incorrect age for his son at the time of the match. Later that month, in an interview with Liverpool's Radio City station, Nuttall clarified that he had not 'lost anyone who was a close personal friend' in the Hillsborough disaster after being shown two press releases on his website which indicated that he had. His press officer took responsibility for the posts and resigned, but these incidents were said to have shaken the new leader's confidence.[13] Nuttall came a relatively poor second in Stoke with 24.7% of the vote and Labour held the seat comfortably. As Farage noted after the vote: 'We failed to get tactical votes from the Conservatives. Theresa May has now taken up the Brexit mantle and people believe her, for now.' After just 12 weeks as party leader, there were already calls for Nuttall to resign.

The personal and ideological feuds that were well known within the party became ever more public.[14] In February 2017, Arron Banks, one of UKIP's main donors, stated that he was considering standing against Carswell in the 2020 general election as part of an ongoing feud between Banks and Carswell—the former vocally supported by Farage—regarding the leadership and direction of the party. The announcement followed allegations that Carswell had blocked attempts for Farage to be awarded a knighthood and was in talks to rejoin the Conservative Party. In March, Banks claimed that he had been suspended by UKIP following comments about the party's leadership, although the party responded that Banks had not renewed his membership and therefore it would not be possible to suspend him.

On 25 March, prior to the triggering of Article 50, Carswell jumped ship, announcing that he had resigned from the party and would sit as an Independent MP. He stated that: 'I switched to UKIP because I desperately wanted us to leave the EU. Now we can be certain that that is going to happen, I have decided that I will be leaving UKIP.' While he had resigned to fight a by-election when he defected to UKIP, he claimed this was not necessary this time: 'I will not be switching parties, nor crossing the floor to the Conservatives, so do not need to call a by-election'. In response, Farage tweeted that Carswell 'jumped before he was pushed'; Nuttall stated Carswell 'was never a comfortable Ukipper'; and Banks tweeted a blushing smiley face emoji with a tick (not a sentence that featured in any earlier volumes in this series). When the election was called in 2017, Carswell declared that he would not be seeking re-election and intended to vote Conservative. Banks initially said that he would stand as a candidate in Clacton despite admitting that he knew 'nothing at all' about the constituency or whether he would be UKIP's representative, only to back away from this pledge a few days later.

Almost uniquely among serious British political parties, UKIP had done next to no preparation for an election, having taken at face value the claims of Theresa May that there would be no contest. 'We were caught completely on the hop', said MEP Patrick O'Flynn, who was brought in to manage the campaign.[15] UKIP went into the 2017 contest unprepared, without a single MP and polling the lowest they had for years.

In May 2016, Natalie Bennett announced that she would not be standing for re-election as leader of the Green Party of England and Wales. Under her leadership, the party had increased its membership fourfold, seen record-breaking performances in the 2014 European elections, its best-ever result in a general election in 2015 (gaining over one million votes and saving 123 deposits) and, days before her announcement, the best performance by a Green in the London mayoral contest, with Siân Berry coming third with 6% of first preference votes. But the 2015 election had not been a happy experience for Bennett. At times, she struggled to perform competently and there were tensions with former leader, and the sole Green MP, Caroline Lucas.[16] Despite the advances the party had made, there were those in the party who felt they had under-performed and held Bennett largely, if not solely, responsible.

In September 2016, Caroline Lucas and Jonathan Bartley were elected to replace Bennett with almost 90% of the vote, in a job-share arrangement. This was not a pairing of equals. Lucas had been in the party for 30 years, had been an elected representative—at council, European or Westminster level—for almost 25 of those years, and had previously served for four years as party leader. Bartley only joined the Greens in 2010. He had stood unsuccessfully in Streatham in 2015 (polling 9%), had lost out in the party's selection to be their London mayoral candidate, and was the party's Work and Pensions spokesperson. There was little doubt who was the more senior player.

For all Lucas's undoubted ability, the irony was that the Greens never returned to the levels of success the party had seen under Bennett's leadership. Of all of the major parties, it was the Greens who were most discombobulated by the arrival of Jeremy Corbyn as Labour leader. Although there were differences between Corbyn's anti-imperialist and Marxist analysis and that of most senior Greens, many Green members and voters could easily imagine Corbyn as one of them. Almost a quarter of those who joined Labour immediately after Corbyn became leader had voted Green in the 2015 general election.[17] Green Party membership fell from its 2015 high, albeit still to a level that previous party leaders would have killed for, if Greens believed in killing.

After Theresa May became Prime Minister, the party had set up a snap election working group, which had done some rudimentary work by the time the election was called. The party also began to consider the idea of standing aside in some seats, as part of a so-called 'progressive alliance' with other parties, an idea that Lucas had supported during the leadership contest. The first obvious manifestation of this came in the Richmond by-election. As part of a progressive alliance with the Women's Equality Party, the Greens chose to support Sarah Olney rather than field a candidate.[18] The Green Party conference in the spring of 2017 supported a motion agreeing to such local electoral pacts in parliamentary election with candidates and parties whose principles 'are broadly in line with the values of the Green Party' and, crucially, where they might help increase support in the House of Commons for proportional representation.

In December 2015, the BBC published a list of political parties to be offered party political broadcasts; outside election periods in England and Wales, the Green Party was given none. After an appeal from the Greens, the BBC ruled that the party 'had not demonstrated substantial levels of past and current electoral support'. Nothing about their performance afterwards proved the BBC wrong, although one party election broadcast they produced in the run-up to the local and London elections, featuring small children as political leaders, was one of the most watched of the Parliament. A homage to the Channel 4 programme *The Secret Life of 5 Year Olds*, it featured small children arguing over politics ('Even your

Mummy doesn't agree with your policies') and attracted nearly 500,000 views across the party's social media accounts within 24 hours and close to 20 million in total. Like previous Green party election broadcasts which have gone viral, it was either a witty satire on politics or sanctimonious, depending on your point of view.

When Plaid Cymru were preparing for the party leader debates in the 2015 general election, one of their main goals was to raise the profile of the party's relatively new leader, Leanne Wood. Despite what were seen by most UK-wide viewers as poor performances in the debates, the strategy appeared to work, with Wood emerging from the election as both well-known and liked by Welsh voters.[19] For the first time since the creation of the National Assembly for Wales, Welsh Labour was facing a party with a rival leader as popular as their own.[20] This did not, at first, appear to translate into high ratings for the party as a whole, but the 2016 Assembly elections saw a modest advance for Plaid, which moved back into second place. It also witnessed a personal triumph for Wood, who took the supposedly safe Labour constituency of Rhondda, defeating an incumbent Labour minister on a remarkable 24.2% swing.[21]

The election saw Labour lose its majority in the Assembly. Just one seat shy of a majority, most people assumed that Labour's leader, Carwyn Jones, would remain as First Minister and lead a minority government. Plaid, however, put forward Wood as a rival candidate. In an Assembly vote on the election of the First Minister on 11 May 2016, both Jones and Wood tied on 29-29, Wood gaining the backing of Plaid Cymru, Conservative and UKIP Assembly Members (AMs). After this unprecedented deadlock, Labour and Plaid Cymru reached an agreement on 17 May that Jones would remain as First Minister and lead a minority government—although the sole remaining Liberal Democrat AM, Kirsty Williams, was appointed to the Cabinet, giving the government a bare majority. As part of its deal with Plaid, Labour agreed to establish three liaison committees on finance, legislation and the constitution, which would comprise a Labour minister and Plaid representative.

Plaid were a resolutely pro-Remain party during the referendum, only to find themselves on the wrong side of the result, both in the UK as a whole and also in Wales, where a majority voted Leave. The result came as a shock to many in the party (and others in the Welsh political

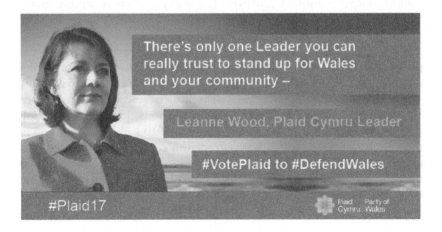

and cultural elite) who had long cherished a view of the Welsh as more progressive and internationalist than the English. But it also undermined Plaid's long-term objective of 'independence in Europe'. The party's 2016 Assembly manifesto had stated that whilst 'independence, of course, remains our long-term aspiration as a party ... we do not plan to hold a referendum on Welsh independence in the near term'. But in the wake of the referendum result, Wood claimed that it was 'time to put independence on the agenda now in order to safeguard Wales's future', and she returned to the theme following Nicola Sturgeon's announcement in March 2017 that she was seeking to hold a second referendum in Scotland, with Wood calling for a 'national debate to explore all of the options, including that of an independent Wales'.

The party was also unsettled by the arrival of Jeremy Corbyn as Labour leader. Corbyn initially enjoyed a slight honeymoon period in Welsh opinion polls, but this faded, and by 2016 he appeared to be less popular in Wales than the Prime Minister. Carwyn Jones had deliberately put distance between Welsh Labour and Corbyn's leadership—which presented Plaid with two targets, neither of them easy. The former emphasised its Welsh distinctiveness, while the latter was a problem for a party which had managed to make hay by being to the left of Labour. 'We didn't know how to deal with them', admitted one of Wood's team. The option chosen was to focus on criticising Welsh Labour, largely ignoring Corbyn. The party's 2016 Assembly manifesto, and its campaigning activity up until 2017, almost never featured Corbyn.

One Plaid staffer described the party as 'deeply unprepared' for the general election, but in early 2017, Plaid had spent some time preparing contingency plans in case the Prime Minister called an election to coincide with the local elections in May. As well as financial reserves, this work consisted of draft timetables for candidate selections, logistics of election addresses and so on. In addition, a draft manifesto had been drawn up in the autumn of 2016, which was refreshed in early 2017. Once the final date for a May election had passed, the party staff relaxed ('she'll not go this year', said one) and attention had instead shifted to the forthcoming local elections. When the general election was announced, Plaid were optimistic that they might be able to increase their number of MPs, such was Labour's apparent weakness in Wales.

In July 2015, the former Respect leader George Galloway said that he would like to rejoin Labour if Jeremy Corbyn was elected leader of the party; in December of the same year, it was reported that Salma Yaqoob, another former Respect leader, had applied to join Labour, only to be blocked by her local party for having previously stood against Labour candidates. Galloway stood as Respect candidate in London in 2016 (calling Sadiq Khan 'a rancid traitor to his faith and to any conceivable definition of Labour'), polling just 1.4% in first preference votes and finishing seventh out of 12 candidates. By January 2016, Respect membership was said to be under 1,000 and in August 2016 the party had 'voluntarily deregistered' from the Electoral Commission's Register of Political Parties.[22]

In January 2016, the British National Party were temporarily removed from the Register of Political Parties for having failed to confirm its registered details. The party reapplied in February 2016 and contested a handful of elections during the Parliament, mostly doing badly. Their best performance came in the Batley & Spen by-election, caused by the murder of Jo Cox, where they polled 2.7%, albeit in a contest where the Conservatives, Liberal Democrats, UKIP and Greens were not standing out of respect to Cox. They were to stand in ten seats in 2017, two up from 2015, but hugely down on the 338 constituencies they had fought in 2010.

The Christian People's Alliance fought in the London elections (1%) and a string of by-elections where they achieved a consistent level of support: Tooting (0.5%), Richmond Park (0.4%) and Stoke-on-Trent Central (0.5%). They were to stand 31 candidates overall. Yorkshire First had launched in April 2014, contesting seats in the 2015 election.[23] They rebranded themselves as the Yorkshire Party in 2016, arguing that the new title would be 'a more positive and inclusive name for our party'. England's most successful regional party, the party stood 21 candidates in 2017. The National Health Action Party (NHA), which had been formed in 2012, contested five constituencies. The most significant of these was South West Surrey, where the Green candidate stood down, and the NHA candidate received support from some Liberal Democrat and

Labour activists as the best chance of defeating the Health Secretary, Jeremy Hunt.

A new entrant in the political marketplace was the Women's Equality Party, which launched in 2015. Set up as an explicitly feminist party by Catherine Mayer and Sandi Toksvig, as of mid-2016, they claimed an impressive 65,000 members. The Reuters journalist Sophie Walker became the party's first leader. It claimed to be 'non-partisan' and said its goal was to put women's issues on the agenda.[24] It proved adept at attracting media coverage, possibly in excess of its success in winning votes. Standing candidates in the London mayoral and Assembly elections, as well as in devolved contests in Scotland and Wales, the party's best performance came in London, where Walker polled 2% for Mayor and the party gained 3.5% on the London-wide list. It was to stand seven candidates in 2017.

Brenda from Bristol would have been even more frustrated had she been Brenda from Belfast: her complaint of 'too much politics' especially applied in Northern Ireland. In addition to the Brexit referendum, there were two assembly elections within a year of each other; the four major political parties all changed leaders, which included changes in the First and Deputy First Ministers; the new First Minister then became embroiled in a bizarre scandal which involved people being paid to heat empty buildings; and the Assembly collapsed again.

The Assembly was teetering on the edge for almost all of the 2015–2017 Parliament. In August 2015, the Ulster Unionist Party (UUP) withdrew from the Northern Ireland Executive, stating it was 'impossible to do business' with Sinn Féin as a result of the latter's attitude to the continuing activities of the Provisional IRA and especially their involvement in the murder of a former IRA member, Kevin McGuigan. First Minister Peter Robinson declared that he wanted to suspend the Executive until the issue had been resolved, but failed to win sufficient support in the Assembly; he then stepped aside as leader of the Democratic Unionist Party (DUP) and First Minister, with Arlene Foster becoming acting First Minister. On 22 September, talks to resolve the situation began, involving the UK government, the Irish government and the five largest Northern Ireland parties. In October, DUP ministers resumed their posts in the Executive, including Robinson returning as First Minister, and in November 2015 an agreement was reached. *A Fresh Start: The Stormont Agreement and*

Implementation Plan included measures on welfare and paramilitarism which managed at least to secure relations until the scheduled Assembly elections in May 2016.

The Social Democratic and Labour Party (SDLP) meanwhile had changed leader, Colum Eastwood—aged just 32—defeating the incumbent Dr Alasdair McDonnell. Following the signing of the *Fresh Start* agreement, the DUP also had a leadership change: Robinson resigned, being replaced by Arlene Foster. She was the first female leader of the DUP and in January 2016 became the first female and youngest First Minister. Originally a UUP member, Foster had defected to the DUP in 2004 over sharing power with Sinn Féin; she was now First Minister sharing power with Sinn Féin.

The 2016 Assembly elections resulted in minimal changes in party composition, and a new power-sharing executive—broadly identical to the last one—was formed. Although entitled to membership, the SDLP and the UUP both declined to nominate ministers and instead formed the first formal opposition in the Assembly. Foster continued as First Minister, with Martin McGuiness continuing as Deputy First Minister. Northern Ireland as a whole voted Remain in the Brexit referendum, by 56% to 44%, with most of the province's parties backing Remain, but with the DUP being officially pro-Brexit. The contrast between the pro-Remain majority in Northern Ireland and the pro-Brexit majority in the UK led to calls from Sinn Féin for a border poll on reunification, a stance swiftly rejected by the Westminster government.

Foster was then to become embroiled in one of the more curious political scandals of recent years. The Renewable Heat Incentive (RHI) scheme introduced in Northern Ireland had provided a financial incentive to increase uptake of renewable heat technologies. Foster had overseen the scheme's introduction as Minister for Enterprise, Trade and Investment. There was initially an under-spend due to a low uptake, but the number of applications began to increase significantly in 2015, as people realised that the amount paid to recipients was greater than the cost of producing the energy. In January 2016, a whistleblower wrote to the Office of the First Minister and Deputy First Minister alleging abuse of the scheme—including one farmer who was heating an empty shed with the aim of collecting approximately £1 million over the next 20 years. The scheme became known as 'cash-for-ash'. It was closed to new applicants on 29 February 2016 when it became clear that it posed a significant financial risk to Northern Ireland's finances. Existing applicants continued to be paid and a report by the Northern Ireland Audit Office in July 2016 found that the scheme had 'no upper limit on the amount of energy that would be paid for' over the 20-year period; later estimates put the total cost at £500 million. The minister who took over from Foster at the Department of Enterprise, Trade and Investment claimed that Foster had attempted to remove her name from documents linked to the scheme and her advisors had delayed its closure.

Under growing political pressure, Foster and McGuiness recalled the Assembly to discuss the scandal in December 2016. Foster survived a vote of no confidence brought by the SDLP and supported by the UUP. She admitted that the failure to include cost controls was the 'greatest political regret of my life', but claimed that she had acted 'with the highest level of integrity'. On 4 January 2017, Foster confirmed that she would not be stepping down and described calls for her to do so as 'misogynistic'. Five days later, McGuinness resigned as Deputy First Minister in protest against Foster's refusal to stand aside whilst an investigation into the scandal was carried out, and under the power-sharing agreement, Foster lost her role of First Minister along with McGuinness's departure.

A deadline for Sinn Féin to nominate a new deputy First Minister was set for 16 January 2017, but the party refused to participate, in order to trigger an election. The result was the Northern Ireland Assembly elections on 2 March 2017, held just 301 days after the previous elections. McGuiness confirmed that he would not be seeking re-election. He had originally intended to stand down in May 2017 to mark the tenth anniversary of the power-sharing Executive, but his health and the current political crisis had 'overtaken the timeframe'; he was to die in March 2017, aged 66. He was replaced as party leader by Michelle O'Neill. She had been first elected to the Assembly in 2007 and had held various senior ministerial positions, including Health Minister, where she ended Northern Ireland's blanket ban on gay men donating blood in 2016.

The 2017 elections proved more consequential than the elections of 2016. With a reduction in the number of seats overall, almost all of the losses came from the DUP (down 10) and the UUP (down 6). The DUP finished less than 1,200 votes ahead of Sinn Fein and no longer had enough Members of the Legislative Assembly (MLAs) to unilaterally use a 'petition of concern', a procedure they had employed 86 times in five years, often to prevent issues like gay marriage progressing.[25] The UUP lost their position as the third-largest party, which they had held since 2007, to the SDLP, with the UUP leader Mike Nesbitt announcing his resignation shortly afterwards. Combined, the unionist parties did not constitute a majority in the Assembly for the first time since the body was created.

The deadline to form a new power-sharing executive was initially for 27 March 2017; negotiations collapsed on 26 March. Foster claimed that Sinn Féin was 'not in agreement-finding mode', whilst O'Neill said the DUP did not have 'the right attitude'. Gerry Adams, Sinn Féin's President, stated that legacy issues from the Northern Ireland Troubles, an Irish Language Act, a Bill of Rights and marriage equality had been the stumbling blocks in negotiations. Rather than calling yet another election immediately, Northern Ireland Secretary James Brokenshire said on 28 March that the government would 'consider all options', including direct rule, if further talks did not succeed.

There was no Northern Ireland executive when the general election was called. Northern Ireland would face its fourth election in 18 months, this time without a devolved government—and the heightened tensions of an election seemed unlikely to help increase the prospects of one being formed.[26]

These 'other' parties matter in their own right, as the choices of millions of voters. At the start of the 2017 campaign, and despite some evidence of UKIP's vote having been in decline since the referendum, around a third of voters in Great Britain said they were intending to vote for a party other than Labour or the Conservatives. They also matter because they can affect election outcomes, especially in close contests, either by taking, or at least threatening to take, votes from the larger parties—and because of the way the larger parties respond to that threat. No one looking at the history of the preceding five or so years could seriously argue that UKIP's rise had been inconsequential, despite only ever winning one seat at a general election. These parties can also help determine the government because of their involvement in post-election deals. This last justification seemed merely theoretical this time around. No one seriously expected any of the parties discussed in this chapter to be involved in the formation of a government once the election was over.

Notes

1. In that same speech, given to the Gladstone Club on 9 June 2015, Farron made it clear that he thought coalition was the right decision in 2010, even if things could have been done differently once it had been formed. Mark

Park argued that Farron was constrained in terms of how much he could disown the Coalition by the party's influx of new members immediately after the 2015 defeat, many of whom were perceived to be supportive of Nick Clegg and the policies undertaken after 2010. See Mark Pack, 'Tim Farron: Coalition was Right and I'd Do it Again', 11 June 2015, https://www.markpack.org.uk/132718/farron-coalition-was-right-and-id-do-it-again.

2. Decca Aitkenhead, 'Tim Farron Interview: "Maybe God's Plan is for Me to Lose a Bunch of Elections and Be Humbled"', *The Guardian*, 26 June 2015, https://www.theguardian.com/politics/2015/jun/26/tim-farron-liberal-democrats-interview-gods-plan-for-me.

3. There was another increase, of around 14,000, in the two weeks following the announcement of the snap general election, and by 3 May there were 101,768 members—the largest figure recorded in the party's history.

4. This was not actually true. The Liberal Democrat 2017 manifesto contained a pledge to develop 'safe, effective, humane and evidence-based ways of controlling bovine TB'—as opposed to the government's badger cull—and there was an almost-identical pledge in the draft of *Opportunity Britain*.

5. Also influential in the discussions was a pamphlet produced by Mark Pack and David Howarth called *The 20% Strategy: Building a Core Vote for the Liberal Democrats* (2015, with a 2016 second edition).

6. Constituency-level estimates by Chris Hanretty estimate that some 71% of voters in Richmond Park voted Remain, making it the thirty-first most pro-Remain constituency in the Great Britain. See Chris Hanretty, 'The EU Referendum: How Did Westminster Constituencies Vote?', *Medium*, 29 June 2016, https://medium.com/@chrishanretty/the-eu-referendum-how-did-westminster-constituencies-vote-283c85cd20e1.

7. In the 2017 general election, the Lib Dems finished fifth in Manchester Gorton, losing their deposit. Labour say this confirms their view that they would have held the seat in any by-election; the Lib Dems, in contrast, say the experience in the general election was very different, as discussed below on p. 166.

8. See Isabel Hardman, 'Exclusive: Nigel Farage "Never Resigned" from UKIP in "Stitch up"', *The Spectator*, 15 May 2015, https://blogs.spectator.co.uk/2015/05/exclusive-nigel-farage-never-resigned-from-ukip-in-stitch-up.

9. Roger Scully and Jac Larner, 'A Successful Defence: The 2016 National Assembly for Wales Election', *Parliamentary Affairs*, 70 (2017): 507–29.

10. Kevin Schofield, 'Analysis: Why Labour MPs Fear Paul Nuttall is "a Clear and Present Danger" to Their Job Prospects', *Politics Home*, 28 November

2016, https://www.politicshome.com/news/uk/political-parties/uk-independence-party/news/81239/analysis-why-labour-mps-fear-paul-nuttall. See also Helen Lewis, 'New UKIP Leader Paul Nuttall Plans to Destroy Labour – Can He Succeed?', *New Statesman*, 1 December 2016, https://www.newstatesman.com/politics/uk/2016/12/new-ukip-leader-paul-nuttall-plans-destroy-labour-can-he-succeed.

11. Katy Balls, 'Paul Nuttall's Election is Bad News for Labour', *The Spectator*, 28 November 2016, https://blogs.spectator.co.uk/2016/11/paul-nuttalls-election-bad-news-labour.

12. Matthew Goodwin, 'Why UKIP Will Face an Uphill Battle to Take Stoke-on-Trent Central from Labour', *Daily Telegraph*, 13 January 2017, www.telegraph.co.uk/news/2017/01/13/ukip-will-face-uphill-battle-take-stoke-on-trent-central-labour.

13. Tim Ross and Tom McTague, *Betting the House*. Biteback, 2017, pp. 353–54.

14. These are well documented in Matthew Goodwin and Caitlin Milazzo's *UKIP: Inside the Campaign to Redraw the Map of British Politics*. Oxford University Press, 2015.

15. Ross and McTague, *Betting the House*, p. 354.

16. See, for example, Philip Cowley and Dennis Kavanagh, *The British General Election of 2015*. Palgrave Macmillan, 2015, pp. 155–56.

17. That is, between Corbyn's election and May 2016. See Tim Bale, 'Jezza's Bezzas: Labour's New Members', *Huffington Post*, 28 June 2016, www.huffingtonpost.co.uk/tim-bale/jeremy-corbyn-labour-membership_b_10713634.html.

18. And, on the other side, both the Conservatives and UKIP both decided not to put up a candidate in the by-election against Goldsmith. In this particular case, it was alleged that the Green Party was offered £250,000 by a donor not to stand; the complaint was investigated by the Metropolitan Police, which found that 'no offence had been committed as the Greens' intended candidate was not formally standing at the time the donation was offered'. The donation was not accepted by the party.

19. Roger Scully, 'New Barometer Poll: The Standing of the Party Leaders in Wales', *Cardiff University Blogs*, 22 April 2015, https://blogs.cardiff.ac.uk/electionsinwales/2015/04/22/new-barometer-poll-the-standing-of-the-party-leaders-in-wales.

20. Roger Scully, 'New Welsh Political Barometer Poll: Party Leader Ratings', *Cardiff University Blogs*, 30 June 2015, http://blogs.cardiff.ac.uk/electionsinwales/2015/06/30/new-welsh-political-barometer-poll-party-leader-ratings. And for later data, see, for example, 'Voters Say Plaid Leader's Doing Well, PM Very Badly', *ITV News*, 25 April 2016, www.itv.com/news/wales/2016-04-25/voters-say-plaid-leaders-doing-well-pm-very-badly.

21. Scully and Larner, 'A Successful Defence', pp. 519–20.
22. Galloway went on to stand, as an independent, in Manchester Gorton, coming third with 5.7% of the vote. Yaqoob stood, also as an independent, in Bradford West, also coming third, but with 13.9% of the vote.
23. A. Giovannini, 'Towards a "New English Regionalism" in the North? The Case of Yorkshire First', *Political Quarterly*, 87 (2016): 590–600.
24. Rainbow Murray, '50,000 Members and Counting: Meet the Political Party Prepared to Lose, to Win', *The Conversation*, 17 February 2016, https://theconversation.com/50-000-members-and-counting-meet-the-political-party-prepared-to-lose-to-win-54677.
25. Peter Geoghegan, '4 Takeaways from Northern Ireland's Snap Election', *Politico*, 3 April 2017, https://www.politico.eu/article/4-takeaways-from-northern-irelands-snap-election-dup-sinn-fein.
26. Peter Geoghegan, 'Brexit Plays into Old Divisions in Northern Ireland', *Politico*, 22 May 2017, https://www.politico.eu/article/brexit-plays-into-old-divisions-in-northern-ireland-general-election-democratic-unionist-party-sinn-fein-ulster.

CHAPTER 6

Still Different, Only Slightly Less So: Scotland

Gerry Hassan

In the period 2014–2017 from, and counting, the independence referendum, Scottish voters have been to the polls on six separate occasions.
The Scottish political environment of the last few years has experienced
dramatic change, turbulence and seismic shocks that have been more
far-reaching than in any era since the 1970s. The period has witnessed
the arrival of the SNP in office as first a minority, then majority government, followed by the 2014 independence referendum. Subsequent
events in 2015–2017—of two UK elections and the 2016 Scottish
Parliament elections (which the SNP won but in which they lost their
overall majority)—have to be seen against this backdrop: of a politics
still in flux on big questions such as independence and Scotland's place
in the UK.

The following assessment of politics north of the border places it in the
context and evolution of 'the Scottish question'—defined as the many
ways in which Scotland has sought influence, voice and autonomy in the
constitutional and political arrangements of the UK.[1] According to one
analysis: 'There has never been a single Scottish question except in the
broadest sense of how Scotland relates to the rest of the UK and the question of how Scotland should be governed.'[2] In the last 50 years this two-
part question has become increasingly focused on the self-government,
devolution and independence debate.

© The Author(s) 2018   125
P. Cowley, D. Kavanagh, *The British General Election of 2017*,
https://doi.org/10.1007/978-3-319-95936-8_6

The academic Bill Miller, writing on Scotland in the Nuffield Study of the 1979 UK election, reflected on the unusually high profile of Scottish politics in the October 1974–1979 UK Parliament:

> The basic problem was that Scottish politics were not purely Scottish in the sense that politics in England are almost exclusively English and politics in Ulster almost exclusively Irish. The Scottish dimension coexisted rather uneasily with a British dimension. With some variations in attitude or emphasis, Scots worried about the same issues and personalities as other Britons…[3]

Miller concluded with an observation nearly as true today as when it was first written: 'So this is not the only Scottish chapter in this book, they all apply to Scotland.'[4] These are salutary words to remember in an environment which is increasingly disunited and missing an over-arching British politics, but in which political debate and power focus around, and are determined in, Westminster.

There are significant differences between the key elections of the two years examined—the 2015 Westminster, 2016 Scottish Parliament and 2017 Westminster contests. There are academic debates about first-order and second-order elections, with state-wide elections in the former, and sub-national and regional contests in the latter.[5] Turnout is usually higher in the first and lower in the second, a pattern which can be seen post-1999 with Westminster elections having higher turnouts than the Scottish Parliament. They are conducted by different electoral systems with a more proportional system for the Scottish Parliament; the role of Scottish-only parties is enhanced by devolution—the SNP mainly, but also the Scottish Greens—while there is a different mix of political dynamics and issues at play in each system.

This latter point does not mean that voters follow a neat, tidy devolved versus reserved distinctions of policy areas for Scottish and Westminster elections, as the politics of Scotland post-1999 shows. The 2003 Scottish Parliament election was influenced by the then recent Iraq war, and the 2007 election by the last days of Tony Blair as UK Prime Minister. Westminster contests have increasingly seen detailed discussion of devolved issues such as education and health.

Steve Bell, *The Guardian*, 3 May 2016 © Steve Bell

The 2015 election in Scotland witnessed a nearly completely altered political map. In one election, Scotland went from a political territory in Westminster representation, where Labour routinely returned a majority of the Westminster seats, to one dominated by the SNP. Between 1964 and 2010, Labour won 13 elections in a row in the Scottish popular vote, while from 1959 to 2010, the party won 14 successive elections in parliamentary representation. All of this changed in the 2015 election, with Scotland undergoing political change unprecedented either in terms of its own experience or indeed that of anywhere else in the UK, with 84.7% of seats changing hands, all SNP gains from the three other main parties.

Scotland's impact was not restricted to the election result. Scotland became a major issue in the campaign, and it remained so in the UK Parliament and politics afterwards. With 56 seats, the SNP became the third-biggest parliamentary party at Westminster. Scottish politics became the subject of a host of epithets—'tsunami', 'tartan tsunami', 'Ulsterisation' and more. Comparisons were even made between the SNP 56 and the election of a mass block of Sinn Fein MPs in 1918, which heralded the independence of Ireland from the UK four years later.[6] Yet, while such over-the-top rhetoric invoked rupture and rebellion, more critical was the expression of Scotland's evolving quasi-independence and the partial autonomy of its public sphere.[7]

The problems of success came to haunt the SNP in a way the party had never before experienced. The sudden influx of resources and energies following the independence referendum which saw SNP membership rise from 25,000 to 120,000 initially surprised the party as much as everyone else. While the party's own internal processes and structures were stretched in the run-up to 2015, this huge wave of enthusiasm turned out to be in many cases conditional with, in subsequent elections, the new membership not engaging and remaining for the most part inactive and invisible.[8] But what it also meant was that one legacy of the unexpected election of 56 SNP MPs was that party monitoring and checking may not have been as thorough as before, building up problems for the future.

The Westminster 56 as the new third force in British politics (with most newly elected to national office) were a major novelty. This resulted in heightened public interest and media scrutiny, something the party had not seen at Westminster since 1974–1979. Angus Robertson, SNP Westminster leader, gained the right to two questions in each week's Prime Minister's Questions, while the party gained more coverage on UK-wide programmes such as BBC *Question Time* and *Any Questions*, in response to their new-found popularity and representation.

This brought with it a downside. Two of the SNP's 56 MPs, Natalie McGarry (Glasgow East) and Michelle Thomson (Edinburgh West), faced serious allegations of misbehaviour shortly after the election. McGarry was implicated in the unauthorised spending of monies belonging to the Women for Independence group and the Glasgow SNP; Thomson was involved in 'alleged irregularities' in relation to buying multiple properties.[9] Both resigned the party whip and sat as independents in the Commons. No charges emerged against Thomson; McGarry was charged by the police authorities.[10]

The SNP group came to Westminster with high expectations, reminiscent of the Labour 'Red Clydesiders' in 1922, and the prospect of shaking the institution to the ground. Maiden speeches by new SNP MPs such as

Mhairi Black, MP for Paisley and Renfrewshire South (elected at the age of 20 years and 237 days, making her the youngest MP at least since 1832) and Tommy Sheppard, MP for Edinburgh East, made a huge impact on social media. But seldom stated was the deeper comparison to the 'Red Clydesiders', of the limits of political rhetoric, and that Westminster was more likely to change the SNP group than they were to profoundly change Westminster.

The politics of class and nation seemed intertwined in the SNP. The 2015 British Election Survey found that 67% of Scots thought the SNP represented the working class, while 34% thought it represented the middle class. But this perception was weakest in the working class: 52% of working-class respondents saw the SNP as a working-class party, compared to nearly 80% among the middle class.[11] The SNP had successfully positioned themselves literally on Scottish Labour's former ground: of speaking for the working class and presenting itself as its champion, but doing so from middle-class interests. This had proven an effective strategy for decades for Scottish Labour.

Adams, *Daily Telegraph*, 28 March 2017 © Adams/Telegraph Media Group Ltd

Scotland's opposition parties—Labour, Conservatives and the Lib Dems—were reduced to a single Westminster MP each in 2015.[12] The Conservatives faced the least disorientation, having had one Scottish MP since the 2001 election. The Lib Dems were in a more perilous place, having lost ten of their 11 seats—their single representative was Alistair Carmichael, outgoing Secretary of State for Scotland in the Coalition. Neither of these travails compare to the collective experience of Scottish Labour. The party had gone over the course of one election from 41 MPs to a mere one. The efforts of Jim Murphy, who became Scottish Labour leader in December 2014, seemingly counted for nothing. He made numerous policy announcements and embraced populist stances (including promising to overturn the ban on alcohol at football matches), all to little avail.

The election result saw moves to unseat Murphy as leader, he having failed to get elected in the East Renfrewshire seat he had held since 1997. He tried to hold on as leader and won a Scottish Labour Executive vote of confidence by 17:14 the second weekend after the election.[13] But the pressure proved too much and after indicating he would remain, he resigned the same day, attempting to seek solace in his advancement of various party reforms.

Scottish Labour's eighth leader of the devolution era was chosen from a contest involving Kezia Dugdale, list MSP for Lothian, and Ken Macintosh, MSP for Eastwood. Dugdale had been Deputy Leader under Murphy and seemed to indicate a dramatic changing of the guard—politically, generationally (she was 33) and culturally. She embodied a different political age and persona compared to Labour's old guard, was not wedded to Labour's detesting of all things SNP and had no investment in the party's previous entitlement culture of giving the impression that they had a divine right to rule. She quickly established herself as the favourite and easily won with 72% of the vote.[14] Alex Rowley, MSP for Cowdenbeath, won the Deputy Leadership.

Dugdale's election was the culmination of a dramatic feminisation of the top of Scottish political parties with women leaders of Scottish Labour, the SNP and the Scottish Conservatives. This triumvirate were of a similar generation, had only experienced Holyrood, having never served at Westminster, and openly got on with each other in public and on social media. All three were to lead their parties through the 2016 and 2017 elections and the EU referendum. This was all the more a shift considering the male-only and aggressive nature of Scottish parties historically, and it left the only major party which had never had a women leader as the Lib Dems (while the Scottish Greens elected a female co-convenor, Maggie Chapman, in November 2015 alongside existing co-convenor Patrick Harvie).

Two of the three women leaders were also part of the lesbian, gay, bisexual and transgender community. Davidson had long been publicly out as gay and Dugdale came out in 2016.[15] Together with Patrick Harvie of the Scottish Greens, who was bisexual, and David Coburn, leader of UKIP in Scotland, who was gay, it meant that four of the country's six parties had individuals who identified as LGBT. Whether related or not, this change happened at the same time that Scotland became a more pro-LGBT country, passing legislation on same-sex marriage in 2014 and being acknowledged internationally as a leader in gay rights and equality.

One month after Dugdale's election, Jeremy Corbyn was elected leader of the British party. The Corbyn effect in Scotland, unlike in England and Wales, did not see any major uplift in members or initially in support. This restricted the potential of Corbyn's appeal, as did the absence of Momentum organising in Scotland, with the left of the party instead organising through the long-established Campaign for Socialism, which reflected traditional socialist and labourist politics.[16]

One consequence of Corbyn's emergence was that it ended the trope in Scotland of stating 'I didn't leave Labour, Labour left me' and targeting more anger towards 'red Tories' rather than real Tories. This had found its most eloquent expression in former communist-turned-SNP-supporter Jimmy Reid in a quote used extensively in the 2014 referendum when he said: 'When New Labour came to power, we got a right-wing Conservative government. I came to realise that voting Labour wasn't in Scotland's interests anymore.'[17] Now the SNP had to switch from this to making the claim that Corbyn's Labour was weak, divided and unelectable—a claim that was predicated on political realities staying as they were and not changing.

The 2016 Scottish elections were the first sign of the limits of the SNP's appeal. Standing on a platform to win a historic third term—something which had not been achieved by any party under devolution—the SNP's campaign was based on their record in government, standing up for Scotland and the appeal of Nicola Sturgeon. This was complicated by the shadow of the impending EU referendum on 23 June, a month and a half after the Scottish election on 5 May.

The SNP manifesto 'Re-elect' (with a front cover featuring Nicola Sturgeon despite the fact she was standing for the first time as First Minister) attempted to galvanise pro-independence opinion, while retaining room for manoeuvre. The message was less empowering than 2015, more presidential than under Salmond in 2011 and less clearly based on the winning formula of five years previously of 'Our Record, Our Team, Our Vision'.[18] There was a concerted #BothVotesSNP strategy on social media which attempted to maximise the party's constituency and regional vote; this enthused loyalists, while annoying those who had hoped for more pluralist politics. Sturgeon's only real misstep in the campaign was to do a photo opportunity holding the front-page endorsement of *The Scottish Sun*, only days after the Hillsborough verdict (which brought back memories of *The Sun*'s coverage), none of which played well in some left-wing pro-independence circles.[19]

The SNP manifesto stated that 'if there is clear and sustained evidence that independence has become the preferred option of a majority of the Scottish people—or if there is a significant change and material change in circumstances that prevailed in 2014, such as Scotland being taken out of the EU against our will',[20] the SNP argued that in such circumstances, they had the right and mandate to hold a second independence referendum.

While the SNP attempted to defend their dominant position and parliamentary majority, significant movement occurred in the opposition parties. Labour were still affected by post-referendum blues, while Kezia Dugdale struggled to make any impact. She was seen as wobbly on independence (for example, saying that it was 'not inconceivable' she would support independence if the UK voted for Brexit and Scotland voted to remain in the EU), made worse by Jeremy Corbyn's own undisciplined messaging on Scotland.[21] At points he seemed open to courting the SNP and independence (stating in March 2017 that he was 'absolutely fine' with a new independence referendum), showed little understanding or interest in Scotland, and gave the impression that post-2015 he had written off Scotland.[22] He also seemed to deliberately show a lack of support for Dugdale on Scottish visits, not inviting her to events he spoke at and not mentioning her on such occasions—and while she was no Blairite like Jim Murphy, nor was she a Corbynite.

The Conservatives under Ruth Davidson's leadership entered the Scottish elections more hopeful than they had been in many years, informed by Davidson's popularity ratings and her adeptness at campaigning. But there was more than that. In post-independence referendum Scotland, politics had become increasingly divided into pro- and anti-independence camps. The Tory message of no second vote and making an unapologetic case for the union came from their core DNA and hit home in comparison with Labour's ambiguous and conflicting signals about independence. For the first time in years, the Scottish Conservatives had an issue which allowed them to unapologetically speak for a majority of voters and which genuinely represented what they stood for.

The 2016 Scottish election saw the comfortable re-election of the SNP in government and Nicola Sturgeon as First Minister, but also a failure to manage expectations. The SNP increased their constituency vote from 45.4% to 46.5%, but in the regional vote their support fell back from 44.0% to 41.7%. This was enough for their parliamentary representation to fall from 69 in 2011 to 63, with the party losing their overall majority. The Conservatives finished with 22.9% of the regional vote to Labour's 19.1%, the first time the party had finished ahead of Labour in the national popular vote since 1959. The Scottish Greens went from two seats in

Table 6.1   Yes and No supporters by party vote 2015–2017

	Yes	No
	%	%
2015		
SNP	90	12
Con	1	25
Lab	4	45
Lib Dem	2	13
2016 (constit. vote)		
SNP	86	14
Con	2	37
Lab	6	35
Lib Dem	2	10
2017		
SNP	73	9
Con	8	44
Lab	17	36
Lib Dem	2	10

Source: British Election Study 2015–2017

2011 to six, supplanting the Lib Dems on five seats as the fourth-biggest party in the Parliament, and contributing to a pro-independence parliamentary majority of SNP and Greens.[23]

In 2015 the SNP had won 90% of Yes supporters supplemented by 12% of No supporters. This fell slightly in 2016 in the constituency vote to 86% of Yes supporters, while their support rose to 14% amongst No voters. Significant movement happened in the other parties and No voters, who split in 2015 45% Labour and 25% Conservative, in 2016 shifted to 37% Conservative and 35% Labour (see Table 6.1).[24]

No sooner was the Scottish election campaign over than the same politicians had to adjust to the pressures of the UK EU referendum. Several Scottish politicians—Nicola Sturgeon and Ruth Davidson in particular—played high-profile roles in the UK campaign. Sturgeon took part in the ITV debate on 9 June, calling the £350 million Vote Leave NHS figure 'a whopper', but the Remain side found she did not go down well with some English voters, who 'responded very badly to Sturgeon'.[25] Davidson took part in the Wembley Arena BBC TV Brexit debate two days before polling, where she passionately put the pro-European Remain case and criticised leavers such as her fellow Conservatives Boris Johnson and Andrea Leadsom (accusing the latter of telling a 'blatant untruth').

There was an overwhelming political class consensus in Scotland for remaining in the EU, with the Scottish Parliament voting in May 2016 by 106 votes to eight to support EU membership.[26] All of Scotland's political parties in the Scottish Parliament were pro-EU, as were all the leaders of all the main parties. The opposition to EU membership in the referendum was made up of UKIP Scotland leader MEP David Coburn, its sole elected representative; ex-Labour MP and Vote Leave Scotland co-ordinator Tom Harris and former SNP MP Jim Sillars. This represented a gap between the political class consensus and public opinion, and one which posed problems for broadcasters. There were some echoes of Scotland's self-proclaimed belief in its progressive values and trumpeting of the politics of difference, which is validated by the more centre-left political discourse evident in the Scottish Parliament, but which is not evidenced in repeated Scottish Social Attitude Surveys.[27]

The EU campaign did not feel like an equal contest in Scotland. It did not come completely as a surprise when on 23 June 2016, while the UK voted to leave the EU, Scotland voted 62% to 38% to remain. Every one of Scotland's 32 council areas returned a Remain vote, but underneath this apparent homogeneity lay many differences. The 32-council uniformity was misleading: Moray, for example, voted 50.1% to 49.9% for Remain, a majority of 122 votes in the area represented by SNP Westminster leader Angus Robertson. Despite the uneven contest in the political classes, 1,018,322 voters in Scotland voted Leave, compared to 1,661,191 for Remain. Critically, SNP voters split 64:36 for Remain, nearly the same proportion as Labour voters across the UK—a divide that led to discontent in Labour about the role of the Corbyn leadership in the referendum.[28] The SNP did not anticipate they would face similar acute pressures: on hearing the result, Nicola Sturgeon commented that it was 'a monumental fuckup'[29]; publicly she declared the day after the vote that another independence referendum was 'highly likely'.[30]

Gordon Brown's role in the independence referendum had a lasting impact on the Brexit campaign. In the 2014 campaign Brown showed his dislike of the Better Together campaign and Labour's alliance with the Conservatives, and set up the United with Labour campaign. He believed the Scottish experience showed that 'the only way a referendum could be won convincingly was if Labour ran its own strong campaign … reaching its own supporters with a Labour case for staying in Britain'.[31] Brown took this experience of cross-party campaigning as proof that Labour had been tainted by the Tory brand in 2014, something widely felt in the party. This reinforced the case for a separate Labour campaign in the EU referendum, which played into the view of the Corbyn Labour leadership. There was rich irony in this. Labour had come full circle, returning to Labour isolationism which had been evident in Helen Liddell's memo (when Scottish Labour General Secretary) for the 1979 devolution referendum forbidding Labour cross-party cooperation with the SNP.[32] That hurt Labour and devolution in 1979, and Labour's Brexit stand-off had even more fatal and damaging consequences, aiding the cause of leaving the EU.

The SNP believed that most of their leave voters would be persuadable to remain in the independence camp, but this proved more complex than first anticipated. The dynamics of up to half a million SNP voters supporting leave proved to be one of the critical cross-currents of politics, cutting across the independence divide. Initial post-Brexit polls showed a sizeable rise in support for independence, with three polls giving it a clear majority, one of which, undertaken by ScotPulse, put it on 59% support.[33] However, this proved to be a temporary blip and support quickly returned to below 50% support and a consistent trend of 43–45%, historically high, but with no sign of growth or a breakthrough since the 2014 referendum level of 44.7%.

This contradicted conventional wisdom north and south of the border which had long held that the UK voting for Brexit and Scotland for the EU would be a gift for the Nationalists. Instead, the aftermath of the Brexit vote, after the short pro-independence spike, showed how the causes of remain and leave were cross-cutting in relation to the independence debate. Thus, two-thirds of Yes voters supported remain, as did 58% of No voters.[34] In a July 2016 YouGov poll, 68% of No voters said they would rather live in a UK outside the EU compared to the 18% who would rather live in an independent Scotland in the EU. Some voters did change their minds, but this did not amount to any move to independence. A total of 93% of No voters who voted leave would vote No again, whereas only 74% of No voters who backed remain would vote No; 86% of Yes voters who supported remain would still vote Yes, while 65% of Yes voters who supported leave would still vote Yes.[35] Thus, the anticipated long-term flip to independence from Brexit has yet to appear.

At the same time, the Scottish Parliament voted 92 to 0 to give the Scottish government a mandate to open direct talks with the EU—with Labour, the Lib Dems and Greens supporting the SNP, and the Conservatives abstaining.[36] At the end of 2016, the Scottish government published its Brexit proposals, *Scotland's Place in Europe*, which made the case for Scotland remaining in the European Single Market and a differentiated Brexit.[37] These proposals were sidelined and never formally engaged with by the UK government, much to the dismay of the Scottish government.

While the Scottish government was engaged in such high-level politics, party politics continued. SNP Depute Leader Stewart Hosie and MP Angus MacNeil were both identified as having had an affair with the same woman, resulting in Hosie resigning as Depute Leader and separating from his wife, Scottish government Health Secretary Shona Robison.[38] The resulting depute leadership contest saw Angus Robertson win with 52.5% of the vote on the first ballot.[39]

At more important levels of state, David Cameron resigned as UK Prime Minister on 24 June, replaced by Theresa May on 13 July. Cameron had been unpopular in Scotland and proven hugely problematic in the 2014 independence campaign, playing into Scottish stereotypes of Tories—English, privileged and privately educated. May came across as more down to earth, and in her first year enjoyed a sustained period of popularity in Scotland as well as the rest of the UK.[40] Combined with Ruth Davidson's popularity, this gave the Conservatives a rare double uplift of popular Scottish and UK leaders.

On 13 March 2017, Nicola Sturgeon announced that as a result of the UK government's refusal to engage seriously with the Scottish government's proposals on Brexit, it was her intention to support a second independence referendum. There were rumours that Sturgeon had not been completely enthused by this approach and felt boxed in by the twin pressures of the UK government, alongside public and private advocacy from former First Minister Alex Salmond.[41]

Three days later, on 16 March, Theresa May replied with a carefully crafted and worded statement (see pp. 61–2) that 'now is not the time' for a second vote. Despite this, on 28 March, the Scottish Parliament voted 69 to 59 to support a second referendum, with the SNP and Greens combining to produce a parliamentary majority. The Scottish vote was formally to request a section 30 order from the UK government to hold a referendum, but the UK government did not formally respond to this request. Instead, the following day, Theresa May triggered Article 50, which began the two-year process of negotiations between the UK and the EU on the terms of the UK's withdrawal.[42]

Thus, the main parties entered the Westminster election in differing moods. The SNP, for so long outsiders and challengers in politics, now had to adjust to the pressures and scrutiny which came with being the leading party and defending seats and support from the high watermark of two years previously, along with ten years of tenure and a track record to defend as the Scottish government.[43] In the previous year, public opinion had become less favourable towards the SNP on devolved areas such as health and education. Asked by YouGov to assess how the Scottish government was handling health in May 2016, respondents split 49% well to 40% badly, while by April 2017 this sat at 42% well and 47% badly. Asked the same on education, respondents split in May 2016 45% well and 38% badly, whereas in April 2017 this shifted to 40% well and 46% badly.[44] This move was reinforced by concerns over the economy, as well as anxiety over Brexit and independence, and presented a more challenging environment for the SNP than they had hitherto encountered.

The Conservatives' long period in the wilderness, where they had been for many the pariahs of Scottish politics, was clearly beginning to draw to a close for many, if not everyone. They were now the main challengers to the SNP in votes, seats and raison d'être, having established themselves in the 2016 Scottish elections in second place ahead of Labour. They were more unambiguous in their defence of the union than Labour and had a popular message with No voters opposing a second independence referendum, alongside a popular leader in Ruth Davidson.

Labour were not in a good place, having been on a downward curve in the Scottish Parliament since its inception, having relented power and the place of the dominant party to the SNP. But if that were not enough, they had suffered a near-wipeout in Westminster in 2015 and, after losing first place to the SNP, had now lost second place to the Tories. The Lib Dems were now resigned to their permanent shrunken status after the Westminster coalition with the Conservatives. Meanwhile, the Scottish Greens and UKIP made great play of their right to be taken seriously as national parties and hence included in election debates, but neither put significant resources into the forthcoming election, with the Greens standing in only three constituencies and UKIP in two.

The year 2017 also reflected the altered state of the party leaders and their popularity—and in particular of Nicola Sturgeon and Ruth Davidson. The phenomenon of Sturgeon mania evident in 2015 and 2016, which had seen her rated 'the most popular and widely appreciated living person among the Scottish public', was now clearly on the wane.[45] Conservative private polling indicated that in parts of Scotland, Sturgeon had become a mobilising factor for their vote. One SNP 2015 voter told a Lord Ashcroft focus group at the onset of the campaign that: 'Every time Nicola Sturgeon is on the television she's banging on about the referendum to go solo, but she wants to be concentrating on things like the NHS, that's in absolute chaos, education, absolutely awful.'[46] Her popularity had fallen from a net of +56% in May 2015 to +26% in May 2016 and then +2 in May 2017 (see Table 6.2).[47]

The more polarised politics post-Brexit vote and the controversies over a second independence referendum saw a marked shift from reverence towards Sturgeon to 'that bloody woman' amongst many non-SNP voters. Ruth Davidson over the same period rose to a peak of popularity of +31% in July 2016, falling back to +11% in June 2017 (see Table 6.3).[48] Focus groups found people recognised her as a different kind of Conservative: 'she's more of a Scottish Conservative, as opposed to an English Conservative in Scotland'.[49] Similarly, the shifts of Yes and No supporters evident post-2014 continued with the SNP vote falling from 86% of Yes supporters in 2016 to 73% in 2017. Meanwhile the dramatic shift of No support continued, with the Conservative vote rising from 37% in 2016 to 44% in 2017 (along with the phenomenon of a small group of Yes former SNP voters voting Conservative, most of whom had voted leave),[50] with Labour at 35% in 2016 and 36% in 2017 (see Table 6.1).[51]

The different parties' attitude to the 2017 election was informed by the topsy-turvy nature of Scottish politics over the last few years. The SNP had

Table 6.2   Do you think Nicola Sturgeon is doing well or badly as First Minister?

	May 2015	May 2016	August 2016	May 2017
	%	%	%	%
Very well	45	23	24	19
Fairly well	30	36	29	27
All well	75	59	53	46
Fairly badly	7	16	14	14
Very badly	12	17	19	30
All badly	19	33	33	44
Don't know	6	9	14	9
Well/badly	+56	+26	+20	+2

Source: YouGov

Table 6.3 Do you think Ruth Davidson is doing well or badly as leader of the Scottish Conservative Party?

	September 2015	May 2016	July 2016	June 2017
	%	%	%	%
Very well	8	9	19	16
Fairly well	30	33	33	30
All well	38	42	52	46
Fairly badly	19	16	11	14
Very badly	19	18	10	21
All badly	38	34	21	35
Don't know	25	23	28	18
Well/badly	=	+8	+31	+11

Source: YouGov

organisation and resources beyond any other party, and had already factored into their calculations the Tory revival and the threat from Ruth Davidson, realising that some of their North East strongholds might be vulnerable. What they did not predict was any kind of Corbyn factor north of the border or new threat from Labour. The party knew from their own private polling from Survation that there was little enthusiasm for a second independence referendum before the end of the Brexit process and that they had left open a flank where opponents could attack them.

Hence, the SNP entered the election with a mix of complacency and nervousness, most sure of what they were not fighting an election on—independence or Brexit—and utilising the time-honoured slogan 'Stronger for Scotland' for the campaign and manifesto, which has been so successful in 2015. That said, they saw their dominance as secure and the only real variable in the election was how many of their 56 seats from 2015 they would hold on to. While more enthusiastic pro-independence voices at the onset of the campaign talked of the SNP holding all their seats, the SNP knew they were in an expectations game. Privately, SNP sources started off by assessing that holding the line at 50 seats or the mid- to high 40s would be a good result and that the circumstances of the 56—immediately after and filled with the hopes and energies of the independence referendum on their side—could not be repeated.

The Conservatives were upbeat for the first time in years. They had to utilise the popularity of Ruth Davidson and new Prime Minister Theresa May, while allowing the Scottish party to establish clear blue water between themselves and the rest of the party. Their pollsters Populus backed up the impression that Ruth Davidson had a distinctive appeal and message, and that the pitch of saying 'not now' to an independence referendum was the right approach, oscillating between flexibility and principle.

Scottish Labour were unsurprisingly nervous and filled with apprehension. The party's strategy was limited and focused first and foremost on defending their solitary MP, Ian Murray in Edinburgh South, to which all else was secondary. Yet, partly because Labour in London had written off their prospects in Scotland, for the first time in many an election, Scottish Labour were left to their own devices, which was an improvement compared to recent contests. The Lib Dems set very specific targets, focusing on areas of local strength they had previously won, and nursed two former Lib Dem seats where the sitting MSP had either got into trouble (Edinburgh West) or was locally unpopular (East Dunbartonshire).

All three opposition parties in Scotland were determined to play down the expectations game, while Labour and the Conservatives had gone from a position where in 2015 they were regarded as indistinguishable by part of the Scottish electorate to maximising the differences between them and attacking the SNP in a pincer movement. None of the four main party leaders (Nicola Sturgeon, Ruth Davidson, Kezia Dugdale and Willie Rennie, all MSPs) were standing in the 2017 election, yet each would dominate their party's coverage, further blurring the distinction between devolved and reserved matters.

Scotland approached the 2017 election in a state of flux, with the shadow of two disruptions—the twin peaks of the independence referendum and Brexit—hanging over its politics. This, combined with the aftermath of the election of the SNP 56 two years earlier, would make this an election like no other that Scotland had experienced.

One example was that this was the first time that the SNP were conducting a Westminster election entirely as a holding exercise, playing a defensive game, and being attacked and vulnerable as incumbents to their opponents. It was not a political environment, despite being in office for ten years in devolved government, which the Nationalists found easy to adjust to. All of their challengers knew that at least part of the political climate was changing in Scotland and that the turbo-charged politics of recent years, after taking its toll on the pro-union parties, was now proving more difficult for the SNP.

There was also the question of how Scotland reacted to the expected emphatic endorsement and prospect of a landslide for the Conservatives. Scotland had been here before between 1979 and 1997, but never with a Scottish Parliament, an entrenched SNP in office and in the aftermath of an independence referendum—and with the question still a live one. The SNP would never admit it, but they knew that the return of a Conservative government would allow them to present a politics of 'Standing up for Scotland' and offer the prospect of returning to a second independence referendum in the context of Brexit and putting together a winning popular majority.

Yet for all the turbulence and upheaval, there was also familiar territory: the claim that the Conservatives were imposing policies on Scotland with 'no mandate', with the SNP, Labour and the Lib Dems competing to who could best speak for non-Tory Scotland, and the politics of who could best defend Scottish interests. Similarly, all three pro-union parties had to carefully project their Scottishness, differentiate themselves from their British operations and attempt the balancing act of establishing clear water between each other, while agreeing on the case for the union.

In an age where prediction has proven to be a hazardous enterprise, it should not be surprising that many of the pre-election assumptions turned out to be erroneous, and Scotland came out of the campaign a different-looking place from that in which it entered. Scotland was the most electorally volatile part of the UK in 2015 and this was to continue into the 2017 election, and may continue to do so in the near future, and with it the salience of the continuation of the Scottish question and debate on Scotland's place in the UK.

Appendix: Timeline of Scottish Politics 2015–2017

2015

7 May: UK general election.

11 May: David Mundell is appointed Secretary of State for Scotland.

16 May: Jim Murphy announces he will stand down as Scottish Labour leader, following a 17 to 14 vote for him to remain in post by the Scottish Labour Executive.

22 May: Lib Dem Alistair Carmichael admits he leaked the Nicola Sturgeon memo known as 'Nikileaks' about Sturgeon meeting with the French Ambassador.

1 June: Former Lib Dem leader Charles Kennedy dies.

24 July: Community Empowerment (Scotland) Act receives Royal Assent.

15 August: Kezia Dugdale is elected Scottish Labour leader.

12 September: Jeremy Corbyn is elected Labour leader.

29 September: Michelle Thomson, MP for Edinburgh West, resigns the SNP whip.

24 November: Natalie McGarry, MP for Glasgow East, resigns the SNP whip.

27 November: Maggie Chapman is re-elected co-convenor of the Scottish Greens, winning 57.7%.

9 December: Alistair Carmichael election court case finds he told a 'blatant lie' when he denied leaking Sturgeon memo, but it is not proven that he committed an 'illegal practice'.

2016

23 March: Scotland Act 2016 receives Royal Assent.

30 March: Scottish Elections (Dates) Act receives Royal Assent, extending the term of the Scottish Parliament from four to five years, with the elections after 2016 to be held on 6 May 2021.

22 April: Land Reform (Scotland) Act receives Royal Assent.

5 May: Scottish Parliament elections sees the SNP win 63 seats compared to the Conservatives 31, Labour 24, Scottish Greens six and Lib Dems five.

17 May: Nicola Sturgeon is re-elected First Minister with 63 votes to Lib Dem Willie Rennie's five.

22 May: Stewart Hosie announces he will not stand again for SNP depute leader post.

26 May: Scottish Parliament votes by 106 votes to eight to support EU membership.

23 June: UK EU referendum.

24 June: David Cameron announces his resignation as UK Prime Minister. Nicola Sturgeon says a second independence referendum is 'highly likely'.

28 June: Scottish Parliament votes 92 to 0 to give the Scottish government a mandate to open EU discussions on the implications of Brexit for Scotland.

28 July: Supreme Court rules against aspects of the Scottish government's named person scheme in the Children and Young People (Scotland) Act.

31 July: Council house sales end.

24 September: Jeremy Corbyn is re-elected British Labour leader.

13 October: Angus Robertson wins the SNP depute leadership.

20 December: Scottish government White Paper *Scotland's Place in Europe* is published.

2017

1 January: First baby boxes in Scotland pilots start in Clackmannanshire and Orkney.

22 February: BBC announces new BBC Scotland TV channel to begin broadcasting in autumn 2018.

13 March: Nicola Sturgeon calls for a second independence referendum in light of the UK's withdrawal from the EU.

16 March: Theresa May says that 'now is not the time' for a second independence referendum.

28 March: Scottish Parliament votes 69 to 59 for a second independence vote.

29 March: UK triggers Article 50 to begin the process of leaving the EU.

Notes

1. James G. Kellas, *The Scottish Political System*, 4th edn. Cambridge University Press, 1989; Michael Keating, *The Government of Scotland: Public Policy Making after Devolution*, 2nd edn. Edinburgh University Press, 2010.
2. James Mitchell, *The Scottish Question*. Oxford University Press, 2014, p. 4.
3. William Miller, 'The Scottish Dimension' in David Butler and Dennis Kavanagh, *The British General Election of 1979*. Macmillan, 1980, p. 98.
4. Ibid., p. 99.
5. Richard Wyn Jones and Roger Scully, 'Devolution and Electoral Politics in Scotland and Wales', *Publius: The Journal of Federalism*, 36(1) (2006): 115–34.
6. Iain Macwhirter, *Tsunami: Scotland's Democratic Revolution*. Freight Books 2015; Aidan Kerr, 'The Ulsterisation of Scottish Politics', 31 December 2014, https://aidankerr.com/2014/12/31/the-ulsterisation-of-scottish-politics; Peter Jones, 'Ireland's Exit a Lesson for Cameron', *The Scotsman*, 11 May 2015; Martin Kettle, 'From Provocation to Power: the SNP's Tricky Road Ahead', *The Guardian*, 28 May 2015.
7. Gerry Hassan, *Independence of the Scottish Mind: Elite Narratives, Public Spaces and the Making of a Modern Nation*. Palgrave Macmillan, 2014.

8. Rob Johns and James Mitchell, *Takeover: Explaining the Extraordinary Rise of the SNP*. Biteback, 2016.
9. See Matt Dathan, 'Natalie McGarry Resigns Party Whip over "Missing Donations" Claims', *The Independent*, 24 November 2015; and 'Probe over Property Deals on Behalf of Michelle Thomson MP', *BBC Scotland News*, 29 September 2015, https://www.bbc.co.uk/news/uk-scotland-scotland-politics-34395392.
10. Mark Aitken, 'Ruthless Nicola Surgeon Axes SNP MP's Natalie McGarry and Michelle Thomson as Parties Get Revved up for General Election', *Daily Record*, 23 April 2017. The surprise 2017 election meant that both were not allowed by the SNP to stand again for the party: Edinburgh West was won by the Lib Dems and Glasgow East was narrowly held by the SNP.
11. Geoffrey Evans and James Tilley, *The New Politics of Class: The Political Exclusion of the British Working Class*. Oxford University Press, 2017, pp. 179–80.
12. The best account by far of the disorientation and inner chaos of the Labour, Conservative and Lib Dem parties over the 2014 referendum and 2015 UK election is by far Joe Pike, *Project Fear: How an Unlikely Alliance Left a Kingdom United But a Country Divided*. Biteback, 2015.
13. 'Scottish Labour Leader Jim Murphy to Resign', *BBC Scotland News*, 16 May 2015, https://www.bbc.co.uk/news/uk-scotland-scotland-politics-32760196.
14. James Cusick, 'Kezia Dugdale: Scottish Labour's New Leader, 33, Claims Optimism of Youth', *The Independent*, 15 August 2015.
15. Mary Riddell, 'The Long Road: Interview with Kezia Dugdale', *Fabian Review*, 1 April 2016. Dugdale subsequently claimed she was outed against her wishes. See Maya Oppenheim, 'Kezia Dugdale: Former Scottish Labour Leader Claims She was Outed as Gay against Her Will', *The Independent*, 31 August 2017.
16. Gerry Hassan, 'The Coming of Caledonian Corbynism' in Mark Perryman (ed.), *The Corbyn Effect*. Lawrence & Wishart, 2017, pp. 81–95.
17. 'Obituary: Jimmy Reid', *The Telegraph*, 11 August 2010.
18. *Re-elect: A Scottish Government Working for Scotland*. Scottish National Party, 2011, p. 2.
19. 'To Boldly Go', editorial, *The Scottish Sun*, 29 April 2016; Neil McLeod, 'Why it's No Surprise SNP'ers are in Denial over Sturgeon and the *Sun*', *CommonSpace*, 4 May 2016, https://www.commonspace.scot/articles/3957/neil-mcleod-why-its-no-surprise-snpers-are-denial-over-sturgeon-and-sun.
20. *Re-elect: SNP Manifesto 2016*. Scottish National Party, 2016, p. 23.
21. 'Kezia Dugdale Clarifies Independence Stance', *BBC Scotland News*, 1 April 2016, http://www.bbc.co.uk/news/uk-scotland-scotland-politics-35948407.

22. Peter Walker, 'Jeremy Corbyn Denies Backing Second Scottish Independence Vote', *The Guardian*, 13 March 2017.
23. Andrew Aiton, Ross Burnside, Allan Campbell, Tom Edwards, Greig Liddell, Iain McIver and Alanis McQuillen, *SPICe Briefing: Election 2016*. Scottish Parliament Information Centre, 2016.
24. British Election Study, private communication from John Curtice.
25. Tim Shipman, *All Out War: The Full Story of How Brexit Sank Britain's Political Class*. William Collins, 2016, p. 334.
26. 'EU Referendum Debate: MSPs Vote Overwhelmingly for UK to Remain in EU', *BBC Scotland News*, 26 May 2016, https://www.bbc.co.uk/news/uk-scotland-scotland-politics-36383590.
27. Alex Massie, 'Scotching a Myth: Scotland is Not as Left-Wing as You Think it is', *Spectator Coffee House*, 21 May 2014, https://blogs.spectator.co.uk/2014/05/scotching-a-myth-scotland-is-not-as-left-wing-as-you-think-it-is.
28. Lord Ashcroft, 'How the United Kingdom Voted on Thursday … and Why', *Lord Ashcroft Polls*, 24 June 2016, http://lordashcroftpolls.com/2016/06/how-the-united-kingdom-voted-and-why.
29. Shipman, *All Out War*, p. 456.
30. 'Brexit: Nicola Sturgeon Says Second Scottish Independence Vote "Highly Likely"', *BBC Scotland News*, 24 June 2016, https://www.bbc.co.uk/news/uk-scotland-scotland-politics-36621030.
31. Gordon Brown, *My Life, Our Times*. Bodley Head, 2017, p. 401.
32. Helen Liddell's memo written in January 1978 in anticipation of the March 1979 Scottish devolution referendum stated that Labour would adopt a 'no collaboration' stance with the SNP and the Liberals. The thinking was, wrote Liddell, that 'the achievement of an Assembly for Scotland will be ours and it would be wrong to allow our consistent opponents … to claim credit for this constitutional advance'. Allan Macartney, 'The Protagonists' in John Bochel, David Denver and Allan Macartney (eds), *The Referendum Experience: Scotland 1979*. Aberdeen University Press, 1981, p. 17.
33. Andrew Picken, 'End of the UK? New Survey Shows 59% Support Scottish Independence after Brexit Vote', *Sunday Post*, 26 June 2016.
34. John Curtice, 'Scottish Public Opinion and Brexit: Not So Clear after All?' in Gerry Hassan and Russell Gunson (eds), *Scotland, the UK and Brexit: A Guide to the Future*. Luath Press, 2017, p. 50.
35. Chris Curtis, 'Why Have the polls Not Shown a Shift to Scottish Independence?', *YouGov*, 27 January 2017, https://yougov.co.uk/news/2017/01/27/why-have-polls-not-shown-shift-towards-scottish-in.
36. Tom Peterkin, 'MSPs Give Nicola Sturgeon Mandate to Hold Direct EU talks', *The Scotsman*, 28 June 2016.

37. *Scotland's Place in Europe*. Scottish Government, 2016.
38. Annie Brown, 'Meet Woman at the Heart of Tawdry Love Triangle that Led to the Breakdown of Two SNP MPs' Marriages', *Daily Record*, 17 May 2016.
39. Angus Robertson won with 52.5% of the vote on the first ballot, to Tommy Sheppard's 25.5%, with Alyn Smith on 18.6% and Chris McEleny on 3.4% on a low turnout of the SNP's enlarged membership: with 35,004 members voting out of an eligible electorate of 103,000, a mere 34%. Patrick Grady, 'SNP Depute Leadership Contest Result', *SNP*, 13 October 2016, https://www.snp.org/depute_leadership_contest_result.
40. Simon Johnson, 'Theresa May and Ruth Davidson More Popular than Nicola Sturgeon in Scotland', *Daily Telegraph*, 15 September 2016.
41. Mark Leftly, 'Alex Salmond: Nicola Sturgeon Should Call a Referendum Even if the Polls are 50/50', *PoliticsHome*, 13 October 2016, https://www.politicshome.com/news/uk/political-parties/snp/alex-salmond/news/79822/alex-salmond-nicola-sturgeon-should-call.
42. 'Scottish Independence: Nicola Sturgeon to Seek Second Referendum', *BBC Scotland News*, 13 March 2017, https://www.bbc.co.uk/news/uk-scotland-scotland-politics-39255181; 'Theresa May: "Now is Not the Time" for Scottish Independence Vote', *BBC Scotland News*, 16 March 2017, https://www.bbc.co.uk/news/av/uk-scotland-scotland-politics-39291860/theresa-may-now-is-not-the-time-for-scotland-independence-vote; 'Scottish Parliament Backs Referendum Call', *BBC Scotland News*, 28 March 2017, https://www.bbc.co.uk/news/uk-scotland-39422747; 'Article 50: UK Set to Formally Trigger Brexit Process', *BBC News*, 29 March 2017, https://www.bbc.co.uk/news/uk-politics-39422353.
43. Gerry Hassan and Simon Barrow (eds), *A Nation Changed? The SNP and Scotland Ten Years on*. Luath Press, 2017.
44. 'How Well or Badly Do You Think the Current Scottish Government is Handling the NHS?', *What Scotland Thinks*, www.whatscotlandthinks.org/questions/how-well-or-badly-do-you-think-the-current-scottish-government-is-handling-the#line; 'How Well or Badly Do You Think the Current Scottish Government is Handling Education?', *What Scotland Thinks*, www.whatscotlandthinks.org/questions/how-well-or-badly-do-you-think-the-current-scottish-govt-is-handling-education#line.
45. Will Dahlgreen, 'Nicola Sturgeon is Scotland's Most Popular Person', *YouGov*, 1 November 2015, https://yougov.co.uk/news/2015/11/01/nicola-sturgeon-scotlands-most-popular-person.
46. Lord Ashcroft, 'Lord Ashcroft Discusses Focus Group Results of Previous SNP, Labour and Lib Dem Voters in Edinburgh and Aberdeen', *Holyrood*, 26 May 2017.

47. 'Do You Think Nicola Sturgeon is Doing Well or Badly as First Minister?', *What Scotland Thinks*, www.whatscotlandthinks.org/questions/do-you-think-nicola-sturgeon-is-doing-well-or-badly-as-first-minister#table.
48. Ibid.
49. Ashcroft, 'Lord Ashcroft Discusses Focus Group Results'.
50. John Curtice, 'The Three Characteristics of the Scottish Conservative Revival', *What Scotland Thinks*, 1 October 2017, http://blog.whatscotlandthinks.org/2017/10/the-three-characteristics-of-the-scottish-conservative-revival.
51. British Election Survey, private communication from John Curtice.

CHAPTER 7

Towards a Landslide

Even by the standards of a normal election campaign, which are not for the lazy, the first few weeks of the 2017 campaign were especially hectic. All those involved speak of the frantic pace at the start of the campaign. The preparatory work that parties would normally undertake before an election over at least a year—drafting manifestoes, planning campaign events, allocating funding and selecting candidates—all had to be shoe-horned into a fortnight or so.

While some of the opposition parties had been actively preparing for a contest, the governing party—the one with the power to call the election—had not been able to give any indication it was considering the election until it was announced, lest it give away its intentions. This ruled out all but the most minimal of preparatory work by the Conservatives; as one Number 10 aide noted: 'We called an election and only the Conservative Party was surprised.' Once discussions about an early election had begun in earnest, a small group, consisting of Stephen Gilbert, Darren Mott and several of Theresa May's aides, had begun to hold private planning meetings, which, for the sake of secrecy, took place not at Conservative Campaign Headquarters (CCHQ), but in the Trafalgar Suite at the St Ermin's Hotel in Westminster.[1] The meetings were scheduled to last for an hour—apparently a rule of Lynton Crosby's, even though he was still abroad when the campaign began—and discussed basic campaign mechanics and arrangements. Plans for the group to meet daily were aborted and no more than a handful were held; Crosby's absence, despite his involvement on the occasional conference call, limited their usefulness. Crosby was in Fiji for his wife's birthday and did not arrive in London

© The Author(s) 2018
P. Cowley, D. Kavanagh, *The British General Election of 2017*,
https://doi.org/10.1007/978-3-319-95936-8_7

until 25 April; Mark Textor arrived on 20 April. 'We were waiting for Lynton to arrive', admitted Nick Timothy later, 'and the advantage of getting a head start on Labour was basically lost.'

'All the work that goes into preparing for an election normally', said one of those at CCHQ, 'none of it was done.' Phone calls over the Easter weekend had managed to reunite many, though not all, of the same people who had been involved in the 2015 campaign. There was a feeling, remarked one, of 'getting the band back together' (although they were to realise quickly that the lead singer had changed). Conservative staff hoped they would catch up as the campaign went on, but they did not. 'We were never ahead of ourselves', said one. There was no proper grid, setting out the campaign plan ('Every day, the programme would change three or four times'); none of the key seats material was ready, so the team were frequently in the office until 2 am preparing material for the next day. Almost none of the policy preparation had been undertaken; special advisers were being asked urgently, before resigning from government to work on the campaign, to gather as much data and material as they could find to bring to CCHQ. For the 2015 election, the Conservative events team had spent two years planning, scouting out venues and sorting out travel logistics; for 2017, they had a standing start. As one of those working in CCHQ noted: 'All of that work, the prep, the data, it just wasn't there this time. So it was more a case of what can we do, in seven and a half weeks, with what we've got left over from the last election.' 'The thing that shocked me most', said another 'was the last-minuteness of it all.'[2]

Moran, *Daily Telegraph*, 22 April 2017 © Bob Moran/Telegraph Media Group Ltd

Labour had suspected the Prime Minister might call an early election to coincide with the local elections due on 4 May; even after the last possible date to trigger a 4 May contest had passed, there was still lingering concern within Southside that she might use the local elections—which were not expected to be good for Labour—as the springboard for a June contest, and the party machine continued to prepare accordingly. On the morning of 18 April, as the Prime Minister briefed the Cabinet on her decision, one of Labour's election coordinators Andrew Gwynne happened to be in Southside, looking through an almost finalised draft of Labour's *Snap General Election Guide*. When it was announced that there would be a prime ministerial statement, Patrick Heneghan received a text message from Jon Ashworth, Labour's Shadow Health Secretary, which summed up the feeling of many in the party: 'Fuck she's not going to call an election is she[?]' The election guide was then circulated to all Labour MPs within two hours of the Prime Minister's announcement—although, as one of those involved in its distribution noted, this was at least partly just to calm people down ('So they know we're on it') rather than because the document was especially useful. More importantly, the more detailed logistical list of the activities required to get the party on an election footing—'Operation Rapid Deployment'—was immediately put into action.

The Leader of the Opposition's Office (LOTO) team moved out of their offices in the parliamentary Norman Shaw buildings and into Southside. The duplication of effort involved in running parallel operations was even more obvious when the two teams were brought together. One of Jeremy Corbyn's team described the new arrangement as like Noah's Ark, with two of everything. Another noted the two rows of press desks—the Southside team and the leader's team—and observed that it was 'like North and South Korea'; 'I know which one you are', muttered one of the party staff. The Southsiders would frequently complain that the LOTO team did not know what they were doing ('Everything's so last minute, so disorganised, they don't have a proper media grid, they're just making it up on the spot'), whilst the leader's team believed the Southsiders continued to frustrate them at every turn. Jon Trickett was given the title of political advisor and was brought back into the fold, much to the surprise of some Southsiders. 'There were plenty at Southside who wanted to run a traditional, Blair-like campaign … We had plenty of resistance', said one of Corbyn's team. 'He was brought in to bolster the numbers against the bureaucracy.'

Seumas Milne presented a quickly written version of Labour's strategy to the NEC on 19 April. Much of the document was vague (as such documents often are), but it identified key aspects of the Labour campaign. It began, crucially, by noting that 'making this a referendum re-run is a trap'. 'Brexit is settled', it argued. 'But what kind of Brexit is not.' In the campaign, Labour should try to draw out the differences between what they called a 'Tory reckless Brexit' and a 'people's Brexit'. The latter would involve 'access to' the Single Market, a carefully written phrase that was not the same as 'membership of'. The presentation predicted that Conservative attacks would primarily focus on how 'Corbyn would bankrupt Britain', with secondary attacks to come over the 'spectre of the SNP', Labour's divisions over leadership and Brexit, and how the party was 'weak and extremist'.

The presentation also listed Labour's 'key targets'. These included 'low and middle-income voters', 'older voters and pensioners', 'young people and students', 'ethnic minorities', 'self-employed and small business owners', 'people with disabilities and carers', 'WASPI women' and 'public service professionals'. These key targets did not exclude much of the population. Not everyone present was convinced.[3]

Noting that the polling advice was that simply attacking the Conservatives only tends to worsen Labour's position (see above, p. 93), Milne argued that Labour's approach could not be 'business as usual'; in order to cut through: 'We have to surprise.' The document gave little evidence of how Labour would do this, but this approach would inform much of what was to follow. As another of Labour's team noted: 'Politics is a gamble. And when you're that far behind, you may as well take risks.'

A campaign plan, drafted by Steve Howell, discussed at a Southside–LOTO meeting a week later, outlined a broad 'narrative arc' for the campaign, beginning with the premise of a rigged system that held people back before moving to demonstrate Labour's alternative. It noted that the election would give Labour a platform and much greater media access. It would maintain momentum with policy announcements, as well as the need to invest in a celebrity-led registration campaign ('on a scale never seen before aimed at students/young people').[4] A draft grid proposed a series of major rallies, including one in the penultimate week of the campaign involving Bernie Sanders.

For all the remaining mistrust and hostility, LOTO and Southside did now share a common enemy. There would be arguments about how best to do it, but it was in all their interests for Labour to do as well as possible. The Southsiders were convinced that Labour were heading for a catastrophic defeat, but they wanted to save as many Labour MPs as possible in order to help rebuild what many of them hoped would be a

Corbyn-free-Labour party afterwards. Within LOTO, although relatively few believed that Labour could win the election, they knew that the better they did, the more chance they had on holding on to the leadership of the party.

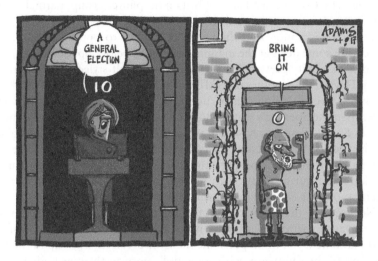

Adams, *Daily Telegraph*, 19 April 2017 © Adams/Telegraph Media Group Ltd

The opening of the campaign saw attempts to redefine the political battle lines. The Greens urged Labour and the Liberal Democrats to join them in combining forces to beat the Conservatives. In a letter to Corbyn and Tim Farron, the Greens' co-leaders said:

> we … continue to believe there is a role for some form of cooperation in a handful of seats to create the best possible chance of beating the Tories and, crucially, of thereby delivering a fairer voting system. The latter is critical if we want to build the better politics to which both of you have said you are committed.

The SNP similarly called for post-election anti-Conservative deals if the numbers supported it. Open Britain—the shell of the 2016 Remain campaign—announced that it would work to support Remain candidates, only to then face a walkout by Conservative MPs who did not want to support from an organisation that was also trying to defeat their Leave colleagues.

Gina Miller, who had been behind the court challenge over Article 50, launched a tactical voting initiative, designed to rally support behind candidates opposed to a hard Brexit.[5]

For the most part, this attempt to create a 'progressive alliance' all came to little. The Communist Party of Britain (a splinter group, naturally) and the Trade Unionist and Socialist Coalition (which had fielded 135 candidates in 2015) announced they were not going to oppose Labour, and there were some deals at the margins (discussed below, pp. 385–386). The Women's Equality Party called for a clear run at self-styled 'Men's Activist' Philip Davies, the Conservative MP in Shipley, with the Greens withdrawing in its favour. Labour, in particular, refused to stand aside anywhere other than the Speaker's seat of Buckingham, and disciplined party members in South West Surrey who wanted the party to stand down to allow the National Health Action Party a clear run at the Health Secretary, Jeremy Hunt. For the most part, the party system remained intact. Farron quickly ruled out not only such pre-election deals but also any form of coalition or post-election agreement with other parties.

No one at that point expected that any configuration of non-Conservative parties would make much of an impact on the shape of the next Parliament. Opinion polls saw the Conservatives track up in the first few days of the campaign, with some polls putting them as high as 48%, with Labour falling as low as 24%. The doubts that some Conservative MPs had had about the calling of the election largely vanished after they spent their first weekend on the doorstep canvassing. With Parliament still sitting, Conservative MPs came back from their constituencies 'cock-a-hoop', according to one member of the government's whips' office. On 24 April, a poll of voting intentions in Wales put the Conservatives on 40%, ten percentage points ahead of Labour, a lead substantial enough to see the Conservatives win a majority of Welsh seats, the first time this would have happened since the 1850s. Wales was, wrote Roger Scully, 'on the brink of an electoral earthquake'.[6] On 26 April, Conservative MPs were called to party HQ at Matthew Parker Street to have photographs taken with the Prime Minister for their campaign material. Repeatedly, she was told how well she was going down on the doorstep.

The mood amongst Labour MPs reflected the flipside of such encounters and the view of the party's field team in Southside was that the result could easily be worse than that of 1983; some insiders even worried that the party could fall short of its catastrophic performance in 1935. At a Southside meeting on 22 April, Steve Howell began a presentation with the words 'we are campaigning to win', only for half the table to burst out laughing. Two days later, an internal Labour polling presentation at Southside predicted that in a worst-case scenario, Labour could end the election below 130 seats; Ian Lavery remarked to a colleague that it was the most depressing meeting he had ever attended. 'It's about limiting the scale of the disaster', said one of Labour's field team at the beginning of the campaign.

For the Conservatives, the assumption of an easy victory was a problem. Their key campaign message was supposed to be about the risks of a Labour government. But if everyone thought the Conservatives were a shoo-in, then it became safe to vote Labour. The Crosby-Textor memo to May before the election was called noted that there were:

> exceptionally high expectations that this [a Conservative majority] will be the outcome of any election held now. Both quantitatively (in Liberal Democrat seats) and qualitatively (in Labour seats) this is leading voters to believe that they can vote for the best local MP, or not reject their current good local MP, while still remaining secure in the knowledge that Jeremy Corbyn will not be Prime Minister. Thus the Conservatives must urgently work to *ensure that any election is seen through a national prism*. (Emphasis in original)

Some Labour politicians saw the opportunity. Early on in the campaign, Helen Goodman, the Labour MP for Bishop Auckland, gave a TV interview in which she declared: 'I don't think that this election is about changing the Government ... I think this election is about preventing the Tories from getting such an overwhelming majority that there is no possibility of dissent in this country.' John Woodcock's candidature for Barrow & Furness briefly seemed in doubt, after he announced that he would 'not countenance ever voting to make Jeremy Corbyn Britain's Prime Minister'. Challenged about this, he responded that it was just hypothetical anyway: 'we're never going to win'. Even Labour's Deputy Leader came close to a similar claim. Addressing USDAW, the shopworkers' union, Tom Watson claimed that 'sometimes the most important question isn't what makes the best PM. It's who makes the best MP'.[7] Other Labour MPs tried in their campaign literature to distance themselves from the party and its leader (see below, pp. 295–6).

The early weeks of the campaign revealed a clear difference between the approaches taken by the two main parties. Largely drawing on policies already scheduled as part of their campaign for the local elections on 4 May, Labour announced a series of policies, including: pay rises for NHS staff, plans for housebuilding, the outlawing of zero hours contacts, a reduction in the threshold for inheritance tax, a 20-point plan for workers' rights and proposals to improve the rights of those renting homes. One early eye-catching initiative was a call for four extra Bank Holidays, one on each of the patron saints' days for England, Wales, Scotland and Northern Ireland; announced during a St George's Day interview Corbyn had with Andrew Marr, the policy was dropped into the party's media grid at 3 pm the day before, when it became clear to everyone involved that otherwise Corbyn had nothing to announce. It was, one of Corbyn's key advisors ruefully admitted, 'media-driven'.

The Conservatives offered little policy in return. The original campaign grid planned for the Conservatives to spend the first week justifying the decision to call the election; the official narrative (the words of which were

posted on the walls of CCHQ) began with the words 'we need this election now...'. The Conservative media grid initially consisted almost solely
of attacks on Labour—and especially on Jeremy Corbyn. Soon after his
arrival at CCHQ, Crosby briefed Conservative Party staff and explained
that they were going to focus on May as a leader; their focus groups had
shown she was a great leader and a huge asset: 'We are framing this election as the choice between her and Jeremy Corbyn.' In another briefing,
Textor claimed that no right-of-centre party across the world had ever had
an electoral asset as strong as May; no left-of-centre party, by contrast, had
ever had an electoral liability like Corbyn. The guidance given to those
constructing Conservative press releases or media briefings therefore
began with three key rules:

1. Always emphasize the need to back Theresa May and her team.
2. Never mention Labour without referencing Jeremy Corbyn—he should be
   the primary focus, not the Labour brand.
3. To the extent possible, re-focus issues to Brexit outcomes—without a
   strong negotiating hand everything is at risk and other's policy proposals
   aren't possible.

The stated aim was to 'Corbynise'—their word—the Labour campaign.
The top line for every press release was to contain a variation of 'another
nonsensical Jeremy Corbyn idea'.

As a result, the positive news stories, policy announcements and pledges
that are the familiar daily grind of elections were largely absent from the
Tory campaign. Some aides pushed to trail positive policies in advance of
the manifesto, but were blocked by Crosby. On 21 April, the Prime
Minister publicly committed her party to continue to support a 0.7% target for foreign aid spending (albeit with the proviso that the government
would ensure that the money was being spent 'in the most effective way').
There were indications from both the Prime Minister and the Chancellor
that David Cameron's tax lock promising no rises in income tax, National
Insurance or VAT would be dropped—although this was hardly likely to
win over swing voters.

The Tory campaign centred almost exclusively on Theresa May and her
ability to deliver 'strong and stable' leadership. The frequency with which
the phrase was heard—from almost every Conservative spokesperson—
was such that journalists and other observers soon started to groan at its
predictability. Tom Watson joked that: 'People are worried about the risk

of robots taking their jobs. I fear with this Prime Minister it's already happened.'

There was also a very obvious difference in the type of events in which the party leaders took part. The plans of the team in Downing Street for a more collegiate approach in which May presented herself as part of the Cabinet and in which she was not always front and centre—and which included the sort of press conferences that had largely vanished from recent British elections—were abandoned in favour of events that were an almost carbon copy of those in which David Cameron had taken part during the 2015 campaign, but with an even greater focus on the leader.[8] The campaign bus on which the Prime Minister travelled was decorated with the words 'Theresa May: For Britain' in huge lettering, with even a faux May signature on side (as if she had signed the bus, lest anyone be confused). The word 'Conservatives' featured in much smaller font. A familiar sight on the evening news would be the Prime Minister giving a talk in front of a backdrop featuring her name (again in huge letters), taking a handful of questions from journalists with a small coterie of supporters behind her—supporters who were often MPs, candidates or party members.

These events were mocked for being so tightly controlled and safe. Writing in *The Guardian*, Marina Hyde noted:

> Each day the Prime Minister is rendered to a sealed regional facility, where she tortures a captive audience with looped repetitions of the phrase 'strong and stable'. After a sustained period of it, people are unsure whether to applaud or confess to a Pakistani embassy bombing they had nothing to with just to make it stop.[9]

David Cameron had been similarly mocked during the 2015 campaign, including by Marina Hyde, only to emerge victorious.[10] However, some of those involved in 2017 soon realised that there were differences. For one thing, Cameron had years of experience of such events, having made an art of 'Cameron Direct' events even before becoming Prime Minister; May was much less experienced. Second, there was the duration: the 2017 campaign went on for longer and the mockery began much earlier. And, third, there was the contrast with the Leader of the Opposition.

Corbyn's team chose to focus his energies and efforts on a format that had brought the best out of the Labour leader in the two leadership campaigns: rallies. Usually outdoors, Corbyn and the local candidates would address hundreds and, as the campaign went on, often thousands of people. These were very different from the events that Labour staff had been organising for most recent previous leaders; the last to take a similar approach was Michael Foot and outside of LOTO, this was not widely seen as an encouraging precedent.' In 1983, *The Guardian* had reported one of Michael Foot's rallies as an 'effusion of love and affection', only for the party to collapse to its worse post-war defeat.[11] Corbyn's critics within the party worried that the same would be true this time. 'No swing voter goes to a rally', complained one Southsider. For the LOTO team, the events were important to show contact, but also to generate a sense of momentum and, as the campaign went on, the crowds got larger, and the contrast with the Prime Minister's smaller events grew more obvious.

Corbyn's stump speech varied relatively little: at its heart was a refrain of public ownership, renewed public services and an 'end to austerity', to which his team would feed in topical additions or local references. To his critics, these were banalities: he was in favour of good things and against bad things. Matthew Flinders notes the left-wing strain of populism in Corbyn speeches, offering 'simple solutions to complex problems … particularly attuned to the plucking of popular emotions'.[12] For his supporters, though, the Labour leader was someone willing to say things that other British politicians were not. Moreover, the Corbyn of 2017 was not the Corbyn of 2015. His speaking style had improved during his leadership, as a result of doing so many similar events, and he had smartened up his appearance. At Prime Minister's Questions in 2016, David Cameron had taunted Corbyn, saying that he should 'put on a proper suit, do up your tie and sing the national anthem'.[13] By 2017, he had complied. He now routinely appeared in a dark blue suit, with a white or blue shirt. He sometimes even wore a tie.[14] His beard had been trimmed. Smartening him up had been a long-term project of his team; they had been trying, slowly, to get him to work on his appearance for months.[15] 'I'm glad I never have to see that yellow sports jacket again', remarked one of his closest aides. Corbyn needed to be persuaded of such things and chivvying him could be counterproductive, but in the end, he was convinced. 'There were two Jeremys during the campaign', one of his team said. 'One is open-necked shirt, no tie, out at the rallies. But we want our guy to look like a Prime Minister as well. Image is everything.' Unlike others who have smartened up their appearance when moving into the front row of politics, Corbyn managed this transformation while avoiding accusations of selling out.

Even one of Corbyn's internal critics at Southside admitted that he had also got better at media interviews: 'He used to ramble on about where he was, and what he'd been doing. He now goes, bang, straight to the message. He's also got much less irritable when challenged.' At a rally in Oxford in May, Corbyn described himself as 'Monsieur Zen', saying he 'never got angry'. This was not the view of those who worked with him; although he rarely completely lost his temper, he could frequently get irritated, especially with journalists, and his early media interviews showed little sign of Zen-like behaviour. But by the time the campaign began, he was much more relaxed and comfortable when dealing with the media.

 ‣ The Conservative campaign attracted criticism for controlling journalists' access to the Prime Minister, yet Conservatives—and some journalists—would note that Corbyn rarely took questions at his rallies and almost never questions from journalists. The Corbyn team decided early on that there was little to gain from attempting to engage with much of the print media during the campaign, with almost the sole exception of the *Daily Mirror*, a position even some Southsiders conceded was understandable (as one said: 'It's probably fair enough. It's just another five questions about the IRA and nothing positive'). In that sense, the Corbyn events were at least as controlled, if not more so, than those run by the Prime Minister, but the contrast in the sort of images generated for television and social media was stark. The Labour leader looked as if he was out and about, meeting normal people; the Prime Minister did not.

Facing criticism that she was not meeting the public in unvarnished settings, it was briefed that May had raged at her team about restrained access and to prove the point was taken door knocking with Ruth Davidson, the Scottish Conservative leader. Door after door went unanswered and a sheepish Prime Minister had to retreat back to her car.[16] For security reasons, police advice was for her to limit the number of walkabouts she conducted, but those she did were not successes. There was also an awkward photocall in Cornwall in which the Prime Minister walked around with a portion of chips in one hand and a cup of tea in the other, giving the impression of someone who had never encountered food or drink before.[17] Later in the campaign, a walkabout in Abingdon Market in Oxfordshire saw her harangued by a voter called Cathy, who wanted to know how she was going to help people with learning disabilities.[18] (As is now customary in such encounters, the person doing the haranguing did not wait for answers before continuing to harangue.) None of these events helped the Prime Minister's image as someone in touch with the people.

On 28 April, Labour launched their election slogan 'For the many, not the few'. It was one of five slogans the party had tested:

1. 'We will build a Britain for the many not the few.'
2. 'We need to end the rigged system that is holding people back.'
3. 'For the people, not the powerful.'
4. 'Don't let the Conservatives hold Britain back.'
5. 'The Conservatives look after the richest, not the rest of us.'

Of these, 'We will build a Britain for the many not the few' performed best in the quantitative polling among the general public and 'Labour Considerers'. It also worked well in the qualitative work the party carried out. The phrase had Blairite connections; it was in the revised Clause IV of the Party Constitution ('to create for each of us the means to realise our true potential and for all of us a community in which power, wealth and opportunity are in the hands of the many, not the few'), to which Corbyn had objected when it was introduced, and was variously used by Tony Blair during the 1997 campaign. But it had much wider antecedents, having been variously used by an eclectic group of politicians including Ramsay MacDonald, Harry Pollitt, Iain Macleod, Merlyn Rees and John Major.[19] Those around Corbyn knew of the Blair connection, but did not care. 'I don't think the electorate really remember political history like that', said one of Corbyn's aides. They liked the phrase because it 'speaks to the universalist approach on education, on pensions, on tax policy. It was broad and universal for the public and members got it too which was important'. Those who follow politics obsessively may have over-stated the extent to which the rest of the country were paying attention; by early May, and despite its almost constant repetition, YouGov found that just 15% of Britons could recall the Conservative 'strong and stable', and even amongst the minority of voters who reported high levels of political attention, the figure was just 39%. The same poll found just 2% could recall Labour's 'For the many'.

One of Labour's early policy announcements—another that had been originally planned for the local elections but quickly cannibalised for the general election campaign—was on police numbers. A media blitz was scheduled on 2 May for Diane Abbott, Labour's Shadow Home Secretary, to announce that Labour would increase police numbers by 10,000, with the funding to come from a partial reversal of cuts to capital gains tax.

Interviewed by Nick Ferrari on LBC Radio, Abbott struggled to respond to basic factual questions about the costs of the policy, contradicting herself repeatedly; at times the only noise being transmitted being the desperate sound of briefing papers rustling.[20] Initial questions about the cost of the policy costings generated a somewhat hesitant answer ('They will cost... It will cost... About... About 80 million pounds...'), after which things went downhill swiftly:

Ferrari: But... I don't understand, if you divide 80 million by 10,000, you get 8,000. Is that what you're going to pay these policemen and women?

Abbott: No, we're talking about, um, a process over four years.

Ferrari: I don't understand. What is he or she getting? 80 million divided by 10,000 equals 8,000. What are these police officers going to be paid?

Abbott: We will be paying them the average...

Ferrari: Has this been thought through?

Abbott: Of course, it's been thought through.

Ferrari: Where are the figures?

Abbott: The figures are that the additional costs in year one when we anticipate recruiting about 250,000 policemen will be £64.3 million.

Ferrari: 250,000 policemen?

Abbott: And women.

Ferrari: So you're getting more than 10,000? You're recruiting 250,000?

Abbott: No, we are recruiting 2,000, and perhaps 250. And the cost...

Ferrari: So where did 250,000 come from?

Abbott: I think you said that, not me.

Ferrari: No, no. I can assure you, you said that figure.

By this point, Abbott had found the correct figures, but the damage had been done. It was at least as painful an interview as Natalie Bennett's in 2015—which was also with Ferrari, also over cost and also involving getting tripped up by arithmetic—but Bennett had been the Green Party leader and no one expected her to end up in government. Abbott was a potential Home Secretary and this was a flagship Labour policy. She continued with her media round, heading over to the BBC's lunchtime political TV programme, *The Daily Politics*. If LBC on radio had been bad, *The*

Daily Politics was perhaps worse: the programme replayed the audio of the LBC interview while the camera focused tightly on Abbott's face. It was an excruciating moment of political television. All elections have their moments of television or radio notoriety, which are often rightly dismissed as ephemera that the public do not know, or care, about. This was an exception. Polling found that the Abbott incident was one of the most noted moments of the opening stages of the election.[21] Lord Ashcroft's polling found that the 'incident was mentioned spontaneously in nearly every one of our focus groups from then until election day' and that 'it crystallised many people's views of Labour basic competence and apparently cavalier attitude to public money'.[22]

Abbott, and those close to Corbyn, complained of 'gotcha' journalism, with journalists trying to trip politicians up over details rather than engaging with a policy, adding that the treatment of Abbott was driven by racism, with her being treated in a way that other politicians were not.[23] It was certainly true that she was not the only politician to slip up during the campaign and yet none of the others attracted the same opprobrium. Later that month, the Chancellor, Philip Hammond, got the cost of the HS2 rail link wrong by a non-trivial £20 billion—during an interview meant to highlight Labour's inability to manage finances—yet the incident generated none of the equivalent coverage; Theresa May managed to confuse tourism and terrorism ('We want to lead the world in combatting tourism'), whilst Jeremy Corbyn similarly endured a painful radio interview much later in the campaign (see p. 221), also without the widespread mockery that Abbott suffered.[24] There was plenty of evidence that much of the dislike of Abbott was driven by racism of the most straightforward kind. Yet at the same time, many within the Labour machine had relatively little sympathy for her, believing that she had a tendency to go on programmes under-briefed—often refusing to take briefings from Southside staff—and on this occasion had been caught out. In particular, there was little sympathy for someone caught out on costings, given that is often the first thing Labour spokespeople are asked by interviewers. 'She loses us votes every time she goes on TV', complained one Southsider.

At Southside, Milne signed off Labour's broadcast appearances—and tried, not entirely successfully, to limit Abbott's media appearances following the debacle.[25] There was a small pool of MPs used for Labour media appearances, not least because relatively few were willing to put themselves forward. The lack of frontbenchers volunteering for media appearances had been raised at a Shadow Cabinet meeting just before the election began, but fear of being associated with what they assumed would be a disastrous campaign held some back. At least five Shadow Cabinet ministers refused to do broadcast media during the campaign; some refused even to leave their constituencies to canvass in other seats. Several of those who did volunteer flourished during the campaign, most notably Emily Thornberry and Barry Gardiner.

The Liberal Democrat campaign also did not get off to a smooth start. On the day that the election was called, Tim Farron gave an interview to Cathy Newman of *Channel 4 News*. She reprised her questions from the day after his leadership election, asking whether he saw homosexuality as a sin; he reprised his evasive answers ('I'm not going to spend my time talking theology or making pronouncements'). Yet unlike after the leadership election in 2015, when relatively few people had noticed his equivocation, this time the story exploded, especially on social media. The issue was to cause Farron personally and the party collectively considerable grief. Farron's private view was that in a theological sense gay sex *was* a sin, but he—and those around him—was aware that to say so explicitly would have been an electoral catastrophe, given the liberal nature of the party's support. He also genuinely did not feel that such questions were the role of a politician. 'He doesn't see it as his role to talk about what sin is', said one of his team, 'it's a theological question, and he's very uncomfortable talking about what is or isn't a sin' and, as another of his team argued, 'once you get into it, where do you stop? We did one interview and there's some bloke asking him about whether it's OK to eat shellfish'.

The next day, 19 April, Farron responded to a similar question in the House of Commons, this time from a Conservative MP, with a more straightforward answer ('no, no I do not'), but on 23 April, he appeared on the *Peston on Sunday* programme on ITV. He dealt easily with the question about whether homosexuality was a sin, but then—just as some of his advisors had feared—Peston moved the questioning onto whether gay *sex* was a sin, at which point the equivocation began again. It took until 25 April before he explicitly said that he did not think gay sex was a sin, in a BBC interview that was designed to put an end to the issue.[26] Yet he still struggled with the subject, and in a later LBC interview, he again equivocated.[27]

Behind the scenes, multiple attempts had been made to try to come up with forms of words that he would be willing to say and which would resolve the issue. On several occasions, those around the leader believed they had done so, only for Farron to change his mind, usually after a trip back to his constituency. As one of those involved said: 'It really matters to him what his church thinks—literally, the people he sees in church.' Or, as another put it: 'He'd travel back to Westmorland, where things were not going well, and he'd go to church and he'd realise how much they mattered to him, and how much it mattered to them, and he'd come back down to London on Monday and everything we thought we'd agreed would have unravelled.' Those around him realised the pressure that this clash between his personal beliefs and the party was placing on him—whenever the subject was raised, he looked stressed and anxious ('Tim's whole shtick, the cheeky chappie, just vanishes; he becomes like a salted snail')—but they were also aware of the problem it was causing for the party.

It could have been worse. The party believed the *Daily Mail* had a two-page spread prepared, featuring assorted comments from those in Farron's church, along with excerpts from sermons that he had sat through, which would have been incendiary had they been released. ('It's a bit like Obama and his Preacher', said one staffer, 'the only problem is: we've not got Obama.') There was also a fear that the questions would start to spread to other areas of policy. A month after the campaign began, an interview that Farron had given to the Salvation Army magazine in 2007—after he became an MP, but before becoming party leader—surfaced, in which he had described abortion as 'wrong'. It led to a series of headlines about whether the Lib Dems were anti-abortion. During a private debate rehearsal session, Farron was asked a question about whether abortion was morally wrong, at which point he started to equivocate. The former Clegg advisor James McGrory was playing Paul Nuttall ('he had a great time, made a much more effective Paul Nuttall than the real Paul Nuttall'), but at this point he broke out of character and exploded: 'For fuck's sake, you just say no—it's not fucking wrong.'

The party had not intended to open the campaign with a theology seminar. 'It spread a nasty stain across the whole of the campaign', one staffer complained. Perhaps worse, this issue was cutting through with the public, whilst the party found its other announcements getting nowhere. When a Labour focus group discovered the reaction of voters to Farron's comments, Labour quickly prepared an attack clip—featuring various Farron interviews on the subject—which they pushed heavily in Labour-Lib Dem constituencies via Facebook. Later in the campaign, Lib Dem party staff ran a focus group of their own with would-be Lib Dem voters, in which they asked what people had heard about the party. 'The only thing that got mentioned was homosexuality', said one of those who organised the groups. 'People said: "That doesn't sound very liberal", and you wanted to scream.' The pro-EU stance that the party had assumed would be such a distinctive position—and which had appeared to be working in by-elections previously—was failing to cut through. 'It was like a door had closed', said one of the party's field team. Those studying the party's canvass returns were in despair. 'They were watching things fade away', said one. At one point, the internal Lib Dem estimate, based on their canvass returns and some very limited polling, was that the party might be reduced to just one MP—Alastair Carmichael in Orkney & Shetland. James Gurling, the head of the party's campaign, found himself thinking that he might well be chairing the last ever Liberal Democrat election campaign.

On 30 April, details of a dinner in Downing Street attended by Jean-Claude Junker, David Davis and the Prime Minister were leaked. The full details were set out in *Frankfurter Allgemeine Sonntagszeitung* and were initially broadcast to the British political establishment in a series of tweets by *The Economist* journalist Jeremy Cliffe. They recounted a dinner at which it had become increasingly clear there was no meeting of minds on the big issues, Juncker reportedly telling May that 'I'm leaving Downing Street ten times more sceptical than I was before'. After the dinner, Juncker had apparently phoned Angela Merkel and described May as 'living in another galaxy'. On 3 May, Parliament was dissolved. Having visited Buckingham Palace, the Prime Minister returned to Number 10 and, on the steps of Downing Street, accused European politicians of meddling in the election:

> The European Commission's negotiating stance has hardened. Threats against Britain have been issued by European politicians and officials. All of these acts have been deliberately timed to affect the result of the general election which will take place on 8 June.

She went on to say that 'the events of the last few days have shown that whatever our wishes, and however reasonable the positions of the Europe's other leaders, there are some in Brussels who do not want these talks to succeed, who do not want Britain to prosper'. The Prime Minister, according to *The Times*, was talking 'fire and brimstone'. Her anger was not synthetic—she was genuinely cross about the leak—but it was also, in the words of one of her team, 'a strategic decision to refocus on Brexit again'. Watching on, Crosby was delighted. It was the highlight of the campaign for him.[28] For Chris Wilkins, by now entirely marginalised in the campaign, it was the low point. As he later remarked, it was the 'point at which the PM became a divisive figure rather than a unifier, and at which we set a course to bang on about Brexit for about 7 weeks'.

Local elections sometimes occur concurrently with general elections or have previously occasionally been used by politicians to test the water before triggering general elections. But they rarely took place during general election campaigns.[29] Speaking before the campaign got under way in earnest, one of Labour's field team thought the local elections on 4 May could 'define the landscape. It'll be a different electoral battleground if the Lib Dems do well, compared to just if the Tories hammer us. It's just different, not better or worse. We're up shit creek either way'.

One consequence of the two elections was a lot of party election broadcasts—with parties putting out both local and general election party election broadcasts (PEBs). Indeed, the day that the election was called saw a Green Party PEB scheduled for the local elections, and from then until the day before polling day, only eight weekdays (out of 37) would not feature a PEB.[30] PEBs are now almost all short by historical British standards (three minutes is the norm), although this still makes them lengthy compared to, say, US spot ads. Most are now produced cheaply with low production values; one of those involved in the Liberal Democrat campaign described theirs as being made on 'a shoestring that was about to snap'. Conservative PEBs featured Theresa May, either directly (speaking to camera or extracts from her speaking) or indirectly (with people saying how good a Prime Minister she was); subject-wise, they majored on Brexit.[31] Labour's broadcasts were more varied—both in cast and message—and included one made by the director Ken Loach. Loach's PEB was the only one to feature in the top 30 most-viewed programmes for any channel, with an audience of 4.1 million.[32]

The Greens produced probably the most imaginative, if hammy, broadcast, with a parody of a family playing 'Game of Life'-style board game and saying it was time to '#ChangeTheGame' of 'the rigged system'. SNP broadcasts focused on opposing Tory Westminster and their attempts to 'tighten their grip' on power and impose austerity on Scotland, but for Labour and the Conservatives, one issue dominated in Scotland, with their broadcasts competing to claim the mantle for the anti-independence party. In Labour's case, Corbyn was given equal billing with Kezia Dugdale, although for the Conservatives, Ruth Davidson was the primary message carrier. In Wales, Plaid Cymru's broadcasts offered a bleak prospect for Wales without a strong Plaid voice, while Labour's spoke of Welsh Labour's record of achievement in government—and put a clear dividing line between Welsh Labour and Jeremy Corbyn. The broadcasts of the Northern Ireland parties by and large relied upon party leaders and leading party figures talking to camera and urging people to support them so that the devolved institutions could be restarted and a fair Brexit deal for Northern Ireland could be achieved.

The local elections saw the Conservatives gain 563 seats, taking control of 11 councils, whilst Labour lost 382 seats and control of seven councils, including Glasgow.[33] Labour won the newly created mayoral posts in Greater Manchester and Liverpool City Region, but suffered a surprising defeat in Teesside and a very bad result in the West Midlands, when former John Lewis Managing Director Andy Street gained the West Midlands mayoralty for the Conservatives. Labour's performance, measured as a national vote, was the worst by an opposition party in local elections for at least 35 years; in terms of net seats won or lost, it was the worst by an opposition party since 1980. The Liberal Democrats—who had been hoping to make gains—ended up losing 42 seats. But equally, the results were not quite the Conservative landslide that the national polls were predicting. Writing for the BBC, John Curtice described the results as 'highly satisfactory' for the Conservatives and noted that 'Labour is in deep trouble', but also pointed out that the national vote share calculation put the Conservatives on 38%, some 11 points ahead of Labour, a less dramatic lead than most opinion polls. It was, he noted, 'only four points above the lead David Cameron had in 2015, which only gave the party an overall majority of 12'.[34]

The Conservative photocall in response to their victory provided yet more evidence of how last minute everything was in their campaign. 'This should be easy', said one of May's aides. 'You go to the most high-profile place you've just won. We'd won in Teesside and the West Midlands. We end up with an event in London—which didn't even have any elections.' Corbyn headed for Manchester, with the aim of being seen with Andy Burnham, who had won the mayoralty convincingly. Burnham had no desire to be seen with Corbyn and so the Labour leader held a victory rally *sans* victor.[35]

One policy not on the Conservative grid was fox hunting. Late on 8 May, the *Daily Mirror* published an email sent by Lord Mancroft, the chair of the Council of Hunting Associations, to hunt masters, in which he had urged them to mobilise support for Conservative candidates in marginal seats. 'A majority of fifty or more', he argued, 'would give us a real opportunity for repeal of the Hunting Act ... This is the chance we have been waiting for.'[36] The following day, in answer to a question at a campaign event in Yorkshire, the Prime Minister confirmed that she expected the Conservative manifesto to contain a pledge to allow Parliament to hold a free vote on whether to repeal the Hunting Act. The Prime Minister's answer was seized upon by Labour and Labour-supporting groups as evidence that a Conservative government would reintroduce fox hunting. For several days, the British Election Study panel of voters found evidence that the issue had cut through; on 10 May, it was the main issue cited by people who said they had changed their mind. Yet this was not a new pledge—the 2015 Conservative manifesto had similarly contained a pledge to allow a free vote on the issue, as indeed had that in 2010—and it did not pledge the government to repeal of the Act, merely to allow a vote on the subject. One of the puzzles of the 2017 campaign was why this issue took off in a way it had not in 2015.[37] May had added that she was personally in favour of hunting (a response that surprised some of her team), although unlike David Cameron she had never actually taken part in a hunt. The Conservatives had expected the subject to come up and later regretted not devoting enough attention to it. 'We knew the question might come up', said one of May's aides. 'We should have used it to close the topic down.'[38]

On 10 May, the Crown Prosecution Service (CPS) confirmed that no criminal charges would be brought against up to 20 MPs over the national party's failure to accurately declare campaign spending on a battlebus tour at the 2015 election. The CPS concluded that there was insufficient evidence to prove dishonesty or bring a criminal case against the MPs and their agents. The CPS head of special crime said: 'By omitting any battlebus costs, the returns may have been inaccurate', but added that because it was clear that agents were told by Conservative Party headquarters that the costs were part of the national campaign, 'it would not be possible to prove any agent acted knowingly or dishonestly'.[39] (The case against one MP, Craig MacKinlay, the MP for Thanet South, was unresolved and on 2 June, the CPS announced that he would be charged for offences under the Representation of the People Act, as would two others, his election agent and a party organiser.)[40] Given some of the apocalyptic claims that had been made in the run-up to the election, though, this was small beer.

For those who had been involved in the Conservative campaign in 2015, one noticeable difference in 2017 was the diminished role played by Lynton Crosby. Having previously said that 2015 would be his last campaign, he was quieter and less energetic. 'In 2015, everything went through Lynton', said one of those with experience on both campaigns. This was not true in 2017. Sat at what was called the 'Pod of Power' in CCHQ were 'the Chiefs' (Fiona Hill and Nick Timothy), along with 'the Australians' (Crosby and Textor) and Alan Mabbut and Stephen Gilbert. It was, said one of those involved in the campaign, 'never clear who was in charge'. 'It felt much more like the Remain campaign', said another, 'where it was also not clear who was in charge.' There were fewer staff meetings than previous elections, and those that did take place were often chaired by Gilbert or Textor rather than Crosby. Indeed, of the two Australians, Textor was more prominent for much of the campaign. Morale at CCHQ, which was high to begin with, began to dip as the campaign progressed. Things were not helped by a flu bug that was working its way through the building. The Prime Minister was almost entirely absent from CCHQ. Eventually, she was persuaded to come in to try to raise morale. She delivered her standard stump speech. Morale did not rise.

However, it was not entirely clear who was in charge of the Labour operation either. Asked to identify one person, most of those present will mention John McDonnell, but the divisions between LOTO and the Southsiders—and the lack of any overall chain of command—meant that it could take excessively long for decisions to be taken. That things were not going entirely to plan within Labour was evidenced in early May when the experienced Andrew Murray, the Chief of Staff to Len McCluskey and a long-time friend of Corbyn, was seconded from Unite to work as yet another adviser to Corbyn. Murray began to work on the campaign on 8 May, joining full time from 15 May. As someone who had been a member of the Communist Party of Great Britain until 2016, his role in running a Labour campaign was itself noteworthy. Bringing Murray on board was primarily McDonnell's idea, the latter becoming increasingly frustrated at the inability of the campaign to function properly. He realised that the LOTO team were inexperienced, but also that the running disputes between LOTO and Southside needed resolving. Murray's arrival is seen as important by almost all of those involved in the Labour campaign, although they differ on precisely why. Some saw his arrival as significant because he had considerable organisational ability and experience. Others, however, point to a more fundamental reason: because Unite was funding large parts of the Labour campaign, Murray was able to wield significant authority in a way that others could not. As one of Corbyn's team noted, 'he was an enforcer and he controlled the money'. Perhaps the single most important thing about Murray's arrival is that he did not arrive until a month into the campaign—and that he arrived because there was an acceptance that things were not working.

In the 1983 election, Labour's vote had fallen by around eight percentage points during the course of the campaign, with the party ending the election dangerously close to third place. Despite the fears of many in Labour that 2017 would be a repeat performance of 1983 and despite the opening weeks of the campaign not going smoothly, there were no signs of Labour's vote crumbling in a similar fashion. Indeed, if anything, Labour's support was increasing very slightly. The opening week's polling had the Conservatives ahead by an average of 20 points. By the weekend of 29–30 April, that lead had closed to 15 points. Noting their small advance in the polls, in late April one senior member of the Shadow Cabinet told a room of journalists that if Labour kept up this rate of progress, the election would end with Jerey Corbyn in Number 10. Everyone, including the Labour MP, laughed.

NOTES

1. One very early meeting took place at Nick Timothy's house in Vauxhall.
2. Although a later story that the party could not locate enough paper for its mailshots (Mark Wallace, 'Our CCHQ Election Audit: The Rusty Machine, Part Two. How and Why the Ground Campaign Failed', *ConservativeHome*, 6 September 2017, https://www.conservativehome.com/majority_conservatism/2017/09/our-cchq-election-audit-the-rusty-machine-part-two-how-and-why-the-ground-campaign-failed.html) is disputed by those involved, who say that suppliers always plead insufficient stocks.

3. See Tim Shipman, *Fall Out*. William Collins, 2017, p. 216. The text of the full presentation is given at pp. 549–52.

4. One of the first things Labour's field team did was to contact branches of Labour students, to check on term dates.

5. In one of his rare interventions during the campaign, Tony Blair explicitly ruled out advocating tactical voting, although he came close to appealing for something that sounded remarkably similar ('as part of this election campaign, we create the capacity for the people to know exactly what the choices are; and elect as many MPs as possible with an open mind on this issue who are prepared to vote according to the quality of the deal and the interests of the British people').

6. Roger Scully, 'The First Welsh Election Poll of the General Election', *Cardiff University Blogs*, 24 April 2017, https://blogs.cardiff.ac.uk/electionsinwales/2017/04/24/the-first-welsh-poll-of-the-general-election.

7. Christopher Hope, 'Tom Watson Appears to Give up on Jeremy Corbyn Becoming Prime Minister', *Daily Telegraph*, 2 May 2017, www.telegraph.co.uk/news/2017/05/02/tom-watson-appears-give-jeremy-corbyn-becoming-prime-minister.

8. One of the few joint events that was organised did not go especially well; appearing with the Chancellor on 17 May, she twice failed to confirm that he would remain as Chancellor if she won the election.

9. Marina Hyde, 'In Stoke, May Marches on with Familiar Neuron-Crushing Dullness', *The Guardian*, 16 May 2017. She added: 'To adapt Dorothy Parker, the PM ran the full gamut of emotion from strong to stable.'

10. See Philip Cowley and Dennis Kavanagh, *The British General Election of 2015*. Palgrave Macmillan, 2015, p. 185.

11. Terry Coleman, 'Foot Starts at the Beginning', *The Guardian*, 18 May 1983. As the then Labour MP John Golding had remarked: 'I would show Footie the opinion polls ... and he'd go "You're wrong. There were a thousand people at my meeting last night and they all cheered". And I'd say, "Yeah. But there are 122,000 outside saying you're crackers".' The Golding quote is from *The Wilderness Years: Comrades at War*, BBC2, 9 December 1995.

12. Matthew Flinders, 'The (Anti-)Politics of the General Election' in Jonathan Tonge, Cristina Leston-Bandeira and Stuart Wilks-Heeg (eds), *Britain Votes 2017*. Oxford, Oxford University Press, 2017, p. 233.

13. HC Debs, 24 Feb 2016, c. 291. More precisely, the retort was what Cameron thought his mother would say to Corbyn.

14. Very early on in Corbyn's leadership, Labour had to organise a pool clip of him for broadcast, and the new leader pulled a tie from his pocket to wipe some sweat from his forehead. 'The best use of a tie', he remarked to the bemused staff.

15. In an interview broadcast in March 2018, Corbyn referred to this pressure: 'People round here [his office] don't like me going out in a tracksuit. They say, look, if you're the leader of the Labour Party you can't go out in your trackies.' From *Nikki Lilly Meets...*, CBBC, 16 March 2018.

16. Other encounters were similarly unsuccessful. The week before on a visit to the Black Country, a 73-year-old man told the Prime Minister not to bother approaching him. 'She asked if she could walk across my lawn and I said, not really, I have just cut it.'

17. How this terrible photo opportunity came to pass is described in Tim Ross and Tom McTague, *Betting the House*. Biteback, 2017, pp. 195–96.

18. Tim Farron had a similar encounter, also in Oxfordshire, with a voter who had voted Leave and complained that the Lib Dem leader thought all Leaver voters are racist.

19. For example, Macleod used the phrase in his 1969 party conference speech when Shadow Chancellor, and Major (an admirer of Macleod) used it in his 1996 conference speech, albeit after Blair had begun to use it. Used slightly differently, 'not for the few but the many', it was employed by Harold Wilson in 1963 (ironically enough while proposing the abolition of university fees) and Margaret Thatcher (in 1976). The first recorded use in *The Times* would appear to be by Sir Robert Wilson, during an election debate in Southwark, in 1820. Another variant—'for the many, and not for the few'—was used by Charles Dickens (see 'Charles Dickens's Speeches', *The Times*, 24 July 1870) and antecedents can be traced back to Thucydides' account of Pericles' Funeral Oration ('we are called a democracy, for the administration is in the hands of the many and not of the few') or Shelley's 'The Masque of Anarchy' ('ye are many, they are few'). The then ex-MP for Derby North, Chris Williamson, had used lines of Shelley's poem at a rally in 2016, saying: 'Let's use that as our battle cry' (Nick Clark, 'Jeremy Corbyn Tells Rally "This is about the Kind of World We Want to Live in"', *Socialist Worker*, 21 July 2016). Although Corbyn was at that rally, knew of the poem and was later to use it on the campaign trail (see p. 225), there is no evidence that the poem was an important justification for the slogan at the time it was chosen.

20. 'The Car-Crash Interview Everyone's Talking About: Diane Abbott on Police Funding', *LBC*, 2 May 2017, www.lbc.co.uk/radio/presenters/nick-ferrari/diane-abbotts-agonising-interview-over-policy-cost.

21. See, for example, Pascale Hughes, 'A Third of People Can't Remember a Single Moment from the General Election Campaign', *i News*, 2 June 2017, https://inews.co.uk/essentials/news/politics/memorable-moment-campaign-far-dont-know (which showed it was the most memorable single incident of the campaign for voters in London even by late May); or Chris Prosser, 'What was it All About? The 2017 Election Campaign in Voters'

Own Words', *British Election Study*, 2 August 2017, www.britishelection-study.com/bes-findings/what-was-it-all-about-the-2017-election-campaign-in-voters-own-words/#.WbFvBLKGOUk (which showed that it was the top issue the British Election Study found for voters who claimed to have changed their mind about the parties up until 9 May).

22. Michael A. Ashcroft, *The Lost Majority*. 2017, Biteback, p. 23.

23. A good discussion of this can be found in Anoosh Chakelian, 'All Politicians Expect Criticism. But Has the Treatment of Diane Abbott Crossed a Line?', *New Statesman*, 7 June 2017, https://www.newstatesman.com/politics/june2017/2017/06/all-politicians-expect-criticism-has-treatment-diane-abbott-crossed-line. For the counter-argument, see Zoe Strimpel, 'It's Not Racist to Point out that Diane Abbott is a Bungling Disappointment', *Daily Telegraph*, 6 June 2017, www.telegraph.co.uk/news/2017/06/06/not-racist-point-diane-abbott-bungling-disappointment.

24. One reason, though not the only reason, why the Abbott interview took off in the way it did was because it took place so early on in the campaign. Had Corbyn's interview over childcare—discussed below—occurred earlier, it is plausible that it too would have been covered in such depth. By the time he endured his moment of embarrassment, everyone was deep in the thick of it.

25. Tim Shipman claims that McDonnell reacted with fury to the interview and declared that Abbott would do no more broadcast interviews (*Fall Out*, p. 222). Given what was to occur later in the campaign, it would not have been possible to keep the Shadow Home Secretary out of the media, even if she had agreed to do so; in any case she did not agree.

26. He would later regret giving this interview. Speaking after the election and having resigned from the leadership of the party, he admitted: 'Foolishly and wrongly, [I] attempted to push it away by giving an answer that, frankly, was not right.'

27. This interview, which attracted less attention than some of the others, was a source of particular ire amongst some of his campaign team, since the question over which he struggled was the generic one—whether homosexuality per se was a sin—one for which there was an easy answer. As one senior member of the campaign team put it: 'This was utterly needless.'

28. Shipman, *Fall Out*, p. 231.

29. The last time there were scheduled—that is, non-by-election—local elections during a general election campaign was 1955, when some local elections in England and Scotland were held two weeks before the general election.

30. Two of these days were the pause after the Manchester attack and three were around polling day for the local elections.

31. There was an intriguing contrast with a PEB put out by the party for the local elections (on 10 April, prior to the announcement of the general election) and which was clearly inspired by the pre-Crosby alternative Number 10 strategy. This featured optimistic and generalist images of the country with a CCHQ scripted narration from May. It is, presumably, what the general election broadcasts would have looked like had it not been run by Lynton Crosby.

32. Vincent Campbell, 'PEBs in 2017: Not Gone, But Largely Forgotten?', *Election Analysis*, www.electionanalysis.uk/uk-election-analysis-2017/section-4-parties-and-the-campaign/pebs-in-2017-not-gone-but-largely-forgotten.

33. 'Local and Mayoral Results: Tories Advance amid Labour Losses', *BBC News*, 5 May 2017, www.bbc.co.uk/news/uk-politics-39810488.

34. John Curtice, 'Local Elections 2017: Six Key Lessons for the General Election', *BBC News*, 5 May 2017, www.bbc.co.uk/news/uk-politics-39822775. The original news story says 2010, but it clearly means 2015. The 38% figure comes from the BBC's Projected National Vote, data for which goes back to 1982. Colin Rallings and Michael Thrasher's alternate National Equivalent Vote, with data back to 1979, put the Conservatives on 39% with Labour on 28%, another 11-point gap. Either method made Labour's performance the worst by any opposition party in any election for which they had data.

35. As Tim Shipman notes, Burnham 'felt he had won in spite of the leader rather than because of him' (*Fall Out*, p. 224). But see Steve Howell, *Game Changer: Eight Weeks that Transformed British Politics*. Accent Press, 2018, p. 133, who claims Burnham's absence was merely because of a prearranged dinner with friends and family.

36. Jack Blanchard, '"This Could Be the Chance We've Been Waiting for": Fox Hunt Bosses' Leaked Tory Campaign Email in Full', *Daily Mirror*, 8 May 2017, https://www.mirror.co.uk/news/politics/this-could-chance-weve-been-10383290.

37. The banal answer to this is 'social media', where the subject was widely discussed, but social media existed, and was widely used, two years before, and yet the subject did not achieve the same resonance with voters. It could be that the public followed Lord Mancroft's logic—that a large Conservative majority, expected in 2017 in a way it was not in 2015, would make repeal more likely—although this does credit the British voter with more understanding of parliamentary cohesion on free votes than seems likely.

38. Indeed, not only did they expect the subject to come up because of stories in that morning's press about the subject, but they had also been given advance warning of the precise question by a journalist. See Ross and McTague, *Betting the House*, p. 193.

39. 'CPS Statement on Election Expenses', *CPS*, 10 May 2017, https://www.cps.gov.uk/cps/news/cps-statement-election-expenses.

40. 'South Thanet Tory Candidate Craig MacKinlay Charged over Expenses', *BBC News*, 2 June 2017, https://www.bbc.co.uk/news/uk-england-kent-40129826.

CHAPTER 8

Everything Changes

With Wes Ball

Few general election manifestoes are remembered. Even fewer make much difference. Labour's 1983 manifesto was famously described as 'the longest suicide note in history'; few others have been anywhere near as memorable. Almost none have materially affected election campaigns. Yet the process of manifesto production is taken seriously by the parties, both as a chance to showcase their policies and—if elected—as giving a mandate for government. It is normally an extended process, taking place over months, sometimes years, with policies carefully trailed and tested, involving extensive consultation with think tanks and campaigning groups. In 2017, by contrast, all the parties rushed to write their manifestoes in weeks. Even under normal circumstances, manifestoes are not usually great works of literature, and given the speed at which they were produced, this was especially true in 2017; yet these hastily produced and cobbled together documents mattered, in a way they rarely do and in a way few would have predicted at the start of the campaign.[1]

The road to Labour's manifesto had begun with a paper taken to the National Executive Committee in September 2016 setting out how the

© The Author(s) 2018   177
P. Cowley, D. Kavanagh, *The British General Election of 2017*,
https://doi.org/10.1007/978-3-319-95936-8_8

party would prepare for an early general election. This established a series of working groups needed for a contest in 2020, but it also put in place arrangements to speed the process up if there was an earlier election. In the Leader of the Opposition's Office (LOTO), Andrew Fisher had begun to prepare policies for the local elections as well as working more generally on a planned industrial strategy and nationalisation policy with an eye on 2020, but the work was all incomplete. Securing additional staff from the trade unions, Fisher and his team produced a draft document in under two weeks, covering a series of significant reforms including major extensions of public ownership. Little detailed work had gone into their development or how they would be delivered. There was no 'first hundred days plan' or draft legislation similar to that prepared before the 2015 election.[2]

Ben Jennings, *The Guardian*, 30 May 2017 © Ben Jennings

Although manifestoes are often discussed as if they have an author (or a couple of authors), the process is in reality usually much more collaborative than this implies; the 'authors' are often much more like 'editors', albeit interventionist editors. With the Labour manifesto, much of the early work was sub-contracted to shadow ministers and their advisors, who were asked to send in submissions. One of those involved described it a crowd-sourced manifesto. Fisher would edit these submissions, as well as drafting the more high-profile policies from scratch. Political management and oversight of the process was cursory. He rarely went back to advisors or shadow ministers for further consultation, and time for fine-tuning was limited. A party source said it was 'a case of looking at what we were already working on and looking at what is popular and going to win votes'. Key for those involved were around a dozen high-profile policies, most of which Fisher drafted himself, which the leadership believed were popular in themselves, as well as being things Labour would like to do in government—although as one of those involved in its drafting admitted, the Labour manifesto was not meant to be a handbook for civil servants; it was a political document, designed for the public.

On the evening of 10 May, word reached LOTO that the *Daily Mirror* and the *Daily Telegraph* were going to publish leaked, and near-final, versions of the draft manifesto.[3] The leak was significant for its novelty and for the effect it had on the campaign—but also for what it said about the state of the Labour Party at the time. When the news broke, everyone blamed everyone else, and everyone was certain they knew who was responsible. The party staffers were convinced the leak had come from within LOTO, either as an attempt to make it harder for people to argue against any of the more radical policies once they had been made public, or as a device to generate yet further criticism of Southside, or simply as a gamble designed to generate coverage. LOTO in turn assumed that the leak was an attempt to sabotage the campaign, to paint the Labour operation as shambolic and to derail the manifesto's launch. Initial LOTO suspicion especially focused on Deputy Leader Tom Watson, as a draft had been sent to him shortly before the leak. Watson was furious, and his staff spent the evening scouring through the leaked text to prove that they had a different version and could have not been responsible.[4] After some initial panic and a long discussion into the early hours of the next day, the Labour campaign team agreed that they needed to attempt to capitalise on the leak. It was decided that Jeremy Corbyn would pull out of a planned poster launch (one of relatively few scheduled by any of the parties during the campaign) and Andrew Gwynne would take the heat in a morning media round. He fended off media criticism by welcoming the fact that people were talking about Labour's policy. The Conservative response perfectly illustrated Crosby's mantra of attacking Corbyn and linking everything to Brexit. It said: 'This is a total shambles. Jeremy Corbyn's plans to unleash chaos on Britain have been revealed. The commitments in this dossier will rack up tens of billions of extra borrowing for our families and will put Brexit negotiations at risk.'

Almost all of the clever conspiracy theories were completely wrong. A later internal inquiry found that the leak had come from within Scottish Labour; the party believed it had identified the individual concerned, who, after the election, no longer worked for Labour. The leak had been intended to damage, but in retrospect almost all those involved in the campaign—on all sides—accept that it generated positive coverage for Labour. Indeed, in an election over which so much is disputed, this is one of the few things about which there is close to a consensus amongst participants. The novelty of the leak meant that journalists gave the manifesto coverage in a way they might not otherwise have done, and it gave Labour an additional round of coverage, allowing them to float the policies one week, before formally launching them the next.

The leak appeared in newspapers on the morning of Labour's Clause V meeting—the meeting of representatives from the membership, unions and Parliament to agree the final manifesto. This had often been a hard-fought final battle between different party factions and groups to secure their key priorities.[5] The 2017 meeting was remarkable, both for its convivial nature and for the extent to which it amended the draft manifesto. Almost all suggestions from attendees were agreed by Shadow Cabinet members, often without discussion. There was, one of those present said, a view that it did not really matter what the party decided 'because we're going to get smashed'. This led to proposals being accepted with more latitude than normal. 'There was a moment', one attendee noted, 'when,

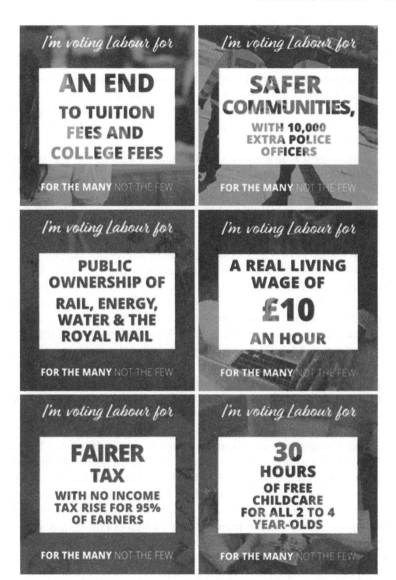

on the health chapter, Jonathan Ashworth responded to a whole series of requests for additions just by going "yep, yep, yep, yep"—accepting all the additions.' This laid-back approach to manifesto drafting meant that the session saw more amendments than anyone involved could remember at a similar Clause V meeting. It also included some fairly fantastical policies being accepted, including one to restore the 1960s Beeching cuts to the rail network (although this was later discreetly dropped before publication).

The meeting was not entirely consensual. A sign of the way in which the manifesto had been produced was that rather than complaints coming from the unions or local parties representatives—who are normally the ones pushing for changes—this time they came from shadow secretaries of state, some of whom were unhappy with their sections of the manifesto, over which they had not been fully consulted. There was a sharp exchange between Shadow Education Secretary Angela Rayner and McDonnell, with the former demanding extra resources for early years education. Keir Starmer made a number of changes to the Brexit section. The policy on Heathrow expansion—Heathrow Airport being in John McDonnell's constituency—was also an issue.

On the way into the meeting, Corbyn's car had run over a BBC cameraman's foot, and Len McCluskey emerged after the meeting only to slip and fall over onto his backside. Had the campaign panned out as many people—including many of those inside the meeting—had expected, these were images that would have been replayed endlessly as totemic of the sort of campaign that Labour had run.

Labour's manifesto was formally unveiled in Bradford on 16 May. Corbyn called it a 'programme of hope'. The two biggest cheers during the leader's speech introducing *For the Many, Not the Few* came when he mentioned rail renationalisation and the scrapping of tuition fees, although the biggest cheer of all came during the Q&A when a journalist from the *Morning Star* (whose involvement was itself a sign of how things were different under the new regime) asked if anything could be done about the 'shockingly biased media'.

The published manifesto had some notable differences from the leak of the previous week. Some compromises with the party were clear. On nuclear weapons, the draft had said that 'any prime minister should be extremely cautious about ordering the use of weapons of mass destruction which would result in the indiscriminate killing of millions of innocent civilians'. This was an equivocation too far for the final manifesto and was deleted; similarly, a commitment to UK membership of NATO was added. The early draft had already included multiple nationalisations, including energy companies, rail companies, bus companies and the Royal Mail; the published manifesto added water nationalisation.[6] The draft had also not included the explicit commitment that 'free movement will end when we leave the European Union'.

Other key policies included rises in income tax for those earning above £80,000 (beginning at a 45p rate and rising to 50p for the highest earners); an end to zero-hours contracts; an expansion of free childcare; a rise in corporation tax; a national investment bank; ending the public sector pay gap; a living wage of £10 per hour; and the building of over 1,000,000 homes. On Brexit, the manifesto promised to accept the referendum result, but to negotiate to retain the 'benefits' of the Single Market and the Customs Union—but without actual membership of either—and to guarantee existing rights for EU nationals living in the UK.

One notable absence, given the role it had played in Corbyn's leadership victory in 2015, was any pledge to repeal the benefit cap. The absence of this promise, which would have benefited some of the poorest in society, sat oddly with the proposal to scrap student fees and reintroduce grants, which was to cost £11.2 billion—the single largest budget item in the entire manifesto—and would disproportionately benefit the wealthiest. Pressed on this during the post-launch Q&A, Corbyn said that 'clearly' the party would not freeze benefits, but he soon had to admit that there was no commitment to this; the party then issued a statement pledging 'an end to the freeze', before Emily Thornberry admitted that although Labour would try to 'offset the impact' of the benefit cap, it would not be reversed. 'I don't think we can reverse it entirely', she said. 'We shouldn't be promising things we can't afford.' This confusion was partly because the Corbyn team believed the manifesto needed to be taken as a whole—and that other policies would at least partly ameliorate the effects of the benefit cap.[7] But it was also simply a product of the haste with which the document was put together; that section was, one of those involved admitted, a 'bodge job'.

One of Corbyn's team argued that the manifesto 'had to be transformational. There had to be a vision, of a different society. One that's not just tinkering. We needed to show that politics does not have to be like this'.

It was, another of those involved in its drafting argued, designed to break the consensus of the last 25 years. Jon Trickett, whose influence was clear here, was fond of quoting R.H. Tawney about how politics should not be about offering 'the largest possible number of carrots to the largest possible number of donkeys'.[8] Yet the manifesto was packed full of carrots, and there was an argument about how radical or transformative it really was. It was clearly not pure Corbynism. Various party sources have described it as 'reheated Milibandism' and a 'radical social democratic package', and plenty of the LOTO team would argue that many of the proposed policies were mainstream in many European countries. Nevertheless, it was clearly more radical than the manifesto of two years before. Until the election, it had been possible to argue that—for all the changes in rhetoric—there was relatively little in Labour's policy platform under Corbyn that was radically dissimilar to the Labour manifesto of 2015.[9] However, the 2017 manifesto marked a clear shift; it was the most leftist Labour manifesto in Britain since at least 1983 and just as significant, perhaps, was the fact that Labour promoted the manifesto as a break from its past rather than as incremental or middle of the road.

Yet not too radical. Corbyn said the manifesto '[w]ill change our country while managing within our means', and alongside the manifesto, Labour also published a short costings document, *Funding Britain's Future*, which claimed to show how the policies would be funded. This document had been the source of considerable dispute, probably more so than most of the policies in the manifesto themselves. At the final Shadow Cabinet meeting, there had been agreement that the answer to questions on costing would be that 'full details will be set out in the manifesto', but not to specify whether proposals would be fully costed. McDonnell was adamant, privately, that they needed to do so, and used various opportunities to try to push this agenda. Plenty of those around Corbyn were not as convinced.[10] For one thing, producing detailed costings in opposition is difficult, especially at such short notice; in normal circumstances, the information necessary would be gathered over time through a series of parliamentary questions, an approach that the snap election prevented. Politically, several of those involved were worried that it would invite Conservative attacks on the costings rather than on the policies, whilst others had concerns about the reliability of the costings themselves. Anticipating possible attacks from the Conservatives and a hostile press, one internal email highlighted some of the problems with Labour's cost estimates, including the lack of detail on capital spending, as well as some individual costings that were implausible or entirely absent. These covered almost every area of the manifesto, including welfare, health, education, the economy, transport, policing and prisons, and collectively came, even conservatively, to billions of unaccounted spending. A prolonged debate including all those around Corbyn and McDonnell as well as longstanding senior party staff was ultimately resolved at McDonnell's insistence, despite the fears of several of Corbyn's aides, including Seumas Milne. As one of those involved noted: 'There were people there who were long in the tooth enough to remember John Smith's shadow budget in 1992. You just don't go there. You don't give them that ammunition. But we knew from polling that there was a large degree of scepticism about our ability to manage the economy, tax and spend, and so on. There was nothing to be lost. We needed to offer a degree of confidence that we could be trusted.' Or, as another argued: 'We knew we needed to be on the pitch on economic credibility.' Releasing costings was seen as crucial in doing so.

Expectations remained low. On the day of the launch, in a nod to the fears not just of recalcitrant MPs, but also of many of Corbyn's close supporters, Len McCluskey told *The Guardian* that winning just 200 seats would constitute success for Labour. Corbyn's critics within Labour feared that this was all part of an expectations game within the party, designed to set the bar for success so low that the leader could not fail to clear it.

Plaid Cymru released their manifesto on the same day as Labour's. Launched by leader Leanne Wood in Penygraig, Rhondda, it was less detailed than normal and carried the proviso that much of the policy in the more detailed 2015 (Westminster) and 2016 (Assembly) manifestoes was still relevant. The *Action Plan 2017* ('Defending Wales') was deliberately more focused on Brexit, promising to give Wales a 'strong voice' during Brexit and demanding that all future trade deals should be signed off by the National Assembly for Wales.

Within the Conservatives, there were calls for Theresa May to emulate Margaret Thatcher's 1979 thematic election manifesto and provide a document with relatively few policy details. At 30,000 words, David Cameron's 2015 manifesto was widely considered to have been too long. Crosby, in particular, was famous for a strategy of 'scraping the barnacles off the boat', removing any policies which distracted from a party's key message. Stephen Gilbert had been known to joke that the ideal campaign would be one featuring no policies. But those working on the Conservative manifesto thought the analogy with 1979 was misplaced, especially given why they were calling the election in the first place. The party no longer had a majority in the Lords and the challenges facing Britain—economic, demographic and Brexit—were such that a mandate for bold policies was required. 'Theresa thinks people want honesty', said one aide. Another added: 'We wanted a mandate for difficult times. We had to be grown up and present the choices to people.' If the Labour manifesto was a political document for the public, the Conservative manifesto was, quite self-consciously, a programme for government. One of those involved in its production called it a 'maximalist' manifesto, one 'like no other'. This turned out to be true, albeit not quite for the reasons its authors intended.

If the campaign overall was a Crosby campaign, the manifesto was not. It was written by Nick Timothy and Ben Gummer (the latter had not been keen on an early election, given that he held a marginal seat), together with John Godfrey and Will Tanner at the Policy Unit. All were committed to May's broader agenda. As with Labour, submissions were sought from Secretaries of State with help from their junior ministers and sometimes from special advisers. Despite mostly calling for short manifestoes, few ministers managed to keep their submissions especially brief. 'Everyone

Martin Rowson, *The Guardian*, 21 May 2017 © Martin Rowson

wanted a short manifesto', noted one of those involved ruefully, 'just expansive in their area'—and at least one of those to argue for a short manifesto when the subject was discussed at Cabinet on 18 April, then submitted over 1,000 words for their own contribution. Justine Greening at the Department for Education, Sajid Javid at the Department for Communities and Local Government and Jeremy Hunt at the Department of Health sent lengthy papers. There was also substantial Policy Unit input on industrial strategy, corporate governance, mental health, technical

Steve Bell, *The Guardian*, 8 June 2017 © Steve Bell

education and workers' rights, but less from the Policy Board headed by George Freeman, although he did suggest cancelling the HS2 railway programme.[11]

Again, as with Labour, shortage of time precluded much opportunity for wider consultation. The authors sent draft manifesto sections to relevant ministers and Gummer liaised with each Secretary of State. He negotiated frequently with Philip Hammond as relations had broken down between the Chancellor and Nick Timothy. Hammond asked to see an early draft and was the only senior minister to see the full draft in advance, albeit only days before publication. The final wording on fiscal policy, public sector investment and industrial strategy were agreed between him and Gummer. Throughout the drafting process, Timothy kept in touch with May, often seeking her approval of the drafts. (Corbyn, by contrast, saw a draft of Labour's manifesto just five days before the Clause V meeting.) All Secretaries of State received their departmental texts five days before the manifesto was sent to the printer, but the manifesto as a whole was kept on a tight leash because of the risk of leaks (especially after Labour's experience); Boris Johnson's request to see the full document was refused. He was not trusted not to leak.

The manifesto was produced at great speed, which at times showed. While the manifesto was being readied at the printers, someone noticed that one paragraph had been repeated, verbatim, and edits had to be called down the phone. The manifesto also contained a policy on television licences that directly contradicted legislation that the government had just passed. One of those involved admitted: 'We had to go around pretending that what it means is no changes in addition to what we've just done ... But everyone knew that was nonsense.'

The lack of time led to several potential ideas being shelved completely, of which the most high profile would have been a proposed shift from Stamp Duty to Capital Gains Tax for house purchases. According to one of those involved, the change had multiple benefits: 'a much fairer and more precise system, taking from the party more likely to have ready cash, a cleaner system for first time buyers, doesn't punish people in negative equity who need to move, means you are hitting unearned wealth rather than transactions, helps make the whole market more liquid, and could give you a way of reforming IHT [Inheritance Tax], so that it is far more transparent, fair and aligned with other taxes'. Yet the idea—which had long been a hobby horse of Will Tanner's—was shelved when it became clear there was insufficient time to model the consequences properly. As a finance measure, which could bypass the Lords, the need for an electoral mandate was also less pressing. One of the things which most concerned those involved was that it was too big a policy change to drop into a manifesto, unannounced, and that they had not properly prepared people 'for such a massive change that would affect people's houses, and therefore was easily misconstrued'.[12]

The one policy that was to cause the largest problems for the Conservatives was one on which there had been considerable preparation—but which was also easily misconstrued. Work on reforming social care for the elderly had been under way for months (see above, pp. 62–3). Given that this work was not fully completed, one option was to delay any decision by promising to deliver a social care Green or White Paper, but Gummer regarded this idea as a cop out, since it would not give the government a mandate for radical action. There was agreement about a 'floor' which allowed people in care to retain some money from the sale of their assets (usually a property), but several, including May, strongly resisted the idea of a ceiling—or 'cap'—on costs. The original draft package would have allowed the elderly receiving care at home to defer the costs and remain in their houses in their lifetimes, and would increase the amount they could keep in savings and assets to £50,000 (compared to the present £23,250), but there would be no ceiling to the costs they could incur. The view taken was that taxpayers, some of whom might have a modest property or not be on the housing ladder at all, should not subsidise the care of wealthy homeowners.

Wanting to concentrate the campaign message on May's leadership and Brexit, Crosby expressed worries about the extent of the policy detail being proposed. However, contrary to later reports, he was aware of the main policies being considered by the manifesto team. In late April, Timothy sent Mark Textor a list of the 'slightly more controversial' policies that the manifesto was planning to include. These included many of the policies that would later cause the party problems, including the changes to pensioner benefits and school meals. The list also included the outlines of what was to be the party's social care policy. The detail of the policy to be tested read:

> We will scrap the Winter Fuel Payment for all but the poorest of pensioners, allowing us to put the proceeds into long-term care for the elderly. We will change the rules so people receiving care at home can defer the costs while they are alive, just as they can already for residential care and guarantee that, no matter how large the cost of care, people will never be left with less than £50,000 in savings and assets after paying for care costs.

This definition was slightly different from the policy eventually contained in the manifesto. The lack of any cap was implicit rather than explicit (as indeed it was to be in the actual manifesto), but equally the tested policy was less generous than the eventual policy—as the 'floor' was to be raised before the manifesto was published.[13] Crosby's company, CTF, thus had more than two weeks' notice of all the key planks of the Conservative manifesto. Nothing in the polling indicated problems, although it did reveal that few members of the public understood social care—that is, either the existing policy or the proposed one.[14] The manifesto authors were pleasantly surprised by the response, as they had expected to be pulled back from some of their more radical proposals.

Yet there were concerns amongst those around May. At a meeting at Sonning on Sunday 14 May, days before the manifesto was to be signed off, Joanna Penn, Fiona Hill, Gilbert and Crosby all expressed unease about the policies on school meals, pensioner benefits and especially social care. An extended discussion led to nuanced amendments in wording covering overseas aid, the environment and Brexit. A proposal to introduce minimum service levels for strikes in transport and key public services was dropped. It had been the subject of much Cabinet discussion; the Transport Minister Chris Grayling was a forceful supporter.[15] The most significant policy change at this point was the suggestion from Gummer and Timothy to lift the social care floor from the initially proposed £50,000 to £100,000, on the basis that this would be the level at which it would do the most to help those 'just-about-managing'. Despite this, Hill remained concerned about the social care policy and refused to let the matter go. Early the following week, and on the day that the manifesto was due to go to the printers, she again raised the matter with Timothy. The pair had what for them was a very rare argument.[16] By now, Timothy told her, it was too late.

Entitled *Forward, Together*, the Conservative manifesto was launched on 18 May in Halifax, just eight miles from where Labour had launched their manifesto. The launch was emblematic of the campaign. For one thing, it was yet another example of how last-minute everything was: 'The day before the manifesto launch we still didn't have a venue', said one of those involved. They also did not have a speech. At short notice, a draft script was prepared based on the old 'Plan for Britain' narrative; Crosby then listed policies he wanted mentioned; Timothy complained that he wanted the speech to focus on different policies, which were then also added. The manifesto contained just one photo—of the Prime Minister. Key policies included an energy price cap, free breakfast clubs for primary schoolchildren (albeit with an end to universal free school meals for children in Key Stage 1), a revival of grammar schools and changes to school admissions, an increase in housebuilding targets, targets for research and development spending, an ambitious programme for digital technology, and increased spending for schools and the NHS. It also continued Cameron-era commitments to 0.7% of GDP being spent on international aid and the continuing promise of a reduction in net immigration to 'the tens of thousands'. On Brexit, the manifesto committed Britain to leaving the Single Market, the Customs Union and jurisdiction of the European Court of Justice, and it pledged to keep agricultural subsidies at EU levels for the forthcoming Parliament while 'taking back control' of British fishing waters. Dropped were George Osborne's tax lock—which prevented the government from raising income tax, National Insurance or VAT for the course of the Parliament—and the Winter Fuel Payment for better-off pensioners.

The manifesto defined the five key issues for the next government as 'a strong economy; Brexit; healing social divisions; the ageing society; and technological change'. The introduction, drafted by Timothy, was heavy on philosophy: 'Conservatism is not and never has been the philosophy described by caricaturists. We do not believe in untrammelled free markets. We reject the cult of selfish individualism. We abhor social division, injustice, unfairness and inequality. We see rigid dogma and ideology not just as needless but dangerous.' The immediate reaction to the manifesto was broadly positive and noted its interventionist approach. It was described as 'a break from Thatcherism' that 'junked much of David Cameron's liberal legacy' by *The Times*. It prompted some on the party's free-market wing to dub the manifesto 'red Toryism'. In *The Guardian*, Matthew d'Ancona thought the manifesto 'represents the most adventurous restatement of Conservatism since Margaret Thatcher and her allies smashed the Butskellite post-war consensus'. 'In an age of verbless sentences and drearily safe political language', he wrote, 'this manifesto reflects a welcome intelligence.'[17]

The social care package was a rare attempt to address the issue of intergenerational inequality, about which all the parties claimed to care deeply but which is always easier to put off than resolve. The proposed policy allowed the elderly to keep their homes in their lifetimes and gave them a fourfold increase in the amount of money they could retain; in practice, for many families, the lack of a cap was irrelevant, given the floor of £100,000.

Yet the policy was complicated and easy to misrepresent, either due to malice or ignorance. Days after it had been launched, Fiona Hill, who was supposed to be one of those responsible for promoting it, was overheard confusing its fundamentals.[18] Jeremy Corbyn at one point claimed that the Conservatives were putting a £100,000 cap on social care costs, which was the exact opposite of what the proposal did. In one televised encounter later on in the campaign, the Prime Minister was asked by a voter how he could be sure that he would not be bankrupted to pay for his social care. The answer should have been very simple—that she could guarantee him that he would be left with at least £100,000—yet she did not seem able to explain the policy. Even its authors thought that the policy was badly presented and that the media had not been properly briefed about its supposed benefits, although those doing the briefing complained they were not given sufficient warning. Others thought that it was just too radical to

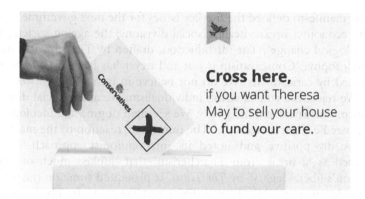

Cross here, if you want Theresa May to sell your house to **fund your care.**

be sprung at short notice on voters. 'We had not rolled the pitch', said one minister.[19]

One of the few people who did understand the policy was Sir Andrew Dilnot, who had devised the social care policy which the Conservative manifesto was rejecting. He had been briefed about the policy the day before, by Jeremy Hunt, and had reacted angrily. Those involved in the manifesto think that Dilnot was misguided. 'Dilnot was expensive, a universal benefit for the better off', said one. But on the morning of the manifesto launch, he gave an interview to the *Today* programme in which complained that the policy would leave people 'helpless, knowing that what will happen is that if they are unlucky enough to suffer the need for care costs they will be entirely on their own until they are down to the last £100,000 of all of their wealth including their house'. He said the proposed policy was 'a bit like saying you can't insure your house against burning down. If it does burn down then you are completely on your own, you have to pay for all of it until you are down to the last £100,000 of all of your assets and income'. Those involved in the manifesto preparation thought this was a ridiculous comparison, given the infrequency with which fire insurance is needed compared to the demands on social care, but Dilnot's opposition meant that a key Conservative policy was undermined from the morning of its launch.

There was a debate about who was responsible for first coining the phrase 'dementia tax' to describe the policy—although the Alzheimer's Society had been using the phrase to refer to the *current* system for years.[20] But the term was in widespread use by lunchtime on the day of the launch.

Conservatives would complain that this was to misrepresent the policy, although there was little sympathy from their political opponents, given that in 2010 the Conservatives had accused Labour of introducing a 'death tax' when they had been attempting to deal with similar issues. The Conservatives digital team soon began to buy Google ads for the phrase in order to steer people towards their explanations of the policy, which led to the claim that they were legitimating the phrase by using it themselves.[21]

During the production of the manifesto, May's economic adviser Douglas McNeill had maintained a spreadsheet of costings, mirroring the Treasury methodology for budgets and spending reviews. Each major policy was cleared through this process, which David Gauke, a Treasury minister, oversaw throughout, and which the Chancellor cleared a few days before the manifesto was published. The result, those involved claim, was that the manifesto was essentially cost neutral. Yet no costings document was published. 'We didn't give figures because we didn't want to get into nit-picking with the media', said one of the manifesto's authors. As well as attacking many of the policies, Labour condemned the Conservative manifesto as an '84 page blank cheque'—with McDonnell repeatedly using a line about how the only numbers contained in the Conservative manifesto were page numbers.[22] Given the Conservatives' standard attacks on the cost of Labour's policy agenda, the lack of Conservative costings—especially when juxtaposed with Labour's supposedly 'fully costed' document—proved problematic. After the election, one of May's aides justified the decision not to publish internal costings: 'It sets a terrible precedent, creates opportunities for mischief, could have led to days of headlines about whether our sums added up—but clearly Labour doing so meant we looked shifty by comparison.' The effect was to disarm the party for an effective attack on the Labour manifesto. Some within Labour could not believe their luck. Talking of their own manifesto, one Southsider declared: 'It didn't add up! It didn't add up! That was obvious to anyone who looked in any detail. I just kept thinking, they'll tear us apart on this. But the attack never came. Their manifesto was so light on numbers that it made it impossible to attack us.' One of those involved in the preparation of Labour's manifesto believed that it would have been possible for the Conservatives to have credibly claimed there was £1 trillion of spending commitments in the Labour manifesto. 'The Tories just didn't attack us on our economic policy', he said. 'It was a huge mistake for them.'[23]

Liberal Democrat manifesto launch podium. Credit: Ned Simons

The Liberal Democrat manifesto, *Change Britain's Future*, was launched the day after Labour's, in London. Manifestoes traditionally offer a programme for government; the Liberal Democrats presented a manifesto for opposition. It began with a foreword entitled 'Your Chance to Change Britain's Future by Changing the Opposition', which effectively conceded that Theresa May was going to win the election and ruled out a coalition with either Labour or the Conservatives. This foreword, which the leader's office had insisted on inserting late on in the drafting process, sat awkwardly with the rest of the document, which was a more conventional manifesto, packed—as Liberal Democrat manifestoes often are—with policy detail. A first draft of the document, loosely based on the unused 2016 manifesto, had been completed two days after May called the election. By the time the party's Federal Policy Committee (FPC) met on 2 May in an eight-hour meeting to sign it off, it was on its fifth draft. Given that the foreword effectively said that none of it was going to be implemented, some of those involved in its production did wonder why they had bothered to work so hard. As one of those involved in writing it noted: 'It was a manifesto for government, even though we said it wasn't.'

The manifesto began with Brexit, with Tim Farron launching the document at a podium surrounded by the 12 gold stars of the EU flag. The manifesto promised to let the 'British people' rather than 'politicians' make the final Brexit decision by offering a referendum on any eventual deal with the EU. This pledge was the subject of some disagreement at the FPC meeting. The meeting began with a presentation from the party's director of campaigns on the electoral realities in some marginal seats: 'It was made clear', said one of those present, 'that we did need Leave voters in marginal seats.' There was a divide between those who wanted an unambiguous message on Europe and those who had concerns about their Leave-leaning voters. Several of the sitting MPs—most notably Norman Lamb—were unhappy with anything that appeared to dismiss the views of those who voted Leave. In particular, Lamb was adamant that there could be no pledge to campaign to Remain in any future referendum without knowing the details of the Brexit settlement, believing it would be unsellable on the doorstep.[24] In the end, the policy on the new referendum—what the party always tried to insist was not a second referendum, but a referendum on any deal—was accepted. Similar electoral considerations entered into the discussion on the 'mansion tax'. The 2015 manifesto had promised a 'High Value Property Levy' on properties worth over £2 million; in 2017, several of the key Liberal Democrat targets in the election were in South West London, where property prices were high, and no such levy made it into the manifesto.[25]

Over the weekend of 20–21 May, Conservative candidates began reporting back a terrible doorstep reaction to the manifesto. It was not just the social care policy that had gone down badly; concerns about it had coalesced with other policies, including the changes to the Winter Fuel Payment and the removal of the pensions triple lock. On social media, there was considerable criticism of the manifesto for the absence of a pledge, present in both 2010 and 2015, to push for a total ban on the sale of ivory; criticism of the Conservatives over this became one of the single most-read stories on Facebook during the campaign.[26] There was also criticism for the absence of any identifiable LGBT policies.[27] But of all of these, it was social care that was the main problem. The Sunday press was terrible. The term 'dementia tax' was by now common currency and a YouGov poll published in the *Sunday Times* had the Conservative lead down to single figures—the first poll in the campaign to do so—with Labour on 35%, four points better than the party had managed in 2015.

The Conservatives faced a choice. They could try to ride the storm out and justify the policy. All of those involved in the manifesto still believed their policy was significantly better than both the status quo or the proposals put forward by Dilnot. It was, in their view, a serious attempt to deal with issues of inter-generational justice and introducing a cap would only benefit the wealthiest. 'We all thought the cap idea was regressive', said one of the team.[28] Or they could change policy, somehow. The problem with changing policy, as one of those involved noted, was that '[i]t completely undermined the core message of the election. We should have held our nerve, and explained the policy properly. This is one of the major challenges of our time. By reversing, you just look ridiculous'. If the core message of the election was 'strong and stable', U-turning risked looking the opposite. By the Sunday evening, however, the pressure had built up to such an extent that those arguing for change (especially Timothy, who was taken aback at the reaction, and Jeremy Hunt) had won the internal argument. Crosby's view by this point was that the policy could cost the party the election.[29] He argued that changing policy would involve taking a hit, but it would pass in a day. At one point, Timothy was overheard joking: 'On the plus side, we've just had an open and honest debate about social care. On the downside, it's been massively damaging to the campaign.' As with so many of the key campaign decisions, May was essentially a passive bystander in this discussion, angry at having to change policy, but providing almost no input into the decision herself and accepting the verdict of her advisors.

In a speech in Wrexham on 22 May, launching the Welsh Conservative manifesto, the Prime Minister announced a change in policy, only then to deny there had been a change in policy. She said that the Conservative social care policy had been misrepresented by Labour, complaining of 'fake claims' and 'fear and scaremongering', and argued that the Conservatives were the only party facing up to the difficult decisions facing the country. She reiterated the basics of the policy, adding that in addition to a floor, there would also be a cap—'an absolute limit'—on the amount of money that anyone would spend on care. The details of this cap were to be resolved later via the Green Paper promised in the manifesto.

The problems began once journalists started to ask her questions:

BBC:	'You have just announced a significant change to what was offered in your manifesto ... That doesn't look so strong and stable, Prime Minister, does it?'
Sky:	'You talk about a coalition of chaos but isn't this a manifesto of chaos now? What else are you going to clarify within in the next few days?'
ITV:	'You have just buckled under pressure over your social care plans. Isn't this U-turn really just a cynical attempt to stop voters leaving you in droves?'
Channel 4:	'Doesn't this show that you are really weak and wobbly, not strong and stable? Can you give us an idea of what the cap will be?'

The Prime Minister's irritation was obvious, and grew more so with each question. In the end, in response to a question from Chris Hope from the *Daily Telegraph* ('Will anything else in the manifesto change between now and June 8th?'), she snapped: 'Nothing has changed! Nothing has changed!'

Her irritation was said to come from her feeling that the journalists were not interested in the detail of the policy, but were instead grandstanding in order to produce good footage for TV.[30] Her argument was that the manifesto had promised a Green Paper, setting out the details, and that any cap could be considered part of the detail, whilst the principles of the policy had remained fundamentally unchanged. It was indeed true that the manifesto had promised a Green Paper (and it had similarly not explicitly ruled out a limit on contributions), but the lack of a cap was more than a detail. It was a fundamental part of the policy and one that had been made explicit both in private briefings to journalists before the manifesto was launched and in various comments by Conservative politicians afterwards.[31]

It might, perhaps, have been possible to try to make an advantage of changing policy, to make a virtue of the pragmatism involved, but instead May ended up changing a flagship policy whilst denying doing so. As one Conservative aide said: 'People don't mind you doing U-turns if it shows you're listening and if you explain what you're doing—so to change the policy and then claim you're not changing it was devastating to the brand. At that point, you're just another politician.'[32] Another of those involved in the policy's development said that 'it completely trashed her brand'.

The media response was immediate. Gary Gibbon of Channel 4 said May's image as 'Gloriana' had been battered; other journalists were less kind.[33] Her aides watching on were under no illusions about how the event had gone. As one said: 'We differed in how badly we thought it went. Some people thought it was horrendous. Others thought it was worse than that.' The public noticed. One poll found that those who noticed the manifestos at all noticed the more popular policies in Labour's—those with public support—such as to remove tuition fees (noted by 32%) or increase NHS funding (21%). But for the Conservatives, only one policy was recalled by more than a fifth of voters, and that was the changes to social care (36%).[34] The British Election Study would regularly ask voters what, if anything, had caused them to change their minds during the campaign. From the point at which Labour's manifesto had leaked, the word 'manifesto' had become the most frequently mentioned response, but from 18 May onwards, 'social care' and 'dementia tax' began to emerge, until 'care' was the single most significant issue on 23 May, remaining important thereafter.[35]

Also on 22 May, the Green Party of England and Wales launched their manifesto—what they called their 'Green Guarantee'.[36] Welsh Labour did the same; First Minister Carwyn Jones, launching Labour's Welsh manifesto, managed not to mention Jeremy Corbyn once.[37] In Edinburgh, Kezia Dugdale launched the Scottish Labour manifesto. A poll found that Labour had moved back into the lead in Wales.[38] Labour also announced that their policy on abolishing student fees would begin in the coming academic year. Following her U-turn in Wales, May endured a difficult interview with Andrew Neil on BBC1, the first of his interviews with the party leaders; 'this must be the first time in modern history', Neil said, 'that a party's actually broken a manifesto policy before the election'. The day also saw the deadline for voter registration, with over 600,000 people accessing the registration website on the final day.[39] Postal votes had begun to arrive on people's doormats.

That evening, in Manchester, just over 14,000 people attended a concert by the pop star Ariana Grande in the MEN Arena. As the concert finished and people were exiting the venue, a Manchester-born suicide bomber detonated an explosive device. He killed 22 other people and injured around 500. Many of the dead were children; the youngest was eight. In the early hours of the morning, the Prime Minister spoke to the Leader of the Opposition and the election campaign was suspended.

Notes

1. For one analysis, see Mish Slade, 'The Party Manifesto Awards for (Mostly) Making a Pig's Ear of Written Communication', *Mortified Cow*, https://blog.mortifiedcow.com/the-party-manifesto-awards-for-mostly-making-a-pigs-ear-of-written-communication-b7d99b2d6848.
2. There is a claim by Alex Nunns (*The Candidate*. OR Books, pp. 316–17) that this was the first time 'in living memory' that Labour had sent their manifesto to the printers on time, thus repudiating the claims of incompetence made against the Leader's Office. Whilst producing the manifesto in such a short time period was an impressive achievement, this particular claim came as news to some of those involved in earlier manifestoes.
3. There are good accounts of the reaction, and the ensuring blame game, in Tim Ross and Tom McTague, *Betting the House*. Biteback, 2017, Chapter 11; and Tim Shipman, *Fall Out*. William Collins, 2017, Chapter 17.
4. There was, for example, a foreword in the version Watson had been sent, which was absent from the leaked version. The draft foreword (which was completely different from the eventually published version) began with 'Britain will prosper when the people of Britain prosper'. Watson's team pointed out the similarity of this line to Ed Miliband's 'Britain will only succeed when working people succeed'. But there were other smaller differences too, which helped to prove that Watson was not responsible; at one point, discussing tuition fees, the leaked version said 'in Britain', whereas the version sent to Watson said 'here'.
5. It was also traditionally chaired by the party leader. It was suggested to Corbyn that it would be better for Glenis Willmott MEP, the National Executive Committee (NEC) Chair, to lead the meeting without informing him that previously the Leader had chaired it. As neither Corbyn nor any of his close team had ever attended a Clause V meeting before, no one seems to have realised that he could chair the meeting.
6. One of the clues that helped Labour eventually identify the source of the leak was the absence of water nationalisation in the leaked version, which narrowed down where it could have come from.
7. This is well explained in Nunns, *The Candidate*, p. 316.
8. The phrase comes from R.H. Tawney's 'The Choice before the Labour Party', *Political Quarterly*, 3(3) (1932): 323–45.
9. See, for example, Stephen Bush's 'Jeremy Corbyn's Policies aren't That Different from Ed Miliband's or Even New Labour. So Why is He Being Attacked?', *New Statesman*, 11 April 2017, https://www.newstatesman.com/politics/welfare/2017/04/jeremy-corbyns-policies-arent-different-ed-milibands-or-even-new-labour-so, published just a week before Theresa May called the election. Bush had previously described Corbynism as 'turbo-charged Milibandism' or 'Milibandism minus dithering'.

10. This argument is sometimes presented as another Southside versus LOTO dispute, but plenty of Corbyn's closest aides were extremely hesitant about publishing any costings.
11. There is a slightly different view on this in Shipman, *Fall Out*, p. 284.
12. Shipman (*Fall Out*, pp. 295–96) claims May blocked the policy, but doubts about its political wisdom were held more widely within the manifesto team.
13. Similarly, the eventual Winter Fuel Payment policy was rather more generous than 'for all but the poorest of pensioners'.
14. Although we cannot confirm this, given what was to unfold almost as soon as the policy was announced, the suspicion must be that the proposal was focus group-tested largely as written rather than as the party's opponents would present it.
15. One of Crosby's suggested changes involved the wording of the pledge of fox hunting. The 2015 manifesto had said: 'We will protect hunting, shooting and fishing ... A Conservative Government will give Parliament the opportunity to repeal the Hunting Act on a free vote, with a government bill in government time.' Crosby suggested flipping the order around in order to lead with the free vote. What ended up in the 2017 manifesto was: 'We will grant a free vote, on a government bill in government time, to give parliament the opportunity to decide the future of the Hunting Act.' Ironically, therefore, the 2017 manifesto was less pro-hunting than that of 2015—there was no reference to protecting hunting, or shooting or recreational fishing, and no explicit mention of repeal—yet the party got much more grief over the issue during the campaign.
16. Shipman, *Fall Out*, p. 293.
17. Matthew d'Ancona, 'We Wanted a Politics of Audacity. May's Manifesto Delivers it', *The Guardian*, 21 May 2017.
18. Ross and McTague, *Betting the House*, p. 271.
19. This metaphor is used by multiple individuals involved in the process.
20. The first individual seems to have been a man called Phil Lewis. But Paul Butters in the Liberal Democrats press team was also quick to use the phrase and probably did more to get it into widespread circulation than anyone else. See Shipman, *Fall Out*, p. 300.
21. Jim Waterson, 'How the Tories' Decision to Buy Google Ads about the "Dementia Tax" Backfired', *BuzzFeed News*, 22 May 2017, https://www. buzzfeed.com/jimwaterson/how-the-tories-decision-to-buy-google-ads-about-the?utm_term=.rawJOQrLR4#.msQm7AZDxN.
22. This line had the merit of being memorable, while not actually being true. There were plenty of numbers in the Conservative manifesto, just not full costings.
23. On the few occasions that the Conservatives did attempt to provide journalists with detailed critiques of Labour's policies, Labour staffers

were surprised by the poor quality of the work. One briefing was described by a Labour staffer as: 'A typical CRD [Conservative Research Department] thing, and I don't mean that in a positive way. They are so lazy. It was properly ropey.' The Labour staffer tasked with responding produced a ten-point rebuttal within an hour and the topic fell off the agenda.

24. Ross, *Betting the House*, p. 350. That said, despite Lamb's objections, the eventual manifesto noted that the Liberal Democrats 'continue to believe that there is no deal as good for the UK outside the EU as the one it already has as a member'. It did not quite rule out voting to leave in any new referendum, but it came close.

25. Although it remained in the manifesto, the fallout from the fuss over Farron's views on homosexuality led to the party abandoning an announcement of its policy to legalise prostitution in advance of the formal manifesto launch. The party had done a similar 'soft launch' with its policy on legalising cannabis on 12 May, but a plan to do the same for prostitution was abandoned, as the 'optics [were] all wrong' according to one of the Lib Dem team. For a more graphic version of the internal Lib Dem discussions, see Shipman, *Fall Out*, p. 257.

26. Following lobbying from the antiques industry, the manifesto included a more vague pledge to 'protect rare species', but there was no mention of ivory, unlike in 2010 and 2015. See Jim Waterson, 'This was the Election Where the Newspapers Lost Their Monopoly on the Political News Agenda', *BuzzFeed News*, 18 June 2017, https://www.buzzfeed.com/jimwaterson/how-newspapers-lost-their-monopoly-on-the-political-agenda?utm_term=.yxy9Zw8oO5#.whBPZQL5nq.

27. There was some LGBT-related policy in the manifesto, albeit not much, but nothing that used the phrase 'LGBT' or similar. As one CCHQ aide said: 'it fails the CTRL-F test'. See Skylar Baker-Jordan, 'What Do the Parties' Manifestos Promise the LGBT Community?', *Huffington Post*, 19 May 2017, https://www.huffingtonpost.co.uk/skylar-bakerjordan/lgbt-general-election-2017_b_16689178.html.

28. The manifesto even included a dig at Dilnot, noting that the proposals in his report would have 'mostly benefited a small number of wealthier people'.

29. Shipman, *Fall Out*, p. 278.

30. Ross and McTague, *Betting the House*, p. 275. The view inside CCHQ was that the problems with the policy were too advanced and serious to attempt to make a virtue of changing policy.

31. For example, during a *Today* interview on the same day that the manifesto was launched, Jeremy Hunt said of the cap 'not only are we dropping it, but we're dropping it ahead of a General Election and we're being completely explicit in our manifesto that we're dropping it, and we're dropping

it because we've looked again at this proposal and we don't think it's fair'. It would have been difficult to be clearer.

32. Ross and McTague, *Betting the House*, p. 275.

33. See Gary Gibbon, 'After Today's U-Turn, Theresa May's "Gloriana Image" is a Little Battered', *Channel 4 News*, 22 May 2017, https://www. channel4.com/news/by/gary-gibbon/blogs/after-todays-u-turn-theresa-mays-gloriana-image-is-a-little-battered.

34. Anthony Wells, 'Manifesto Destinies', *YouGov*, 25 May 2017, https:// yougov.co.uk/news/2017/05/25/manifesto-destinies.

35. Chris Prosser, 'What was it All About? The 2017 Election Campaign in Voters' Own Words', *British Election Study*, 2 August 2017, www.britishe-lectionstudy.com/bes-findings/what-was-it-all-about-the-2017-election-campaign-in-voters-own-words/#.WrO67WrFJhF.

36. The full title of the document was the much less snappy *The Green Party for a Confident and Caring Britain*. The Scottish Greens would launch their manifesto a week later.

37. The same had been true when Labour launched their campaign in Wales. In a 45-minute rally, the Party Leader was not mentioned a single time. See Martin Shipton, 'Welsh Labour Held a 45-Minute General Election Launch and Didn't Mention Jeremy Corbyn Once', *Wales Online*, 8 May 2017, https://www.walesonline.co.uk/news/politics/welsh-labour-held-45-minute-13003959.

38. 'Poll Shows Labour Reclaiming Lead in Wales', *ITV News*, 22 May 2017, www.itv.com/news/wales/2017-05-22/poll-shows-labour-reclaiming-lead-in-wales.

39. In total, 2.9 million applications to register to vote were made between the Prime Minister's announcement on 18 April and the deadline; more than 96% of these were made using the online service, including 612,000 which were submitted on the last day for applications. Of the online applications, over two-thirds were made by people aged under 34. However, as in previous elections, many of these merely duplicated entries already on the register. Estimates of duplication ranged from 30% to 70% in some areas. See the Electoral Commission's *Electoral Registration at the June 2017 UK General Election* (2017).

CHAPTER 9

Horrors and Hopes

The bombing in Manchester on 22 May 2017 was the worst terrorist attack in the UK since 2005. The country woke the next morning to shocking pictures of bloodied concert-goers being helped out of the Manchester Arena by members of the emergency services. The Prime Minister chaired an early morning meeting of COBR, the government's emergency response committee.[1] She then gave a statement outside Number 10, in which she described the attack as 'among the worst terrorist incidents we have ever experienced in the United Kingdom'.[2] She announced that she would be travelling to Manchester to meet with the Chief Constable and the newly elected Mayor of Greater Manchester, Andy Burnham, as well as the emergency services.

A vigil was held in Manchester later that day, attended by Jeremy Corbyn, Tim Farron and the Commons Speaker John Bercow. The Prime Minister, having visited victims of the bombing at Manchester Children's Hospital, had returned to London to chair a second meeting of COBR and sent Amber Rudd in her place. Her absence from the vigil resulted in some criticism, both from the crowd and elsewhere.[3] That evening she announced that the independent Joint Terrorism Analysis Centre (JTAC) had raised the security threat to 'Critical' for the first time in ten years—indicating that further attacks might be imminent—and that 'Operation Temperer' had been launched, deploying troops to augment the police on the streets of Britain.

© The Author(s) 2018
P. Cowley, D. Kavanagh, *The British General Election of 2017*,
https://doi.org/10.1007/978-3-319-95936-8_9

   Campaigning remained suspended for a second day. On the third day, 25 May, a national minute's silence was held. Most parties continued their campaign suspension, although UKIP broke ranks, launching their manifesto, entitled *Britain Together*. Paul Nuttall defended the event, saying: 'We took the decision that the best way to show these people they will be beaten and they will not win is to get back into the saddle and launch our manifesto.' Media questions about whether UKIP were trying to capitalise on the bombing did not go down well with the audience at the manifesto launch, with journalists variously abused by UKIP members. The party's policy announcements were largely overshadowed by comments made by the party's deputy leader, Suzanne Evans, who implied that the Prime Minister bore some responsibility for the Manchester attack as a result of her time as Home Secretary, since she had cut police numbers. *The Spectator*'s report on the comments thought this line of attack 'might be a step too far'.[4] Later that day, after the minute's silence had been observed, many election candidates across the country resumed low-key campaigning—and the decision to restart national campaigning the following day was announced by the major parties after three full days' halt.

Ben Jennings, *i*, 27 May 2017 © Ben Jennings

   For the most part, the cessation had held. There were occasional stories of leaflets being delivered or activity on social media, but these isolated events were nearly always pre-booked activities—such as direct mail—which it had been too late to stop being delivered, despite the frantic efforts of party staff to cancel as many as possible.

The immediate reaction of most involved in the campaign was to assume that, insofar as there would be political consequences from the attack, these would be positive for the Conservatives. The widespread assumption was that a terrorist attack would re-emphasise issues of law and order—as well as Corbyn's past links—whilst drawing attention away from the Conservatives' social care debacle. (On the conspiracist fringes of the left, there were even occasional claims that this was *why* the attack had taken place.) Moreover, the longer the campaign pause went on, the more the Prime Minister would appear on television, giving statements and appearing prime ministerial, exactly the image she liked to project— 'getting on with the job'—but which the events of the campaign had done so much to undermine. For precisely this reason, Labour were not keen on a lengthy pause in campaigning. Corbyn had taken the decision to agree to the suspension alone when he had spoken to the Prime Minister; not all of the Labour campaign team believed it should have been taken, were desperate to get back to campaigning and resisted any attempts by the Conservatives to extend the campaign pause.[5] 'I almost felt dirty thinking it', admitted one of the Labour team, when asked about the political impact of the bombing. 'It's horrific. But then you think, we are in an election campaign.'

However, not all Conservatives were convinced that the pause would benefit them. Although the parties stopped campaigning, many satellite organisations did not. At one point, Stephen Gilbert asked Conservative staff to identify groups that were still active on social media. They found 40 organisations. 'Without exception', said one of the Conservative team, 'they all hate the Tories.' Also, because the Manchester bombing took place immediately after the manifesto debacle, it prevented any Conservative fightback on the issue. 'It froze the debate at the worst possible time', said one of those involved in the Conservative campaign, 'with a visibly angry Prime Minister shouting at journalists. We never returned to the substance [of social care].'

The bombings led to a major diplomatic row with the US after intelligence information shared between the countries' intelligence services began to be published in the US. It also, in different ways, triggered major rows within the two main political parties. Within the Conservatives, there was a heated internal argument about how the Prime Minister should respond to the bombing publicly—and in particular whether to use social media to do so. Nick Timothy and Fiona Hill were adamant that this was not the correct way for a Prime Minister to behave, and that there needed to be a clear distinction between the way Theresa May responded as Prime Minister and the way she would behave as a campaigning party leader. Apart from a brief press statement around 2.20 am, there was no official response from Number 10 until she gave her first statement in Downing Street just after 11 am on the morning after the bombing. Others argued that her absence from social media merely created a vacuum for others to fill; Corbyn, for example, had tweeted his sympathies to all those involved at around midnight.[6] But Hill and Timothy won out.[7]

The row within Labour—which was much more visceral—concerned the role that Corbyn should play in any events in Manchester. According to multiple accounts (although still denied by some in LOTO), the leader's office repeatedly pushed for Corbyn's involvement in events in ways that many of those dealing with the aftermath of the bombing felt were inappropriate—including a proposed photocall with all the Labour candidates from Manchester along with members of the emergency services.[8] Some of the local MPs were 'incandescent' (according to one) at what was being suggested. Corbyn arrived in Manchester accompanied by Karie Murphy and Ian Lavery; the very presence of the latter, as the party's campaign coordinator, was seen as inappropriate by some. At a meeting in the Manchester Midland Hotel, a short time before a mass vigil was held, there was what one of Corbyn's team admitted was a 'huge row' and the LOTO team backed off.

ꞌ No polls were published while the campaign was suspended. Polls released on 26 May, however, all had the Conservative lead down to single figures, with leads lower than anything seen so far in the campaign. YouGov had Labour on 38%, the party's best polling since late 2014, with the Conservative lead as low as five points. This would represent a Conservative majority of just two seats.

Labour re-entered the national campaign on 26 May with a speech by Corbyn directly engaging with the Manchester bombing. Labour had always intended for him to give a major speech on security during the campaign, which he had delivered at Chatham House on 12 May. Slightly hyperbolically, Steve Howell had wanted the Chatham House speech to be Corbyn's 'Philadelphia moment', a reference to Barack Obama's speech on race in March 2008 when he answered attacks on him over his links with the Reverend Jeremiah Wright.[9] Some of the themes of the Manchester speech were similar to the speech given at Chatham House—the War on Terror had failed, causing destabilisation abroad—yet the post-Manchester speech went further, explicitly linking what had happened in Manchester with British foreign policy.

Corbyn said that to protect people, a Labour government would require 'change at home and change abroad'. At home, this meant reversing cuts to emergency services and police. 'Austerity has to stop at the A&E ward and at the police station door. We cannot be protected and cared for on the cheap', he said. The more controversial parts of the speech came once he moved on to 'change abroad'. 'Many experts,' he argued, 'including professionals in our intelligence and security services have pointed to the connections between wars our government has supported or fought in other countries, such as Libya, and terrorism here at home.'

Martin Rowson, *Daily Mirror*, 15 May 2017 © Martin Rowson

A carefully worded part of the speech tried to make clear that he was not excusing the attack:

> That assessment in no way reduces the guilt of those who attack our children. Those terrorists will forever be reviled and implacably held to account for their actions. But an informed understanding of the causes of terrorism is an essential part of an effective response that will protect the security of our people, that fights rather than fuels terrorism.

He went on:

> No government can prevent every terrorist attack. If an individual is determined enough and callous enough, sometimes they will get through. But the responsibility of government is to minimise that chance, to ensure the police have the resources they need, that our foreign policy reduces rather than increases the threat to this country, and that at home we never surrender the freedoms we have won, and that terrorists are so determined to take away.

Giving the speech in the aftermath of Manchester, before the dead had even been buried, was a gamble. The risk was that—even if people agreed with the content, and there was no guarantee they would—they might disagree with the timing. Not all of Corbyn's team supported him giving the speech, although Corbyn himself was strongly in favour of doing so. Like so many of the campaign decisions, the division was not one that neatly separated LOTO and Southside. Andrew Gwynne was initially sceptical, for example; Ian Lavery was more supportive.

The backlash was quick in coming. Speaking from the G7 summit in Sicily, the Prime Minister hit back at the Labour leader:

> I have been here with the G7, working with other international leaders to fight terrorism. At the same time, Jeremy Corbyn has said that terror attacks in Britain are our own fault and he has chosen to do that a few days after one of the worst terrorist atrocities we have experienced in the United Kingdom. I want to make something clear to Jeremy Corbyn and to you: there can never be an excuse for terrorism, there can be no excuse for what happened in Manchester.

Amber Rudd described Corbyn's comments as 'absolutely outrageous'; Michael Fallon said they showed 'dangerous thinking' and Boris Johnson called the speech 'monstrous', claiming that Corbyn had 'spent a political career sticking up for terrorists, sympathising with the IRA, with Hamas, with Hezbollah, and blocking every single piece of anti-terrorist legislation in the last 30 years'. However, Conservative attacks on Corbyn's speech soon faltered when polling found that many of Corbyn's views were widely shared (see below, p. 265) and when journalists started to repeat similar claims made by Conservative politicians.[10] On *Channel 4 News*, for example, Fallon found himself condemning what he thought were excerpts from the Corbyn speech, only to be told they were in fact previous comments made by the Foreign Secretary.

The resumption of the campaign also brought the response of the Institute for Fiscal Studies (IFS) on the party manifestoes. It was not complimentary. 'The shame of the two big parties' manifestos', they said 'is that neither sets out an honest set of choices. Neither addresses the long-term challenges we face.' According to the IFS, May's plans failed to address 'risks to the quality of public services and tough choices over spending' and there was therefore a danger that the Prime Minister 'would not be able to deliver the promised spending cuts either at all, or at least without serious damage to the quality of public services'. The verdict on Labour was every bit as critical. It was misleading to claim the huge public spending increases proposed 'can be funded by faceless corporations and "the rich"'. Rather than £49 billion a year, Labour were unlikely to raise more than £40 billion in the short term and 'considerably less in the longer term'.

That evening, Corbyn was interviewed by Andrew Neil on BBC One and defended his comments on terrorism, arguing that they were similar to those made by Boris Johnson, two heads of MI5 and the Foreign Affairs Select Committee. It was one of multiple one-on-one interviews that the party leaders would give during the campaign. None were disasters for either major party leader, but—whether they were more combative (such as Neil's) or more chatty (such as those on *The One Show*)—May's were widely judged to be the less convincing performances. All of the issues with her ability to communicate, of which her close team were well aware—her lack of dexterity when questioned, the apparent lack of empathy, especially when dealing with members of the public, her inability to stay on message without sounding robotic—were clear in almost all of her media appearances (see Chapter 13). In contrast, Corbyn emerged relatively well, seeming more relaxed and comfortable in the format, and mostly doing well at deflecting the more difficult or aggressive questioning. The one exception was a Radio 4 *Women's Hour* interview with Emma

Liberal Democrat debate rehearsal, Ministry of Sound, 29 May

Barnett, towards the end of the campaign, in which he was caught out by a question over costings—('It will cost ... erm ... it will obviously cost a lot')—and endured a painful few minutes as he searched for the correct information. He apologised afterwards to his team for letting them down. But in general, no one watching or listening to the televised interviews would have been able to identify the candidate who was supposed to be a political titan and the one who—until the campaign had begun—had been widely considered incompetent and unelectable.

A mistake in a Conservative briefing document led to *Schools Week* breaking the story that the party's pledge for free breakfasts in schools had been priced at just seven pence per meal.[11] (Labour had, just in time, spotted a similar mistake in its costings document which had led to the entire document being reprinted before release.) It took time for Conservative Campaign Headquarters (CCHQ) to begin to land similar blows on Labour, although they slowly began to work their way through the Labour

BREAKFAST
CLEARLY
DOESN'T
MEAN
BREAKFAST

manifesto, identifying weaknesses. The experienced special adviser Sheridan Westlake repackaged Labour's proposal to consider replacing council tax with a Land Value Tax as a 'garden tax'. The party found that this attack worked—'this was more potent than people realise', said one of those involved in the Conservatives' social media team. Given that Labour were only committed to considering the policy, it was a pretty tenuous attack, but probably no more tenuous than some of the claims made about the dementia tax. The Conservatives also eventually noticed Labour's proposal to abolish the marriage allowance, which would have affected around a million households and which appeared to contradict Corbyn's claim that only the top 5% would pay increased tax.[12]

As the weekend began, investigations by the security services led the JTAC to reduce the terror threat to 'severe'.

The SNP manifesto, *Stronger for Scotland*, was launched in Perth on 30 May. The launch had originally been planned for 23 May and had been delayed as a result of the Manchester attack. The manifesto's title was exactly the same as in 2015, but whereas in 2015 the front cover had consisted solely of a portrait of the First Minister, the political world had moved on. This was less a presidential document—no First Minister on the cover—and whereas the launch in 2015 had had the feel of a revivalist meeting, in 2017 it felt more like that of a conventional political party.[13] In her launch speech, Nicola Sturgeon said that the manifesto set out a plan 'to end Tory cuts, protect Scottish jobs, and strengthen Scotland's hand'. The manifesto contained plenty of policies designed to try to stop the party being outflanked by Labour, including £80 billion of spending commitments, along with relatively little on independence, so as not to alienate those opposed to or annoyed by the subject. If anyone was talking a lot about independence, it was not the SNP. As Sturgeon said: 'Ruth Davidson is going around Scotland saying I talk about nothing other than independence. She talks about it so much that I don't get a chance.' The manifesto promised no immediate independence referendum, but linked it to Brexit, with any referendum to take place 'when the terms of the deal are known'. 'There is just too much at stake for Brexit simply to be imposed on Scotland, no matter how damaging it turns out to be', said Sturgeon. 'Our future must be decided by us, not for us.'

• Earlier in the campaign, and when there was a need to avoid Conservative complacency, Theresa May had asserted that if she lost just six seats 'I will lose this election and Jeremy Corbyn will be sitting down to negotiate with Europe'.[14] At the time, this claim was greeted with incredulity, both because a loss of six seats would in any case not automatically lead to a Labour-led government and because it did not seem very likely, given the Conservative poll leads.[15] But late on 30 May, word that YouGov were about to release a 'dramatic poll' began to leak out on Twitter. When the embargo broke at midnight, there was astonishment at its prediction of a hung parliament, with the Conservatives losing seats. As discussed below (p. 267), this was not, strictly speaking, a poll, but a model based on polling, and on the same day other polls put the Tory lead as high as ten points.

The Conservatives had ruled out the Prime Minister's participation in any televised leaders debates from the very first day of the campaign. Given the commanding opinion poll lead, there seemed little reason to risk participating. They all remembered 2010, when the televised debates had derailed the Conservative campaign by helping to create 'Cleggmania'. Lynton Crosby was adamantly opposed. Plus, nothing in the Prime Minister's televised interviews during the campaign had convinced anyone in CCHQ that she was an undiscovered media star who would be well suited to the format.

Labour had criticised May for refusing to take part, but declared that if she was not going to be there, then nor would Corbyn. The Labour team were more than happy to sit out the debate of opposition leaders—what they dismissively termed 'the losers' debate'—on 19 May. As one of

Peter Brookes, *The Times*, 1 June 2017 © News UK/News Licensing

Corbyn's team said, 'we'd seen what had happened to Ed Miliband [in 2015]—they just all gang up on you'. The idea of flipping their position and taking part in the seven-way main debate on BBC on 31 May was first floated by Andrew Murray during the morning campaign meeting the day before.[16] As was so often the case, there was no consensus amongst the campaign team—and again, this was not a straightforward LOTO/ Southside split. Those arguing against participating thought that it was too great a risk. Although his stump speeches had been going well and he was getting better at one-to-one interviews, Corbyn had undertaken no preparation for the debates—the team had been busy rehearsing Emily Thornberry as his stand in—and there were lots of ways in which multi-person debates could go wrong. A poor performance at this stage of the campaign could destabilise the party for the final stages of the campaign. Labour had momentum. Why risk it? Those arguing in favour responded that for all their achievements, if they were to have any chance of hitting the desired 40% mark, then, as one put it, 'we've got to take a risk'. Corbyn's participation was also seen as an excellent chance to destabilise the Prime Minister. The mere fact of his taking part, especially at short notice, drew attention to her absence, undercutting yet further any claims that she was strong or authoritative. The meeting ended with no decision and when he was told about it, Corbyn—who was not initially keen—agreed to think about it overnight. That evening he sent texts to a wide range of close friends and contacts. One responded that however hostile the audience, it would not be as bad as facing the Parliamentary Labour Party (PLP) 'on a Monday night in Committee Room 14'.

The final decision was made the next morning, and at a rally in Reading, Corbyn announced that would be taking part in the debate. There was no time for formal rehearsals, although some last-minute preparation was done in the car en route. 'You know what the questions are going to be, and what they're going to throw at you', said one of those involved. 'He knows what his message is. He's comfortable doing that sort of stuff.' As the team left the hotel in which they were staying to head to the venue, they found people lining the streets cheering them.

The Liberal Democrats, for whom leaders' debates are a rare chance to make an impact, had taken preparation much more seriously, including two full rehearsals. As one Lib Dem said: 'We all agreed at the last one that Corbyn would definitely come. We all said: if we were Labour, what would we advise? It was a no brainer.'[17] Sean Kemp, who had worked for Nick Clegg in Downing Street, played Corbyn during the final Lib Dem rehearsal. He was struck by 'how easy and enjoyable it was'. He said: 'It felt a lot like doing the briefings for Lib Dem frontbenchers before Question Time in, say, 2008 or 2009. Five or six good clap lines. It just felt easy.'[18]

May was, by now, in an impossible position. As one Lib Dem staffer noted: 'There was a case for her taking part in a head-to-head debate, but not a seven-way; it would just be a pile on, with everyone attacking her. No matter how good you are, you can't come out of that well. And by that point, it was clear that she wasn't good at this sort of stuff.' Moreover, to change her mind now and to be appearing to follow Corbyn's lead would hardly demonstrate leadership. No one at CCHQ seriously considered her participation.

Amber Rudd, who had been rehearsing extensively, deputised for the Prime Minister. Most Conservatives thought Rudd did well—all the more so given that her father had died just days before, something not made public before the debate—but she was hamstrung by being the monkey, not the organ grinder. In her absence, May was attacked five times for not turning up (see below, p. 333). That things were not going well was made clear when a plea from Rudd to 'judge us on our record' was greeted with dismissive laughter.

One curiosity about the 2017 campaign is how few polls there were of the leaders' debates (unlike in 2010, say, where the debates were heavily polled, or even in 2015), and so it is difficult to be sure about who did well or badly in the eyes of the public.[19] Corbyn did not especially shine (and in places the lack of debate preparation showed), but nor did he mess up, and his attendance achieved its strategic objective—of drawing attention to the Prime Minister's absence. One participant in an Ashcroft focus group complained: 'She called the snap election, and now she can't be bothered turning up to it.'[20]

. On 1 June, a week before polling day, a poll in the *Evening Standard* showed Labour a full 17 percentage points ahead in London, with, for the first time, more voters in London thinking that Corbyn would make a better Prime Minister than May.[21] In March, the Conservatives had just been just three points behind in London. The same day, a poll in Wales had the Labour lead up by a point to 11, confirming the complete reversal from the ten-point Conservative lead at the start of the campaign. In both Wales and London, such poll figures would indicate Labour gaining rather than losing seats.[22] The rise in both Labour and Corbyn's standing in Wales came as a particular shock to Plaid Cymru, which had been hoping to benefit from Corbyn's unpopularity and did not know how to respond. 'What you ended up with', said one of the Plaid team, 'was people who liked Carwyn Jones voting Labour and people who liked Jeremy Corbyn voting Labour. Rather than causing division, it managed to appeal to both centre and hard-left and hoover up everybody in the middle.' Leanne Wood earned ridicule for a tweet arguing that people should vote for Plaid to get Corbyn's policies.[23] 'It was sign of how we didn't know how to deal with them', admitted one of her advisers.

The narrowing polls gave questions about post-election deals a new relevance. Corbyn told a rally in Basildon on 1 June: 'We are not doing deals, we are not doing coalitions, we are not doing any of these things. We are fighting to win this election.' Emily Thornberry went further:

> We are fighting to win and we are fighting to win a majority. If we end up in a position where we are in a minority, then we will go ahead and put forward a Queen's speech and a budget and, if people want to vote for it, then good, but if people don't want to vote for it, then they are going to

have to go back and speak to their constituents and explain to them why we have a Tory government instead. Those are the conversations we have had. No deals.

The Conservatives had always planned for May to make a keynote speech with a week to go. Its contents were informed by a note from Mark Textor on 31 May, based on his focus groups, which read: 'New themes are excitement/enthusiasm about the bright future after Brexit (but only if we get it right). Other mob have a dimmer/darker view. Speech to lift TM out of the fog of war without diminishing risk or core framing. But the risk is now framed as the bright future that could be at risk rather than just stuffing up Brexit.'[24] The resulting speech—'the Promise of Brexit'—was seen by some journalists as a switch in tone to a more positive campaign. 'If we get Brexit right', the Prime Minister declared in Teesside, 'then together we can do great things. We can build a Britain beyond Brexit that is stronger, fairer and more prosperous than it is today.' She added: 'You can only deliver Brexit if you believe in Brexit.' The remark was curious, given she had voted to Remain (and that Jeremy Corbyn was hardly an ardent supporter of the EU himself), but the overall message of the speech was essentially what the Downing Street team's vision of the campaign had been all along and was markedly different from what Crosby had pre-scribed and implemented. According to one of her team, it 'basically was the speech she had been making for ages before the campaign started. We had come full circle'.[25]

Relations within CCHQ were now distinctly strained. Timothy was angry at the briefing that had already begun against him over his role in the manifesto. He felt that he had been unfairly singled out over the social care package and detected the hand of CTF in the briefing. Crosby and Textor began to be referred to, increasingly, and not approvingly, as 'the Australians'. As one of the campaign team noted: 'the D minus grid, typi-cally used as a countdown to election day ... became the countdown to the day that we no longer had the Australians in our lives'. Hill had realised sooner than most that things were going wrong and had wanted to revert to their original strategy, with May less centre stage, giving occasional set piece speeches and focusing on policies that could help those struggling, a theme that had hardly figured so far. She was already aware of Chris Wilkinson's view—as one of the architects of the original strategy—but she could not persuade Timothy to join in an approach to Crosby to change tack. At the Chequers away day in February, she had been Crosby's biggest advocate, but now she said to one of her colleagues: 'these Australians are just so much more right-wing than we are'.

The *Question Time Leaders Special* on 2 June was one of only two occasions during the campaign when both May and Corbyn appeared on the same programme, albeit sequentially rather than face-to-face. As Stephen Cushion and Charlie Beckett note (below, p. 334) 'neither had a meltdown moment or blundered badly', but both endured awkward spells during their questioning, which were emblematic of broader issues with their campaigns. The Prime Minister was the first to be questioned and struggled both over her failure to participate in the earlier debates and over domestic policy. There were, one of her team admitted, several 'head in hands' moments.* Faced with a nurse who complained about her pay not rising, May responded that she was 'being honest ... there isn't a magic money tree that we can shake that suddenly provides for everything that people want'. Faced with a woman who had had problems with mental health care and who was almost in tears as she asked her question, the Prime Minister seemed unable to engage on anything more than a logical level. The bluntness of her responses was partly down to her own lack of dexterity, but it was also based on advice from her team not to back down or to give any ground.[26] ·

Corbyn had a more enthusiastic response from the audience, with cheers at the beginning and end of the appearance, prompting complaints from the Conservatives about its composition (see below p. 338). But problems emerged once he faced sustained questioning over the IRA and over nuclear weapons, where he was clearly discomforted by the line of questioning—not least because he was giving answers he did not really believe in. He ruled out first the use of any nuclear weapon, but struggled when he was pushed over any retaliatory second use, at which point he began to be heckled and laughed at. He was rescued by another audience member, who asked (to cheers from Corbyn supporters) why so many people in the audience seemed keen on nuclear warfare. Even Alex Nunns' highly sympathetic account of the Labour campaign describes the seven minutes of questioning on the topic as 'excruciating' and notes that her intervention 'saved Corbyn's skin'.[27]

The Conservative team felt they had survived the *Question Time* debate intact and maybe even had begun to land some blows. 'She wasn't great', one of her advisers said, 'but she was better than him. It's all relative.'[28] The media on the Saturday had been good for the party; the Sunday press was even better. There were stories of planned Labour tax rises in the *Sunday Telegraph* and *Sunday Times* (a 'triple tax whammy', according to the *Sunday Times*). The *Mail on Sunday* had a tape recording of Seumas Milne in conversation with Corbyn discussing how the *Question Time* debate had gone. Whilst recognising he had done well overall, Milne noted the problems over nuclear weapons. 'We need to find [a way]', he said, 'without looking defensive of trying to seal down the Trident thing so it doesn't keep intruding in the next few days … We just need a form of words.' In itself, it was evidence that Milne knew that Labour would not always be able to rely on audience members to dig them out of holes, but the conversation also included him describing the idea of a retaliatory attack as 'bonkers' and 'completely off the wall', and calling the deterrent 'a complete Emperor's new clothes', adding: 'If there has been a first strike, what is the point of the second strike?' This was the very question Corbyn had been so desperate to avoid answering.

The recording had been made by a Conservative staffer who happened to find himself on a train with Milne when the latter, incautiously, was on the phone to the Labour Party leader—a lesson that almost everyone is now armed with a video camera and audio recorder. It was then passed by CCHQ to the *Mail on Sunday*. Indeed, as one of the Conservative team admitted: 'Almost every story on that Sunday was a story we'd planted.' The papers also reported a fresh batch of polls, showing the election continuing to be closer than most had expected. Conservative leads reached as high as 11 or 12 points in two polls (ComRes and ICM), but Survation's poll for the *Mail on Sunday* had the Conservative lead as low as one point, the lowest of any poll so far during the campaign, and two other companies had the lead at just four points. The Conservative plan was to spend most of the rest of the campaign focussed remorselessly on Brexit and the economy.

Just after 10 pm on Saturday 3 June came the second terrorist attack of the campaign. A van was driven at high speed into pedestrians on London Bridge. After crashing, its occupants ran to nearby Borough Market, where, armed with foot-long kitchen knives, they began to attack anyone they encountered. In total, they killed eight people, injuring another 48. The three attackers, all of whom were wearing fake explosive vests to heighten any panic, were then shot dead by police.

This time there was no lengthy or complete cessation of campaigning. Most of the major parties suspended national-level (but not local) campaigning for a day. The decision to pause their campaign was taken by the Conservatives (against Crosby's advice) without consulting Labour, and the Conservatives did not coordinate their response with Labour.[29] Labour were in any case desperate not to stop campaigning and would have resisted any lengthy break. 'We couldn't afford not to campaign', admitted one of the Labour team. 'We couldn't afford to. So close to polling day.' Again, UKIP stood outside the consensus. Nuttall said that UKIP would not suspend campaigning at all, 'because this is precisely what the extremists would want us to do'.

On the Sunday morning, the Prime Minister yet again delivered a statement from behind a podium outside of Number 10. It began by outlining the facts of the attack and paying tribute to the police and emergency services. It noted that this was the third terrorist attack in Britain in three months and that in that time, the security services had disrupted five other 'credible plots'. It then shifted in tone. 'Things need to change', she said. Although the recent attacks were not connected by common networks, she claimed they were 'bound together by the single, evil ideology of Islamist extremism that preaches hatred, sows division, and promotes sectarianism'. As well as promising changes to the regulation of cyberspace and a review of counter-terrorism policy, the Prime Minister said 'there is, to be frank, far too much tolerance of extremism in our country, so we need to become far more robust in identifying it and stamping it out across the public sector and across society'. 'It is time', she said, 'to say "Enough is enough".' She confirmed that the election would go ahead as planned. Violence, she said, 'can never be allowed to disrupt the democratic process. So those campaigns will resume in full tomorrow. And the general election will go ahead as planned on Thursday'.[30]

The speech was widely considered a more hard-line response than the one given after the attack in Manchester. It was, thought one of her team, a 'great speech' (although he added, 'no policy flowed from it. It almost wouldn't have mattered what that was. But nothing…') and it infuriated many in Labour, who felt it was a deliberately political intervention, delivered whilst they were unable to respond. Various outriders for Labour were under no obligation to cease campaigning, however, and multiple responses to May's speech began to circulate online. One of the most widely circulated was a clip of a former Metropolitan Police officer who, in an interview with *Sky News*, said the government were 'lying' about the number of armed police available; that clip, circulated on social media, was seen at least 7.5 million times.[31] Another clip, from 2015, of May as Home

Secretary telling the Police Federation they were 'scaremongering' about the impact of spending cuts on the police also went viral.

The campaign suspension lasted less than 24 hours, with Corbyn restarting Labour's campaign with a speech in Carlisle on the Sunday evening. The speech had been intended to focus on the NHS, but instead, just like after Manchester, the party chose to go on the attack over the issue of terrorism. Corbyn avoided directly linking the attacks to the reduction in police numbers, but declared: 'You cannot protect the public on the cheap. The police and security services must get the resources they need, not 20,000 police cuts. Theresa May was warned by the Police Federation but she accused them of "crying wolf".'

The speech also attempted to close down areas of Conservative attack, offering to look again at the powers the police needed and making it clear that Corbyn was in favour of them having the powers to 'shoot-to-kill' when necessary ('whatever force is necessary to protect and save life'). The former, while not a blank cheque for the security services, was a sentence the backbench Corbyn would never have uttered; the latter was a response to a claim, based on an earlier interview (widely used by the Conservatives in their campaign material), that he was not in favour of allowing the police the power to 'shoot-to-kill'.[32]

The London attack led to the cancellation of a large rally the Conservatives had planned, ironically in the London Bridge area, the only such event the party had planned for the campaign. It also fundamentally shifted the focus of the rest of the campaign. After the election, many in the Conservative campaign believed that the incident in London—whilst involving fewer casualties—was more important politically than the one in Manchester. The Manchester attack was perhaps more shocking, but after London, the agenda shifted firmly onto police cuts in a way it did not after Manchester.[33]

This was the policy on which Diane Abbott had got into so much trouble at the beginning of the campaign. It now returned with a vengeance. On the Monday (5 June), after a speech in London, the Prime Minister was repeatedly questioned by journalists over police numbers. She was not helped by the comments of the head of the Metropolitan Police, Cressida Dick, who had said that morning on ITV's *Good Morning Britain* that she would be seeking 'more resourcing obviously'. 'We were doing alright until Cressida Dick decided she needed more resources', said one of May's team; 'It also allowed Sadiq [Khan] to get involved.' The Mayor of

London had been keeping a deliberately low profile during most of the election ('diligently canvassing', in the words of one of his team). After the London attack, he did a full media round, attacking the Conservatives over police spending in London. Karen Bradley, the Secretary of State for Culture, Media and Sport, endured a painful interview on *Good Morning Britain* on 5 June, in which she erroneously claimed the number of armed police had not fallen ('as soon as she'd said it, she knew she'd got it wrong' said one Conservative aide).

Even the US President managed to make matters worse for the Prime Minister, attacking the Mayor of London for saying that people should try not to be alarmed by the increase in police on the streets. 'At least 7 dead and 48 wounded in terror attack and Mayor of London says there is "no reason to be alarmed!"', Donald Trump tweeted.[34] The Prime Minister found herself repeatedly asked by journalists if she condemned Trump's comments, questions she did her best to evade, provoking the pointed question from one journalist: 'What would Donald Trump have to say for you to criticise him publicly?' Steve Hilton, David Cameron's former adviser, got involved, calling for the Prime Minister to resign, calls that Jeremy Corbyn then appeared to endorse. The idea that the Prime Minister would resign three days before a general election was a bizarre one—earning Corbyn some ridicule—but it all had the effect of keeping the attention on May's tenure at the Home Office rather than on what the Conservatives had intended to be discussing.[35]

Many of the Conservative team considered Labour's linking of the attacks to police cuts specious. As one Cabinet Minister put it: 'They were shot dead in eight minutes. If we'd had another 10,000 police, they wouldn't have been shot dead in seven minutes.' Some of them thought it tasteless. But they all recognised that it was an effective political move. It was not just that it connected security policy with the consequences of austerity, but also that this was an area of policy where the Prime Minister herself had been in charge for five years under the Coalition. 'We had no good rebuttal', admitted one Conservative aide. 'Because there was no good rebuttal. As Home Secretary, she'd cut police numbers. It's a fact.' 'We never returned to the economy', bemoaned one of her team. The result was that the election went into its final week focusing on security and terrorism, with the Conservatives facing a Labour Party led by Jeremy Corbyn and with Diane Abbott as Shadow Home Secretary—and, remarkably, it was the Conservative Party that was on the back foot.

During the final week of the campaign, four of Corbyn's key aides—Murphy, Andrew Fisher, Milne and Murray—met in a hotel in Victoria to discuss post-election outcomes. They drew up four scenarios: (a) the worst, in which Labour polled less than in 2015; (b) an increase in votes while losing some seats; (c) an increase in votes to around 36–38%, with more seats; or (d) a hung parliament. Under (a), they accepted that Corbyn would probably have to resign. The plan would have been to announce a timetable for his resignation, but with his staying in post until a new leader was elected at the party's annual conference. The aim was to stop Labour's deputy leader taking office, even as an interim position. 'We did not want Tom Watson becoming acting leader', said one of Corbyn's closest aides. Both Fisher and Murphy were cross that they were even discussing the first option—and when Corbyn was later told of the conversation, he told them they had been wasting their time. By this point in the campaign, unless the polls were badly inflating Labour's vote, outcome (a) seemed unlikely anyway. Instead, they spent most of the meeting discussing scenarios (b) and (c), and the resulting possibility of a leadership challenge. Almost no time was spent discussing option (d).

Murphy had long been the most optimistic of Corbyn's closest aides. She had drawn up a full Labour Cabinet list, along with designated advisers and notes on the required changes to the staffing of Number 10, which she presented to Corbyn. She was said to have bought a new dress ready for when Corbyn would be called to the Palace. This was only half-correct—she had chosen her favourite dress and she had discussed travel arrangements with civil servants. She also tried to get Corbyn to think about what he would need to wear. Such was her confidence that Labour Party staff inside Southside circulated a spoof Number 10 seating plan, with various left-wing journalists and bloggers in key positions. However, channels of communication between LOTO and the Cabinet Secretary's team had been opened in secret, and Murphy and others had been invited to the Cabinet Office for a meeting early on in the last week of the campaign.[36] Two further meetings had followed, one of which took place on polling day itself. These meetings had indeed included discussing the seating plan in Number 10, as well as talking about Labour's proposals for the reorganisation of government, such as a Ministry of Labour. To much amusement amongst the LOTO team, it was explained that the office hierarchy in Number 10 mattered greatly; the most senior person in the team should sit at the desk closest to the Prime Minister.

One remaining problem was Diane Abbott. Despite the campaign team trying to keep her away from the media—a curious position for the Shadow Home Secretary, given the debate in the country—she had refused to follow their instructions and had been booking herself on to media appearances, phoning broadcasters personally. Even her aides often did not know what she was doing. One such appearance was *The Andrew Marr Show* on 28 May; challenged about comments she had made about the IRA in the 1980s ('every defeat of the British state is a victory for all of us'), she replied: 'It was 34 years ago, I had a rather splendid afro at the time, I don't have the same hairstyle and I don't have the same views. It is 34 years on. The hairstyle has gone, and some of the views have gone.' When pushed on whether she regretted the comments, she merely repeated that she had moved on. It was not the comments that caused anger in LOTO circles, but that Abbott was on the programme at all.[37]

On Monday 5 June, Abbott endured another painful interview, this time on *Sky News* (another interview she had organised herself), during which she struggled to answer questions over the Harris Review that had been commissioned by the Mayor of London. After a series of vague answers, it became clear that she was able to recall next to no details of the document. 'Have you actually read the report?', asked the presenter, Dermot Murnaghan. To some of her defenders, this was yet another example of 'gotcha' journalism—although she was the Shadow Home Secretary, the interview was taking place just days after a terrorist attack in London and the subject of the review had been anti-terrorism measures in London.

The following day, at very short notice, Abbott pulled out of an interview on *Woman's Hour* after being 'taken ill' and missed an *Evening Standard* hustings event that evening. On 7 June, the day before polling, Labour announced that she was temporarily standing down while she dealt with what was described as a period of 'ill health'. She was replaced by Lyn Brown, the Shadow Minister for Policing. Barry Gardiner said that Abbott had been 'diagnosed with a serious, long-term condition' and he hoped there would be less 'cynicism' about Abbott's condition. (Cynics did note that within ten days of the election, she had recovered sufficiently to return to her role as Shadow Home Secretary.) Publicly, Corbyn defended Abbott, claiming she was the victim of 'totally unfair attacks', but the LOTO team had lost patience with her. As one of Corbyn's team noted: 'She wasn't taking instructions from anyone, Southside or

LOTO. She was booking herself onto programmes.'[38] Corbyn had to phone her. Given their political and personal closeness, it was a difficult conversation. It was later revealed that she had Type 2 diabetes, although it became clear that this was not the whole story when she fell victim to a hoax email, to which she responded that she was 'worried about telling untruths about my health which are easily disproved'.[39] With less than 24 hours before polling opened, Labour's Shadow Home Secretary was an MP who just a year earlier had described Corbyn's leadership as 'untenable' and called on him to resign for the good of the country.

On 20 May, Corbyn had spoken at the Wirral Live music festival in Prenton Park, before an audience of around 20,000. Few politicians could speak at a music festival without fear of heckling and booing. But his team had few doubts about his appearance. They knew how well he was going down on the road. 'By that point we were riding high', said one. Midway through his speech, the crowd had begun to chant his name, to the rhythm of 'Five Nation Army' by the White Stripes—'Oooh Je-re-mee Corrr-byn'. Corbyn was taken aback at first, unsure of what he was hearing. The *Liverpool Echo* described it as a 'rock star welcome'.[40] Earlier that day, Corbyn had in any case in his own right attracted a crowd of 2,000 to a rally in West Kirby. By the end of the campaign, the crowds had become even more impressive. In Gateshead on 5 June, in terrible weather, there were around 10,000. In Birmingham on 6 June, there was a crowd of nearly 6,000. John Prescott noted that these crowds were larger than those which New Labour had attracted even at its peak in 1997.

Corbyn's final speech of the campaign came back on home turf, at the Union Chapel in Islington.[41] The venue was packed with 800 supporters; hundreds more lined the roads, cheering and chanting as the Labour campaign bus approached. The *Islington Gazette* said it felt 'like a world famous rock band's glorious homecoming show, rather than a political rally'.[42] The warm up act was the Shadow Foreign Secretary, Emily Thornberry, whose barnstorming speech opened with a sarcastic: 'How's it going Theresa? How's that strong and stable worked out for you?' To enormous cheers, she introduced Corbyn as 'the next Prime Minister'. He received a near-two-minute standing ovation—again with obligatory 'Oh Jeremy Corbyns'—before saying a word.

Towards the end of his speech, Corbyn quoted from Shelley's 1819 'The Masque of Anarchy':

> Rise like Lions after slumber
> In unvanquishable number
> Shake your chains to earth like dew
> Which in sleep had fallen on you-
> Ye are many—they are few.[43]

The crowd chanted the final words along with him, then roared their approval.

Outside of Islington, though, expectations of anything other than a Conservative victory remained low. One poll found 58% of people expecting a Conservative victory, just 9% a Labour win and 13% a hung parliament.[44] These figures were not all that different from those at the beginning of the campaign (see pp. 17–18). The final polls from the members of the British Polling Council all put the Conservatives ahead, albeit by significantly smaller margins than at the start of the campaign. Survation had the lead at just one point—clearly in hung parliament territory—but others had Conservative leads as high as 13 percentage points.[45] *The Guardian*'s report of Corbyn's Islington speech noted that, for all the euphoria, it was different from those given at the end of his leadership contests in one important way. 'Then he had known he had won. But this time he had to sound as passionate as he had on those two occasions, only this time knowing he had almost certainly lost.'[46]

NOTES

1. COBR stands for Cabinet Office Briefing Room, where the meetings take place. It is often referred to as COBRA, because there is a meeting room A, because cobra is an actual word and because it sounds more like something from James Bond—but Downing Street refer to it as COBR.
2. In her statement, the Prime Minister added: 'And although it is not the first time Manchester has suffered in this way, it is the worst attack the city has experienced, and the worst ever to hit the north of England.' This reference to the IRA's 1996 bombing of Manchester annoyed some in the Leader of the Opposition's Office (LOTO) team, who felt it was a deliberate attempt to draw attention to Corbyn's links with Irish republicanism.
3. See Tim Ross and Tom McTague, *Betting the House*. Biteback, 2017, pp. 292–93.
4. Tom Goodenough, 'Ukip's Tough Talk on Terror Comes with a Big Risk', *The Spectator*, 25 May 2017, https://blogs.spectator.co.uk/2017/05/ukips-tough-talk-terror-comes-big-risk.

5. Tim Shipman, *Fall Out*. William Collins, 2017, p. 321; Ross and McTague, *Betting the House*, pp. 297–99.

6. https://twitter.com/jeremycorbyn/status/866792385333911555?lang=en.

7. The various arguments are well documented in Ross and McTague, *Betting the House*, pp. 284–85.

8. There are, for example, details of this row in both Ross and McTague, *Betting the House*, pp. 289–90 and Shipman, *Fall Out*, pp. 322–23.

9. See his *Game Changer*. Accent Press, 2018, p. 95.

10. Although polling found Corbyn's position to be widely shared, some focus groups did detect unease at the timing of the speech—and some candidates reported negative doorstep feedback. See, for example, Shipman, *Fall Out*, p. 328.

11. Jess Staufenberg, 'Conservatives' Free Breakfast Pledge "Costed at Just 7p per Meal"', *Schools Week*, 23 May 2017, https://schoolsweek.co.uk/conservatives-free-breakfast-pledge-costed-at-just-7p-per-meal.

12. See Owen Bennett, 'Labour "Breaks" Flagship Manifesto Pledge Not to Raise Taxes on Those Earning Less than £80k', 6 June 2017, https://www.huffingtonpost.co.uk/entry/labour-manifesto-tax-rises_uk_593666e0e4b0099e7faecf55.

13. For 2015, see Philip Cowley and Dennis Kavanagh, *The British General Election of 2015*. Palgrave Macmillan, 2015, p. 189.

14. https://twitter.com/theresa_may/status/865855578454806529?lang=en.

15. Georgina Lee, 'Is Theresa May Six Seats from Losing the Election?', *Channel 4 News*, 22 May 2017, https://www.channel4.com/news/factcheck/is-theresa-may-six-seats-from-losing-the-election.

16. Tim Shipman has the idea coming from Patrick Heneghan (*Fall Out*, p. 343).

17. They also predicted that the Conservatives would send Amber Rudd.

18. Kemp is also quoted by Shipman (*Fall Out*, p. 346) saying that Corbyn is 'totally unencumbered by self-doubt. Most opposition leaders worry about going too far or striking a balance. Corbyn just says "X is terrible. People are suffering. That's why I want Y, which the rich will pay for" … If you don't want to agonise about what your policies mean in practice, you can hoover up applause lines.' This mirrors the remarks made by a Labour observer of the party's leadership contests (see above, p. 72).

19. In a pre-debate poll, YouGov found that the public wanted May to participate (by 56% to 20%).

20. Michael A. Ashcroft, *The Lost Majority*. Biteback, 2017, p. 30.

21. Joe Murphy, 'UK General Election Polls: Jeremy Corbyn in Shock Surge as Labour Leader Now More Popular than Theresa May in London', *Evening Standard*, 1 June 2017.

22. See Roger Scully, 'One Week to Go ... The Latest Welsh Poll', *Cardiff University Blogs*, 1 June 2017, https://blogs.cardiff.ac.uk/electionsin-wales/2017/06/01/one-week-to-go-the-latest-welsh-poll. The Welsh poll confirmed that the rise in support seen in Wales earlier in May had not been a temporary blip, caused (for example) from sympathy following the death of the well-liked former First Minister Rhodri Morgan on 17 May.

23. See https://twitter.com/LeanneWood/status/870736320980758529.

24. We have corrected the multiple spelling errors.

25. He added 'but it was too late by that point'.

26. Shipman, *Fall Out*, pp. 349–50.

27. Alex Nunns, *The Candidate*. OR Books, pp. 360–61.

28. This is moot. The one poll, by Survation conducted on 3 June, which asked about the programme found that respondents who had seen any of the programme or read about it saying they were slightly more likely to vote Labour as a result than not (by 36% to 24%) and less likely to vote Conservative (by 24% to 32%). The same poll found unhappiness with several of Corbyn's responses, especially over the IRA, although it lacked similar questions about May's answers.

29. The claim that the Conservatives were reluctant to discuss arrangements is in Ross and McTague, *Betting the House*, pp. 361–62; the Crosby claim is in Shipman, *Fall Out*, p. 396. The latter also notes that even people within the Conservative campaign found it hard to get answers about the campaign suspension at the time, as the May/Hill/Timothy triumvirate were too busy coordinating the response to the attack, which may also explain the lack of response to Labour's calls.

30. In her statement, she said that 'the two political parties have suspended our national campaigns for today', although the temporary pause in campaigning also included the Liberal Democrats, the SNP, Plaid Cymru and the Greens.

31. Nunns, *The Candidate*, pp. 363–65.

32. Less noticed in the mainstream media, but picked up online, was his linking of terrorism to British links with Saudi Arabia: 'We do need to have some difficult conversations starting with Saudi Arabia and other Gulf states that have funded and fuelled extremist ideology. It is no good Theresa May suppressing a report into the foreign funding of extremist groups. We have to get serious about cutting off the funding to these terror networks.'

33. Amongst others, this was the view of Crosby (McTague and Ross, *Betting the House*, p. 369), but it was more widely shared. It is true that there had been some discussion of police cuts after Manchester, but it became more dominant after London Bridge.

34. https://twitter.com/realdonaldtrump/status/871328428963901440?la ng=en. Khan's actual words were: 'My message to Londoners and visitors to our great city is to be calm and vigilant today. You will see an increased police presence today, including armed officers and uniformed officers. There is no reason to be alarmed by this.' The response from the Mayor's office was that he had 'more important things to do than respond to Donald Trump's ill-informed tweet that deliberately takes out of context his remarks', provoking yet more criticism from the US President ('Pathetic excuse by London Mayor Sadiq Khan'). None of this was helpful to the Conservatives.

35. Corbyn's comment was a sloppy response to a question, which he had corrected even within the same interview. Asked whether he agreed with calls for the Prime Minister to resign, he replied that he did; when then asked 'to be clear, you'd like to see her resign over this?', he responded 'we've got an election on Thursday and that's perhaps the best opportunity to deal with it'.

36. Murphy and Fisher were at all three meetings; Jon Trickett was at the first and Milne was at the last two.

37. See, for example, Sam Coates and Lucy Fisher, 'Labour Frontbench Fury as Diane Abbott Goes Rogue', *The Times*, 3 June 2017.

38. Even after she had stood down, several people in LOTO were worried that she would book herself onto programmes on election night.

39. Anushka Asthana and Heather Stewart, 'Diane Abbott Reveals Illness and Hits out at "Vicious" Tory Campaign', *The Guardian*, 13 June 2017; and Scott Campbell, 'Yet ANOTHER Blow for Under-Fire Diane Abbott as She is Fooled by Prankster Pretending to Be Jeremy Corbyn Adviser in Email Hoax', *Daily Mail*, 6 June 2017.

40. Liam Thorp and Amy Coles, 'Jeremy Corbyn Given Rock Star Reception as He Declares Merseyside "Music Capital of UK"', *Liverpool Echo*, 20 May 2017, https://www.liverpoolecho.co.uk/news/liverpool-news/jeremy-corbyn-given-rock-star-13066662.

41. The rally is sometimes referred to as occurring in his constituency, although the venue is in fact in the neighbouring Islington South & Finsbury, which Thornberry was defending.

42. James Morris, '"Jez We Can!" Wild Support for Corbyn at Islington Homecoming Rally', *Islington Gazette*, 7 June 2017, www.islingtongazette.co.uk/news/politics/jezza-s-coming-home-wild-support-for-corbyn-at-islington-homecoming-rally-1-5053061.

43. In his Islington speech, Corbyn used 'That in sleep', although the original is 'Which'.

44. The percentage expecting a Conservative majority was down by eight points, while those expecting a Labour majority or a hung parliament were

both up by five. The figures come from the Ashcroft post-election poll, which asked about people's recollections of what they had expected before they heard the result—but if anything, we might expect such a poll to over-state the percentage saying they expected the hung parliament, given the well-documented tendency of people to alter their own memories to rec-oncile with inconvenient facts.

45. As discussed below (p. 263), one company not in the British Polling Council published a poll showing Labour ahead by two points.

46. Ewan MacAskill, 'Jeremy Corbyn Gathers the Faithful for Upbeat Final Rally on Home Turf', *The Guardian*, 8 June 2017, https://www.the-guardian.com/politics/2017/jun/08/jeremy-corbyn-gathers-the-faith-ful-for-upbeat-final-rally-on-home-turf.

CHAPTER 10

Election Night and Its Aftermath

For most voters, election day was warm (the warmest since 1997), if wet (with some of the heaviest rain since the election of February 1974, especially in Scotland).[1] The usual reporting restrictions limited discussion of the election on conventional media to stilted accounts of polling stations opening and politicians casting their votes, although on social media—here as elsewhere driving a coach and horses through much of existing electoral law—there were claims of unusually long queues at some polling stations, along with a larger than normal presence of younger voters, especially in some university towns and cities. In Newcastle-under-Lyme, there were reports of newly registered students being turned away at Keele University despite having polling cards, until council staff were forced to produce up-to-date registers. However, claims of high turnout had frequently been made in the past, only to turn out to be exaggerated, and rumours about the high participation of young voters and students failed to dent private predictions in all the political parties that the election would result in a comfortable Conservative majority.

Internal Conservative predictions suggested a majority of between 50 and 60; this was not the landslide that some had expected at the beginning of the campaign, but it was enough of an increase to have justified calling an election. Conservative intelligence on election day—which in 2015 had proved astonishingly accurate—was that, if anything, their position was getting stronger throughout the day.[2] Labour's internal estimate based on its polling was for an 8% Conservative lead, with Labour down to around

© The Author(s) 2018
P. Cowley, D. Kavanagh, *The British General Election of 2017*,
https://doi.org/10.1007/978-3-319-95936-8_10

203 seats. At lunchtime, Theresa May visited Conservative Campaign Headquarters (CCHQ) and was told that she had nothing to worry about. About half an hour before polls closed, in a text to Nick Timothy, Lynton Crosby expressed concern about 'any Labour ground effort we are not picking up the impact of', but said they still expected to do well.[3] As the close of poll approached, the mood became even more buoyant and a celebratory staff party began on one floor of Conservative headquarters.

The release of the exit poll at 10 pm—published simultaneously on the BBC, ITV and Sky—therefore came as a something of shock. It predicted the Conservatives to be the biggest party, but short of an overall majority. The precise breakdown was:

Conservative	314
Labour	266
SNP	34
Liberal Democrat	14
Plaid Cymru	3
Green	1
UKIP	0
Others	18

If correct, it meant that Labour had gained dozens of seats, wiping out the Conservative majority in the process—with the SNP also suffering significant losses. Tom Bradby, fronting ITV's election night programme, called it a 'simply stunning result'. David Dimbleby, announcing the poll on the BBC's TV programme, noted that the Prime Minister had called the election because she wanted certainty and stability—'and this doesn't seem, at this stage, to look like certainty and stability'.

Despite the high degree of accuracy the exit polls had enjoyed in 2010 and 2015, there seemed grounds for scepticism. The poll came with the explicit caveat that it was possible the Conservatives would end the night with an overall majority, especially as in 2015 the exit poll had similarly initially predicted the Conservatives to be in a minority—on 316 seats, almost identical to the 2017 prediction—only for the party to outperform the poll and end the election with a small majority. (The wording used by the broadcasters when announcing the exit poll is very carefully chosen. The three broadcasting organisations involved agreed ten variants to describe possible outcomes. That the wording used in 2017 did not include the words 'hung parliament' was because there was at this stage a realistic chance of a majority Conservative government.) The figures for Scotland also seemed on the high side for SNP losses and many of the predictions for the Scottish seats were very close to call, with a much higher margin of error; this was the part of the exit poll that those involved in it were most concerned by, a point that was emphasised privately to broadcasters.[4] These caveats notwithstanding, prior to the poll's publication, the bookmakers were offering 5/1 on a hung parliament; immediately after its publication, those odds tumbled to 4/6.[5] The final result may still have been unclear at this point, but even if the exit poll proved to be wrong, it would have needed to be wildly wrong for any resulting Conservative majority to be anything other than tiny. It already seemed obvious that Theresa May's gamble had backfired.

At CCHQ, the poll's announcement was greeted with a stunned silence, save only for the sound of someone retching. The poll had leaked to Fiona Hill shortly before broadcast and she had shared the figures with Nick Timothy, both of them aghast at what they had been told.[6] Whilst most staff had gathered around television sets waiting for the poll's broadcast, those in charge of the campaign—including Stephen Gilbert, Jim Messina and Crosby—had retreated to a small private room, just as they had done two years before; Crosby's initial reaction to the exit poll was that it must be wrong. Gilbert was more sceptical, telling his colleagues why he thought it could be off, but adding that exit polls were not normally wrong. Crosby then toured the office, trying to keep morale up, telling people why they should not worry too much ('The BBC's never been right about anything in their lives').[7] 'I've never seen Lynton so unconvincing', said one of those present.

A few hundred yards away, in Southside, there was a more mixed reaction. The exit poll had similarly leaked, to Labour's media team, but in too cryptic a form to be of much use ('"shocking"—what the hell did that mean?', said one of those who received the message). The poll's broadcast was met with cheers, although not from everyone. The core Leader of the Opposition's Office (LOTO) team, crowded in one office, was jubilant. But some of the party's staff elsewhere in the building watched in silence, torn between the tribal pleasure of seeing Labour do well—and at the prospect of seeing some MPs they had assumed were defeated hold on—and being well aware of what this would mean for any hopes of prising the leadership out of the hands of Jeremy Corbyn and the left.[8] It was a sign of how divided the Labour operation had been that those who had planned for election night had a serious concern about fights breaking out amongst staff once alcohol-fuelled recriminations began. Those involved in the field team shared Crosby's scepticism about the poll's accuracy. 'Total incomprehension', said one staffer. 'I didn't believe it. I mean, I did believe it, because I know that these polls are right. But I couldn't work out how it could be right on the basis of everything I knew to be true.'

Polling station sign, London. Credit: Richard Cracknell

The first seat to declare, at 11.01 pm, was Newcastle upon Tyne Central, held by Chi Onwurah for Labour. Six minutes later came Houghton & Sunderland South. It was the first election since 1992 in which Sunderland South (or some variant thereof) had not been the first seat to declare; it was also the first ever election in which the first MP returned to the Commons was a black woman.[9] Labour comfortably held the first four seats to declare, all in the North East, but the Conservatives outperformed the expectations of the exit poll—including swings from Labour to Conservative in the two Sunderland seats. Both in the media and privately within the parties, this prompted discussion as to whether the exit poll had indeed under-estimated how well the Conservatives were going to do. At CCHQ, Messina was heard to say: 'I told you so.' At Labour HQ, Patrick Heneghan was similarly still unconvinced. 'Miles out', said one of the field team.

Almost on the stroke of midnight, however, came Swindon North: a Conservative hold, it saw a swing to Labour much more in line with the predictions of the exit poll. This was the point at which those around the Labour leader began truly to believe the exit poll. Just before 1 am came Darlington, a key Conservative target. The result was a Labour majority of

7.3%, barely denting the 7.7% majority of 2015. Around ten minutes later, Wrexham declared, one of the top Conservative targets in Wales, also with a barely reduced Labour majority, along with Swindon South, held by the Conservatives but where Labour cut a 12% majority down to 4.8%. This was the third general election in a row in which publication of the exit poll had been greeted with shock and disbelief—yet by now it was clear that it was the third in a row that turned out to be broadly accurate.

The first seat to change hands was Rutherglen & Hamilton West, Labour recapturing a seat they had lost to the SNP in 2015. A narrow Labour majority of 265 wiped away an SNP majority of almost 10,000. It had been the twentieth most marginal seat in Scotland and its changing hands demonstrated that lots of SNP seats were indeed in play. Just before 2 am, the Conservatives gained Angus, held by the SNP since the seat's creation in 1997.[10] The Scottish part of the exit poll suddenly did not seem unbelievable either. A total of 21 seats were to change hands in Scotland, with the SNP losing seats to all three of their unionist rivals. Casualties included the party's depute leader Angus Robertson, who lost Moray, a seat the party had held since 1987, and the former party leader and First Minister Alex Salmond, who lost Gordon. Of the nine largest majorities to be overturned on 8 June, all were in seats that had been held by the SNP, the largest of all being Salmond's former seat of Banff & Buchan, where a SNP majority of over 14,000 was transformed into a Conservative majority of more than 3,500.

At 1.40 am, Labour retook Vale of Clwyd, which had been lost to the Conservatives in 2015. Chris Ruane, the Labour MP for the seat between 1997 and 2015, became the first of 12 former MPs—so-called re-treads—to return to the Commons. Just after 2 am, Labour took Stockton South, James Wharton being the first government minister to lose a seat. The first four seats to change hands therefore involved Labour gaining constituencies in England, Scotland and Wales. By 1 am, the bookies were offering 1/3 for a hung parliament; by 1.30 am, that had moved to 1/6. The odds on a Conservative majority were now out to 5/1, exactly the same as the odds on a Labour majority.

Early results in London looked especially encouraging for Labour. The first London constituency to declare was Tooting, where Labour increased a 6,000 or so majority in the 2016 by-election to one of over 15,000 in a seat which the Conservatives had hoped to take just two years before. Next came Putney, where the Education Secretary Justine Greening saw her majority slashed to just over 1,500, and at just gone 2 am came

Battersea, which Labour had been hopeful of taking in 2015 only to fail miserably—but which in 2017 they won on a swing of 10%. Four minutes later, Ealing Central & Acton transformed from the most marginal Labour-held seat in London into a Labour majority of almost 14,000. London saw the biggest Conservative to Labour swing anywhere in Britain in 2017, with the Conservatives losing another five constituencies, three more to Labour and two to the Liberal Democrats.[11] It was not much compensation for the Conservatives when shortly after 7 am on Friday morning, Zac Goldsmith retook Richmond Park—lost to the Liberal Democrats in the 2016 by-election—by just 45 votes.

The first three Conservative gains of the night all came in Scotland. The party was to end the night with 13 seats north of the border, more than in any Westminster election since 1983 and with the best share of the vote since 1979. In six of their 12 gains, the Conservatives came from third place to win, in Gordon doing so on an astonishing 20% swing. It soon became clear that if Theresa May was to remain Prime Minister, it would only be because of the strength of the Conservative revival in Scotland. For a party that had had at most a single MP in Scotland for the last 20 years, it was a dramatic change in fortunes. South of the border, the

#dogsatpollingstations. Credit: Freida Moore

Conservatives did not make any gains at all until just after 2.30 am, when the party captured Southport from the Lib Dems; the first Conservative gain from Labour did not come until around 3 am, when the party won Walsall North, unseating David Winnick who had held the seat for Labour since 1979. This was one of just six seats the Conservatives would take from Labour all night. All were in England, all had experienced sizeable Brexit votes in the referendum the year before and all had vintage Labour pedigree. They included Copeland, which the Conservatives had won in the by-election earlier in the year (and which under different nomenclature had been a Labour seat since 1935), along with Middlesbrough South and East Cleveland (held by Labour since 1997), Stoke-on-Trent South (Labour since 1950), North East Derbyshire (Labour since 1935) and Mansfield (Labour-held since 1923 and never previously Conservative going back as far back as the seat's creation in 1885).[12] Many of the more surprising Labour gains—such as Canterbury, discussed below—were later held up as totemic of the election, but whilst fewer in number, these Conservative gains were just as revealing in their own way.

It soon became clear that turnout was up, rising in all but one of the first 20 seats to declare. It was the fourth consecutive election to see a rise in turnout. Yet for all the talk of queues at polling stations, at 68.8% and up 2.5% on 2015, turnout was still below the 71% seen in 1997, and that was an election noted at the time as seeing unusually low participation.[13]

It was the first election since 1997 in which the phrase 'Labour Gain' was routinely heard throughout election night. Between 2 am and 4 am, Labour took a string of Conservative-held seats—such as Bury North, Cardiff North, Derby North, High Peak, Bedford, Ipswich, Bristol North West and Weaver Vale. In Stroud, the former MP, David Drew, beat the Conservative incumbent Neil Carmichael; it was the fifth consecutive election in which Drew and Carmichael had both contested the seat.[14] Although these seats were surprises to most people on the night ('get in your fucking car and get here', one Labour organiser was ordered, once the ballot boxes in Stroud began to be opened), most of the gains were not in any wider sense unprecedented. All were constituencies which had fairly recently been held by Labour and were the sort of seats that Labour would have to take were it to have any realistic change of government. Labour ended up taking seven of their top 10 targets and 14 of their top 20.

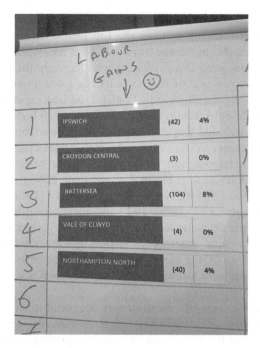

Labour Gains board, Southside. Credit: Iain McNicol

Just before 3.30 am came more of a shock: Labour took Canterbury—a seat that had returned a Conservative MP since its creation in 1918.[15] Containing two universities, it seemed emblematic of one story already being told about the election, even if—as discussed variously below—the impact made on the election by young people (and students in particular) was much less dramatic than many supposed. A few minutes earlier, but to less fanfare, came Labour's gain in Portsmouth South, another seat that had never returned a Labour MP in a general election, but that saw an even larger increase in the Labour vote than in Canterbury, with Labour coming from third place to win.

Around 2.45 am, Labour captured Sheffield Hallam—yet another seat with a large student population and another that had never previously returned a Labour MP—defeating the former Liberal Democrat leader and Deputy Prime Minister Nick Clegg. Not a single member of the

Martin Rowson, *Chartist Magazine*, 25 June 2017 © Martin Rowson

all-powerful Quad that had effectively run the Coalition government between 2010 and 2015 now remained in the House of Commons. In addition to Southport (see above) and Leeds North West, which they lost to the Conservatives and Labour respectively, the party also lost Ceredigion to Plaid Cymru, leaving the party without a single MP in Wales for the first time since the formation of the Liberal Party in the nineteenth century. In return came three Liberal Democrat gains in Scotland as well as five in England. All the English gains came from the Conservatives, all recapturing seats the Lib Dems had lost in 2010 or 2015: Oxford West & Abingdon, Eastbourne, Kingston & Surbiton, Bath, and Twickenham, the last won by the returning Sir Vince Cable with a majority of almost 10,000. Given the party's dire internal predictions during the campaign, the modest gain in seats came as a considerable relief—yet it masked yet another fall in the party's vote nationally. The Lib Dems lost 375 deposits, even more than in the catastrophe of 2015. At just before 3.30 am, the party leader Tim Farron held on in Westmorland & Lonsdale by a mere 777 votes.

Plaid Cymru's gain in Ceredigion, by just 104 votes, took them to four seats, despite their vote share falling by almost two percentage points across Wales to the lowest level for 20 years. They failed to take Ynys Môn, where they had been less than one percentage point behind Labour in 2015, but were now pushed into third place by the Conservatives. They held Arfon by just 92 votes. The result was the party's equal best-ever haul in seats, on a par with 1992, 1997 and 2001—but was just a hair's breadth away from the worst since 1983. Labour made three gains in Wales, all from the Conservatives. They included Gower—previously the most marginal seat in the UK with a majority of 27, now transformed into a Labour majority of over 3,000. The Conservatives saw their vote share in Wales rise to 33.6%, the best they had achieved in Wales since the introduction of universal suffrage, yet lost seats, down to eight.[16]

Shortly after 3 am, UKIP lost Clacton to the Conservatives, their former MP, Douglas Carswell, having endorsed the victorious Conservative candidate. Nationally, UKIP fell from almost four million votes in 2015 down to under 600,000. Their best performance came in Thurrock, a seat they had been hopeful of winning in 2015, but where two years later they came a poor third, polling just 20%.[17] The party achieved not a single second place throughout Britain. At 3.30 am, Paul Nuttall failed in his attempt to be returned as MP for Boston & Skegness, coming third.

This was the first general election for 25 years to be held without other concurrent elections taking place on the same day—and so a quicker count had been widely expected. In 2015, just five seats had declared by 1 am; in 1992, the last election with no concurrent election, some 121 had done so. In 2017, although things were not as slow as in 2015, they were not as quick as in 1992 either, as a result of the need to verify last-minute postal votes. Fewer than half of all constituencies had declared by 3 am. The circulation of political intelligence on social media, however, often meant that rumours of unexpected or close results were widely known long before any actual result, with the result that the moment of declaration was often not quite as shocking or dramatic as had previously been the case. One of the factors that kept the exit poll team confident despite the early results not quite going in line with their prediction was that there was so much talk on social media of strong Labour performances in constituencies in London and the South East, exactly as they expected.

Such rumours were not always correct. Early in the night, left-wing social media went into ecstasy over claims that the right-wing Conservative Philip Davies had lost Shipley, only for Davies to hang on fairly comfortably later in the night. The Women's Equality Party (WEP) candidate in Shipley came a poor fourth, on just 2% of the vote; this was the best performance of the WEP's seven candidates. More impressive was the National Health Action party candidate standing against the Health Secretary Jeremy Hunt, who polled 20% of the vote and came second in South West Surrey. In East Devon, the independent candidate Claire Wright managed second place for the second consecutive election, polling more than 20,000 votes.

The political parties were aware of the state of play even earlier. The major parties organise for feedback from the counts to be systematically returned to head office, where it is analysed, providing them with a running total of boxes opened and approximate vote share. Parties claim to be about two hours ahead of most broadcasters in being able to call the outcome of most seats; the first marginal seat Labour claimed internally was Ipswich, which did not declare formally until 3 am and where Ben Gummer, one of the authors of the Conservative manifesto, was defeated. Shortly after 1 am—with just 15 seats formally declared—Jeremy Corbyn was told by staff at Southside that there was no chance that Theresa May would be able to achieve a Commons majority. The Cabinet Office sent an email to both Andrew Fisher and Karie Murphy in Corbyn's team, opening a line of communication in case Labour became able to form a government, with Murphy taking a phone call to check on expected numbers. For a brief period after 2 am, the returns from opened ballot boxes were so good that Labour's field team even thought there was a slim chance they would emerge as the largest party, ahead of the Conservatives. Even when it became clear that was not going to happen—once postal votes, which were more positive for the Conservatives, had been included in counts—it still seemed plausible that Labour might emerge at the head of a minority government. It began to dawn on people within Southside that unlike in 2015, they had done almost no preparation for the sort of negotiations that would be required.

Jeremy Corbyn watched the exit poll at his home in Islington. He had not watched one before and had to be persuaded that it was important to do so, as he may have needed to make decisions based on what it predicted. Before it was broadcast, Corbyn handed those with him scraps of paper and told them to write down their predictions. Whilst others went for Conservative majorities but with Labour increasing their vote share a little, Karie Murphy went for 39.2%, almost certainly a hung parliament.[18] There are claims that when the exit poll was announced, Corbyn took it all in his stride and simply carried on drinking his tea. The reality is more understandable. For all the talk of Monsieur Zen on the campaign trail, Corbyn's reaction when the exit poll was announced was one single, and un-Zen-like, word.

After a flurry of phone calls, Corbyn then travelled to his count, where the Islington North declaration came shortly after 3 am. In his victory speech he noted that it was the highest turnout of any election in Islington since 1951 and the largest vote received for a winning candidate in the history of the borough. 'The Prime Minister called the election because she wanted a mandate', he said, 'well, the mandate she's got is lost Conservative seats, lost votes, lost support and lost confidence.' He added: 'I would have thought that's enough to go, actually, and make way for a government that will be truly representative of the people of this country.' It was a good line, if not entirely true—the Conservatives were gaining votes, just not at the rate Labour were doing—and it was not clear who would be able to form any alternative administration 'representative of the country', given that by now it was clear that Labour were going to finish the night behind the Conservatives.

Labour's position had always been that in the event of a hung parliament, they would do no deals with other parties and would put forward a Queen's Speech which other parties could vote for if they wanted to. Yet such an approach still required the party to think about the process of getting the incumbent out of Downing Street—and getting other parties on board. In 2015, Labour had done extensive preparatory work on both, and its representatives had headed to broadcast studios on election night prepped to the eyeballs with helpful precedents about what would happen in the event of a hung parliament, with the goal of driving the narrative of the election in a way that would make it difficult for David Cameron to cling on to power in a hung parliament, only, very quickly, to realise that all such material was redundant. Two years later, exactly that situation had materialised—and yet no one had prepared for it. During the campaign, one political advisor, with knowledge of the 2015 experience, had offered to do work on the subject but was told it was a waste of resources—and so in the early hours of the morning requests began to go out from Southside and the Leader's team to those who had been involved in 2015: could they share their earlier work? 'Yes', came one reply, 'but I'm on holiday in Menorca.'

Theresa May's declaration came around quarter of an hour after Corbyn's—with the media coverage of a jubilant Leader of the Opposition offering a sharp contrast to a sombre and clearly shaken Prime Minister. She had heard the result of the exit poll at home in Sonning. Her husband had watched it for her, before breaking the bad news. Once what he was telling her had sunk in, she cried.[19] She then travelled to her count, where on arrival she was greeted by journalists asking her if she intended to resign.[20] This was not how she had imagined election night would play out.

May too set records in her own seat, winning Maidenhead with the highest vote on the highest turnout since the seat had been created in 1997. She shared the stage with 12 rival candidates, including one dressed as Elmo from Sesame Street and another known as Lord Buckethead who claimed to be an intergalactic space lord and who wore—as his name implied—a large bucket on his head.[21] Depending on one's perspective, there was something either poignant or funny about seeing the grim-faced and heavily made-up Prime Minister stood with a man wearing a black bucket. Elmo secured just three votes, the lowest for any candidate in the entire election.[22] In her acceptance speech, the Prime Minister said that while results were still coming in, 'we have yet to see the full picture emerging', although the truth was that by now the picture was pretty clear. She argued the country needed stability and that if it turned out the Conservatives were the largest party, then it was incumbent on them to provide that stability—although here, as with Corbyn's offer of an alternative government, it was not obvious how this was going to happen.

In Northern Ireland, which was, eventually, to provide a solution to that puzzle, the first seat to change hands was South Antrim, gained by the Democratic Unionist Party (DUP) from the Ulster Unionist Party (UUP). The second was Foyle, taken by Sinn Féin from the Social Democratic and Labour Party (SDLP). That set the pattern for the night. Sinn Féin went on to gain three seats in total, including South Down (from the SDLP) and Fermanagh & South Tyrone (from the UUP). The DUP also took Belfast South from the SDLP. The election saw the final collapse of the old order. With the exception of North Down, held by the independent unionist Lady Sylvia Hermon, all the other seats in Northern Ireland were won by either the DUP or Sinn Féin. The UUP—once so dominant—the SDLP and the Alliance Party of Northern Ireland all failed to win a single seat. Both the Sinn Féin and DUP gains were good news for the Conservatives. By refusing to take their seats, the former lowered the number of seats the Conservatives needed to achieve a majority in the Commons, whilst the latter were seen as more likely to do a deal with the Conservatives than any of their rival parties.[23]

In total, nine government ministers lost their seats. From very early on in the night, there had been rumours that these might include one high-profile scalp when it emerged that the Home Secretary, Amber Rudd, was in trouble in Hastings & Rye. Had she lost, she would have been the first serving Home Secretary to have been defeated since Donald Somervell in 1945, but at just before 5 am, she narrowly held on, after a full recount, winning by just 346 votes. She was helped by a disgruntled Labour Party member who stood as an independent and who received 412 votes. There was to be no Portillo moment in 2017.

The Prime Minister returned to CCHQ around 4.30 am. She spent around 45 minutes with her closest advisors—including Crosby and Mark Textor—closeted in the boardroom. The atmosphere was strained.[24] May complained that she had done what they had told her. She had said what they had advised her to say and had visited places they said they could win—only to see almost none of those seats fall to the Conservatives, whilst Labour made gains in places she had been assured were safe. After just over an hour, the Prime Minister emerged and addressed her party staff. 'The Conservative Party is the best political party in the world', she told them. 'We continue to be the best political party in the world and live to fight another day.'[25] Just before 6 am, it became confirmed that the UK had a hung parliament when Labour held Southampton Test, making it arithmetically impossible for the Conservatives to win enough seats for a majority.

The Green co-leader Caroline Lucas held her Brighton Pavilion seat at just after 6 am. When she first won the seat in 2010, it was with a majority of just over 2%; that had now increased to more than 25%, with the Greens gaining more than half of the votes cast. Elsewhere, however, the night was not a good one for the party. Their only second-place finish came in Buckingham, where the Speaker John Bercow was re-elected, but where the other major parties did not stand. In most other seats in which the Greens had previously been in contention, their vote was squeezed by Labour. In Bristol West—seen as a three-way marginal just two years before—Labour's vote went up by more than 30 percentage points with the Green vote collapsing by 14 points, pushing the party into third. In two of the seats in which the Greens were second in 2015, they lost deposits in 2017.

Further Labour gains came after 4 am, the party re-taking yet more seats it had lost between 2005 and 2010, such as: Reading East; Lincoln; Enfield, Southgate; Crewe & Nantwich; Colne Valley; Plymouth, Sutton & Devonport; Brighton, Kemptown; and Keighley—the last seeing John Grogan returned some seven years after losing Selby.[26] At around 6.15 am, in Newcastle-under-Lyme, where there had been the squabbles about student registration, Paul Farrelly held on for Labour by 30 votes—almost certainly the result of students who had initially been turned away from the polls returning and insisting on being allowed to vote.[27] The last seat to declare was Kensington, close to 24 hours after polls had closed and after three recounts.[28] It was taken by Labour by just 20 votes, making it the most marginal seat in England. Much of the commentary on the event equated Kensington solely with wealth and affluence—and it was true that it was a constituency where more than half of the children in it were educated in private schools—but the seat also contains much of the poorer parts of north Kensington, horrifically illustrated less than a week later when a fire broke out in a tower block in the constituency and 72 people were killed. It was also a constituency in which 69% were estimated to have voted Remain, but where the Conservative incumbent, Victoria Borwick, had campaigned for Brexit. Borwick was one of those Conservative MPs who had not wanted an election, and on the day it was announced had burst into the whips' office complaining that it would cost her the seat—and it did. Victory in Kensington left Labour with a total of 262 seats, up 30. The Conservatives were on 317 (that is, excluding the Speaker's seat), down 13 on 2015 and short of an overall majority.

Things could have easily been different. The election saw 97 constituencies won by a margin of 5% or less.[29] Theresa May would end the night just seven seats short of a bare Commons majority—and there were four constituencies that the Conservatives lost with majorities of between just 20 and 30 votes.[30] Just 51 people voting differently in those four seats could have been enough to produce a one-seat Conservative majority in the House of Commons.[31] Equally, however, Jeremy Corbyn was much closer to power than most people—including those in Labour—had expected. Although Labour remained a long way off a Commons majority, had they taken another eight seats from the Conservatives, they may have been able to form an anti-Conservative blocking group in the Commons, at least enough to vote down a Conservative Queen's Speech.[32] There were eight Conservative seats with majorities of between 31 and 609 in which Labour came second; just over 1,420 people voting differently in those seats could have put Jeremy Corbyn into Number 10.[33] Indeed, fewer than 1,000 votes changing hands in the eight most marginal Conservative-held seats could have been enough to have created such an anti-Conservative block.[34] Such calculations are always somewhat hypothetical—they require these particular votes to change hands in this particular way, whilst holding everything else about the election constant—but they are an indication of just how much of a knife edge the election ended on.

For the Liberal Democrats, the night could have been worse in several ways. They missed winning a handful of seats by small margins, missing four by fewer than 350 votes each. Most of these additional gains would have involved winning more seats from the Conservatives. Had they done so (or, indeed, had Labour done marginally better against the Conservatives), there would have been the possibility of the Liberal Democrats having to choose whether to support a Corbyn or May premiership, or neither, thus triggering a fresh election.[35] Under normal circumstances, being able to play kingmaker is the sort of position in which minor parties want to find themselves, but with such a polarised electorate and after the experience of 2010, it was not one the party sought or had prepared for. 'Thank God we didn't win any more seats', noted one Liberal Democrat campaigner. 'If you think 2010 was bad…'[36] It could also easily have been an even worse night for the SNP. They held North East Fife by just two votes—the closest result of the night and the closest anywhere since Winchester in 1997 or Ilkeston in 1931, both also decided by two votes. They held another seven seats by under 500 votes. True, they only lost some seats by small margins as well and they remained the largest party in Scotland, and with a number of MPs that would have been unimaginable before late 2014, but just two years after their near-clean sweep of Scotland, the party came within 1,000 votes of losing half of its Westminster MPs.

Almost from the point at which the exit poll was announced, there was discussion as to whether the Prime Minister would resign. Since the election, there have been constant rumours that she seriously considered doing so during the night and had to be persuaded to remain in office. These accounts often vary somewhat. In some versions of events, she is persuaded to stay by her husband, while in others it is David Davis who phones Philip May to persuade him that he needs to persuade his wife. In yet others, it is the Cabinet Secretary who applies the pressure, concerned that the Brexit negotiations are about to start. Some versions of events have these conversations happening while she is in Sonning, others while she is at CCHQ, others once she is back in Downing Street. That the details of such stories vary so much does not generate confidence in their veracity. It would hardly be surprising if the Prime Minister did not at least privately consider resigning given the circumstances (and it may yet emerge that she did so seriously). Many of with her on the night deny that there were any such conversations or that she had to be persuaded to remain in office.[37] Certainly, by the time she had reached CCHQ at around 4.30 am, she had resolved to try to stay on.

By 7 am, May had met both the Cabinet Secretary, Sir Jeremy Heywood, and the Chief Whip, Gavin Williamson. The former had been in contact with Sir Christopher Geidt, the Queen's Private Secretary. Given the parliamentary arithmetic, Heywood advised the Prime Minister that before the Queen could invite her to form a government, she needed to be sure that she had the support of the Cabinet. There was already evidence of supporters of potential rivals beginning to mobilise—but in a series of meetings and calls, her two most obvious potential rivals, David Davis and Boris Johnson, both formally pledged their support.[38] Separately, the Chief Whip told her that the only way she could expect to govern was to do a deal with the DUP, whose ten seats would be sufficient to enable her to command a narrow Commons majority. She told Williamson to arrange it.

Labour claimed to be willing to form an alternative administration. 'In the interests of the country', said John McDonnell, 'we are willing to form a government—a minority government—to put forward a programme, a Queen's speech, as well as an alternative budget and an alternative programme for the Brexit negotiations. And then it is up to other parties if they want to support us.' There was also talk of an alternative Queen's Speech.[39] But this was mostly for show. Privately Labour knew they had little chance, given the parliamentary arithmetic. 'It would be absurd to have tried to form a government', said one of Corbyn's closest aides. Several of Corbyn's aides later regretted not having been better prepared for the scenario of a hung parliament in order to at least have attempted to put serious pressure on the Prime Minister to resign. That they had not done so was evidence of how few of them had seriously anticipated it to arise as a possibility.

By 12.50 pm on Friday 9 June, Theresa May had been to the Palace and, standing outside Number 10, declared herself willing to form a government to provide the stability and certainty she said Britain needed— and for which she had justified the election being called. 'Having secured the largest number of votes and the greatest number of seats in the General Election', she said, 'it is clear that only the Conservative and Unionist Party has the legitimacy and ability to provide that certainty.' The inclusion of the words 'and Unionist Party' was no accident. She went on to stress that the Conservatives would 'work with our friends and allies in the Democratic Unionist Party in particular … Our two parties have enjoyed a strong relationship over many years, and this gives me the confidence to believe that we will be able to work together in the interests of the whole United Kingdom'. At this point there was no agreement with the DUP. On paper, at least, May could not command the majority of the Commons, but there had already been private conversations between the DUP and the Conservatives to ensure that there was at least the possibility of a deal.[40]

With just minimal tinkering, it was essentially a speech that May could have delivered had she secured an outright majority and it was immediately criticised for being politically tone-deaf.[41] It included no acknowledgement of what had happened in the election and nothing about listening to the message the voters had sent. The *London Evening Standard*'s front-page headline read: 'Queen of Denial'. The speech was the most obvious manifestation of the state of the Downing Street operation at that point. 'Politically, it had all collapsed' said one of those who visited the Prime Minister early on 9 June. 'Chaos' said another. No one had planned for this outcome. Hill and Timothy—who had been so important to the Number 10 operation previously—had both left, never to return.[42] Everyone who remained was shell-shocked. The speech 'was the product of everyone being exhausted' said one of those involved. 'We had planned to do a read through, and if we had, someone—everyone!—

would have noticed what was wrong. But then we get into the [Cabinet] room, and all the civil service are interested in is getting her to the Palace, and getting back again, and the speech got overlooked.' The speech, and especially any absence of mention of defeated MPs, went down extremely badly with Conservative MPs, many of whom began to make their feelings known. As one senior member of the 1922 Committee noted: 'This was the speech of a party that had just been returned with a majority of 140. It didn't strike the right tone.' This point was relayed firmly to the Prime Minister by the Chair of the 1922 Committee, Graham Brady, and she recorded a hasty additional interview in which she expressed regret for the election outcome: 'I'm sorry for all those candidates and hard-working party workers who weren't successful, but also for those colleagues who were MPs and ministers and contributed so much to our country and who lost their seats and who didn't deserve to lose their seats.'

The process of coalition formation in the five days following the 2010 election was the subject of intense media scrutiny. There followed three books which focused solely on the coalition's formation as well as TV documentaries and even dramas.[43] Seven years later, the process of conducting a deal between the Conservatives and the DUP took significantly longer—it was not signed until 26 June—but it attracted nothing like the same coverage. In part, this was because it lacked the same will-they-won't-they drama. In 2010, even if the parliamentary arithmetic made it a somewhat asymmetric choice, the Liberal Democrats could have chosen to go into power with either Labour or the Conservatives. In 2017, the DUP were only ever going to do a deal with one party. Whilst they had been prepared to talk to Labour in both 2010 and 2015, Corbyn's support for Irish republicanism and his links with Sinn Féin now ruled that option out entirely. (The Conservatives had been frustrated during the election campaign that their attacks on Corbyn's links with Sinn Féin were not having quite the impact they had hoped with the electorate, but one group who really did care about the issue were the DUP.) But the difference was also that the meetings held by the parties were deliberately more low-key. In 2010, whilst there had been some secret meetings, others had seen doorstep press conferences given by the various negotiating teams. By contrast, in 2017 not only were there no comparable formal negotiating teams, but all of the meetings were also held behind the scenes and with as much secrecy as possible.

On the Friday immediately after the election, May despatched the Chief Whip to Belfast to meet with the DUP. Williamson flew out that afternoon, from Northolt, still in the same clothes he had been wearing at his election count and accompanied by two civil servants—one with a background in Northern Ireland, the other an expert on the constitution—and a Number 10 special adviser. Negotiations started that night in a hotel in Stormont, but for the next day's meeting they travelled to another hotel, in the rural constituency of the DUP Chief Whip Sir Jeffrey Donaldson, in an effort to be more discreet.

Before the Chief Whip left for Belfast, there had been a long meeting in the Cabinet room to discuss what could be offered to the DUP. The room was hot, there were too many participants and everyone—including the Prime Minister—was exhausted. Eventually, it was agreed that the DUP could be offered either a confidence-and-supply arrangement, by which they would support the government on key votes, or a full coalition, in which they would also sit in the government as ministers. Everyone involved in the discussions knew there would be plenty of Conservative MPs unhappy about any formal coalition, but several argued that they had at least to offer it. 'You've got to show them that you're serious', said one, 'and not to patronise them.' By the Saturday morning, however, with unrest building up amongst some backbenchers, Number 10 had had second thoughts, and there were several phone calls between London and Belfast, in which Williamson was told he had to row back. He was resistant. If the argument for offering a coalition was to show that the DUP were not being taken for granted, to have offered and then withdrawn an offer of coalition would be counterproductive. The discussion on Saturday began by focusing on the broad nature of any deal, during which the DUP in any case confirmed that they preferred a confidence-and-supply arrangement.

Neither party was in a strong negotiating position. The DUP did not want to see a Corbyn government or another election (which might lead to a Corbyn government), whilst the Conservatives had no alternate partners to secure a majority. All other political parties had ruled out supporting them.[44] Given this, some Conservatives wondered why they could not just call the DUP's bluff. The view taken by those negotiating was that whilst the DUP would not vote to bring down the government, their lack of support on day-to-day votes—and especially over the Brexit legislation—would have hobbled the government from the beginning. The Conservatives could perhaps have remained in government without the formal support of the DUP, but they could not have attempted to govern.[45]

Nobody involved expected negotiations with the DUP to be easy. 'They're pros at this sort of stuff' said one Conservative. When Williamson and his team arrived at Stormont, they were made to wait several hours before the first meeting began, a delay none of them thought was accidental. The process almost derailed on the Saturday evening when a draft statement was put out by Downing Street saying that a deal had been concluded and would be put to the Cabinet on Monday. The DUP thought that this was a not-so-subtle attempt to bounce them into an agreement and immediately denied it. Those involved on the Conservative side argued that it was a cock-up—the premature release of a draft that had been meant to be agreed by the DUP before release—but it knocked the negotiations back. Meetings then continued in London, in a variety of offices in or around Westminster, including in Number 10 when the Prime Minister was involved.[46] There was a rolling cast list of attendees. For the Conservatives, Williamson was occasionally joined by the First Secretary of State, Damian Green, and by the Prime Minister. On the DUP side, most discussion was led by the party's deputy leader Nigel Dodds and Chief Whip Donaldson, with party leader Arlene Foster joining occasionally. But a further week of discussions had produced relatively little progress, until a long, four-hour meeting, about a week and a half after polling day, in the government chief whip's office and focusing on matters on which they knew they could agree, brought matters back on track.

Dealing with the DUP caused concern amongst some Conservatives, who feared that being linked with them—and especially their attitudes towards abortion and homosexuality—would damage the party in the medium term by 'retoxifying' its image. Labour made much of this, conveniently overlooking the fact that they had been willing to do similar deals with the DUP in both 2010 and 2015. One positive of dealing with the DUP was that they were upfront about what they wanted. In the run-up to 2015, they had produced a 'Northern Ireland Plan', ready for the expected post-election negotiations; as one Labour staffer tasked with negotiating with the DUP at the time had noted: 'It was basically a shopping list ... It even had the prices marked up.' As one of the Conservatives involved in 2017 argued: 'They will deliver. If you pay the price, they will deliver the goods.'

The formal signing of the agreement came on 26 June. It was frequently referred to as a confidence-and-supply agreement, although its scope went wider than that, if not as wide as the Lib-Lab pact of 1976–78. The DUP pledged support for the Conservatives on votes of confidence, finance measures, including the Budget, and legislation on Brexit and national security.[47] In return, there was approximately £1 billion of additional funding for Northern Ireland.[48] The agreement was to remain in place for the whole Parliament, but was to be reviewed after every parliamentary session. The signing ceremony in Number 10 was conducted by the two party chief whips, watched by the party leaders and their deputies. Donaldson, in particular, was tickled by a sketch in *The Times* by Patrick Kidd, which began:

> Announcements: Mr Gavin Williamson, a chief whip from Staffordshire, and Sir Jeffrey Donaldson, an exporter of oranges from the Lagan Valley, celebrated their civil partnership yesterday at the Whitehall register office witnessed by Mr Williamson's parents, two of Sir Jeffrey's business associates, the cabinet secretary and a Mr Larry Cat. The flowers, costing £1 billion, were donated by Mr Philip Hammond.[49]

Contra some of the media discussion, the DUP's focus in negotiations was always on additional resources for Northern Ireland rather than on policy issues such as abortion—although the agreement did include the Conservatives pledging no changes in either the pensions triple lock or the winter fuel payment. The extra revenue for Northern Ireland represented around £100 million per DUP MP. The end product of these negotiations was that on the areas covered by the agreement, a government about to undertake the most significant international negotiations in post-war history had a majority in the Commons of just 13. On all other matters, it was a minority administration.

NOTES

1. House of Commons library, Briefing Paper CBP 7979, *General Election 2017: Results and Analysis*, 11 July 1997, pp. 78–79.
2. Those conducting the exit poll found no such effect—with relative levels of support mostly unchanging throughout the day.
3. We discuss below (p. 276) the claims that by the end of the campaign, some of the Conservative polling and modelling was pointing to a potential hung parliament. Suffice it to note here that these claims were all made after the election result was known and nothing any of the participants did or said on polling day up until the exit poll was released indicated they had

any serious doubts that the Conservatives were heading towards a majority.

4. This was a result both of a limited number of sampling points north of the border (itself a reflection of how, historically, Scottish seats were not overly important in election outcomes) and a relatively evenly spread SNP vote, making seat predictions very sensitive to small changes in vote share.

5. Odds used in this chapter all come from Ladbrokes. Other bookmakers were all offering very similar odds.

6. The timing of this leak is disputed. Tim Ross and Tom McTague (*Betting the House*. Biteback, 2017, p. 384) imply the leak came from Andrew Marr, phoning Hill up for a reaction shortly before the poll's broadcast at 10 pm—and Marr admits doing this 'seconds' before broadcast. Yet following the conversation, Hill and Timothy had time to brief Alex Dawson from the Research Department and to prepare the party's response, and Ross and McTague also claim that Labour in turn heard that the Conservatives had the exit poll—all of which would indicate a significantly longer passage of time than mere seconds. Tim Shipman (*Fall Out*. William Collins, 2017, pp. 406–7) has the leak to the Conservatives timed at 9.56 pm, but with Labour hearing rumours of the poll *before* the Conservatives, with another leak as early as 8 pm. Besides, there was certainly other well-informed discussion of a leak, outside of the party HQs, at least 15 minutes before the poll was broadcast.

7. Ross and McTague, *Betting the House*, p. 387.

8. In November 2017, the BBC broadcast a programme called *Labour—The Summer That Changed Everything*, which followed several Corbyn-sceptic MPs and showed their response to the exit poll. None cheered.

9. At 11.45 pm came Sunderland Central, the first three seats to declare all returning women MPs. Onwurah was also one of the MPs who had nominated Jeremy Corbyn for the leadership in 2015 despite supporting another candidate.

10. It largely replaced East Angus, similarly held by the SNP since 1987.

11. Whereas the Conservative share of the vote mostly rose throughout Britain, if not always by as much as the rise in Labour's, it fell in London. The result could easily have been even worse for the Conservatives: Chipping Barnet—a Conservative seat since 1974—was held by just 353 votes and Hendon by just over 1,000.

12. The same applies to some of the Conservatives' near-misses: such as Dudley North, Newcastle-under-Lyme and Ashfield, all seats with a long Labour pedigree and all where Labour clung on with majorities of 1% or less.

13. This is turnout as a percentage of those on the electoral register. Turnout as a percentage of eligible voters is almost certainly higher (see below, note 17, on p. 445).

14. Drew had previously emerged victorious in 2001 and 2005, and Carmichael in 2010 and 2015. Enfield North similarly witnessed the fifth consecutive contest between Joan Ryan for Labour and Nick de Bois for the Conservatives, albeit a less balanced one, Ryan emerging with her fourth victory to de Bois' victory in 2010.

15. Or, with a brief exception, since its predecessor seat was created in 1885.

16. That is, counting votes just for Conservative candidates and excluding the broader alliances in 1931 and 1935.

17. UKIP's vote share fell in every seat, bar one. The exception was Cumbernauld, Kilsyth & Kirkintilloch East, where the party had not stood in 2015 and where it managed 1.4% of the vote in 2017.

18. There is a slightly different version of events in John Rentoul, 'Yes, I Got it Wrong Where Corbyn was Concerned—But That Doesn't Mean the Opinion Polls were Off-Target', *The Independent*, 19 July 2017, www.independent.co.uk/voices/jeremy-corbyn-general-election-i-was-wrong-opinion-polls-labour-conservatives-a7847676.html.

19. When her husband told her the result, 'it took a few minutes for it to sort of sink in, what that was telling me', she later admitted (interview with Emma Barnett, Radio 5, 13 July 2017) and when it did, she felt 'devastated'. She admits to shedding 'a little tear'; Ross and McTague (*Betting the House*, p. 386) say she 'broke down and wept'.

20. All three of the main UK party leaders had their counts at leisure centres— the Magnet Leisure Centre (May), the Sobell Leisure Centre (Corbyn) and the Kendal Leisure Centre (Farron)—which just goes to show that politics is not always quite as they portray it in *The West Wing*.

21. His real name was Jonathan David Harvey.

22. Both Maidenhead and Islington North were notable for seeing the worst electoral performances of the whole election. In the former, Bobby Smith, the Elmo-suited independent, polled the lowest of any candidate in the entire election. In the latter, Andres Mendoza of the Communist League Election Campaign secured just seven votes, the worst by any candidate formally representing a party. Indeed, the worst *four* performances were seen in the two leaders' constituencies—with another independent candidate in Maidenhead polling just 16 votes and a representative of the Socialist Party of Great Britain in Islington North managing 21.

23. Another effect of the result in Northern Ireland was that a part of the UK that had voted to Remain in the EU was represented at Westminster almost entirely by politicians who supported Britain leaving the EU. The only exception was Lady Sylvia Hermon, who voted Remain.

24. There is a good account of this meeting in Shipman, *Fall Out*, p. 423.

25. Ross and McTague, *Betting the House*, p. 400.

26. Technically, Plymouth, Sutton & Devonport was a new seat in 2010 when it was won by the Conservatives, but its two predecessor seats had both been Labour. In 2017, the seat was noteworthy for being wrongly declared on the night; a spreadsheet error resulted in one ward's votes not being included in the total. The later inclusion of the missing ward increased the Labour majority from 6,002 (declared) to 6,807 (actual).

27. After the election a report on Newcastle-under-Lyme by the Association of Electoral Administrators found that over 500 postal voters in the constituency were disenfranchised, that almost 1,000 potential electors were not included on the register and that two non-eligible voters were allowed to vote in error. It concluded that given the eventual majority was just 30, 'it is impossible not to question the result for the constituency'. See Andrew Scallan, *Independent Report into Issues Faced by Voters in Newcastle-under-Lyme at the 8 June 2017 General Election*, November 2017, https://www. newcastle-staffs.gov.uk/sites/default/files/IMCE/News/NBC_News/ NBC_Election_Report_November_2017_%282%29.pdf.

28. The second and third recounts were separated by a break, with the count suspended, to allow council staff to recuperate.

29. Up from 56 in 2015. At the same time, there was also a rise in the number of very safe seats.

30. As is frequently the case, there was debate immediately after the election about the precise size of the government's majority. Often such calculations exclude the Speaker, but forget to make similar allowances for the three Deputy Speakers (understandably perhaps, given that they fight seats under their normal party labels—indeed, in 2017, one Deputy Speaker, Natascha Engel, lost her seat) or the Sinn Féin MPs who do not take their seats. The figure in the text is the figure excluding Sinn Féin MPs and excluding both the Speaker and Deputy Speakers.

31. That is, assuming the Conservatives attracted half the majority plus one additional vote in each seat.

32. By this is meant a combination of Labour, Liberal Democrat, Green and SNP/Plaid Cymru MPs. It would have taken seven Labour gains to prevent a deal with the DUP being able to provide the Conservatives with a majority, and eight to prevent a combination of the DUP and Lady Sylvia Hermon doing so.

33. Again, that is assuming Labour attracted half the majority plus one additional vote in each seat.

34. In the eight most marginal Conservative-held seats after the election, 944 votes changing hands could have produced a sufficiently large anti-Conservative block, with five seats going to Labour, two to the Liberal Democrats and one to the SNP.

35. Of the most 11 marginal Lib Dem misses, all but four are held by the Conservatives.

36. This point is well made in Mark Pack, 'How the 2017 General Election was Nearly Far, Far Worse for the Liberal Democrats', 13 August 2017, https://www.markpack.org.uk/151078/2017-general-election-nearly-far-far-worse-liberal-democrats. At the other end of the spectrum, total Liberal Democrat majorities sum to just over 42,500 votes, so it would only have required just over 21,000 people to have voted differently to wipe out the parliamentary party entirely.

37. Ross and McTague (*Betting the House*, p. 394) are sceptical about claims she intended to stand down; Shipman (*Fall Out*, p. 419) credits Philip May with persuading his wife to remain in office.

38. These manoeuvrings are dealt with well by Shipman (*Fall Out*, Chapter 26) and Ross and McTague (*Betting the House*, Chapter 20).

39. Labour later published an amendment to the Queen's Speech, which they claimed was—and some outlets reported as—an alternative Queen's Speech, even though it was clearly nothing of the sort.

40. Often forgotten is the fact that in 2010, David Cameron had been invited to the Palace before the Liberal Democrats had formally agreed to support the Conservatives.

41. There was, however, no truth in the rumour that it was the speech she had in fact prepared for victory, minimally amended.

42. Their departures were formally announced over the weekend.

43. For example, Rob Wilson, *5 Days to Power* (Biteback, 2010); David Laws, *22 Days in May* (Biteback, 2010); and Andrew Adonis, *5 Days in May* (Biteback, 2013). For the documentary, see *Five Days That Changed Britain* (BBC One, 29 July 2010) and for the drama, *Coalition* (Channel 4, 28 March 2015).

44. The idea of at least offering to consult with the other political parties was not seriously considered. The belief was that they wanted a five-year deal and so needed to play it straight—'not be too clever by half'.

45. Indeed, the very first vote in the Commons after the election, on public sector pay restraint, was won by just 14, with ten DUP votes. Without the deal, the government could have lost the first vote of the Parliament, establishing the narrative that the government was in crisis even before the Queen's Speech had been passed. Even with the DUP support, those involved were under no illusions about how difficult life was going to be.

46. Other locations included the offices of the Government Chief Whip and Nigel Dodds of the DUP, and in the Cabinet Office.

47. See Jon Tonge, 'Supplying Confidence or Trouble? The Deal between the Democratic Unionist Party and the Conservative Party', *Political Quarterly*, 88(3) (2017): 412–16.

48. Prime Minister's Office, *UK Government Financial Support for Northern Ireland*,   https://www.gov.uk/government/publications/conservative-and-dup-agreement-and-uk-government-financial-support-for-northern-ireland/uk-government-financial-support-for-northern-ireland.
49. Patrick Kidd, 'It Was All Pretty Shameless but Elegantly Done', *The Times*, 27 June 2017.

CHAPTER 11

Wrong-Footed Again: The Polls

Having been spectacularly wrong about the 2015 general election—when they had predicted that Labour and the Conservatives were too close to call in terms of vote share, only for the latter to end up 7% ahead—the opinion pollsters knew they were on trial in 2017. Since the 2015 debacle, they had enjoyed some success with predictions for Corbyn's leadership election in 2015 and 2016, Sadiq Khan's victory in the London mayoralty race, and in the devolved elections in Wales and Scotland. Their performance in the 2016 referendum, however, was more mixed. In the last month of the campaign, marginally more polls predicted a Leave outcome than Remain, although most of the final polls predicted a win for Remain.[1]

Yet despite the scepticism that many had expressed about polls after the debacle of 2015 (some doing so in vehement terms) and the subsequent problems in 2016, it was noticeable how important opinion polls remained in 2017. For all that there were other motivations for calling the election, had the polls not showed the Conservatives comfortably ahead, there would have been no election in the first place. Polling, both public and private, then encouraged Conservative Campaign Headquarters (CCHQ) to mount an ambitious attack on Labour held-seats and Labour to mount a defensive campaign, hoping to limit the scale of the expected defeat. Whereas in 2015 the polls had pointed overwhelmingly to a hung parliament and the media coverage had been dominated by speculation about coalitions and deals, in 2017 the speculation was instead about how Theresa May would use her enhanced authority to re-shape her Cabinet and on whether Jeremy Corbyn would face a leadership challenge or not.

© The Author(s) 2018
P. Cowley, D. Kavanagh, *The British General Election of 2017*,
https://doi.org/10.1007/978-3-319-95936-8_11

'My dad's an opinion pollster. I hope he never loses that sense of wonder and surprise at election results'

Matt, *Daily Telegraph*, 8 June 2017 © Matt/Telegraph Media Group Ltd

Had the polls, this time accurately, pointed to a hung parliament, the narrative at least towards the end of the campaign would instead have been about May's disastrous decision to call an election, her loss of authority and the leadership positioning of colleagues. It could have also been more about the realistic prospect of a Prime Minister Corbyn and Labour's policy programme—and an intensive scrutiny of both—as well as discussion of the consequences of a hung parliament. As in 2015, one of the biggest shocks of the 2017 election was the exit poll and, just as two years before, once it was announced, all the previous poll-driven commentary became water under the bridge. Almost all of it had been wrong.

The scale of the public polling was down on 2015. There were 87 Great Britain-wide polls over the 51 days between the calling of the election and polling day. Over the six weeks of the 2015 election, there were 92, but over a comparable 51 days there were 118, as well as far more constituency polls. The anticipation of a clear winner, compared to the expected close result in 2015, removed one incentive for the media and interested groups to commission more. Rather than releasing daily polls, as they had done in 2010 and 2015, and which had been one of the main drivers behind the recent explosion in the quantity of polling, YouGov published just two a week (although the company still continued to poll daily for internal consumption). At almost two polls per day, the level of polling was still noticeably up compared to most post-war elections.

During the campaign, there were also three polls in Northern Ireland, five in Wales, 13 in Scotland and three in London. There were noticeably fewer published constituency polls and focus groups (only five of the former), largely because of the reduced activity of Lord Ashcroft, who had been responsible for the majority of the constituency polling in 2015. Given how poorly constituency polls had functioned in 2015 (or how badly the handful of constituency polls that were conducted in 2017 fared), few bemoaned their absence.[2]

There was some re-alignment of media outlets for published polling. Opinium continued with *The Observer*, ICM remained with *The Guardian*, but also began to publish in the *Sun on Sunday*, Ipsos MORI remained with the *London Evening Standard*, and YouGov with *The Times* and the *Sunday Times*. ComRes published simultaneously with the *Mail on Sunday* and the *Independent on Sunday* (publishing their final poll in *The Independent*), Survation published with ITV and the *Mail on Sunday* (and with the *Daily Record* and *Sunday Post* in Scotland), ORB with the *Sunday Telegraph*. BMG published its one public poll of the campaign in *The Herald*, Norstat published twice in the *Sunday Express*, and *The Sun* published three SurveyMonkey polls—a far cry from its daily YouGov polling in 2015—with one YouGov poll in the *Scottish Sun*. In 2015, the seeming inevitability of a hung parliament based on the polls had driven much (pointless) 'coalitionology' analysis; in 2017, both the press and broadcast media vowed to learn lessons from that experience. The seeming inevitability, this time, of a Conservative majority and a deliberate decision not to give the polls so much prominence meant less coverage in 2017. Among the dailies, there was only one front-page lead based on the polls (see below).

The report of the British Polling Council (BPC) into what had gone wrong in 2015 was eagerly awaited prior to its publication in March 2016.[3] It pointed to two main errors concerning sampling and weighting.

First, the samples used by pollsters were not fully representative of the whole electorate; the samples of young people had too many who were politically engaged and not enough politically disengaged. The effect was to have too many Labour supporters and not enough non-voters. Second, there was a problem with adjustments made or not made for likely turnout among different age groups. Insufficient allowance was not made for older voters being more likely to vote than younger ones. This factor again worked to boost Labour and depress Conservative support in the polls. The report also recommended that current methods for allocating respondents who were don't knows or who refused to declare a vote intention should be reviewed.

Following the BPC report, the pollsters made changes in their demographic quotas and in their statistical modelling. The key area of disagreement between pollsters was on likely turnout and what to do about the young. While ICM, MORI and ComRes made significant adjustments to their original findings, Survation and YouGov made relatively few.[4] Aware that in 2015 over 60% of those aged 18–24 said they would vote, but only 43% did so, and that something similar happened in the referendum, ComRes (which found during the campaign that over 70% of 18–24s said they were 'absolutely certain' to vote) and ICM decided that the age group would vote in similar numbers in 2017.[5] Opinium, Ipsos MORI and YouGov still used declared intention to vote, but the last two weighted down those who had not voted in the past.[6] To meet the recommendation to reduce the numbers in each poll interested in and engaged in politics, some pollsters also weighted respondents by level of education or newspaper readership. But not all pollsters were comfortable with the scale of the turnout adjustments. One experienced pollster complained that the adjustments were little more than historically grounded guesswork—'creating a number you feel comfortable with'.

Figure 11.1 shows the polling estimates for the whole of the 2015–2017 Parliament, based on pooling all of the published polls. It updates the similar figure used in Chapter 1. The dramatic upturn in Labour support during the campaign is obvious. The average of the first ten polls of the campaign was 46-26 in favour of the Conservatives; the average for the ten polls between 19 and 29 May was 44-35 in favour. The 20%-plus Conservative lead in the early polls was reduced to an average of 7% by 8 June, and even that proved to be an over-estimate, as discussed below. There was, as is clear, a downward trend in Conservative support towards

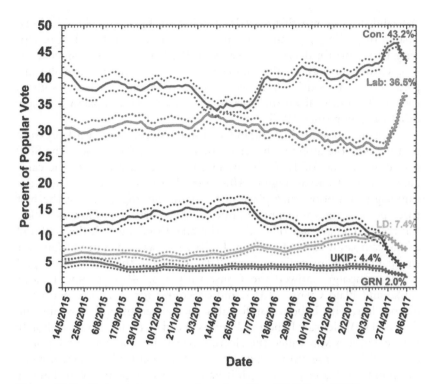

Figure 11.1 Estimated party vote intention, May 2015–June 2017.
Source: Polling Observatory

the end of the campaign, but the Conservatives essentially ended the campaign polling pretty much what they did at the beginning. Despite these changes, only one poll—by Qriously, a relatively new entrant to political polling and not in the BPC—showed Conservative support on less than 40% or Labour's above 40%.[7] The campaign polls also identified the related squeezing of the other parties during the campaign, as the combined vote for the two major parties rose inexorably during the seven-week period. The changes in the relative standing of Labour and the Conservatives represent one of the largest shifts in the poll positions of parties during an election campaign since polling in Britain began. The record for the largest variation in polling during a campaign remains Liberal Democrat support in 2010 as caused by 'Cleggmania' (an 18-point variation between the party's lowest and highest poll), compared to a 16-point range for Labour in 2017.[8] The crucial difference was that in 2010, the Liberal Democrat surge had dissipated by polling day—the party moving from third to first, before slipping back into third place—whereas in 2017, Labour maintained their momentum throughout the campaign. In terms of the net overall campaign effect, Labour's 2017 performance represented a larger shift in their poll position from the start to the end of the campaign than any other campaign since 1945.

Campaign polling in Scotland identified slight downward pressure on the SNP vote along with a clear rise in support for Labour. The SNP polled an average of 42.7% in the first three Scottish polls of the campaign, falling to an average of 40% in the last three. Labour began the campaign in a poor third place in Scotland, polling 19.7% in the first three polls of the campaign—in one poll the party fell as low as 13%—but reached an average of 25.3% in the final three; indeed, the final poll of the campaign had Labour ahead of the Conservatives in Scotland for the first time in any poll since late 2015. In Wales, the first YouGov poll of the campaign showed the Conservatives on 40%, leading Labour (30%) and Plaid Cymru (13%), and on course for a historic victory. It did not last, with Labour comfortably back ahead by mid-May, and the final poll in Wales saw Labour 12 points ahead. A poll in London shortly before Theresa May called the election had Labour a mere three points ahead of the Conservatives, but by early May that lead had extended to five points and later that month it had risen to 17 points, with Labour polling at 50%. Northern Ireland was the exception to this story of change: the three polls there—conducted by Lucid Talk—all showed the DUP marginally ahead of Sinn Féin by gaps of between 0.8 and 1.7 percentage points, with relatively little variation elsewhere.

As well as identifying the narrowing Conservative poll lead, at various points in the campaign the polls helped shape the nature of debate. When Labour's manifesto leaked, polling soon identified that far from repelling voters—as some Conservatives had hoped and some of Corbyn's party critics had feared—many of its policies were popular. ComRes found clear majorities for protecting the pension age (74% support), banning zero-hours contracts, increasing income tax for the higher paid (65%) and renationalising the railways (52%), along with plurality support for renationalising the energy companies (49%).[9] YouGov similarly found significant support for capping rents (65%), increasing income tax (57%), abolishing tuition fees (50%) and renationalising the national grid, railway companies and the Royal Mail (45%).[10] There was a similar finding following the Manchester bombing. Despite a fear amongst some Labour staff—including members of his own team—that Corbyn's speech linking the attack to British foreign policy would be seen as out of touch with public sentiment, polling soon found that large proportions of the British public agreed with its central propositions. An ORB survey for *The Independent* found that 75% of people believed Britain's various military interventions in Iraq, Afghanistan and Libya had made terrorist attacks in Britain more likely—this included 68% of Conservative voters.[11] YouGov similarly found majority support (53%) for the claim that wars that the UK had supported or fought were 'at least in part' responsible for terror attacks in the UK.[12] Indeed, when asked about specific conflicts—and Corbyn's claim that the last just conflict Britain had fought in was the Second World War—more of the public agreed with Corbyn over Libya, Iraq (both in 1991 and 2003) and Afghanistan than did not.[13]

However, when ComRes first published findings showing the support for policies in the leaked Labour manifesto, they also found that 56% said Corbyn would be 'a disaster as Prime Minister' and perhaps the most striking thing about the polls during the campaign—other than the change in party support—was the rising approval of Labour's leader from such a low base, particularly among Labour supporters. Some political scientists have argued that, given the problems associated with predicting elections on the basis of a voter's declared voting intention, the ratings of party leaders are a better indicator.[14] This was supposed to be the Conservatives' key advantage entering the election. Ipsos MORI reported on 26 April that May's score of 61% on its question of being capable as a Prime Minister was the highest the company had ever recorded since they first asked the question in 1979.[15] In the same survey, Corbyn scored 23%. Even a quarter of those intending to vote Labour then preferred to have May as Prime Minister. At the beginning of the campaign, one Labour staffer described their leader as 'electorally toxic' and yet by polling day, May was down to 47% and Corbyn had risen to 36%. YouGov found a similar trend, with May's initial lead of 35% over Corbyn cut down to 13% by the end. The Conservative determination to make the election presidential and relentlessly attack Corbyn had not worked. Yet, for all that, even at the end of the campaign, May was still ahead as best Prime Minister, no matter how the question was asked and whichever company was asking it.

This shift in sentiment came through in other polling questions. The final ComRes poll found that that when people were asked how they would feel waking up to a Corbyn-led or a May-led government, 50% said they would be delighted with either.[16] Some 52% said they would be terrified if Corbyn won, but then 48% said the same about May. This represented a significant shift in attitudes from a YouGov finding on 16 May that voters by 64-36, including a fifth of Labour voters, wanted the Conservatives to win the election.[17] There was a similarly even split when people were asked how favourable their views of the parties were. The Conservatives also lost their reputation for honesty over the course of the campaign. At the start of the campaign, YouGov found that voters were equally sceptical of the honesty of both parties. By the end, the Conservatives had an 'honesty deficit' of 27%, while Labour was level-pegging.[18] Labour also made significant advances when asked about the issues facing Britain, especially domestic issues.

Matt Singh, the former City trader and founder of Number Cruncher Politics, had gained fame by warning on the eve of the 2015 election that the polls were wrong and was proved correct. He pointed to the more reliable 'fundamentals' of voters' ratings of the parties on leadership and economic trust, and on both the Conservatives were decisively ahead. He also drew on the historical record, noting—as others did—that the polls usually under-estimated the Conservative vote share and over-estimated that of Labour. Singh wrote in his regular column for the *Financial Times* that he expected a clear Conservative victory.[19] *The Independent*'s John Rentoul wrote a balanced column about the reasons why the polls forecasts of a clear Tory majority might be wrong, but concluded that if the pollsters' adjustments for their errors last time were wrong again, 'it is more still more likely to be by overestimating Labour and underestimating the Conservatives'.[20]

Commentators' general confidence about a decisive Conservative victory was based not only on the consensus of the polls, polling history and the changes that pollsters had made in their methods, but was also encouraged by the reports of the parties' canvass returns and the gloomy expectations of many Labour candidates and organisers. On 4 June, *The Observer*'s Michael Savage reported on Labour organisers' scepticism about claims that an army of new and non-voters was riding to its rescue: 'It's complete fucking nonsense', he quoted a senior party insider and campaigner as saying, who had not met anyone 'who thinks we're going to gain a single seat, never mind getting rid of the Tory majority'.[21]

One notable innovation in 2017 was YouGov's use of a technique called Multilevel Regression and Post-stratification analysis (MRP) to attempt to model constituency outcomes more accurately. It was a technique the company had used during the Brexit referendum and which had shown Leave ahead throughout.[22] Crudely put, it pooled large amounts of polling data to try to identify the way in which different types of voters were behaving. It then used this information to predict constituency outcomes based on the demographics of each seat. It represented a significant investment by the company, since in order to be done properly, the technique requires large amounts of data; in addition to pooling their polls of 2,000 voters per day, YouGov carried out polling solely for the MRP procedure containing an extra 5,000–7,000 respondents each day.

The Times ran the model's first public outing on its front page on 31 May ('Shock Poll Predicts Tory Losses'). The model had the Conservatives to lose seats, ending up on 310, with Labour on 257 and the SNP on 50, and with the Prime Minister lacking a majority. The forecast caused some consternation, even disbelief, among pollsters and commentators. Peter Kellner thought it 'brave stuff' and Martin Boon of ICM added: 'Splashing this on the front page is even braver than YouGov doing it in the first place.' Not to be outdone, the Conservatives' Jim Messina tweeted that he was 'laughing at yet another stupid poll from YouGov', a comment that would come back to haunt him.[23] There was some nervousness within YouGov about the model's forecast. The company stressed that the estimates were mid-points, ones with fairly sizeable confidence intervals, and that even based on their data, it was still possible that the Conservatives could end up with a good majority or indeed that Labour end up as the largest party, although without a majority. As a senior Conservative strategist acidly commented at the time, 'it's impossible for YouGov to lose'. As the campaign continued—and with few other polls predicting anything close to the forecasts of YouGov's model—the company made less of the model, although the team involved continued to produce it and revised estimates were still published. Formally, YouGov said they should be judged on their final conventional poll.

The model's final estimate had the Conservatives on 302, Labour on 269, along with 12 Lib Dems, 44 SNP, five others and 18 (non-forecast) seats in Northern Ireland, albeit again with very wide confidence intervals. Using the mid-point estimates enabled YouGov to correctly call 93% of the seats—including some that few others had believed would change hands, such as Canterbury and Kensington.[24] That said, despite all the praise it attracted after the event, the model was not perfect, especially in Scotland, where it under-estimated the SNP slump and the Conservative advance, and although it correctly predicted a hung parliament, had its estimates been accurate, it is unlikely that the Conservatives would have been able to put together a government. Moreover, YouGov continued to release conventional polls, the last of which had the Conservatives seven percentage points clear.

For all these caveats, the YouGov MRP model did at least show the Conservatives set to lose their Commons majority. Almost all other published forecasts—by a wide variety of academics and pollsters—had the Conservatives heading for a clear overall majority, ranging from 48 to landslides of over 100. This uniformity in outcome, if not magnitude, applied across all types of approaches, regardless of the methodology or type of data used. The average prediction of the Political Studies Association's poll of 'experts' produced an implied Conservative lead of 14 percentage points, with the party heading for a landslide, although most respondents completed the exercise before the Conservative manifesto launch.[25] Those who claim that the betting markets offer a better predictor than the polls—although after recent events no one has much excuse for making such a claim anymore—similarly found themselves confounded; on almost every measure, the betting markets were more bullish for the Conservatives than either the polls or various forecasts derived from the polls.[26]

The normal mantra of pollsters is that opinion polls are merely snapshots of public opinion at the time they are taken, not predictions of what will necessarily happen in the election. This get-out clause does not apply to companies' final polls, which—if the exercise is to have value—should fairly accurately correlate to the actual election result, within margins of error.

There was little 'herding' in the findings of the final polls in 2017. Nine companies in the BPC reported Conservative leads ranging up to 13%, with three showing leads in double figures. In addition, there were polls from SurveyMonkey (for *The Sun*) and Qriously (for *Wired*), neither of which are members of the BPC. SurveyMonkey had the Conservative lead at four percentage points. Qriously reported a two-point lead for Labour (41%) over the Conservatives (39%), the only poll of the entire campaign to do so.[27]

Of the BPC polling companies, the outlier was Survation, whose fore-cast of a narrow lead of 1% and a hung parliament was derided by some other pollsters, just as YouGov's model had been. From 14 May onwards, the Conservative leads shown in Survation polls were clearly and consistently below the average of other polls. Survation made minimal adjustments to their raw data for turnout, a step that gave greater weight to young voters than other polls. They were one of just two BPC-registered companies in the entire campaign to report Labour reaching 40%, which they did in their final poll when the others ranged from 33% to 38%. The company would look like either a hero or a fool when the votes were counted and the polling industry, if it had a collective voice, would have backed the second. Survation's position as an outlier had history. On the eve of poll in the 2015 general election, they had conducted a phone poll, in which it named the local candidates and insisted on speaking to the named person from the data set. Its 5% lead for the Conservatives was out of line with the other polls, but proved close to the final result. Sceptical about the finding, the company did not release the poll, and the chief executive latter bitterly regretted that he had lacked the confidence to back his own poll and go against the trend.[28] He was now gambling with his final poll.

Table 11.1 shows the publicly released findings of the final BPC polls. All correctly predicted the winning party. They were also pretty much spot-on in predicting the Conservative vote share, an average of just 0.2% higher than the actual result. The problem came with Labour, with the average figure under-estimating Labour's vote by 5.2%. Although rare, it was not unknown for polls to under-estimate Labour; they had done so in 2010, 1983 and in February 1974.[29] But never before had the polls under-estimated the Labour vote share by quite so much.[30] The mean average error across the parties may not have been quite on the scale of 1970, 1992 or even 2015, but the outcome still felt like a collective failure because only one BPC poll showed the parties so evenly matched that there would clearly be a hung parliament.

In Scotland and Wales, the final polls were relatively accurate, although the eventual SNP lead of 8.3 percentage points was smaller than any poll had predicted in the campaign, whilst the Labour lead of 15.3% in Wales was larger than had been shown in any campaign poll.

It was not hard to find the main source of the problem, at least after the fact. The final figures reported in a poll can often vary markedly from those initially collected. Many pollsters in 2017 reported that by the end

Table 11.1 Final polls by BPC companies

Polster	Con	Lab	LD	UKIP	Green	Other	Con lead	Method	Sample size	Fieldwork
Opinium	43	36	8	5	2	6	7	Online	3,002	4 June
Survation	41	40	8	2	2	6	1	Telephone	2,798	6–7 June
Ipsos MORI	44	36	7	4	2	6	8	Telephone	1,291	6–7 June
ICM	46	34	7	5	2	6	12	Online	1,532	6–7 June
ComRes	44	34	9	5	2	5	10	Online	2,051	5–7 June
YouGov	42	35	10	5	2	6	7	Online	2,130	5–7 June
Panelbase	44	36	7	5	2	6	8	Online	3,018	2–7 June
Kantar Public	43	38	7	4	2	6	5	Online	2,159	1–7 June
BMG	46	33	8	5	3	6	13	Telephone/online	1,199	6–7 June
Average	43.7	35.8	7.9	4.4	2.1	5.9	7.9			
Result (GB)	43.5	41.0	7.6	1.9	1.6	4.4	2.5			
Difference	0.2	–5.2	0.3	2.5	0.5	1.5	5.4			

Source: British Polling Council

of the campaign, their unadjusted figures showed little difference between the two main parties; it was the turnout adjustments which had the effect of increasing the Conservative lead. On average, these effects increased the Conservative lead by around five points and in some cases more.[31] Without turnout adjustments, no polling company would have put the Conservatives more than five points ahead—and the mean average lead would have been 2.6 points, almost identical to the actual result.[32]

Yet the companies had not introduced turnout adjustments on a whim, but because turnout had been crucial in previous elections. ComRes, for example, found that when they retrospectively applied their new model to their 2015 data, it produced vote shares for both the Conservatives and Labour within just one percentage point of the actual result. But in 2017 their final poll had both parties on 39% before turnout adjustments were made; it was the turnout model that resulted in the company reporting a ten-point Conservative lead.[33] In other words, many of the methods employed in 2017 would have worked better in 2015, but those employed in 2015 would have performed better in 2017.

Television sponsorship of exit polls for British general elections dates back to October 1974. The process has undergone many changes since then—perhaps the most important of which is that they have become considerably more accurate. In October 1974, the BBC's exit poll—there were then separate polls for the BBC and ITN—under-estimated the Conservatives by 77 seats and over-estimated Labour by 61. Having predicted a Labour majority of 132, the actual majority turned out to be just three. In 1987, the BBC's poll under-estimated the Conservatives by 38 seats (and over-estimated Labour by 32), whilst in 1992, both ITN and the BBC under-estimated the Conservatives by more than 30 (31 for ITN, 35 for the BBC).

Since the 2010 general election, the exit poll has been financed jointly by a triumvirate of the BBC, ITV and Sky, and fieldwork conducted by the polling teams of Ipsos MORI and GfK. Moreover, from 2005 onwards, they have used a very different methodology from earlier work.[34] In 2017, the teams interviewed some 30,000 voters at 144 polling stations across Great Britain. As far as possible, they interviewed in the same polling stations as in 2015, so that they could measure changes in voting data between the two elections. A sample of voters leaving each polling station are asked to complete a mock ballot paper reporting who they had voted for—which they then drop into a mock ballot box. This gives the exit poll

Table 11.2   Record of exit poll seat predictions 2005–2017

2005: Conservatives over-estimated by 11. Correct for Labour
2010: Correct for Conservatives. Labour under-estimated by 3
2015: Conservatives under-estimated by 11. Labour over-estimated by 7
2017: Conservatives under-estimated by 4. Labour over-estimated by 4

team 144 estimates of the levels of change in party support since 2015 in the chosen constituencies. Regression analysis is then used to identify statistically significant differences between different types of constituencies; this produces a model which gives each constituency a probability of which party will win it, with these probabilities then summed to give the national totals. The exit poll does not attempt to predict national vote shares or to identify types of voters and their behaviour; the process is explicitly designed purely to predict seat outcomes. Since 2005, and the new methodology, the polls have been remarkably accurate, as Table 11.2 shows.

As noted in the previous chapter, the exit poll was treated with some scepticism when it was first broadcast, although it soon proved to be broadly accurate. The exit poll has gained a deserved reputation for accuracy, but it differs from a conventional poll both because it involves asking people how they have voted as they leave voting booths, thus avoiding the pollster's two perennial problems of calculating whether they will turn out and whether they will vote as they have indicated.[35] One potential methodological issue is that the exit poll does not take any account of postal votes, even though these now account for more than one in five of the votes cast in Britain. Since the poll works by measuring change rather than absolute levels of support, this does not present a problem so long as the change in standing of the parties amongst those voting by post is the same as the change amongst polling station voters. However, in 2017 several of those involved in the exit poll's production had been concerned that if it erred, it was more likely to err in a pro-Labour way, because many postal votes would have been cast earlier in the campaign when Labour were doing less well. In the event, the poll was one of the more accurate exit polls in recent elections.

In addition to the large quantity of published polling, political parties often commission their own polling. Such private polling is often referred to in hushed tones, as if it is of a higher level, revealing truths that conventional polling somehow misses. Yet it is not as if there is some clever technique or advanced methodology that the parties can uti-lise that has otherwise passed pollsters by. The truth is that political par-ties and politicians are mostly keen users of polling, despite various hackneyed protestations to the contrary. They make extensive use of pub-lished polling—especially where data sets are available, such as with the British Election Study—and there is then little point in them merely rep-licating the sort of questions that published polling asks. Instead, they tend to use polling to test messages, policies or personalities, to try out ideas or to poll in specific places and among specific groups. Moreover, although all major parties commission some private polling, such work is expensive and, as we show below, only one party—the Conservatives—really invested in large-scale polling in 2017 and, given the result, it is not entirely clear how much value it generated.

The Conservative Party again relied on CTF for its political polling. As noted above (p. 59), it showed little interest in the private polling con-ducted by Number 10's political team or the work undertaken by Populus in Scotland. CTF's findings immediately before the election was called, drawn from both quantitative and qualitative work, inspired the presiden-tial emphasis on May and the relegation of the party's name in the first half of the campaign. It is, in retrospect, remarkable how an entire election strategy was built on not much more than a single 1,000 person poll and a handful of focus groups.

Once the election was under way, the party conducted a nightly tracker poll across 50 marginal constituencies, a mix of defensive and attacking seats, producing a rolling average from clusters of small polls every three or four days. A key tracker question asked voters what might cause them 'the biggest hesitation' for voting Labour or Conservative; another was which party 'is on your side'. The tracker quickly identified the unpopular-ity of the manifesto's social care package—although identifying this hardly required the party to spend money on private polling. The feedback from Conservative candidates and organisers was overwhelming and the *Mail on Sunday*'s front-page headline 'Dementia Tax Backlash' drew on a Survation poll which found the policy to be unpopular.[36]

As in 2015, Lynton Crosby and Mark Textor's questions and findings were made available to only a handful of senior campaign members in CCHQ. Textor gave a brief daily review of the polling ('usually evasive' said one attendee), a couple of briefings to May ('not useful' said the same source), and Crosby and Textor discussed the implications of the focus group and poll findings with Stephen Gilbert, Messina and a couple of field directors. At the time, the restricted group sharing the polling did not cause much concern; after all, 2015 had been a poll-driven campaign, in which hardly anybody saw the data, and it had been successful. After 8 June, however, sceptics wondered if some of the findings might have been shaped by the kind of questions asked. As one Conservative insider reflected: 'No one really asked serious questions about the data, partly because we trusted them. Right up to 9.59 pm on election day and beyond that as they were saying the exit poll was wrong.' Another bluntly said of the secrecy that it was a case of 'marking your own homework'.

Populus conducted over 20 focus groups for the Scottish Conservative Party before the election. They found little response when they asked potential Conservative voters if they could mention what ten years of SNP government had done for Scotland and mixed views about the party's fixation on a second referendum.

In October 2016, Labour appointed BMG, a Birmingham-based polling company, to conduct their surveys and advise on strategy. BMG conducted fortnightly polls in Great Britain and monthly polls in Scotland (the results were passed on to Edinburgh once). From January 2017, they reported their findings directly to John McDonnell and shared only with a few highly trusted members of the leader's team, Seumas Milne, Steve Howell, Andrew Fisher and Madeleine Williams, McDonnell's chief of staff, along with Cynthia Pinto, McDonnell's wife who had experience of dealing with polling and data. Also usually in attendance were at least one of the campaign coordinators, Andrew Gwynne and Ian Lavery. As noted in Chapter 4, there were no polling presentations to the parliamentary party or national executive, although three were made to the Shadow Cabinet, and BMG were involved in testing policies for Andrew Fisher's work on the manifesto.

Once the campaign started, it was planned that BMG would make a weekly polling presentation to senior Southside staff and members of the Leader of the Opposition's Office (LOTO). After a few sessions, these meetings petered out and the LOTO team commissioned work on target voters for their own use. Some of its findings were hardly encouraging about Corbyn and his stance on defence. For example, although one set of interviews with ex-Labour voters in the North found close to unanimous agreement that Labour 'look after working people' and are 'for the many not the few', it also noted:

Leadership and associated policy differences, economic competence and reduced 'toxicity' of the Conservative Party appear to be the three main motivating factors for switching or distancing from Labour party. As well as changing leader, participants cited defence and immigration as examples of areas in which a change in policy could persuade them to vote Labour.

'Most participants', it reported, 'were critical of the Labour leadership. These concerns related to both style and substance, notably on the issue of defence'; they were positive about the manifesto, but worried about Labour's ability to deliver it ('Participants were not convinced that plans were fully costed'). McDonnell and his team who attended the meetings in the first couple of weeks at times joined in the gallows humour about the negativity of the findings.

BMG recommended that in the national campaign Labour should attack May's character on account of her policy U-turns and broken promises: 'She needs to be skewered.' When the company reported on Labour's lines, they found close to unanimity on 'Jeremy Corbyn's Labour Party will look after working people', 'is for the many not the few' and 'Theresa May's Tory party protects the wealthy', but division about claims that the Conservative Party 'is still the nasty party' and 'is running down the country'.

The agency reported that the groups helping Labour's recovery in the polls in the campaign were disproportionately the 18–44s employed in the public sector, former Green and Lib Dem voters, and the undecideds (often 2015 Labour voters and with anti-austerity views). As the polls narrowed, BMG concentrated their research more on the 'soft' Labour voters, asking what held them back from voting Labour (the most commons responses were: Corbyn, Diane Abbott and 'where's the money coming from?') and what attracted them (often the party's policy offers). But, in contrast to the Conservative campaign, Labour's was not poll-driven. BMG's relationship was not on a par with the central role Mark Textor and colleagues played day after day in CCHQ during the campaign.

BMG's private polling-day forecast for Labour was an 8% Conservative lead, more comforting than their published one of 13%, but still disappointing for some of Corbyn's team. Afterwards, some of Corbyn's closest allies were very critical of BMG's polling for being excessively negative. 'They came in their suits, just telling us their view', said one of Corbyn's team. 'They just didn't have a clue what was going on out there.' Steve Howell was later to describe BMG's presentations as 'one doom-laden slide after another'.[37] Yet BMG's negative findings were similar to other polls and were largely borne out in the local elections, while they reported an improvement for Labour in mid-May.

It is naïve of politicians and strategists to judge private pollsters primarily on their accuracy in predicting the result, although they often do. It is equally naïve of private pollsters to boast about their forecasting accuracy as proof of their superior quality, not least when the findings are not available to more than a handful of colleagues. There are numerous public polls already making predictions and, crucially, reporting sample size, weighting, questions and the type of seats polled. The private pollsters are recruited to provide data and advice which help a party craft its communications and strategy. But there is a strong commercial and reputational incentive for them to be reported after the event as having been 'correct', without being open to the same scrutiny that public polls receive.

Although the parties' private pollsters are not appointed primarily to forecast the result, it is worth noting that in neither party did all the private polling and data analysis ever predict anything other than a clear Conservative majority of seats. Some sources close to CTF now claim to have seen what was coming, although insiders who were present in CCHQ on 8 June have been startled by what they regard as a re-writing of history in interviews given by some of the principals since. Messina's gibe about the YouGov prediction of a hung parliament, based on its model, and Crosby and Textor's more general—and longstanding—dismissal of the quality of British polling turned out to bite them.[38] After the election, it was claimed that Messina's final model was said to predict the Conservatives to win between 303 seats (short of a majority) and 354 (a majority of 58), with a mid-point prediction of a majority of just eight, and Textor's final poll apparently showed the party on course for a hung parliament. As Tim Shipman notes, it was 'strange' that Messina did not share this information with other key strategists.[39] Yet, as discussed in the previous chapter, senior figures in CCHQ insist that CTF informed them on polling day that the party was heading for a majority of over 50 and Messina and others dismissed the exit poll prediction. A May aide bluntly dismissed their claims to have foreseen a hung parliament: 'They went round mouthing "it's wrong" about the exit poll and did so after the first few results, saying "see? Told you it was wrong".' Shipman acidly comments that whereas others may have accepted their part in the flawed Conservative campaign, 'the consultants were not so frank about their own role'.[40]

Parties continued to use focus groups to test and refine their election messages, themes and policies. They can be a salutary reminder of how little attention is paid to politics outside the Westminster bubble. When asked, potential Liberal Democrat voters said they had never heard of Tim Farron, when another group was asked to say which party leader was 'strong and stable', the convenor was met with blank faces, and the Conservative pledge of a cap on energy prices was assumed to be a Labour one. A convenor of Conservative groups noted the increasing scepticism voters have about some slogans. He added that: '"Strong and stable" was vacuous and too static, whereas "long term economic plan" in 2015 worked because it was positive.'

During the campaign, Textor drew on the reactions in the groups in marginal seats to craft passages for May's speech-writers and to monitor reactions to policies. The Prime Minister followed to the letter the instructions of her campaign managers to deliver the message about the need for strong and stable leadership for Brexit, even when it had run its course. Only right at the end of the campaign (see p. 216) did it drive a brief change in tone.

Labour's focus groups consisted of 'soft' or potentially defecting 2015 supporters in marginal seats. At the start of the campaign, they were depressing, showing that many who had been undecided between Labour and the Conservatives were moving to the latter, although there was some recovery in the second half of the campaign. In mid-May, BMG held sessions with a more challenging set of voters—former supporters in northern seats; not surprisingly, they were pretty discouraging. Voters mentioned their fears over Corbyn's leadership and the party's economic competence as reasons for defecting. While conceding that the Conservative Party was still on the side of the wealthy, they thought that it had become more moderate and was 'now more in line with the needs/aspirations of the working class'. They were more positive about Labour's manifesto ('I'm not a Corbyn supporter, but I do like what he's saying at the moment'), although sceptical about the idea of extra government spending.

At the beginning of the campaign, Survation polling for the Liberal Democrats in key constituencies prompted party managers to withdraw resources from some seats (see below, p. 292), and the party carried out a handful of constituency polls and some focus groups during the campaign. Focus groups were depressing. Members of groups in Manchester agreed with most of the party's policies, but would add that they would have to vote Labour to stop the Conservatives. For the most part, the party had such limited resources that it was relying on publicly available data and its canvass returns. One of those responsible for running the campaign wondered how much difference it had made, noting ruefully that 'spotting trends only matters if you can do something about it'. In the case of the Lib Dems, he added, it was 'not so much pulling levers and finding nothing happening, but not even really having levers to pull'.

It is difficult to make a strong case for the vote-catching influence of the parties' private polls in 2017. No party had the extensive and long-term pre-election polling as Labour and the Conservatives had commissioned before 2015 to shape their strategy. No pollster in 2017 had the frequent access to, or at least contact with, the leader that Crosby had with Cameron before 2015, or Philip Gould used to have with Tony Blair. Crosby had only a couple of meetings with May before the campaign and minimal contact during it; BMG's Michael Turner had three meetings with Corbyn in a group and never one on one.

There was a big difference, however, in the resources the two parties invested in polling. For the seven weeks of the campaign, Labour spent around £250,000 with BMG and £50,000 with ICM. CTF were reportedly paid £1.7 million for the campaign polling and the final figure, including fees to the partners, brought the total Conservative spend to some £4 million. At times, CTF had up to 30 people at any one time working in CCHQ. It is possible that Labour, allegedly led by ideologues with limited polling resources, were no worse served by the data than the better-resourced and supposedly pragmatic Conservatives. The dominant position of CTF may be seen in its contract with CCHQ, which also provided for the pollster to do post-election polling to analyse the result, which in turn was then used for the CCHQ 'inquiry' or post-mortem into what went wrong; one insider, surprised by the arrangement, commented that it was a case of 'Marking your own homework squared'.

Although there is no evidence that polls, in general, are becoming less accurate than they used to be, the last two general elections have seen the opinion polls move from one disaster to another.[41] The errors of 2015 (sampling) were not the problems of 2017 (turnout adjustments). The assumptions and methodology operating for one election clearly do not necessarily hold for the next. The turnout corrections for the young voters, based on the 2015 experience, proved faulty. John Curtice's expectation that the post-2015 changes in methods would 'mean that they at least have a better chance of getting the broad picture on June 8 roughly right' was confounded.[42] Pollsters may have to regard elections as distinctive events, each one challenging established methodologies.

One success was the MRP modelling introduced by YouGov. When those involved later released data for the entire campaign, it revealed that the Conservatives had been on course for below 325 seats from 22 May onwards—or, in other words, immediately after the launch of, and retreat over, the Conservative social care policy. In future, the clients and readers of the polls who are primarily interested in forecasts may place more credence on the model. Yet there are two caveats. The first is that the model is much more expensive to produce and takes more time. The second is that that no methodological innovation can guarantee success. Lord Ashcroft, who used an MRP model similar to that employed by YouGov, fared no better than most conventional pollsters. The Ashcroft model drew on around 40,000 interviews in which he asked voters questions about their personal economic optimism, identity and whether the country was heading in the right or wrong direction. He updated the finding during the campaign and yet still predicted a 'probable' Conservative total of 363 seats and an overall majority of 76.

Readers of the polls may also look beyond the headline voting intention figures and take more note of the rich contextual information many polls provide. One experienced but disillusioned pollster dismissed the traditional vote intention poll, surrounded by so much uncertainty, as 'a crap product'. We have long known that an expression of an opinion to a pollster is not the same as an action. And, drawing on the 2017 experience, the media and pollsters may also learn to be more tolerant of the outlier poll(s).

However, it was not only the polls that took a battering in 2017. The feedback from canvassers for Labour and Conservatives confirmed the thrust of the polls—that the Conservatives were comfortably ahead. In 2015, both polling and canvassing had erred in the same direction, showing Labour doing better than proved to be the case when the votes were counted. That outcome had reinforced belief in the importance of the 'fundamentals' of the parties' relative ratings on leadership and economic competence and on the polls' history of over-estimating Labour's vote. But in 2017, these also erred.

Immediately after the election, the BPC ruled out holding an inquiry on the scale of 2015 into what had gone wrong, but for the pollsters—and backers of other proxy indicators—it was back to the drawing board to decide if 2017 is the new norm or an anomaly.

NOTES

1. John Curtice, 'EU Referendum – How the Polls Got it Wrong Again', *The Conversation*, 26 June 2016, https://theconversation.com/eu-referendum-how-the-polls-got-it-wrong-again-61639.

2. Of the constituency polls conducted in 2017, three correctly identified the winning party—although given that two of these polls were in Tatton and Brighton Pavilion, this was not an especially onerous task. The poll conducted in Battersea would not have helped identify Labour's eventual gain; ditto for the one poll conducted in Kensington, which had the Conservatives 17 points ahead in a seat Labour went on to win.

3. P. Sturgis, N. Baker, M. Callegaro, S. Fisher, J. Green, W. Jennings, J. Kuha, B. Lauderdale and P. Smith, *Report of the Inquiry into the 2015 British General Election Opinion Polls*. Market Research Society and British Polling Council, 2016.

4. For a good discussion on the changes, see Anthony Wells, 'How the Polls Have Changed since 2015', *UK Polling Report*, 27 May 2017, http://ukpollingreport.co.uk/blog/archives/9895.

5. Andrew Hawkins, 'Why the Huge Disparity in This Election's Opinion Polls?', *The Times*, 8 June 2017.

6. For example, a Survation poll in late May 2017 for ITV's *Good Morning Britain* reported that 82% of those aged 18–25 would vote and was greeted with disbelief.

7. Qriously use a technique they call 'programmatic sampling', which involves mobile phone users responding to questions whilst using apps. Their poll was published in *Wired*, which later ran an article examining how Qriously had been so accurate (see Joao Medeiros, 'Remember the Poll That Predicted the Labour Surge? We Explain the Methodology', *Wired*, 9 June 2017, www.wired.co.uk/article/labour-election-result-poll-qriously), based on the fact that the poll had accurately predicted the Labour vote share. The article spent less time on the fact that the poll predicted a two percentage point Labour lead in an election which the Conservatives won by 2.5 points.

8. Will Jennings, 'The Polls in 2017' in Dominic Wring, Roger Mortimore and Simon Atkinson (eds), *Political Communications: The General Election of 2017*. Palgrave Macmillan, 2017. Jennings excludes the Qriously poll from his calculations, but even with this included, the Labour range only rises one point and the conclusion remains the same.

9. 'Daily Mirror GE2017 Poll', *ComRes*, 11 May 2017, www.comresglobal.com/polls/daily-mirror-ge2017-poll.

10. Matthew Smith, 'How Popular are the Parties' Manifesto Policies?', *YouGov*, 22 May 2017.

11. Andrew Grice, 'Majority of British Voters Agree with Corbyn's Claim UK Foreign Policy Increases Rise of Terrorism', *The Independent*, 6 June 2017.www.independent.co.uk/news/uk/politics/jeremy-corbyn-poll-foreign-policy-terrorism-british-voters-agree-majority-latest-a7776276.html.

12. Matthew Smith, 'Jeremy Corbyn is on the Right Side of Public Opinion on Foreign Policy: Except for the Falklands', *YouGov*, 30 May 2017, https://yougov.co.uk/news/2017/05/30/jeremy-corbyn-right-side-public-opinion-foreign-po.

13. The only conflict on which Corbyn was in a minority was the Falklands War.

14. For just one example, see Amanda Bittner, *Personality or Platform: The Role of Party Leaders in Elections*. Oxford University Press, 2011.

15. Gideon Skinner and Glenn Gottfried, 'Theresa May Has Big Lead as Most Capable Prime Minister', *Ipsos MORI*, 26 April 2017, https://www.ipsos.com/ipsos-mori/en-uk/theresa-may-has-big-lead-most-capable-prime-minister. There had, however, sometimes been bigger leads—such as Tony Blair's over William Hague in 2001.

16. 'The Independent Eve of Election Poll', *ComRes*, 7 June 2017, www.comresglobal.com/polls/the-independent-eve-of-election-poll.

17. Stephan Shakespeare, 'A Fifth of Would-Be Labour Voters Want a Tory Government', *YouGov*, 16 May 2017, https://yougov.co.uk/news/2017/05/16/one-five-those-who-intend-vote-labour-want-conserv.

18. Peter Kellner, 'Why is Labour Surging – And How Worried Should the Tories Be?', *Prospect*, https://www.prospectmagazine.co.uk/blogs/peter-kellner/why-is-labour-surging-and-how-worried-should-the-tories-be.

19. See, for example, Matt Singh, 'History Points to a Convincing Conservative Victory', *Financial Times*, 24 May 2017; and 'Theresa May's Lead Has Dipped But is Stronger than Polls Suggest', *Financial Times*, 7 June 2017.

20. John Rentoul, 'Be Careful with Your Election Predictions, the Opinion Polls Could Be Very Wrong. Again', *The Independent*, 29 May 2017.

21. Michael Savage, 'From NME to No 10 – Could the Youth Vote Win Corbyn the Election?', *The Observer*, 4 June, 2017. See also Anne Perkins, 'Building Your Hopes up, Corbyn Supporters? Have You Forgotten 2015?', *The Guardian*, 7 June 2017.

22. See Doug Rivers, 'Introducing the YouGov Referendum Model', *YouGov*, 21 June 2016, https://yougov.co.uk/news/2016/06/21/yougov-referendum-model.

23. https://twitter.com/messina2012/status/869928746974949378?lang=en.

24. Despite an 11-point Conservative lead in 2015, Kensington was predicted by the YouGov model to be a toss-up with both Labour and Conservatives on 43%; election day saw both parties on 42%, with 20 votes between them.

25. As the press release rather dryly noted, 'the results of this survey should be interpreted in light of the … poor forecasting performance of similar expert surveys of predictions for the 2015 general election and the 2016 EU referendum'. See 'Expert Predictions of the 2017 General Election: A Survey by Stephen Fisher, Chris Hanretty and Will Jennings on Behalf of the U.K. Political Studies Association', *Political Studies Association*, 2 June 2017, https://www.psa.ac.uk/psa/news/expert-predictions-2017-general-election-survey-stephen-fisher-chris-hanretty-and-will.

26. See Stephen Fisher, John Kenny and Rosalind Shorrocks, 'A Post-mortem on Forecasts for the 2017 British General Election', presented at the EPOP Conference 2017. The one caveat is that the betting markets did marginally better when it came to the Liberal Democrats.

27. This poll attracted relatively little attention at the time, partly because it was not by a BPC member and partly because of its methodology—using an app on mobile phones.

28. See Philip Cowley and Dennis Kavanagh, *The British General Election of 2015*. Palgrave Macmillan, 2015, p. 239.

29. As they had, albeit with much more limited polling, between 1945 and 1955.

30. Indeed, that scale of error on any one party was exceptionally rare—on a par with the Conservative vote share in 1992.

31. This is discussed in Patrick Sturgis and Will Jennings, 'Will Turnout Weighting Prove to Be the Pollsters' Achilles Heel in #GE2017?', *Soton Politics*, https://sotonpolitics.org/2017/06/04/will-turnout-weighting-prove-to-be-the-pollsters-achilles-heel-in-ge2017.

32. See Will Jennings, Evidence submitted to the House of Lords Select Committee on Political Polling and Digital Media, 31 August 2017.

33. ComRes, 'GE2017: Our Take'.

34. Described in John Curtice and David Firth, 'Exit Polling in a Cold Climate: The BBC-ITV Experience in Britain in 2005', *Journal of the Royal Statistical Society A*, 171 (2008): 509–39.

35. John Curtice, Stephen Fisher, Jouni Kuha and Jonathan Mellon, 'Surprise, Surprise! (Again). The 2017 British General Election Exit Poll', *Significance*, August 2017.

36. Some 47% said they opposed the policy, compared to just 28% who said they supported it (and 26% who did not know). In addition, majorities of respondents said that they would be more anxious about getting older, more anxious about securing a future for their children, caring for older relatives and owning a house (52%). See Survation, *General Election 2017 Poll*, 21 May 2017, http://survation.com/wp-content/uploads/2017/05/Final-MoS-Poll-190517GOCH-1c0d1h7.pdf.

37. Steve Howell, *Game Changer*. Accent Press, 2018, p. 2.

38. See, for example, Textor's claim that British polling was 'hopeless' (Cowley and Kavanagh, *The British General Election of 2015*, p. 63) or in 2017 that it was 'shit' (Tim Shipman, *Fall Out*. William Collins, 2017, p. 373).
39. See Shipman, *Fall Out*, pp. 403–4 and 527.
40. Ibid., p. 527.
41. See Chris Prosser and Jon Mellon, 'The Twilight of the Polls? A Review of Trends in Polling Accuracy and the Causes of Polling Misses', *Government and Opposition* (2018): 1–34. See also the conclusions of the House of Lord Select Committee on Political Polling and Digital Media, *The Politics of Polling*, Report of Session 2017–2019, HL Paper 106.
42. John Curtice, 'How Pollsters Have Changed Their Tactics', *The Times*, 29 May 2017.

CHAPTER 12

Targeted (and Untargeted) Local Campaigning

Constituency campaigning has been transformed in recent elections. Many of the more traditional methods, such as volunteers knocking on doors and delivering leaflets, still take place, but increasingly there has been more direction and control from national party headquarters, more use of technology and more sophisticated targeting of individual voters. All three of these changes were in evidence in 2017 and probably to a greater degree than in recent elections, along with a larger spend than ever on digital messaging. But there were also widespread complaints about the inaccuracy of much targeting and the failure of central direction. The 2017 election was also notable for the number of candidates who complained of intimidation and abuse, often (though not solely) on social media.

'Early money works best' has long been the local campaigner's watchword. Local and regional party organisers usually estimate that they need at least 12 months to plan for fundraising, recruiting staff, direct mail, booking venues, canvassing and targeting voters. Ideally, parties hope to have selected candidates even longer in advance to establish themselves in the constituency, particularly in target seats. In recent general elections, the Parliament has run into its fourth or even (as in 1992, 1997 and 2010) its fifth and final year, and in 2015 parties had known the probable date of the general election well in advance because of the provisions of the Fixed-term Parliaments Act. In 2017, by contrast, although some local parties

© The Author(s) 2018
P. Cowley, D. Kavanagh, *The British General Election of 2017*,
https://doi.org/10.1007/978-3-319-95936-8_12

'He spent 20 minutes telling
me what a disaster Corbyn
would be. I assume he's the
Labour candidate'

Matt, *Daily Telegraph*, 23 April 2017 © Matt/Telegraph Media Group Ltd

were preparing for the local and mayoral elections on 4 May, the general election caught almost all of them by surprise.

Some of the plans originally made for a 2020 general election had been abandoned. Lord Feldman, the Conservative Chairman, had wanted to build on his party's victory in 2015 and floated radical reforms to the way in which the constituency parties operated. Nothing came of his suggestions for merging weaker associations and pooling their resources or about measures to professionalise the voluntary party. Feldman resigned, along with David Cameron, after the EU referendum result and was succeeded by Sir Patrick McLoughlin. Plans for the continued employment in key seats of the 100-plus campaign directors beyond the 2015 general election—a statement of intent of becoming a year-round campaigning party—were also dashed; all but a score were released. The databases for the digital operation were not updated, a painful contrast to the party's large investment in digital activity before the 2015 election. The combination of the party's large opinion poll lead and the widespread expectation that there would not be an election until 2020 seems to have weakened the battle-readiness of Conservative Campaign Headquarters

(CCHQ). Mark Wallace, a longstanding critic of CCHQ's campaign readiness, had complained that the Copeland by-election in February 2017 had been won despite, not because of, the party machine.[1] Many of the party's 2015 key campaign personnel were recalled for the campaign, at short notice, but the machine was far from ready. A senior figure returning after a two-year absence complained: 'It was as if CCHQ had gone into meltdown. You don't have four years of peace time and one year of campaigning. The world's changed.' After the campaign, another consultant added: 'To call an election when you are not in any way, shape or form ready (as now seems to have been the case) is highly reckless and irresponsible.' Labour's plans to employ up to 40 campaign organisers in key seats, with the costs shared between the sitting MP and the national party, had also not been implemented. But thanks to the increase in membership after 2015, Labour were at least flush with a campaign war chest of over £3 million and were prepared for the logistical side of any election.

Perhaps in no area is ample time more important than for selecting and supporting the candidate in target seats. Inevitably the activity that over many months had preceded the 2015 election had not taken place. Aware that some opinion polls showed the party 20% or more behind the Conservatives, the pressure on Labour's professional staff at Southside was to compile a defensive list of seats. With Parliament still sitting, the group was aware that if some MPs learnt that their seats had been written off, morale might collapse and the media might report that the party had already conceded the election. The initial decision was therefore taken to support candidates in all Labour-held seats, except the 75 safest. This list was then adjusted further over the next few days, in light of feedback from regional organisers, and a handful of even safer Labour seats were added.

The parties had until Parliament was dissolved in which to spend money before it would count against local campaign spending limits, so one early priority was to get money and direct mails to the constituencies as quickly as possible. With Unite providing £250,000 on the first day to help with direct mail, Southside spent some £3.4 million in the first few days alone, with around £1.5 million going to support candidates with campaign costs. Candidates in Labour-held seats received an average of £8,000 each. There was little disagreement at this initial meeting that the list should be a defensive one; the polls were pointing only in one direction. In any case, it was harder to spend the money attacking Conservative seats because at this point, there were no Labour candidates in place to support in these seats. The agreement did not last and Leader of the Opposition's Office (LOTO) staff were soon complaining about the list being too defensive.

The longstanding tensions between LOTO and Southside abated somewhat for the campaign, but in no way was there an integrated Labour campaign. Southside directors, who were used to having a few weeks' notice of the campaign grid, often learnt from LOTO only a couple of days in advance about Jeremy Corbyn's visits and scheduled themes and media interviews. Corbyn had a separate social media operation and Momentum, the grassroots organisation organised after his election as leader and dedicated to supporting him, liaised with LOTO rather than Southside in choosing seats to canvass. The leader's team claim that had they been more open about their plans, there would have been unhelpful leaking from Southside; as it was, Southside repeatedly leaked during the campaign. In turn, Southside, as well as the greater campaign experience of its senior staff, also had a digital team, and had separate teams responsible for direct mail, leaflets and press advertising.

Of all the disagreements, the biggest was to come over which seats to target. There was a continuing power struggle, before and during the early stages of the campaign, between senior Southside staff and more ambitious members of Corbyn's team over the number and choice of target seats.[2] This was a clash about strategy, politics and resources. Corbyn's team complained that Southside was defeatist, seeking merely to stop Labour losing seats; they aimed higher and wanted to allocate resources to candidates who were challenging Conservative seats. It was true that Southside, guided by the polls and feedback from MPs and organisers, was primarily working to minimise the scale of losses and was running an operation that was different from what Corbyn's team wanted. Patrick Heneghan, aware of the gloomy findings from the BMG polling, decided, without consulting LOTO, to commission a large 20,000 sample survey from ICM to help identify target seats, at a cost of around £50,000. The findings were as gloomy as those of BGM. But there was also a political angle to the battle over resources. LOTO suspected that some Southside directors were supporting certain candidates because they were hostile to Corbyn and were looking forward to a change of leader following a likely election defeat. Equally, many of the party's professional staff suspected that LOTO would happily throw anti-Corbyn MPs overboard. As one Southsider said: 'We want to save the Labour Party.'

However, on 18 May, one month into the campaign, the newly arrived Unite official Andrew Murray intervened to press Heneghan to add another 50 offensive seats to the target list; if all were captured, that number would be enough to deny the Conservatives a majority. His opinion carried weight, given that Unite had recently contributed £2.25 million to the campaign; LOTO staff, particularly Karie Murphy and Steve Howell, claimed that Unite insisted this money be used to attack Conservative seats. Internally, these were categorised as OF1 and OF2 (the former very marginal, the latter longer shots); they included seats like Leeds North West, Croydon Central, Brighton Kemptown and Sheffield Hallam, which were now to receive more support. Some seats, including Angela Eagle's Wallasey (with a majority of over 16,000) and Dan Jarvis's Barnsley Central (with a majority of over 12,000) were taken off the list. In contrast to 2015, when it had gradually narrowed the number of target seats during the campaign, Labour in 2017 were expanding the number. By the last week of the campaign, the national Labour campaign was providing help in some form to over 200 constituencies, enough—if all were won—to form a majority government.

With Darren Mott, the Conservative Director of Campaigning, ill for part of the campaign, his predecessor Stephen Gilbert effectively oversaw the party's target seats exercise. He had done this in 2015, when the choice had been driven by analysis of the seats' marginality, local demographic factors (informed in particular by the modelling of Jim Messina), quality of the candidate and whether the opponent was a sitting MP. These key players were again in place in CCHQ, although they lacked the rich canvassing and other data that had been gathered before 2015. At short notice in 2017, Gilbert initially designated 22 defensive and 35 attack

VOTE THERESA MAY

Because your children deserve worse X

seats; the latter, largely Labour, were based mostly on having voted Leave in the referendum, a Remain-voting MP and a substantial 2015 UKIP vote to squeeze.[3] The attack figure was then increased during the campaign, largely on the back of the favourable local election results and the low poll ratings of the Liberal Democrats. One week into the campaign, the list of Labour seats considered 'in play' by the Conservatives included all of the seats in West Yorkshire and Nottinghamshire, all of the seats in Stoke and dozens more. By the end of the campaign, the Conservative digital team were putting out material in 200 constituencies, a remarkably similar number to Labour's. However, these were not all offensive seats. 'The campaign was facing two ways [by the end]', said one of those involved. 'We were being both defensive and very ambitious.' He added: 'The exit poll was a shock, but anyone who says it took them completely by surprise wasn't aware of our data. We knew the outcomes ranged from a hung parliament at one end and the Promised Land at the other.'

Messina's team analysed a raft of political and commercial data to identify the types of voters who might switch to the party in the marginals and these voters were bombarded with direct mail, social media and phone canvassing. In 2015, this had been successful in micro-targeting and capturing Liberal Democrat voters in South West England. The main targets in 2017 were different, including Labour Leave voters and 2015 UKIP supporters, with a Number 10 aide talking about the election being an opportunity to add to the Cameron coalition. But unlike 2015, CCHQ was short of canvass data on such voters and was more reliant on demographic data.

CCHQ support to target seats came in the form of salaries for the short-term employment of a dozen local campaign managers and a free mailshot, as well as the usual centrally created direct mail and digital messaging. The Prime Minister also paid visits, however fleeting, to many of these seats. If Labour optimists were aiming to hold the party's number of seats (and exceed Ed Miliband's vote share in 2015), the Conservatives were bidding to capture Labour seats. A CCHQ strategist commented: 'We know Labour's battleground; it's largely the same as ours.' The knowledge gave him confidence that they were fighting the appropriate target seats.

In Scotland, Labour and the Conservatives were largely left alone by the respective London leaderships. All sides were aware that any hint of influence from Westminster would have played into SNP hands. In truth, neither Labour nor the Conservatives initially had high hopes for Scotland. CTF conducted a single focus group—in the constituency of the Conservatives' sole Scottish MP. The Scottish Labour leader, Kezia Dugdale, distanced herself from the Corbyn agenda, despite polling evidence of his popularity.[4] At the same time, the LOTO team had little faith in Dugdale either.

If Dugdale trailed Corbyn in the popularity stakes in Scotland, Davidson ran ahead of May. Leaving aside Davidson's personal qualities, her support for Trident, tax cuts, remaining in the EU and opposing independence extended her appeal beyond the Conservative core. Where the SNP, aware of the lack of majority support for a second independence referendum, were cautious on the issue, Davidson played the Unionist card with fervour.

For this, Davidson's campaign chief Mark McInnes drew on the polling of Populus' Andrew Cooper and the data analytic work of James Kanagasooriam. The latter's analysis of census data and voting showed that both Labour and the Conservatives had dominant heartlands on what he called a diversity/security model ('diversity' largely equating to ethnic and cultural differences, population density and other factors; 'security' mainly covering income, education, home ownership, health and other factors). Labour polled well in postcode areas scoring high on diversity and low on security, with the Conservatives doing well in areas scoring low on diversity but high on security. Kanagasooriam found that the issue that united likely Tory voters was opposition to a second referendum, and the Conservative campaign material was remorseless in banging the Unionist drum. Early in the campaign, Davidson and McInnes attended a meeting in CCHQ with Textor, Gilbert and Crosby, who joined in for the last few minutes. The meeting was the brainchild of May's chief of staff Fiona Hill, who had wanted to align the Scottish campaign with CTF's south of the border. Hill, apparently acting on her own initiative, did not turn up, and the CCHQ chiefs accepted Davidson's case for a different Scottish focus and a more ambitious campaign.

After the election, a myth developed that Crosby and others in London had been dismissive of Davidson's optimism. While it is true that the very first list of Conservative targets only included the most obviously winnable three or four seats in Scotland, the first wave of research conducted by CCHQ produced much more optimistic findings. McInnes' view was that the Scottish party could win up to 22 seats; at that stage, CCHQ's modelling was producing a similar outcome.

As well as the nine seats the party held, the Liberal Democrats had originally intended to support around 50 seats in any election. These were what they rather grandly called 'Tier 1+ seats', although this was a limited classification, given that there was no Tier 2. The aim was not necessarily to win all 50, but to at least rebuild support in seats 'in which there were signs of life', as well as making some gains. However, very early on in the campaign, they cut 20 of the 50 loose, including Bristol West, Cardiff Central and Manchester Withington—all held by the party until 2015—realising that they were wasting scarce resources. This led to some awkward conversations, as in some cases the central party had recently been urging the local candidates to stand again ('please do it, it'll really help'), followed by another phone call a few days later ('sorry, this isn't working'). At one point during the campaign, the party feared it was going to be wiped out in mainland Britain (see above, p. 166), although by the second half of the campaign, it had 28 seats 'in play' (albeit of varying degrees of seriousness and support) However, there were increasing concerns about Tim Farron's seat in Westmorland & Lonsdale, where canvass returns were poor.[5] The concern was such that an experienced organiser was transferred from Nick Clegg's contest in Sheffield Hallam—where the party thought the seat was relatively safe—to help Farron. The leader was to hang on; the former leader was not.

At the start of the campaign, with Labour apparently in the doldrums, there had been internal arguments about whether the Liberal Democrats should make more of an effort to target Labour-held seats. By the end, however, almost all of the Labour-facing seats were clearly out of contention.[6] Yet other seats, previously thought to be pretty hopeless, came back into play, including Oxford West & Abingdon (always known to party insiders as OxWAb). By the end of the campaign, the internal party estimate was that they might fall as low as three, but rise as high as 13. The result therefore came as a relief.

A serious issue for all the parties was a lack of reliable canvass data, which normally takes years to acquire. In many hitherto safe Labour seats—now targeted by the confident Conservatives—Labour had little voter ID data, both because less than active local parties had not felt the need to collect it in previous elections and because local party workers had often been encouraged to campaign in nearby marginal seats. As one of Labour's field team noted: 'Even if the MP was conscientious and hard-working, these are the sort of places where we have been asking them to send their activists elsewhere.' Equally, the Conservatives were effectively flying blind in many of their target seats, with next to no local organisation or data in many. The snap election meant that there was no time to build up such data and, to make matters worse, the changing nature of support during the campaign—with Labour support rising so dramatically—meant that even canvass data collected at the start of the campaign was often out of date by the end. As one of the Lib Dem team noted after the election: 'Some of our canvasing must have been 100% wrong.'

Lynton Crosby's decision to frame the election as a choice between the Conservative and Labour leaders, a Conservative strength versus a Labour weakness, met with little dissent once the campaign began. Much of the party's campaign literature, social media and canvassing hammered home the merits of May and the dangers of a Corbyn premiership. One senior Conservative MP joked that 'the manifesto should just have a picture of Theresa May on the front, Corbyn on the back'. Centrally designed election leaflets for candidates contained at least three photos of May, two mentions of the key slogan 'Strong, Stable Leadership in the National Interest', a full page on Brexit and only a brief statement from the local candidate who declared that he or she was 'Standing with Theresa May' (also mentioned twice). Other leaflets and posters referred to 'Theresa May's Team' rather than the party.

This emphasis on the Prime Minister may have been CCHQ-generated, but most candidates also initially regarded her as box office. A plan for the election addresses of candidates in target seats to include a photo of May and a message from her was extended after CCHQ was inundated with requests from other candidates to have a photo with the leader and a message on their leaflets. Yet the shortage of space to allow significant local input meant that some election addresses were poorly targeted. The Brexit emphasis, for example, was hardly calculated to appeal to Remain-voting Conservatives. In Remain-voting South West London, for example, one Conservative candidate was given leaflets detailing how Theresa May was going to implement Brexit. 'I can't put this out', he said.

To coincide with the local elections—but carefully chosen so that they also covered key Conservative targets in the general election—the Conservatives purchased four-page wrap-around adverts on a series of local newspapers, from the *Westmorland Gazette* to the *Exeter Express and Echo*, in which the Conservative material replaced the front page. These all carried the slogan 'Theresa May for Britain' and promised the holy trinity of strong and stable leadership, a stronger economy and Brexit.[7] The word 'Conservative' did not appear on the front cover at all. By not mentioning the local candidate, such advertisements came under 'party' (or national) spending limits rather than 'candidate' (local) limits, as did much of the parties' direct mail and social media activity. In the period between the dissolution of Parliament and polling day, candidates are allowed to spend £8,700 plus 6p or 9p per voter depending on whether it is a borough or a county constituency. However, the national limits are much higher, allowing for parties to flood individual constituencies with 'party' material. The parties all privately admit that the distinction is now a flawed one and has been made even worse by the decision of the Electoral Commission to allow material to mention a specific constituency and yet still be classified as national. As one Labour campaigner noted: 'It makes even more of a mockery of the idea of local spending limits than before. But there you go. We will follow the rules, and if they allow us to do it, we will do it.' One Lib Dem staffer noted the irony of increasingly stringent policing of local limits, whilst allowing widespread national spending: 'They police the local expenditure so rigorously now, you can't get away with anything, the sort of tricks all the parties used to do won't fly anymore. Yet you're allowed to spend £100,000 nationally on the same seat. It makes no sense.' Another member of the Lib Dem team worked out that in one week alone, in each of the party's key seats, the party would spend on digital campaigning something close to the whole of that seat's local spending limit.

In recent general elections, a party's central headquarters have distributed questionnaire scripts for canvassers to ask target voters in battleground seats, a sign of the centre's increasing oversight of local campaigning. Conservative scripts would avoid asking directly how the respondent would vote, but would ask other attitudinal questions from which campaigners could deduce which party the voter would support on polling day and which messages would be most likely to work to persuade them. Conservative canvassers were instructed to ask whether Theresa May was a factor in deciding the voter's choice, how important strong leadership was, 'Does Theresa May being leader of the Conservative Party make you more or less likely to vote Conservative?', and to rate the parties on a scale of 1 to 10. They were also told how to introduce themselves: 'I am here on behalf of Theresa May's candidate.' In 2015, a crucial part of the canvassing exercise had been to identify the voter's second preferred party, information that could be used to 'squeeze' UKIP or Liberal Democrat voters who wanted to stop Labour winning a key seat (and Ed Miliband becoming Prime Minister). Such questions were omitted in

2017 both because of time constraints and because CCHQ calculated that the election was now a binary choice between the Conservatives and Labour. For the first half of the campaign, the feedback about voters' attitude to May was positive.

Voters' doorstep reactions to Corbyn were a problem for many Labour candidates and canvassers. Labour candidates reported that Corbyn was liked by some supporters, but they often added that it was a 'struggle' with other voters to make the case for him, given the complaints that he was 'too radical' or 'not a leader', often echoing the attacks of the right-wing press. Within days of the announcement of the election, Andy Burnham, Labour's candidate in the Greater Manchester mayoral election, was taken aback when visiting longstanding party voters who announced they were now 'unsure'. Many other candidates reported similar unsettling feedback. One incumbent MP said she was campaigning with 'a millstone round my neck'. Another recounted being chased down the road by angry Labour voters. A Conservative candidate in the North East was leaving a previously Labour-supporting household when a man followed and holding a finger aloft, said 'Corbyn can swivel on this'.

There developed an understanding, sometimes explicit and sometimes implicit, about how local parties could respond to voters' concerns about Corbyn and distance themselves from him. A strategy note from the party's private pollster recommended: 'Local campaigns should be laser-focused and be about sending local representatives to Westminster to hold Tories to account', and the party's field team helped candidates draw up material in which candidates would be packaged 'as a good local Labour candidate'. This would include canvassers emphasising the need to stop the Tories having too big a majority, voting for the local candidate or even suggesting that there was no chance of Labour winning and Corbyn becoming Prime Minister. One Conservative Facebook ad said: 'A Vote for Labour is a Vote for Jeremy Corbyn', whereas Labour candidates were often keen to stress the opposite. Phil Wilson (Sedgefield) said he was 'for Labour—not Corbyn' and John Woodcock (Barrow & Furness) declared he could not support Corbyn. Ben Bradshaw wrote to his Exeter constituents that the election was not about electing a party leader. Another Labour MP replied to an anti-Corbyn supporter on the doorstep: 'Look, I hate him even more than you.' Candidates' feedback on voters' concerns about the leader (and, frequently, Diane Abbott) forced regional organisers and the campaigners in London to come up with advice which usually took the form of recommending candidates to run on their own merits and that of the manifesto, and to talk around the leadership question. Steve Howell addressed some 160 candidates in a conference call on 17 May and, when asked about how to deal with voters who 'openly criticise' the leader, gave similar advice. One candidate made a recording of the session to a newspaper, which headlined its report as 'Don't Mention Corbyn, Aide Tells Labour Candidates'.[8]

For the first half of the campaign, candidates, particularly where they had been MPs, rarely mentioned Corbyn.[9] 'We are fighting a localised incumbent campaign', said one organiser. Another said: 'Normally, the message to the candidate is: "it's not about you. You are just the representative of the party. We'll help you, but you might think you are the most important person, but it's not the case". Now it's the other way around.' A study of election leaflets revealed that whereas nearly 75% of Conservative leaflets carried a photo of May, less than 5% of Labour's had one of Corbyn.[10] After a day campaigning in Derby North, the Conservative Chairman Sir Patrick McLoughlin came back to CCHQ with one of Chris Williamson's leaflets. 'Look, I've found one!' he exclaimed—meaning a Labour leaflet featuring a picture of Corbyn. Corbyn figured more prominently in Conservative Facebook ads and local election addresses, as well as in the air war.

Campaign resources are, in the words of one party staffer, 'stickier' than many commentators realise and are harder to adjust quickly to the changing fortunes of a campaign. Personnel are especially hard to shift. 'If you try to move staff, you've got a real political problem', said one Labour staffer. 'If that person wins, they will forever claim they won despite you. If they lose, they will have lost because of you.' At the other end of the spectrum, social media advertising can be adjusted very quickly—one of several advantages it has over conventional campaigning material. Direct mail and leaflets fall somewhere in between. Much of the printed campaign material was produced early on in the campaign, and by the end, with May less of an asset and Corbyn attracting enthusiastic crowds, no doubt different material would have been produced. One Conservative candidate is convinced that he only saved his seat because his agent locked the centrally produced material—all about May—in a car and refused to give people access to it. Still, it is striking how few members even of the Shadow Cabinet had a photo of their leader on any their campaign material. As one of the Southside team remarked after the result: 'How many candidates in winnable seats can you find who put pictures of Jeremy on

their leaflets? It wasn't just us who thought he was an electoral liability…
We weren't making this stuff up.'

In recent elections, the parties have become aware of the so-called
incumbency bonus, where first-term MPs outperform their party. This was
notable for the Conservative Party in 2015. New MPs tend to work harder
and hope to build up a personal vote. The trend was evident again.
Appendix 1 (see below, p. 459) shows that where a Labour MP had first
been elected in 2015 and stood again, his or her vote share increased by
an average of 3.6 percentage points more than a Labour MP first elected
in 2010 or earlier. For a Conservative MP first elected in 2015, the average
extra gain was 2.4 points. The short Parliament meant that there had been
little earlier central input to such seats in terms of leafleting and targeting
of voters; the new MPs had been left largely to their own devices. Yet even
in two years, they had managed to build up a personal vote.

Candidates usually look forward to a party's manifesto as something
they can present as an additional reason for voters to back them. Labour
campaigners claimed that voters appeared enthused by the party's offer-
ings of higher taxes on the better-off, public ownership of privatised utili-
ties, and protecting pensioner benefits. 'We had something positive to talk
about to voters', said one candidate in a marginal seat. This was useful
ammunition for the Momentum activists visiting seats; often lacking local
knowledge, they could promote relevant policies during discussions with
voters. As already noted from the day when the manifesto was launched,
Conservative campaigners found themselves on the defensive, particularly
over the social care package. A senior CCHQ figure later complained: 'We
had been making converts from Labour until the manifesto. Our feedback
from the regional officers and our phone canvassing showed that the converts suddenly stopped.' Other Conservative activists complained that the
policies on school lunches, and means-testing of some pensioner benefits
and social care all fed into the image of the Tories as 'nasty', and one
added that 'we had no offers to make on the doorstep'. A consultant at
CCHQ said: 'We gave up trying to get moderate Labour voters.'[11]

The snap election presented a challenge for organisers of the party leaders' visits. Usually the leader's staff visit target seats well in advance to liaise
with the local candidate, choose suitable venues such as schools and hospitals for events, line up media coverage, arrange the leader's transport,

including aircraft, and liaise with security. There was much less time to do this on the scale of previous campaigns. For both leaders, some visits were arranged on the same day. Visits cover a range of activities, from a five-minute visit for a local newspaper interview to a full afternoon or evening rally. The preparations, criss-crossing the country, and media engagements take up a good part of the leader's day, but parties are still convinced that, when combined with TV coverage, the visits are an effective means of delivering a national message.

Organisers usually welcomed the visits, although some complained of their disruptive effects on the local campaign when they were made nearer to polling day.[12] May visited, however briefly, 73 constituencies, 43 of them held by other parties, mostly Labour; many of the latter were in the North and the Midlands and had voted Leave in the referendum. Yet just six of those she visited were won by the party: three from Labour and three from the SNP. On 6 and 7 June, for example, she made hurried visits to ten seats, eight of them held by Labour and two by the Conservatives, a reflection of the plan to make gains from Labour. But just one Labour seat, Stoke-on-Trent South, was captured. There was no difference in the rise (from 2015) in the Conservative share of the vote between seats May visited and seats she did not.[13] At the end of the campaign, May pointedly asked her CCHQ strategists why they had sent her to so many of the seats for such a poor return—and not to those which Labour were to capture. The May camp's view about the seats selected by Messina and CTF was blunt: 'The data were wrong.'

As noted earlier, May's visits were often small-scale and tightly controlled; Corbyn, by contrast, had made a point of addressing gatherings of supporters around the country before the election—an approach he carried into the campaign. His office manager Karie Murphy liaised with local Momentum contacts to spread the word about his visits, often selected at short notice, and to areas of strong local activity, but often avoiding seats in which the local candidate was thought to be opposed to the leader. A number of Labour MPs declined offers of a Corbyn visit to their constituencies (and after the events at the beginning of the campaign, not all Lib Dem candidates wanted a visit from Tim Farron either). This ensured good crowds and positive coverage for the regional and local media, covering a range of seats. Murphy used Momentum to outflank what she regarded as Southside's defensive strategy of not attacking Conservative seats, often working independently of the regional organisers. On a wall in Corbyn's office was a large snake-like map of all the places he was visiting.

Party leaders' visits can boost supporters' morale, contribute to a 'feel-good' mood and generate good pictures for television; a Corbyn aide described the rallies as 'life-affirming' and a Momentum member talked of campaigning now being about 'big rallies and making great videos'. Alex Nunns' insider account of the Corbyn and Momentum visits plausibly claims that they 'gave a psychological boost to the movement on the ground' and enhanced Corbyn's image.[14] However, it is possible to exaggerate their effect in switching votes. The enthusiastic crowds at the rallies led some to claim that there had been a 'Corbyn effect' and a significant increase in the Labour vote in the seats he visited.[15] Of the 30 seats Labour gained, Corbyn visited 13. Yet even allowing for the conflation of causation and correlation, there was in fact very little visible effect in terms of votes; the difference in the rise in Labour's vote share between seats visited and not visited was less than 1%.[16] It is likely that the voters attending the rallies were predominantly already party supporters rather than swing voters.

There have been similar bold claims made for the role of Momentum. Using the group's My Nearest Marginal website, activists could key in their postcode and be directed to their nearest marginal seat. The site also listed campaign events, mobile phone numbers for local party organisers, and contacts for car sharing. Momentum claimed that over 100,000 used the software during the campaign and hosted canvassing workshops for volunteers. Volunteers from the Bernie Sanders team visited from the US to conduct seminars on the lessons they had learnt from their work in the 2016 Democrat presidential primaries. They advised activists about the importance of striking a relationship with the voters and talking about the issues which interested them rather than box-ticking a list of questions. Its members flooded seats such as Leeds North West, Derby North, Croydon Central, Hampstead & Kilburn, Sheffield Hallam and Lancaster & Fleetwood, all of which were to fall to Labour. In Derby North, Chris Williamson, a Corbyn supporter, fought and won on an anti-austerity message and regarded his campaign as a 'test case' for the leader's politics.[17] Momentum claimed that 25 of the 30 non-Labour seats it targeted were captured.[18] Yet there were also big swings to Labour in seats where the Labour candidate was overtly hostile to Corbyn. Joan Ryan in Enfield North achieved a 9% swing, Wes Streeting in Ilford North 8.5%, Chuka Umunna in Streatham 9.5%, Chris Matheson in Chester 8% and Peter Kyle in Hove 15%. It is, as that list illustrates, very difficult to differentiate the Momentum effect from the more general London/Remain vote effect across the country, as well as the campaigning efforts of candidates and their party members and supporters.

The Conservatives had nothing similar. In 2015, the party co-chairman Grant Shapps had utilised the party's youth wing Conservative Future to send young party workers on his Battlebus 2015 into marginal seats. But the group was closed down after scandals, including allegations of bullying leading to the suicide of a young activist and incorrect declarations of election expenses. According to one Number 10 official, the combination of charges hanging over candidates at the start of the campaign and the uncertainty as to whether spending should be charged to local or national accounts had left CCHQ 'cowed'. Already short of activists, the Conservative Party had no replacement for the Battlebus. Within Labour and the Liberal Democrats—both of which had experienced large increases in membership—there were also issues, with members being inexperienced and keen to help but unsure of the best way to campaign. One Lib Dem local constituency party in London, largely run by post-Brexit arrivals, decided to have its post-election drinks party at 7 pm on polling day, as none of them knew they were supposed to continue campaigning until the polls had closed.

Faced by Labour's 500,000-plus members, the Conservatives (estimated at some 100,000 members, with four in ten aged over 65) were in any case always going to be outgunned on the ground. Yet a study of the campaign activities of party members reports that most relative levels of activity within parties were down on 2015.[19] Some organisers talked of 'election fatigue', with the election following on the referendum and local elections all within 12 months. Another factor may have been the lack of time to make adequate preparations. Approximately a third of Conservative, Labour and SNP members claimed to have done some leafleting. For canvassing by phone or face to face, the figure was around a quarter. Nearly half displayed a poster, with the SNP (two-thirds) leading the way, followed by Labour and the Liberal Democrats (a half) and the Conservatives (a quarter). Around a quarter of Conservatives and UKIP members admitted they had not been active at all in the campaign, compared to less than 10% for Labour and the SNP. Labour's larger membership, combined with their higher activity rate, meant that overall there was noticeably more activity by Labour members, and in absolute terms Labour's campaigning was up on 2015. One study multiplied the average number of separate types of activities claimed by each party by its total number of members: Labour members led the way, by far, with over 1.3 million 'activities', followed by 323,000 for the SNP (within Scotland), 264,000 for the Liberal Democrats and only 262,000 for the Conservatives.[20]

Table 12.1, drawing on data from the British Election Study (BES), gives the view from the voters' perspective. It shows the type and extent of campaigning that voters claim they received from the parties. The study asked about six types of contact, from phone calls to social media. The parties are sceptical about the absolute values in such data, suggesting that such self-reporting almost certainly under-estimates levels of contact; even in the most marginal constituencies, in which every voter will have received multiple forms of contact from the parties, the percentage reporting doing so is always remarkably low. But the data are still useful in relative terms, allowing us to compare different types of contact across the parties and across different elections.

Voters' reported contacts were down across the board from 2015. Overall, 39% of voters claimed to have received some contact from one or more of the parties, a figure that is noticeably lower than the 52% who reported hearing from the parties two years before, despite the 2017 campaign being longer. This pattern was similar across all of the parties. In 2015, for example, 43% said they had heard from Labour, down to 29% in 2017, and there are similar falls—less dramatic in the case of Plaid Cymru and unsurprisingly much more dramatic in the case of UKIP—for every party listed in the table. As in previous elections, the importance played by

Table 12.1 Types of voter contact during the campaign (%)

	Con	Lab	LD	SNP	PC	UKIP	Green
	1	2	1	2	1	–	–
A leaflet/letter delivered to your home	25	26	15	33	22	4	4
A visit to your home	3	6	2	7	4	–	–
Contact in the street	1	2	1	4	1	–	–
Email	4	6	2	6	2	–	1
Social media (e.g., Facebook, Twitter)	2	4	1	4	2	–	–
Overall	27	29	16	36	24	4	5
On day	2	5	1	5	2	–	–

Source: BES, Wave 13, weighted. Polling conducted 9–23 June. The figures in each row do not sum to the overall figure because some people may have been contacted in more than one way; figures for the SNP and Plaid Cymru (PC) are for Scotland and Wales only respectively; the final row relates to a different question, 'Thinking about those parties that contacted you, did any of them do so on the day of the election?'; – indicates >0 and <1.0

leaflets and letters as a method of communication is striking. Indeed, for UKIP and the Greens, they are basically the sole method of communication noticed by voters. Even here, though, the level reported was lower than two years before for all the parties. The most impressive levels of such contact once again were achieved by the SNP, within Scotland, although on almost every measure, they were still less than at their 2015 peak. Analysis of the contents of Labour leaflets shows that health, the economy and education, in that order, were the most frequently mentioned (all over 70%). Just over half mentioned Brexit. For the Conservatives, the most frequently mentioned topics were the economy, followed by Brexit and health. For the Liberal Democrats, it was health, followed by Brexit and the economy. UKIP's leading issue was, predictably, immigration and for the Greens, also predictably, the environment.[21]

The lack of any marked differences between Labour and the Conservatives here may be surprising, given the reports of a massive ground campaign by Labour as a result of the large expansion in its membership and the Momentum effect. In part, this may be a methodological issue.[22] The BES data, for example, do not distinguish between a leaflet delivered by hand and one delivered by a contractor; nor do they measure the quantity of material received or the number of conversations with canvassers. It may also be that such data under-estimate the work done by groups such as Momentum, distinct from but working with Labour, although we are sceptical as to whether large numbers of respondents—faced with a knock at the door from a stranger—would have drawn much of a distinction.

That said, there are some signs of the effects of Labour's operation in the data, particularly on the more labour-intensive measures of activity, at least within England and Wales. On canvassing, for example, 3% of respondents said they had had a visit from the Conservatives, compared to 6% for Labour. The figures for contact on the street and telephone calls (although some of the latter work can be contracted out) are also higher for Labour. Moreover, the final row reports a separate question about being contacted by the parties on the day—another labour-intensive activity. Although the absolute figures are low, albeit higher in marginal seats, more than twice as many people recall being contacted by Labour on election day as by the Conservatives. Indeed, according to the BES data, Labour contacted more voters on the day of the election than all the other British political parties combined. The figure for the SNP (5% within Scotland) equals Labour's in relative size, even if it is obviously smaller in absolute terms.

Rates of voter contact in marginal seats were, as expected, higher. In marginal seats, with majorities of 10% or less, almost 60% of people said they were contacted by at least one of the parties; in seats with majorities of 20% or more, that figure fell to 39%. Similarly, on polling day, in marginal seats 5% of voters were contacted by the Conservatives and 10% by Labour. This chimes with estimates from a survey of party agents, which found Labour had twice as many campaign workers as the Conservatives in marginal seats—including twice as many on polling day.[23] The assessment in that study of the impact of local campaigning is that it produced a significant electoral benefit for Labour, enough to have gained them at least 20 seats, compared to what would have been likely to occur had they campaigned at a minimal level. On this basis, then, the ground war probably prevented a Conservative majority government.

Signing up supporters for postal votes is now a major part of campaign activity, as parties know that they are more likely to be returned than conventional votes. Although not counted before polling day, postal votes are opened for verification, which gives party observers a clue as to how well the campaign is going.[24] For most of the campaign, feedback from postal votes gave the Conservatives no reason to be concerned, nor Labour any reason to hope. Even allowing for the differential nature of postal voters—who tend to be older on average—things were looking bad for Labour in most constituencies.[25] 'In some coal mining seats', reported one of Labour's staffers, 'there was a 20% swing away from us'. Polling companies, who monitor but are not allowed by law to report figures for those who have voted by post, also found heavy Conservative support amongst postal votes. ComRes, for example, had a 16-point Conservative lead among postal voters even in early June. Only right at the end of the campaign did the Conservatives (and the pollsters) note any signs of postal votes becoming more pro-Labour.[26]

A week before polling day, Jim Messina's analysis had Labour to fall to 207 seats, with the Conservatives on course to win 371. Even then, there were some concerning signs, especially in London. Battersea and Croydon Central were already identified as probable losses to Labour. Both Putney and Kensington were seen as very tight—with just one point between the parties in both—and other seats in London such as Ealing Central & Acton, which should have been marginal, were clearly going to stay Labour. A member of the Conservative targeting team noted later: 'We knew Kensington was an issue from a long way out.' However, one of the other big surprise results of election night—Canterbury—was more of a shock, since at this point the Conservative modelling had it to be held with a majority of over 20%. But the party still seemed on course to take almost 30 Labour-held seats—mostly in the North and the Midlands. They included constituencies such as Durham North West, Bassetlaw, Rother Valley, Hartlepool and Ashfield. Expected Conservative gains included some totemic places covering both New and Old Labour, such as Sedgefield (Tony Blair's former seat) and Bolsover (Dennis Skinner's constituency). Although Labour's two campaign coordinators, Andrew Gwynne (Denton & Reddish) and Ian Lavery (Wansbeck), were now regarded as safe, the predicted Conservative gains at this point included Jon Trickett's Hemsworth. The Conservatives also expected to make seven gains from the Liberal Democrats, almost wiping out the party in the House of Commons, including taking Westmorland & Lonsdale. Expected Conservative gains from the Lib Dems at this point also included Sheffield Hallam and Leeds North West, both of which were indeed lost by the Lib Dems—but to Labour. However, in addition to over-estimating Conservative success in England and Wales, Messina's modelling also under-estimated the forthcoming Conservative advance in Scotland; at this point, it was predicting just five Conservative gains from the SNP instead of the 12 that did occur.

Labour's overall feedback was gloomy, although more positive in London. The views reported by many long-established MPs, union organisers and party workers were largely downbeat, with one forecasting 'a nuclear winter' outside of London.[27] Labour's deputy leader Tom Watson campaigned across 50 seats. The feedback he received replicated what was being conveyed to headquarters. 'Overwhelmingly it was negative. Virtually all of the candidates thought they would lose and so did we', said one of his aides. Yet many Labour marginals that had been written off were held, often with increased majorities. In both main parties, experienced directors of local campaigning were left dumbfounded by the result, as were many candidates, some of whom had no idea what was happening until the ballot boxes began to be opened. If feedback to Labour headquarters had been too optimistic in 2015, it now turned out to be too pessimistic. Reflecting on the error, one Labour organiser noted that the reliability of canvassing from election to election 'is undermined now when there is so much volatility'. Labour's canvassing was too negative essentially because it focused on people who had previously voted Labour (many of whom were not now doing so), but missed those who had not backed Labour before (or in some cases any parties) and who were now voting Labour. As another said, the parties missed those 'about whom we had no prior information'. This judgement was echoed by many other Labour campaigners.

Yet Labour complaints were as nothing compared to Conservative criticisms. On ConservativeHome, Mark Wallace presented a devastating account of how the targeting of voters and constituencies went awry, with party workers sent to people who were never going to vote Conservative and away from seats that were presumed safe but were lost in a vain attempt to capture seats which remained Labour, often with increased majorities.[28] One of those involved in CCHQ said: 'Overly optimistic targeting does appear to have stretched resources of all kinds (from doorstep campaigners right through to where our Facebook ads went) far too thin and left us potentially speaking to the wrong people in the wrong constituencies.' Another said: 'We were too specific. The level of granularity we ended up in 2015 was the level we began with in 2017; there is a point at which you become too specific, and you lose sight of the bigger picture.' This misdirection of some party workers combined with local dissatisfaction with the national campaign and the inadequate consultation angered some local associations. The contrast with two years before was stark. On polling day in 2015, Amber Rudd had been given a list of constituents who had said they would vote Conservative if they spoke to her in person. She travelled around her constituency, ticking them off the list, each one promising their support after they had had some of her time. In 2017, the party was not even sending people to the right seats.

One telling example of how parties are often working with imperfect information comes from election day itself, where Lib Dem feedback from polling station tellers had both of the two neighbouring constituencies of Twickenham and Richmond Park too close to call. The former went on to be won by almost 10,000 votes, the latter was lost by 45. Had the information been more accurate, the party could have easily redeployed activists across the constituency border, almost certainly gaining an extra seat.

The role of social media in elections has been steadily increasing; in 2015, it had been more significant than in 2010, and in 2017, its impact was greater again. The advantages for political parties are obvious. Parties can contact thousands of voters, persuade users to donate money, pledge to volunteer and share messages with friends; they can respond to events and changes in public mood quickly and, perhaps above all, relatively inexpensively. As one of Labour's field team noted: 'This is another election where there has been a real shift in how we conduct elections... You can get a lot of impressions for the cost of a direct mail.'[29] Given the decline of press readership, especially among the young, the new forms of social media are a way for politicians to communicate with a group which has hitherto been difficult to reach. For minor parties, it can overcome their neglect by the mass media and for Corbyn's team in particular, it was an alternative outlet to the largely hostile mainstream press.[30]

The lesson of the 2015 election appeared to be that what worked best online was highly targeted paid advertising and that there were limits to what could be achieved simply by letting supporters share content. While users are more likely to engage with content shared with trusted or close friends, whereas paid content is more likely to be regarded as advertising and usually generates less engagement, such 'organic' reach could not guarantee that material reached the right people at the right time. It may be free, but it may not be effective. As one Labour internal briefing document noted dryly: 'The issues that motivate and inspire Labour Party supporters to back the Labour Party are not always the issues which persuade undecided electors that voting Labour is the right choice for them.' Yet just two years later, the 2017 election appeared to overturn much of this wisdom. Conservative targeting appeared much less successful, whilst Labour enjoyed considerable success as a result of material shared peer to peer.

In part, this was because the Conservative digital operation was less polished. As in 2015, the party relied on Craig Elder and Tom Edmonds. But whereas before 2015, the two had been able to build up their own digital team, this time they had to work with one largely recruited by CCHQ. In 2015, they had been able to draw on at least 18 months of preparation, in which they had had time to test video and messaging, as well as to build up data from emails and doorstep conversations. In 2017, they returned, only to find that almost none of the necessary preparatory work had been done; the subsequent digital campaign, one noted, was 'like driving the car at the same time as you are building it'.[31] They also knew that they began firmly in second place; Corbyn already had three times as many followers as May on platforms such as Facebook and Twitter.

The CCHQ team continued to regard Facebook, in the words of one, as 'the bread and butter of digital communications'. They also found preroll ads on YouTube (which appear before video is played) and Google AdWords extremely useful. (Over half of those who saw a Conservative ad explaining the 'dementia tax' clicked through for further information—although this may reflect just how worried many people were by the issue.) Twitter was much less useful ('garbage', as one Tory put it). Defenders of the operation can point to some local successes, including its effectiveness in repelling a potential Lib Dem resurgence in the South West and winning votes in Scotland (albeit under the direction of the Scottish campaign). One video attacking Corbyn's record on defence policy attracted over eight million views and was, the team claimed, 'the most watched video in British political history'. The Conservatives' digital team found that images featuring Diane Abbott as part of the 'coalition of chaos' were more widely shared than images with other politicians. ('It's crazy', said one of the Conservatives' staff. 'She's the Shadow Home Secretary. How is that a Coalition of Chaos? But it worked'.)

Conservative critics of the party's digital operation have argued that it was too negative and leader-focused, although this was the campaign strategy. Theresa May's Facebook account issued largely positive messages, particularly on Brexit, and left the party's main page to transmit attack messages. 'The Conservatives' videos', wrote one journalist, 'didn't offer people a reason to share other than they supported May.'[32] Their material was much less often shared, or liked, but in itself this did not overly matter—as long as they were targeting the right voters.

In 2015, the Conservatives had managed to carry out much of this activity largely unnoticed. Their success then made life harder in 2017 because—helped by sites such as Who Targets Me—journalists now reported the digital campaign in real time. Digital staff on all sides of the political divide were frustrated by much of the coverage, which often had a tendency to be over the top and conspiratorial (with talk of 'dark ads', a phrase which usually just meant 'ads'). Campaigners were particularly annoyed by much of the coverage of Cambridge Analytica's activities during the Brexit referendum, after which the company had boasted about the sophistication of its targeting. As one digital campaigner noted, companies were 'significantly over claiming'. Another, from a rival party, commented that: 'People now expect miracles, and digital campaigning can't deliver miracles. And if you do believe it, it makes us look like Bond Villains.'

After the 2015 election, the Labour digital team had looked on in some frustration as the Conservatives were lavished with praise for the sophistication of their operation; Labour staffers believed they had been doing essentially the same, just with far lower resources.[33] A widespread myth developed that Labour had spent just £16,000 on Facebook advertising in 2015 because the election receipts contained just one invoice from Facebook; the reality was that Labour bought most of their digital advertising through intermediaries, especially data companies, in much the same way that most of us do not buy our household products direct from Procter & Gamble—and this significantly under-estimated Labour's spend on social media. But still, the party knew it had been outgunned digitally in 2015 and had spent too long talking to its base and not enough time engaging with floating voters. After the election, it split its digital operation into two, an outward-facing team, led by Tom Lavelle, and a supporters' mobilisation team, led by Ben Nolan. In addition, the LOTO operation ran Corbyn's separate social media operation. Labour had been slowly developing its digital operation, including using the London mayoral elections to test some techniques. Like the Conservatives, their work was dominated by Facebook, because of its reach and ease of use, although they also used other platforms more than the Conservatives, including pre-roll adverts (for which the optimum duration is 30 seconds). Of Labour's total digital spend of £1.2 million, around half was spent on Facebook. Their big innovation in 2017 was Snapchat, which the Conservatives had experimented with but soon abandoned when the results were so poor ('we realised that didn't work even quicker than Twitter', as one of the Conservative digital team put it). By contrast, Labour's Snapchat filter—allowing people to share photos with a message saying they were voting Labour—had 36 million views and was used by a total of 7.7 million people. Each use cost Labour just £0.004. Labour also ran Snap Ads as polling day reminders; of the 1.2 million people who visited their polling station finder—which gave everyone a personalised visit to their nearest polling station—half came via Snapchat. On polling day itself, the party used Twitter's First View service—which allows organisations to ensure their tweet is the first in anyone's feed—to remind people to vote.[34]

One of Labour's team believed there was a false distinction drawn between paid online campaigning and organic spread. 'Last time, it was all about paid advertising', they said. 'But it's not really either/or. Paid and organic reach are complementary.' Perhaps the best example of this came from Labour's investment at the beginning of the campaign to expand the reach of their Facebook page, which was done largely through paid advertising. Spending around £35,000, Labour added around 230,000 followers to their Facebook page (another 220,000 joined during the campaign organically). Once people had liked the page, this then increased the reach of any further publicity, because once someone on Facebook has liked a page, it increases the number of adverts that can be pushed at them, and whenever they like an advert, their friends will see it, which they hope works by association. In the final ten days of the campaign, Labour claim that an astonishing 23 million people saw their Facebook page.

A key part of Labour's approach was its Promote software, work on which was completed just days before the election was called and which facilitated local campaigns in purchasing Facebook advertising. Promote represented a deliberate break with the approach the party had taken in 2015, when targeting was directed from the centre. Many of those involved with it worried that it had not been sufficiently road-tested for the rigours of a campaign, and there were some early teething problems as well as a lack of time to train people in how best to use it.[35] It contained models of voter types and the Southside data team developed generic messages for local parties to use in targeting messages to particular groups. It did not enable local activists to do very much they theoretically could not already do, but there was a recognition within the campaign team that the process of buying online adverts was complicated, that most people do not know how best to do it and—unlike, say, a local print shop when producing a leaflet or direct mail—there is no obvious place to go to ask for help.[36] Some constituency parties used it extensively, while others did not, but local feedback was generally positive.[37]

Promote was especially useful for A/B testing—sending different versions of ads, emails and graphics to samples of voters to see which attracted the greatest response. It could send five different images, with five different texts, targeting five different groups, which automatically generated 125 different markets, allowing campaigners to track different metrics within different groups. Indeed, as well as its local use, Labour also ran much of their national social media advertising through Promote because of the ease with which A/B testing could be carried out. Promote was fundamentally just a media-buying tool, originally designed by a private sector company to help organisations like pizza restaurants target their online ads, although it required some development and reskinning before it could be used for politics. ('Political parties are the only people who care what constituency you live in', as one of those involved put it. 'Tesco's don't.') It suited Southside's localist strategy. Braced for attacks on the Labour leadership, they had assumed they would require more advertising than normal to mention the candidate's name, which would automatically come under local expenditure, and so they needed a mechanism to enable local parties to campaign online. As one official explained at the start of the campaign: 'The leader isn't exactly our strongest card, so we can't talk about him', but, instancing the Labour MP for Gedling, 'They can't get away with saying Vernon Coaker is a security risk, because no one believes that.'

When Jeremy Corbyn is asked about the election, he is always keen to stress the role of what he calls 'the outriders', those groups who were Labour- or Corbyn-supporting but not formally affiliated.[38] In terms of the ground operation, the most significant of these was Momentum, but online there were dozens of others, some groups, some merely individuals, working to support Labour, and who achieved quite phenomenal levels of contact, often for negligible amounts of money. They included groups such as 38 Degrees, the People's Assembly Against Austerity, Hope not Hate, trade unions and charities.[39] In addition, LOTO amplified its messages by working closely with alt-left sites like The Canary, Novara Media, Evolve Politics and Skwawkbox, written by sympathetic journalists and bloggers. The organic reach of such groups was massive in 2017, far outstripping anything seen in 2015, and it was almost all Labour-supporting. As one Conservative campaigner said: 'Before the next campaign we need to figure out who our friends are. We can't go into another one relying on just the Taxpayers' Alliance and the Countryside Alliance. Seven weeks before an election, you can't just find some more friends.'

These groups campaigned with verve and imagination, pushing boundaries in a way that political parties would have been wary of doing. For precisely this reason, Labour's digital team deliberately kept a fairly hands-off approach with outriders, although links with LOTO were well established. Momentum produced the most striking video of the campaign: 'Daddy why do you hate me?' It was widely shared and viewed more than seven million times. The video, a mock-party election broadcast, shows a father discussing life in 'Tory Britain' in 2030 with his young daughter. The girl asks why her school meals aren't free, why class sizes are so big, whether she can go to university—and why he got all of this and yet she does not. When he replies: 'Because I voted for Theresa May', the girl asks: 'Dad, do you hate me?' 'Obviously', he replies. 'VOTE THERESA MAY', said one graphic. 'Because your children deserve worse.' The outriders were also able to reach groups that political parties would traditionally struggle with, as with the #grimeforcobyn movement, with grime artists supporting Corbyn and encouraging voter registration amongst the young.[40] They also promoted stories that might otherwise not have been picked up—such as the ivory ban, LGBT policies and fox hunting—all of which were significant stories on social media, but were largely ignored in the mainstream media.

These highly partisan blogs and groups could never compete with the sheer weight of the anti-Labour and anti-Corbyn coverage in much of the national press, but they had a greater viral impact than the mainstream media. A study by BuzzFeed revealed the very limited sharing of the stories on Twitter and Facebook from the Conservative-supporting press. Those pieces that were shared were predominantly anti-Corbyn and anti-Labour; the most popular was the charge that Labour's mooted land value tax would result in homeowners paying a 'garden tax'. By contrast, there was significantly more sharing of stories from the alt-left sites that were more supportive of Labour policies and Corbyn.[41] The most viral piece of the whole election was on Facebook and was Another Angry Voice's 'How many of Jeremy Corbyn's policies do you actually disagree with?'[42]

Much of the political messaging on social media was, as expected, to the already converted; this was the very opposite of targeted campaigning, but its reach was so wide that this did not especially matter, and in a campaign where the key battlegrounds were shifting, it was beneficial not to be micro-targeting. When you are trying to hit a moving target, a shotgun is not a bad weapon to have.

There is little doubt about Labour's victory on the social media front.[43] An analysis of the conversations on social media outlets (largely on Twitter) by Impact Social showed that positive comments about May hardly rose (from 9% to 10%), but negative ones climbed from 14% to 30%; she suffered from missing the leaders' debate as well as the party's policies on social care and supporting a free vote on ending the ban on fox hunting (anti-hunting ads often featured a charming picture of a fox). Although Corbyn never overtook May in the opinion polls on preferred choice for Prime Minister, the balance between his positive and negative conversations moved in the former direction, while the opposite was the case for May. In CCHQ, Messina's team were conducting a similar operation, called 'social listening', to measure the momentum of the campaign. They found voters expressing concern over police cuts, particularly after the Manchester and London attacks, and the manifestoes.[44]

Other studies show that of the top 20 most popular political subjects talked about on Facebook, most of the topics referring to Labour and Corbyn were supportive, while six out of the seven most popular topics about the Conservatives were negative. The BuzzFeed News Social Barometer reported the frequency of viral stories about Corbyn, the NHS and fox hunting, but almost nothing about how the parties would approach Brexit. On social media, at least, this was not a Brexit election.[45]

Yet claims by social media cheerleaders that it was better at detecting the political trends and patterns than the opinion polls go too far. After all, the polls also reported the rise in support for Labour and Corbyn and mounting dissatisfaction with the Conservative campaign.[46] The figures in Table 12.1 also put some of the claims in perspective. The highest figure for contact—by Labour and the SNP—was just 4%, significantly lower than most traditional forms of campaigning.[47] A separate survey conducted by Harold Clarke and colleagues generated broadly similar recall for the more conventional measures of campaigning, but larger measures of 'electronic' contact than the BES, with Labour outperforming the other parties: 12.5% of respondents were contacted 'electronically' by Labour, close to double the 6.8% who said they were contacted by the Conservatives.[48] With the Clarke et al. data, this type of contact was more important than home visits, although mostly still a considerable way behind leaflets and letters.[49]

In total, some 10% of people during the campaign claimed to have seen information put out by parties or candidates on Facebook.[50] Some 20% claimed to have seen political information shared by someone they knew personally and 12% by people other commentators, journalists or activists. In total, 28% saw some political content on Facebook. Another 42% used Facebook, but said that they did not use it for politics—although just because you may not use Facebook for politics, politics may still use Facebook for you.[51]

One in ten said that they had shared political content on Facebook (and 5% had done so on Twitter). They were not a representative sample of the electorate.[52] As shown in Table 12.2, Labour and SNP supporters were much more likely to have done so than Conservative supporters. This was largely not a consequence of their age or lack of technological sophistication.[53] It is not that Conservatives are much less likely to use social media, but that they are much less likely to use social media for politics. As Table 12.2 shows, Conservative voters were also significantly less likely to display a poster or to try to convince other people how to vote. Almost a quarter of Labour voters claim to have done the last, nearly three times the figure for Conservative voters.

Table 12.2   Political activities by voters during the campaign (%)

	Con	Lab	LD	SNP	PC	UKIP	Green
Displayed an election poster	1	6	4	7	11	2	5
Tried to persuade somebody which party they should vote for	8	22	17	19	14	7	10
Done any work on behalf of a political party or action group	1	3	3	3	6	1	2
Shared political content on Facebook	5	18	12	21	12	6	11
Shared political content on Twitter	2	9	7	9	7	2	7

Source: BES, Wave 12, weighted. Polling conducted 5 May–7 June 2017

Yet for all the attention and the influence attributed to digital operations, the party expenditure on social media still lags behind direct mail and, notably in the case of CCHQ, market research. Analysis of social media trends by Laurence Stellings at Populus during the campaign (covering the most-used hashtags on Twitter, top search trends on Google and biggest-trending videos on YouTube) are sobering. His daily tracker of the biggest stories on each social network trends showed that politics and the election gained traction on Twitter, but had little presence on YouTube or Google.[54] As with much exposure to political communications, the new media often reinforce rather than change attitudes. Supporters are likely to follow their party's politicians, commentators and thinkers on Twitter and interpret stories, campaigns and images in ways that reinforce their views. According to a YouGov survey, British voters still get more of their political news from traditional media (television and newspapers) and credit it with more influence on how they vote than social media. Compared to the 60% mentioning the BBC, just 15% mention Facebook, 8% Twitter and 4% BuzzFeed. Age is a big divide in responses, with social media mentioned more frequently by 18–24 year olds (unsurprisingly), although even among that group, more of them still use traditional news sources. When asked about media that influenced them, television (42%) and newspapers and magazines (32%) were ranked ahead of social media (26%) as influencing their vote in 2017, although half of 18–24 year olds claimed that social media influenced them, only narrowly trailing television.[55]

Labour's remarkable campaign effort was also not without its critics, largely about the professional staff in Southside. Supporters of the Corbyn campaign complained they had been let down by the initial negative posture of Southside—defending seats rather than trying to make gains from the Conservatives. 'It was defeatist and we should have poured resources into attacking Tory seats and we could have got another thirty seats', said one of the LOTO team. Writing in *Jacobin*, Frederick Cotton had Southside in mind when he complained that 'key powerbrokers in the party prevented them [Labour] from winning'.[56]

Yet there is some retrospective wisdom at work here; some candidates who claimed post-election that the party should have spent more resources attacking Tory seats had been saying the opposite early on in the campaign. When the list of target seats was first compiled, Labour were trailing badly in private and public polls, and the pessimism was confirmed by much local and regional feedback and then by poor local election results. Andrew Gwynne was heard in Labour headquarters early on in the campaign warning that the aim was to save as many Labour seats as possible. Several of those who have since gone public to argue that Labour should have been fighting a more offensive campaign were calling for more aid to be given to their own (defensive) seats, even during the later stages of the campaign. One Southsider, when challenged about why they had not initially adopted a more offensive targeting strategy, suggested looking at the freepost electoral communications, sent out on behalf of each candidate, and which had to be signed off in early to mid-May: 'You weren't saying all this in May!' The sharp disagreement between LOTO and the Southside staff about the campaign and how it could have been more successful meant that the two sides could not present an agreed internal report on the lessons of the 2017 election.

One striking feature of the election was the large number of candidates who claimed that they had not enjoyed the campaign. Aside from 'election fatigue', a significant element was the scale of allegations by candidates, campaigners and their families of harassment, including online abuse and intimidation. Apart from the rise in recent years of aggressive internet trolling, the killing of the Labour MP Jo Cox in 2016 had heightened fears about safety even before the campaign began. The complaints variously covered racist, anti-Semitic, misogynistic and Islamophobic messages, threats of death or sexual violence, and the defacement of campaign materials or other vandalism.

An analysis of the election abuse on Twitter by BuzzFeed and Sheffield University researchers found that prominent politicians were the most frequently targeted online, with Jeremy Corbyn narrowly ahead of Theresa May, Boris Johnson, Sadiq Khan and Jeremy Hunt, and with, in general, male Conservative candidates receiving the most abuse. The study also found spikes in abuse following both the Manchester and London Bridge attacks.[57] A separate study by Amnesty International found that Diane Abbott was a particular target for online abuse, receiving nearly half of all abusive tweets sent to female MPs in its sample and ten times the abuse received by any other female MP.[58] Claims of intimidation came (unprompted) from just 4% of candidates in the Electoral Commission's post-election survey, but when asked specifically about a wider range of inappropriate behaviour—including harassment and threats—another survey found around one-third of candidates identifying such behaviour.[59] There were notable party differences, with more than two-thirds of Conservative candidates, compared to 36% of Labour candidates, reporting such actions.[60] Around a third of those who were targeted said they were 'moderately' or 'very' fearful as a result.

The subject was raised at the first Prime Minister's Questions of the new Parliament, when Sheryll Murray, the Conservative MP for South East Cornwall, talked of the abuse she had suffered during the campaign, including having swastikas carved into campaign posters.[61] A debate in Westminster Hall followed in July, during which one MP described the last election as 'the most brutal I can imagine', while another said it was 'by a long chalk the most unpleasant one in which I have ever participated'.[62]

Such concerns prompted a post-election inquiry by the Committee on Standards in Public Life. Its report warned of the coarsening and violent tone of some political debate in recent years and argued that the 2017 election had exacerbated it. It blamed social media as 'the most significant factor accelerating and enabling intimidatory behaviour in recent years'.[63] The claim that the problem was worse in 2017 than before was not actually proven by the Committee, although it was a widespread belief among experienced candidates.[64] We lack much comparative data—and whilst the absence of such data can sometimes indicate that there was not previously considered to be a problem, it is not itself proof that no such problem existed. What evidence we do have shows that the problem certainly did not begin in 2017, even if it has become worse recently.[65] The Committee called for legislation to make social media companies liable for illegal online content and a new offence in electoral law of intimidation of parliamentary candidates and party campaigners.

The long-term decline in party membership prior to the 2015 election, more scientific feedback about voters' views, the growing impact of technology and the dominant role of the campaign chiefs in party HQ had all combined to transform local campaigning in British elections.[66] But in 2017, some old-style activities were revived, notably the mass rallies which had virtually disappeared and the practice of flooding seats with supporters knocking on doors. Members of Corbyn's team believed that the enthusiasm of the large crowds at his rallies better reflected the public mood than opinion polls and organisers' canvass returns. The true believers in Corbyn's team were confident that their campaign approach was superior to what they regarded as the tried and failed methods of Southside. It has long been believed that effective local campaigning makes only a marginal difference to a local outcome—a couple of thousand votes at best—and that it is the national campaign that is decisive and that higher voter contact rates did not always correlate with higher swings. The 2017 experience may have altered that belief. The result of the election meant that the campaign equivalents of 'the man in Whitehall' or in party HQ did not know best—in 2017 at least—and his (only rarely her) reputation took a knock. It remains to be seen whether 2017 was a one-off or a portent of what is to come. Parties will continue to adapt to and exploit the rapid changes in social media and technology. A Labour staffer stressed the need to keep abreast of change: 'What worked six months ago doesn't work now.'

Notes

1. See Mark Wallace, 'In Copeland, the Campaign is Exposing Problems with the Tory Ground Operation', 16 February 2017, https://www.conservativehome.com/thetorydiary/2017/02/copeland-byelection-tory-ground-campaign-problems.html.
2. See, for example, Steve Howell's *Game Changer*. Accent Press, 2018, pp. 139–41.
3. This figure differs slightly from that in Tim Shipman's *Fall Out*. William Collins, 2017, pp. 240–41.
4. Ailsa Henderson and James Mitchell, 'Referendums as Critical Junctures? Scottish Voting in British Elections' in Jonathan Tonge, Cristina Leston-Bandeira and Stewart Wilks-Hegg (eds), *Britain Votes 2017*. Oxford University Press, 2018, p. 121.
5. Farron believed that one reason he was doing badly locally was that local voters saw him as having deserted them to go and be a big-name politician in London. He therefore did not want to be seen in the campaign bus going into or out of the constituency, so the party had to arrange for the bus to

stop outside the constituency boundary, at which point he was transferred into a car, complicating an already tortuous set of travel arrangements.

6. In the final weeks, the party believed just two Lib Dem-Labour contests were even plausible: Cambridge (although, as one Lib Dem campaigner noted, 'a week out and we knew that had gone') and Bermondsey & Old Southwark ('reasonable, but only because of Simon Hughes'). Both were lost by majorities of more than 12,000.

7. Jim Waterson and Tom Phillips, 'How the Conservatives are Using Local Adverts to Get around Election Spending Rules', *BuzzFeed*, 5 May 2017, https://www.buzzfeed.com/jimwaterson/how-the-conservatives-are-using-local-adverts-to-get-around?utm_term=.oanz2dXVNO#.sin-Q2ERoPk.

8. Tim Shipman, 'Don't Mention Corbyn, Aide Tells Labour Candidates', *Sunday Times*, 21 May 2017. See also Howell, *Game Changer*, pp. 178–79.

9. Robert Booth, 'Conservatives Launch Online Offensive against Corbyn', *The Guardian*, 16 May 2017.

10. Caitlin Milazzo, Jesse Hammond and Joshua Townsley, 'Leaflet Messaging in the 2017 and 2015 General Elections', paper presented at the Elections, Public Opinion and Parties (EPOP) Conference, 2017.

11. If so, no one told the team responsible for May's campaign visits, since she carried on visiting Labour seats. 'The two were out of sync', one of the Conservative team admitted.

12. Alia Middleton, '"For the Many, Not the Few": Strategising the Campaign Trail at the 2017 UK General Election', *Parliamentary Affairs* (forthcoming).

13. See Alia Middleton, 'Criss-crossing the Country: Did Corbyn and May's Constituency Visits Impact on Their GE17 Performance?', *London School of Economics British Politics and Policy Blog*, 9 August 2017, https://archive.is/MaCv7.

14. Alex Nunns, *The Candidate*, OR Books, 2018, p. 343.

15. For example, ibid., p. 322.

16. Here we differ from the claims made in Middleton, 'Criss-crossing the Country' (see also footnote 18 in Appendix 1, below).

17. See also Lewis Bassett, 'How Corbyn's Message Helped Labour Reclaim a Key Marginal Seat', *Labour List*, 19 June 2017, https://archive.is/TiuVI.

18. Tim Ross and Tom McTague, *Betting the House*. Biteback, 2017, p. 133.

19. Tim Bale, Paul Webb and Monica Poletti, 'Twice in a Row? UK Party Members' Campaign Activities in the 2015 and 2017 General Elections Compared', paper presented at the EPOP Conference, 2017. The exception is Facebook usage, largely because of the efforts of Labour and Lib Dem members.

20. Tim Bale, Paul Webb and Monica Poletti, *Grassroots: Who They are, What They Think and What They Do*. Mile End Institute, 2018; and Tim Bale and Paul Webb, 'We Didn't see it Coming' in Tonge, Leston-Bandeira and Wilks-Hegg (eds), *Britain Votes 2017*. p. 49.
21. Milazzo et al., 'Leaflet Messaging in the 2017 and 2015 General Elections'.
22. The BES changed the question response slightly, replacing the (rather quaint) 'text message' option with a social media option. If anything, this should have had the effect of raising the overall contact levels, given how much money the parties invested in social media, but it does not appear to have done so.
23. Justin Fisher, David Cutts, Edward Fieldhouse and Yohanna Sällberg, 'The Impact of Constituency Campaigning on the 2017 General Election', presentation at 'Election Campaigning Laid Bare: New Research on the Nature and Impact of Election Campaigns', PSA Event at the Institute for Government, October 2017.
24. The legal position of this activity is discussed in Philip Cowley and Dennis Kavanagh, *The British General Election of 2015*. Palgrave Macmillan, 2015, p. 199.
25. Though not all. Some of the London constituencies were looking good for Labour almost immediately.
26. By eve of poll, ComRes had only a five-point Conservative lead among postal voters, as a result of a surge in postal voting by Labour-backers aged under 35.
27. Quoted in Lucy Fisher, 'Labour Set to Lose Seats Everywhere But London', *The Times*, 7 June 2017.
28. Mark Wallace, 'Our CCHQ Election Audit: The Rusty Machine, Part Two. How and Why the Ground Campaign Failed', *ConservativeHome*, 6 September 2017, https://www.conservativehome.com/majority_conservatism/2017/09/our-cchq-election-audit-the-rusty-machine-part-two-how-and-why-the-ground-campaign-failed.html.
29. See the Electoral Commission's *Digital Campaining: Increasing Transparency for Voters* (2018), which traces the rise of digital advertising as a proportion of total advertising spend, including a jump of almost 20 percentage points between 2015 and 2017. As one Lib Dem campaigner put it rather prosaically: 'Stamps have got a lot more expensive in recent years.'
30. Jim Waterson, 'Corbyn's Media Gamble: The Labour Leader Has Ditched Newspaper Journalists in the Campaign Trail', *BuzzFeed*, 4 May 2017, https://www.buzzfeed.com/jimwaterson/jeremy-corbyn-has-ditched-newspaper-journalists-on-the?utm_term=.annNW4XmE#.wbyyvzY4O.
31. One other difference was that since 2015, Edmonds and Elder had set up a digital consultancy. For the 2017 campaign, Edmonds was seconded to CCHQ full time, whereas Elder split his time between CCHQ and the consultancy.

32. Joe Wade, 'How Labour Won the Social Media Battle', *The Times*, 24 June 2017.
33. See Cowley and Kavanagh, *The British General Election of 2015*, p. 266.
34. Christopher Hope, 'Revealed: Twitter Admits How it Helped Labour Win the Social Media General Election Battle', *Daily Telegraph*, 28 December 2017. In general, however, digital staff of all parties are fairly dismissive of Twitter, which they see as a platform inhabited by journalists and commentators rather than swing voters.
35. After the election, a member of the team said: 'Hardly out of its cradle, and we made it sit its A levels.'
36. There was also—just as importantly—a need to ensure that all spending was compliant with the law, and so built into Promote were procedures to record and limit spending to the permitted level.
37. By the end of the campaign, about 60% of Labour MPs in the North East, for example, were using Promote to send out local targeted Facebook adverts.
38. There is a good discussion of how Labour affiliated with 'outriders' in Howell, *Game Changer*, pp. 68–69.
39. Katharine Dommett and Luke Temple, 'The Rise of Facebook and Satellite Campaigns' in Tonge, Leston-Bandeira and Wilks-Heeg (eds), *Britain Votes 2017*.
40. Philip Maughan, 'How Grime Music Fell in Love with Jeremy Corbyn', *New Statesman*, 8 August 2017.
41. Tom Phillips and Jim Waterson, 'Not Even Right-Wingers are Sharing Positive Stories about Theresa May on Facebook', *BuzzFeed*, 3 June 2017, https://www.buzzfeed.com/tomphillips/not-even-right-wingers-are-sharing-positive-stories-about?utm_term=.ccK7Xa5yAp#.swZwn6gqkX.
42. See Thomas G. Clark, 'How Many of Jeremy Corbyn's Policies Do You Actually Disagree with?', *Another Angry Voice*, 20 April 2017, http://anotherangryvoice.blogspot.com/2017/04/how-many-of-jeremy-corbyns-policies-do.html.
43. Robert Booth and Alex Hern, '"Labour Win Social Media Election", Digital Strategists Say', *The Guardian*, 10 June 2017; and Nicholas Cecil, 'How Jeremy Corbyn Beat Theresa May in the Social Media Election War', *Evening Standard*, 14 June 2017.
44. Ross and McTague, *Betting the House*, pp. 320–21.
45. On the most popular topics, see Tom Phillips, 'People on Facebook Didn't Think This was the "Brexit Election"', *BuzzFeed*, 8 June 2017, https://www.buzzfeed.com/tomphillips/social-barometer-final-week?utm_term=.lqjv2Z5Lr#.emw3QlaXG. See also Freddy Mayhew, 'General Election: Only Five out of Top 100 Most-Shared Stories on Social Media were Pro-Tory', *Press Gazette*, 12 June 2017.

46. As claimed by Jimmy Leach, 'Polling Asks Questions, Social Media Analysis is about Listening. That's Why the Polls were Wrong', *The Times*, 16 June 2017.

47. This may be an artefact of the way in which the BES asks the question—first asking people if they've been contacted and only then how. It is possible that people who have seen, say, Facebook adverts do not initially see this as 'contact'.

48. The SNP were on 9.6% and the Liberal Democrats on 3.6%. See https://twitter.com/GoodwinMJ/status/899900238114291713.

49. Both surveys were conducted online, which will have skewed the responses, ignoring the minority of people who now have no online presence at all.

50. This paragraph draws on Wave 12 of the BES, conducted during the campaign.

51. The figures for Twitter are lower: 6% had seen information from candidates or parties, 6% from those they knew personally and 9% from others.

52. As they were not in 2015. See Jonathan Mellon and Christopher Prosser, 'Twitter and Facebook are Not Representative of the General Population: Political Attitudes and Demographics of British Social Media Users', *Research & Politics*, 4(3) (2017): 1–9.

53. Conservative (and UKIP) supporters were slightly less likely than the supporters of the other parties to be users of social media (64% of Conservative supporters used Facebook, compared to 78% for Labour supporters, for example), but even controlling for usage of Facebook (or Twitter) produces an almost identical effect. Of those who used Facebook, for example, 8% of Conservative voters shared political content compared to 23% of Labour voters.

54. Note that the data exclude the largest social network, Facebook.

55. Darren Yaxley, 'Brits Believe Traditional Media Mattered More in the 2017 General Election', *YouGov*, 4 August 2017, https://yougov.co.uk/news/2017/08/04/brits-believe-traditional-media-mattered-more-2017. See also Freddy Mayhew, 'Survey Reveals the Extent to Which Newspapers and Social Media Influenced Voting Decisions at the 2017 General Election', *Press Gazette*, 31 July 2017.

56. See 'What Could Have Been' *Jacobin*, 2017; and Nunns, *The Candidate*, p. 340. Cotton criticised, among others, the campaign in Worsley & Eccles South (where Barbara Keeley defended a 6,000 majority, which she increased to 8,000) for not directing workers to nearby marginals. But in 2015, UKIP had polled over 7,500 votes in the constituency, and there was no UKIP candidate standing in 2017. Hindsight is a wonderful thing.

57. Tom Phillips, 'This is What the Twitter Abuse of Politicians during the Election Really Looked Like', *BuzzFeed*, 23 July 2017, https://www.

buzzfeed.com/tomphillips/twitter-abuse-of-mps-during-the-election-doubled-after-the?utm_term=.ja9KDJl1V3#.oe8X3O5EZw.

58. Jessica Elgot, 'Diane Abbott More Abused Than Any Other MPs during Election', *The Guardian*, 5 September 2017.

59. See Electoral Commission, *Standing for Office in 2017*. Electoral Commission, 2017; and Sofia Delmar, Jennifer Hudson, Wolfgang Rudig and Rosie Campbell, 'Inappropriate Behaviour: Experiences of 2017 Parliamentary Candidates: Evidence from the Representative Audit of Britain Study', submitted to the Committee on Standards in Public Life, 19 September 2017.

60. The other figures variously ranged from 62% (the SNP) to 10% (Green), although some of the sub-samples are based on very low numbers of respondents (just eight in the case of the SNP).

61. HC Debs, 28 June 2017, c. 585.

62. HC Debs, 12 July 2017, cc. 152WH–170WH. The topic was also discussed in the Commons on 14 September 2017, cc. 1041–1083.

63. Committee on Standards in Public Life, *Intimidation in Public Life: A Review by the Committee on Standards in Public Life*, December 2017.

64. See also the comments in the Conservatives' post-election review (*Eric Pickles' General Election Review 2017*), which noted that such 'levels of intimidation and abuse have not been experienced before' (p. 6).

65. For example, one study of the 2005 Parliament, solely of MPs rather than candidates and in general rather than just at election time, found that 81% of respondents had experienced what it called 'intrusive/aggressive behaviours', including 53% who had been stalked or harassed. See David V. James, Seema Sukhwal, Frank R. Farnham, Julie Evans, Claire Barrie, Alice Taylor and Simon P. Wilson, 'Harassment and Stalking of Members of the United Kingdom Parliament: Associations and Consequences', *Journal of Forensic Psychiatry & Psychology*, 27(3) (2016): 309–30.

66. For a discussion of the trends in local campaigning, see Justin Fisher et al., 'The Evolution of District-Level Campaigning in Britain: The Resilience of Traditional Campaigning?', paper presented at the EPOP Conference 2016.

CHAPTER 13

Campaign Coverage and Editorial Judgements: Broadcasting

Stephen Cushion and Charlie Beckett

If this was an election where the campaign made a difference, then the media—and especially broadcasters—played a critical role. On television, still the most influential medium for the majority of voters, broadcasters challenged the parties' approach as politicians discovered that their robotic soundbites and stage-management could backfire. Like politicians, journalists found that social media was now a vital factor in helping shape what became an unexpectedly dynamic broadcast campaign. The result challenged the conventional wisdom of many Westminster journalists, and prompted new questions about the role, relevance and authority of the mainstream media during election campaigns.

Despite the growth of online and social media, TV was considered the source most likely to influence people's voting decisions.[1] UK broadcasters have to remain impartial in terms of their coverage of politics and public affairs, a regulatory duty which is put under even closer scrutiny during an election campaign. Ahead of most recent election campaigns, Ofcom—the media regulator—has provided guidance for broadcasters (excluding the BBC) about which party should be considered 'major' or 'minor' during the campaign. The aim was to help broadcasters interpret their 'due impartiality' requirements, balancing coverage between an increasingly diverse bunch of parties across England, Scotland, Wales and Northern Ireland. After the publication of an Ofcom review, typically the focus of attention would be on which parties were considered minor and which were major (prompting fierce debate about the methodology

© The Author(s) 2018
P. Cowley, D. Kavanagh, *The British General Election of 2017*,
https://doi.org/10.1007/978-3-319-95936-8_13

behind these decisions, such as current poll ratings, past electoral performances, sitting MPs, etc.). However, Ofcom—which from 2017 is now also responsible for the regulation of BBC *and* commercial news—changed its regulatory guidance to allow broadcasters greater discretion, no longer issuing parties with a minor or major status. This represents a longer-term trend in lightening the regulatory obligations of public service broadcasters.[2]

Although impartiality is difficult to define, let alone put into practice, broadly speaking the aim is to ensure that parties receive fair and balanced treatment across different programmes.[3] As we will explore in this chapter, there was little evidence of any sustained or flagrant breaches of impartiality in election coverage on the late-evening UK national television news bulletins or on the live TV debate-type programmes, the format of which were largely determined by the major political parties rather than broadcasters. But in following the political agenda and relying on the consensus of most opinion polls, the television news agenda centred on the two-horse race between the Conservative Party and Labour. While the smaller parties had a platform during live televised TV debates, in day-to-day television news they were squeezed out by the narrative focus on Theresa May's faltering, over-controlling campaign versus Jeremy Corbyn's buoyant rallies and less scripted campaigning style.

TELEVISION NEWS: HOW WAS THE ELECTION CAMPAIGN REPORTED?

Although political parties increasingly rely on social media to convey their messaging, the battle for the 'air war' in UK election campaigns still centres on gaining favourable coverage on the UK's flagship television news bulletins—little wonder, since the BBC's *News at Ten* attracts, on average, about four million viewers each night, many of whom are highly likely to vote. ITV *News at Ten* audiences are approximately 1.6 million.[4] Fewer viewers regularly tune into Channel 4's 7 pm and Channel 5's 5 pm bulletins, although both attract different demographics. Channel 5, for example, has the highest proportion of viewers in the DE social economic groups.[5]

A content analysis of these bulletins—including Sky News at 10 pm—during the campaign revealed that 45.7% of television news airtime was spent reporting on the general election (see Table 13.1).[6] This was roughly

Table 13.1 Proportion of news about the 2015 and 2017 general election campaigns (by percentage time, with total number in brackets)

	2015	2017
BBC News at Ten	49.8%	42.4%
ITV News at Ten	43.5%	42.0%
Channel 4 News at 7 pm	49.0%	51.2%
Channel 5 News at 5 pm	52.4%	43.0%
Sky News at Ten	41.2%	46.3%
Total	47.1% (843)	45.7% (840)

Table 13.2 Proportion of lead election news items in the 2015 and 2017 general election campaigns (by percentage)

	2015	2017
BBC News at Ten	63%	50%
ITV News at Ten	61%	58%
Channel 4 News at 7 pm	37%	55%
Channel 5 News at 5 pm	50%	47%
Sky News at Ten	53%	55%
Average	53%	53%

in line with the level of coverage during the 2015 election campaign, but there were some differences in the volume of news between bulletins. In the 2017 campaign, Channel 4 spent the highest proportion of its bulletins—over half in total—focused on the election, with *BBC News* and ITV reporting the least amount of coverage (about 42%).

The average number of lead election items was the same (53%) in both the 2015 and 2017 campaigns (see Table 13.2). However, there was greater variation between bulletins in the 2015 campaign, with 63% of lead items on the BBC, for example, focusing on the election, compared to 37% on Channel 4. In the 2017 campaign, while 47% of Channel 5 lead items were about the election, they made up 50% or more on the other bulletins examined. There was little difference between the types of stories at the top of the bulletin, with both campaigns including more lead items about the process of the election campaign than policy issues.

Perhaps more so than the 2015 campaign, election news had to compete with other newsworthy events, in particular the terrorist attacks in Manchester and London. The government was understandably given a platform to respond to each attack, providing updates on fast-moving events. However, at times the terrorist attacks became politicised, with the Labour focus on police cuts by the government given prominent coverage, as well as new Conservative proposals to boost security measures. The Corbyn speech about foreign policy put Labour back into the spotlight a few days after the Manchester attack, while UKIP's manifesto launch towards the end of that week and the comments by its leader, Paul Nuttall, also captured media attention.

As Table 13.3 shows, the issue of terrorism was a prominent part of the news agenda, particularly in weeks 4 and 6 of the campaign. Political leaders reacting to the Manchester and London attacks made up 5% of all election coverage (this excluded news related to the police investigation, victims or commemoration events in Manchester), and terrorism, discussed in the context of wider issues involving defence, foreign affairs and police, made up another 11.5% of the agenda. In other words, terrorism overshadowed key moments of the campaign, pushing other issues off the news agenda. For example, on the night of the terrorist attack in Manchester, the Conservative Party's problems with the 'dementia tax' was the lead item on all bulletins, but social policy as an issue received very little airtime after this point in the campaign.

Although the Conservative Party attempted to make the campaign the 'Brexit election' and post-election polls suggested that many thought Europe was top of the agenda, items about the EU made up less than 10% of total airtime. Broadcasters appeared to push back against the Conservatives' agenda-setting and broadened the editorial selection of issues, as Jonathan Munro, the BBC's Head of Newsgathering, made plain: 'Our first decision on the first day was that we would not call it a

Table 13.3 Top ten subjects in election news (by percentage time)

Horse race	14.4%
Terror/defence/foreign affairs/police	11.5%
Campaigning strategies/launch	10.9%
EU/Brexit	9.1%
Manifesto/general policy	7.9%
TV leader debates	5.3%
NHS	5.1%
Manchester/London attacks	5.0%
Social policy	4.2%
Taxation	3.7%

Brexit election though May wanted to do that in the first 24 hours'. Meanwhile, one news editor acknowledged that:

> On Brexit this election was supposed to be all about it and about giving her [May] a mandate and I was clear that we shouldn't buy that spin. We weren't given any detail about Brexit policy at all. So we had to report the fact that there wasn't anything to talk about with Brexit—important to highlight to viewers that we weren't being told.

Given the complexity of Brexit, Channel 4's Gary Gibbon conceded that broadcasters struggled to make sense of the issue for viewers. In his words, 'when it came to saying what will Brexit actually look like. I think we tried to do that—but we probably all could have done better—you saw in the referendum coverage—we could have done better then'.

Overall, few other 'issues' dominated the television news agenda, with stories about education, the economy, housing, the environment, transport, jobs and employment all given limited airtime. Consistent with previous election campaigns, the most reported topic was 'horse race'-type stories, which primarily related to exploring the everyday dynamics of the electoral competition. This included stories on: the local election results, where the focus was on how the results may impact on general election; people's voting intentions via 'vox pops'; journalists or reporters commenting on the race between leaders; or official polls and final predictions (e.g. the gap has narrowed). In this, the 2017 general election was no different from most other elections in the UK or elsewhere. As a comprehensive review of international election studies recently found, horse-race news is by far the most dominant type of campaign story in the majority of Western democracies.[7]

However, unlike the 2015 general election, a greater proportion of time was spent reporting policy issues rather than news about the campaigns, the horse race or other process-type stories. In 2015, 37.6% of airtime across all broadcasters was spent reporting policy, whereas this rose to 53.3% in 2017. The 2015 election news agenda, of course, was dominated by the prospect of a hung parliament. The then head of BBC News, James Harding, acknowledged that a 'coalitionology' had infected journalistic thinking during the election campaign.[8] Coverage of the 2015 election campaign was fuelled by a reliance on opinion polls, which turned out to be driving a misleading narrative about a Labour/SNP coalition government. As the BBC's Jonathan Munro pointed out: 'A number of the interviews we did in 2015 included questions about red lines on coalition and those questions proved to be redundant so editorial direction in 15 was a misrepresentation of public opinion and of the reality.' By contrast, given the outcome, it could be argued that broadcasters should have spent more time in 2017 considering the possibility of a hung parliament; despite some opinion polls, at the very end of the campaign, suggesting the outcome could be close between the Conservatives and Labour, the prospect of some kind of coalition or confidence-and-supply deal was not widely debated on television news.

Ahead of the 2017 campaign, some of our interviewees signalled a reluctance to rely on opinion polls, in particular ITV's editors, who did not commission any. Alex Chandler, ITV's editor, claimed:

> Because we weren't focused on polls there was much more policy investment. So, we did go around and ask people in particular places what their policy concerns were. The What Matters series identified what people cared about around the country. That delivered depth when the policies were launched on what people thought about them.

As Table 13.4 shows, there was a remarkable degree of consistency in the volume of policy coverage, with all bulletins dedicating between 50% and 55.7% of airtime towards issues.

However, when the degree of policy information was examined more carefully, ITV's coverage was not as detailed as that of the BBC, Channel 4 or Sky News (see Table 13.5). In order to determine whether an election item had detailed policy coverage, it generally had to provide one of five features:

- context surrounding the policy provided;
- comparison between parties;
- comparison with previous policies or past election pledges;
- figures/statistics/graphs showing trends;
- impact of the policy on businesses, citizens, etc.

Table 13.4 Proportion of policy versus process news in the 2017 election campaign (by percentage time, with the total number in brackets)

	BBC	ITV	Channel 4	Channel 5	Sky	Total
Policy	53.5%	52.5%	55.7%	50.0%	51.5%	53.3% (461)
Process	46.5%	47.5%	44.3%	50.0%	48.5%	46.7% (379)
Total	100% (168)	100% (177)	100% (190)	100% (139)	100% (166)	100% (840)

Table 13.5 Level of policy information in the 2017 election coverage (by percentage time, with the total number in brackets)

	BBC	ITV	Channel 4	Channel 5	Sky	Total
None	22.5%	23.1%	19.7%	34.1%	23.2%	24.5% (213)
Some	53.6%	57.8%	55.2%	55.2%	55.8%	55.5% (476)
Detailed	23.9%	19.1%	25.0%	10.7%	21.0%	19.9% (151)
Total	100% (168)	100% (177)	100% (190)	100% (139)	100% (166)	100% (840)

If policy information was presented or mentioned in the story but only in a descriptive way, rather than analysing or scrutinising an issue, it was not classified as being detailed. So, for example, election items often involved a reporter on the campaign trail, who might reference policy pledges of particular parties without really explaining them. Similarly, live two-ways with political correspondents would often engage with policies, but in relatively brief pieces, introducing and describing them rather than scrutinising them in any detail.

ITV's Alex Chandler acknowledged that the *News at Ten* 'didn't go into the manifestos in fine detail, we came to it when it was newsworthy. We did a lot ahead of Labour's manifesto launch because of the leak but there wasn't actually that much in the Tory manifesto'. Indeed, ITV spent a lot of time exploring citizens' perspectives on policy issues and identifying policy issues relevant to voters. Meanwhile, according to its head, John Ryley, Sky News focused its resources on analysing and critically interpreting issues: 'We did actually spend quite a lot of time crunching policy—Ed Conway [Economics Editor], for example, had a series of special items where he crunched manifesto numbers—in a way not having a cabinet minister makes no difference—they would simply defend their policy. It was more important to try to unravel policies.' This feature was labelled 'Election Forensics', with stories such as the Conservative social care policy being carefully scrutinised, with a studio reporter illustrating trends and figures with graphs and charts (for example, how the policy has changed over the past few weeks, and individual costs and governments costs compared). Perhaps due to its lengthier format and distinctive reporting style, Channel 4 supplied the most detailed policy analysis—25% of its election items—during the 2017 campaign. On 26 May, for example, a package included detailed Institute for Fiscal Studies (IFS) analysis of both the Labour and Conservative manifestos, comparing the spending plans and economic consequences of their pledges on education and the NHS. More generally, the IFS was the most dominant expert voice during the campaign, supplying instant responses to the parties' spending commitments.

THE ROLE OF ELECTION TV DEBATES AND LEADERS' APPEARANCES ON TELEVISION

Unlike the 2010 and 2015 election campaigns, there were limited negotiations between broadcasters and political parties about televised leaders' debates. Calling a snap election meant that there was less time for discussions between the broadcasters and the parties. What 'negotiations' there were were perfunctory. The Conservative Party was adamant that May would not appear one-on-one with Corbyn or debate with other party leaders. According to one news editor: 'In our negotiations with the Tories about the debates they made it clear that they would not come. This time around "we're not doing it and that's the end of it".'[9] The BBC's head of newsgathering, who was involved in negotiating TV debates with party representatives, also pointed out that May's team was 'very clear that they would not appear in any studio with any rival—they would do *Question Time* [the BBC's *Question Time* programme] sequentially but not head to head'. 'In the end', as John Ryley, Head of Sky News, conceded, 'there were election programmes but not proper debates between the leaders'.

The result was that during the 2017 election campaign, there were no television programmes where the main party leaders—May and Corbyn—engaged in direct debate with one another on the same platform. There were, as in 2015, a series of programmes where the two main leaders appeared and took questions from a journalist and/or members of the public (see Table 13.6). The viewing figures for these election special programmes were significantly lower than in the previous two campaigns. It is difficult to make direct comparisons as the formats were different. However, to take one comparable case, despite the late surge in interest of the fortunes of May and Corbyn, the BBC *Question Time Leaders Special* featuring the two leaders in 2017 received an average audience of 3.8 million, compared to 4.7 million for Miliband and Cameron in 2015. The TV programmes did not remotely dominate the wider news media agenda as they had in 2010, when they were still a novelty. They did not generate any particular policy concerns, nor did they create exchanges that meaningfully shifted the dynamics of the campaign in the way that they arguably had done in 2010 or 2015. There are, perhaps, two exceptions. In the

Table 13.6 The main televised leaders' debates/election programmes during the 2017 general election campaign

Date	Time	Channel	Show title	Participants
Thursday 18 May	8 pm	ITV	*ITV Leaders' Debate*	Tim Farron Nicola Sturgeon Paul Nuttall Leanne Wood Caroline Lucas
Monday 29 May	8.30 pm	Sky/ Channel 4	*May v Corbyn: The Battle for Number 10*	Theresa May Jeremy Corbyn
Wednesday 31 May	7.30 pm	BBC1	*The BBC Election Debate* (party spokespeople)	Jeremy Corbyn Amber Rudd Tim Farron Angus Robertson Paul Nuttall Leanne Wood Caroline Lucas
Friday 2 June	8.30 pm	BBC1	*Question Time Leaders Special*	Theresa May Jeremy Corbyn
Monday 5 June	9 pm	BBC1	*Question Time Leaders Special*	Tim Farron Nicola Sturgeon

later stages of the campaign, the *BBC Election Debate* with all of the leaders, bar Theresa May, helped crystallise the idea that the Prime Minister was running from open questioning, while supporting the image of Corbyn as open and 'honest'. The final BBC *Question Time Leaders Special* featuring the two leaders compounded that contrast.

The ITV Leaders' Debate

The first *ITV Leaders' Debate* on 19 May, hosted by Julie Etchingham and featuring all the minor party leaders, helped lower expectations about the significance of televised election debates. Both Corbyn and May declined invitations to appear. Unlike in 2015, the public and the media appeared less interested in the characters of the leaders of the minor parties, and opinion polls were suggesting that they would have less of an impact on the campaign. With an average viewing figure of 1.6 million, marginally fewer people tuned in than watched a programme about vets on Channel 4 at the same time.[10] The new UKIP leader, Paul Nuttall, despite an exuberant performance, was put under attack by all the others; his repeated failure to get Plaid Cymru's Leanne Wood's name right—he called her 'Natalie'—was perhaps the most noteworthy part of the low-key debate. Liberal Democrat leader Tim Farron used the programme to push his party's demand for another EU referendum. All of them attacked the Prime Minister for failing to 'show leadership' by her non-appearance.

The Battle for Number 10

Sky and Channel 4's joint 29 May programme with the two party leaders facing separate questioning from the audience moderated by Sky Political Editor Faisal Islam and then a 15-minute grilling from Jeremy Paxman generated more interest. Channel 4's viewing figures of 2.9 million was supplemented by 400,000 on Sky and another 400,000 via live feeds on Facebook and YouTube.[11] Corbyn came under sustained attack from the public and Paxman on issues such as security, Brexit and his leadership. Paxman also focused on the Labour leader's past statements on terrorism, foreign policy, the monarchy and banks. Even commentators for the Conservative-supporting *Daily Telegraph* acknowledged that the audience seemed surprisingly 'sympathetic' to Corbyn, who was a 'natural communicator' who remained calm under fire from Paxman.[12] May, by contrast, according to the *Daily Telegraph*, was 'Prime Ministerial' but also 'dull, professional and on message'. She came under fire from the audience questioners on Brexit, but also on domestic issues such as health, social care and her leadership style. Paxman majored on Brexit, but also touched on the increasingly sensitive issues of social care, which she defended despite increasing criticisms. Both avoided any gaffes and got their core messages across. But in terms of the visual and personal impact that matters so much on television, it gave the first indications that the public were less frightened by what they saw of Corbyn and less engaged by May as a character.

The BBC Election Debate

By the time of the *BBC Election Debate* hosted by Mishal Husain on 31 May, the perceived momentum of the campaign had shifted. The terrorist incidents had temporarily halted but not swamped the campaign. The polls had narrowed and a consensus was building that Corbyn was exceeding many people's low expectations. Just 24 hours before the broadcast,

Corbyn agreed to take part in the *BBC Election Debate*. The opening part of the statement read 'I have never been afraid of a debate in my life', but it went on to reveal the real strategic motive for his change of heart:

> The Tories have been conducting a stage-managed arm's-length campaign and have treated the public with contempt. Refusing to join me in Cambridge tonight would be another sign of Theresa May's weakness, not strength.

The other leaders were happy to adopt the same tactic and, during the debate, May was attacked directly five times for not taking part and accused of being 'afraid'. The Green Party's Caroline Lucas pointed out that 'the first rule of leadership is showing up', while Plaid Cymru's Leanne Wood suggested that May's 'campaign of soundbites was falling apart'. Home Secretary Amber Rudd defended Conservative policies competently, but the absence of her leader left a lasting impression. The Liberal Democrats' Tim Farron even suggested that viewers should tune into *The Great British Bake Off* rather than bother listening to her closing statement. This sense of the Conservatives being embattled led to party complaints about 'biased' audience selection. The BBC had asked pollsters ComRes to vet the audience and had given 'rough equivalence' to Labour and Conservative supporters. But with supporters of the other parties also lining up against Amber Rudd, the atmosphere in the studio enforced the sense of Conservative isolation.

The audience of 3.5 million was not particularly big in itself, but Corbyn's decision to take part helped shift the focus onto the gathering doubts about May's campaign competence and generated wider media interest in the debate. The questions from Husain had covered the economy, climate change and foreign policy, but it was the leadership exchanges that hit home. It appeared to enhance the sense that Corbyn was at least prepared to engage, while his team's tactical shift gave his campaign an aura of political credibility at last.

The BBC Question Time Leaders Special

The final election debate programme, moderated by David Dimbleby, secured the highest viewing figure at just over four million and was the liveliest on-screen event. It brought both leaders into direct and often hostile contact with members of the public for 45 minutes each, with May in the preferred first slot. Again, Conservative supporters subsequently questioned the composition of the York audience, which, judging by noise levels, seemed more enthusiastic about Corbyn and, at times, more hostile to May. However, the BBC insisted that statistically it was proportionate, with two-thirds allocated to supporters and one-third 'undecided'. The questions were also equally critical, attacking each leader from the left and right. One BBC executive we interviewed suggested that the impression of an imbalanced audience response may have reflected the degree of overt enthusiasm their supporters were feeling. Early questions to May focused on her own credibility, on her change of heart on Europe and on calling an election she had previously ruled out. It moved on to wider issues around health, climate change and even foreign aid.

Questions to Corbyn also began by challenging his leadership ability, specifically on Brexit. He was also asked about his nuclear defence policy and public spending as well as tuition fees, business and zero-hours contracts. He was heckled at one point over the IRA, but deflected the angry challenge with a calm generalisation that 'all deaths are wrong, all killing is wrong'. Neither had a meltdown moment or blundered badly. Corbyn stuck to his non-committal stance on pressing the nuclear button while hinting at a softer Brexit stance. May was focused and assertive, saying that she had shown 'balls' to call the election and in a tough question from a nurse insisted there was no 'magic money tree' to relieve austerity. For once, the phrase 'strong and stable' did not cross her lips. One survey of viewers suggested that Corbyn had scored marginally higher in his performance than May, especially on the measure of 'understands people like me' and particularly with younger people.[13] With under a week left to campaign, it did not appear to have changed much, but it might have confirmed that Corbyn was, at least, competitive.

Other Set-Piece Programmes and Overall Debate Impact

There was a range of other non-bulletin special programming, including a series of election debates featuring local politicians in every BBC nation and region. The BBC also put on a separate leaders' debate for the Liberal Democrats' Tim Farron and the SNP's Nicola Sturgeon. Two one-off Theresa May interviews produced a couple of the more cited if less momentous quotes. During a bland BBC *The One Show* interview, her husband Philip admitted he was the one to put the bins out—prompting the Prime Minister to remark that there were 'boy jobs and girl jobs'. During her interview with ITV's Julie Etchingham, May admitted that the naughtiest thing she had done as a child was 'running through fields of wheat'. The BBC's Andrew Neil interviewed five of the party leaders, but while the half-hour programmes were typically thorough, even his persistent style was unable to gather any serious news-making lines. ITV's Robert Peston also interviewed Theresa May for a Facebook live event that covered a lot of ground. The highlight was probably Peston reading out a question from 'Jeremy from Islington' asking why the Prime Minister would not debate with Mr Corbyn.

Paradoxically, perhaps the main impact of the debates was the decision of one leader to avoid them. Despite their reduced importance in themselves, the programmes (and those featuring Corbyn especially) made visual to a relatively large audience a key late dynamic of a campaign where perceptions of the leaders seem to have shifted significantly close to the vote. While the viewing figures may have been down and press coverage of them also reduced compared to 2015, the programmes still reached millions of people. In 2017 especially, the TV leaders' debates provoked extensive reaction on social media, stimulated further by the broadcasters' own efforts to spread their impact via online networks such as Twitter, Facebook and YouTube. Broadcasters accepted that with such short notice, there was always going to be little leeway for bargaining. They hope that for the next election, there should be a more coherent approach, perhaps even including some sort of formal debate planning body. However, the broadcasters themselves have different interests at stake and the parties, especially the government, will always resist surrendering control over media management.

Questions asked by journalists and the public during these programmes covered a wide range of topics overall (Table 13.7). Clearly, Brexit was the most popular, but the NHS was not far behind. Immigration was raised less than education. In an election where the character of the two main party leaders became a real issue, this topic was mentioned in all but one of the programmes.

BALANCE, BIAS AND TONE: A TWO-HORSE RACE AND EDITORIAL (MIS)JUDGEMENTS

All the major broadcasters were sensitive about their impartiality requirements ahead of the election not just because of the regulatory requirements, but also because of a professional commitment to report in a fair and balanced way. This was not just at the BBC, which attracts most critical

Table 13.7 The questions asked in the main televised leaders' debates/election programmes during the 2017 UK general election campaign

Topic	18 May: ITV Leaders' Debate	29 May: Sky/Channel 4 May v Corbyn: The Battle for Number 10	31 May: BBC Election Debate	2 June: BBC Question Time Leader Special (May and Corbyn)	5 June: BBC Question Time Leader Special (Sturgeon and Farron)
Brexit	1	2		2	1
Leadership	1	2	1	1	1
NHS and social care	1	2		2	
Education	1	1		1	1
Terrorism and foreign policy	1	1	1		1
Cost of living			1		
Immigration		1	1		
Nuclear weapons		1		1	
Public spending			1	1	
Climate change			1	1	
Inter-generational fairness	1				
Tax					2
IRA		1			
Economy		1			
Police		1			
Winter Fuel Payment		1			
Foreign aid				1	
Business				1	
Zero-hours contracts				1	
Tuition fees				1	
Surveillance					1
Scottish independence					1
Coalition making					1

Notes: This includes questions asked by members of the public only. Follow-ups from moderators are not included. For *Question Time* shows, only questions by named members of the public were included attention about its coverage despite regularly commissioning impartiality reviews and refining its editorial codes; ITV, for example, took seriously the need to balance the views of competing parties in the context of the UK's political system, as Alex Chandler explained:

> We are very conscious about giving minority views although Ofcom guidelines have relaxed. We were mindful this time around not to over-cover UKIP because they'd gone down in the polls and they'd lost their only MP. The difficulty with UKIP is they shout loudly and they are engaging because of what they say but there's a danger of giving them more coverage than, say, the Liberal Democrats. We always aim to be balanced as possible. We didn't count minutes and seconds but we did log appearances. If there were times when we thought we hadn't heard from one party then we could adjust.

Overall, a systematic review of airtime granted to parties over the six-week campaign confirmed that, broadly speaking, equal time was granted to the Conservatives and Labour across the UK national bulletins (see Table 13.8). The Conservatives' greater airtime is consistent with the 'incumbency bonus' most parties receive when campaigning in office. But during the 2017 campaign, this might especially be explained by prominent appearances by government spokespeople in the aftermath of the London and Manchester terrorist attacks.

During the campaign, there is, as the BBC's former television news editor Roger Mosey acknowledged, a fine balance between the government updating viewers about the latest news and campaigning about new anti-

Table 13.8 Share of party political airtime on UK television news evening bulletins (by percentage time)

	BBC	ITV	Channel 4	Channel 5	Sky	Total
Conservatives	38.4%	36.0%	41.2%	39.8%	37.0%	39.4%
Labour	33.7%	33.9%	36.4%	29.2%	37.5%	35.3%
Liberal Democrats	8.5%	11.5%	9.8%	11.0%	11.1%	10.1%
UKIP	4.8%	6.6%	3.0%	6.2%	3.2%	4.0%
SNP	10.1%	6.1%	4.3%	7.8%	8.7%	6.3%
Green Party	1.7%	2.6%	1.5%	1.6%	0.2%	1.5%
Plaid Cymru	1.1%	1.5%	1.5%	0.4%	0.0%	1.2%
Other	1.7%	1.8%	2.3%	4.0%	2.2%	2.3%
Total	100%	100%	100%	100%	100%	100%

terrorism policy.[14] A few days after the terrorist attack in Manchester, the Conservatives still outweighed Labour voices by a small but significant margin between 25 and 28 May (37.5% versus 31.6%).[15] Nevertheless, overall the Labour Party clearly benefited from receiving more balanced coverage during the election campaign. Previous studies have shown that since Corbyn was elected in 2015, he has often been reported in the context of leading a divided party. Under Corbyn, Labour substantially increased their number of party members, but the media focus tended to be on MPs who were critical of their leader.[16] During the campaign, particularly after the local election results, some Labour MPs remained sceptical of Corbyn's leadership. But as election day drew closer, fewer Labour MPs were publicly critical of their leader. The UK's broadcasting rules about impartiality may have also contributed to more balanced coverage of Corbyn during the campaign.[17] Since much of the media focus had previously been centred on Labour's internal divisions, the party's policy agenda and Corbyn's campaigning strengths were not widely discussed. However, once the election campaign was called, broadcasters struck more rigidly to balancing the parties' competing perspectives and, in doing so, gave Corbyn a platform he had previously not enjoyed.

Over the six-week campaign, while almost all broadcasters balanced the two main parties more evenly, Channel 5's coverage was the most imbalanced (with roughly 10% more coverage of the Conservative Party). A similar disparity in Channel 5 coverage was discovered during the 2015 general election (again, favouring Conservative voices by 8.7%), which suggests the editorial team may not monitor the allocation of party political airtime as closely as the other UK broadcasters. Given that the final general election result revealed that over 80% of voters opted for the Conservatives and Labour, overall broadcasters could conclude that their stop-watch balanced the main parties appropriately. However, this overlooks the role they may have played in helping to construct—not just reflect—public opinion towards the parties over the six weeks.

Over recent local, European and general election campaigns, UKIP's prominence in broadcast media has often been a point of debate, but post-Brexit (and Farage) the party's coverage during the 2017 campaign fell (down by 7.3% across the UK national bulletins compared to the 2015 election). With the exception of the televised leaders' debates, there was limited time for the smaller parties, such as the Green Party, on the national bulletins. Indeed, the DUP—which agreed a confidence-and-supply agreement with the Conservatives after the election—made up just one or two appearances across each of the evening bulletins. The narrative focus was instead on the two-horse race between the Conservatives and Labour and, in particular, the battle between the leaders of the two parties.

As Table 13.9 shows, over 70% of airtime granted to the party leaders was taken up by May and Corbyn, leaving limited airtime for other parties, such as UKIP's Paul Nuttall or the Green Party's Caroline Lucas and Jonathan Bartley.[18] Once again, there was an imbalance in the time allocated for Conservative and Labour party leaders to speak on television news. This is consistent with previous academic studies showing that the party in power often enjoys an incumbency bonus to make announcements, most notably about terrorism in 2017.[19] While May accounted for 40.3% of airtime dedicated to all party leaders, Corbyn made up 30.7%. As shares of the total cover of their parties, May constituted 47.9% of Conservative Party airtime; that of Corbyn made up 40.7% of Labour airtime.

May's appearances on television news were not particularly effective. The Conservatives sought to run a presidential-style campaign, focusing on May's 'strong and stable' offer of leadership for the challenges ahead. Her media performances and unwillingness to engage with journalists at campaign 'walkabouts' soon undermined this strategy and influenced how she was portrayed in broadcast news. As ITV's Alex Chandler explained: 'We vox popped early on in the campaign and people were regurgitating the "strong and stable" line but it wasn't long before it became clear that it was a veneer and there was nothing behind it.' When asked to name one thing about the Conservatives' campaign, one poll found that 23% said 'bad campaign', while 11% stated (unprompted) 'strong and stable campaign'.[20] In other words, the Conservatives' strategy of stonewalling the campaign with a well-rehearsed soundbite appeared to have backfired with voters.

Table 13.9 Share of party leaders' airtime on UK television news (by percentage time)

Theresa May	40.3%
Jeremy Corbyn	30.7%
Tim Farron	10.8%
Nicola Sturgeon	8.5%
Paul Nuttall	4.4%
Caroline Lucas/Jonathan Bartley	3.0%
Leanne Wood	2.3%
Total	100%

Corbyn, by contrast, had a more relaxed campaigning style. He appeared prepared to meet and chat with 'ordinary people', whereas May was rarely seen to engage directly with the public. Often the Labour leader appeared on television news in front of large crowds of people, from well-attended rallies to 'walkabouts' where he was filmed taking selfies with voters and listening to their concerns. However, the Labour leader's apparent openness with the public did not necessarily mean that he was more accessible to journalistic questioning than May. Channel 4's Gary Gibbon, for instance, suggested that while the media exposed May's attempt to control the agenda, Corbyn was often left unchallenged. In his words: 'He [Corbyn] didn't take any questions when he was at those rallies—he just picked up the old 1970s megaphone and broadcast to the adoring crowd and somehow that was a cleverer image that made him look down and with the people.'

While the image of Corbyn touring the country may have helped Labour's campaign, the media commentary towards the Labour leader was less complimentary. At times journalists questioned the significance of attracting large numbers of people to rallies—most memorably Channel 4's Michael Crick, who compared Corbyn's rallies to Michael Foot's ineffective 1983 campaign. While Labour was gradually closing the gap in the opinion polls, there was little recognition throughout the campaign of Corbyn's electoral appeal. Indeed, notably after the local elections, journalists often cast doubt on Corbyn's ability to win over voters and questioned whether Labour's policy agenda would appeal to the public. In vox pops—an editorial construction of public opinion—there was often a focus on disgruntled Labour voters, which was not counterbalanced by disaffected Tory supporters. So, for example, one study found that while the vast majority of vox pops did not express a clear party political preference, there was an imbalance in coverage about people's *former* voter preferences, with 60.6% focused on Labour compared to just 12.8% on the Conservatives.[21] As one vox pop put it: 'I still believe in Labour [but not] plonker Corbyn.' How far Corbyn was the crucial factor in Labour's surge remains open to debate, but his personal ratings increased over the course of the campaign.

On the eve of election day, some journalists acknowledged that Corbyn was picking up public support.[22] Yet, despite the popularity of many of Labour's policies and the party's rise in public support during the campaign, most commentators did not anticipate Corbyn's electoral success or the prospect of a hung parliament. This was recognised by Channel 4's anchor Jon Snow the day after the election when he began the programme by stating: 'I know nothing, we the media, the pundits and experts, know nothing.'

Given that the polls indicated a comfortable Conservative victory throughout most of the campaign, it is perhaps understandable why broadcasters misjudged 'the mood' of the electorate. But since one in five news election items were live two-ways involving correspondents often asked to interpret the 'horse race', the editorial focus of so much campaign coverage almost encouraged journalists to act as pseudo-psephologists. As Roger Mosey put it, 'there have been times in this campaign when ... we learn too much too quickly about a correspondent's view of the agenda'.[23]

In a political culture where the left-right consensus is difficult to interpret, electoral predictions not only appear risky, they seem unnecessary. Although broadcasters spent more airtime reporting on policy than the previous campaign, a great deal of time was still spent forecasting the election. As several of our interviewees acknowledged, this could be due to a broader structural problem within the journalism industry that affects how election campaigns are understood and reported. This was well summed up the BBC's Jonathan Munro: 'In the wake of the exit poll and the actual result the question we have to ask ourselves is—what is it about our reporting which is missing the point here ... we don't employ enough people from the background where the Corbyn or Brexit supporters come from.' In other words, editorial judgements might be improved if newsrooms were more socially diverse.

WHEN SOUNDBITES BACKFIRE

Despite it appearing to be a relatively undramatic election at first, broadcasters fulfilled their public service responsibility by giving a substantial volume of coverage to the election campaign and broadly balancing the airtime of the major parties. While this was evident on the UK's main evening bulletins, broadcasters struggled to stage televised debates between party leaders because of the Conservative Party's reluctance to participate in them. Having called a snap election with a commanding lead in the polls, the Conservatives attempted to put Brexit at the centre of the campaign. But broadcasters resisted following this agenda-setting too closely, reporting other election issues as well as two terrorist attacks that occurred during the campaign.

While the main political parties were criticised for limiting access to their rallies and walkabouts in the previous election, in 2017 their campaigns continued to exercise tight control over their media appearances.[24] Corbyn's team was shrewder in this respect, controlling his appearances in front of large crowds of enthusiastic supporters and giving the impression of spontaneity during the campaign, which, at times, restricted journalistic scrutiny and questioning. Instead, the more prominent subtext of much campaign coverage was May's attempt to tightly control her appearances and stick rigidly to a soundbite about 'strong and stable' leadership that quickly backfired. It became a symbol of May's robotic campaigning style, which contrasted with Corbyn's more open and accessible approach. As Sky's John Ryley put it, 'the PM's team was obsessive about fixing shots, holding mics, calling journalists', while the BBC's Jonathan Munro complained that the 'stage management was ridiculous. We got one shot of her [May] in front of her bus surrounded by people or so it appeared but there was not a real person present and the wide shot showed she was just talking to cameras'. While broadcasters felt they exposed moments where parties displayed too much media manipulation, there was also a sense—at the risk of losing access to senior politicians—they could have 'called out' more instances.

It is becoming increasingly difficult to assess the impact of broadcasters alone given the fast-changing ecology of social media and digital campaigning. The way in which journalists reported the parties' campaigns, for example, may not have been driven by pre-planned editorial judgements, but by 'pack journalism'. Some issues appeared to be shaped by 'real-time' events such as when the Prime Minister's spin doctors limited access to local journalists in Cornwall. Word soon spread online and on platforms such as Twitter, sparking debates among journalists how they should report the parties' election campaigning. It also prompted journalistic introspection, with reporters aware of their own coverage being critiqued on social media. So, for example, when ITV's Paul Brand tweeted 'Terrified workers at GSK have clearly been briefed to within an inch of their lives not to speak to media. Won't even open their mouths' after the Prime Minister's highly staged walkabout at a factory, *The Guardian* journalist John Harris replied by asking why this was not mentioned on ITV's 10.30 pm news bulletin.

Although the previous election was only two years ago, broadcasters during the 2017 campaign coverage appeared more integrated with the brave new world of online and social media platforms. They were more assiduous in repackaging their material for social networks such as Facebook, while correspondents such as Robert Peston or Laura Kuenssberg, who often had large followings on networks such as Twitter, were also high profile and active on social media. There were also many new online news sites such as the Corbyn-supporting *The Canary* that achieved high levels of traffic and spent a lot of time critiquing and recycling broadcast news content, much of which was shared in turn by their users online.[25] Newspapers, for instance, did not set the agenda to the same degree as the 2015 election campaign.[26] In a wider news culture increasingly defined by partisan information and online commentary, broadcasters are redefining how they interpret balance and impartiality during election campaigns. Given that journalists were committed to exposing May's style of electioneering, the adversarial nature of political coverage has not been undermined by past government attempts to intimidate broadcasters. Political parties may be reluctant to centre their campaigns on cheap soundbites in future election campaigns or to so flagrantly avoid debating other party leaders on television.

However, broadcasters have acknowledged that they found it challenging to report the UK's political landscape during the campaign, attempting to balance right- and left-wing perspectives in ways that did not always connect to people's concerns and anxieties. The conventional wisdom of many commentators—that Corbyn's brand of politics would not attract voters—had been exposed, as it had been after Brexit and Trump's electoral success in the US.[27] Finding the UK's political gravity is hard to comprehend, let alone interpret in television news. And yet the editorial approach to so much political news continues to rest on professional judgements about the positioning of the mainstream parties. Following how parties campaign or interact at Westminster may help broadcasters interpret the UK's impartiality guidelines. But engaging with voters' concerns beyond the narrow parameters set by political parties might represent a more effective way of reporting future election campaigns.

NOTES

1. 'New Poll Unpacks Social Media and GE2017', *Weber Shandwick*, 31 May 2017, http://webershandwick.co.uk/social-media-ge2017.
2. Stephen Cushion, *The Democratic Value of News: Why Public Service Media Matter*. Palgrave Macmillan, 2012.

3. Stephen Cushion and Richard Thomas, 'From Quantitative Precision to Qualitative Judgements: Professional Perspectives about the Impartiality of Television News during the 2015 UK General Election', *Journalism*, 23 January 2017, http://journals.sagepub.com/doi/pdf/10.1177/1464884916685909.

4. Jasper Jackson 'ITV's The Nightly Show Pulls Almost 3m Viewers But News at Ten Suffers', *The Guardian*, 28 February 2017, https://www.theguardian.com/media/2017/feb/28/itvs-nightly-show-pulls-3m-viewers-news-at-ten-suffers.

5. See Ofcom, 'Licensing of Channel 3 and Channel 5', 2012, http://stakeholders.ofcom.org.uk/binaries/broadcast/tv-ops/c3_c5_licensing.pdf.

6. Stephen Cushion, who carried out the content analysis part of the study, would like to acknowledge the excellent support of his research assistants. They were funded, in part, by an ESRC project 'Television News and Impartiality: Reporting the 2017 UK General Election Campaign', which was supported through the ESRC Cardiff University Impact Acceleration Account (ES/M500422/1). This included Marina Morani, Harriet Lloyd, Sophie Puet, Stephanie Frost and Rob Callaghan. The content analysis examined 2222 news items and 840 election items between 30 April and 7 June 2017 (the timeframe was selected so that the same number of days were examined as in the 2015 election campaign). An intercoder reliability test was carried on all variables, with 10% of the sample recoded. Overall, the level of agreement for each variable was between 81.9% and 99.5%, while Kripendorff Alpha scores were between 0.73 and 0.99. Percentage totals may not add up to 100% due to rounding up.

7. Stephen Cushion and Richard Thomas, *Reporting Elections: Rethinking the Logic of Campaign Coverage*. Polity, 2018.

8. See the full speech by James Harding at the VLV Conference on 2 June 2015 at: www.bbc.co.uk/mediacentre/speeches/2015/james-harding-speech-vlv-2-june-2015.

9. Some interviewees have asked to remain anonymous.

10. Steve Hawkes, *The Sun*, 19 May 2017, https://www.thesun.co.uk/news/3602557/last-nights-tv-election-debate-drew-smaller-audience-than-a-documentary-about-a-vet.

11. Freddy Mayhew, 'May vs Corbyn Live Q&A Attracts Combined Audience of 3.3m Viewers across Channel 4 and Sky News', *Press Gazette*, 30 May 2017, www.pressgazette.co.uk/may-vs-corbyn-live-qa-attracts-combined-audience-of-3-3m-viewers-across-channel-4-and-sky-news.

12. 'Theresa May vs Jeremy Corbyn: Who Won? Our Writers Give Their Verdict', *The Telegraph*, 30 May 2017, www.telegraph.co.uk/news/2017/05/29/theresa-may-vs-jeremy-corbyn-won-writers-give-verdict/#premiumConfirmationComponent.

13. J. Blumler, S. Coleman, and C. Birchall, *Debating the TV Debates: How Voters saw the Question Time Special.* Electoral Reform Society, 2017.
14. Roger Mosey, 'The Manchester Attack Will Define This Election: Broadcasters Have a Careful Line to Tread', *New Statesman*, 25 May 2017, www.newstatesman.com/2017/05/manchester-attack-will-define-election-broadcasters-have-careful-line-tread.
15. Stephen Cushion, 'Amid the Fallout from Manchester, the Tories Dominated News Coverage', *New Statesman*, 1 June 2017, www.newstatesman.com/politics/staggers/2017/06/amid-fallout-manchester-tories-dominated-news-coverage-0.
16. Justin Schlosberg, 'Should He Stay or Should He Go? Television and Online News Coverage of the Labour Party in Crisis', Media Reform Coalition, 2016, www.mediareform.org.uk/wp-content/uploads/2016/07/Corbyn research.pdf.
17. Stephen Cushion and Justin Lewis, 'Equal Time Helped Labour Defy Predictions, But Election Coverage Could Have Been More Balanced and Impartial' in J. Mair et al. (eds), *Brexit, Trump and the Media.* Abramis, pp. 378–85.
18. Party leaders in Northern Ireland made few appearances on UK TV news reports, so they have been excluded from Table 13.9.
19. Cushion and Thomas, *Reporting Elections.*
20. Matthew Smith, 'What People Recall about the Tory and Labour Election Campaigns', *YouGov*, 12 July 2017, https://yougov.co.uk/news/2017/07/12/what-were-britons-main-memories-conservative-and-l.
21. Stephen Cushion, 'Using public opinion to serve journalistic narratives: Rethinking vox pops and live two-way reporting in five UK election campaigns (2009–2017)', *European Journal of Communication, Ifirst* (2018).
22. Sky News's Faisal Islam made reference to growing Labour support: https://twitter.com/faisalislam/status/887087104072855552?refsrc=email&s=11.
23. Roger Mosey, 'Does the Media's Herd Instinct Risk Them Missing the Real Story Yet Again?', *New Statesman*, 23 May 2017, www.newstatesman.com/politics/media/2017/05/does-medias-herd-instinct-risk-them-missing-real-story-yet-again.
24. Stephen Cushion et al., 'Interpreting the Media Logic behind Editorial Decisions: Television News Coverage of the 2015 UK General Election Campaign', *International Journal of Press Politics*, 21(4) (2016): 472–89.
25. Jim Waterson, 'The Rise of the Alt-Left British Media', *BuzzFeed News*, 6 May 2017, https://www.buzzfeed.com/jimwaterson/the-rise-of-the-alt-left?utm_term=.iyVbkee0rX#.qdrYZkkDg9.

26. Stephen Cushion et al., 'Newspapers, Impartiality and Television News: Intermedia Agenda-Setting during the 2015 UK General Election Campaign', *Journalism Studies* (2016), https://doi.org/10.1080/14616 70X.2016.1171163.

27. Cushion, 'Using public opinion to serve journalistic narrative'.

CHAPTER 14

A Bad Press: Newspapers

Dominic Wring and David Deacon

Like Theresa May, many in the print media will want to forget the 2017 general election. The outcome of the campaign came as a particular shock to those newspapers that have long prided themselves on being able to understand and represent the public mood. Even as recently as the 2015 election and the 2016 referendum, there was much commentary on the supposed ability of the press to make a critical intervention in major votes. But 2017 has challenged this and many other assumptions about electoral politics in Britain. The 'Tory press', which is the overwhelming majority of titles, did still contribute to a pro-Conservative effort that saw the party achieve its largest vote share in any election since 1983 and it is plausible that these newspapers helped reinforce, if not necessarily change, their readers' opinions during a campaign in which they relentlessly attacked and in some cases vilified Jeremy Corbyn and Labour. What very few commentators appeared to realise at the outset of this election was the extent to which, in the words of Peter Hitchens, '[p]olitics in this country are a good deal less solid and stable than they seem' (*Mail on Sunday*, 23 April).[1]

© The Author(s) 2018
P. Cowley, D. Kavanagh, *The British General Election of 2017*,
https://doi.org/10.1007/978-3-319-95936-8_14

Contrary to the dominant press narrative throughout the campaign, Theresa May was not on course to win a decisive victory and nor were Labour in the process of disintegrating. This was reflected in polling, although print media reporting of this trend was more limited and sceptical when compared with the 2015 election. Various newspapers' predispositions coloured their perceptions of what was happening in this campaign. Such a phenomenon is not new. But the fact that the final result was so at variance with what much of the press had both anticipated and wanted highlights the apparent disconnect between them and the electorate at large. This reflects the ageing profile of diminishing newspaper readerships.[2] It is noticeable how past events were often invoked in this election to provide historical parallels, thereby further reinforcing the distance between the press and younger potential consumers, many of whom were increasingly registering to vote. Readers (such as they existed) aged under 50 would not have readily appreciated the references to Theresa 'Maggie' May being on her way to a 1983-style landslide victory, accompanied by references to the IRA, industrial discontent and a divided opposition party led by another leader perceived to be out of touch with the country. But like so much other newspaper comment and analysis about this election, print journalists largely missed the real story of the campaign as it unfolded.

ELECTORAL ENGAGEMENT AND FALLING READERSHIPS

One clear indication of the growing disconnect between the national press and the British public is offered by the continued decline in print circulation and readership figures, election by election (see Tables 14.1 and 14.2). A comparison of available circulation figures for daily newspapers in 2017 shows a 10.7% decline compared to the 2015 campaign and a 37.4% reduction compared to the 2010 election. The equivalent figures for Sunday titles reveal a 12.8% decline compared to 2015 and a 43.7% drop compared to 2010. National daily press readership tells a similar tale, with a 15.4% reduction since 2015 and a 45.8% fall since 2010. There is doubt that the political reach of these newspapers is being compensated by the growth of their online readership. National Readership and Comm Score data track a 16.6% drop in print and online readership between 2015 and 2017.

Table 14.1   Daily newspapers' partisanship and circulation

Title (Proprietor/Chair) Editor	Declaration (2015)	Circulation[a] 2017 (2015) (000s)	Print readership[b] (000s)	Print and online[c]
Daily Mirror Trinity Mirror (David Grigson) Lloyd Embley	Strong Labour (Very strong Labour)	687 (882)	1,691 (2,211)	2,083
Daily Express Northern and Shell (Richard Desmond) Hugh Whittow	Very strong Conservative (Very strong UKIP)	386 (438)	838 (993)	1,216
Daily Star Northern and Shell (Richard Desmond) Dawn Neesom	No declaration (No declaration)	438 (420)	769 (943)	980
The Sun News UK (Rupert Murdoch) Tony Gallagher	Very strong Conservative (Very strong Conservative)	1,617 (1,858)	3,653 (5,178)	3,998
Daily Mail Associated Newspapers (Lord Rothermere) Paul Dacre	Very strong Conservative (Very strong Conservative)	1,454 (1,631)	3,215 (3,704)	4,443
Daily Telegraph Telegraph Group (Barclay Brothers) Chris Evans	Strong Conservative (Very strong Conservative)	467 (486)	1,171 (1,119)	1,768
The Guardian Scott Trust (Alex Graham) Katherine Viner	Moderate Labour (Moderate Labour)	154 (176)	898 (761)	2,015

(continued)

Table 14.1   (continued)

Title (Proprietor/Chair) Editor	Declaration (2015)	Circulation[a] 2017 (2015) (000s)	Print readership[b] (000s)	Print and online[c]
The Times News UK (Rupert Murdoch) John Witherow	Moderate Conservative (Moderate Conservative– Liberal Democrat Coalition)	446 (394)	1,049 (788)	1,168
i Johnston Press (Camilla Rhodes) Oliver Duff	No declaration (Weak Conservative–Liberal Democrat Coalition)	263 (276)	475 (518)	491
Financial Times Nikkei (Tsuneo Kita) Lionel Barber	Weak Conservative (Weak Conservative–Liberal Democrat Coalition)	197 (212)	Not available	Not available

Notes: Changes introduced into this calculation in June 2015 prevent a direct comparison with figures for April 2014–March 2015. The equivalent figures for 2015 are taken from the chapter on the press in Cowley and Kavanagh, *The British General Election of 2015*. The assignment of partisanship is based on analysis of each title's formal endorsement (see David Deacon and Dominic Wring, 'Partisan Dealignment and the British Press' in John Bartle, Ivor Crewe and Brian Gosschalk (eds), *Political Communications: The British General Election of 2001*. Frank Cass, 2002, pp. 197–211). [a]Audit Bureau of Circulation (April 2017); [b]National Readership Survey (April 2016–March 2017); [c]National Readership Survey and Comm Score (April 2016–March 2017)

Table 14.3 lists the front-page lead items in the daily press between 1 May and 7 June, and it might be tempting to conclude that this ever-bleaker commercial situation encouraged the most popular titles to focus less attention on the election in their bid to shore up readership. There were several major news events during the last weeks of the campaign that provided ample justification for a redirection of focus, including two terrorist attacks in Manchester and London, and the death of the infamous 'Moors murderer' Ian Brady. In total, under a third (30.6%) of the front-page leads (in Table 14.3) in the *Daily Mail*, the *Daily Express*, *The Sun*, the *Daily Star* and the *Daily Mirror* were focused on the election campaign, although this proportion is identical to that found for the

Table 14.2   Sunday newspapers' partisanship and circulation

Title	Declaration	Circulation[a] 2017 (2015) (000s)	Readership[b] 2017 (2015) (000s)
Sunday Mirror	Moderate Labour	585	1,761
	(Strong Labour)	(833)	(2,401)
Sunday Express	Very strong Conservative	335	893
	(Very strong UKIP)	(385)	(1,150)
Sun on Sunday	Strong Conservative	1,358	3,847
	(Very strong Conservative)	(1,474)	(4,207)
Sunday People	Strong anti-Conservative	228	Not available
	(None)	(324)	(674)
Mail on Sunday	Strong Conservative	1,239	3,399
	(Strong Conservative)	(1,447)	(4,007)
Star on Sunday	No declaration	252	804
	(No declaration)	(254)	(825)
Sunday Telegraph	Strong Conservative	355	1,219
	(Strong Conservative)	(371)	(1,150)
The Observer	Strong anti-Conservative	181	947
	(Moderate Liberal Democrat)	(196)	(723)
Sunday Times	Moderate Conservative	780	1,219
	(Strong Conservative)	(809)	(2,010)

Notes: [a]Audit Bureau of Circulation (April 2015); [b]National Readership Survey (April 2016–March 2017)

same period of the 2015 campaign.[3] The biggest change in press engagement by this measure came with the 'quality' press, with 56% of lead items in 2017 focused on the election, down from 73% for the same period in 2015.

But front pages only tell part of the story about the extent of press engagement with the election. Further examination of media content analysis data sets carried out by Loughborough University's Centre for Research in Communication and Culture reveals significant reductions in the amount of space given to the election in the last 20 weekdays of the 2017 campaign across all sectors compared with the same period for 2015. In the 'quality' papers, total space reduced by 25.2%, in the 'mid-market' papers (the *Daily Mail* and the *Daily Express*) by 19.8% and in the 'red tops' by 26.1%.[4]

Table 14.3 Front-page lead stories, 19 April–8 June

	Daily Mirror	Daily Express	The Sun	Daily Mail	Daily Star	Daily Telegraph	The Guardian	The Times	i	Financial Times
19 April	(You did us proud)	Vote for me and I'll deliver EU Brexit	Blue murder	Crush the saboteurs	Brexit serial continues: Snap, cackle and pop!	May's bolt from the blue	May: give me my mandate	May heads for election landslide	Stunned Britain heads to the polls	May calls snap election in bid to strengthen hand in Brexit talks
20 April	Fowl play! Chicken Theresa May still refuses to take part in live TV debates	(New drugs to beat dementia)	(Terror drivers will be shot dead)	Theresa's cast-iron Brexit pledge	(Exorcist called in to Corrie haunting)	SNP plots a 'coalition of chaos'	Lives at risk if Tories cut aid, Gates warns	May forced to weaken key targets on migrants	Battle begins	(Brussels starts to shut British companies out of contracts)
21 April	(15 dead babies and 3 dead mums ...and a scandal to terrify EVERY parent)	(Diet drinks health alert)	(I wish I'd raped schoolgirl)	(New terrorist attack in Paris)	(Maddie: shock new evidence revealed)	(Terror on the Champs-Elysees)	(It's not too late to avert Brexit, says EU leader)	(Britain told to keep EU laws)	Corbyn's message to Remainers: no second Brexit referendum	(Trump fires protectionist warning over steel industry)
22 April	Tories' VAT bombshell	Migrant worker madness	Pay and DisMay	(Mortgage rates hit record low)	(Real ghost caught on film for first time)	May risks backlash over tax and foreign aid	(France heads for poll on high alert)	(Trump puts EU ahead of Britain in trade queue)	Pensions face pinch	Fears of Hammond 'tax bombshell'

(continued)

Table 14.3 (continued)

	Daily Mirror	Daily Express	The Sun	Daily Mail	Daily Star	Daily Telegraph	The Guardian	The Times	i	Financial Times
24 April	(Maddies 'was snatched for rich family'?)	(New foreign aid outrage)	(Cops taser Ferne fella in his pants)	(New French Revolution)	(Maddie: MI5 hid her body)	Labour's nuclear implosion	(It's Macron versus Le Pen)	(New French revolution as outsiders sweep to victory)	Forget party allegiances, says Blair	(Macron and Le Pen to face-off in contest for French presidency)
25 April	(Husband beat up a shark to save my life)	(Exercises to beat dementia)	(Have a go hero Hardy)	(GPs failing thousands of cancer patients)	(Moaning Rhys killer: prison's too tough)	(Students told not to obsess over finding job)	Remain group seek to oust pro-Brexit MPs	(Brussels to hit Britain with $2bn fraud claim)	Labour unveils Brexit Strategy	(Relief sweeps market as Macron secures place in French run-off)
26 April	(We have a major line of inquiry … it could provide an answer)	(Vital new clues in Maddy hunt)	(Who bun it)	(Maddie police chasing 'critical lead')	(New Rhys horror: kid shot as TV drama screened)	Britain faces EU bill until 2020	(MPs condemn 'wasteful' schools policy)	(Borrowing falls to lowest level since Brown years)	We want May in TV debates, say voters	(Arnault tightens grip on LVMH as luxury assets become scarcer)
27 April	(51 investigations at baby death NHS trust)	(Turning down heating can beat diabetes)	(The fraud squads)	(Millions failed by GPs who shut in the afternoon)	(John Terry in vile sex tape fury)	May keeps Britain tied to Europe's human rights law	(Foreign fighter exodus leaves Isis weakened)	(Drug giants threaten to quit Britain)	(Taxman tackles football elite)	(White House pledges biggest ever tax cut to unleash US economy)

(continued)

Table 14.3 (continued)

	Daily Mirror	Daily Express	The Sun	Daily Mail	Daily Star	Daily Telegraph	The Guardian	The Times	i	Financial Times
28 April	500 school heads: Tory cuts are damaging our schools	(New Whitehall knife terror)	(Knife one lads)	(Seized, with a sackful of knives)	(Smirk of a jerk)	(Downing Street terror plot)	(Police swoop on suspected terrorist near Westminster)	(Hit internet giants over danger to child safety)	(Westminster terror suspect thwarted by police)	(EU signal over united Ireland stokes fear for post-Brexit Britain)
29 April	(Butcher surgeon's 1,000 victims)	(Evil cancer doctor played god)	(Louise and Jamie on rocks)	(Why did NHS fail to stop butcher surgeon?)	(Billion-dollar beefcake)	Tory tax pledge to high earners	(NHS pays £9m to victims of rogue surgeon)	(Isis suspect seized in raid)	(Surgeon guilty of mutilating patients)	(Growth slows as rising prices hit households)
1 May	Blair: I'm back	(Your £15m goes up in smoke)	(I'll make a billion ... and pay my bill at the laundrette)	Elderly care tax breaks lifeline	(Joshua: the movie)	(Facebook 'must pay to police internet')	PM paves way to end key tax commitments	(Social media giants fail to tackle hatred, says MPs)	Corbyn pledges £3bn to close education gap	(Interest-free credit cards are a 'ticking time-bomb', bankers warn)
2 May	(Brits facing Spanish holiday ban)	May's outrage at EU's dirty tricks	(Terrorist's cushty life on benefits in Peckham)	(Exploited by cash-for-eggs IVF clinics)	(Mel B tug of love hell)	EU plots to block May's deal on expats	May fights accusation of botched and humiliating start to Brexit talks	(Fears for car market amid loan mis-selling)	(Tax bills that don't add up)	(Brussels poised for power grab on London's euro-clearing market)
3 May	(Kate demands £1.3m over topless pics)	(Keep taking your statins)	(Quids on the skids)	(IVF clinics peddling false hope over egg freezing)	(Maddie: parents kept info from the cops)	Tory cash handouts to scrap diesel cars	I'll be bloody difficult in EU talks, says MP	You can't lead Brexit talks, EU tells May	(Statins: don't believe the scare stories)	(EU raises Brexit bill to €100bn as Paris and Berlin harden stance)

(continued)

Table 14.3 (continued)

	Daily Mirror	Daily Express	The Sun	Daily Mail	Daily Star	Daily Telegraph	The Guardian	The Times	i	Financial Times
4 May	May plotting snap vote on bombing Syria	Don't meddle with our election	Nuclear Juncker	Hands off our election	(Cops talked stressed footie ace back from brink)	May unleashes fire at Europe	May declares war on Brussels	Brussels is meddling in our election, warns May	EU trying to rig election, warns May	May accuses Brussels of election sabotage and ramping up tension
5 May	(Beeb fury at Cliff's £1m legal bill)	(Thank you sir!)	(He's had his Phil)	(The nation salutes you, sir)	(Fears for 62 more Prem stars)	(Service with a smile)	(Show respect in Brexit talks, Tusk tells May)	(Duke retires rather than grow frail in public)	(I can't stand up much longer! Duke of Edinburgh retires aged 95)	(Slide in prices casts shadow over buoyant oil earnings)
6 May	(Zoe Ball's torment as lover 'kills himself')	Theresa's the new Maggie	(Zoe's lover found hanged)	Theresa on the march!	(Zoe Ball's lover 'kills himself')	Great Tory rebirth as the Right unites	May crushes UKIP as Corbyn admits: 'we face historic challenge'	May on course for a landslide	Blue tide	Tories triumph in local elections
8 May	(England star bet on his own transfer)	(Broccoli pill to save your life)	(118 calls costs £9)	(Shame of the insurance giants)	(Summer starts today)	(France's new hope puts cloud over Brexit)	(Macron wins French presidency—but a country remains divided)	(Landslide for Macron)	(Macron marches to victory)	(Macron sweeps to victory in French presidential election)
9 May	Secret Tory plot to bring back fox hunting	May vows to slash migration	(Why I tried to kill Trump)	£100 off your energy bill	(Katie Price steamy clinch with mystery man)	(Anger as energy bills rise by 37pc)	Corbyn pins election hopes on housing reform pledges	May faces backlash over energy cap	(UK border could move from Calais)	May to renew Tories' broken promises on immigration

(continued)

Table 14.3 (continued)

	Daily Mirror	Daily Express	The Sun	Daily Mail	Daily Star	Daily Telegraph	The Guardian	The Times	i	Financial Times
10 May	(School trip girl, 11, dies at theme park)	(Ibuprofen: new heart danger)	Danczuk rape quiz	(Girl, 11, dies in theme park)	(Horror on the rapids: Girl 11 dead)	Labour faces historic party split	Corbyn: business tax rise will pay for £6bn boost for schools	(Stop splitting up elderly couples)	(Millions to miss out on full state pension)	May manifesto chief held talks with former Miliband aide
11 May	Corbyn will nationalise energy, rail and mail	(Britain's facing drought disaster)	(I warned park over death raft ride)	Labour's manifesto to drag us back to the 1970s	(Hotter than Ibiza)	Revealed: Corbyn's manifesto to take Britain back to 1970s	Corbyn's plans to nationalise rail, mail and energy firms	Cracks widen between Chancellor and No 10	(Stroke epidemic to hit UK)	(Defiant Trump calls for closer Moscow ties after firing FBI chief)
12 May	Dear PM, you're destroying nursing	(Dementia crisis out of control)	Crash, Jez runs over TV man, Bang, Red Len on backside, Wallies! Manifesto launch is shambles	Corbyn's fantasy land	(Enders axes Danni for good)	Labour MPs ditch Corbyn manifesto	Corbyn vows to 'transform lives' as party backs radical manifesto	Labour fights civil war over hard-Left manifesto	Labour's £50bn wish list	(Boost for British tech as Softbank invests $500m in software start-up)
13 May	(Hackers hold NHS to ransom)	(NHS chaos after hacker attack)	(National Hacked Service)	(Cyber hackers cripple the NHS)	(Fear of a clown: Cowell's new terror)	(Hackers hold NHS to ransom)	(NHS targeted in global cyber-attack)	(Huge hack attack hits hospitals)	(Huge NHS cyber attack paralyses hospitals)	(NHS hackers used stolen cyber weapons from US spy agency)

(continued)

Table 14.3 (continued)

	Daily Mirror	Daily Express	The Sun	Daily Mail	Daily Star	Daily Telegraph	The Guardian	The Times	i	Financial Times
15 May	(Web hackers to strike Britain again)	May: I'll boost rights for the worker	(Brady on deathbed)	Your right to time off if relative needs care	(Gambler Roo in £140m China crisis)	Workers get leave to care for elderly	Labour and Tories step up the fight to win working-class votes	May gives all workers new rights to time off	Workers offered new deal by Tories	(Businesses around the world told to prepare for fresh cyber attacks)
16 May	(Burn in hell, Brady)	(Moors killer Brady is dead)	(Monster Brady is dead)	(Monster of the moors is dead)	(Tragic Zoe: I'll keep loving)	Labour plan to pull 1m into top tax bracket	Labour 'fat cat' tax to rein in excessive pay	(Drug firm faces fine of £220m for hiking prices)	Labour's tax grab on the rich	(Hackers have second US weapon primed for attack, warns analyst)
17 May	(Scatter my ashes over Moors with my victims)	(Why was £10.4m wasted keeping monster Brady alive?)	(Too brainy to be jailed)	Corbyn plan to bankrupt UK	(Evil Brady wanted ashes scattered on moors)	(Family of shot WPC are denied justice)	Labour won't win, says top union backer	Labour's tax raid in shatters	Corbyn's sharp left turn	Labour pledges £49bn tax rise to fund huge spending push
18 May	(100 Rochdale paedos still walk the streets)	May's plans for a fairer Britain	RIP to rip-offs	You won't have to sell your house to pay for care	(Cowell facing quiz on Mel B threesomes)	Middle-class lose winter fuel payments to fund social care	PM gambles on making elderly pay their way	Thousands hit be new care costs	Millions of pensioners to lose winter fuel funding	(Trump faces escalating crisis after Congress demands Comey memo)

(continued)

Table 14.3 (continued)

	Daily Mirror	Daily Express	The Sun	Daily Mail	Daily Star	Daily Telegraph	The Guardian	The Times	i	Financial Times
19 May	10 million OAPs to lose winter fuel cash	We'll put Juncker back in his box	Blue Labour	At last, a PM not afraid to be honest with you	(Pippa's sexy Ann Summers wedding)	May's manifesto for the mainstream	May manifesto rejects legacy of Cameron era	Mainstream May reaches out to Labour heartlands	May's vision for Britain	May break with Thatcherite faith in centrist pitch to Labour voters
20 May	('BBC stars had sex in woods and asked kids to join in')	(Alzheimer's cure hope)	(Wedding of the rears)	(What a creep)	(Harry and Meghan's bi (bum) day)	Scottish to keep winter fuel benefit (because it's colder)	('The war's just begun': Assange defiant after rape case dropped)	(Tough new controls on web giants)	(RBS justice denied)	(Trump turmoil erases dollar gains)
22 May	PM's election guru in tax scandal	(Ten days of sun on way)	(I walked plank over Jolly Roger with Orlando)	Corbyn's kick in teeth for IRA victims	(Meg's yes to Harry after all-night wedding booze-up)	Corbyn engulfed in IRA furore	(Revealed: Facebook's secret rules on sex, violence, hate speech and terror)	Care crisis threatens to scupper May reform	Tories stand firm after care wobble	Senior Tories were kept in the dark over May's 'dementia tax'
23 May	How can we ever trust Mrs U-turn?	(Dementia runs in the family)	Blood on his hands: ex-IRA killer's Corbyn verdict	(Facebook lets teens see porn)	(Blooming Kell it's a scorcher)	Care cost chaos after May U-turn on key pledge	May's manifesto meltdown: U-turn on 'dementia tax' leaves PM on back foot	Pensioners to pay for May's social care U-turn	'Dementia tax' U-turn	May's U-turn on social care costs rattles Tory campaign

(continued)

Table 14.3 (continued)

	Daily Mirror	Daily Express	The Sun	Daily Mail	Daily Star	Daily Telegraph	The Guardian	The Times	i	Financial Times
24 May	(Killed by evil)	(Evil beyond belief)	(Pure evil)	(Soldiers on the streets)	(Slaughter of the innocents)	(Troops on the streets in race to foil second terror attack)	(Young lives stolen by terror)	(Libya terror link)	(The girls who will never go home)	(Manchester man identified as concert bomber who killed 22)
25 May	('Bomber brother planning his own attack')	(Hunt for the bomb maker)	(Find the bomb gang)	(The jihadi family)	('My boy is innocent. He was about to become an uncle')	(Five missed chances to foil bombers)	(May to confront Trump as US leaks crucial bombing evidence)	(MI5 was warned)	(Terror network active in the UK)	(Police hunt terror network linked to Manchester concert bomber)
26 May	(Bank holiday bomb alert)	(Bombing was 'very wicked')	(Inside the bomb factory)	(Curb web giants that give terror a voice)	(Trash takes out the trash)	Corbyn: UK wars to blame for terror	(May: technology giants must lead fight against extremism)	(Bomber planned for a year)	(Net closes on Manchester terror gang)	(OPEC strikes deal to extend supply squeeze into 2018)
27 May	(Terror chief: go out and enjoy yourselves!)	(Net closes in on evil bombers)	('Mass murder terror targets')	(Bank holiday ring of steel)	(Sup for the cup)	Corbyn is making excuses for terror attacks, says May	May puts bombing at heart of the election with attack on Corbyn	(UK home to 23,000 jihadists)	(Police urge public: 'go out and enjoy yourselves')	May puts Manchester bombing at centre of election campaign

(continued)

Table 14.3 (continued)

	Daily Mirror	Daily Express	The Sun	Daily Mail	Daily Star	Daily Telegraph	The Guardian	The Times	i	Financial Times
29 May	(We are not afraid)	(UK faces wave of Libyan terror)	(7/7 hero is '23rd bomber victim')	(BA chaos: was cost cutting to blame?)	(We are not afraid)	Corbyn accused of honouring Palestinian terror chief	(MI5 launches two inquiries into missed terror warnings)	(Power to ban UK jihadis has been used 'just once')	10 days to decide the PM	(Asset managers Brexit-proof their businesses; fund houses bolster presence in Europe)
30 May	(Cop hunt for the bomber's suitcase)	(Oily fish can beat dementia)	(Tiger kills keeper Rosa)	(Zoo girl mauled to death by tiger)	(The heat is on)	Corbyn ducks terror challenge	Corbyn tells Paxman: 'I'm no dictator' in TV debate	May woos working class with tough line on Brexit	May and Corbyn endure bruising TV debate	(Subprime-scarred banks retreat from $1.2tn US car load market)
31 May	(Diana 'death car' outrage)	Migrant summer chaos	(Death trap)	Labour's plan to open doors to Britain even wider	(Megastars come out for Manchester)	Labour's secret plan to increase migration	May intensifies personal attack as polls narrow	Shock poll predict Tory losses	Hunt: bad Brexit will damage NHS	(US shoppers put economy back on course to lead global recovery)
1 June	NHS: the money has run out	Corbyn's plot to bring in migrant workers	(B.B. Seedy)	Fury at bias on BBC TV debate	(Black panther stalks mum in UK woods)	Record number hit by 45p top rate of tax	Corbyn confronts Rudd on cuts in fractious TV debate	Have faith in me: May fights back with Brexit	Ambush	(China and EU seal climate pact as doubts rise over US commitment)

(continued)

Table 14.3 (continued)

	Daily Mirror	Daily Express	The Sun	Daily Mail	Daily Star	Daily Telegraph	The Guardian	The Times	i	Financial Times
2 June	(Shame of the 10,000 bomb concert ticket leeches)	Corbyn doesn't believe in Britain	Leaf it out	Corbyn's sly death tax trap	(TV Caroline Love Isle lesbian romps)	Fake web accounts boosting Labour vote	(Anger at US as Trump rejects climate accord)	We will use SNP to give us power, says Labour	Rivals clash over Brexit	May offers Brexit vow as Corbyn surge dims hope of landslide victory
3 June	Tory MP charged over election expenses	Sturgeon: I'll help Corbyn	(100 celebs in tax dodge)	Corbyn's nuclear meltdown	(Amanda's boobs win BGT)	Tory tax pledge to high earners	Labour accuses Tories of using fake news stories to attack Corbyn	('Myths' by Muslims hit anti-terror campaign)	Tory shock at criminal charges	May reaches out to business as Brexit tensions escalate
5 June	(Monsters and heroes)	(Enough is enough)	(Jihadi killer in an Arsenal shirt)	(Bloody day all of Britain said: enough is enough)	(Heroes)	(Police uncover YouTube link to London terror attack)	(Seven dead, 21 critically hurt: May says 'enough is enough')	(Massacre in the market)	(Defiant)	'Enough is enough' declares May in vow to ramp up war on extremism
6 June	(So how the hell did he slip through?)	May: trust me to keep you safe	(Why didn't they stop TV jihadi?)	(MI5: we had him—and let him go)	(How did we let him walk the streets?)	(Brazen jihadist who was free to parade his extremism on TV)	(Britain faces 'completely different' level of terror threat, police warn)	(London attacker linked to 7/7 bombing suspect)	('We will not be dragged into hatred')	(London attacker was known member of extremist group)

(continued)

Table 14.3 (continued)

	Daily Mirror	Daily Express	The Sun	Daily Mail	Daily Star	Daily Telegraph	The Guardian	The Times	i	Financial Times
7 June	(I'm going to be a terrorist)	Vote May or we face disaster	Jezza's jihadi comrades	Apologists for terror	(Burning in hell forever)	(I'm going to be a terrorist)	May threatens to dismantle human rights law in wake of terror attacks	(MI5 warned attacker 'wanted to be a terrorist')	(The nurse who ran towards danger)	May targets Labour heartlands and ramps up anti-terror rhetoric
8 June	Lies, damned lies and Theresa May	Vote for May today	Don't chuck Britain in the Cor-bin	Let's reignite British spirit	Tezza vs Jezza	Your country needs you	Corbyn and May make last pitch for votes after bruising campaign	(Midnight terror plot five days before attack)	X marks the spot	(Santander buys Popular for €1 after ECB triggers bailout)

Note: Headlines in brackets refer to non-election-related stories

Whether this reduction was the result of commercial judgements or the crowding effect of other major news events is a moot point. It may well be that complacency also played a part in some quarters. Theresa May's announcement of the election proved a welcome surprise for many of her press supporters. Stephen Pollard applauded it as being 'right to call' (*Daily Express*, 19 April), whilst Trevor Kavanagh agreed that '[t]here'll never be a better time to strike' alongside an editorial in *The Sun* arguing that 'Britain needs this new vote' (19 April). Predictably the anti-Conservative *Daily Mirror* took a different view, declaring 'The Lady is for U-Turning' (19 April), a reference to the Prime Minister reneging on her promise not to hold a snap election. This alleged deceit would be an issue for the *Daily Mirror* to the end, when it portrayed May as Pinocchio (8 June). But this was a minority view and rival newspapers preferred to speculate about what was likely to happen on polling day.

The Times' front-page headline 'May Heads for Election Landslide' reflected an early press consensus as to the likely result (19 April). *The Sun* reinforced this narrative with a striking cover headline 'Blue Murder' and accompanying story that claimed the 'PM's Snap Poll Will Kill off Labour' (19 April). Notable opponents of the government agreed. For Jonathan Freedland, May's decision was a 'gamble', but 'only in the sense that the risk is ultra-low' (*The Guardian*, 19 April). The *Daily Mirror* also quoted Labour Party sources saying they faced 'disaster' ('We Fear Bloodbath', 20 April). Reporting a poll taken following the calling of the election, a front-page headline in the *Daily Express* claimed '1 in 7 Labour Voters Turns Tory' (23 April). Stories of this kind encouraged a view that, in the words of Andrew Rawnsley, the coming campaign would make little difference and a 'thumping' Conservative 'triumph looks unstoppable' (*The Observer*, 7 May).

Anticipation of a decisive outcome informed press reporting through-out the election, particularly among the Tory-supporting papers. Similarly, Trevor Kavanagh hoped that 'the promised election day landslide could yet become a tsunami' (*Sun on Sunday*, 15 May), estimating that she would 'do much better' than the majority of 94 seats initially projected by pollsters (*The Sun*, 22 May). Even after the Prime Minister's difficulties over her so-called 'dementia tax' in the middle of the campaign, many in the press remained confident that she would easily win the election. Writing in the aftermath of the hiatus, Macer Hall predicted 'May is Still on Course for a Massive Majority' (*Daily Express*, 27 May). Likewise, a reported narrowing in the polls was met with scepticism by *The Observer*, which commented that 'many are bewildered by figures showing Labour has closed the gap to within five points' (28 May). When another company's findings appeared to confirm this trend a few days later, John Rentoul also expressed doubts: 'Why I Wouldn't Trust the Poll Predicting a Hung Parliament' (*i*, 1 June). Conservative strategist Jim Messina's dismissive response to the same research (see p. 267) was widely quoted.

There was considerable doubt about the apparent shift in public opinion as the campaign drew to a close. Dominic Lawson, for instance, concluded: 'Don't Panic about Polls, May is Way Ahead' (*Sunday Times*, 4 June). Heightened expectations of a convincing victory did, however, create a potential problem for the Prime Minister, as Mary Dejevsky noted: 'Anything Less Than a Thumping Majority Will Be a Failure for May' (*i*, 2 June). This comment hinted at another possible outcome that few commentators had considered, specifically that the Tories were not on course for victory. *The Times*' Rachel Sylvester was one observer who, at the beginning of the campaign, questioned the prevailing consensus that the Conservatives would win because 'nothing is certain', given the fraught situation caused by Brexit (22 April). Andrew Marr also believed the issue might be detrimental to the government and warned: 'The PM has alienated the "48 per centers", and it could cost her dear' (*Sunday Times*, 23 April). Having speculatively linked May's decision to call the election to the potential prosecution of some of her colleagues over their 2015 electoral expenses, Peter Hitchens presciently observed that 'the Tory campaign this time will have to be a good deal more cautious about such things, which may weaken it, especially if the campaign goes wrong—and this is not impossible' (*Mail on Sunday*, 23 April).

There was a discernible tendency for press commentators to draw on historical comparisons in their analyses of the election's potential outcome. Professor Vernon Bogdanor suggested Labour was 'maybe heading for its worst humiliation since 1935' (*The Times*, 20 May). The expectation of a landslide victory for the Conservatives also rekindled memories of their 1983 triumph. Harold Wilson's former Press Secretary Joe Haines referenced that result when comparing current party policies to those of the then leader and the foremost comedy act from the time: 'Corbyn's Morecambe & Wise manifesto is madder than Michael Foot's' (*Daily Mail*, 12 May). The *Daily Mail* explicitly mentioned the 1983 document to dismiss its contemporary as 'Labour's New Suicide Note' (11 May). A *Financial Times* editorial was also critical and, conscious of historical precedent, described the party's programme as a 'misguided bid to turn the clock back' (12 May). Dominic Sandbrook agreed with this, observing: 'Mr Corbyn and Co increasingly remind me of one of those deranged Californian cults of the Seventies' (*Daily Mail*, 10 May). An American example from the same decade provided the basis for another colourful attack, albeit in this case by Aditya Chakrabortty on Theresa May: 'Britain risks becoming a one-party state following June's election with a PM who is an heir to Nixon' (*The Guardian*, 25 April). Chakrabortty would not have imagined that weeks later, his comparison would be apt, but for very different reasons relating to the prospect of a once-powerful incumbent having to resign.

THERESAMAYNIA

The sitting Prime Minister is normally the most prominent figure in the reporting of an election and 2017 proved no exception in this respect.[5] In 2017, this focus on the leader rather than her colleagues was frequently remarked upon. As Dominic Lawson noted: 'There are No Tories—Only Theresa' (*Sunday Times*, 14 May). Similarly, James Forsyth predicted: 'On June 8, Theresa May will be the queen of all she surveys' (*The Sun*, 29 April). Even the idiosyncratic Peter Oborne embraced the prevailing wisdom: 'History Beckons: This Election Gives Mrs May What Every Conservative Leader since Churchill Has Dreamed of—Putting an End to Labour for Ever...' (*Daily Mail*, 19 April). May had enjoyed nearly a year in Downing Street, during which time favourable press coverage had helped establish her credentials. According to Tim Shipman, the 'Ronseal PM' and her 'cult of personality, rather than Toryism, is helping Theresa May in the left's heartlands' (*Sunday Times*, 14 May). The local election results confirmed what the *Daily Telegraph* heralded as the 'Great Tory Rebirth' (6 May), a phenomenon encouraged by 'Theresamaynia' (*The Sun*, 6 May). Leo McKinstry believed that the Tories' performance had been helped by May being 'a superb political strategist'. Moreover, he linked her abilities to an upbringing that had helped make her 'a quintessentially English figure who exudes the respectability, trustworthy values of her upbringing as a vicar's daughter from the Home Counties' (*Daily Express*, 8 May).

   Some commentators questioned the assumption that the Prime Minister was as strong and stable figure as suggested by her soon-to-become notorious campaign slogan. Aside from Peter Hitchens, such critics tended to be on the left and included Paul Mason, who argued that May 'doesn't understand' contemporary Britain (*The Guardian*, 23 May). Similarly, Polly Toynbee contended that a certain newspaper had had more impact on the Prime Minister than her own formative experiences: 'The *Daily Mail*, not her father's church, is her spiritual guide, its editor, Paul Dacre, her compass. She never challenges its warped version of middle England' (*The Guardian*, 6 June). Other newspapers strongly disagreed, with the *Daily Telegraph* believing that in the election 'This Mrs May's Chance to Become as Dominant a Figure as Mrs Thatcher' (19 April). The *Daily Express* went further, using a front-page headline to declare this transformation was complete: 'Theresa the New Maggie' (6 May). Such observations were encouraged by May's admission, reported by the *Daily Mail*, that 'I'll Be a Bloody Difficult Woman' (3 May) in her dealings with the UK's European partners. The choice of words revived memories of Thatcher's approach to her EU counterparts and led *Daily Express* columnist Judy Finnigan to complement the current Prime Minister as a 'British battle-axe' (6 May).

Whereas her supporters characterized May as steadfast, others detected weakness in her reluctance to answer questions. This began when the election was announced after she refused to participate in face-to-face debates with her rivals ('May Accused of Dodging TV Showdowns', *The Times*, 19 April; similarly, a *Daily Telegraph* editorial later lamented the decision 'hardly spoke to confidence in her' (1 June)). The Conservative leader also appeared uncomfortable on a rare public walkabout in Oxfordshire when directly confronted over disability benefit cuts by voter Kathy Mohan, who subsequently told *The Guardian*: 'I wanted to have my say. I just came out with it' (17 May). Observing her early election engagements, Stephen Bush commented: 'You have more chance of bumping into a swing voter at Tory conference than you do at the PM's campaign events' (*i*, 4 May). For *Mail on Sunday* correspondent Andrew Gimson, this was a facet of Conservative strategy: 'Our Supreme Leader Will Bore Her Way to Victory' (23 April). Before re-using the nickname 'Maybot' (6 June) he had coined, *The Guardian* sketch writer John Crace picked up on Gimson's theme to liken the Prime Minister's speeches to those of the notorious North Korean dictator ('Kim Jong-May', 26 April).

May's apparent reluctance to freely engage with the public was mocked by various publications, including some sympathetic to the Conservatives. *The Times* even used the term 'Maybot' to describe her leaden performance in response to a local reporter while visiting Plymouth (2 June). Similarly, *Daily Telegraph* correspondent Michael Deacon referred to the

Prime Minister's 'stiffly unrevealing answers' on another occasion (9 May). May's perceived lack of charisma became a persistent feature in the reporting of her campaign. Matt Chorley was even more explicit in his unflattering assessment: 'Except for calling a snap election, Mrs May has barely said or done anything interesting for 11 months and yet is the subject of fevered fan-worship usually reserved for One Direction or Kim Kardashian's bottom' (*The Times*, 6 May).

This echoed critic Marina Hyde's labelling of the Tory leader as 'Groundhog May' (*The Guardian*, 18 May). Hyde had earlier warned that such a risk-averse approach could yet rebound: 'With May the snowflake in charge, this is health and safety gone mad: Dalek soundbites and dodging debates may secure a Tory win, but contempt for voters can backfire' (*The Guardian*, 29 April). Despite her refusal to debate with her opponents, the Prime Minister did make some scheduled broadcast appearances. One of her most memorable was an interview she gave alongside husband Philip on BBC1's primetime *The One Show*. Press reaction to this was mixed. In her highly sympathetic profile, Jan Moir praised the couple for appearing the epitome of normality and decency ('Theresa: Behind the Mask', *Daily Mail*, 13 May), with the paper later featuring them in a photograph doing their own shopping at Waitrose (20 May). Conversely, Elizabeth Day bemoaned the interview as a 'dreary' attempt to 'humanize' them (*Daily Telegraph*, 15 May), whilst John Crace dismissed the pair as boring, concluding that the Mays produced 'pure valium' (*The Guardian*, 10 May). The Prime Minister's apparent awkwardness in public registered in other ways. A photo opportunity involving her eating chips led to comparisons with the infamous image of Ed Miliband devouring a bacon sandwich (*The Guardian*, 3 May). Following the controversy over the Conservative manifesto, critics such as Zoe Williams mocked campaign branding that had positioned May as 'strong' and 'stable': 'A woman who changes her mind on everything is running as the immovable rock in a turbulent world' (*The Guardian*, 29 May). A *Daily Telegraph* editorial response to the crisis was less damning but nonetheless telling when it suggested: 'We should see more of the PM's team' (2 June).

Theresa May's failure to assert herself when challenged over her manifesto proved the turning point in the campaign. The hiatus emboldened press critics and reinforced a growing public perception that she was a brittle politician who was out of her depth. As Tony Blair's former speechwriter turned columnist Philip Collins put it, 'Mrs May has been rumbled as not very good' (*The Times*, 26 May). Various newspapers blamed May's close aide Nick Timothy for the fateful decision to include social care reform in the Conservative manifesto, with an editorial in the *Daily Telegraph* lamenting the way in which 'bad politics can thwart good policies' (23 May). Reports suggested that the controversial measure had been approved without the knowledge of the Cabinet or the party's returning election strategist Lynton Crosby (*The Times*, 23 May). Prior to this Timothy, along with his colleague Fiona Hill, had what Dominic Lawson called a 'fearsome' reputation (*Sunday Times*, 14 May). And it was pointedly Timothy's humble Birmingham origins that were cited as the inspiration for the so-called 'Erdington modernisation' plan to broaden the Conservatives' appeal to working-class voters (*Financial Times*, 6 May).

Mr Zen

The election proved as momentous for the Labour leader as his Conservative counterpart, and, as with Theresa May, the campaign would alter public perceptions of Jeremy Corbyn. This would be a change that also ended the newspaper speculation that had continually plagued what Andrew Rawnsley dismissed as his 'abysmal leadership' (*The Observer*, 9 May). From the announcement of the election, poor expectations framed press analysis of Labour's chances. The party in turn limited print journalists access to its campaign (*Financial Times*, 9 May), although exceptions were made for correspondents from the *Daily Mirror* and *The Guardian*. This, of course, hardly stopped newspapers from commenting on Labour's predicament. Former Labour MP Tom Harris expected his former party would be 'crushed, but perhaps, in numerical terms, not by quite the margin it deserves' (*Daily Telegraph*, 19 April). Polly Toynbee used similarly apocalyptic terms, believing that the Labour leader's 'every impulse is to make the wrong call on everything'. Toynbee excoriated her target: 'Corbyn is Rushing to Embrace Labour's Annihilation' (*The Guardian*, 19 April). She drastically altered her view after the election, commenting that 'Corbyn Has Rescued Britain from the Chaos of Austerity. This is His Moment' (*The Guardian*, 13 June).

Labour-sympathising columnist Janice Turner in *The Times* was downbeat at the beginning of the campaign, saying she felt like 'a powerless spectator at your party's probable destruction' (22 April). Stephen Pollard argued that this fate could still be averted if MPs acclaimed former Shadow Home Secretary Yvette Cooper as their leader as 'Only Yvette Can Save Her Party from Oblivion' (*Mail on Sunday*, 23 April). Labour losses in the local elections further concentrated minds on what lay ahead. Jonathan Freedland, fearing Pollard's prediction was now becoming reality, suggested one person was responsible: 'No More Excuses: Corbyn is to Blame for This Meltdown' (*The Guardian*, 6 May). The adverse council results also prompted *i* contributor Sarah Ditum to comment: 'We had the fiction that a "truly left-wing" leader could win by recruiting non-voters... If there's any wickedness in politics, it's not in Tory voters: it's in the self-righteous leftist ninnies who've given up on their own nation' (*i*, 6 May).

Similarly, offering the kind of counsel normally delivered in an electoral post-mortem, former Cabinet member Peter Mandelson criticised what he called the 'populists offer(ing) false promise' now in control of his party. He lamented how 'the hard left leadership wants to build a socialist movement instead of an election-winning force' (*Financial Times*, 22 April). Invoking memories of 1983's 'longest suicide note', Philip Collins denounced the party's current programme as 'This is Labour's Ticket to the Dignitas Clinic' (*The Times*, 12 May).

Daniel Finkelstein predicted that the Labour manifesto would 'haunt' the 'party's moderates long after he [Corbyn] has been defeated' (*The Times*, 17 May). On the day of its manifesto launch, *The Sun* mocked the party for a series of mishaps ('Crash Bang Wallies!', 12 May). Reporting of this kind added to a sense that Labour was heading towards disaster, although the paper was hardly devoid of a bias that would continue to inform its coverage throughout the campaign. For instance, overlooking the Prime Minister's non-appearance in the major face-to-face leaders' debate, *The Sun* claimed 'Corbyn [had been] walloped by all six opponents' ('Weakest Link Jez', 1 June), whereas the view of *The Times*' correspondent Lucy Fisher was more typical of others' reporting in concluding that the Labour leader had performed reasonably well (1 June).

The widespread expectation that Labour was facing oblivion encouraged speculation as to what would happen after polling day. Debate intensified following reports that former party deputy leader Roy Hattersley had already called for a 'campaign to oust Corbyn and "reclaim" Labour' (*Daily Telegraph*, 5 May). In characteristically blunt terms, the *Sunday Express* predicted that the leader 'will face Labour attack dogs after he is defeated' (15 May). Anticipating such a scenario, Sebastian Payne advised candidates to promote their own rather than their presumed-to-be-tainted party's credentials as part of 'A local approach [that] will help Labour moderates take back control' (*Financial Times*, 26 April). Speculation also turned to who might succeed Corbyn prior to polling day, with Jim

Pickard identifying Yvette Cooper and Chuka Umunna as two of the most likely contenders (*Financial Times*, 6 June).

Some journalists raised the possibility of a new centre party forming following reports that there could be a significant 'breakaway' from the Parliamentary Labour Party after the election (*Financial Times*, 6 June). The *Daily Telegraph* had earlier reported that as many as 100 MPs were planning to leave and set themselves up as the official Opposition in the event of an electoral rout (10 May). Rachel Sylvester welcomed such a prospect, urging: 'It's Time for Labour Moderates to Jump Ship' (*The Times*, 9 May). Drawing inspiration from the new French President Emmanuel Macron, Sylvester argued: 'With deluded extremists in firm control of the party, the centre left must take inspiration from Macron's path to power... Centrists in this country need to show their courage. There is nothing to lose any more. Labour is drowning—it's time for moderates to take the plunge and break away' (*The Times*, 9 May). The party's improving poll figures diminished but failed to end such talk. Rather, believing 'Corbyn's Surge Marks a New Low for Labour', Philip Collins suggested that the leader remaining in place after the election could even turn out to be 'an act of accidental strategic genius by a lucky Conservative Party' (*The Times*, 2 June).

Jeremy Corbyn was routinely portrayed by the press as a revolutionary figure, but often in language designed to undermine and attack him, sometimes in the most graphic of ways. The *Mail on Sunday* 'Election Guru' Dan Hodges was unequivocal as to the threat posed: 'On June 8, Labour must face its reckoning. Jeremy Corbyn must be crushed' (23 April). Tony Parsons agreed, portraying the party as one that 'despises' the 'instinctive patriotism of our people' (*Sun on Sunday*, 23 April). In his column, Richard Madeley railed against the 'Marxists, Leninists and Trotskyists who now control Labour' (13 May), whilst a fellow *Daily Express* contributor likened Corbyn to a famous Vietnamese revolutionary, calling him 'Britain's Ho Chi Minh' (22 April). Some journalists took a particular interest in those advising the Labour leader. The *Daily Mail* ran unflattering profiles of Corbyn aides, 'privately educated' James Schneider (22 April) and 'Hardline socialist' Andrew Fisher, the author of Labour's manifesto (25 April). But the greatest opprobrium was afforded to Andrew Murray, whose appointment *The Times* reported thus: 'Ex-communist who defended Stalin will lead Corbyn's team' (16 May). The announcement provoked an editorial, 'Stalin's Sycophant', denouncing Murray as 'an enemy of democratic politics' (*The Times*, 16 May). By contrast, there was noticeably little coverage of Corbyn's sons or wife Laura Alvarez, reflecting one aspect of press reporting that the leader would have appreciated.

During the election, some in the press challenged the consensus that Corbyn was a disastrous candidate. These observers included leading *Daily Mail* journalist Peter Oborne, who drew a favourable comparison between Corbyn and Tony Blair, claiming the former had 'restored honest politics to Britain' (20 May). For Aditya Chakrabortty, the leader's misfortune was to be condemned by his predecessors' abandonment of their core supporters: 'With its Bedrock Smashed to Pieces, Labour Cannot Win' (*The Guardian*, 9 May). Others praised the displays of calmness by a politician who John Crace referred to as 'Mr Zen', a name Corbyn had used to describe himself the previous week (*The Guardian*, 13 May). The *Sunday Mirror*, a sympathetic paper, reported that voters who had come into direct contact felt him to be a 'lovely person' (4 June). Having accompanied Corbyn during the closing stages of the election, Ewen MacAskill of an increasingly supportive *The Guardian* came to a similarly positive conclusion when he praised the politician's campaign as 'dignified, assured and positive' (3 June). Fellow contributor George Monbiot even went as far as suggesting 'A Labour win isn't an impossible dream. We have Corbyn to thank' (7 June).

A STARK DIVIDE

The snap election led to parallels being made with 1983, the most obvious of which was that an incumbent female Conservative leader would win a landslide victory. But although the press was similarly overwhelmingly pro-Tory, there were differences, notably in the case of the *Daily Star*, which had long abandoned its once trenchant right-wing position. The paper had subsequently adopted a policy of not publishing editorials about politics (or anything else). Where it mentioned the election, it was to lament the need for the vote to be taking place at all ('Election: 47 Ruddy Days to Go', *Daily Star*, 22 April), and one edition of the *Star on Sunday* (21 May) even managed to avoid making any mention of the campaign. The other title that opted not to endorse a party was the *i*, which, like its *Independent* forerunner, had not existed in 1983. This self-styled 'quality tabloid' promoted its lack of partisanship as a virtue against rivals it pointedly called 'the newspapers that tried to tell you how to vote' (*i*, 9 June).

The Guardian and the *Daily Mirror*, the two daily newspapers that had been against the Conservatives in 1983, restated their opposition in 2017 (see Table 14.1 above). Both had also supported Remain in the EU referendum. The *Daily Mirror* and its Sunday sister paper endorsed Labour as they had traditionally done for decades. During the campaign, support for the party and Jeremy Corbyn became more enthusiastic, culminating in a formal endorsement on polling day itself (*Daily Mirror*, 8 June). The sister paper was more reticent, restating doubts about Corbyn, but nonetheless clearly preferring him to his Conservative rival (*Sunday Mirror*, 4 June). *The Guardian* also warmed to Corbyn, having criticised him prior to the election. Applauding the manifesto 'as a genuine attempt to address a failing social and economic model', the relevant editorial declared 'The Tories Run on Fear and Do Not Deserve Our Vote. Labour Does Because it Offers Hope' (*The Guardian*, 3 June). Its sister paper *The Observer*, mindful of Brexit, stopped short of endorsing a party, but made clear its opposition to the Conservatives and urged readers to vote likewise (4 June). The other Trinity Mirror title, the *Sunday People*, adopted a very similar position in a personalised attack on the Prime Minister ('Beware Bucket Shop Boudicca May', 4 June) (see Table 14.2 above for the Sunday editorials).

Six of the ten national dailies endorsed the Conservatives, but with varying degrees of enthusiasm. Aside from the degree of their hostility towards Labour, Brexit was a factor in this, with the *Financial Times* warning that 'Liberal cosmopolitanism does not have an active voice at present' (8 May), before later backing the Tories (1 June). Like the *Financial Times*, *The Times* had supported Remain, but ultimately endorsed the government, having called May 'wooden' (7 June). The *Sunday Times* came out for the Conservatives, but was similarly critical, focusing its ire on the deficiencies of May's fiscal policies alongside the obligatory attacks on Labour (4 June).

The *Daily Telegraph* was the most enthusiastic pro-Conservative title among the party-supporting qualities. It had also been the only one of the three to support Leave in the 2016 referendum. Nevertheless, the *Daily Telegraph*, like its Sunday sister paper (4 June), shared its rivals' concern about May's economic policies and this slightly tempered a still-clear endorsement: 'Britain Has a Stark Choice—A Corbyn Government Would Be a Calamity' (7 June). The three other dailies (the *Daily Mail*, the *Daily Express* and *The Sun*), the populars (or what used to be called 'tabloids' before *The Times* adopted the format), had all campaigned in favour of Leave and now enthusiastically endorsed the Conservatives to deliver Brexit. The *Daily Express* had been so preoccupied with the European issue that it had supported UKIP in 2015, but now switched its allegiances back to the government: 'Vote May or We Face Disaster' (7 June). It featured some of the rare print advertising by the Conservatives, predictably about the EU (*Daily Express*, 7 June). And though this marked a change of partisanship, the EU issue was still the paramount concern, as its sister paper made clear: 'Five Days to Save Brexit' (*Sunday Express*, 4 June).

The *Daily Mail* attacked Labour using the strongest language in an endorsement, 'Apologists for Terror', that denounced the party's leadership as totally unfit to lead the country (7 June). The same editorial also unequivocally supported May and her plans. The *Mail on Sunday* enthusiastically endorsed the Conservatives, though it drew attention to the party's campaigning mistakes before focusing on the deficiencies of the Labour leadership (4 June). The *Sun on Sunday* did pretty much the same (4 June). For its part, *The Sun* was unequivocally for the Tories, but focused its headline on Labour, declaring 'Don't Chuck Britain in the Cor-Bin' above a photograph depicting the politician sitting in a bin with its lid on Corbyn's head (8 June).

Marginal Factors

During the campaign, there was noticeably little coverage about parties other than the Conservatives and Labour. Plaid Cymru and the Green Party once again barely featured in terms of print coverage (0.9% and 0.2% of all party sources, respectively). The Liberal Democrats, the SNP and UKIP fared better, although none of these received the amount of press interest afforded to them in 2015. The Liberal Democrat news presence fell from 10% in 2015 to 6% in 2017, the SNP from 9% to 2.4% and UKIP from 8% to 3%. And where they were reported, the coverage tended to be critical in nature. Reviewing the Liberal Democrats' early campaign performance, for instance, Matt Chorley dismissively concluded: 'This is a party which seems to be returning to its gloriously bonkers past' (*The Times*, 29 April). Macer Hall in the *Sunday Express* attacked the Liberal Democrats as the 'yellow peril' (22 April). Even one of the more balanced accounts by Sebastian Payne midway through the campaign provided little encouragement: 'The Lib Dems' Yellow Bird is Failing to Take Flight' (*Financial Times*, 17 May).

Tim Farron did not fare well in this, his first election as Liberal Democrat leader. *The Guardian*, a paper that had endorsed the party as recently as 2010, raised questions about his credentials with headlines such as 'Abortion is Wrong at Any Time, Farron Said in Interview with Salvation Army' (17 May) in a piece revisiting past statements. The *Mail on Sunday* was one of the few national newspapers to take the Liberal Democrats seriously, with an editorial suggesting that the election could help revive the party, given the 'concerns of those who—like this newspaper—supported Remain' (7 May). And in a perhaps surprise move, the paper's pro-Brexit daily sister even urged a tactical vote for Nick Clegg in Sheffield Hallam (*Daily Mail*, 7 June).

The SNP had received unprecedented press coverage during the 2015 campaign. Despite widespread expectations that Labour was now on course for defeat, some commentators warned that the party might play a role in a 'progressive alliance' government and this helped raise its print media profile, at least in the early stages of this election (*Daily Mail*, 21 April). The *Daily Mail* attacked such a scenario, believing that a minority Labour government supported by the SNP would create a 'Coalition of Chaos' (22 April). This fear had provided a major campaign narrative in 2015 and *The Sun* duly revived a prominent image from that election to again portray a diminutive Labour leader under the control of First Minister Sturgeon: 'Jezza in My Pocket: Corbyn Would Be Nic Puppet' (20 April 2017).

Some in the print media remained sympathetic to UKIP, notably the *Express* newspapers, which had both endorsed the party in 2015. Following UKIP's rout in the local elections, the *Sunday Express* demonstrated its residual sympathy by attacking 'the schadenfreude shown by the liberal elite at Ukip's poor results' (7 May). By contrast, a *Daily Mail* editorial argued that the realities of the British electoral system meant the party had effectively run its course: 'Rest in Peace Ukip, Now it's up to Mrs May' (6 May). Following a similar logic, *The Sun* urged party supporters living in 35 key seats to vote Tory in order to 'Do Corbyn up Like a Kipper' (7 June). UKIP leader Paul Nuttall was not on this list, and his reluctance to confirm if and where he would stand in the election led to mockery if it elicited any reaction. The *Daily Telegraph* sketch writer Michael Deacon ridiculed Nuttall: 'Chicken? Maybe, But He Can Duck a Question' (25 April). Aside from this adverse commentary, the *Daily Star* harked back to better times for the party when it pointedly headlined its coverage by making reference to the previous leader rather than his successor: 'Nigel: UKIP Still Has Brexit Role: "We Will Be Here to Bash Brussels"' (8 May).

The 2017 election saw a significant decrease in so-called 'process' coverage devoted to 'horse race' aspects of the campaign involving personalities, intrigue and other non-policy-related matters, much of which have been the focus of the preceding discussion (from 44.5% of all themes in 2015 to 33.6% in 2017; see Table 14.4). Integral to this was the relative lack of press attention devoted to the polls some newspapers had commissioned and which collectively identified the shift of public opinion. Nor was there much prominence given to the role and influence of social media. The election was therefore more preoccupied with substantive issues than had been the case in 2015 and this in turn concentrated greater media attention on the rival manifestoes.

The leaking of a full draft of Labour's manifesto plans in advance of its publication intensified the debate over its contents. But few could have predicted the drama about to unfold surrounding the government's proposals. When David Cameron's former Director of Communications Craig Oliver observed: 'Think this week's Tory manifesto scarcely matters? You couldn't be more wrong', he was writing in expectation that the document would make a wholly positive contribution to the campaign (*Mail on Sunday*, 14 May). Initially at least, the soon-to-be controversial Conservative proposals were sympathetically received even in the normally

Table 14.4   Campaign issues: top ten in the press (%)

Rank/topic	2017	2015 (rank)
1. Electoral process	33.6	44.5 (1)
2. EU/Brexit	10.4	3.4 (8)
3. Health and healthcare provision	6.9	3.7 (6)
4. Defence/military/security	6.8	–
5. Taxation	6.1	6.5 (3)
6. Social security	5.3	–
7. Business/economics	5.1	13.1 (2)
8. Immigration	4.3	3.5 (7)
9. Standards	3.6	3.8 (4)
10. Education	2.7	–

Source: Loughborough University Communication and Culture Research Centre ('General Elections', *Loughborough University Centre for Research in Communication and Culture*, http://blog.lboro.ac.uk/crcc/general-election).

Notes: Up to three themes could be coded per election item. Percentages are frequency of theme appearance/total theme appearances.

antagonistic *Daily Mirror* ('Care Revolution', 18 May), which reported '[o]nly those with £100k+ will have to pay [in] ... sweeping changes'.

The subsequent debate surrounding a social care policy critics quickly attacked as the 'dementia tax' proved hugely embarrassing for the Prime Minister: 'The Lady is for Turning: May Backs off on Care' (*Daily Star*, 23 May). For Polly Toynbee, the Tory leader inflamed the situation through her seemingly inept handling of the crisis: 'After May's "Dementia Tax" U-turn She Can't Accuse Anybody of Weakness' (*The Guardian*, 23 May). The *Sunday Express* leapt to the defence: 'Prime Minister is Right to Listen to Voters' Concerns', claiming she had 'shown her flexibility' (23 May). But the episode did considerable damage, given that May had hitherto enjoyed a relatively good press.

Health and social care was a major issue in the campaign, but its importance was greatly inflated by the debacle over the dementia tax. The remainder of this chapter focuses on the issues that routinely featured in newspaper coverage throughout the election—Brexit, security plus tax together with the economy—that attracted substantial interest (Table 14.4). It is worth noting that other substantive, so-called 'bread and butter' issues such as education and housing, were comparatively marginalised in terms of press reporting, and typically it was the anti-Conservative *Daily Mirror* that tended to highlight related stories (for example, '500 School Heads: Tory Cuts are Damaging Our Kids', 28 April).

THE BREXIT CAMPAIGN?

Although acknowledging Europe would be an issue, commentators differed over the degree to which they thought it would make the headlines. Whilst Stephen Pollard doubted the subject would dominate the campaign (*Daily Express*, 19 April), Polly Toynbee emphatically disagreed: 'This election will be pure Brexit, up to the blood and guts hilts' (*The Guardian*, 19 April). Pro-Leave newspapers relished this prospect and one of them, the *Daily Mail*, produced the most (in)famous front-page headline of the campaign: 'Crush the Saboteurs' (19 April). The targets of the paper's ire were those it was claimed were impeding the UK's orderly exit from the EU. The 'saboteurs' included Gina Miller, a fund manager who had organised a successful legal case for Parliament to have a vote before the Brexit process began. Miller featured prominently in reports in the *Daily Star*, among other papers: 'Gina Will Back the Remain Fighters' (20 April).

Welcoming the campaign, the front page of *The Sun* declared the election was a 'Bid for clear Brexit mandate' that would enable the 'PM' to 'smash rebel Tories'. The fate of these EU-supporting MPs exercised the *Mail on Sunday*, which, unlike its daily sister paper, had campaigned against Leave. The newspaper reported, with apparent concern, a 'Plot to Purge the Remainers' following allegations that certain Conservative MPs were under threat of being deselected (23 April). Stories like this suggested UK–EU relations might become the major issue throughout the election, as some had predicted. This expectation increased following a private meeting between Theresa May and EU President Jean-Claude Juncker.

When the *Frankfurter Allgemeine Sonntagszeitung* broke the story about the meeting between May and Juncker, the pro-Brexit *The Sun* identified Juncker's 'Rasputin'-like adviser Martin Selmyr as the culprit responsible for the leak. The *Daily Mail* sketch writer Quentin Letts went on the counter-attack: 'Who'd Want to Be Ruled by the Risible Juncker and His Poison-Spreading Brussels Sidekick?' (3 May). Responding to the leak, Theresa May warned what the *Daily Mail* called the Commission 'plotters' against interfering in domestic British politics (4 May). The potential long-term damage of the episode led the *Financial Times* to argue: 'One Rotten Dinner Must Not Poison Brexit Talks' (3 May). But a more typical reaction came from the *Daily Star*: 'Theresa: EU Can't Bully Us', a story which reported that the Prime Minister 'gave Brussels both barrels [to] meddling eurocrats' (4 May). Drawing parallels with Margaret Thatcher's approach to European negotiations, Letts believed the 'May handbag' had been similarly effective and concluded there had been only one winner from this encounter: 'Whack, Whack, Whack! Medical Orderlies for Mr Juncker Please!' (*Daily Mail*, 4 May).

Like the Juncker leak, a public altercation between Tim Farron and a 'Brexiteer' was taken up by a *Daily Telegraph* editorial (4 May) and again hinted at the way in which the EU yet might still dominate press coverage of the election. But commenting towards the end of the campaign, Charles Grant expressed dismay that there had been 'virtually no discussion of the key issues' relating to Brexit during the preceding weeks (*The Observer*, 4 June). Grant was likely referring to the 759 agreements the *Financial Times* estimated the UK would need with 168 countries (31 May). Other Brexit-related commentary focused on the respective parties' stances and in particular on what Andrew Pierce of the *Daily Mail* dismissed as Labour's 'muddled' position (26 April). Pierce ridiculed spokesperson

Keir Starmer's attempts to set out his party's position: 'Humiliation of Sir Flip-Flop, the Luvvie Left's Darling Tipped to Topple Corbyn'. The *Daily Express* took a similar view, believing 'Corbyn's Lack of a Brexit Plan is an Insult to Voters' (10 May). By contrast, the Remain-supporting *The Guardian* applauded a seemingly nuanced approach: 'Labour Takes the World as it is, Not as it Wants it to Be' (26 April).

It has already been noted that the key Brexit-supporting newspapers pledged allegiance to the Conservatives as the best choice to deliver British withdrawal. They also believed that the party, in doing so, would be able to restrict EU citizens' freedom of movement. So whereas the *Daily Express* hopefully reported 'May Vows to Slash Migration' (9 May), it also published warnings such as 'Corbyn's Plot to Bring in Migrant Workers' (1 June). Similarly, the *Daily Mail* provided leading pro-Leave Tory Iain Duncan Smith with the opportunity to set out 'Why We Have to Take Back Control of Our Borders' (8 June). And whilst it endorsed the Conservatives, the Remain-supporting *Financial Times* still continued to provide the counter-argument, warning 'Britain Need Not Slam its Doors to Limit Migration' because of 'Mrs May's clampdown' (10 May).

SECURITY MATTERS

Prior to the terrorist attacks in Manchester and London, the issue of security had already featured in extensive press coverage and, more specifically, allegations relating to Jeremy Corbyn's longstanding involvement in Northern Irish politics. In one of the more dispassionate newspaper accounts, the *Financial Times* acknowledged that the Labour leader was 'dogged by past links to Irish republicans' (31 May). Similarly rare was a piece by Kevin Lynch defending the politician: 'It's absurd to criticise Corbyn for talking to the IRA... The British establishment has talked to Irish rebels for centuries' (*i*, 23 May). But overwhelmingly, print coverage of the issue was unrelentingly hostile about Corbyn's record of meetings with Sinn Féin politicians. This included a *Daily Mail* cartoon featuring two balaclava-wearing men carrying guns, coming up the pathway of an elderly couple, peering at them from their window, with the caption reading: 'Oh dear. Will you answer the door? I think they're canvassing for Jeremy Corbyn' (23 May).

In its front-page denunciation, *The Sun* claimed Jeremy Corbyn had 'Blood on His Hands' and featured him in a photograph with Sinn Féin President Gerry Adams (23 May). The paper drew on the testimony of former Provisional member Sean O'Callaghan, who denounced Corbyn and John McDonnell for being 'unambiguous supporters of the armed struggle'. An editorial accused the pair of being 'snivelling IRA fanboys'. This story coincided with the Manchester bombing, an attack that had already happened by the time the edition had gone to press. Most newspapers abandoned their coverage of the election following this, an atrocity that claimed multiple victims. The *Daily Telegraph*, however, took exception to what it perceived to be the Labour leader's slowness to respond: 'Corbyn Condemned for Delay before Calling Attack "Terror"' (24 May). A week later, *The Sun* returned to the veteran MP's record. In 'He's Talking the Peace', the historian Ruth Dudley Edwards alleged that the Labour leader was lying about his past record of involvement in what she called 'pro-IRA circles' such as the Troops Out Movement (31 May).

Following the Manchester attack, the *Daily Mail* accused Corbyn of being 'The Terrorists' Friend' (27 May) and repeated the allegation in follow-up editions. Inside the paper, Guy Adams pointedly drew parallels between the Manchester Arena attack and the Provisionals' bombing of the city in 1996, and excoriated the Labour leader for being 'a shameless apologist for the world's men of evil', before calling his 'support for the IRA most nauseating'. Adams' indictment came in response to Corbyn's speech following the Manchester attack, an intervention the veteran foreign affairs correspondent Patrick Cockburn had welcomed: 'Corbyn is Correct: The War on Terror Puts Us All at Risk' (*i*, 27 May). Others strongly disagreed: 'Hogwash: He's Tried to Block All Anti-terror Laws … and Now He Blames the West' (*The Sun*, 26 May). Inside, columnist Iain Martin articulated the paper's concerns: 'There is no better time to ask if Corbyn would keep Britain secure.' Colonel Richard Kemp was even more trenchant: 'Corbyn is Calling All Our Boys Murderers' (*Sunday Express*, 28 May). In its following edition, the paper returned to the question of the Labour leader's ability to defend the country. It superimposed his head on a photograph of Neville Chamberlain holding the Munich Agreement and captioned: '"Don't Trust That Appeaser Corbyn", Expert Warns' (4 June). The following day's sister paper took up this theme, linking it to the Labour leader's lifelong unilateralism and alleged attempts by the party to downplay this ('Spin Doctor is Secretly Recorded Telling Corbyn How to "Shut Down" Outrage over Refusing to Use Trident', *Express*, 5 June).

In the aftermath of the Manchester attack, there were some press criticisms of the government's record on security. Former Deputy Prime

Minister-turned-columnist John Prescott suggested the tragedy had serious resource implications: 'Cuts Making Terror Battle Harder' (*Sunday Mirror*, 28 May). Peter Hitchens was also dismissive of the government's deployment of the army in response to the crisis: 'Put away Your Pointless Troops, PM—Only Beat Bobbies Can Stop Terror' (*Mail on Sunday*, 28 May). Such criticisms intensified following the shocking events at London Bridge. Following these attacks, newspapers considered the security implications, with the *Daily Mail* raising questions about the prior monitoring of those responsible for the killings: 'MI5 and Yard: We Had Him—and Let Him Go' (6 June). The *Sunday People* returned to the issue of policing—'Thinner Blue Line'—and repeated Labour claims that 16,000 officers were in the process of being cut (4 June). This made for particularly uncomfortable reading for former Home Secretary May. The Prime Minister also came under direct attack from Jason Beattie, who accused her of making a 'nakedly partisan' speech in response to the London outrage in contrast to her 'pitch perfect' reaction to Manchester ('Tory's Get-Tough Message Turned into Campaigning', *Daily Mirror*, 5 June). Beattie's colleague Alison Philips was more blunt. Declaring 'Enough is Enough of Terror Flop May', she dismissed the Prime Minister's denials that cuts had not undermined public safety as 'a crock of arrogant, disrespectful horse dung' (*Daily Mirror*, 7 June).

Following the London Bridge attacks, the denunciations of 'Corbyn the Hypocrite' continued, with Guy Adams accusing him of '30 years cosying up to terrorists' and only belatedly supporting the police's right to 'shoot to kill' (*Daily Mail*, 5 June). The *Daily Mail* also gave prominence to Lord Carlile's insistence cuts had not exacerbated the terror crisis, whilst columnist Richard Littlejohn ridiculed Labour on the same subject, sarcastically asking 'Corbyn the Coppers' Friend?' (6 June). Criticism of the Labour leader's record broadened beyond Northern Ireland to his involvement in Middle Eastern affairs. The *Sun* used a front-page image of Corbyn addressing a protest meeting, 'Jezza's Jihadi Comrades', in an attempt to associate him with extremists (7 June).

The most memorable intervention in this debate came with the front-page headline 'Apologists for Terror: The *Mail* Accuses This Troika of Befriending Britain's Enemies and Scorning the Institutions That Keep Us Safe' (7 June). Inside, the paper went into considerable detail, using 13 pages to explain why, among other things, Jeremy Corbyn, Diane Abbott and John McDonnell were wholly unsuitable to take office. Corbyn later mocked the *Daily Mail* in his 2017 Party Conference speech: 'The day before the election, one paper devoted 14 pages to attacking the Labour party. And our vote went up nearly 10%. Never have so many trees died in vain. The British people saw right through it. So this is a message to the *Daily Mail's* editor: next time, please could you make it 28 pages?' Abbott, the Shadow Home Secretary, featured prominently in this *Daily Mail* attack, having earlier come in for particular criticism following her performance on LBC radio that the paper reported as the 'worst interview ever?' and that sketch writer Quentin Letts likened to 'a frogman wading into cow manure'; even the *Daily Star* picked up on the story with a rare election related front-page story mocking 'Diane's Dumb Maths' (3 May).

ECONOMIC AND TAX POLICIES

Several specialist contributors believed that the campaign marked an important watershed in terms of fiscal policy. Observing the more interventionist policies of May (and Donald Trump), Martin Wolf concluded: 'Conservatism Buries Reagan and Thatcher' (*Financial Times*, 24 May). John Kay concurred with Wolf, noting: 'The retreat from economic liberalism is most striking in the Tory manifesto' (*Financial Times*, 20 May). Anti-Conservatives such as Larry Elliott also agreed that the programme marked a serious re-evaluation of the party's economic strategy, likening it to a 'clause IV moment' (*The Guardian*, 19 May). In an interview in *The Sun*, May explained that what the *Financial Times* called her 'manifesto for Middle England' was designed with the 'people who can just about manage' in mind (18 May). Using a phrase associated with her rivals, she pointedly added 'I'll help you all, not just the few'. *The Sun* enthusiastically embraced this vision on its front page: 'Blue Labour—May's "Red Tory" Manifesto: Bold PM Bid to Win over Socialist Voters' (19 May).

Emblematic of the Conservatives' more interventionist policies were plans to regulate energy prices. The measure had previously been associated with Labour and this link brought criticism from Philip Collins, who dismissed the initiative: 'May's Price Cap as Marxist as Miliband's' (*The Times*, 28 April). Nevertheless, *The Sun* now promoted the measures on its front page: 'R.I.P. to Rip-offs: Consumer Champ May Targets Fatcats', welcoming them as emblematic of her 'new centre ground policies' (18 May). The prospect of this and other 'Red Tory' initiatives on workers' rights was not universally welcomed by other Conservative-leaning newspapers ('Leading Tories Fear Manifesto Shift away from Free Markets', *Financial Times*, 6 May). A *Sunday Telegraph* cover story, 'Tories: Don't

Ditch Thatcher', featured quotes from those closely associated with the late Prime Minister (14 May). Replying to Tom Harris' claim 'Now We Socialists Have a Real Leader: Theresa May', Andrew Roberts professed that the Conservatives' repositioning was 'alarming traditional Tories like me' (*Mail on Sunday*, 21 May). Comments like this led the Prime Minister to reassure core supporters in a *Sunday Telegraph* interview: 'I'm not abandoning Thatcherism: I just get in there, do the best I can and get on with it' (21 May).

If some in the Tory press were concerned about May's economic policy, this was nothing compared to their fear of what the *Daily Mail* dismissively called 'Corbyn's La-La Land Economics' (1 June). Tom Newton-Dunn used a front page of the *Sun* to develop the metaphor: 'Leaf it out: Corbyn's Magic Money Tree Will Cost Families Extra £3.5K-a-Year' (2 June). The notion of false promises had already been taken up by *Sunday Express* editor Martin Townshend, who depicted the Labour leader as an untrustworthy figure preying on the young: 'Devious Corbyn is like the Child Catcher, offering treats galore to ensnare voters' (4 May). The *Daily Mail* likened the party's economic plans to another kind of fantasy: a 'Marxist' one (8 May). Tory papers also offered practical examples of what they believed might follow should Labour take office: 'Venezuela Chaos... The Future We Would Face under Corbyn' (*Sunday Express*, 15 May). Similarly, the *Daily Mail* attacked a 'bombshell' it called the 'Marxist Labour garden tax [that] would hit 10 million families' (5 June).

The 'Marxist' description of Labour's tax and economic plans was further popularised following a BBC interview with John McDonnell in which the Shadow Chancellor discussed the continuing significance of *Das Kapital*. The *Sun* mocked the revolutionary basis for McDonnell's financial profligacy ('Marx & Spender', 8 May). But Larry Elliott defended Labour's economic strategy, arguing that they were practical as well as far-sighted: 'What McDonnell proposes is more Keynesian than Marxist: these essentially social-democratic ideas will seem even more mainstream if—as is entirely possible—there is another crisis' (*The Guardian*, 15 May). Others defended the party's policies as 'modest' (*Sunday People*, 14 May), a word that might have characterised Corbyn's own explanation of his plans to a sympathetic Nigel Nelson when he commented: 'Those with broad shoulders should bear the greatest burden and our taxation system doesn't do that' (*Sunday Mirror*, 23 April).

CONCLUSION

This campaign marked an important watershed for the print media in exposing a divergence between the press and a public they have often claimed to represent. This was obvious in the terms of the newspapers' partisan disposition and, linked to this, their pursuit of certain topics to the exclusion of others. The latter included so-called 'bread and butter' issues such as schools, hospitals, housing and assorted perennial voter concerns. Even Brexit, or more precisely its implications, failed to attract the kind of incessant press scrutiny some had predicted. Economics and business were also noticeably pushed down the print agenda. By contrast, press coverage of security-related matters, especially after the Manchester and London atrocities, was pronounced, although often bound up with past conflicts rather than the factors behind the devastation that so directly impacted on this campaign. These tragedies, together with the snap election itself, were unforeseen events that, together with the ongoing speculation over Brexit, stoked an already-volatile political environment that few newspaper commentators really understood, despite the near-certainty with which many of them made their various pronouncements.

Hitherto, newspapers' preferential treatment of a given party has been seen as a potentially important contributory factor to their ultimate success. But 2017 has challenged this assumption like no other election in recent times, particularly in view of the remarkable vehemence with which some of the press had attacked Jeremy Corbyn, only to see his party's support dramatically rise in the polls. But it should be noted that the 'Tory press' was far from uniform in their endorsement of the government. Whereas *The Sun* and the *Daily Express* were staunch in their support, *The Times* and the *Financial Times* were markedly less impressed by the Conservatives' 'hard' Brexit and economic policies. It is also noteworthy that the *Daily Star*, which consciously avoided endorsing a party, has maintained circulation compared with its more opinionated rivals, most notably *The Sun*. The latter, in particular, has become politicised to an extent that editorialising (not to mention the paper's form and other content) threatens to undermine its profitability: fierce pro-Conservative partisanship is unlikely to appeal to the younger audiences the daily needs to survive, let alone prosper. In terms of its once-formidable position of influence, this campaign may yet come to be seen as the one in which 'it was *The Sun* that lost it'.

NOTES

1. All newspapers cited in this chapter refer to hardcopy editions published in 2017.
2. Half of those aged 65 or over regularly read a printed newspaper compared to just 14% of 16–24 year olds (Ofcom, *News Consumption in the UK: 2016*, 27 June 2017, p. 9, https://www.ofcom.org.uk/__data/assets/pdf_file/0017/103625/news-consumption-uk-2016.pdf).
3. David Deacon and Dominic Wring, 'Still Life in the Old Attack Dogs: The Press' in Philip Cowley and Dennis Kavanagh, *The British General Election of 2015*. Palgrave, 2016, pp. 314–21.
4. In 2015 and 2017, the Loughborough Communication and Culture Research Centre studies coded all election-related news items that appeared on the front page, the first two pages of the domestic news section, the first two pages of any specialist section assigned to the coverage of the campaign and the pages containing and facing papers' leader editorials.
5. 'General Elections', *Loughborough University Centre for Research in Communication and Culture*, http://blog.lboro.ac.uk/crcc/general-election.

CHAPTER 15

Political Recruitment Under Pressure: MPs and Candidates

Rosie Campbell and Jennifer Hudson

A total of 3,304 candidates stood in the 2017 general election, down from 3,971 in 2015 and far fewer than the 4,150—the highest number ever recorded—who stood in 2010. An average of 5.1 candidates stood per constituency in 2017; they represented 71 parties along with 187 independent candidates and the Speaker.[1] Nearly half of these candidates (1,568) lost their £500 deposit, failing to meet the 5% minimum vote share threshold, and the Treasury's lost deposit fund was £784,000 better off after the election.[2]

The Conservatives contested 638 seats (including seven in Northern Ireland), Labour 631 (all seats in Great Britain save the Speaker's seat in Buckingham) and the Liberal Democrats 629. The SNP contested all 59 seats in Scotland and Plaid Cymru all 40 in Wales. UKIP contested 378 seats, considerably down on the 624 they fought in 2015 or the 558 in 2010. The Green Party also contested significantly fewer seats in 2017, with 467 candidates standing, down from 573 in 2015, but still higher than the 335 who stood in 2010. In the short run-up to the election, there had been much speculation about a possible progressive alliance between parties on the left, but in the end the impact was limited and one party, the Greens, did most of the heavy lifting. The Progressive Alliance website listed 41 seats where a candidate stood down to boost the chances of another candidate of the left's election.[3] But there were few reciprocal agreements, all between the Liberal Democrats and the Greens or the Greens and the Women's Equality Party. In Brighton Pavilion, the Liberal Democrats did not challenge the Green MP Caroline Lucas and, in turn,

© The Author(s) 2018
P. Cowley, D. Kavanagh, *The British General Election of 2017*,
https://doi.org/10.1007/978-3-319-95936-8_15

the Greens did not contest Brighton Kemptown. They came to a similar arrangement in Skipton & Ripon, which the Liberal Democrats did not contest, and in Harrogate & Knaresborough, where the Green candidate stood down.

There were 31 seats not contested by an incumbent in 2017.[4] They included: 14 Labour MPs standing down, as well as Simon Danczuk (Rochdale), who had been suspended from the party following allegations that he had sent explicit messages to a 17-year-old girl, along with 12 Conservatives; two former SNP MPs (subsequently independent) who had lost the party whip due to allegations of financial impropriety, the former UKIP and subsequently independent MP Douglas Carswell, the Liberal Democrat John Pugh and Sinn Féin's Pat Doherty. Given that only two years had passed since the previous election, it is unsurprising that the total number of retirements was noticeably down from the 86—on average—at each election between 1979 and 2015.[5] The last time there were so few retirements was October 1974, when just 19 MPs stood down having been elected in February of the same year. In 1974, 69% of the candidates in the October contest stood in the same or a nearby seat as in February; in 2017, on average half (50%) of Conservative, Labour, Liberal Democrat and SNP candidates stood in the same seat as they had in 2015.[6]

There were three Conservative retirees under the age of 60. The highest-profile of these was the former Chancellor George Osborne. Since being sacked by Theresa May in 2016, Osborne had received substantial criticism for taking on the role of editor of the London *Evening Standard* and also working one day a week as an advisor to BlackRock on a salary of £650,000, whilst still serving as an MP. His constituency of Tatton was also due to be scrapped in the forthcoming boundary review and his departure was not a surprise. Karen Lumley (Redditch) cited ill-health as the reason for her departure and David Mackintosh (Northampton South) announced his decision not to stand in advance of a local constituency meeting where he was expected to be opposed because of allegations about financial misconduct involving public funds at Northampton Town Football Club.[7]

Five Labour MPs under the age of 60 stood down. Former Shadow Home Secretary and leadership contender Andy Burnham (Leigh) stepped down to fight a successful campaign as Greater Manchester's Metro Mayor. Steve Rotheram (Liverpool Walton) similarly stood for Mayor for the Liverpool City Region, also successfully. Michael Dugher (Barnsley East), former spokesman for Gordon Brown who had been vocally hostile to the Corbyn leadership and had been sacked from the Shadow Cabinet, announced his retirement, saying that he wanted 'nothing but the best for the future' of Labour, but that it must be a party 'that can get into government so we can actually do something to really help people'. Tom Blenkinsop (Middlesbrough South & East Cleveland) was another critic of Jeremy Corbyn. Announcing his decision, he said that his 'significant and irreconcilable differences with the current Labour leadership' meant that he could not in good faith stand as the party's candidate.[8] Iain Wright (Hartlepool) had similarly opted to serve as Chair of the Business, Innovation and Skills Select Committee rather than joining Corbyn's Shadow Cabinet, and was reported as wanting to take on new challenges outside of Parliament.

Other retirees included the former Labour Home Secretary Alan Johnson, the former Secretary of State for Communities and Local Government Eric Pickles and the former Conservative Treasury committee chairman Andrew Tyrie. Douglas Carswell, UKIP's only incumbent MP after the 2015 election, announced that he would not be standing again just weeks after renouncing UKIP and declaring himself as an independent.

Of the 618 sitting MPs who stood again, 551 were re-elected (285 Conservatives, 211 Labour, four Liberal Democrats, three Plaid Cymru, 34 SNP, one Green, eight DUP, three Sinn Féin, one independent and the Speaker). Overall, 43 candidates who were previously MPs but not current incumbents stood for election in 2017, and 12 were returned. Nearly half (20) of the former group were Liberal Democrats, reflecting the devastation wreaked on the party's parliamentary representation in 2015. Perhaps surprisingly, only one former Scottish Labour MP stood again; instead of contesting his former seat of Glasgow South West, Ian Davidson stood in Berwickshire, Roxburgh & Selkirk, which has not been held by the Labour Party in any of its various incarnations since 1983. The unwillingness of former Scottish Labour MPs to stand again suggests that they, like many others, underestimated the chances of Labour gains in Scotland.

Among the ranks of returners were Liberal Democrat former Secretary of State for Business, Innovation and Skills (and soon to be party leader) Vince Cable, Liberal Democrat former Secretary of State for Energy and Climate Change Ed Davey, Conservative former Minister of State for Employment Esther McVey (replacing George Osborne in Tatton rather than for her former seat of Wirral West), Conservative Zac Goldsmith, who stepped down over Heathrow expansion in 2016, precipitating the by-election in Richmond Park which he lost (discussed on pp. 104–5) and Liberal Democrat Jo Swinson (soon to be party deputy leader). The 67 incumbent MPs who did not make it back into the Commons included former Liberal Democrat leader Nick Clegg (Sheffield Hallam), Angus Robertson, the SNP depute leader and leader of the SNP in the House of Commons (Moray), and former SNP leader Alex Salmond (Gordon).

Among the new intake were a number of parliamentary firsts. Preet Gill (Birmingham Edgbaston) was the first Sikh women to be elected to the Commons, and Tanmanjeet Singh Dhesi (Slough) was the first turban-wearing Sikh MP. Layla Moran (Oxford West & Abingdon) became the first MP of Palestinian descent and the first woman Liberal Democrat MP from a minority background.

The election was a difficult one for party selectorates, with just over seven weeks between the Prime Minister's announcement on 18 April and polling day on 8 June. Candidate selection was only in the earliest of stages in most parties, save for the Liberal Democrats, who had begun in earnest following their near-wipeout in 2015. While the 2017 election resembles the October 1974 election in some ways, candidate selection was more of an issue in 2017. Although in 1974 the parties had less than a month between Harold Wilson's announcement and the election itself, the widely recognised vulnerability of the newly formed minority government meant that the parties had begun efforts to 'short-circuit normal selection procedures' very shortly thereafter in anticipation of another election.[9] In 2017, they were taken much more by surprise.

As noted above (pp. 149–50), the party machinery that was least ready for a snap election was the Conservatives. The usual Conservative selection process involves about two selections a week for two years preceding an election, but in 2017 selection of over 300 non-incumbent Conservative candidates had to take place within a three-week period.[10] The Conservative Party runs an approved candidates list for non-incumbents from which local constituency associations must select; to join the list, candidates must usually pass a day-long parliamentary assessment board (PAB). When the election was called, the 2015 list had been sifted, but the process of adding approved candidates was not complete. To meet the challenge of completing the list, the central party overrode usual procedures by making use of a clause in the party's constitution (part IV, clause 17), which allows the party board 'to do anything' it sees fit in the interests of the party, and putting in place special rules agreed by the party board.[11] Emergency PABs were arranged, comprising a 45-minute interview with a senior party officer, with a pass or fail decision made on the day. Aspirant candidates were asked where they hoped to be selected, a handful of policy and campaigning questions, and questions about their approach to working with different groups of voters. All of the emergency PABs were conducted within a five-day period. In addition to the selection procedures for new candidates, incumbent Conservative MPs who chose to stand again were required to secure a majority of their local association's executive council or, if not, a majority of local association members.[12]

The most contentious change was the decision not to allow candidates to apply directly to winnable seats (that is, retirement seats—where the incumbent is standing down—and target seats, which the party hopes to take), thus taking control over selection away from local associations. Instead, associations were usually offered a choice of three candidates (decided by the central party candidates' team in consultation with the officers of the local association) at a general meeting of the local party.[13] In seats in which the party felt it had no chance at all (i.e. neither retirements nor targets), a candidate was selected by the chairman of the party and the chairman of the national Conservative convention, after consultation with officers from the local party. Any consultation with local parties was often minimal.[14]

The party focused on shortlisting a diverse slate of candidates in retirement and target constituencies, adopting a policy of including at least one woman on all retirement and target shortlists, and a black and minority ethnic (BAME) candidate on shortlists in safe seats. Innovations employed in recent elections such as using open or closed primaries (constituency-level elections of all voters or Conservative supporters) and open meetings were not used at all in 2017. The Scottish Conservative Party set its own selection rules and utilised a centralised process in most seats. Officially the Conservatives in Wales were due to follow the same rules as applied to the English seats, but the shortlists in target seats sometimes contained fewer than three names, and in some instances only one candidate was offered; the justification was the need to return at least one Welsh woman MP, given that the Conservatives had never returned a woman MP in Wales (and indeed still have not).

Mark Wallace, of ConservativeHome, described the party's job as 'the wedding seating plan from hell' and the resulting selection arrangements resulted in considerable disaffection among aspirant candidates.[15] Conservative Party Headquarters (CCHQ) allocated candidates to constituency shortlists and a few withdrew when told which seats they were to be put forward to. The difficulties some candidates experienced included being asked to stand without any previous knowledge of the constituency or being sent to stand in rural constituencies without means of transport, leaving them stuck in B&Bs and unable to campaign effectively. Several candidates were included on the shortlists for winnable seats, even though they had only planned to campaign in an unwinnable constituency as a dry run in advance of 2020, and were not able to take up the role of MP if elected. Some 2015 candidates were not automatically reselected and were never told why.

When the election was called, Labour had formally selected just one candidate, Afzal Khan, for the Manchester Gorton by-election. It did not have an agreed list of target seats and the Leader of the Opposition's Office (LOTO) did not have a cadre of their preferred candidates primed and ready to seek selection. The party leadership was not well placed to dominate the selection process and, rather than parachuting allies of Corbyn into retirement seats, the strategy was to try to maximise the election of candidates from the left of the party generally. Given that both the paid party officials and many of LOTO anticipated Labour losses, identifying candidates to fill target seats was not their focus; instead, the priority was safe retirement seats and shoring up against losses.

A meeting of National Executive Committee (NEC) officers agreed selection procedures on 18 April, on the same day as the election was announced, and decided that given the time constraints, any sitting MP would automatically be endorsed by the NEC and other selections would be made using the 'exceptional selections procedure'. Rumours had been circulating that incumbent MPs would face 'trigger ballots' if they wished to stand again in 2017. Trigger ballots are a mechanism for establishing whether a sitting MP has the support of more than half of their local constituency party; if the sitting MP does not enjoy such support, then the constituency selection process is opened up to other potential candidates. The fear amongst many Labour MPs was that trigger ballots would be used to unseat MPs hostile to the leadership and that they would be a distraction from the general election. Trigger votes were ultimately ruled out by the party leadership because of the foreshortened campaigning period. It was felt that it would be impossible to implement one member one vote, or even the more truncated trigger ballot process, within the timeframe without drastically diminishing the resources available for campaigning (not least the national and regional staff time which could have involved hundreds of hours in selection activities). Had trigger ballots been in operation, a number of sitting MPs would most likely have been deselected, but instead incumbent Labour MPs were effectively nodded through by the NEC. There were only two Labour MPs who faced possible deselection. The pro-Trident John Woodcock's (Barrow & Furness) candidacy was challenged by a motion put forward by Corbyn supporters on the NEC shortly after the election was announced in response to Woodcock's statement that he would 'not countenance ever' voting for Corbyn to be Prime Minister. The motion was, however, voted down. The suspended MP for Rochdale, Simon Danczuk, did not receive endorsement. Corbyn demanded that Danczuk be barred following allegations of sexual impropriety and a unanimous vote of the NEC banned him from standing as a Labour candidate.[16] Thus, within the parliamentary party, some senior MPs got their way and there was no mandatory reselection of incumbent MPs, whilst LOTO was free to expend its energies on brokering deals with the unions over candidates in retirement seats.

All other sitting MPs were required to confirm whether they wished to stand again by 6 pm on Thursday 20 April. Applications to stand in the 13 seats where Labour MPs stood down were opened the following day and closed on Sunday 23 April at noon. A background check was conducted by the party investigating prospective candidates' social media history, their history within the party and whether they were otherwise eligible to stand, although this was also done in a very expedited fashion. Longlisting was then conducted by an NEC panel made up of the most senior NEC officers. Incumbent MPs could not sit on the panels and as a result the trade unions were strongly represented. The panel sifted through CVs and listed 6–10 candidates for interview. The interview panels consisted of three NEC members and a member of staff acting as a secretary to consider 13 seats or between 78 and 130 candidates. There was one late retirement, Steve Rotheram, the MP for Liverpool Walton who was elected to be Mayor of the Liverpool City Region on 4 May 2017, which required an even more expedited process and brought the total number of Labour retirements to 14.

There was a push from individual unions and the leader's office for their 'favourites' to be installed in retirement seats, although there is little evidence that the party leadership was able to take control of the selection process to promote its own candidates. There were no reported examples of Corbyn insiders being parachuted into safe Labour seats, and several of Corbyn's key allies who sought selection were not successful.[17] LOTO tried to find a retirement seat for Corbyn's political secretary and former Scottish

MP Katy Clark; however, Clark's efforts to be nominated for the safe seats of Leigh (vacated by Andy Burnham) and Rochdale failed. Yet Corbyn's allies were not defeated everywhere and Corbyn loyalist former MP Chris Williamson was selected to fight the Derby North seat he had lost in 2015.

By contrast, the trade unions were well placed to take advantage of the expedited process and the lack of local input. In the late retirement seat of Liverpool Walton, Dan Carden, a former aide to Len McCluskey, General Secretary of Unite, was selected, causing a backlash among many local Labour Party members, who supported Mayor of Liverpool Joe Anderson's bid for the seat. Steve Rotheram, the retiring MP, argued that there was strong support for the selection of a local candidate and had tried to convey this to the central party: 'I believe that the failure of the Labour Party to allow local representation on the panels to select candidates is a significant misjudgement.'[18]

However, this is not simply a story of a union carve-up. The unions were extremely influential in the selection process, but there was also a pragmatic element of claiming candidates as their own, without facing resistance from LOTO because they were also candidates of the left. Carden probably would not have won the selection if a vote of the local party had been in operation, but it is likely that there would have been greater resistance from the local constituency towards a candidate who had come directly from the leader's office.

For all other seats in England not held by Labour, applications opened on 21 April and were publicly advertised; they closed on 23 April at noon. Because gains were not expected, the selection of candidates in non-held seats was less contentious. Candidates were required to write to declare the seats they were applying to, with no limit on the number. This produced more than 3,000 applications. Again, the standard social media and party history checks were undertaken, but this time interviews were not conducted and the candidates were not always well known to Southside or LOTO; no local selection hustings were held. The basic background checks and CV assessments were the only opportunities for candidates' weaknesses to be identified. For each English European Parliament region (Wales and Scotland ran their own processes), the party formed a panel consisting of two NEC members and a member of the regional board. A meeting or conference call was conducted for each regional panel. Candidates who stood in 2015 were considered first and the process was the same for all non-held seats. It is striking that the shortlisting did not result in a local party vote, even in retirement seats.

Paradoxically, having started a process where giving ordinary members a say was an avowed priority, Labour's 2017 selections became one of the greatest backroom selection deals ever seen. When it came to a choice between focusing on delivering an effective campaign (within 51 days) or party democracy, securing votes took precedence. The end result was that 38 Labour MPs were elected in seats gained from other parties with no oral scrutiny whatsoever. Of the 38, four had previously been MPs (but not current incumbents) and nine had stood in the 2015 election. That left 25 who were only vetted through the examination of CVs and basic background checks. Within the party, there is a sense that this was worthwhile, given the trade-off between devoting resources to campaigning or selection processes in a snap election, but it was still less than ideal, and some of the consequences became clear after the election.[19]

The Liberal Democrats were still licking their wounds from the 2015 electoral cycle when they had been caught out by waiting for the boundary review to be finalised and were behind with their selections as a result. Having candidates in situ ready to fight a campaign was, they concluded, critical and warranted an expedited selection process. In 2016, they contacted all candidates who stood the previous year, saying that they would be assumed to be standing again, unless they explicitly stated otherwise. They then undertook an accelerated selection process for other seats based on their by-election procedure. More than 400 candidates were in place by the end of 2016, with the majority selected by September; the party was more relaxed about selecting candidates in the seats where they knew they had no chance. There was little controversy surrounding the selection of Liberal Democrat candidates, with the exception of David Ward. Ward was formerly the Liberal Democrat MP for Bradford East before losing in 2015. He was selected to stand as the Liberal Democrat candidate again in 2017, but was subsequently barred by the then party leader Tim Farron, after Theresa May had questioned his suitability, given that he had been temporarily suspended from the party for anti-Semitic comments.

One criticism of the shortened selection window was that it reduced the amount of time that candidates had to garner support among local members, favouring incumbents and well-known candidates, but was considered to be worth the cost, given the potential electoral benefits. The process also reduced opportunities for new members, of which there were many following surges after the 2015 election and post-Brexit; new members could vote, but not stand. Hustings were held in only the top 60 seats and only in contested selections (no other candidates applied to stand against Vince Cable in Twickenham or Ed Davey in Kingston & Surbiton, for example). In the vast majority of other seats, candidates were appointed through an agreement between the regional party and local party chair.

Selection was far easier for the SNP, whose 54 sitting MPs were all re-selected. This left just five candidates to choose through the SNP's normal general election selection process, covering the three seats they failed to win in 2015 and two where the SNP MPs elected in 2015 had subsequently been suspended by the party. Plaid Cymru had done some early selections in 2016, in case they faced an early election. These selections had mostly expired and the party had to start again. They stuck to their normal selection process, with local party members selecting candidates in all seats across Wales that they did not hold. Despite the snap election, the Green Party used its usual local selection procedures based on a vote of local groups of party members.

Within UKIP, the issue of where to stand provoked a huge row. One faction believed that the party should mostly stand aside and allow Theresa May to get on with Brexit, but the party's deputy leader, Peter Whittle, wanted to stand candidates everywhere. Initially a compromise was agreed whereby UKIP would not stand against Brexit-supporting MPs. The party's executive produced a list of 100 mostly Conservative-held seats that they would not contest, but grassroots pressure later pushed the total number of seats contested down further, to 378.[20] There was also some internal conflict over individual candidate selections, most obviously in Clacton, where Douglas Carswell had been the only UKIP MP before he resigned from the party. Jeff Bray, a local councillor, supported by party donor Arron Banks, was selected to stand by local party members before the *Huffington Post* accused him of posting offensive tweets. Bray's selection was then overruled by the party's headquarters and he was replaced by Paul Oakley, a member of the party's National Executive Committee.[21] Anne Marie Walters was originally selected as the candidate for Lewisham East, but she was deselected on the instructions of party leader Paul Nuttall, as he felt her views were too extreme for the party.

Some 973 women candidates stood for election in 2017, the greatest proportion (29.4%) ever.[22] Of these, 208 were elected, comprising 32% of the House of Commons. This is the highest ever proportion, and up three percentage points from 2015, although still 117 MPs short of 50%.[23] Table 15.1 shows the number and percentage of women MPs elected by party.

Table 15.1 The number (and percentage) of women elected by party in 2015 and 2017

Party	2015	2017
Conservative	68 (21)	67 (21)
Labour	99 (43)	119 (45)
SNP	20 (36)	12 (34)
Liberal Democrat	0	4 (33)
Plaid Cymru	1 (33)	1 (25)

The Labour Party remains far ahead of the other parties in terms of the election of women candidates. In 2017, it did not use all-women shortlists in any constituencies for the first time since 2001. However, as the selection was done by committee in batches, the party could consider the diversity of the full slate of candidates when making selection decisions, and the various factions of the party were all agreed on the shared goal of continuing to increase the diversity of its political representation. This unanimity led to selection decisions that increased the proportion of women Labour MPs from 43% (99) in 2015 to 45% (119) in 2017. An initial decision was taken that where a woman MP stood down, she should be replaced by another woman candidate. However, there was a lobby for this rule to be relaxed where other 'protected' characteristics were concerned. This led, for example, to the decision to select Tanmanjeet Singh Dhesi in Slough, a decision the outgoing MP, Fiona Mactaggart, challenged. Despite this relaxation of the rule, 11 men and three women MPs who stood down were replaced by ten women and four men in the first round of retirement seats.

There were 67 Conservative women MPs elected in 2017, one fewer than in 2015, and the percentage of women in the parliamentary party remained static at 21%. From January 2017, the Conservative Party's Women2Win organisation had started to prepare for a 2020 election; it had identified potential candidates and had begun to undertake mock selections with them—but selections had not yet begun. Overall, the Conservatives selected 29% women candidates in 2017, up from 26% in 2017; they selected 50% women in their retirement seats, with six out of 12 seats going to a woman candidate. Thirty women candidates had been selected to stand in the party's top 100 winnable seats. Had both the Labour and Conservative Parties performed as early polls expected, the Conservatives would have made a significant breakthrough on the number of women MPs in Parliament, replacing Labour as the party with the most women MPs. One forecast estimated that 98 Conservative women MPs would be elected, compared to just 73 Labour women MPs, an increase of 30 Conservative women MPs and a loss of 26 Labour women MPs from 2015.[24] The SNP's diminished parliamentary party resulted in a slight dent in the proportion of SNP women MPs elected, 34% (12), down from 36% (20). The SNP selected two men to stand in the seats vacated by the two former SNP women MPs who lost the party whip.

Following the outcome in the 2015 election which left the Liberal Democrats with a solely male parliamentary party, the party had taken significant steps to increase the diversity of future parliamentary candidates. It appointed a Candidate Diversity Task Force and Candidate Diversity Champion for the anticipated 2020 elections. It also agreed a significant shift in policy, adopting the use of all-women shortlists (AWS) for any seat vacated by a sitting MP. In 2017, only one Liberal Democrat MP, John Pugh MP for Southport, retired; Southport selected a woman candidate via AWS, although she was not successful in the election.[25] Given that fewer MPs retired than would have been expected in 2020, the snap election reduced the Liberal Democrats' options for increasing the diversity of its parliamentary party, although the party still increased the number of women Liberal Democrat MPs from zero to four (33%).

Eleven new BAME MPs were elected, making a total of 52 BAME MPs in the new Parliament. Broken down by party, 12% of Labour MPs (32), 6% (19) of Conservative MPs, plus one Liberal Democrat are from BAME backgrounds. In total, five BAME candidates were selected to stand in retirement seats, two in Conservative and three in Labour-held seats, and all five were elected: Bim Afolami (Conservative, Hitchin & Harpenden); Kemi Badenoch (Conservative, Saffron Walden); Tanmanjeet Singh Dhesi (Labour, Slough); Preet Gill (Labour, Birmingham Edgbaston) and Eleanor Smith (Labour, Wolverhampton South West), the last being elected for Enoch Powell's former constituency.

Both new Conservative BAME MPs represent constituencies where more than 90% of the population (according to the 2011 census) is white. There is much more variation in the ethnic make-up of the constituencies represented by new BAME Labour MPs than those of new Conservatives; in Tanmanjeet Singh Dhesi's constituency, 45% of the residents are white, compared to Faisal Rashid's Warrington South constituency, where 95% of the residents are white. Of the candidates for which we have data, across the main parties, 10% (63) of Labour candidates, 7% (43) of Conservative candidates, 7% (41) of Liberal Democrat candidates, 6% (21) of UKIP candidates and 2% (1) of SNP candidates were from BAME backgrounds.[26]

A record 15 Muslim MPs (12 Labour, three Conservatives) were elected in 2017, three more than in 2015. The number of Muslim MPs has gradually increased from one in 1997, two in 2001, four in 2005, eight in 2010 and 12 in 2015 to 15 in 2017.[27] Muslim MPs currently make up approximately 2% of the House of Commons, whilst according to the 2011 census, Muslims comprised approximately 4% of the British population.[28]

The Father of the House, the MP who has the longest unbroken service, is now jazz-loving former Chancellor Kenneth Clarke, who first entered Parliament in 1970. Clarke had previously announced his intention to stand down at the next election, but changed his mind when the early election was called. Born in 1932 and aged 85 at the election, Dennis Skinner is the oldest member of the Commons. Skinner also entered Parliament in 1970, but was sworn in after Clarke. More generally, Table 15.2 shows the year first elected for the 2017 cohort of MPs, and the relative inexperience of both Conservative and Labour MPs: 65% of Conservative MPs and 60% of Labour MPs have been elected since 2010, resulting in majorities on both sides knowing either only (coalition) government or opposition. The table also underscores how 2017 MPs break with the past: less than 1% of MPs sat in Parliament before Margaret Thatcher was first elected as Prime Minister in 1979 and just 9% preceded

Table 15.2 2017 MPs by year first elected and party

	Con		Lab		SNP		LD		Other		Total	
	N	%	N	%	N	%	N	%	N	%	N	%
1970	1	0	1	0	0	0	0	0	0	0	2	0
1974 (Oct)	1	0	2	1	0	0	0	0	0	0	3	0
1979	0	0	4	2	0	0	0	0	0	0	4	1
1983	12	4	6	2	0	0	0	0	0	0	18	3
1987	4	1	5	2	0	0	0	0	0	0	9	1
1992	13	4	11	4	0	0	0	0	0	0	24	4
1997	19	6	41	16	0	0	3	25	2	8	65	10
2001	14	4	13	5	1	3	2	17	5	21	35	5
2005	46	15	23	9	2	6	2	17	2	8	75	12
2010	112	35	56	21	0	0	1	8	6	25	175	27
2015	65	21	54	21	31	89	0	0	3	13	153	24
2017	30	9	46	18	1	3	4	33	6	25	87	13

Source: C. Barton and L. Audickas, 'Social Background of MPs, 1979–2017', House of Commons Library, Briefing Paper 748, 28 September 2016. Figures include by-elections; MPs are counted in the first general election for which they are elected

Tony Blair's election in 1997. The only party with less Westminster parliamentary experience is the SNP, with more than 90% of MPs elected in 2015 or 2017.

The average (arithmetic mean) age of MPs elected in 2017 was 51, a figure that has only changed marginally since 1979—between a low of 48.8 (1983) and a high of 51.2 (2005). Yet while average age has changed little, there has been some change in the range or distribution of age, seeing greater numbers of both younger and, particularly, older MPs elected. As shown in Table 15.3, this was particularly true for Labour in 2017, with 15% of MPs elected aged 65+, compared to just 9% for the Conservatives. The ages of the 99 'new' MPs who entered the House ranged from 24 to 74, with an average age of 45.[29] There was little difference in the average age of new Conservative (42) and new Labour MPs (44). The average age of 'new' Liberal Democrat MPs was 55, but of the eight elected in 2017, four had previously been MPs, including Vince Cable (74). There are five Conservative, two Labour, two SNP and one Plaid Cymru MPs under the age of 30, whilst there are three times as many Labour MPs over 70 (18) than Conservatives (6). All three of the MPs who are in their eighties sit on the Labour benches.

Aged 23 at the time of the election, SNP MP Mhairi Black remains the youngest Member. Nine teenage candidates stood in the election. The youngest was Robbie McMinn Lee, the 18-year-old Green candidate in Hazel Grove.[30]

There are some 50 MPs who are closely related to previous MPs, compared to 53 in 2015.[31] Elected in 2017 were four married couples (compared to three in 2015): Jenny Chapman and Nick Smith; John Cryer and Ellie Reeves; Caroline Dinenage and Mark Lancaster; and Jack Dromey

Table 15.3 MPs' ages by party

	18–24	25–34	35–44	45–54	55–64	65+	Total
Conservative	0	17 (5)	67 (21)	124 (39)	81 (26)	28 (9)	317
Labour	0	19 (7)	51 (20)	68 (26)	85 (32)	39 (15)	262
SNP	1 (3)	6 (17)	6 (17)	12 (34)	8 (23)	2 (6)	35
Liberal Democrat	0	0	2 (17)	3 (25)	6 (50)	1 (8)	12
DUP	0	1	1	2	6	0	10
Sinn Féin	0	1	1	3	0	2	7
Plaid Cymru	1	0	1	1	1	0	4

Note: Numbers in parenthesis are percentages

and Harriet Harman.[32] There are two sets of sisters, Ellie and Rachel Reeves and Maria and Angela Eagle, and one pair of brothers, Jo and Boris Johnson. Ellie Reeves' election to represent Lewisham West & Penge in 2017 was an addition to an already impressive political lineage: as well as joining her sister and husband on the green benches, her husband, John Cryer, is the son of Ann and Bob Cryer, who were both former Labour MPs. There are currently 16 MPs who are the sons or daughters of former MPs; in 2015 there were 17.

At 29%, the percentage of MPs in the House of Commons who had attended a fee-paying school hit a historic low, down 1% from 2015.[33] Of the MPs who attended fee-paying schools, one in ten went to Eton College. Overall, the proportion of Conservative MPs who were privately educated fell from 48% in 2015 to 44%, the lowest ever proportion (down from 72% in 1979). On the Labour benches, the proportion of privately educated MPs was 16% in 2015 and 13% in 2017. Few SNP MPs attended fee-paying schools, just 6% in 2017 and 7% in 2015. In 2017, 30% of Liberal Democrat MPs attended fee-paying schools, up from 13% in 2015. Given the decline in MPs who attended fee-paying schools, the proportion of MPs who attended state schools has increased; in 2017, 50% of MPs went to comprehensive schools compared to 49% in 2015 (Table 15.4).[34]

In addition, 82% of MPs are graduates, with 24% having attended Oxbridge. These figures have not changed measurably since 2015, where 85% of MPs were university educated and 26% had attended Oxbridge, but they reflect two trends since 1979: first, the percentage of MPs attending university has steadily increased (in the 1980s, 60% of MPs had gone

Table 15.4 Candidates' school type (percentage)

	Comprehensive (or secondary modern)		Selective		Fee-paying	
	MPs	Candidates	MPs	Candidates	MPs	Candidates
Conservative	101 (34)	74 (48)	66 (23)	32 (21)	129 (44)	48 (31)
Labour	149 (65)	95 (75)	51 (22)	22 (17)	31 (13)	10 (8)
SNP	30 (88)	18 (95)	2 (6)	–	2 (6)	1 (5)
Liberal Democrat	6 (60)	113 (52)	1 (10)	50 (23)	3 (30)	55 (25)

Note: The data is for schooling of 588 MPs and 737 unsuccessful candidates

to university); and, second, the percentage of MPs attending Oxbridge has declined (compared to 36% of Conservative, Labour and Liberal MPs in 1979). Of all candidates, 15% did not have a university degree, 85% had an undergraduate degree and 35% had a postgraduate degree.

Table 15.5 shows the number and percentage of candidates' highest educational qualification by party. There is little difference here between Conservative, Labour, Liberal Democrat and Green candidates, with the proportion without degrees ranging from nearly 4% to about 14%. Plaid Cymru candidates were slightly less likely to have attended university, but the most conspicuous group are the UKIP candidates, nearly 44% of whom have not attended university, a finding that is consistent with previous research on UKIP.[35] Among unsuccessful candidates, 20% of Conservative, 13% of Labour, 15% of Liberal Democrat, 11% of Green, 5% of Plaid Cymru, 7% of UKIP and no unsuccessful SNP candidates attended Oxford or Cambridge.

Table 15.6 below shows the immediate previous occupation and occupation type of MPs elected in 2017. Routes into politics have changed significantly over the last century. Traditional 'brokerage occupations' (such as law or education, which provide skills relevant for a political career, but are not overtly political) have declined as avenues for pursuing a political career, whilst more narrowly political 'instrumental' tracks have become more prominent. This has led to significant criticism about the rise of the professional politicians, particularly when special advisers (SpAds) were seen to be 'parachuted' into safe seats with which they had

Table 15.5 Candidates' highest educational qualification (percentage)

	No degree		Undergraduate		Oxbridge		Postgraduate	
	MPs	Cands	MPs	Cands[a]	MPs	Cands[b]	MPs	Cands
Conservative	17	9	55	53	34	20	28	38
Labour	17	14	52	47	20	13	32	39
SNP	37	4	49	78	0	0	13	17
Lib Dem	8	10	50	50	17	15	42	40
Plaid Cymru	–	22	–	30	–	5	–	48
Green	–	10	–	53	–	11	–	37
UKIP	–	44	–	33	–	7	–	23

Note: [a]Data for university education of 1,426 unsuccessful candidates; [b]Data for university attended is based on 1,259 unsuccessful candidates. We do not provide percentages for Plaid, Green or UKIP MPs due to low numbers

Table 15.6 2017 MPs' occupation immediately prior to the election

	Conservative		Labour		Liberal Democrat		SNP	
	MPs	Cands	MPs	Cands	MPs	Cands	MPs	Cands
Brokerage	55 (17%)	57 (20%)	50 (19%)	69 (21%)	4 (33%)	112 (20%)	7 (20%)	4 (17%)
Legal profession	38 (12%)	25 (8.6%)	25 (9.5%)	17 (5.1%)	2 (16.7%)	25 (4.4%)	1 (2.9%)	3 (12.5%)
Education	6 (1.9%)	16 (5.5%)	20 (7.6%)	39 (11.7%)	2 (16.7%)	62 (10.8%)	3 (8.6%)	0
Physicians/dentists	7 (2.2%)	10 (3.4%)	3 (1.1%)	6 (1.8%)	0	9 (1.6%)	2 (5.7%)	0
Architects/surveyors/engineers	4 (1.3%)	6 (2.1%)	2 (<1%)	7 (2.1%)	0	16 (2.8%)	1 (2.9%)	1 (4.2%)
Instrumental	101 (32%)	85 (29%)	129 (49%)	92 (28%)	3 (25%)	133 (23%)	13 (37%)	11 (46%)
Councillor/other elected office	28 (8.8%)	34 (11.7)	47 (17.9%)	51 (15.3%)	2 (16.7%)	70 (12.2%)	5 (14.3%)	3 (12.5%)
Political/social/policy research	30 (9.5%)	24 (8.3%)	27 (10.3%)	9 (2.7%)	0	23 (4%)	5 (14.3%)	6 (25%)
Party official	14 (4.4%)	10 (3.4%)	14 (5.3%)	6 (1.8%)	1 (8.3%)	23 (4%)	2 (5.7%)	0
Journalism/broadcast/media	10 (3.2%)	5 (1.7%)	6 (2.3%)	6 (1.8%)	0	8 (1.4%)	1 (2.9%)	2 (8.3%)
Trade union official	0	0	30 (11.5%)	17 (5.1%)	0	0	0	0
Lobbyist	19 (6%)	12 (4.1%)	5 (1.9%)	3 (<1%)	0	9 (1.6%)	0	0
Business/commerce	130 (41%)	87 (30%)	15 (6%)	52 (16%)	4 (33%)	137 (24%)	6 (17%)	3 (13%)
Other	29 (9%)	60 (21%)	64 (24%)	115 (34%)	1 (8%)	189 (33%)	8 (23%)	6 (25%)
Agriculture/farmers	6 (1.9%)	2 (<1%)	0	1 (<1%)	0	4 (<1%)	0	0
Armed services	2 (<1%)	1 (<1%)	2 (<1%)	0	0	0	0	0
Civil service/local authority	5 (1.6%)	8 (2.8%)	3 (1.1%)	4 (1.2%)	0	8 (1.4%)	1 (2.9%)	1 (4.2%)
Clergy	0	1 (<1%)	1 (<1%)	2 (<1%)	0	0	0	0
NHS	2 (<1%)	4 (1.4%)	7 (2.7%)	9 (2.7%)	0	7 (1.2%)	0	0
Other	0	3 (1%)	4 (1.5%)	19 (5.7%)	1 (8.3%)	28 (4.9%)	0	0
Other white collar	6 (1.9%)	20 (6.9%)	8 (3.1%)	34 (10.2%)	0	75 (13.1%)	2 (5.7%)	1 (4.2%)
Retired	2 (<1%)	4 (1.4%)	0	13 (3.9%)	0	20 (3.5%)	1 (2.9%)	0
Social worker	0	1 (<1%)	5 (1.9%)	5 (1.5%)	0	5 (<1%)	0	0
Voluntary sector	5 (1.6%)	13 (4.5%)	32 (12.2)	25 (7.5%)	0	35 (6.1%)	2 (5.7%)	4 (16.7%)
Writer/literary/artist	1 (<1%)	3 (1%)	2 (<1%)	3 (<1%)	0	7 (1.2%)	0	1 (4.2%)
Manual	2 (<1%)	1 (<1%)	4 (2%)	5 (2%)	0	3 (<1%)	1 (3%)	0

no connection. However, there has been a notable decline in the number of SpAds elected to the House of Commons in recent years. In 2015, only one new SpAd was elected, and whilst 11 SpAds stood as candidates in 2017, few were successful. Alex Burghart, an advisor to Theresa May, was elected in Brentwood & Ongar, vacated by Eric Pickles' retirement; Neil O'Brien, another SpAd to Theresa May and George Osborne, was elected to Parliament for Harborough. However, SpAds are not the only politics-facilitating or 'instrumental' routes taken by aspirant candidates.

Nearly half of all Labour MPs (49%) were in instrumental occupations immediately prior to election, most likely as a councillor or other elected official. For Conservative MPs, just under a third (32%) were in instrumental occupations prior to being elected. Both are small increases on 2015, where 47% of Labour and 29% of Conservative MPs were employed in an instrumental occupation immediately prior to their first election to the Commons. A quarter of Liberal Democrat (no change from 2015) and 37% of SNP MPs worked in instrumental or 'politics facilitating' jobs prior to election (for the SNP, this was down from 43% in 2015). The Conservative Party continues to recruit more of its MPs from commerce, management, business and finance than the other parties; 41% of Conservative MPs were employed in business or commerce immediately prior to their first election, compared to 6% of Labour, 33% of Liberal Democrat and 17% of SNP MPs.

There are very few MPs on any of the Commons benches who were manual workers immediately before their election—one Conservative MP, four Labour MPs and one SNP MP were employed in a manual job immediately before entering Parliament (at 0.9%, this is very similar to the 1.1% proportion we found in 2015).[36] Whereas previous efforts at estimating the percentage of candidates and MPs from manual backgrounds have used a politician's first occupation as an indicator of occupational class, our data is collected identifying MPs' occupation immediately prior to entering the Commons. This approach risks missing information that is harder to find, and it is likely that our figures represent a low(er) estimate of the true number of aspirants from manual backgrounds. Greater social mobility has meant that even as many have started off in manual occupations, their classification changed by the time they stood. For example, in 2015, Criddle (2016) estimates that there were 19 (3%) Labour and Conservative MPs from manual backgrounds compared to our estimated 1% for 2017. Nonetheless, both figures reflect the continuation of the trends identified in previous elections, which show the decline of MPs entering the Commons from manual occupations, although the figures cannot be directly compared. Finally, given their historical links, only the Labour Party has a significant proportion of MPs entering Parliament immediately from a role as a trade union official (12%).

Unsuccessful Conservative (20%), Labour (21%), Liberal Democrat (20%) and SNP (17%) candidates all have very similar occupational profiles in 2017 with respect to the percentage in brokerage occupations. Conservative (29%) and Labour (28%) candidates are also similarly matched with respect to instrumental occupations, with Liberal Democrat (23%) and SNP (46%) candidates falling below and above the Labour/Conservative average respectively. Significant differences emerge across 'business/commerce' and 'other' occupational categories, with unsuccessful Conservative candidates considerably more likely to come from the former. The Conservatives have the largest proportion of candidates with business backgrounds (30%), although the difference between parties is less stark than among elected MPs.

At least 47 'out' lesbian, gay, bisexual, trans or queer (LGBTQ) MPs were elected to the House of Commons, the highest ever publicly recorded number, up by six from 2015. Among the SNP MPs were seven out LGBTQ MPs, constituting 20% of the parliamentary party. The remaining out LGBTQ MPs were made up of 19 Conservatives and 19 Labour members. Overall, at least 147 LGBTQ candidates stood in the election (4.5% of the total), including 42 Conservative, 42 Labour, 30 Liberal Democrat, 11 Green, 10 SNP, six UKIP, two Plaid Cymru, two SDLP and two Alliance Party of Northern Ireland candidates.[37]

In 2017, five MPs with publicly recorded disabilities were elected to the Commons, up from three in 2015, taking the proportion of disabled MPs up to 1%. The two new MPs—Jared O'Mara (Sheffield Hallam) and Marsha de Cordova (Battersea)—both joined the Labour benches.

CONCLUSION

Given that the election was unexpected, we might have anticipated that the parties' equality machineries would have malfunctioned and that 2017 could have signalled a backwards step in terms of the increasing diversity of the House of Commons. However, progress on diversity continued, albeit incrementally and partially. The centralisation of the selection process in the Conservative and Labour Parties meant that the rapidly formed selectorates could consider the full slate of candidates and ensure the better representation of women and ethnic minority MPs. In the Labour Party, the result was a slight increase in the proportion of women elected, but a flatline in relation to the incremental progress the Conservatives have made in terms of women's representation in recent elections. Both parties improved the ethnic diversity of their benches partly through a repeat of the strategy employed in 2017 of selecting BAME candidates in retirement seats. The Conservatives and Labour continued to improve the representation of LGBTQ MPs on their benches, with the highest ever recorded number of LGBTQ MPs elected in 2017. The small rise in the number of Liberal Democrat women had nothing to do with the party's first use of all-women shortlists, but given their adoption of the procedure, we should expect to see the proportion of Liberal Democrat women MPs rise in the future.

The expedited and centralised processes employed by the two largest parties allowed them to fill candidacies quickly. However, there were associated costs. In the Conservative Party, there were a considerable number of disaffected aspirant candidates who felt overlooked and sometimes illtreated. Candidate selection is always a beautiful baby contest with mostly unhappy parents, but the grumbles were far greater than normal in 2017. Local associations were not seriously involved in the shortlisting process for any seats, and in seats that were neither retirements nor targets, there was no final vote of the local association. The right to have the final say in the selection of parliamentary candidates is one that is jealously guarded by local associations. And whilst there was an understanding that the snap election required an expedited process, there was groundswell of opinion that the process had not been well-managed and that local associations could have been given more input. Such widespread dissatisfaction with the selection process among candidates, aspirant candidates and the grassroots of the party was later acknowledged by Theresa May when she tasked Eric Pickles with undertaking a review of the election.[38]

There was less public evidence of a backlash among Labour candidates or local associations, although the divided nature of the party perhaps means that there is less confidence about giving internal wrangles a public airing. However, the view that it was crucial to move quickly and devote resources to campaigning rather than selection was widely shared. The accelerated selection processes necessarily reduced the time available to vet candidates, and some of the signs of this became clear soon after the election. Unlike the Conservatives, the final decision for Labour candidates in retirement and target seats was not taken by a vote of the local party, and in the case of candidates who were standing in seats not held by the party, interviews were not even conducted. As a result, dozens of Labour MPs entered the House of Commons with the most minimal of internal scrutiny.

NOTES

1. 'Briefing Paper. General Election 2017: Results and Analysis', *House of Commons Library*, 3 April 2018, http://researchbriefings.parliament.uk/ResearchBriefing/Summary/CBP-7979.
2. Noel Dempsey, 'Lost Deposits', *House of Commons Library*, 22 June 2017, https://secondreading.uk/elections/lost-deposits.
3. 'Local Alliances', *Progressive Alliance*, http://www.progressivealliance.org.uk/alliances.
4. Three MPs departed from Parliament in 2017 before the election was announced. Tristram Hunt, the historian and Labour MP for Stoke-on-Trent Central, exited the Commons in January 2017 to become director of the Victoria and Albert Museum; Jamie Reed, the MP for Copeland since 2005, said that his departure had 'absolutely nothing to do with Jeremy Corbyn', although he had been an outspoken critic of the Labour leader. Another by-election was due to be held on 4 May 2017 in Manchester Gorton following the death of Labour MP Gerald Kaufman, but it was cancelled when the general election was announced (the first by-election to be cancelled since 1924).
5. 'General Election 2017: Results and Analysis', http://researchbriefings.parliament.uk/ResearchBriefing/Summary/CBP-7979.
6. David Butler and Dennis Kavanagh, *The British General Election of October 1974*. Macmillan, 1975, p. 208.
7. Jack Lopresti, MP for Filton & Bradley Stoke, faced the possibility of deselection as supporters of his ex-wife allegedly sought to have him deselected, but he hung on. See 'Lopresti Calls Cops on Tories Trying to Deselect Him', *Guido Fawkes*, 28 April 2017, https://order-order.com/2017/04/28/lopresti-calls-cops-on-tories-trying-to-deselect-him.
8. Emma Bean, 'Corbynsceptic MPs Alan Johnson and Tom Blenkinsop to Stand Down at Election', *LabourList*, 18 April 2017, https://labourlist.org/2017/04/tom-blenkinsop-will-not-stand-for-re-election-in-snap-general.
9. Butler and Kavanagh, *The British General Election of October 1974*, p. 210.
10. Mark Wallace, 'Our CCHQ Election Audit: The Rusty Machine, Part Two. How and Why the Ground Campaign Failed', *ConservativeHome*, 6 September 2017, https://www.conservativehome.com/majority_conservatism/2017/09/our-cchq-election-audit-the-rusty-machine-part-two-how-and-why-the-ground-campaign-failed.html.

11. Part IV, clause 17 of the Conservative Party Constitution reads: 'The Board shall have power to do anything which in its opinion relates to the management and administration of the Party ...'

12. Alan Haselhurst, the MP for Saffron Walden, who was nearly 80 years old and had been an MP for almost 40 years, was facing pressure to retire; he cited the decision to reselect sitting MPs as part of his motivation for standing down. See Angela Singer, 'Sir Alan Haselhurst Steps Down after 40 Years as Saffron Walden MP', *Dunmow Broadcast*, 25 April 2017, www. dunmowbroadcast.co.uk/news/sir-alan-haselhurst-steps-down-after-40-years-as-saffron-walden-mp-1-4989811.

13. Mark Wallace, 'Exclusive: CCHQ Will Shortlist Candidates for Target Seats without Even Inviting Applications', *ConservativeHome*, 20 April 2017, https://www.conservativehome.com/parliament/2017/04/exclusive-cchq-will-shortlist-candidates-for-target-seats-without-even-inviting-applications.html.

14. Mark Wallace, 'Centralisation and Chaos—Inside the Rush to Select Conservative Candidates in Time for the Election', *ConservativeHome*, 9 May 2017, www.conservativehome.com/thetorydiary/2017/05/centralisation-and-chaos-inside-the-rush-to-select-conservative-candidates-in-time-for-the-election.html.

15. Ibid.

16. Danczuk stood as an independent and received 1.8% of the vote in Rochdale.

17. They were Corbyn's political secretary Katy Clark; Sam Tarry, who played an important role in Corbyn's second leadership campaign; and David Prescott, son of Lord Prescott and former Corbyn speechwriter, both of whom failed to be selected in Alan Johnson's former seat of Hull West & Hessle.

18. Steve Rotheram, 'I Have Tried My Utmost for a Local Candidate in Liverpool Walton', *LabourList*, 7 May 2017, https://labourlist. org/2017/05/steve-rotheram-i-have-tried-my-utmost-for-a-local-candidate-in-liverpool-walton.

19. For example, shortly after the election, it was revealed that Jared O'Mara, who had won Sheffield Hallam, had made a series of sexist and homophobic comments online, in addition to a series of other allegations about his behaviour, which led to his suspension from the party.

20. Tim Ross and Tom McTague. *Betting the House: The Inside Story of the 2017 Election*, Biteback, 2017.

21. 'UKIP's Clacton Candidate Dropped in "Shambolic" Move', *BBC News*, 10 May 2017, www.bbc.co.uk/news/uk-england-essex-39870009.

22. 'General Election 2017: Results and Analysis', http://researchbriefings. parliament.uk/ResearchBriefing/Summary/CBP-7979, p. 46.

23. We are extremely grateful to Linda Hein, Agnes Magyar, Naveen Saini and Nikki Soo for their outstanding help with 2017 data collection for this chapter.

24. See Agnes Magyar and Jennifer Hudson, 'More Female Candidates Selected, But the Gender Balance of the House of Commons is Likely to Be Little Changed after June 8', *Constitution Unit*, 24 May 2017, https://constitution-unit.com/2017/05/24/more-female-candidates-have-been-selected-but-the-gender-balance-of-the-house-of-commons-is-likely-to-be-little-changed-after-june-8/#more-5832.

25. Mark Pack, 'Details of Lib Dem All-Women Shortlists Plans Released, and They're Not Just about Women', 6 February 2016, https://www.markpack.org.uk/137338/lib-dem-all-women-shortlist-plans.

26. We collect data on parliamentary candidates from public/available sources. We do not survey or contact candidates for sociodemographic data, hence there is missing data, which varies by party.

27. Hamed Chapman, 'Record Number of Muslim MPs Selected', *Muslim News*, 23 June 2017, http://muslimnews.co.uk/newspaper/home-news/record-number-muslim-mps-elected.

28. The Muslim Council of Britain's Research & Documentation Committee, *British Muslims in Numbers. A Demographic, Socio-Economic and Health Profile of Muslims in Britain Drawing on the 2011 Census*, 2015, https://www.mcb.org.uk/wp-content/uploads/2015/02/MCBCensusReport_2015.pdf.

29. In 2015, the average age of newly elected MPs was 43.9, continuing the trend of newly elected MPs to be older, rather than younger, on average. See Chrysa Lamprinakou, Marco Morucci, Rosie Campbell and Jennifer van Heerde-Hudson, 'All Change in the House? The Profile of Candidates and MPs in the 2015 British General Election', *Parliamentary Affairs*, 70 (2016): 207–32.

30. Three more teenage Greens were 19-year-olds: Benjamin Smith, who stood in Cardiff Central, Alice Kiff in Birmingham Edgbaston and Lawrence McNally in Cities of London & Westminster. Two Labour candidates were 19 years old: Eli Aldridge in Westmorland & Lonsdale and Christopher Rimicans in North Ayrshire & Arran. Rory Daniels, aged 19, stood for the Liberal Democrats in Llanelli. One UKIP candidate was 19 years old, Nathan Ryding standing in Wigan. Finally, Jack Render, also aged 19, stood for the Yorkshire Party in Skipton & Ripon.

31. Sarah Priddy, 'Briefing Paper. MPs Related to Other Current or Former Members in the 2017 Parliament', *House of Commons Library*, 26 September 2017, https://researchbriefings.parliament.uk/ResearchBriefing/Summary/SN04809#fullreport.

32. Andrea Jenkyns and Jack Lopresti married in December 2017, bringing the total to five.
33. Rebecca Montacute and Tim Carr, 'Research Brief. Parliamentary Privilege—The MPs in 2017', *Sutton Trust*, 18 June 2017, https://www. suttontrust.com/wp-content/uploads/2017/06/Parliamentary-privilege-2017_FINAL_V2.pdf.
34. For reasons explained above (Note 26), there is missing data, which varies by party.
35. See Lamprinakou et al., 'All Change in the House?'
36. Ibid.
37. Andrew Reynolds, 'UK Set to Break Record for Highest Number of LGBTQ MPs after General Election', *Pink News*, 5 June 2017, www. pinknews.co.uk/2017/06/05/uk-set-to-break-record-for-highest-number-of-lgbtq-mps-after-general-election.
38. Eric Pickles, 'Eric Pickles' General Election Review 2017', *Conservatives*, September 2017, https://www.conservatives.com/gereview. The Pickles review suggests selecting candidates early for the next election to avoid the short-cutting of the selection process that removed local associations from the shortlisting process.

CHAPTER 16

The Election in Retrospect

Calling a general election has traditionally been considered one of the key powers exercised by a prime minister. It is a politically consequential decision. Harold Wilson in 1970 and Ted Heath in 1974 both called elections earlier than needed—and both lost. Indeed, there were striking similarities between Theresa May in 2017 and Heath's snap ('Who Governs?') general election in February 1974. Heath, also backed by opinion poll leads, had reluctantly called the election to give him a stronger hand to reinforce his statutory incomes policy against the coal miners' industrial action. But his party was ill-prepared, the public mood was volatile and he lost. In 2017, May's party had clear poll leads but was ill-prepared, the mood was volatile and the voters baulked at the invitation to back her.

Deciding not to call an election, though, can be just as consequential. James Callaghan in 1978 and Gordon Brown in 2007 were criticised for contemplating but then pulling back from going to the country, avoiding contests they might have won. Whilst neither might like the comparison, there were multiple similarities between May and Brown. One was a son of the manse, the other a vicar's daughter; both had a belief in public service and in trying to do what they thought was right for their country; both had enhanced their reputations with extended periods of ministerial office in one department; both followed prime ministers who they and especially members of their teams saw as superficial; both had loyal, perhaps excessively loyal, consiglieres who had dysfunctional relationships with others in their

© The Author(s) 2018
P. Cowley, D. Kavanagh, *The British General Election of 2017*,
https://doi.org/10.1007/978-3-319-95936-8_16

party; both experienced honeymoon periods after taking office, in which they enjoyed high levels of public popularity (often to the surprise of those who knew them well), after which both then struggled to articulate their vision; both appeared to suffer from a lack of emotional intelligence, often failing to connect or at least appear to empathise with the public; and both—in different ways—were to come a cropper over snap elections.

Either way, it is a lonely decision, as Harold Wilson once said.[1] In the private election planning meeting, held in April 2017 at the Prime Minister's house in Sonning, the party chairman Sir Patrick McLoughlin reminded the group that Margaret Thatcher used to say that this was a decision only the Prime Minister could take. Plenty of people were urging May to go to the country—all of her key aides, the Chancellor, the Brexit Secretary, as well as many political journalists—but the decision remained hers alone. Had she won handsomely, as most people expected when the campaign began, she would have been hailed as a political titan, as, indeed, much coverage of her did when she called the election. Instead, it diminished her. Rather than delivering a 'strong and stable' government, the nation ended up with a minority government and a weakened Prime Minister about to embark on the most important and complex negotiations the UK had entered in living memory.

Steve Bright, *Sun*, 12 June 2017 © News UK/News Licensing

The election saw an unusually long campaign—of almost seven weeks, although it felt longer—punctuated by two terrorist attacks, in Manchester and London, which between them left a total of 30 victims dead, including children, and led to the campaign being suspended twice. Even allowing for the unusual circumstances, the campaign did not get a good press. *The Economist* said the choice on offer was 'dismal'; *The Observer* complained that the challenges Britain faced required 'innovative and radical thinking, of which we have seen too little throughout this campaign'.[2] The verdict of the Institute for Fiscal Studies on the parties' manifestoes (see above, p. 210) was damning. Much of this has become par for the course; you will search in vain for a recent election during which commentators have praised the parties' serious and well-developed proposals, and during which there was an honest debate about the challenges facing the nation. Levels of interest amongst the public were up—the British Social Attitudes survey found a higher level of interest in politics in 2017 than in any election since the data began in the early 1990s—although the rise appeared to have occurred as a result of the 2016 referendum rather than being triggered by the election per se.[3] Commentators struggled to cope with the extent to which much modern campaigning now takes place below the radar, in the form of postal votes (21.6% of all votes in 2017, up from 20.5% in 2015) and digital communications.[4] Traditional and more visible activities, such as daily press conferences, posters and billboards, have declined almost to the point of total absence—almost all poster 'launches' are now what Daniel Boorstin in 1961 termed 'pseudo-events', designed solely for the purpose of generating publicity rather than ever actually seeing a billboard—and unlike in 2010 and 2015, there were no head-to-head debates between the main party leaders to compensate. The audience figures for broadcast coverage of the election were down compared to 2015, as was the space the press devoted to it. According to Populus, although the election was the single most-noticed story for the first three weeks of the campaign, the percentage of people naming it never rose over 30%. Perhaps the lack of excitement in the first half of the campaign was because of the widespread expectation of a clear winner for the first time since 2005, and probably a landslide, the first since 2001. Understandably, voters reported that the Manchester and London attacks were the most-noticed events in the final three weeks of the campaign (see Table 16.1).

One of the truisms of election campaigns is that the formal, 'short' campaign does not matter very much. For all the sound and fury, campaigns rarely affect election outcomes. The party ahead in the polls at the

Table 16.1   Stories the public noticed

Week ending	Most-noticed story		Second most-noticed story	
5 May 2017	General election	30%	Brexit	12%
12 May 2017	General election	23%	Dismissal of James Comey	14%
19 May 2017	General election	27%	NHS cyber attack	18%
26 May 2017	Manchester attack	90%	General election	2%
2 June 2017	Manchester attack	43%	General election	19%
9 June 2017	London attack	58%	General election	23%

Source: Populus

beginning is almost always ahead at the end, often by roughly the same amount, and when this is not true, it is usually because of errors in the polls rather than any change in the standing of the parties. All the things that obsess journalists and excite politicians—the leaders' tours, the debates, any 'gaffes', the parties' manifestoes—are all electorally trivial. When a party wins or loses an election, it is not because of what it did in the weeks of the campaign, but because of more fundamental perceptions about the parties, their policies and their leaders which have built up over the preceding years of a parliament, or in some cases even longer.

The 2017 campaign presented a serious challenge to such a view of politics, because what happened between 18 April and 8 June 2017 profoundly mattered and had a material impact on the outcome of the election. Labour began the campaign staring down the barrel at one of its worst election performances in its history, but ended just a few thousand votes away from Downing Street. On leadership, Jeremy Corbyn narrowed his considerable starting deficit against May on the question of being considered a capable Prime Minister (see Table 16.2). Labour also caught up with the Conservatives on which party could best handle some major issues. YouGov showed Labour overtaking the Conservatives on education and housing to add to its long-established lead on the NHS, and narrowing its deficit on managing the economy.

Voters gave higher marks to Labour's campaign on positivity, honesty, clarity and talking about the issues they cared about.[5] The British Election Study (BES) estimated that 19% of voters changed their mind during the campaign (or, more precisely, between its surveys in April and May and its post-election survey). This was slightly lower than the churn seen in 2005 and 2010, if two percentage points higher than 2015. Normally such switchers (mostly) cancel each other out, as do late-deciders. But in 2017,

Table 16.2 The most capable Prime Minister (%)

Date	May	Corbyn	None/neither	Don't know	May lead
21–25 April	61	23	6	7	+38
15–17 May	56	29	7	6	+27
30 May–1 June	50	35	6	8	+15
6–7 June	47	36	7	8	+11

Source: Ipsos MORI

Labour won more than half of those who changed their minds during the campaign (compared to just 19% who ended up with the Conservatives) and more than a half of those who had not decided before the campaign began.[6] In 2017, the changes in voting intentions had not cancelled out by polling day, with Labour managing to recover many of the voters it had lost since 2015. Campaigns clearly can matter—particularly if one party campaigns so badly that it allows the other to land a series of blows almost without retaliation.

Yet for all Labour's impressive progress, the party ahead at the beginning of the campaign remained ahead at the end; the 2017 election remains the latest in a line of elections about which this can be said dating back to 1964.[7] Those who noted, when the Prime Minister called the election, that no party had ever come from as far behind as Labour and still gone on to win were not proved wrong. The party ahead at the beginning of the campaign again went on to form the government. Nor should 2017 be seen as a complete dismissal of other well-rehearsed maxims about the importance of competence and leadership—what political scientists call 'valence' politics. Corbyn's ratings improved during the campaign, but even at the end he still trailed May as the person seen as making the best Prime Minister. For all that Labour's standing improved, the final polls still showed the Conservatives ahead on economic competence and on their ability to handle the most important issue facing the country. In other words, the party led by the person considered the most competent, which was ahead on the economy and on the issues considered most important to voters, went on to form the government. To note this is not to downplay the transformation in Labour's standing. It affected the outcome significantly, far more than almost everyone expected. As a result of the campaign, Britain ended up with a minority Conservative government rather than a majority Conservative government, let alone one with a landslide majority, but it did not end up with a Labour government. Labour won the campaign; it did not win the election.

Steve Bell, *The Guardian*, 31 May 2017 © Steve Bell

The result challenged other common assumptions about British electoral politics. The 84.5% share of the British vote (82.5% of the UK vote) captured by the two major parties in 2017 was the highest it had been since 1970 and compared with the two-thirds or so of recent elections.[8] Both Labour and the Conservatives profited from the decline in support for the nationalists in Wales and Scotland, the Liberal Democrats, the Greens and, above all, UKIP. Excluding the Speaker, the combined total of seats not held by Labour or the Conservatives fell to 70 from the 87 in 2015, although that figure was still higher than in any of the elections between 1945 and 1992.

The Liberal Democrats increased their seat total from eight to 12, but the party's vote share fell slightly, to 7.4%, and from being a substantial third party and a party in government until 2015, it was now firmly in minor party status. The party did at least survive, which at one point during the campaign did not seem guaranteed, but a mere four constituencies had returned Liberal Democrat MPs in both 2015 and 2017, demonstrating how precarious its position was. The party's offer of another referendum, this time on the terms of Brexit, failed to strike a chord with many of the 48% who had voted Remain, although eight of its 12 seats voted

Remain and the sharp decline of the Conservative vote in Remain-voting Bath and Twickenham clearly helped it. But Labour scooped most of the Remain Conservative defectors. Having recently been in government, the Liberal Democrats were hardly the natural home for an anti-establishment or protest vote, particularly with Corbyn on offer. The party found itself outflanked on the left for the first time, and with a manifesto that contained relatively few policies with popular appeal.[9]

The percentage of voters perceiving a 'great difference' between the Labour and Conservative parties rose from 27% in 2015 to 45%.[10] The Liberal Democrats failed to take advantage. The party's private polling showed that it lacked a clear identity or ownership of important issues, and it was bedevilled during the campaign by the amount of precious media time spent debating the morality of sexual activity. Some candidates felt angst as the student and youth vote flocked to Labour, not least as a result of Labour's promise to abolish tuition fees. Such a pledge had been an electoral plus in 2010, but became an albatross when the party reneged on it during the coalition.[11] The party's decline and the expectation of a clear Conservative victory ruled out much of the talk about possible post-election deals that had figured in the 2010 and 2015 general elections.

UKIP had the third-largest vote in the 2015 election and the decline in its support fuelled Conservative hopes and Labour fears about where most UKIP voters would go. The Conservatives, as the more Brexit-inclined party, targeted UKIP voters, particularly in Labour seats which had voted Leave and where UKIP was not standing a candidate. Over half of the 2015 UKIP vote went Conservative, compared to under a fifth to Labour.[12] Former UKIP voters may have been attracted by Labour's anti-austerity policies and some were returning to the party. They helped Labour to hold a number of seats it feared it would lose. The party's vote in Great Britain declined from 12.9% in 2015 to 1.9% (or 3.3% on average where it stood a candidate). It lost deposits in 337 seats. The Greens, down from 3.9% to 1.7%, did even worse, losing 456 deposits, more than either UKIP or the Liberal Democrats, as many of its supporters flocked to Labour.

Scotland serves as a salutary lesson in how quickly political moods can change. Entering the 2015 general election, Labour held 41 of the 59 seats in Scotland, many with rock-solid majorities, only for the SNP to come close to capturing every seat in Scotland. After 2015, the SNP held 56 seats, many with seemingly impregnable majorities. Yet two years later, not only did the SNP lose 21 seats, but many they held were transformed from safe to marginal. Over a mere four years, then, Scottish parliamentary constituencies went from (a) (mostly) safe Labour to (b) (mostly) safe SNP to (c) becoming a key electoral battleground at the next election. The 2010 election, when not a single seat changed hands in Scotland, seems like something from another era.

An SNP decline was anticipated from such a peak, but not on the scale seen in 2017, a fall of 13%, larger even than UKIP's. An Ipsos MORI poll a week before polling day had the SNP holding 50 of its seats, losing six to the Conservatives, with Labour and the Liberal Democrats rooted on one each.[13] Almost a quarter of SNP voters from 2015 stayed at home.[14] Seats which had increased the most in turnout and had the highest SNP vote in 2015 suffered the biggest falls in turnout. The turnout of 66% compared with 85% for the referendum in 2014. Young former SNP voters turned to Labour, just as the young were doing south of the border, and of those who voted for the SNP in 2015 and switched to the Conservatives in 2017, over 80% had voted to leave the EU.[15] The result was not a boost for the SNP's hopes of a second independence referendum. Two years before, despite having been in government for eight years, the SNP had been able to campaign almost as if they were an opposition party; in 2017, they suddenly found that they had a record to defend.

Of the two main pro-Union parties in Scotland, the Conservatives reversed their long-term decline to add 12 seats to the one they started with and Labour added six to their one. Labour's vote increased from 2015 by 9,900, but was dwarfed by the Conservative increase of 324,000. Had the party increased its vote share only by the same amount as it did in England and Wales, it would have had just two Scottish seats rather than 13. The Liberal Democrats lost vote share in Scotland, but regained three seats lost in 2015, also profiting from the SNP decline. As Appendix 1 shows, the party best placed to oust the SNP candidate gained the most in Scotland.

Wales was not exempt from the return to Labour-Conservative dominance. The 49-34 Labour Conservative vote split compared with 37-27 in 2015. The Conservatives achieved their best ever share of the Welsh vote for a century but still lost three seats, the Liberal Democrats were wiped out, and Plaid Cymru's vote share was their worst since 1997, although the party gained one seat.

Yet to see all this as a return to two-party politics was misleading. For one thing, it ignores stark geographical differences. As in 2015, there were different leading parties in the different nations: the Conservatives in England, Labour in Wales, the SNP in Scotland and the DUP in Northern Ireland. In Scotland (and despite an election setback that would have seemed unthinkable two years before), the SNP still commanded the majority of seats (unthinkable four years before)—despite under-performing by recent standards in the Scottish elections in 2016, they still remained in office at Holyrood. With 35 seats in Scotland held by the SNP and with the distinct party system in Northern Ireland, two-party dominance in the House of Commons was largely an Anglo-Welsh phenomenon.

In England, the two parties' share of the vote was as high as 87.5% (peaking in the Midlands at over 91%), but even here it is best not to get carried away, because the concept of two-party politics was always about more than just a sum of vote shares; it was, fundamentally, about what caused those vote shares—that the parties' support was buttressed by strong levels of class and partisan alignment. This gave both major parties a significant core vote—so loyal that it could almost be taken for granted—on which they could depend, election after election. These foundations have not returned; what emerged in 2017 is merely an ersatz form of two-party politics.[16] As we discuss below, the parties now have new and perhaps uneasy coalitions of support: a more middle-class, socially liberal, better-educated and younger Labour and a more working-class, elderly and more socially and culturally conservative Tory party. But it is far too early to know how stable these coalitions will prove; they could well collapse just as speedily as they seemed to arrive.

The two-party squeeze on the vote was seen in the election coverage. In 2015, 55.7% of politicians' television appearances were from the two main parties; in 2017, it was 67.1%. In the press, the figure was 69.7% in 2015, but 84.3% in 2017. The amount of press coverage for the Liberal Democrats, UKIP and the SNP was less than half what it had been in 2015. The same perception of a two-horse race was reflected among broadcasters. May received just over 40% of the airtime for party leaders and Corbyn just over 30%. As Cushion and Beckett note in Chapter 13, May received the usual 'incumbency bonus'. That the press coverage of Corbyn was very negative—as it had been throughout his leadership—did not seem to bother his team; they had largely written off most of the so-called 'mainstream media' and trusted rallies and social media as a means of getting their message across and of tapping the public mood.

'It turns out the voters are
bloody difficult as well'

Matt, *Daily Telegraph*, 9 June 2017 © Matt/Telegraph Media Group Ltd

Turnout at 68.8% of registered voters was 2.5% above that for 2015, but noticeably down on the 72.4% in the referendum a year earlier.[17] Turnout fell most in Scotland (down by 4.6%) and in seats where UKIP had done well in 2015. Turnout and its effect on Labour's fortunes soon sparked intense debate among election analysts.

During election night, a claim started to circulate that the turnout of those aged 18–24 had risen to an astonishing 72%. The campaign appeared to have energised young people like never before, something consistent with the enthusiastic crowds of young voters at Corbyn's rallies. Yet this statistic, which soon took on a life of its own, appears to have been entirely made up.[18] Estimates from polling companies reported rises in the turnout of those aged 18–24 of between 12 and 21 percentage points, less dramatic, although still an apparent vindication of the Leader of the Opposition's Office (LOTO) electoral strategy.[19] Moreover, almost every study found this age group overwhelmingly voting Labour. Corbyn appeared to have managed to persuade young people both to vote *and* to vote Labour.

Yet two pieces of later analysis by the BES and the British Social Attitudes survey contradicted claims of this so-called 'youthquake'.[20] Based on a face-to-face probability sample and checking claims against marked electoral registers, the BES found no evidence of a rise in turnout amongst the young—although there was still a clear swing to Labour amongst those who did vote. Indeed, based on the validated votes in both 2015 and 2017, the BES team found that turnout amongst those aged 18–24 had actually fallen somewhat (by around six percentage points).[21] The British Social Attitudes research found that the turnout among 18–24 year olds rose by a modest five percentage points, only marginally more than the rise amongst other age groups.[22] Such conclusions provoked some scepticism, mostly based on the sample size involved; the BES study, for example, included just 109 validated responses from those aged 18–24 in 2017.[23] An internal Labour Party estimate, based on analysis of several million records from marked electoral registers, did indeed find an increase in the involvement of those aged 18–24, of about ten percentage points, still significant if not as substantial as the wilder claims made about youth turnout.

However, perhaps the most significant point made by the BES team was that even if they were wrong, it was, by definition, impossible for a rise in youth turnout to have been anything other than a relatively minor part of the story of the election—simply as a result of demography. As they wrote:

> people aged 18 to 24 make up 11% of the electorate, about 5.2 million people in total. Labour won 3.5 million more votes in 2017 than in 2015. If we are wrong about the level of turnout amongst young people and it was in fact as high as 72% … this would be about 1.2 million more young voters than 2015. Even if every single one of these new voters voted Labour (an absurdly strong assumption) this would only account for about one third of Labour's vote gains in 2017 and does not take into account countervailing flows away from Labour.[24]

In other words, even if there had been a massive increase in youth turnout, this can only ever be a relatively small part of the story of the election.

More important than the rise in turnout amongst different age groups was the extent to which age had replaced social class as the main division between the two main parties. As the over-50s swung to the Conservatives, the under-40s swung to Labour, producing the biggest age gap since polling records were compiled. Table 16.3 shows that the pro-Labour swing among those aged 18–29 was 13.5%, but the pro-Conservative swing among over-70s was 8.5%. Much research has shown that incomes rose

Table 16.3   How Britain voted in 2017

	Con	Lab	Lib Dem	UKIP	Green	Con lead	Change since 2015			Swing Con-Lab
	%	%	%	%	%		Con	Lab	LD	
All	44	41	8	2	2	3	6	10	0	2
Men	45	39	8	2	2	6	8	10	0	1
Women	43	43	7	1	2	0	5	11	−1	3
Age 18–29	22	63	9	1	2	−41	−6	21	0	13.5
Age 30–39	29	55	8	1	2	−26	−2	15	−1	8.5
Age 40–49	39	44	8	2	2	−5	6	9	0	1.5
Age 50–59	47	37	7	3	2	10	11	7	0	−2
Age 60–69	58	27	7	2	1	31	8	10	−1	1
Age 70+	69	19	7	2	1	50	17	0	−1	−8.5
AB social grade (professional/managerial)	46	38	10	1	2	8	1	8	0	3.5
C1 (white collar)	41	43	8	1	2	−2	3	13	−1	5
C2 (skilled manual)	47	40	6	2	1	7	11	11	−1	0
DE (semi-/unskilled)	41	44	6	3	1	−3	13	8	−1	−2.5
Remain voters—ABC1	26	53	13	0	2	−27	−6	12	1	9
Remain voters—C2DE	23	60	9	0	2	−37	−3	14	0	8.5
Leave voters—ABC1	70	21	3	3	1	49	15	5	−2	−5
Leave voters—C2DE	59	28	3	5	1	31	23	5	−2	−9
Highest education: GCSE or lower	55	33	5	3	1	22	17	5	−1	−6
Highest education: A-Level	45	39	7	2	1	6	5	10	−1	2.5
University graduates	32	49	11	1	2	−17	−1	12	−1	6.5
Own home	53	31	8	2	1	22	9	5	0	−2

(continued)

Table 16.3 (continued)

	Con	Lab	Lib Dem	UKIP	Green	Con lead	Change since 2015			Swing Con-Lab
	%	%	%	%	%		Con	Lab	LD	
Renting home	32	51	6	3	2	−19	7	11	−2	2
Work in private sector	47	37	8	2	2	10	6	10	0	2
Work in public sector	34	49	8	2	2	−15	−1	13	−1	7
Unemployed	28	54	6	4	2	−26	11	9	−1	−1
Full-time students	19	64	10	1	2	−45	−5	21	2	13
Household income less than £20 k per year	41	42	6	3	2	−1	11	8	−1	−1.5
Household income £20–39 k p.a	47	38	7	2	1	9	8	10	−2	1
Household income £40–59 k p.a	46	39	8	1	2	7	6	8	0	1
Household income more than £60 k per year	47	36	11	1	2	11	1	7	2	3
Daily Telegraph readers	79	12	6	1	1	67	9	3	−1	−3
Daily Mail readers	74	17	3	3	1	57	13	2	−2	−5.5
The Times readers	58	24	14	1	2	34	−1	4	2	2.5
Daily Express readers	77	17	2	3	2	60	26	3	−3	−11.5
The Sun readers	59	30	3	3	1	29	15	5	0	−5
Daily Mirror readers	19	68	3	2	1	−49	2	10	−2	4
The Guardian readers	6	73	12	0	3	−67	−3	14	1	8.5

Source: YouGov, 9–13 June 2017. N=52,615

fastest in pensioner households since 2008 and that the young had borne the brunt of benefit cuts, stagnant real incomes and had difficulty getting on the housing ladder.[25] Too much of the discussion of the election focused on those aged 18–24. Had the Conservatives lost just this age group, they would have been sanguine. The more significant group were those aged in their thirties and forties, who also swung towards Labour. YouGov identified 47 as the precise cut-off point at which someone became more likely to vote Conservative than Labour; it had been 34 at the start of the campaign.[26]

At the same time, the election saw a dramatic weakening of the relationship between social class and vote, as Labour's share of the middle-class vote and Conservative share of the working-class vote reached their highest levels since 1979, when Mrs. Thatcher was first elected.[27] Although the Conservatives had an 8% lead among ABC1s, Labour increased their share among this group by 12%, and while Labour led by 4% among C2DE voters, the Conservatives increased their share amongst this group by 12%. Within the last group, Labour did better among the DEs (semi-skilled and unskilled manual workers and the unemployed) and the Conservatives among the C2s (skilled manual workers).

The findings about education were also notable. The Conservatives led by 22% among those educated to GCSE or below, while Labour had a commanding 17% lead among graduates and an even bigger one (over 40%) among full-time students in higher education, among whom the swing to Labour was 13%. Labour remained strong among BAME voters and increased their lead over the Conservatives in the group to 54%, compared to a six-point Conservative lead amongst white voters.[28] At the start of the campaign, when the party's prospects looked bleak, one Labour MP described the BAME vote as 'our firewall'. The election led to concern within some parts of the Labour Party about the extent to which it was losing ground amongst those for whom the party had been originally set up to represent, by which was usually meant the white working class. Such comments had a tendency to ignore Britain's growing BAME communities—still disproportionately Labour-supporting and still disproportionately working class. Conversely, some Conservatives worried about the extent to which the party was still failing to make inroads—indeed, losing ground—amongst BAME voters. This was the second consecutive election in which the Conservatives had increased their share of the vote, whilst falling behind among BAME voters. Conservatives are a diminishing proportion of a growing share of the electorate.[29]

While the two main parties held on to about 80% of their 2015 voters, the Liberal Democrats held on to around 50%. Labour did better in attracting the approximately 2.5 million who had not voted in 2015; of these, 1.9 million voted Labour and 0.5 million voted Conservative.[30] The rise, however modest, of first-time voters and previous non-voters explains, at least in part, why it was not picked up by the ground campaigns of the two main parties whose canvass records largely comprise voters' past voting.

Table 16.3 also reveals a remarkable diversity of swings, apart from age and class. The readerships of the Leave-supporting newspapers (*The Sun*, the *Daily Mail*, the *Daily Telegraph* and the *Daily Express*) all swung to the Conservatives. The swing among *Daily Express* readers (many of whom voted for UKIP in 2015) was 11.5%. But among *Guardian* readers the pro-Labour swing was 8.5%. What emerges from both survey (Table 16.3) and geographical (Appendix 1) analyses is that the 2016 referendum cast a long shadow over the election, loosening the party loyalties of both former Conservative and Labour voters. A significant minority of voters shifted to align their party vote with their referendum vote and in the process sharpened the age and educational differences between the parties. Jennings and Stoker argue that the 2015 election, the referendum vote and the 2017 election are all the outcomes of a gradual bifurcation of English politics, between metropolitan and cosmopolitan areas of economic growth whose inhabitants are comfortable with diversity and are outward-looking, and backwater areas, often provincial and coastal parts, whose inhabitants are negative about immigration and Europe.[31] The outcomes of both the referendum and the 2017 election have clearly been shaped by social and economic changes that have been building for some years.

The main parties continued to be the preferred choice on their traditional strong policy areas. As Table 16.4 shows, Labour led on housing, education and health, while the Conservatives led on the economy, law and order, and security, as well as the exit from the EU. Yet it was extraordinary how little attention was paid to the economy during the campaign and how minor a role the Chancellor of the Exchequer, Philip Hammond, played. This contrasted with the prominent roles as election strategists and economic spokesmen of Gordon Brown and George Osborne in recent elections. According to the BES, less than 5% of voters considered the economy 'the single most important issue facing the country at this time'—so much for the golden election rule of 'It's the economy stupid'. Yet this is to define 'economic policy' too narrowly. The cost of living

Table 16.4   Preferred party on issues (%)

Issue	Con	Lab	LD	Others	None	Don't know	Con lead over Lab
National Health Service	22	41	4	3	8	22	−19
Asylum and immigration	30	20	5	17	8	20	+10
Law and order	36	26	4	5	6	23	+10
Education and schools	25	36	6	4	7	23	−11
Taxation	30	30	5	4	7	24	0
Unemployment	29	30	2	4	8	26	−1
The economy in general	39	25	4	4	7	23	+14
Housing	21	35	4	4	9	27	−14
Britain's exit from the EU	37	19	7	8	8	21	+18
Defence and security	37	22	3	6	7	25	+15

Source: YouGov, 5–7 June 2017

loomed large when voters were asked which issues mattered to themselves and their families, and that fed into concerns about stagnant incomes and the public sector pay cap. In 2010 tackling the deficit and in 2015 the 'long-term economic plan' had played a major role in the Conservative campaigns, yet in 2017 the few mentions of the deficit were overshadowed by Labour's campaign against austerity and for boosting spending on public services. In two years, the mood had changed; compared to 2015, there were fewer takers for tackling the deficit and continuing with austerity and spending curbs.[32] As one Shadow Cabinet minister put it: 'It used to be community centres in council estates closing. Well, not many floating voters went to those anyway. But now it was middle class parents getting begging letters off their schools, because there was no enough money'. A British Social Attitudes survey in 2017 found that 48% favoured higher taxes to pay for more spending on public services and over 40% favoured the redistribution of wealth from the rich to the poor. Dissatisfaction with years of austerity had reached a tipping point.[33]

Policy areas neglected by the main parties included defence, climate change, public service reform—and immigration. The relative absence of the last of these from the campaign, so prominent only a year earlier in the referendum, was a remarkable comment on how quickly political debate can change. The result of the referendum was that the parties accepted an end to freedom of movement; Labour were fighting on their most restrictive immigration policy for decades, and the decision to leave the EU had shot UKIP's fox. The issue of inter-generational inequality—so often ignored—was covered, both with Labour's promise on tuition fees and the Conservatives' pledges on social care and cutting back some benefits for the elderly.

The polls reported other divisions on values in modern Britain aside from Brexit. As in 2015, the Conservatives were still less positive than Labour about the environmental movement, feminism, immigrants and multi-culturalism, but more positive about capitalism and believing that by working hard, anybody can be successful regardless of their background.[34] The party's brand took a hit during the election. Its commanding lead over Labour on competence was reduced to just 3%, a substantial fall from a year earlier, and it saw no improvement on its ratings for fairness and 'being on the side or people like them', as Labour increased its lead on both. If an aim of party modernisation under both David Cameron and May had been to make the party's support more socially representative, that had been achieved, but Cameron had also wanted the party to be seen as more socially liberal, 'fair' and at ease with modern Britain. This second aim had not been achieved.

Advised by her campaign strategists, Theresa May asked voters for their backing to strengthen her hand in the Brexit negotiations. By design or not, this meant ditching the 'burning injustices' approach that her Number 10 aides had planned for her. But one problem in her trying to make 2017 into a 'Brexit election' was that over the course of a seven-week campaign, she had little concrete to say—or that she was willing to say—about the trade-offs involved in her Brexit plans. Having held her cards close to her chest before the election, it was unclear how she would answer questions about her Brexit plans in the campaign. There was much talk of a soft or a hard Brexit, although the differences probably meant little to most voters and the election produced little clarification on such key issues as the numbers and types of immigrants who would be allowed in, rules regarding the access to the Single Market or Customs Union, and the role of the European Court of Justice in areas of post-Brexit cooperation. Instead, as a despairing aide said, 'she just repeated "back me" ad nauseam'.

Yet Brexit clearly had shaped the views of a substantial number of voters and disrupted the traditional bases of the parties. When asked about the single most-important issue facing the country, the BES found that more than a third mentioned Brexit. It also reported that before the campaign began, the Conservatives had already converted a good number of Leave voters, often from UKIP (whose collapse was also one of the most obvious consequences of Brexit), and that Labour had already lost many of their Leave voters. An Ashcroft election day poll of 14,000 voters found that when asked unprompted questions about reasons for their vote, Conservatives mentioned Brexit (48%) and their confidence in May as the best to lead the negotiations.[35] It therefore should have been game, set and match to the Conservatives.

It was not, and the same poll suggests that may have been because for Labour voters, defending the NHS and public services against cuts greatly outweighed Brexit (mentioned by only 8%). Later and more nuanced analysis in Ashcroft's *The Lost Majority* found that while 29% (the highest figure) of voters regarded negotiating Britain's exit from the EU as the most important issue facing the country, when they were asked what mattered most to 'me and my family', the issue fell to third place behind the NHS and the cost of living.[36] When voters were asked to recall the policies or themes of the two main parties in the campaign, Brexit was most mentioned by Conservatives (nearly a third) followed by social care, or 'the dementia tax' and 'strong and stable', but for Labour, the most remembered was the abolition of tuition fees followed by the NHS and 'spending too much'.[37]

Despite Conservative pressure, the media, particularly the broadcasters, did not treat it as a Brexit election (see p. 326). Conservative post-election research also challenges the BES claim that it was a Brexit election insofar as other issues were also at work to drive away the party's Remain supporters. A Number 10 aide wrote to us: 'It was because they *happened to be* Remain voters rather than *because* they were Remain voters; they were also worried about domestic issues and public services' (emphasis in original). In that case, Labour's domestic agenda compensated for its losses among its 2015 voters who were Leavers. The perceived stances of Labour and Conservatives on Brexit may have influenced a good number of voters, but there was too much cross-cutting traffic for it to have determined the result. Some anti-Brexit Conservatives seized on Labour's capture of a number of Conservative Remain seats in England to make the case for a soft Brexit. Labour's stance was perhaps too ambiguous, too dependent on who the party's spokesperson was to read much into it. But given that the Conservatives were clearly the party for Leave, Labour became the default option for many Remainers. Their so-called 'constructive ambiguity', motivated largely by electoral concerns and intra-party divisions, paid off.

It is striking that the 2015–17 period saw the highest amount of switching between the two major parties of any election since 1966. More than one in ten voters switched direct from Conservative to Labour or vice versa; a full 12% of 2015 Conservative voters, for example, switched direct to a Corbyn-led Labour Party.[38] According to YouGov, 22% of Labour/ Brexit voters who voted in 2017 switched to the Conservatives, while 17% of Conservative/Remain voters switched to Labour. But the turnout was higher (88%) among the Remainers than among the Leavers (79%). On 8 June, 14 million Remainers voted, but only 13 million Leavers. In 2016, the figures had been 16 million and 17 million respectively. The Conservatives had cause to regret that some four million Leave voters in the referendum did not turn out in the election; for the most part, these were 2015 UKIP and non-voters. The Conservatives campaign clearly failed to attract many of those who were outside the political mainstream in 2015 but had been energised by the referendum. On the basis of the large (52,000) YouGov post-election survey, Peter Kellner argues that that had they voted in the same way as other pro-Brexit supporters, the Conservatives would have gained an extra 30 seats.[39] But there were also 2015 Labour Leave voters who remained with Labour because other domestic issues mattered to them.[40]

The Conservatives may have under-estimated the softness of their Remainer votes and as John Curtice cautioned: 'In appealing to the Brexiters, May seems to have forgotten that she needed to carry with her the half of the country that voted remain.'[41] He might have added that a good number of them were Conservatives, often young, well-educated and socially liberal, and who were prepared to defect to Labour. These were the Conservative 'Leaners' that the Number 10 strategists had always feared might be lost. Brexit helped them on their way.

Once the votes had been counted, the Conservatives had 55 more seats than Labour, their highest vote share since 1983 and had increased their share at each general election since 1997. They had done so for the last two elections despite being in government and, as noted in Appendix 1, the increase in the Conservative vote in 2017 was, remarkably, the largest increase in support enjoyed by an incumbent government that had won the previous election since 1832. The party achieved its highest share in Wales in a century and, in reversing a long period of decline in Scotland, ran ahead of Labour for first time since 1959. Its share of the C2 (or skilled working-class) vote was its highest ever and was an increase of 11% compared to 2015, and was very slightly bigger than its share among the middle class. May's Conservatives were a more cross-class party, something Cameron's modernisation of the party had aspired to. The party gained vote shares in the North, the Midlands and Scotland, although it still held only 40 of the 158 constituencies in the North of England, a net loss of four.

The increase in the Conservatives' vote share of nearly six percentage points was reasonably expected to deliver a majority of seats for the party. A similar vote share had gained Margaret Thatcher a landslide victory in 1983. What was not anticipated and upset the calculations was that Labour's vote would increase by almost ten percentage points, resulting in a 2% swing in Labour's favour. May's post-election admission that she had not seen Labour's advance coming could have been said by many in Conservative Campaign Headquarters (CCHQ).[42] The verdict of one of the campaign consultants makes the point:

> There is a case to be made that if our job was to increase the Tory vote in these seats (in the North and Midlands) to a level higher than Labour's 2015 (by bringing together a coalition of voters around the 'best Brexit deal') we succeeded in a lot of cases. However, we did not expect this 'red tide' of Corbyn support to go over the top of us—meaning the targets we'd set ourselves in terms of raw vote to take these seats were in fact met (in some cases exceeded) but proved to be insufficient.

Few Conservatives were consoled by such arguments or statistics. The party had called an election to increase its majority (and until the exit poll thought it was on course to do so) and ended by losing it. It had overwhelming press support, clearly outspent Labour (£18.6 million compared to Labour's £11 million) and always led in the polls.

Not for the first time, an election defeat—or in this case what felt very similar to a defeat—was an orphan. It was remarkable how rapidly key figures appeared to disown the Conservative campaign. Within days, we learnt that May herself had been unhappy with the campaign's focus on her, the sidelining of colleagues and the neglect of policy, but had deferred to her experienced campaign advisers.[43] In a post-election radio interview, she expressed regret at failing to get across the vision she had set out on the steps of Number 10.[44] Lynton Crosby, according to 'sources close to Sir Lynton', blamed, variously, the manifesto which he said came as a surprise to him, his lack of control and the decision to call the election in the first place.[45] Nick Timothy accepted his share of the blame for the manifesto, but regretted that Number 10 plans to present May's 'positive plan for the future' had been submerged by the CTF strategy.[46]

It is easy enough to identify the problems with the campaign. It was, as one study of the campaign noted, 'an election at which everything that could go wrong for the Conservatives did go wrong'.[47] There was the self-inflicted wound of the lack of preparation and planning, which made the polling, narrative and digital operations—all prepared at short notice—less impressive than in 2015. If one of the lessons of Gordon Brown's non-election in 2007 was that the preparations required for an election can make it difficult to prepare for snap elections in secret, one of the lessons of 2017 was that the secrecy required for a snap election prevents the necessary preparation required for a campaign. Number 10 aides had wanted to avoid doing 'a Brown'; in future, aides will want to avoid doing 'a May'.

There was the lack of day-to-day leadership. As discussed in Chapter 7, no one person was continually in charge of the campaign. Lynton Crosby was not the central dominating presence he had been in 2015. He had made it clear he did not want play the central role; Stephen Gilbert was nominally—and reluctantly—in charge, but he effectively handed over to Crosby once he joined the campaign. Fiona Hill (often accompanying May on her travels) and Nick Timothy (working on the manifesto) were the main—and in effect only—regular contacts with May, and Sir Patrick McLoughlin was often absent from CCHQ, visiting constituencies (McLoughlin's absence was largely mirrored on the Labour side by the General Secretary, Iain McNicol, who was also often out visiting constituencies. The days when the Conservative chairman or Labour general secretary ran their election seem long gone). As one key Conservative aide stated: 'Neither Gilbert nor Crosby really wanted to run the campaign and Timothy just wanted to write the manifesto. And in truth no one ran the campaign. There was a complete absence of leadership or direction.'

Then there was the campaign strategy. Even if he was not running it with the same degree of control as he had in 2015, the campaign strategy followed the Crosby playbook, with poll-driven messages and message discipline exercised from the centre. In 2015, the messages had been leadership (Cameron versus Miliband), economic competence (the long-term economic plan) and the rejection of a coalition of chaos (Labour's dependence on the SNP), all backed by research. In 2017, it was again leadership (May versus Corbyn) allied with Brexit. Critics complained that it was negative and personal, although as Chapter 14 shows, this was reinforced by the anti-Corbyn coverage from the right-wing papers.[48] Negative campaigning often works, particularly when it highlights the risk of voting for the other side, but in 2017 it also served to accentuate the 'positive' offers from Labour and Corbyn's refusal to engage in personal attacks.[49] Ironically, the on-message approach may also have emphasised Corbyn's authenticity. Many Labour strategists wondered why the Conservatives neglected so many Labour weaknesses, including the costing of its policies, and divisions in the Parliamentary Labour Party (PLP) over Corbyn's leadership.

Similarly, May's Number 10 strategist Chris Wilkins, who had wanted to campaign on a policy-rich programme, complained that the campaign's failure to connect Brexit with a domestic agenda of improving people's lives allowed Corbyn to be the change candidate and address voters' concerns, some of which had led to the Brexit vote. He also attacked the focus on the Brexit process:

> This was a big negative. Months of research had shown us that talking about Brexit as a process rather than an opportunity would turn people off. What people wanted was for us to explain our policies through the prism of Brexit. In other words, when talking about what you wanted to do with education for example, explain why it was important in the context of Brexit and the kind of country we wanted to be as we emerged from Brexit.

Then there was the manifesto. Campaigners complained they had few retail offers for the voters and were having to explain away policies. Top of the list of complaints was the social care package with its lack of a cap on costs. The dementia tax joined the poll tax and the bedroom tax in the lexicon of politically damaging taxes, none of which were actually taxes. A senior member of the campaign team said that the proposal was 'an unmitigated fucking disaster'.

The manifesto authors had consciously written what they regarded as a 'grown-up' document setting out the challenges the country faced. It made a contrast what they saw as the 'free stuff' on offer from Labour. (As one Shadow Cabinet minister put it: 'people like free stuff'). Yet there is little point in writing a manifesto for government without first being sure of forming the government. One lesson from 2017 might be that even with a big lead in the polls, it is risky for a party to offer tough choices to the voters, particularly after a long period of austerity and without preparing the ground properly. As a Conservative election strategist said almost 50 years ago: 'You don't shoot Santa Claus.' If British general elections are sometimes criticised for being superficial and not engaging properly with the choices faced by the country, nothing in the events of 2017 is likely to make them less superficial in future. But another lesson might be that if there are to be difficult choices, the ground needs to be prepared. Margaret Thatcher once remarked that a good policy should be only slightly ahead of public opinion. 'If a political leader floated an idea five years ahead of its time he could effectively kill that idea', she said. But floating the idea just two years ahead of time would be seen as 'real political leadership'. When reminded of this, one of the 2017 Conservative manifesto team replied: 'That's a very wise dictum and one I wish I had respected.'[50]

Others argued that May's clumsy U-turn ('nothing has changed') was more damaging than the policy itself—yet the U-turn would not have been necessary but for the manifesto. YouGov reported that before the manifesto launch, 35% agreed that the party had well-thought-through policies; afterwards, just 19% did. Before Labour's manifesto launch, 25% thought that the party had well-thought-through policies, but that figure rose to 31% afterwards. Labour support was already rising before the manifesto and it is a convenient excuse to ignore the many other shortcomings of the campaign, but the YouGov Multilevel Regression and Post-stratification analysis model, which would later prove so accurate, had the Conservatives clearly ahead until the launch of the manifesto.

In trying to sort out the claims and counterclaims of the principals, we have to allow for their different perspectives, but also how these might be shaped by political and sometimes commercial interests. In our interviews, frequent complaints of 'arse covering' were heard. As noted in our chapters on the campaign, the tensions in the Labour camp between LOTO and Southside were matched on the Conservative side. If Hill and Timothy were known as 'the Chiefs', Crosby and Textor were called 'the Australians'—the appellations were not always meant warmly—and the bad blood between them was evident in the post-election briefings. Yet many of the claims are clearly wrong. On calling the election, Crosby did indeed present some potential risks, as would be expected, but, contrary to some press reports, he did not say 'Don't' and later he was reported in Australia as approving of the timing.[51] The more controversial manifesto policies, including removing the triple lock, the social care package, and restricting the winter fuel allowance, were tested in CTF polling weeks before the manifesto was launched. As for control of the campaign, decisions about May's prominence, campaign message, the minor role of Cabinet ministers, May's script for speeches and even interviews, the U-turn over the social care package and not pre-releasing any attractive policies were all made by the campaign management team.

'Everyone thought Lynton had worked magic in 2015', said one of those involved, 'and thought it would work again.' The team that had basked in the applause for the victory in 2015 now faced brickbats for 2017. To what extent, some asked, were they like generals who prepared to fight the battles of the last war rather than the next? The judgement of Paul Goodman, on the influential ConservativeHome site, was severe: 'Above all, the myth of Lynton Crosby and Jim Messina's infallible research, social media targeting and data has been exploded.'[52] Perhaps the most wounding indictment of the failure to craft a compelling narrative, in contrast to 2015, was that of a senior CCHQ figure who said: 'In 2017 I had no idea what Theresa May stood for or what she was trying to do, so I don't blame the voters for not knowing either!'

As variously noted above, May's aides, notably Timothy and Wilkins, had hoped to run a different Conservative campaign, based on the themes she had spoken of when she became Prime Minister. This had, they noted, given the party a polling lead of over 20 points. Any prospect of promoting May as the 'change candidate' and forging a new Conservatism were buried under CTF's 'strong and stable' slogan, a decision which at the time nobody appeared to challenge directly. One Number 10 aide complained: 'CTF were only supposed to be involved to run the mechanics of the campaign, not the strategy.' May herself would later regret that she had not managed to get her message across: 'When I came into Downing Street I stood on the steps and I set out my platform for the future, that didn't come through in the election.'[53] This view was echoed in public by Timothy and Wilkins, and in private by others. They regretted that they had not fought harder for their view and regard it as one of the key failings of the campaign. Timothy wrote that the mistake was not to have campaigned 'in accordance with the insight that took Theresa to Downing Street in the first place', adding that if the referendum was a vote to leave the EU, 'it was also a vote for change'.[54]

Yet it is not self-evident that an alternative campaign would have worked. Just because the approach had yielded a large poll lead in government did not automatically mean that it would withstand the stress test of a campaign. Although some thinking and policy work to help the 'JAMS' was under way in May's Policy Unit, there had been too little time to finesse relevant policies; the government was still committed to austerity and much ministerial and Whitehall attention was devoted to Brexit. If there was a popular mood for change, it probably was for an end to austerity and not for more hard choices, and Corbyn was more successful in tapping into that sentiment. There had also not been the groundwork to prepare support across the party or the public for radical polices; as it was, the manifesto's themes like the proposed regulation of energy prices, advancing workers' rights, reforming social care and willingness to intervene if necessary to correct abuses in the free market alarmed some Conservative commentators, who saw such policies as an abandonment of Thatcherism and caused unease among the party's free market wing. There is also some doubt about how united the Cabinet would have been with a more radical programme. (When pressed as to whether ministers would have rallied to such an election programme, one Cabinet minister paused and said 'most would'). However, what is clear is that running two parallel campaigns did not work. 'What in the end happened', said one of May's Cabinet colleagues, 'was that we launched the manifesto into a different campaign.' This incoherence had been prefigured in the Chequers meeting in February 2017 and was fatally never resolved.

But above all, there was the Prime Minister. For Theresa May, this was a personal failure. She had called the election. She had been the focus of the party's campaign, in which role she had been found wanting. Whilst many of the decisions taken about the campaign had not been hers, she had been willing, perhaps too willing, to acquiesce to the judgement of others, and some of the key decisions, most obviously the decision on social care, were indeed hers, taken despite the doubts of others in her team.

As a campaigner, she had demonstrated serious limitations. In modern election campaigns, the party leader is the chief message carrier, not least when the leader *is* the message. But by the end of the campaign, the theme of May's strong leadership had run into the ground. The slogan conveyed no vision or sense of direction, and it was in any case directly contradicted by the Prime Minister's behaviour during the campaign. The characterisation of May as 'bloody difficult' (with echoes of 'battling Maggie') was originally associated with strength and qualities that would be useful in fighting the British corner during the Brexit negotiations. But during the campaign, she came across as wooden and over-scripted, robotically mouthing soundbites. Her chief speechwriter described his role in writing the lines Mark Textor instructed him to craft on the basis of his focus groups as 'soul-destroying'. *The Guardian*'s John Crace captured the mood with his 'Maybot' caricature, suggesting a lack of warmth and engagement and an inability to think on her feet.[55] She sounded scripted even when she was not.

May's avoidance of TV debates and her appearances before small groups of supporters may have suited her reserved personality, but it did not demonstrate someone who was at ease mixing with the public. These limitations were accentuated as Corbyn, a lifelong campaigner who clearly revelled in his contact with supportive crowds. He had polished his skills during two recent leadership contests. May had played little or no role in the referendum campaign, her election as leader had been a coronation and she was relatively untried as a national campaigner. The analogy of May as a submarine used earlier in her career remained apt, if now for different reasons; for all their power when submerged, submarines are vulnerable once they surface. In the full glare of an election campaign and with no place to hide, her limitations as a campaigner became painfully obvious. During one party election broadcast, she said that with her 'what you see is what you get'; this turned out to be part of the problem.

Long before 8 June, it was clear that May was not suited for a leader-based campaign. Crosby was reported to have received a message the day after the election from an Australian politician, consoling him on having a 'crap candidate', yet May's aides, aware of her strengths and weaknesses, blamed CTF for miscasting her. Will Tanner, deputy head of her Policy Unit, said he could not 'fathom that choice': 'You have to ask how a politician who had made her name through quiet competence and by not pushing herself forward as an individual ended up touring the country in a bus with her name plastered over the side of it! Idiotic.'

Some Conservatives wistfully looked to the campaigning joie de vivre of Ruth Davidson, the Scottish Tory leader. She pointedly ran a different, non-Crosby informed campaign, not emphasising May's leadership. She combined a vigorous defence of Unionism with opposition to any change on fox hunting and social care, or cuts to the winter fuel payment for pensioners, and advocated an open Brexit. Her warmth and enthusiasm made a painful contrast with what the party offered south of the border and raised a 'what if?' query even among some Number 10 aides.

This was Theresa May's election. It was her failure. Addressing the 1922 Committee after the election, she claimed: 'I got us into this mess, and I'm going to get us out of it.'[56] Her MPs had little doubt about the first half of the statement; they were much less sure about the second. Yet for all the criticism of the party's campaign, some of it savage and often from within the party, Conservative optimists argue that although it did not improve its vote share in the campaign, it effectively held on to the share it started with and achieved the highest share since 1979. They reflect on what they might have done with a more inspiring leader and a better judged and voter-friendly campaign. The party's pessimists look beyond the campaign and note that they have won a majority in only two of the seven general elections held since 1987, and those by just 21 and 12 seats, and worry that the voting analysis shows that age, education and ethnicity are now working firmly against them. Yet in the 1960s, Sir Michael Fraser, an architect of the party's 1959 election victory, gloomily pointed to the demographics then working against the Conservatives, what he described as 'Death, Youth and the Working Class': older Conservatives voters dying off, the Labour leanings of the young, the tendency for political loyalties to be passed on and for the working class to be more numerous than the middle. Demography is not destiny, though, and the Conservatives won the 1970 general election and four in succession from 1979. Parties are not passive bystanders and by their choices can help to shape their own electoral fortunes.

When the campaign began, there was much speculation about whether Labour would emerge as a credible political force—and several members of the PLP were positioning themselves for the post-election fight for the party leadership. Many doubted that its unpopular leader and left-wing programme would defy electoral conventional wisdom about the importance of a party's leadership and occupying a so-called middle ground. Yet Labour improved their 2015 vote share by almost ten percentage points, winning over former Greens, UKIPers, Nationalists, Liberal Democrats and an estimated 700,000 Conservatives. Although both main parties made gains from each other and from other parties, Labour were more successful in hoovering them up as well as recapturing many of their 2015 voters who had abandoned the party before the campaign.[57] The party made a net gain of 30 seats, with especially big swings in university towns and in Remain-voting seats in London. The swing to the party across England, except for the North East, meant that it was extending its support in its weak regions of the South East and the South West, although it still had less than 30% of the vote and only 18 of the two regions' 174 seats outside of London. The swing to Labour declined as one travelled north from London and the South and reversed in the North East and Scotland. The party gained Canterbury, but lost Stoke-on-Trent South. It was now an electoral coalition of the professional middle class, well-educated (49% of graduates voted Labour), the young and early middle aged, BAME and public sector workers. How stable this alliance will prove to be remains to be seen.

Labour did all this despite having started with a strategy which even one of the campaign team described as 'a leap of faith', and despite the frosty relationship and minimal cooperation between Corbyn's aides and the party's professional staff at Southside. Even after the result, some

Southside staff still dismissed the Corbyn operation: 'It was a disaster', said one. 'I cannot stress to you enough how anyone who had been involved in previous election campaigns would not be able to recognise this as a general election campaign. It was a mess.' Although some of his internal critics would acknowledge Corbyn's success on the campaign trail, on their reading Labour and Corbyn mostly just got lucky, as a result of a poor Conservative campaign. Not surprisingly, Corbyn aides disagree, saying they had no intention of following Southside's campaign model and that they had been vindicated by the party gaining seats for the first time since 1997. They also argued that the Conservative mistakes were not all unforced errors, but that at least in part they came about as a result of Labour's more aggressive campaign. Corbyn's team also complained that Southside were letting him down by not pursuing a more aggressive and offensive targeting strategy.

As reported in Chapter 12, Labour clearly won the ground war; their much larger and more active membership out-canvassed and out-leafleted the Conservatives. There had been much praise for the Conservatives' use of social media to target key swing voters in 2015, but in 2017 Labour not only caught up with but also overtook CCHQ. The Conservatives may have spent £2.1 million buying space on Facebook compared to Labour's £577,000, but more Labour ads and videos were shared organically. Labour also used social media more effectively to encourage registration, to remind people to attend rallies and vote and to generally boost morale. As Dominic Wring and David Deacon report in Chapter 14, the reputation of the print media as a reliable guide to the public mood and to the result took a battering in 2017. The approval ratings for Corbyn and Labour rose impressively despite the onslaught from much of the press. The two forms of media seemed to live in different worlds, with readers of the press elderly, negative and anti-Labour, and those using social media younger, more pro-Corbyn and pro-Labour. Nearly one in five Labour voters said that social media was their main source of news in the election, compared to just six in 100 Conservatives.[58] As a close ally of Corbyn looked back on the terrible press the leader endured since 2015, he reflected how little of it mattered. The same was true with the bad press in the election. 'This was the first post-press general election', he observed, talking of 'the decline of the press barons and the rise of the algorithm'. One of the Conservative team similarly argued it was 'the first election where papers didn't really matter'.

'The star of the show', claimed Emily Thornberry after the election, 'was the manifesto. People think it was Jeremy, and I love Jeremy, but the star of the show was the manifesto.'[59] Policies certainly attracted more media coverage than in 2015, thanks to Labour's manifesto—said to have been downloaded an astonishing six million times from the Labour website—and the controversy over the Conservative social care package. Yet voters rarely decide on policies without taking into account the priority they accord them and the perceived competence and trustworthiness of the parties, and Labour trailed on both. The manifesto was also extremely popular among party supporters and campaigners; candidates and local organisers talked of how the policies had energised party workers and had given them something to offer voters.[60] Separating out the impact of Corbyn (as party leader) and the party manifesto (which only existed in that form because of Corbyn's leadership) is close to impossible, but the two are analytically separable. Would an identical manifesto have had the same reaction with a different leader? It is difficult to imagine that another candidate from the Labour left would have boosted the membership so much. Corbyn showed courage and self-belief in his determination to project a vision that was not derived from campaign strategists and experienced field managers. He appealed to the young (18–24 year olds) who preferred him over May as Prime Minister by more than three to one. In contrast to May, he emerged from the election with enhanced status and challenged many long-held nostrums of campaign wisdom. Yet it is not clear how much of this, compared to the policies, translated into votes. We have noted above that a good number of Labour candidates thought that Corbyn was a handicap on the doorstep and there was no positive 'Corbyn effect' from his visits. Insofar as we can separate Labour's leadership and policy in the campaign, the latter would appear to trump the former.

Some (Tony Blair, for example) have tried to explain the Labour surge by claiming that many Labour voters were only voting Labour because they knew the party could not win. Certainly, versions of 'Jeremy is not going to be Prime Minister, so vote for me and ensure that the Conservatives don't have a huge majority' was a pitch many Labour candidates made to hesitant Labour voters. Two separate pieces of post-election analysis appeared to argue that such voters were relatively few in number. First, the BES found that perceptions of how well Labour would do on polling day rose during the campaign and that voters were *more* likely to switch to Labour if they thought the party could win. Second, *The Lost Majority* reported that Labour voters were in fact the happiest about the outcome of the election.[61] Against this, unreleased private polling commissioned by an organisation close to Labour found more than a third of Labour's voters (38%) thought that the party had little or no chance of becoming the next government, and a quarter (24%) of this group said that this had made them more likely to vote Labour. In other words, just under one in ten of the party's vote may have been contingent on it being unlikely to form the next government.[62] Moreover, Charlie Cadywould's analysis of BES data on voters who switched to Labour during the campaign shows among so-called Homecomers (who voted Labour in 2015 and only returned by polling day) and what he calls Johnny Come Latelys (who had not voted Labour in 2015, but switched during the campaign), only a minority preferred a Corbyn premiership or expected Labour to win a majority of seats.[63] These groups are a minority of Labour voters and were certainly not representative of the more positive reasons others felt for voting Labour, but they are certainly large enough to have denied Theresa May a majority. Of more consequence was that the election as a whole was fought on the premise that Labour would not win. Even most of LOTO did not think so, despite some considerable post-election rewriting of history. The result was that Labour's manifesto was barely scrutinised, to much surprise in Southside.

That Labour lost the election but was widely seen as a winner said much about the importance of expectations. As one of the Southside team remarked: 'Blair in 2005, Brown and Miliband were all crushed by election results. Corbyn is the first leader since 2005 to be happy, although he lost. It's all about expectations.' However, once the elation had died away, Labour was still 64 seats short of an absolute majority. If the Conservatives need a swing of 0.5% to gain a majority of seats next time, Labour's task is more challenging, needing a swing of nearly 5%. The seats where they are vulnerable (with the smallest majorities) are different from those they gained in 2017, as are the targets; they contain fewer voters who are young, graduates and BAME, and more who are older, white, working class and have not gone to university.[64] Given how close to power the party came in 2017, a minority Labour government, propped up by other parties, is clearly more easily achieved, although as soon as that appears to be a realistic prospect, the party again becomes vulnerable—at least in England—to attacks that it would be unstable, blackmailed by the SNP and so on, just as it was in 2015, although since the Conservatives were willing to be propped up by the DUP in 2017, this argument may perhaps have less purchase than it used to have.

It is not difficult to imagine an alternative election outcome to 2017, one in which Labour launched an under-prepared manifesto, consisting of an expensive wish list with implausible costings and which soon unravelled under a forensic Conservative attack on its affordability. This alternative campaign saw a Labour leader who preferred talking to the faithful at rallies rather than engaging with swing voters and a disciplined Conservative campaign, mocked by some at the time for its robotic tendencies, but which kept ruthlessly on message, focusing on the key issues of competence and credibility. On social media, Labour campaigners preferred talking to one another, persuading themselves of their own moral superiority rather than running the targeted digital campaign which had brought success for the Conservatives in 2015. The terrorist attacks in Manchester and London refocused attention on Jeremy Corbyn's past affiliations, not helped by a speech in which he appeared to be arguing that the attacks were justified. Labour's Southside offices contained a deeply divided campaign operation, where it was never clear who was in charge, and with an inexperienced LOTO team refusing to take advice from more experienced professionals. Having ruled out participating in any of the leaders' debates, a last-minute decision to engage in the final debate backfired, as an under-prepared Corbyn struggled in front of the audience. A naïve strategy to engage non-voters and the young failed, as almost all of those involved in politics had predicted it would.

In reality, almost all of Labour's gambles paid off and the leap of faith came closer to succeeding that any of its protagonists had expected. Yet that does not alter the fact that they were still gambles.

Every British general election invites analysis of the working of the first-past-the-post electoral system. In recent years, supporters of a more proportional system had become emboldened by the growth of multi-party politics to call for a change to the system to make it more representative of the parties' shares of votes. In 2015, for example, UKIP's 12.9% share of the vote had returned a single MP, whilst in Scotland the SNP's 50% of the vote had returned more than 90% of the country's MPs. In 2017, thanks to the rise in support for both Labour and the Conservatives, the discrepancies between vote and seat share narrowed somewhat. By the standard measure of disproportionality, the Gallagher index, the 2017 election was the least disproportional since 1955 'and by far the least disproportional since 1974'.[65]

Table 16.5   Alternative projections of the 2017 election

	FPTP	AV	AMS	STV
Conservatives	317	304	274	282
Lab	262	286	274	297
Lib Dem	12	11	39	29
UKIP	0	0	11	1
Greens	1	1	8	1
SNP	35	27	21	18
Plaid Cymru	4	2	4	3

Source: Jess Garland and Chris Terry, *The 2017 General Election: Volatile Voting and Random Results*. Electoral Reform Society, 2017

What had been a long-standing pro-Labour bias in the electoral system had been reversed in 2015, and again in 2017 it was the Conservatives who benefited. The gap between the two main parties' combined vote share (82.5%) and seat share (89.2%) was relatively close. Labour's share of votes (40.0%) and seats (40.3%) were almost identical, while for Conservatives the vote share of 42.5% produced a seat share of 48.9%. In terms of votes per seats, or what campaigners might call vote efficiency, the SNP required 27,931 votes to elect an SNP MP, compared to around 43,000 for a Conservative and just over 49,000 for a Labour MP. For the Liberal Democrats, the figure was 197,665. The Greens attracted over half a million votes but elected a sole MP, and UKIP, also with over half a million, returned none.[66]

Table 16.5 shows how the parties would have fared under different proportional systems. Labour would have benefited under almost any alternate system and would have been the largest party under the single transferable vote (STV) system, because of the second and third preferences of Liberal Democrat and Green voters.[67] In 2015, the Conservatives and UKIP together won 50.5% of the (Great Britain) vote. In 2017, their combined share fell to 45.3%. In contrast, the total vote for Labour, the Liberal Democrats, the SNP, the Greens and Plaid Cymru rose from 48.6% to 53.9%. Although the failure of the Conservatives to win a clear majority of seats was a surprise, it is striking to reflect that while the left-of-centre parties secured a clear 8.6% aggregate lead in the popular vote, they won fewer seats than the right in the new Parliament: 314 (262 Labour and 52 other left-of-centre parties) compared with 317 (all Conservative, excluding the Speaker). And while the Conservatives won 96% of the right-of-centre vote (up from 74% in 2015), Labour won just 76% of the left-of-centre vote (up from 64%).

Yet perhaps the most striking feature of the way in which the electoral system functioned in 2017 was that the traditional defence of the electoral system in Britain—that it produced stable single-party majority government—did not apply, yet again. Indeed, just one of the last three general elections has produced a single-party majority government, and that was a majority of just 12 seats and a short-lived parliament. Psephologists had previously argued that it was the decline of the two-party system, in terms of votes and, crucially, seats that had made hung parliaments more likely. Yet despite a notable rise in the two-party share, the 2017 election *still* ended with a hung parliament. Appendix 1 shows how the decline in the number of marginal seats and the electoral system now combine to make one-party majority government less likely, even with a significant rise in the two-party share.

The election outcome radically reshaped the political terrain, if not in the ways anticipated at the outset of the campaign. Within days, Labour were preparing to build on their advances and the Conservatives had appointed an official working group to report on what had gone wrong. May emerged without a parliamentary majority, facing a reinvigorated Labour opposition. Having been so dominant, she was now in a weak position in Cabinet, not least over her scope to make appointments, faced disaffected Tory MPs, had lost her long-serving advisers and other Number 10 aides. George Osborne's ungallant remark that she was 'a dead woman walking' met with some distaste but little dissent.

The Conservatives quickly reached an arrangement with the DUP, to last for an initial two years. Doubters wondered if even with this, the slim majority would be enough to carry the government through possible by-election losses, defections and rebellions until the next general election, scheduled for June 2022. In 1992, John Major's initial majority of 21 seats had disappeared by 1996. The hand-to-mouth existence of previous minority governments, Labour in 1974 and 1976–79 and the Conservatives in 1996–97, was hardly encouraging. With her Brexit strategy now clouded in uncertainty, critics complained that the Prime Minister had wasted almost seven weeks that could have been spent on the Brexit negotiations—negotiations that were strictly time-limited. That is only partly true. The negotiations were not scheduled to start until the week following the election and the civil service maintained some contact during the campaign, although ministers still lost time when they could have been preparing.

Although May's gamble failed, this does not mean that it was wrong to gamble. All life, especially political life, involves uncertainty, and the arguments for calling an early election were compelling. It is more sensible to separate out the decision to call the election from the preparation for and conduct of the election. The need for a larger Commons majority to facilitate the passage of the Brexit legislation alone justified calling an election. That the Prime Minister failed to articulate this convincingly during the campaign—along with many other failings of the Conservative campaign—does not diminish its importance. The election had, in theory, tied Conservative MPs to a manifesto which explicitly promised both to leave the Single Market and the Customs Union, although any gain from this was more than wiped out by the loss of the Prime Minister's majority and—less quantifiably, but still crucially—her authority. Speaking after the election, and with the Brexit legislation on the horizon, one of May's whips remarked that forthcoming events would justify her decision. 'You are about to see why we needed an election', he said.

The Fixed-term Parliaments Act constrains the power of the Prime Minister in calling an election, but, as 2017 showed, it is difficult for opposition parties to resist if a Prime Minister wishes to go to the country. However, those who said that the election proved the irrelevance of the Act under-play its importance. As we showed in Chapter 1, by introducing an element of uncertainty into the process, the Act was a factor leading to such a lengthy election campaign, one much longer than the Conservatives would have liked—and one which almost certainly prevented them from winning a majority. Ironically, by doing so, the Act saved itself from repeal; the Conservative manifesto pledged its abolition, but it remains on the statute book at the time of writing, and the lack of any Conservative majority now makes it unlikely it will be removed in the near future. By putting on a statutory basis the conditions for a general election following the loss of an explicitly worded motion of no confidence, one consequence of the Act has been to remove from governments the ability to treat votes on legislation as votes of confidence.[68] This thus removes from the whips a tactic used to good effect by John Major when he was trying to navigate difficult European matters with a divided party and a small majority. The role of the party whips is now even harder. As a senior member of the whips' office said in late 2017, looking ahead to the government's legislative agenda: 'It's only going to get more miserable.'

For Labour, the opposite seemed true. There was no more talk of a leadership challenge or of Corbyn's unelectability. His aides seemed vindicated in their belief that his personality, the party's popular policies and the more balanced coverage of the broadcasters would see the party gain an election bounce. By placing so much of their critique on Corbyn's supposed unpopularity, his internal critics found themselves undone by the campaign. Building on his election gains and backed by his committed membership, Corbyn's team were now better placed to reshape the party. Within the next 12 months, the four most senior staff in party headquarters—none of whom were Corbyn supporters—had resigned, elections to the ruling national executive gave Corbyn a majority, and he could proceed with his plans for further party reform and consolidating his policy changes. Before the election, the left's hold on the Labour Party was tentative and contingent; afterwards, it was firmly in charge. Sensing that the political mood was in their favour, Corbyn's team were impatient for another general election—although, privately, several of them doubted one was likely ('It'll go for the full five years', said one of Corbyn's closest aides. 'Why would they just give up?')—and for much the same reasons, the Conservatives were desperate to avoid one. Corbyn's rise as a direct result of the election had been as remarkable as May's decline. The prospect of a Corbyn premiership was no longer a joke and Labour were now preparing for government. Yet given that Corbyn, more than anybody, must realise that a key lesson of 2017 is how expectations can be swiftly confounded, any Labour optimism should be tempered with caution.

Notes

1. Harold Wilson, *A Personal Record: The Labour Government 1964–1970*. Michael Joseph, 1971, p. 201.
2. 'Britain's Missing Middle', *The Economist*, 3 June 2017; 'The Observer View on the General Election', *The Observer*, 4 June 2017.
3. John Curtice and Ian Simpson, *Why Turnout Increased in the 2017 General Election. And The Increase Did Not Help Labour*. NatCen, 2018, p. 5. But see also the Hansard Society's *Audit of Political Engagement 15* (2018). Conducted around six months after the election, it found levels of interest in politics (at 57%) roughly similar to every other post-election year since the *Audit* began in 2004.
4. The Electoral Commission, *UK Parliamentary General Election, June 2017*. 2017, p. 9.
5. Michael A. Ashcroft, *The Lost Majority*. Biteback, 2017, p. 43.
6. From Ed Fieldhouse and Chris Prosser, 'The Brexit Election? The 2017 General Election in Ten Charts', *British Election Study*, 1 August 2017,

www.britishelectionstudy.com/bes-impact/the-brexit-election-the-2017-general-election-in-ten-charts/#.WeC_9VtSxhE.

7. See Mark Pack, 'Turn over, Tune out and Log off: The Irrelevance of Campaigns', in Philip Cowley and Robert Ford (eds), *More Sex Lies and the Ballot Box*. Biteback, 2017. One exception which Pack notes is 2015, but that is because—as we later discovered—the polls had been wrong all along rather than because of any campaign effect.

8. Christopher Prosser, 'The Strange Death of Multi-party Britain: The UK General Election of 2017', *West European Politics*, 39 (2018): 1–12.

9. For example, of the five Lib Dem policies that YouGov tested, for example, only one (increasing the basic rate of income tax by 1% to spend on social care and the NHS) polled above 50%. See Matthew Smith, 'How Popular are the Parties' Manifesto Promises?', *YouGov*, 22 May 2017, https://yougov.co.uk/news/2017/05/22/how-popular-are-parties-manifesto-policies.

10. Curtice and Simpson, *Why Turnout Increased*, p. 7. For all the discussion of how radical Labour's manifesto was, it was striking that this figure is still lower than in the elections between 1979 and 1992. In 1983, a full 88% thought that there was a great deal of difference between the parties.

11. The manifesto was left noting that what it called a 'fairer' system of funding introduced under the Coalition had led to the 'highest university application rates ever, including from disadvantaged students'.

12. Ashcroft, *The Lost Majority*, p. 61.

13. 'STV Election Poll: SNP to Hold 50 Seats amid Tory Gains', *STV News*, 31 May 2017, https://stv.tv/news/politics/1390009-stv-election-poll-snp-to-hold-50-seats-amid-tory-gains.

14. Chris Curtis and Matthew Smith, 'How Did 2015 Voters Cast Their Ballots in the 2017 General Election?', *YouGov*, 22 June 2017, https://yougov.co.uk/news/2017/06/22/how-did-2015-voters-cast-their-ballot-2017-general.

15. John Curtice, 'The Three Characteristics of the Scottish Conservative Revival', *What Scotland Thinks*, 1 October 2017, http://blog.whatscotlandthinks.org/2017/10/the-three-characteristics-of-the-scottish-conservative-revival.

16. Despite the rise in the vote shares, the level of attachment to the two main parties remained roughly stable between 2015 and 2017; indeed, the percentage of the population with no attachment at all rose. See Jonathan Mellon, Geoffrey Evans, Edward Fieldhouse, Jane Green and Christopher Prosser, 'Brexit or Corbyn? Campaign and Inter-election Vote Switching in the 2017 UK General Election', 17 November 2017, https://ssrn.com/abstract=3073203.

17. However, see Jonathan Mellon, Geoffrey Evans, Edward Fieldhouse, Jane Green and Christopher Prosser, 'Opening the Can of Worms: Most Existing Studies of Aggregate-Level Turnout are Meaningless', 8 January 2018, https://ssrn.com/abstract=3098436. Their research argues that measured against the number of eligible voters, as opposed to the electoral roll, the turnout was actually in the range of 76–80%.

18. Ikran Dahir, 'We Don't Actually Know How Many Young People Voted in the General Election Yet', *BuzzFeed News*, 9 June 2017, https://www.buzzfeed.com/ikrd/we-dont-actually-know-how-many-young-people-turned-out-to?utm_term=.ceMoYqwWpm#.xvqp6evd5Y.

19. There is a problem with comparability of some of these studies, as some use turnout as a percentage of registered voters, whilst others (including the BES) use eligible voters.

20. See Christopher Prosser, Edward Fieldhouse, Jane Green, Jonathan Mellon and Geoffrey Evans, 'Tremors But No Youthquake: Measuring Changes in the Age and Turnout Gradients at the 2015 and 2017 British General Elections', 6 February 2018, https://papers.ssrn.com/sol3/papers.cfm?abstract_id=3111839.

21. The paper setting out this conclusion also contained an excellent illustration of the problems of using aggregate-level data, noting that whilst there was an apparent link between the types of seats which saw large rises in turnout and those which contain larger number of young people, there was also an even larger relationship between the number those aged under four in a constituency and the rise in turnout—yet no one would talk about a 'toddlerquake'.

22. Curtice and Simpson, *Why Turnout Increased*.

23. See, for example, the articles by Peter Kellner ('The British Election Study Claims There Was No "Youthquake" Last June. It's Wrong', *Prospect Magazine*, 30 January 2018, https://www.prospectmagazine.co.uk/blogs/peter-kellner/the-british-election-study-claims-there-was-no-youthquake-last-june-its-wrong) and Marianne Stewart et al. ('Yes, There was a "Youthquake" in the 2017 Snap Election—and it Mattered', *New Statesman*, 5 February 2018, https://www.newstatesman.com/politics/staggers/2018/02/yes-there-was-youthquake-2017-snap-election-and-it-mattered).

24. See 'Youthquake—a Reply to Our Critics', *British Election Study*, 12 February 2018, www.britishelectionstudy.com/bes-impact/youthquake-a-reply-to-our-critics/#.WoLnbq5l9hG.

25. For one example amongst many, see the work of the Resolution Foundation's Intergenerational Commission, which showed that whereas the average household incomes of households aged 25–44 were still below pre-2008 levels, the incomes of pensioner household had increased.

26. Chris Curtis, 'How Britain Voted at the 2017 General Election', *YouGov*, https://yougov.co.uk/news/2017/06/13/how-britain-voted-2017-general-election.

27. Gideon Skinner, 'How Britain Voted in the 2017 Election', *Ipsos MORI*, 2017, https://www.ipsos.com/en/how-britain-voted-2017-election.

28. Skinner, 'How Britain Voted'; Ashcroft, *The Lost Majority* has a smaller lead, but a similar swing. In addition, Appendix 1 reports that where the Conservatives stood a BAME candidate, the party under-performed by 4.7%, but that Labour outperformed where it fielded such candidates in seats with a large ethnic population.

29. In 1987, there was no constituency with at least 30% or more BAME voters; by 2022, it is estimated there will be 120 such seats. Andrew Cooper, 'On Diversity, Conservatives are Losing the Generation Game', in Steve Ballinger (ed.), *Many Rivers Crossed*. British Future, 2018, p. 47.

30. A poll for the TUC found Labour won 63% of those who had not voted in 2015, while the Conservatives won just 27%. See '2017 TUC Post-election Poll', Greenberg Quinlan Rosner Research, June 2017.

31. See Will Jennings and Gerry Stoker, 'The Bifurcation of Politics; The Two Englands', *Political Quarterly*, 87 (2016); 372–382; and Will Jennings and Gerry Stoker, 'Tilting towards the Cosmopolitan Axis? Political Change in England and the 2017 General Election', *Political Quarterly*, 88 (2017): 359–69. See also Geoffrey Evans and Anand Menon, *Brexit and British Politics*. Polity, 2017.

32. Ashcroft, *The Lost Majority*, pp. 74–76.

33. See *British Social Attitudes* 34 (2017), www.bsa.natcen.ac.uk/latest-report/british-social-attitudes-34/key-findings/context.aspx.

34. Lord Ashcroft, 'How Did This Result Happen? My Post-vote Survey', *Lord Ashcroft Polls*, 9 June 2017, https://lordashcroftpolls.com/2017/06/result-happen-post-vote-survey.

35. Ibid.

36. Ashcroft, *The Lost Majority*, pp. 58–60.

37. Ibid., pp. 48–50.

38. See Mellon et al., 'Brexit or Corbyn?' Moreover, other periods of high levels of switching took place when the parties were close together; what was remarkable about 2017 was that this occurred when the parties were perceived to be relatively far apart ideology.

39. Peter Kellner, 'Why Did So Many Voters Switch Parties between 2015 and 2017?', *New Statesman*, 29 September 2017.

40. Ashcroft, *The Lost Majority*, p. 60.

41. John Curtice, 'Labour's Strategy Delivered—Up to a Point', *The Times*, 9 June 2017. See also his blog post, 'Why Did Brexit Not Work for the

Conservatives?', 24 October 2017, http://natcen.ac.uk/blog/why-did-brexit-not-work-for-the-conservatives; and Ashcroft, *The Lost Majority*, p. 63.

42. Interview with Emma Barnett, Radio 5 Live, 13 July 2017.

43. Tim Shipman, 'I Look Stupid, Not Strong and Stable, May Said', *Sunday Times*, 11 June 2017; and Henry Zeffman and Sam Coates, 'May Wanted to Drop Hated "Strong and Stable" Slogan', *The Times*, 12 June 2017.

44. Interview with Emma Barnett, Radio 5 Live, 13 July 2017.

45. For the polling consultants' claims that they were ignored and that the manifesto was damaging, see Joe Murphy, 'Revealed: How Theresa May's Two Aides Seized Control of the Tory Campaign to Calamitous Effect', *Evening Standard*, 16 June 2017.

46. Nick Timothy, 'Where We Went Wrong', *The Spectator*, 17 June 2017; and his interview with the *Daily Telegraph*, 5 August 2017.

47. Tim Bale and Paul Webb, '"We Didn't See it Coming": The Conservatives', in Jonathan Tonge, Cristina Leston-Bandeira and Stuart Wilks-Heeg (eds), *Britain Votes 2017*. Oxford University Press, 2018.

48. See also Rachel Sylvester, 'Attacks on Corbyn Do the Tories No Favours', *The Times*, 30 May 2017.

49. Ashcroft, *The Lost Majority*, p. 43.

50. This was said in an interview carried out with Thatcher, then Leader of the Opposition, 9 August 1978, as part of the preparation for David Butler and Dennis Kavanagh's *The British General Election of 1979*. Macmillan, 1979.

51. Christopher Knaus, 'Tory Pollster Lynton Crosby Says Theresa May Right to Call Early Election', *The Guardian*, 11 July 2017.

52. 'Conservative MPs Do Not Believe That May Can Lead Them into the Next Election. Nor, Reluctantly, Do We', 11 June 2017, https://www.conservativehome.com/thetorydiary/2017/06/conservative-mps-do-not-believe-that-may-can-lead-them-into-the-next-election-nor-reluctantly-are-we.html.

53. 'Theresa May: "We've got to make the case for free markets all over again. That message has been lost"' (interview with Lord Howard), *The House Magazine*, 28 September 2017.

54. Timothy, 'Where We Went Wrong'.

55. Crace had coined the phrase in November 2016, six months before the election. See John Crace, 'Theresa Struggles to Take Back Control—from Her Own Maybot', *The Guardian*, 8 November 2016, https://www.theguardian.com/politics/2016/nov/08/theresa-may-struggles-take-back-control-maybot-india-brexit.

56. There are different claims about the precise words used (such as 'I'm the person who got us into this mess, and I'm the one who will get us out of it'), but no disagreement about the sentiment.

57. Mellon et al., 'Brexit or Corbyn?'
58. Ashcroft, *The Lost Majority*, p. 51.
59. Heather Stewart, 'Emily Thornberry Accuses Chuka Umunna of Virtue Signalling on EU Vote', *The Guardian*, 30 June 2017, https://www.theguardian.com/politics/2017/jun/30/emily-thornberry-accuses-chuka-umunna-of-virtue-signalling-on-eu-vote.
60. Alex Nunns, *The Candidate*. OR Books, 2017, p. 317; and Eunice Goes, '"Jez, We Can!" Labour's Campaign. Defeat with a Taste of Victory', in Tonge, Leston-Bandeira and Wilks-Heeg (eds), *Britain Votes 2017*, p. 65.
61. Ashcroft, *The Lost Majority*, p. xiii. Neither piece of research quite demolishes the idea that some Labour voters were doing so safe in the belief that Corbyn could not become Prime Minister. The BES asked about whether voters expected a Labour majority, but a Labour *majority* was never on the cards; the Ashcroft survey found Labour voters happiest with the outcome, but since Labour-Not-Corbyn voters wanted to vote Labour and yet not get Jeremy Corbyn as Prime Minister, and since this was exactly the outcome they ended up with, why would we expect them not to be happy?
62. This evidence too is inconclusive; post-election surveys are prone to people rationalising their behaviour in ways that were not necessarily true at the time. Plus, asking whether someone is 'more' likely to do something is fairly imprecise. Of the 24%, half said they were 'much' more likely to vote Labour because they thought Labour had no chance of forming the government, whereas half were 'somewhat' more likely, but even this does not tell us what proportions might not have voted Labour under different circumstances.
63. Charlie Cadywould, *Labour's Campaign Comeback*. Policy Network, 2018.
64. See Paula Surridge, 'Marginal Gains', in Mark Perryman (ed.), *The Corbyn Effect*. Lawrence & Wishart, 2017, p. 250.
65. Alan Renwick, 'The Performance of the Electoral System', *Election Analysis*, www.electionanalysis.uk/uk-election-analysis-2017/section-1-context/the-performance-of-the-electoral-system.
66. Rod McInnes, 'General Election 2017: Turning Votes into Seats', 11 July 2017, https://commonslibrary.parliament.uk/insights/general-election-2017-turning-votes-into-seats.
67. Jess Garland and Chris Terry, *The 2017 General Election: Volatile Voting and Random Results*. Electoral Reform Society, 2017, p. 34.
68. Philip Norton, 'The Fixed-Term Parliaments Act and Votes of Confidence', *Parliamentary Affairs*, 69(1) (2016): 3–18; and James Strong, 'Confidence and Caretakers: Some Less-Obvious Implications of the Fixed Term Parliaments Act', *Political Quarterly*, 2018 (Early View).

Appendix 1: The Results Analysed

John Curtice, Stephen Fisher, Robert Ford and
Patrick English

The outcome of the 2017 election seems to pose a serious challenge to claims about the decline of Britain's two-party system. No less than 84.5% of the UK-wide vote was cast for either the Conservatives or Labour, well above the proportion at any election since 1970. At 2.88, the effective number of parties in the electorate (as conventionally calculated) is still somewhat above two, but is now well down on the figure of 3.71 that pertained as recently as 2010.[1] But the term 'two-party system', is often used to imply more than two parties dominating the vote. Amongst other things, it is also taken to refer to a system in which power and ministerial office alternate between the Conservatives and Labour, one of whom, thanks to the electoral system, always enjoys an overall majority in the House of Commons. But in 2017 no single party secured an overall majority, and the election resulted in a minority Conservative government backed by a 'confidence and supply' arrangement with the DUP. This follows an election in 2010 which also resulted in a hung parliament (and the formation of the country's first post-war coalition) and another in 2015 that gave the Conservatives a majority of just 12, a majority that in precipitating the early 2017 ballot Theresa May indicated was too small.

There is another reason to question whether the outcome of the 2017 election necessarily represented a return to some kind of 'normality'. The ballot took place just 12 months after a deeply disruptive referendum on the UK's membership of the EU in which many voters failed to follow the advice of their party or party leader as to how they should vote. In seeking

© The Author(s) 2018
P. Cowley, D. Kavanagh, *The British General Election of 2017*,
https://doi.org/10.1007/978-3-319-95936-8

an enlarged majority, the Prime Minister stated that her purpose was to seek a mandate for her vision of Brexit. If, as a result, voters were inclined to align their vote in the election with their preference in the 2016 referendum, the pattern of support for the parties might well have changed substantially and look rather different from what we might once have anticipated.

The aim of this appendix is to examine how the pattern of support for the parties changed between 2015 and 2017. We focus in particular on how far the parties' performances reflect the pattern of voting in the 2016 EU referendum and on the extent to which those performances did or did not represent a departure from the past. We also assess how the way people voted was reflected and refracted by the electoral system, and why it once again did not provide any party with an overall majority. Our evidence is derived from an analysis of the rises and falls in party support since 2015 across the 632 constituencies in Great Britain (for a brief discussion of the outcome in Northern Ireland, where the party system is very different, see p. 244).

MEASURING CHANGE

Our principal measure of a party's performance in a constituency is the change in its share of the vote, that is, the difference between the percentage of the vote it won this time and the share it won in 2015. We usually calculate this change wherever a party contested the constituency at both elections. The Speaker's seat (Buckingham) was not contested by either Labour or the Liberal Democrats and is thus excluded from all our analyses of change in party support. On this occasion, the Liberal Democrats also did not fight Brighton Pavilion or Skipton & Ripon, so these two seats are also excluded in our analysis of Liberal Democrat performance. Meanwhile, after having fought 614 of the 632 seats in Great Britain in 2015 (including every seat in England and Wales), UKIP only contested 378 constituencies this time. This dramatic reduction requires us on occasion to take into account in our analysis the drop in the UKIP vote occasioned as a result of the party's decision not to fight a seat again, as well as the change in the party's share of the vote in the 376 comparable constituencies where the party stood in both 2015 and 2017. The Greens, too, fought rather fewer seats, but in their case the drop was less dramatic, from 568 seats in 2015 to 460 this time.

Table A1.1 summarises the level and distribution (across all constituencies in Great Britain) of the change in the share of the vote for those parties that fought all or most of the seats in 2015 or 2017. It shows the change in each party's overall share of the vote across Britain as a whole, together with: (1) the average (mean) change across all of the seats the party contested in 2015 and 2017; and (2) the median change across constituencies (that is, the value which divides the constituency changes into two equally sized groups). At this election, these various figures are in most instances very similar to each other. In the case of UKIP, we both summarise what happened in those seats that the party fought both times and across all constituencies, irrespective of the pattern of UKIP candidature. The table also shows two measures of the relative performance of the Conservatives and Labour known as 'swing'. These have often featured prominently in previous appendices in this series, but we will make only occasional reference to either measure in this appendix.[2]

Whichever measure of change we examine, this was clearly an election at which the fortunes of many parties changed dramatically. According to the Pedersen Index, a summary measure of the extent of the change in party support between two elections, this was the second election in a row

Table A1.1   Measures of change since 2015

	Overall	Mean	Median	Standard deviation
Change in Con vote	+5.8	+5.9	+6.0	5.9
Change in Lab vote	+9.8	+9.5	+9.8	4.6
Change in Lib Dem vote	−0.5	−0.6	−0.5	3.8
Change in UKIP vote (seat fought both times)		−11.8	−12.0	4.6
Change in UKIP vote (regardless of candidature)	−11.0	−11.1	−11.7	5.3
Change in Green vote	−2.2	−2.4	−1.9	2.0
Total vote swing	−2.0	−1.8	−2.0	4.4
Two-party swing	−3.3	−2.1	−3.9	7.5
Change in turnout	+2.4	+2.4	+2.8	3.1

Notes: Buckingham (no Labour or Liberal Democrat candidates in 2015 and 2017) is excluded from the calculation of the mean, median and standard deviation of all statistics apart from turnout. The seat is also excluded from all analysis of party performance in this appendix. Total vote swing is the average of the change in the Conservative share of the vote and the Labour share of the vote. Two-party swing is the change in the Conservative share of the votes cast for Conservative and Labour only (that is, the two-party vote). In both cases a plus sign indicates a swing to the Conservatives, and a minus sign a swing to Labour that was more volatile than any of the contests between 1945 and 2010.[3] The increase in Labour's share of the vote was the biggest the party had enjoyed since the 1945 election, while the increase in Conservative support was the largest increase in support enjoyed by any incumbent government that had won the previous election since the 1832 Reform Act. In contrast, thanks primarily to a collapse in UKIP support, the combined level of support for parties other than the Conservatives, Labour and the Liberal Democrats dropped markedly from the all-time high of 23% that it reached in 2015 to just 8%, the lowest level since 2005.

Table A1.1 also shows the standard deviation, a measure of the extent to which the change in a party's vote share varied from one constituency to another. From this we can see that it was the Conservatives' performance that varied most across the country. In previous appendices in this series we have consistently reported that the Conservatives' performance varied least from one place to another. However, at this election, at 5.9, the standard deviation statistic for the change in the Conservatives' share of the vote is higher than at any previous post-war contest.

Typically, we do not expect, because historically it has not normally been the case, that the change in a party's share of the vote will be proportional to (or in any other way related to) the share of the vote it won at the last election.[4] However, there have been some recent noticeable exceptions. The sharp fall in Labour's vote in 2010 (and, equally, the dramatic drop in its support in Scotland in 2015) together with the collapse in the Liberal Democrat vote in 2015 were both more limited in those places where the party in question had previously been weaker—because, arithmetically, its support could not fall as heavily in such seats. The sharp drop in the UKIP vote this time creates a similar situation. The Greens too suffered a major loss of support relative to their prior share of the vote. This feature of the decline in UKIP and Green support will inevitably have consequences for the patterns of change in Conservative and Labour support of which we will need to be aware, though not necessarily for the relative performance of the two.

As in 2015, and as can be seen from Table A2.4, the result of the election in Scotland deviated sharply from that in England and Wales. Support for the SNP collapsed from the record 50% vote the party won in 2015, while it was the Conservatives, not Labour, who advanced more strongly north of the border. We thus initially confine our attention to the outcome in England and Wales. We begin by looking at the performance of the two parties that comprise the country's traditional two-party system. We then turn to the outcome for the party that has traditionally donned the mantle of Britain's third party, the Liberal Democrats. Thereafter, we examine the performance of all three parties in Scotland together with that of the SNP. Our attention then turns to the other parties that had enjoyed some representation in the last parliament, UKIP, the Greens and Plaid Cymru, before examining the pattern of turnout across the country as a whole. We conclude by assessing how the electoral system turned votes cast into seats won.

Conservatives and Labour in England and Wales

If voters agreed with the Prime Minister that the election was about Brexit, then given that her vision of Britain's future relationship with the EU was widely regarded as representing a 'hard' Brexit that prioritised securing control of immigration over continued membership of the EU Single Market, we might expect her party to have advanced more strongly in places where the previous year a relatively high proportion had voted to leave the EU. As Table A1.2 shows, this is precisely what happened. The higher the estimated vote for Leave in 2016, the more the Conservative vote increased, while support for the party actually fell back on average where Leave failed to secure at least 45% of the vote.[5]

The link between Labour's performance and the strength of the Leave vote in 2016 is much weaker, a finding that might be thought to reflect the party's relatively ambiguous position on Brexit. There was only a three-point difference between the increase in the Labour vote in places where 60% or more voted to Leave and the equivalent figure for

Table A1.2 Change in Conservative and Labour share of the vote 2015–17 by 2016 Leave vote

	Mean change in % 2015–17		
Estimated Leave vote 2016	*Con*	*Lab*	*No. of seats*
Less than 45%	−1.7	+11.5	100
45–55%	+3.3	+10.8	184
55–60%	+6.9	+10.2	127
More than 60%	+10.2	+8.6	161
All seats	+5.1	+10.2	572

Note: Based on seats in England and Wales only

constituencies where less than 45% voted to Leave, far less than the corresponding difference of 12 points in the Conservative performance. Even so, between them these two patterns are sufficiently strong that in seats where more than 60% voted to Leave, there was on average a net (total vote) swing of 0.8% from Labour to the Conservatives, even though everywhere else in England and Wales Labour's vote increased more than that of the Conservatives.

A key reason why the link between the Conservative performance and the strength of the Leave vote is much stronger than that for Labour lies in the impact on the two parties' performances of the collapse in the UKIP vote. UKIP's share of the vote in 2015 was much larger in areas where Leave did well in the referendum. Meanwhile, as we show below (see pp. 472–3), the decline in UKIP support was almost invariably greatest where the party had previously been strongest. If, given the Prime Minister's stance on Brexit, those who voted UKIP in 2015 (nearly all of whom voted to Leave in 2016) were now particularly inclined to switch to the Conservatives, this could have served to boost the Conservative performance in constituencies that voted heavily to Leave.

This possibility is analysed in Table A1.3, which shows the mean change in Conservative and Labour support broken down both by how much UKIP's vote fell between 2015 and 2017 and by the size of the Leave vote in 2016. The table confirms that, for any given share of the Leave vote (that is, within each row of the table), the Conservatives advanced more strongly the more UKIP support fell. True, Labour also performed somewhat better where UKIP support dropped most heavily—but not to the same extent. While Labour appear to have won some of the voters that UKIP lost, the Conservatives apparently gained many more.

Nevertheless, the fact that Labour gained some ground where UKIP's vote fell most—typically places with a high Leave vote—can be seen to have reduced the strength of the relationship between Labour's performance and how a constituency voted in the 2016 referendum. The differences in the change in Labour's share of the vote between the first and the third rows of the three parts of Table A1.3 are between four and eight points, much sharper than the difference in Labour's performance between predominantly Remain and heavily Leave-voting areas we saw in Table A1.2. Indeed, once we take into account the extent of the fall in UKIP support, the relationship between Labour performance and the size of the Leave vote now begins to look more or less as strong as it is for the Conservatives.

Table A1.3 Change in Conservative and Labour share of the vote 2015–17 by 2016 Leave vote and drop in UKIP vote 2015–17

Mean change in % vote 2015–2017	Drop in UKIP support 2015–17								
	Less than 10 points			10–14 points			More than 14 points		
Estimated Leave vote 2016	Con	Lab	No. of seats	Con	Lab	No. of seats	Con	Lab	No. of seats
Less than 50%	−1.1	+11.0	131	+3.1	+12.1	43	+5.9	+16.6	3
50–60%	+2.8	+9.4	36	+5.5	+10.3	134	+7.5	+11.4	38
More than 60%	+5.6	+6.0	3	+8.2	+7.8	64	+10.8	+8.9	122
All seats	−0.2	+10.6	175	+5.6	+10.2	208	+9.6	+9.9	189

Notes: Seats that UKIP fought in 2015 but not in 2017 are classified according to the share of the vote the party won in 2015. Based on seats in England and Wales only

Although the Conservative performance in constituencies with a large Leave vote was boosted by the collapse in UKIP support in such constituencies, this is far from being the whole explanation for the strong Conservative performance in areas keenest on leaving the EU. If we look down the columns of Table A1.3, we can see that, even when we take into account how heavily UKIP support fell, the Conservatives still performed better the stronger the Leave vote in 2016. The Conservative Party did not do well in places where Leave was strong in 2016 only because of the pattern of switching amongst former UKIP voters; rather, Leave voters more generally seem to have been drawn into voting Conservative at this election, while Remain voters tilted towards Labour.[6]

For all that, it is not clear that the Conservatives derived any net benefit in terms of seats from the impact (alone) of a particularly large or small decline in UKIP support. There is only one seat where the sharp decline in the UKIP vote locally might have been decisive in enabling the Conservatives to win.[7] In contrast, there are at least two and maybe as many as five seats where Labour won narrowly and where a relatively small decline in UKIP support may have played a key role in enabling the party to win the seat.[8]

Support for UKIP in 2015 and for Leave in 2016 varied substantially by age and educational background. Both were particularly popular with older people and those with few or no formal educational qualifications, while younger people and graduates tended to shun UKIP and vote Remain.[9] Given our findings so far, we therefore might anticipate that the Conservatives advanced more strongly in 2017 in constituencies that contain a relatively high proportion of older people and where many voters do not have any formal educational qualifications, while Labour's vote increased most in seats with a relatively large proportion of younger people and of university graduates.

These expectations are largely fulfilled. Table A1.4 shows that the Conservatives tended to do better where there were more people without any educational qualifications.[10] There is a corresponding, though much weaker tendency in the opposite direction for Labour. At the same time, the Conservatives performed less well and Labour better in seats with more young adults—though once we take this into account, there is no indication, despite the prominence given to Labour's manifesto promise to scrap tuition fees for students at English universities, that constituencies with large numbers of students were particularly likely to swing towards the party. Meanwhile, we would acquire the mirror image of the findings

Table A1.4 Change in Conservative and Labour support 2015–17 by percentage without any educational qualifications and percentage aged 18–24

% with no qualifications	Change in % vote 2015–17		Seats	% aged 18–24	Change in % vote 2015–17		Seats
	Con	Lab			Con	Lab	
Less than 20	+0.6	+10.7	178	Less than 8	+5.5	+9.4	237
20–27	+5.8	+10.5	257	8–10	+6.4	+9.9	214
More than 27	+9.8	+9.0	137	More than 10	+2.1	+12.3	121

Note: Based on seats in England and Wales only

in the table if, instead, we looked at the proportion of graduates or of older people in a constituency. However, irrespective of the measure we use, the evidence that either the age or the educational profile of a constituency made a difference to either party's performance is much weaker, though not eliminated, once we take into account the size of the Leave vote in 2016 and the UKIP vote in 2015.[11] The social geography of Conservative and Labour performance at this election was primarily, albeit not entirely, a consequence of the role played by attitudes towards Brexit in shaping how people voted.

Traditionally, the state of the economy has played a central role in how people vote. In 2015, for example, the Conservatives clearly performed worse where unemployment was highest or had increased most, and where household incomes were relatively low.[12] At this election, however, if anything the opposite was the case. The worse local economic circumstances were, the better the Conservatives did and the worse Labour did. For instance, Conservative support increased on average by 5.8 points where the constituency unemployment rate increased between 2015 and 2017, compared with 4.9 points where it fell.[13] The equivalent figures for Labour were 9.8 points and 10.4 points respectively. Moreover, despite a continued squeeze on public spending and a promise from the Conservatives of more austerity to come that could mean cuts in public sector jobs, there was, in contrast to 2015, no particular relationship between Conservative or Labour performance and the local prevalence of public sector employees.[14]

Not that the focus on Brexit meant that nothing else mattered. Jeremy Corbyn's views on the Middle East have attracted particular controversy, with critics accusing the Labour leader of being too sympathetic to individuals and groups opposed to Israel, including some widely regarded as extremist. There were related accusations that, under Corbyn's leadership, the Labour Party had dealt inadequately with allegations that some party members have made anti-Semitic statements. These issues appear to have made a difference. On average Labour's vote increased by 11.6 points in constituencies where more than 4% are Muslim, compared with an average increase of 9.6 points elsewhere in England and Wales. This difference is not accounted for by the tendency of the Leave vote to be lower in seats with more Muslims. Meanwhile, and by contrast, the Labour vote only rose by 8.8 points on average across the ten constituencies with the largest Jewish populations, even though seven of these ten seats are in London, where Labour generally performed relatively well.

The tendency in previous elections for some of the characteristics of individual candidates to make a difference to party performance was again in evidence.[15] A perennial pattern at recent elections has been for incumbent MPs to develop a personal vote and for a party to perform less well where the incumbent MP has opted to stand down. The impact of incumbency often becomes particularly apparent when an MP who captured a seat from another party at the last election defends their newly acquired (marginal) constituency for the first time. Such an MP often records a better performance than their party does nationally, not least perhaps because they have been assiduous in making themselves known locally and in pursuing the interests of both the constituency as a whole and of individual constituents in particular.

No fewer than 71 of the 331 seats that the Conservatives were defending in 2017 were seats where the local MP was first elected in 2015. In these seats the Conservative vote increased on average by 6.5 points; in contrast, it increased by just 4.1 points in seats where the incumbent MP was first elected in 2010 or earlier, while it also only increased by 4.0 points in the 11 instances where the incumbent MP stood down. In short, new incumbent Conservatives MPs generally performed just over two points better than their parliamentary colleagues, a difference that cannot be accounted for by the level of support for Leave or the fall in the UKIP vote in their constituency.

There were, though, only eight Conservative MPs who were defending a seat they had captured from Labour in 2015. Their vote increased on average by 8.2 points, a performance that was only about a point better than might have been expected, given the level of the Leave vote and the scale of the fall in UKIP support in these seats.[16] Indeed, it is far from clear that what Americans call the sophomore surge was crucial in enabling these particular new incumbent MPs to defend their highly marginal seats. Three of them still lost. More generally, although there are as many as 13 constituencies where an incumbent Conservative MP (old or new) only retained their seat against a Labour challenge by less than two points, at 3.6 points the average increase in the Conservative vote in these seats was not particularly remarkable. In summary, it is difficult to identify any seat where an incumbency bonus was pivotal for the Conservatives.

The 51 Labour MPs defending their seat for the first time also generally outperformed their colleagues. On average their share of the vote increased by 13.8 points compared with just 10.2 points for MPs first elected in

2010 or earlier and just 8.5 points where a Labour-held seat was not being defended by the incumbent MP. The nine Labour MPs who were defending a seat they had captured from the Conservatives in 2015 were amongst those who profited from this pattern; on average, they saw their vote increase by 13.9 points.[17] None of these differences can be accounted for by the level of the Leave vote locally. However, given that Labour were advancing more strongly than the Conservatives, in practice most new incumbent Labour MPs did not need a personal vote in order to retain their seat. Nevertheless, there were a few seats where the Labour incumbent only won by a narrow margin, but as it happens all were ones where the increase in the Labour vote locally was relatively low. All in all, although the presence or otherwise of an incumbent had an impact on party performance, on this occasion—in contrast to 2015—it seems not to have had a decisive impact on the outcome in terms of seats.[18]

The second candidate characteristic that, as in previous elections, made some difference to party performance was ethnic background.[19] Fielding an ethnic minority candidate once again tended to prove disadvantageous for the Conservatives. Where the party fielded an ethnic minority candidate this time but not in 2015, its share of the vote rose on average by just 1.6 points, well down on the 5.2 point increase recorded where there was no change in the ethnicity of the party's nominee, and implying an apparent 3.6 point ethnic penalty. Furthermore, where the Conservatives fielded an ethnic minority candidate in 2015 but not this time, their vote increased by 6.5 points, just over a point above the party's average performance elsewhere.

Analysis of both the 2010 and 2015 elections indicated that Labour tended to benefit when they fielded an ethnic minority candidate in an area with a relatively large ethnic minority population.[20] This time around, no fewer than 37 of the 61 ethnic minority candidates nominated by the party in England and Wales contested an ethnically diverse constituency (defined as a seat where less than 78% classified themselves in the 2011 Census as white). Labour tended to perform better in such diverse constituencies at this election irrespective of the ethnic origin of their candidate. On average the party's share of the vote increased by 11.8 points in ethnically diverse seats, compared with 9.8 points elsewhere (after all, on average only 43.9% had voted Leave in these diverse seats in the EU referendum). And the average increase in a diverse seat where an ethnic minority candidate stood was in fact no different from the outcome where a white candidate did.[21] However, where, among less ethnically diverse seats, Labour fielded an ethnic minority candidate in 2017 after not having done so in 2015, the party's vote increased by only 7.5 points, a weaker performance that cannot be explained by the level of the Leave vote in such seats in 2016.

But although patterns of candidature might have made some difference to Conservative and Labour performance, it is clear that this was an election where the geography of Conservative and Labour performance was shaped above all by the fallout from the EU referendum. Moreover, in so doing, the contest served to reduce some of the traditional divisions in British elections. For example, although working-class voters had traditionally been the bedrock of Labour support, they had also been more likely to vote Leave and to vote for UKIP. Thus, thanks to its gains among such voters, at this election Conservative support increased by as much as 9.4 points in seats where more than 13% are engaged in a routine manual occupation, compared with just 1.3 points where less than 10% have a routine job. Conversely, Labour's support increased by just 9.1 points in relatively working-class seats, but by 10.7 points where relatively few have a routine job.[22]

Equally, the North/South divide in Britain's electoral geography also narrowed somewhat, the first time it has done so since 1997. A relatively weak Conservative performance and a relatively strong Labour performance across the largely more pro-Remain South of England[23] meant that on average there was as much as a 3.9-point swing from Conservative to Labour there. In contrast, the swing to Labour was only 1.3 in the North of England (albeit, as Table A2.4 shows, it was rather higher in the North West—which was also somewhat less pro-Leave—than in either Yorkshire & Humberside or the North East) and 0.7 in the heavily pro-Leave Midlands.[24] One striking consequence of this divergence is that Conservative support is now higher in the Midlands than in the South of England, not least, but also not solely, because pro-Remain and ethnically diverse London has now become something of a Labour citadel. Despite initial appearances, therefore, this clearly was not an election that heralded a return to the familiar patterns of two-party politics.

THE LIBERAL DEMOCRATS IN ENGLAND AND WALES

The Liberal Democrats fought the election on a distinctive platform, arguing that another referendum should be held on the UK's membership of the EU once the terms of withdrawal were known. The result was an even smaller, albeit only slightly smaller, share of the overall vote (7.6%) than two years before, putting the party in its worst position since 1970. However, it did fare a little better in those seats where Remain had been most popular in the EU referendum. On average (see Table A1.5 below) the Liberal Democrat vote increased by 0.9 of a point in those constituencies in England and Wales where over 55% of the vote was estimated to have been cast for Remain, but it fell back by 0.6 of a point where between 45% and 55% of the vote went to Remain, and dropped even more, by 1.1 point, where less than 45% had voted Remain.[25] Therefore, the party's distinctive stance on the EU does seem to have helped it make at least a little headway amongst voters living in strongly pro-Remain parts of the country.

This stance may also have helped the Liberal Democrats amongst those living in constituencies with a relatively large number of graduates, a group which voted heavily for Remain and amongst whom the party has traditionally been relatively successful. The Liberal Democrat vote increased on average by 1.7 points in constituencies where more than one in three of the adult population have a university degree, whereas elsewhere it fell back by a point. This pattern is not simply a reflection of the fact that support for Remain was higher in constituencies with more graduates—the party performed somewhat better in seats with a relatively large graduate population irrespective of the outcome locally in the EU referendum.[26] It represents the continuation of a pattern that was also in evidence in the 2015 election, and consequently the party is now noticeably even more reliant on the support of voters in seats with many graduates than it was hitherto.

Table A1.5   Change in Liberal Democrat share of the vote 2015–17 by proportion of graduates and EU referendum vote

Mean change in % Liberal Democrat vote 2015–17	Con seats	Lab seats	All seats
Remain vote 2016			
Less than 55%	−0.5 (165)	−2.0 (120)	−1.1 (288)
45–55%	−0.1 (125)	−1.3 (53)	−0.6 (183)
More than 55%	+5.0 (38)	−1.6 (58)	+0.9 (99)
Graduates			
Less than 25%	−0.5 (113)	−1.9 (145)	−1.3 (260)
25–33%	−0.4 (151)	−1.6 (53)	−0.8 (212)
More than 33%	+3.3 (64)	−1.3 (53)	+1.7 (98)
All seats	+0.3 (260)	−1.8 (212)	−0.6 (98)

Notes: Con seats: seats won by the Conservatives in 2015. Lab seats: seats won by Labour in 2015. Figures in parentheses represent the number of seats in that category. Based on seats in England and Wales only

As Table A2.4 (p. 500) illustrates, the party also performed better in London and the South East—and to a lesser extent in the South West and the Eastern region—regions where graduates and Remain voters are relatively numerous (especially so in the case of London). This difference cannot simply be accounted for by the distinctive demography or referendum voting patterns of these regions, but it does help explain why all of the four seats that the party lost were in the North of England or Wales, while all the Liberal Democrat gains (outside of Scotland) were in constituencies located in London and the South. Meanwhile, Table A1.5 shows how the change in support for the Liberal Democrats not only varied according to how many graduates and how many Remain voters there were in a constituency, but also depended on whether the constituency in question was being defended by the Conservatives or by Labour. For any given proportion of graduates or Remain voters, the party performed better in Conservative-held seats than in Labour-held ones. All five gains made by the Liberal Democrats in England were secured at the expense of the Conservatives, while two of the three losses in England were to Labour.

This distinction between Conservative and Labour strongholds is also in evidence when we look at another aspect of the party's performance, that is, how far it depended on whether or not the party was being represented by a current or former incumbent MP. The ability of the Liberal Democrats to win individual seats has often been dependent on the personal popularity of their local candidate, and in 2015 the loss of support was smaller in seats that were being defended by the then incumbent Liberal Democrat MP rather than by a new candidate.[27] We therefore might anticipate that Liberal Democrat support would have held up better this time in those seats where the incumbent who was defeated in 2015 was trying to regain their seat.

In seats where the party was principally in competition locally with the Conservatives, this expectation was realised (see Table A1.6): where the former Liberal Democrat MP stood once again, the party's vote increased on average by as much as 5.6 points, well above what the party managed in seats where the former incumbent was not standing (a drop of 0.6 of a point), and especially better than in the 11 seats where the former incumbent had stood in 2015, but did not do so this time around (a fall of 3.1 points). At the same time, the three incumbent MPs who were fending off a Conservative challenge on average saw their vote increase by 3.3 points. Conversely, the party's vote fell by 4.6 points in the one seat (Southport) where the Liberal Democrat incumbent stood down.

Table A1.6   Change in Liberal Democrat share of the vote 2015–17 by status of Liberal Democrat candidate and the Liberal Democrats' principal challenger

Mean change in % Liberal Democrat vote 2015–17	*Principal challenger*		
Seat being fought for Lib Dems by:	*Conservatives*	*Labour*	*All seats*
Incumbent MP	+3.3 (3)	−3.6 (2)	−0.7 (6)
Ex-incumbent MP	+5.6 (10)	−11.2 (7)	−1.3 (17)
New candidate in seat lost in 2015	−0.6 (17)	−10.6 (5)	−2.9 (22)
New or old candidate in seat not won in 2010	+0.1 (300)	−1.3 (219)	−0.5 (523)

Notes: Principal challenger: The party that won the seat in 2015 or that was second to a Liberal Democrat victor at that election. Based on seats in England and Wales only. Richmond Park, which was won by the Liberal Democrats in a by-election in December 2016, is excluded from this table

However, the pattern in seats where the party's principal opponent was Labour was very different. Here the willingness of the former incumbent MP to stand again made no difference. The party's vote fell heavily in seats it had lost in 2015, both where the former incumbent did stand and where they did not. The party's vote also dropped somewhat in the two seats where the incumbent MP was being challenged locally by Labour; indeed, in both cases, the MP in question, one of whom was the former party leader, Nick Clegg, lost. It would seem the largely new-found ability the Liberal Democrats had demonstrated at recent elections in being competitive in areas where Labour had previously been strong, and which had enabled the party to gain a record haul of 12 seats from Labour in 2005 and five in 2010, has now fizzled out.

But why were the Liberal Democrats rather more successful where they were in competition with the Conservatives rather than Labour? Table A1.7 shows the average change in support for all three main parties broken down both by the incumbency status of the Liberal Democrat candidate and whether that candidate was primarily in competition with the Conservatives or Labour. So far as the Conservative performance is concerned, it made little difference whether the seat in question was one in which the Liberal Democrats were competing locally with the Conservatives or with Labour. The same is not true, however, of Labour. The increase in

Table A1.7 Mean change in parties' share of the vote 2015–17 by status of Liberal Democrat candidate and the Liberal Democrats' principal challenger

Seat being fought for Lib Dems by:	Change in % vote since 2015 in Lib Dem/ Con battlegrounds			No. of seats	Change in % vote since 2015 in Lib Dem/ Lab battlegrounds			No. of seats
	Con	Lab	Lib Dem		Con	Lab	Lib Dem	
Incumbent or ex-incumbent MP	+4.7	+4.1	+5.1	13	+4.9	+14.9	−9.5	9
New candidate in seat won in 2010	+7.7	+8.5	−0.8	18	+6.8	+16.2	−10.6	5
New or old candidate in seat not won in 2010	+4.4	+10.1	+0.1	301	+5.8	+10.6	−1.3	219

Notes: Lib Dem/Con battlegrounds: All seats won by the Conservatives in 2015 or where the Liberal Democrats were first and the Conservatives second
Lib Dem/Lab battlegrounds: All seats won by Labour in 2015 or where the Liberal Democrats were first and Labour second. Based on seats in England and Wales only

Labour support was well below average—only just over four points—in those Conservative/Liberal Democrat battlegrounds where the current or former incumbent Liberal Democrat MP was standing, while it was well above average—nearly 15 points—in Labour/Liberal Democrat battleground seats where the Liberal Democrats were being represented by a current or former incumbent. Labour's advance was much weaker too (8.5 points) in seats that the Liberal Democrats lost to the Conservatives in 2015 and had not nominated the former MP this time than it was in the equivalent seats the Liberal Democrats had lost in 2015 to Labour (16.2 points).

In short, it appears that the Liberal Democrats had some success in stemming Labour's advance in seats where they appeared better placed locally to defeat the Conservatives. Liberal Democrat candidates have long been able to secure tactical support in such circumstances from those who might otherwise have voted Labour, a phenomenon that did not appear to unravel in 2015 even though the Liberal Democrats had just spent five years in coalition with the Conservatives.[28] It appears that such behaviour was in evidence once again, fuelled this time not only by the traditional antipathy that some Labour supporters have for the Conservatives, but also seemingly because the Liberal Democrats' support for another EU referendum may have made the party appear relatively attractive to Remain supporters who might otherwise have backed Labour.

This pattern was crucial to the party's ability to recapture two seats, Kingston & Surbiton and (despite its strong Leave vote in 2016) Eastbourne. It was also central to the party's success in gaining a strongly pro-Remain seat with a large proportion of graduates, Oxford West & Abingdon, that had been lost as long ago as 2010, but where the party was starting off in second place. The increase in the Labour vote was also stemmed in Twickenham, regained by Sir Vince Cable, though here it was a sharp fall in the Conservative vote in a heavily pro-Remain seat that proved decisive. This was also the case in Bath, regained by the Liberal Democrats even though the ex-MP was not contesting the seat.

There was one constituency, Ceredigion, where the Liberal Democrats were in contention locally with Plaid Cymru rather than the Conservatives or Labour. In practice, the outcome was similar to that in Labour/Liberal Democrat battleground seats. The Liberal Democrat vote fell by 6.9 points, while Labour's advanced by 10.5 points. Together with a small 1.6 point increase in Plaid Cymru support, this enabled the Welsh nationalists to recapture a seat they had previously held between 1992 and 2005. As a result, the Liberal Democrats were left for the first time ever without any representation in Wales.

SCOTLAND

As discussed in Chapter 6, the election in Scotland took place in the wake of not just one major referendum, but two. Scotland's 2014 independence referendum had already had a profound impact on the country's electoral politics, leaving its electoral contours looking very different from those in England and Wales. To that remarkable mix was now added the outcome of the EU referendum, in which Scotland again voted differently from England and Wales. This added a new twist to the debate about Scotland's constitutional status. The SNP (and the Greens) argued that a second independence referendum should be held once the Brexit negotiations had concluded, a proposal the Conservatives in particular opposed vigorously. This inter-linking of the Brexit debate and the question of Scotland's constitutional status meant there was good reason to anticipate that the outcome of the 2017 election would look different north of the border too.

That, indeed, proved to be the case. Even though Scotland voted strongly to Remain, the Conservatives advanced much more strongly north of the border than in England and Wales. After having failed to secure more than 17% of the vote in any UK election since 1997, the party enjoyed a 13.2 point average increase in its support and won 28.6% of the overall Scottish vote, its highest share since 1979. Conversely, the SNP, which campaigned strongly in favour of Remain, suffered an average drop of no less than 13 points, though, at 36.9%, the party's share of the overall vote was still well above that in any previous Westminster election before 2015. Although Labour's support increased, it did so by far less—on average by just 3.2 points—than it did south of the border. With just 27.1% of the vote, the party was outpolled by the Conservatives for the first time in a Westminster election in Scotland since 1959, while it was the first time that Labour had come third since it first started fighting general elections on a widespread basis in 1918. As in 2015, only the Liberal Democrat performance was similar to that in England and Wales: the party's vote fell on average by 0.8 of a point and its overall total of 6.8% was its lowest share since 1970.

Nevertheless, there are echoes of the patterns that we have already seen were in evidence in England and Wales. Within Scotland, Conservative support increased most in constituencies where support for Leave had been highest the previous year. In seats where more than 42% voted Leave, support for the Conservatives increased on average by 15.8 points, while in those where between 35% and 42% voted Leave, the average increase was 12.9 points, and where Leave won less than 35% of the vote, the Conservative vote increased by 10.5 points.[29] In short, as in England and Wales, those living in Leave-voting areas in Scotland were more likely to switch to the Conservatives.

However, the division between supporters of the Union and those who wished Scotland to become independent was also in evidence in the pattern of the Conservative performance. It was not that the Conservatives generally did better in those parts of Scotland that had voted No most heavily in 2014[30]; rather, this division manifested itself in tactical voting for whichever of the three pro-Union parties—the Conservatives, Labour and the Liberal Democrats—now seemed best placed to win locally. In 2015 the Conservative vote in particular had appeared to have been squeezed as a result of voters switching to the Liberal Democrats (especially) or Labour, and now some of that vote might be expected to return to the Conservative fold in seats where the incumbent Liberal Democrat and Labour MPs had come nowhere close to fending off the SNP challenge two years previously.[31] Conversely, the Conservatives might have lost out in places where voters reckoned either Labour or the Liberal Democrats were still better able to challenge the SNP.

In some instances, the Conservatives do indeed seem to have profited from tactical switching. Perhaps the most striking examples arose in two seats[32] where in 2015 the Liberal Democrats fell from first place to third, leaving the Conservatives as now the best placed of the unionist parties. Conservative support increased on average by 18.4 point in these seats, five points above the Scotland-wide average, while the Liberal Democrat vote fell by 13.4 points.

However, there were also signs of tactical switching in eight seats that the Liberal Democrats lost in 2015, but where the Conservatives had still come third and in many of which the Conservative vote had apparently been squeezed tactically last time around.[33] These seats divided into two groups. In the four where the SNP lead over the Liberal Democrats was the smallest, the Liberal Democrat vote edged up on average by 1.9 points,[34] while support for the Conservatives increased by just 9.8 points, somewhat less than the Scotland-wide average. But in the four seats where the SNP lead was greatest, support for the Liberal Democrats fell away, on average by as much as 16.2 points, while the Conservative vote increased by no less than 22.7 points.[35] Apparently in this latter group of seats, voters decided that the Liberal Democrats were no longer a credible challenger locally and switched from the Liberal Democrats to the Conservatives in droves.

Meanwhile, Labour saw its vote squeezed (a drop of 3.8 points) in the one seat (Dumfries & Galloway) where it had fallen from first to third in 2015, though here the Conservative advance (13.4 points) was more modest. But in addition, there were also signs of switching from Labour to the Conservatives in all but one of seven seats where, although the Conservatives had still trailed Labour in 2015, they had won at least 19% of the vote and had been within 12.5% of the second-placed Labour candidate. These were all places where, given the prior evidence of a Conservative advance in both the opinion polls and the 2016 Scottish Parliament election, voters may well have been inclined to regard the party as now the more credible challenger to the SNP locally. Certainly, in the six seats in question, the Conservative vote increased on average by 17.6 points, while Labour's vote fell by 4.9 points—a pattern that cannot be accounted for by the level of Leave support in these seats.[36]

But if the newly reinvigorated independence debate apparently had an impact on the willingness of some voters to switch to the Conservatives, it apparently did little to help the SNP retain the high tide of support they won in 2015. The SNP's advance had been strongest in what had hitherto been Labour strongholds with a substantial working-class population—and a relatively high Yes vote in the 2014 referendum on independence.[37] It was in these very places that the SNP vote tended to fall most heavily in 2017. The SNP vote fell on average by 15.0 points in seats where Labour had won more than 48% of the vote in 2010 and by 16.4 points in seats where more than 15% of the working-age population was engaged in a routine occupation. In contrast, the party's support fell by 11.1 points in seats where Labour won less than 35% of the vote in 2010 and by 10.4 points in seats where less than 12% are engaged in a routine occupation. This pattern meant, in turn, that SNP support fell on average by 9.9 points in constituencies located in a local authority area where less than 42% voted Yes in 2014, but by 15.4 points in constituencies where the local authority had registered 48% or more support for Yes. The impetus amongst voters in traditional Labour strongholds to follow up a Yes vote in 2014 with a vote for the SNP in 2015 election seems to have weakened.[38]

However, the SNP's performance did not simply reflect the apparently waning influence of the 2014 independence referendum; it also reflected the outcome of the EU referendum. Even when we take into account the level of support for Yes locally, the SNP performed rather better in seats where there were fewer Leave voters. For example, in those constituencies lying in a local authority area where fewer than 45% voted Yes to independence in 2014, support for the SNP fell by 10.5 points on average where less than 38% voted to Leave, but by 11.8 points where more than 38% voted that way. The equivalent statistics amongst those seats located in areas where more than 45% voted Yes are 14.2 and 15.2 respectively. This pattern also helps explain why SNP support fell most heavily in seats with more routine workers (there tended to be a higher Leave vote in such seats in 2016) and it certainly suggests that the SNP may have lost ground in particular amongst the one in three or so of the party's 2015 supporters that voted to leave the EU.[39] The clearest demonstration of this pattern was in Banff & Buchan, the constituency with the highest estimated Leave vote in 2016, where the party's former leader and First Minister of Scotland, Alex Salmond, lost his seat to his Conservative challenger in the wake of a 21.1 point fall in his vote.

As we might anticipate, given the pattern of the SNP's performance, Labour's modest advance was slightly less modest in seats with the most routine workers (4.3 points) and in those seats located in a strongly Yes-voting local authority (4.7 points). The party's vote also often rose quite strongly in seats where the Liberal Democrat vote fell (on average by 5.8 points) as the party enjoyed its share of the spoils created locally by very sharp falls in Liberal Democrat support in some of the seats the Liberal Democrats had lost in 2015. The party's best result by far, however, was in the one seat that it was attempting to defend, Edinburgh South, where there was as much as a 15.8 point increase in Labour support, an increase seemingly boosted by yet further tactical switching by Conservative voters above what had already been evident in the seat in 2015.[40] So, while in some seats Labour performed particularly well as a result of winning back support from the SNP, in others it was the beneficiary of relatively poor performances by one of the other two pro-Union parties. What was more or less entirely missing was any sign of the tendency south of the border for the party to do better in seats with more Remain voters and graduates.

Although the Liberal Democrat vote fell heavily in those seats that the party had held until 2015 but where it was now so far behind that it no longer appeared to be a credible challenger locally, elsewhere the party's vote increased in all but five seats (on average by 0.9 of a point). It thus could be said that in most of Scotland, in contrast to the position in England and Wales, the Liberal Democrats recorded a small recovery from the very low level to which they had sunk in 2015. But, as was the case south of the border, incumbency mattered. The party's two best performances were in Orkney & Shetland (up 7.2 points), the one seat the party was defending, and in East Dunbartonshire (up 4.3 points), where the former MP, Jo Swinson, regained the seat she had only narrowly lost in 2015.[41]

Despite initial appearances, therefore, the debate about Brexit does seem to have influenced the pattern of party performance in Scotland. The Conservatives advanced more strongly in constituencies with a larger Leave vote, although it was the SNP rather than Labour that seem to have lost out as a result. There may have been many fewer Leave voters in Scotland, but they behaved in a similar fashion to their fellow Brexiteers in the rest of Britain. However, the outcome also reflected the fallout from the continuing and distinctive debate about Scotland's constitutional status. Some voters were apparently willing to back whichever unionist party was best placed locally to defeat the SNP, a willingness that may well have played a crucial role in enabling the Conservatives to win up to four of the dozen seats that they gained.[42] At the same time, the impetus amongst Yes voters to underline their support for independence by voting for the SNP seems to have weakened. The key forces at play in the election in Scotland were (once again) distinct from those in England and Wales.

One important consequence of these various patterns was to create an electoral geography dominated by marginal seats. The SNP vote has always been relatively evenly spread in Scotland, but at this election it became even more so. The standard deviation of the party's share of the vote across the country's 59 seats had been 8.7 in 2010 and 7.0 in 2015, but now it stood at just 4.8, a result of the party tending to lose ground more in seats where it had previously been strongest. There were just five seats at this election in which the SNP won either less than 30% of the vote or more than 45%. Consequently, the party was in close contention in most seats, but well ahead in very few. No fewer than 22 of the 59 Scottish seats, including 15 of the 35 won by the SNP, were won by majorities of less than five percentage points. This represents a dramatic change in Scotland's electoral geography—as recently as 2010, only four seats were won by so narrow a margin. It means that relatively small changes in the popularity of the parties north of the border could in future result in substantial changes in their level of representation at Westminster.

UKIP

UKIP's 12.9% share of the vote in 2015 represented the best performance ever by a minor party fighting a general election as a wholly independent entity. But just two years on—and shortly after its principal objective of winning a majority Leave vote in a referendum had been achieved—its support imploded, not least, as we showed earlier, as a result of many former UKIP voters switching to the Conservatives. UKIP won just 1.8% of the overall vote.

In part the drop was occasioned by the party's decision to fight far fewer seats than in 2015. Unsurprisingly, the party was more likely to stand down where it had previously been weaker—it fought a little under half of the seats where it won less than 12.5% of the vote in 2015, just under two-thirds of those where it won between 12.5% and 17.5%, but 83% of those where it won more than 17.5%. For any given share of the vote last time, the party was also a little less likely to stand down if it had come second in the constituency last time. More importantly, perhaps, in those seats the party had won between 12.5% and 17.5% in 2015, it was more likely to stand down in seats being defended by the Conservatives than in those won last time by Labour, in some instances in the hope that this would help the incumbent Conservative to defend their seat. One slightly paradoxical consequence of this pattern is that in seats where UKIP performed moderately well last time, it was somewhat more likely to stand down where the Leave vote had been relatively high in the EU referendum.

Where the party did stand again, its support fell an average of 11.8 points and it won 3.3% of the vote on average, its worst performance on that measure since 2005. As we noted earlier, given the party's vote was falling so heavily, this inevitably meant the fall was greater the higher its vote in 2015. Figure A1.1 illustrates this point by plotting the change in UKIP support in England and Wales in the 2017 election against the level of the party's vote in 2015. It shows that the size of the drop in the party's vote in seats in England and Wales is almost entirely a function of the share of the vote that the party won last time. Nearly every dot in the figure (each of which represents a constituency) lies on or close to a straight line

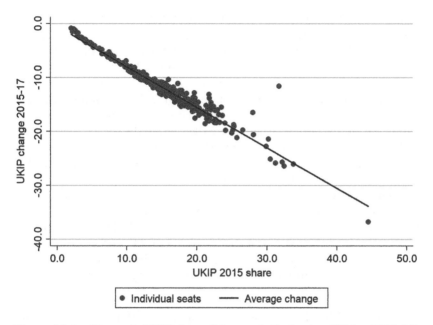

Figure A1.1   Change in UKIP share of the vote in England and Wales, 2015–17, by UKIP share of the vote, 2015

that says that on average the party lost nearly four-fifths of the support it had won in the seat two years earlier.[43]

UKIP managed to buck this trend in just one seat, Thurrock, one of the few seats where the party could present itself as a credible local challenger, having come within 1,000 votes of victory in a tight three-way contest in 2015. But there is no consistent evidence of UKIP support holding up better in seats where the party came second last time around. UKIP's performance in the only seat they won last time—Clacton—was even worse than average, with the party's vote slumping from 44.4% to 7.6%.

The consistency of the pattern of UKIP's retreat is reflected in the demographic character of the seats where the party's vote fell most heavily. UKIP had performed best in 2015 in seats where fewer people have a formal educational qualification, those that contain more older people and those with a relatively small ethnic minority population, and so those were the kinds of seats where the drop in UKIP support now was greatest.[44] For example, the party's vote fell by an average of 8.3 points in those seats in

England and Wales where less than 19% of adults have no formal qualification, whereas in those where more than 27% do not have any qualifications, the fall was 14.9 points. Similarly, in seats where less than 14% were aged 65 or over at the time of the 2011 census, UKIP's vote dropped by 8.4 points, whereas in constituencies where more than 20% were of that age, the average fall was 13.6 points. Meanwhile, UKIP support fell back by 9.1 points where less than 85% identified themselves in the census as white, but by 12.7 points where more than 95% did so.[45]

However, although the pattern of the fall in UKIP support was for the most part a mirror image of the increase in the party's support in 2015, between them the last two elections have left something of a mark on the distribution of the party's vote. In Table A1.8 we show the average level of support for UKIP at each of the last three elections broken down by the level of support for Leave in the EU referendum and who won the seat in 2010, together with the class and educational profile of the constituency. Although in 2010 UKIP already performed rather better in seats that eventually went on to vote heavily for Leave, the gap now is somewhat

Table A1.8 UKIP share of the vote in England and Wales, 2010, 2015 and 2017 by Leave vote 2016, winning party 2010, proportion with no qualifications and proportion in routine manual occupations

	Mean UKIP vote share (no. of seats)		
	2010	*2015*	*2017*
% Leave 2016			
Less than 50%	2.7 (154)	8.8 (171)	1.9 (95)
50–60%	3.8 (230)	14.4 (241)	3.0 (147)
More than 60%	4.5 (146)	20.0 (161)	4.8 (126)
Winning party 2010			
Conservative	4.0 (292)	14.5 (306)	3.2 (193)
Labour	3.2 (192)	14.8 (217)	3.7 (153)
Liberal Democrat	3.2 (42)	9.0 (46)	2.3 (19)
Share with no qualifications			
Low (19% or less)	3.0 (131)	9.6 (141)	2.0 (82)
Medium (19–27%)	3.7 (274)	14.4 (294)	3.1 (178)
High (27% or higher)	4.0 (124)	18.8 (137)	4.7 (107)
Share in routine manual occupations			
Low (9% or less)	3.1 (150)	10.2 (162)	2.2 (91)
Medium (9–14%)	3.8 (253)	14.5 (269)	3.0 (168)
High (14% or higher)	4.0 (126)	18.5 (141)	4.7 (108)

wider. Even more strikingly, in 2010 UKIP performed rather better in seats won by the Conservatives, but now the party does slightly better in those constituencies that seven years ago were won by Labour. In particular, UKIP now performs best in 2010 Labour seats that voted heavily for Leave in 2016 (on average winning 5.3% of the vote), whereas seven years ago it was in Conservative-held Leave-inclined seats in which the party marginally performed best.

Meanwhile, although UKIP has always polled somewhat better in constituencies that have larger concentrations of voters with no formal qualifications or who are engaged in routine manual occupations, this relationship has strengthened. In 2010, UKIP won about one point more of the vote in seats with the highest proportions of voters with no qualifications or routine manual jobs than it did in those with the lowest proportions. Now the gap is 2.5 points. Consequently, UKIP's vote is more clearly concentrated in constituencies containing relatively large proportions of voters that are sometimes characterised as 'left behind'.

UKIP's shift towards more economically deprived 'Leave'-voting seats, and particularly those with Labour incumbents, suggests that the party is developing a more 'radical right' electoral profile, similar to that of anti-immigrant nationalist parties elsewhere in Europe.[46] The pattern of the party's support nowadays also seems to overlap with that of the British National Party (BNP), an earlier and more extreme party whose support peaked in 2010.[47] UKIP benefited from the collapse of the BNP in 2015.[48] Now in 2017, once we take into account the share of the vote the party won in 2015, UKIP's vote can be shown to have fallen by about a point less where the BNP did best in 2010. Partly as a result, in 2017 UKIP still won as much as 5% of the vote on average where the BNP secured 4% or more of the vote in 2010, more than two points above the share UKIP secured elsewhere (2.7%).

THE GREEN PARTY

Having won a record 3.8% of the vote in 2015, the Greens' share of the overall vote fell to just 1.6% this time around. As with UKIP, this was in part a consequence of the party's decision to fight fewer seats. The retrenchment was particularly sharp in the case of the Scottish Greens; they fought just three seats, down from 31 in 2015. Otherwise, the party was somewhat more likely to stand down where it had performed less well in 2015; on average, it had won 3.2% of the vote in 2015 in the seats in

England and Wales in which it stood down this time, compared with 4.5% where it did appear on the ballot paper again.

Even where the party did stand again, its vote fell almost everywhere, on average by 2.3 points. It posted an average share of just 2.1 points, well down on the record 4.2% that it had achieved in 2015. This was still better than the average 1.8% vote the party secured where it stood in 2010 (and, indeed, where the party stood in both 2010 and 2017, its vote was on average 0.5 of a point higher), but it was well down on the 3.4% average share that the party secured in 2005. Much like UKIP, the bloom of the 2015 election faded all too quickly for the Greens.

Given that the drop in the party's support represented around half of the vote that the party had won in 2015, the party's vote was arithmetically bound to fall more heavily where it was previously strongest. As Figure A1.2 illustrates, the decline in the Green vote followed a similar pattern to the decline of the UKIP vote—while UKIP lost four-fifths of its 2015 vote in practically every seat where it stood on both occasions,

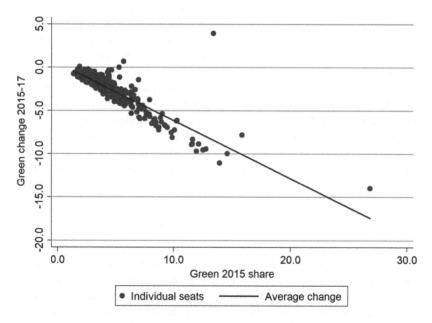

Figure A1.2   Change in Green share of the vote in England and Wales, 2015–17, by Green share of the vote, 2015 (excluding Brighton Pavilion)

the Greens lost two-thirds of their support, with very few seats (dots on the graph) deviating from this average (shown by the black line).[49] On average the party's vote fell by 4.7 points where it had previously won more than 5.5% of the vote, compared with just 0.9 of a point where it had won less than 2.5%. The Greens fell by as much as 14 points in Bristol West, which had seemingly been the party's best chance of winning a second seat. As the party had previously performed relatively well in constituencies that had voted for Remain in 2016, this pattern meant that, despite their opposition to leaving the EU, the Greens' vote fell most where Remain had polled relatively well. The only two notable exceptions to the general decline were the Isle of Wight, where the party's vote increased by four points on the 13.4% share won in 2015, and, above all, in Brighton Pavilion, where Caroline Lucas posted a 10.4 point increase in her support.

The principal beneficiaries of the Greens' decline—and decisions to stand down—appear to have been Labour, even after we have taken into account (see above, pp. 454–6) the link between Labour's performance and: (a) the outcome of the EU referendum; and (b) the fall in UKIP support.[50] For example, if we take those seats in which Leave won between 50% and 60% of the vote in 2017 and where the fall in UKIP support was between 10% and 14%, Labour's vote increased on average by 9.1 points where there was no more than a two point fall in Green support, while it rose by 11.5 points where the Green vote dropped by more than two points.[51] In contrast, the Conservative performance was actually slightly worse where Green support fell more. As a result, it looks possible that the Greens' decision to stand down helped Labour to retain at least one and perhaps both of the Newcastle-under-Lyme and Bishop Auckland seats, both of which Labour won only narrowly against a local swing to the Conservatives. But apart from the additional possibility that the Greens' decision to stand down in favour of the Liberal Democrats in Oxford West & Abingdon may have also helped secure the defeat of the Conservatives there, there was little else to show for the Greens' attempt to forge a 'progressive alliance'.

Plaid Cymru

Plaid Cymru's overall share of the vote fell from 12.1% in 2015 to 10.4% in 2017, its lowest share in a general election since 1997. Its vote fell in all but six constituencies, five of which were highly rural seats, that is, where more than 5% are employed in agriculture. Although three of these contain a large proportion of Welsh speakers, amongst whom the party always finds it easiest to secure support, the other two do not. This, perhaps, helps explain why the party fell back by 3.1 points in its target seat of Ynys Môn (57% Welsh speaking but only 3% employed in agriculture), even though Plaid Cymru was represented there by its former party leader, Ieuan Wyn Jones, but advanced by 1.6 points in Ceredigion (47% Welsh speaking, 7% employed in agriculture) and thereby very narrowly took the seat from the Liberal Democrats. Otherwise, the only other highlight for the party was in Blaenau Gwent, a seat in which Labour has had more than its fair share of local difficulty, including losing control of the local council in elections held shortly before the 2017 election, and where Plaid's vote increased by as much as 12.3 points.

Electoral Registration and Turnout

This election was the first to be held since the full introduction, in December 2015, of a system of individual electoral registration, which replaced the household-based system previously in use. The change was intended both to increase the accuracy of the electoral register, by reducing the number of redundant entries, and to improve its completeness, by ensuring those who should be registered were duly listed. The more immediate consequence seemed to be to improve the register's accuracy rather than its completeness—the total number of names on the December 2015 register was found to be 614,000 below that on the previous register, which itself had nearly 829,000 fewer names than the register before that.[52] Research undertaken by the Electoral Commission suggested that younger people in particular were now even less likely to be registered than hitherto.[53]

However, electoral registration is now a continuous process. Those excluded from the annually compiled register—or who have changed their address—can apply to be added as late as 13 working days before polling day, and such applications can be made online. This process can have a substantial effect on the size of the electorate. For example, the interest sparked by the EU referendum in June 2016 ensured that by the time of that poll, 1.75 million more names had been added (though when the December 2016 register appeared, the increase was only a little over a million).[54]

At this election, many voters again took advantage of the facility to add their name to the register. As a result, by polling day nearly 1.2 million more names appeared on the register in Great Britain than had done six months previously—similar to the increase recorded in the run-up to the 2015 election.[55] In total, a record number of nearly 45.6 million people, 475,000 more than in the 2015 election, were registered to vote in Great Britain.

Applications made via the online rolling registration process came disproportionately from younger people.[56] Consequently, amongst those constituencies where less than 7% of the adult population is aged between 18 and 24, on average only 1,500 more names were added to the register in the six months leading up to the election. In contrast, not far short of 3,200 names were added in constituencies where younger people comprised more than 10% of the population.

Yet if we compare the electorate in 2017 with that at the 2015 election, we find it grew less rapidly over the longer term in constituencies with more younger people. The electorate increased by just over 500 people on average where more than 10% are aged between 18 and 24, compared with an average increase of nearly 1,200 in seats where less than 7% fall into that age bracket. The explanation may lie in the impact of individual electoral registration on students in particular, who used, for example, to be registered automatically by their university if they were living in a hall of residence. The electorate increased on average by 850 in seats where more than 9% of adults are students, but by more than 1,400 where less than 6% are in full-time education. In fact, once we take the size of the student population into account, then, within England and Wales at least, there is some tendency for the electorate to have grown somewhat more where younger people are more numerous. Nevertheless, it appears that much of the disproportionate use of rolling registration by younger people arose because they were much less likely to be on the register in the first place rather than because of a new wave of youthful enthusiasm to vote.

Turnout, defined as the total number of valid votes cast expressed as a percentage of the registered electorate, increased on average by 2.4 points, resulting in an overall figure of 68.9%. Although this was the fourth time in a row that turnout increased, it was still lower than at any election between 1922 and 1997, and indeed was noticeably down on the 72.4% turnout recorded in the EU referendum 12 months earlier.

Within this broad picture, two patterns are immediately evident. First, turnout actually fell in Scotland, on average by as much as 4.6 points. For the most part—although not entirely—this drop simply represents a reversal of the marked increase in turnout north of the border in the wake of the 2014 Scottish independence referendum, in which no less than 84.6% turned out to vote.[57] Turnout was still 2.6 points higher than in 2010, although this is somewhat lower than the equivalent increases of 3.6 points for England and 3.8 for Wales. Meanwhile, within Scotland itself, turnout tended to fall most where it had increased most between 2010 and 2015, many of which were places where the SNP vote rose most dramatically in 2015.

Second, within England and Wales, turnout increased least in constituencies where UKIP had been strongest in 2015. Where UKIP won less than 7.5% of the vote in 2015, turnout increased on average by 4.7 points. In contrast, it increased by 3.3 points where UKIP won between 7.5% and 15% and by just 2.4 points where UKIP won more than 15%. This pattern is consistent with the claim that some UKIP voters stayed at home rather than switched to another party, doubtless in some instances because they did not have a UKIP candidate to support. Conversely (though only partly as a result), turnout increased rather more in constituencies in England and Wales with a younger age profile and those with a more highly educationally qualified population, that is, in the kinds of places where UKIP—and leaving the EU—tended to be less popular. For example, turnout increased by 4.4 points in constituencies where less than 14% are aged over 65, compared with just 2.4 points where more than 20% fall into that category. Whereas previous research has suggested that in the referendum, turnout increased most amongst those who voted Leave,[58] it seems that in the general election the roles may have been reversed.

As we established earlier, constituencies that voted relatively heavily for Remain also often saw larger increases in Labour support. One of the ways that Labour sought to increase its support under Jeremy Corbyn's leadership was by mobilising previous non-voters, including, in particular, young people. We thus might wonder whether the pattern of turnout means Labour's strategy enjoyed a measure of success. To address this question, we can examine whether Labour support increased more where turnout increased more even after taking into account the level of Leave support and the scale of UKIP's decline in a constituency. There is some sign of this, as can be seen if we look, for example, at those seats where support for Leave was between 50% and 60% and where the UKIP vote in 2017 had been between 10 and 14 points lower than in 2015 (i.e. fairly average seats). Amongst this subset, Labour's vote increased by an average of 9.1 points where turnout increased by less than two points, by 10.6 points where turnout increased by between two and four points, and by 10.9 points where turnout went up by more than 4 points. Still, this is no more than a modest association, and most of the above-average increases in turnout occurred in constituencies that Labour already held. In seats that the party gained from the Conservatives, turnout increased on average by 3.4 points, only slightly above the 3.1 point increase across all seats in England and Wales (bar Buckingham). Thus, it is far from clear whether the party's ability to mobilise voters played a key role in Labour's success in winning Conservative-held seats.

THE ELECTORAL SYSTEM

Surprising though the failure of the Conservatives to win an overall majority might have seemed, was the tally of seats won by each party significantly different from what we might have anticipated given the shares of the vote each of them secured? The traditional way of addressing this question has been to compare the actual outcome in seats with what would have happened if in every constituency each party's share of the vote had increased or fallen in line with the change in its overall share of the vote across Britain as a whole (that is, uniform change). However, as we noted after the 2015 election, applying this method becomes difficult when, as happened in 2015 and again this time, there is a substantial change in the level of support for a party, such as the SNP, that only fights elections in one part of the country but wins plenty of seats there.[59] In these circumstances the change in that party's share of the Britain-wide vote will inevitably be but a pale reflection of the actual rise or fall in its support in the part of the UK where it stood.

It is therefore better to use as our initial benchmark what would have happened if support for all of the main Britain-wide parties had increased or fallen in every constituency in England and Wales in line with the overall change in their support in those two parts of the UK combined, while for each seat in Scotland we calculate what would have happened if the rise or fall in each party's support had been in line with the change in its share of the Scotland-wide total.[60] On the basis of these assumptions, the Conservatives would have won 323 seats, Labour 259, the SNP 37, the Liberal Democrat nine, Plaid Cymru three and the Greens one, while, of course, there would be 18 other MPs from Northern Ireland. None of these figures is very different from what actually transpired and, above all, the Conservatives would still have failed to secure an overall majority—albeit they would have been only three rather than eight seats short.

That projected Conservative tally includes 11 seats in Scotland. However, if the increase in the Conservative vote north of the border had been in line with the lower increase in England and Wales—and the fall in SNP support had not happened—the Conservatives would have won only two Scottish seats. Thus, in the absence of the distinctive outcome in Scotland, the Conservatives would have won only 314 seats—and in those circumstances even a confidence and supply arrangement with the DUP would have been insufficient to guarantee them a majority on key votes in the House of Commons. To that extent, the distinctive result in Scotland proved to be crucial to the arithmetic of the new House of Commons.

However, although the overall tally of seats for each party was more or less in line with what might have been expected given the changes in their overall shares of the vote, there were lots of seats where the outcome was at variance with what would have happened if the movements in party support had been the same everywhere. No fewer than 36 seats changed hands that would not have done so under those circumstances, while 16 constituencies were held against the tide.[61] Most of these outcomes can in fact be accounted for by one or other of the systematic patterns of variation our analysis has identified, including the tendency for the Conservatives to perform better in seats with a relatively large Leave vote and Labour to do so in seats where Remain polled relatively well, the Conservatives' ability on occasion to squeeze the other unionist parties in Scotland, and the willingness of some of those who might otherwise have voted Labour to make a tactical switch to the (pro-Remain) Liberal Democrats. In short, much of the significant variation in party performance was linked in some way or other to the fallout from either the 2016 EU referendum or the 2014 Scottish independence referendum.

This still leaves us with the observation that for the third time in a row, the electoral system failed to deliver the winning party a substantial overall majority (and, indeed, on two occasions any majority at all). The system's ability to generate safe overall majorities has long been regarded as a hallmark of the single-member plurality system (often referred to as first past the post) and the resulting clarity of the link between the outcome of an election and who forms the government is often cited as a major justification for its continued use.[62]

It might be thought the explanation is that, at 2.5 points, the Conservative lead over Labour in terms of votes across Great Britain as a whole was a relatively narrow one. It was certainly much narrower than the seven point leads that the Conservatives enjoyed in 2010 and 2015. Yet it was larger than the leads (in Great Britain) that the Conservatives enjoyed in 1955 (1.9 points) and 1970 (2.3 points) or Labour did in 1964 (1.9 points), yet those three contests all resulted in an overall majority, including in two instances a relatively safe one.[63] Historical precedent apparently suggests that the Conservative lead should have been sufficient to give the party an overall majority.

Maybe the electoral system was biased in some way or another against the Conservatives? One consequence of the Prime Minister's decision to secure a Commons vote for an early election is that the contest had to be fought on the same constituency boundaries as in 2015 and not on the new boundaries the various parliamentary boundary commissions were in the midst of preparing in readiness for an election in 2020. The resulting inequality in the sizes of constituencies was certainly a disadvantage for the Conservatives. The average electorate in constituencies they won at this election was 74,451, whereas in seats won by Labour it was 70,529. The difference of some 3,920 people was around 520 bigger than it had been two years previously. The gap may have been increased somewhat by the government's decision in 2015 to speed up the introduction of individual electoral registration, which, as noted earlier, resulted in particularly sharp drops in registration in some typically Labour-held constituencies with large numbers of students. But the gap was then narrowed somewhat by the applications to be added to the register many (and especially younger) voters made after its initial compilation in December 2016. These added 2,300 names on average to the register in constituencies that Labour won, compared with just 1,600 on average in seats won by the Conservatives.

However, inequalities in the registered electorate are not the only consideration that we have to bear in mind in considering the sizes of constituencies. Bias might also arise if turnout is lower in seats held by one party than it is in those won by its opponents. Indeed, turnout was on average some four points lower on average in seats won by Labour at this election (66.5%) than it was in those won by the Conservatives (70.7%). That said, this was a noticeably smaller gap than in 2015, for turnout increased on average by 3.8 points in seats Labour won, but by only 2.0 points in those won by the Conservatives. As a result, at 5,675 votes, the difference between Conservative and Labour-held seats in terms of the total number of votes cast was actually smaller at this election than it had been in the same two sets of seats two years previously (6,541).

To this we need to add one other consideration. The relative success of the Conservatives in seats with a relatively high Leave vote meant that the increase in the party's vote was often greater in more working-class seats outside of London and the South of England, whose populations have grown less rapidly and thus tend to have lower than average electorates. For example, Conservative support increased on average by as much as 7.3 points in seats in which fewer than 72,000 people were registered to vote, compared with just 4.3 points where more than 77,000 names appeared on the register. Similarly, while the Conservative vote increased on average by 9.7 points where turnout was less than 65%, it increased by just 3.2 points where turnout was above 71%. As a result, there was a noticeable reduction in the extent to which the Conservative vote was concentrated in constituencies where more people turned out to vote.

In short, while inequalities in the sizes of constituencies were disadvantageous to the Conservatives at this election, the pattern of the party's performance, together with changes in the pattern of turnout, reduced this disadvantage compared with 2015. Such inequalities are not, though, the only potential reason why the single-member plurality electoral system might treat one of the two largest parties more favourably than the other; a party can also be advantaged if its vote is more efficiently distributed, that is, if it wins seats by small majorities rather than large ones. The Conservatives profited from this feature at this election, as indeed they had done in 2015, primarily because Labour won more seats by large majorities. The Labour Party was ahead of the Conservatives by more than 40 points in 27% of seats that it won, while the Conservative Party was that far ahead of Labour in just 12% of the constituencies that it won. In short, whatever disadvantage the Conservatives suffered as a result of inequalities in the sizes of constituencies tended to be compensated by them having a more efficiently distributed vote.

To understand why the electoral system failed to deliver the Conservatives an overall majority, we have to look at two other aspects of its operation. One is its treatment of the votes cast for smaller parties. The other is how the electoral geography of Conservative and Labour support is markedly different now from what it was in the 1950s and 1960s.

As we remarked at the beginning of this appendix, one of the remarkable features of the 2017 election is the decline in support for parties other than the Conservatives and Labour. At 17.6% their share of the vote fell to its lowest level since 1970. Yet whereas in 1970 just a dozen MPs were elected for parties other than the Conservatives or Labour, at this election no fewer than 70 were. Although this represents a drop of 17 on the equivalent figure for 2015, the total number of third-party MPs in the new House of Commons is still well above the figure recorded at any election between 1945 and 1992.

In short, the electoral system once again proved relatively ineffective at denying third parties representation. The single-member plurality system only denies representation to smaller parties if their vote is geographically evenly spread. The Liberal Democrat vote is relatively evenly spread, albeit that the party managed this time to convert a few more of its isolated pockets of support into seats won. As a result, the party's 7.4% share of the UK-wide vote was rewarded with just 1.8% of the seats. The SNP vote is now also very evenly spread within Scotland, but at the same time it is wholly concentrated in that one part of the UK. Thus, although the party lost 21 seats, at 5.4% its share of seats in the House of Commons was still well above the 3.0% of the UK-wide vote its performance represented. Meanwhile, in stark contrast to the position in 1970 (and beforehand), all of the 18 MPs from Northern Ireland continue to represent parties without any formal link to the Conservatives or Labour. The DUP, which won 0.9% of the UK-wide vote, were rewarded with 1.5% of the seats, while, similarly, Sinn Féin secured 0.7% of the vote and 1.1% of the seats. At the same time, thanks to the continued concentration of Plaid Cymru support in constituencies with many Welsh speakers, its 0.5% of the UK vote was rewarded with 0.6% of the seats.

The relatively generous treatment the electoral system affords political parties with specific geographical concentrations of support and that primarily represent particular territorial interests has two consequences. The first, inevitably, is that the resulting substantial phalanx of third-party MPs makes it more difficult for any party to secure a safe overall majority. All other things being equal, the more third-party MPs there are in the House of Commons, the greater the probability of a 'hung' parliament in which no party has an overall majority. The second consequence is that, in the event of a hung parliament, parties that represent specific territorial interests within the UK can find themselves with more bargaining power than a third party that wins a much bigger share of the popular vote that is obtained across the UK as a whole, as was clearly demonstrated after this election.[64]

But apart from its reduced effectiveness at denying representation to third parties, there is a second reason why the electoral system is nowadays less likely to deliver an overall majority for any party. This is a long-term decline in the number of seats that are marginal between Conservative and Labour, that is, seats which are likely to change hands in the event of a swing from a small nationwide Conservative lead in the popular vote to a small Labour lead (or vice versa). We can define these as those seats in which the Conservative share of the vote cast for the Conservatives and Labour alone would lie between 45% and 55% in the event that the two parties won the same share of the vote nationally. The fewer such seats that there are, the less likely it is that sufficient seats will change hands to give the winning party an overall majority.

As has been shown elsewhere, in 1970 there were still as many as 149 seats that could be defined as marginal, a figure not untypical of the position throughout the 1950s and 1960s.[65] But by 2010, that number had fallen to 85 and it fell even further—to a record low of just 74—in 2015. This decline was the product of long-term changes in electoral geography, whereby Labour's vote became increasingly concentrated in the northern half of the country and in more urban constituencies, whereas the Conservatives advanced in the southern half and in more rural and suburban seats, leaving far fewer constituencies closely contested by the two parties. In fact, the pattern of movement at this election whereby the Conservatives typically performed best in seats with a relatively large Leave vote in 2016, and thus seats with more working-class voters and constituencies located in the North and Midlands of England—and also enjoyed a revival in Scotland—reduced this tendency somewhat. It meant that the Conservative vote increased more in seats Labour won in 2015 (5.8) than it did in those the Conservatives themselves had won (4.6). But even so, the number of marginal seats still only stands at 89, with the result that the electoral system remains much less likely to convert relatively small leads of the kind the Conservatives enjoyed in 2017 into a safe overall majority.

There is, then, little reason to believe the failure of the Conservatives to win an overall majority is an indication that the electoral system treated the party particularly harshly. While inequalities in constituency sizes did disadvantage the party, they did so rather less than in 2015 and the party was compensated (as in 2015) by having a more efficiently distributed vote. Rather, the relative inability of the electoral system to deny representation to third parties and the continued scarcity of seats that are marginal between Conservative and Labour meant that it continued to be relatively difficult for either party to win a safe overall majority, as the outcomes of the 2010 and 2015 elections had already amply illustrated.

Indeed, overall, the electoral system is inclined to treat the Conservatives more kindly than Labour, albeit less so than in 2015. This is illustrated in Table A1.9, which shows what the outcome in seats would be for each of a set of uniform swings between Conservative and Labour. The table can be read by looking first at the seventh row, where no swing has been applied, and where we show the actual outcome of the 2017 election. If we then examine the row immediately above, this shows what the outcome would be if the Conservative vote were to increase by 0.3 of a point in every seat across Great Britain as compared with 2017, while Labour's vote is assumed to have fallen by 0.3 of a point everywhere (that is, a 0.3 point swing to the Conservatives). We also assume that the level of turnout, the size of the electorate in every seat and the level of support for third parties all remain exactly as they were in 2017. This means we are also assuming that the overall share of the vote won by the Conservatives is 0.3 of a point higher than in 2017 and Labour's share 0.3 higher, thereby producing the overall vote tallies shown in the second and third columns of the table. And as we can see, under these assumptions, which, as the fourth column shows, imply a 3.1 point Conservative lead in votes, the Conservatives would win the 326 seats needed for a minimal overall majority of two.

Table A1.9 Relationship between votes and seats following the 2017 election

Swing to Con from 2017 result	% vote (GB)			Seats (UK)			
	Con	Lab	Con lead	Con	Lab	Others	Majority
+5.0	48.5	36.0	12.5	374	209	67	Con 98
+4.0	47.5	37.0	10.5	364	219	67	Con 78
+3.0	46.5	38.0	8.5	355	230	65	Con 60
+2.0	45.5	39.0	6.5	341	239	70	Con 32
+1.0	44.5	40.0	4.5	335	244	71	Con 20
+0.3	43.8	40.7	3.1	326	255	69	Con 2
0.0	43.5	41.0	2.5	318	262	69	None
−1.0	42.5	42.0	0.5	301	283	66	None
−1.25	42.25	42.25	0.0	298	286	66	None
−1.6	41.9	42.6	−0.7	292	292	66	None
−2.0	41.5	43.0	−1.5	287	298	65	None
−3.0	40.5	44.0	−3.5	277	309	64	None
−4.0	39.5	45.0	−5.5	268	319	63	None
−4.9	38.6	45.9	−7.3	259	327	64	Lab 4
−5.0	38.5	46.0	−7.5	259	327	64	Lab 4

We can then look further down the table, where we show (making the same assumptions) what would happen as a result of various uniform swings to Labour, to see what kind of swing—and thus what overall lead—Labour would need to win an overall majority. The answer is a 4.9 point swing, or a lead of no less than 7.3 points, far higher than the 3.1 point lead the Conservatives would require.[66] The table also shows that if the two parties were to win the same share of the vote, the Conservatives would still have 12 more seats than Labour, and that Labour would need to be more than 0.7 of a point ahead of the Conservatives to become the largest party. Both figures are lower than the equivalent statistics for the 2015 election (when the Conservatives would have been as many as 46 seats ahead if the two parties enjoyed the same share of the vote),[67] but they still indicate that, overall, the electoral system was inclined to treat the Conservatives more favourably than Labour. Meanwhile, although less wide than it was after the last three elections,[68] the range of results that would result in no overall majority (anything between a Conservative lead of 3.1 points and a Labour one of 7.3 points) is still quite large.

There is one other important feature of the table. The Prime Minister went into the election in the hope and expectation of winning a landslide, a target that was widely interpreted as winning a three-figure majority. This was, in truth, a bold ambition. As the first row of the table shows, given the electoral geography that actually transpired in the election, the Conservatives would have needed a 12.5 point lead—and no less than 48.5% of the vote—just to be on the cusp of a three-figure majority. Such a lead has only been secured twice in the post-war period (in 1983 and 1997), while no party has managed to win more than 48.5% of the vote since Labour won 48.8% in 1966. Against a backdrop of continued significant third-party representation and a relative paucity of marginal seats, the Conservatives needed to put in a very strong performance indeed to win a landslide. In the event, even though the party's stance on Brexit did seemingly win over many a voter who voted Leave, it also apparently had the opposite effect amongst Remain supporters, thereby inevitably leaving the Prime Minister far short of her ambitious target.

NOTES

1. A. Clark, *Political Parties in the UK*. Palgrave Macmillan, 2012, p. 12.
2. J. Curtice, S. Fisher and R. Ford, 'Appendix 1: The Results Analysed' in P. Cowley and D. Kavanagh, *The British General Election of 2015*. Palgrave Macmillan, 2015 and previous appendices to *The British General Election* series.

3. In 2017, the index, calculated across the UK as a whole, was 15.6. This is second only to the 17.7 figure recorded in 2015. M. Pedersen, 'The Dynamics of European Party Systems: Changing Patterns of Electoral Volatility', *European Journal of Political Research*, 7(1) (1979): 1–26; Clark, *Political Parties in the UK*, p. 12.

4. I. McLean, 'The Problem of Proportionate Swing', *Political Studies*, 21(1) (1973): 57–63.

5. The 2016 referendum was counted by local authority rather than parliamentary constituency. However, estimates of the Leave vote in 2016 by constituency were calculated by Chris Hanretty and these are used throughout this appendix. For further details, see C. Hanretty, 'Areal Interpolation and the UK's Referendum on EU Membership', *Journal of Elections, Public Opinion and Parties*, 27(4) (2017): 466–83.

6. If we regress the change in Conservative support against both estimated Leave share and the change in UKIP support, we obtain a coefficient of 0.22 for estimated Leave share. Undertaking the same exercise for Labour produces an almost exact mirror-image result with a coefficient of −0.24. Both coefficients are significant at the 0.000 level.

7. Comparing the middle and the last set of columns in the penultimate row of Table A1.3 shows that the Conservative vote typically increased by 1.5 points more than Labour did in heavily pro-Leave seats where there was more than a 14 point drop in UKIP support. This suggests that a heavy drop in UKIP support could have been decisive locally in any seat that the Conservatives won against a Labour challenge with less than a 1.5 point majority. There was in fact no seat where the Conservatives defeated Labour by less than 1.5 points and the drop in UKIP support locally was more than 14 points. However, in Stoke South, the Conservative majority was only 1.6 points, and at 21.2 points the drop in the UKIP vote (occasioned by the party's decision to stand down) was especially sharp. It is perhaps also possible that the Conservatives were helped in Telford, where, again, there was just a 1.6 point lead, though here the drop in UKIP (again occasioned by UKIP's decision to withdrawal) was, at 18.0 points, rather lower.

8. Comparing the first and the middle set of columns in the first row of Table A1.3 shows that, on average, the Conservatives performed 4.2 points less well on average where UKIP's vote fell by less than 10 points, while Labour performed just 1.1 points less well. This suggests that a pro-Remain seat won by Labour with less than a three-point lead over the Conservatives and where there was a relatively small drop in UKIP support may have been one where Labour's success was facilitated by that small drop. A similar calculation across the second row of the table suggests a net benefit to Labour of 1.6 points in seats that were moderately pro-Leave. There are two seats where there was a small drop in UKIP support and where Labour

won with less than a 1.6 point majority: Kensington (0.1% majority) and Stroud (1.1% majority). Meanwhile, in Warwick & Leamington, there was only a 2.2% majority and just a 6.8 point drop in UKIP support in what was a pro-Remain seat in 2016. There are also a number of more marginal possibilities in seats where the drop in UKIP support was only a little below 10 points, of which the most likely are Barrow in Furness and Keighley, which Labour won with a 0.4% and a 0.5% majority respectively.

9. J. Curtice, 'Why Leave Won the UK's EU Referendum', *Journal of Common Market Studies*, 55(S1) (2017): 19–37; R. Ford and M. Goodwin, *Revolt on the Right*. Routledge, 2014.

10. Data on the social and demographic character of a constituency are taken from the 2011 Census unless otherwise stated.

11. For instance, in regressions of the Labour to Conservative (total vote) swing, the coefficients for the percentage without any qualifications and the percentage aged 18–24 drop, after controlling for the Leave vote share and fall in the UKIP vote, from 0.37 to 0.11 and from −0.29 to −0.11 respectively.

12. Curtice et al., 'Appendix 1: The Results Analysed', pp. 393–95.

13. Unemployment is measured using data on the claimant count by constituency published each month by the House of Commons Library.

14. Curtice et al., 'Appendix 1: The Results Analysed', pp. 395–96.

15. Some, but not all. We also examined whether there was any evidence that the gender of a candidate made any difference, but in this instance there is no indication that it did so.

16. The increase was, at 9.1 points, larger in the five seats where the former Labour MP did not stand again than in the three where they did (6.7), but the latter had a lower level of Leave support in 2016. Meanwhile, although the vote of first-term Conservative incumbents increased by only 6.0 points in seats captured from the Liberal Democrats, given that these seats recorded an average Leave vote of 52%, the new MPs' performances were well above the average for such seats. However, it is not obvious that these incumbency bonuses helped the Tories save any seats; the only possible case is St Ives, but even here there was only a 4.9 point increase in the new Conservative MP's vote in a seat where 55% voted for Leave, not a particularly outstanding performance.

17. The decision of the former Conservative MP to fight again made no difference—the increase in Labour support was on average 13.7 points where the former MP fought again, only slightly below the 14.0 figure in seats where the new incumbent faced a fresh candidate. The increase in Labour's vote was substantially larger (16.6 points) in seats won from the Liberal Democrats in 2015, but in none of these cases was the outcome close.

18. There is also no evidence that either party performed particularly well in marginal seats that they were defending or attacking, even though such seats are usually the focus of more intense campaigning, including visits from the party leaders. However, receiving such a visit during the 2017 campaign also does not seem to have made any difference to a candidate's performance. We are grateful to Chris Cook and Alia Middleton for sharing their data on which constituencies the leaders visited.

19. S. Fisher, 'Racism at the Ballot Box: Ethnic Minority Candidates' in P. Cowley and R. Ford (eds), *More Sex Lies and the Ballot Box*. Biteback, 2016; Curtice et al., 'Appendix 1: The Results Analysed', p. 396 and references therein. We are grateful to Jennifer Hudson for her help in identifying ethnic minority candidates.

20. Curtice et al., 'Appendix 1: The Results Analysed', p. 396; J. Curtice, S. Fisher and R. Ford, 'Appendix 2: An Analysis of the Results' in D. Kavanagh and P. Cowley, *The British General Election of 2010*. Palgrave Macmillan, 2010, p. 394.

21. The increase in the 14 such diverse seats that were fought by an ethnic minority candidate in 2017 but not in 2015 was just 10.9 points, only slightly above the average for other Labour candidates in ethnically diverse seats that were not already incumbent MPs. Nevertheless, these patterns still meant that Labour were able to increase the number of ethnic minority MPs on their benches by nominating more ethnic minority candidates to stand in ethnically diverse areas. In total, eight of the nine seats that Labour won while fielding a minority candidate this time, but not last time, were ethnically diverse.

22. This difference is mainly but not wholly a consequence of the different levels of Leave and UKIP support in the two kinds of constituency.

23. Defined as London, the South East, the South West (where Labour did especially well in Devon and Cornwall, despite the substantial Leave vote there) and Eastern government regions.

24. Defined as the East and West Midlands government regions. Note though that despite the majority for Leave in Wales, there was a 2.8 point swing to Labour there.

25. Once we have taken into account the proportion in a constituency who voted Leave in 2016, there is no consistent relationship between the size of the fall in the UKIP vote and the Liberal Democrats' performance.

26. However, there is no consistent evidence of the party doing better in seats with large proportions of younger voters, who also voted heavily for Remain. Nor indeed is there any evidence of the party's performance being linked—in either direction—to the proportion of students in a constituency.

27. See T. Smith, 'Are You Sitting Comfortably? Estimating Incumbency Advantage in the UK: 1983–2010', *Electoral Studies*, 21(1) (2013): 167–73 and citations therein; Curtice et al., 'Appendix 1: The Results Analysed', pp. 401–2.

28. Curtice et al., 'Appendix 1: The Results Analysed', pp. 409–10.

29. Given the weakness of UKIP's performance north of the border in 2015, there is, unsurprisingly, no relationship between the fall in UKIP support and the rise in Conservative support (after taking into account the size of the Leave vote locally in 2016).

30. As in the case of the EU referendum, the independence referendum was counted by local authority rather than parliamentary constituency. In this instance, however, no estimates of the outcome in each parliamentary constituency have been produced. Our measure of the level of support for independence in each constituency is simply the share of the vote for Yes in the local authority district in which the constituency lies or, in the case of constituencies that cross a local authority boundary, an amalgam of the result in the relevant councils. Inevitably, this means that our measure is relatively crude for constituencies located in the largest local council areas.

31. Curtice et al., 'Appendix 1: The Results Analysed', pp. 413–14.

32. Aberdeenshire West & Kincardine and Berwickshire, Roxburgh & Selkirk.

33. Curtice et al., 'Appendix 1: The Results Analysed', p. 414.

34. These seats are East Dunbartonshire, Fife North East, Edinburgh West, and Caithness, Sutherland & Easter Ross.

35. These seats are Argyll & Bute; Ross, Skye & Lochaber; Inverness, Nairn, Badenoch & Strathspey; and Gordon.

36. The one exception, East Lothian, was a seat in which the local Labour vote had been shown to be unusually resilient in the previous year's Scottish Parliament election. See J. Curtice, *The 2016 Scottish Election: Getting to Minority Government*. Electoral Reform Society Scotland, 2016.

37. Curtice et al., 'Appendix 1: The Results Analysed', p. 413.

38. In addition, turnout rose more between 2010 and 2015 in areas with a higher Yes vote in 2014, while at this election it fell more in such constituencies. Turnout fell on average by as much as 5.5 points on average in those constituencies lying in council areas in which more than 45% voted Yes, compared with 3.7 points elsewhere. Some of the decline in SNP support in places with a relatively high Yes vote may thus have been occasioned by a tendency for some of the party's supporters in 2015 to stay at home.

39. J. Curtice, 'Why Did Scotland Vote to Remain?', http://blog.whatscotlandthinks.org/2016/10/why-did-scotland-vote-to-remain.

40. Curtice et al., 'Appendix 1: The Results Analysed', p. 414. The 2.2 point increase in Conservative support in the constituency in 2017 was well below that recorded anywhere else in mainland Scotland.

41. The one other former Liberal Democrat MP who tried to get re-elected, Alan Reid in Argyll & Bute, was not so fortunate. His share of the vote dropped by 9.7 points, though this drop was less than that in the other three seats where the Liberal Democrats started off more than 12 points behind the SNP.

42. The drop in the Liberal Democrat vote in Gordon and that in Labour support in Ayr, Carrick & Cumnock and in Stirling certainly looks to have been decisive in enabling the Conservatives to win narrowly in those seats, while the drop in Labour support may have also been crucial in East Renfrewshire. Note that all of these seats are ones where the Conservatives had been in third place in 2015.

43. There is no evidence that the size of the Leave vote locally in 2016 made any difference to this pattern. In other words, for any given share of the vote won by UKIP in 2015, the drop in the UKIP vote between 2015 and 2017 was the same irrespective of how well Leave performed in 2016.

44. Curtice et al., 'Appendix 1: The Results Analysed', p. 403.

45. Intriguingly, despite the prominence given to the issue by the party, there is no evidence that its vote held up any better in constituencies where voters are more inclined to express concern about the consequences of immigration; indeed, if anything, the opposite was the case. This analysis is based on estimates of attitudes the cultural consequences of immigration in each constituency produced by Chris Hanretty using data collected from the 2015 British Election Study internet panel. For further details, see C. Hanretty and N. Vivyian, *Estimating Constituency Opinion in Britain: Technical Report*, http://constituencyopinion.org.uk/wp-content/uploads/2016/09/constituency-estimates-technical-report.pdf.

46. C. Mudde, *Populist Radical Right Parties in Europe*. Cambridge University Press, 2007.

47. Curtice et al., 'Appendix 2: An Analysis of the Results', p. 405.

48. Curtice et al., 'Appendix 1: The Results Analysed', p. 405.

49. Brighton Pavilion, which deviates strongly from this pattern both in terms of total Green vote share and Green performance, is excluded from the graph.

50. There is a partial correlation of 0.16 between the (total vote) swing from Labour to the Conservatives in a constituency and the change in Green support after controlling for the Leave share of the vote in 2016 and the change in the UKIP vote between 2015 and 2017. The figure is significant at the 0.000 level. Seats that the Greens fought in 2015 but not in 2017 are included in this calculation and are categorised according to the Greens' share of the vote in 2015. Seats that the Greens fought in 2017 but not in 2015 are also included; they are all classified as seats where the Green vote fell by no more than two points.

51. The previous footnote also applies to this calculation.
52. Electoral Commission, *Assessment of the December 2015 Electoral Registers in Great Britain.* Electoral Commission, 2016.
53. Electoral Commission, *The December 2015 Electoral Registers in Great Britain.* Electoral Commission, 2016.
54. Electoral Commission, *Analysis of the December 2016 Electoral Registers in the United Kingdom.* Electoral Commission, 2017.
55. Cowley and Kavanagh, *The British General Election of 2015*, p. 40.
56. Electoral Commission, *Electoral Registration at the June 2017 UK General Election.* Electoral Commission, 2016.
57. A similar reversal also occurred in Scotland in respect of electoral registration which had been boosted by the 2014 independence referendum. On average, nearly 1900 fewer people were registered to vote in constituencies in Scotland, with the drop generally greater the bigger the increase had been between 2010 and 2015.
58. K. Swales, *Understanding the Leave Vote.* NatCen Social Research, 2016.
59. Curtice et al., 'Appendix 1: The Results Analysed', pp. 417–18.
60. We assume no change in support for Plaid Cymru, though this is not material to the result of our calculation.
61. The 36 seats that would not have changed hands comprise: 15 that Labour won from the Conservatives and five from the SNP; six the Conservatives won from Labour and four from the SNP; five the Liberal Democrats won from the Conservatives; and one Plaid Cymru gained from the Liberal Democrats. The 16 seats that would have changed hands but did not comprise: eight that the Conservatives did not lose to Labour; three the SNP did not lose to Labour, two to the Conservatives and two to the Liberal Democrats; and one the Liberal Democrats did not lose to the Conservatives.
62. G. Bingham Powell, Jr., *Elections as Instruments of Democracy: Majoritarian and Proportional Visions.* Yale University Press, 2000.
63. Note that in 1955 and 1970, the government would still have had a majority even if we leave aside the Conservative MPs elected at those elections for constituencies in Northern Ireland. In addition, the Conservatives won an overall majority in 1951 even though the party was actually 1.6 points behind Labour in the share of the vote won across Great Britain.
64. J. Curtice and M. Steed, 'Electoral Choice and the Production of Government: The Changing Operation of the Electoral System in the United Kingdom since 1955', *British Journal of Political Science*, 12(3) (1982): 249–98, p. 289.
65. J. Curtice, 'Neither Representative nor Accountable: First Past the Post in Britain' in B. Grofman, A. Blais and S. Bowler (eds), *Duverger's Law of Plurality Voting.* Springer, 2009; J. Curtice, 'A Return to Normality? How

the Electoral System Operated', *Parliamentary Affairs*, 68(S1) (2015): 25–40.

66. It should be noted, however, that because of the large number of closely contested seats in Scotland, this calculation is very sensitive to the assumptions that we make about the SNP's performance. For example, if we were to assume that SNP support were to drop by just two points, with the Conservatives and Labour benefiting equally from this fall, the swing required for Labour to win an overall majority falls to just 3.8 points. Under the same assumptions, the swing required for the Conservatives to secure an overall majority is just 0.1 of a point.

67. Curtice et al., 'Appendix 1: The Results Analysed', p. 423.

68. See the equivalent tables in J. Curtice and M. Steed, 'Appendix 2: An Analysis of the Results' in D. Butler and D. Kavanagh, *The British General Election of 2001*. Palgrave, 2001, p. 331; J. Curtice, S. Fisher and M. Steed, 'Appendix 2: An Analysis of the Results' in D. Kavanagh and D. Butler, *The British General Election of 2005*. Palgrave Macmillan, 2005, p. 251; Curtice et al., 'Appendix 2: An Analysis of the Results', p. 416; Curtice et al., 'Appendix 1: The Results Analysed', p. 423.

APPENDIX 2: THE VOTING STATISTICS

Table A2.1 Votes and seats, 1945–2017

	Turnout/ electorate	Seats/ votes	Conservative[a]	Labour	Liberal (Democrats)[b]	Scottish and Welsh Nationalists	Other
1945[c]	73.3%	640	39.8%–213	48.3%–393	9.1%–12	0.2%	2.5%–22
	32,836,419	24,082,612	9,577,667	11,632,191	2,197,191	46,612	628,251
1950	84.0%	625	43.5%–299	46.1%–315	9.1%–9	0.1%	1.2%–2
	34,269,770	28,772,671	12,502,567	13,266,592	2,621,548	27,288	354,676
1951	82.5%	625	48.0%–321	48.8%–295	2.5%–6	0.1%	0.6%–3
	34,645,573	28,595,668	13,717,538	13,948,605	730,556	18,219	180,750
1955	76.8%	630	49.7%–345	46.4%–277	2.7%–6	0.2%	0.9%–2
	34,858,263	26,760,493	13,311,936	12,404,970	722,405	57,231	263,951
1959	78.7%	630	49.4%–365	43.8%–258	5.9%–6	0.4%	0.6%–1
	35,397,080	27,859,241	13,749,830	12,215,538	1,638,571	99,309	175,987
1964	77.1%	630	43.4%–304	44.1%–317	11.2%–9	0.5%	0.8%–0
	35,892,572	27,655,374	12,001,396	12,205,814	3,092,878	133,551	215,363
1966	75.8%	630	41.9%–253	47.9%–363	8.5%–12	0.7%	0.9%–2
	35,964,684	27,263,606	11,418,433	13,064,951	2,327,533	189,545	263,144
1970	72.0%	630	46.4%–330	43.0%–288	7.5%–6	1.3%–1	1.8%–5
	39,342,013	28,344,798	13,145,123	12,178,295	2,117,033	381,819	524,527
Feb 1974	78.1%	635	37.8%–297	37.1%–301	19.3%–14	2.6%–9	3.2%–14
	39,770,724	31,340,162	11,872,180	11,646,391	6,058,744	804,554	991,036
Oct 1974	72.8%	635	35.8%–277	39.2%–319	18.3%–13	3.5%–14	3.2%–12
	40,072,971	29,189,178	10,464,817	11,457,079	5,346,754	1,005,938	914,590
1979	76.0%	635	43.9%–339	37%–269	13.8%–11	2.0%–4	3.3%–12
	41,093,264	31,221,361	13,697,923	11,532,218	4,313,804	636,890	1,039,563

Year	Turnout	Electorate	Total votes	Seats									
1983	72.7%	42,197,344	30,671,136	650	42.4%–397	13,012,315	27.6%–209	8,456,934	25.4%–23	7,780,949	1.5%–4	457,676	3.1%–17	144,723
1987	75.3%	43,181,321	32,536,137	650	42.3%–376	13,763,066	30.8%–229	10,029,778	22.6%–22	7,341,290	1.7%–6	543,559	2.6%–17	852,368
1992	77.7%	43,249,721	33,612,693	651	41.9%–336	14,092,891	34.4%–271	11,559,735	17.8%–20	5,999,384	2.3%–7	783,991	3.5%–17	1,176,692
1997	71.5%	43,757,478	31,286,597	659	30.7%–165	9,602,857	43.2%–418	13,516,632	16.8%–46	5,242,894	2.5%–10	782,570	6.8%–20	2,141,644
2001	59.4%	44,403,238	26,368,798	659	31.7%–166	8,357,622	40.7%–412	10,724,895	18.3%–52	4,812,833	2.5%–9	660,197	6.8%–20	1,813,251
2005	61.2%	44,261,545	27,123,652	646	32.4%–198	8,772,473	35.2%–356	9,547,944	22.0%–62	5,981,874	2.2%–9	567,105	8.2%–22	2,234,267
2010	65.1%	45,610,369	29,687,409	650	36.1%–307	10,726,555	29.0%–258	8,606,518	23.0%–57	6,836,188	2.2%–9	656,780	9.6%–19	2,861,368
2015	66.2%	46,354,197	30,697,279	650	36.9%–331	11,334,226	30.4%–232	9,347,033	7.9%–8	2,415,916	5.3%–59	1,636,140	19.4%–20	5,963,964
2017	68.8%	46,835,836	32,204,124	650	42.5%–318	13,670,983	40.0%–262	12,877,858	7.4%–12	2,371,861	3.5%–39	1,142,034	6.8%–19	2,175,687

Notes:
[a] Includes Ulster Unionists 1945–70
[b] Liberals 1945–79; Liberal–SDP Alliance 1983–87; Liberal Democrats 1992–
[c] The 1945 figures exclude university seats and are adjusted for double counting in the 15 two-member seats

Table A2.2 Party performance (UK)

Party	Votes	% share (change)	Average % share	Seats (change)	Candidates	Lost deposits
Conservative	13,670,983	42.5 (+5.5)	42.1	318 (−13)	639	7
Labour	12,877,858	40.0 (+9.5)	41.9	262 (+30)	631	0
Liberal Democrats	2,371,861	7.4 (−0.5)	7.2	12 (+4)	629	375
Scottish National Party (SNP)	977,568	3.0 (−1.7)	37.1	35 (−21)	59	0
United Kingdom Independence Party (UKIP)	594,068	1.8 (−10.8)	3.3	0 (−1)	378	337
Green	525,665	1.6 (−2.1)	2.1	1 (0)	467	456
Democratic Unionist Party (DUP)	292,316	0.9 (+0.3)	39.0	10 (+2)	17	0
Sinn Féin	238,915	0.7 (+0.2)	28.5	7 (+3)	18	4
Plaid Cymru	164,466	0.5 (−0.1)	11.2	4 (+1)	40	16
Social Democratic and Labour Party (SDLP)	95,419	0.3 (0)	11.4	0 (−3)	18	5
Ulster Unionist Party (UUP)	83,280	0.3 (−0.1)	12.7	0 (−2)	14	3
Alliance Party of Northern Ireland (APNI)	64,553	0.2 (0)	8.3	–	18	8
Yorkshire Party	20,958	0.1 (0)	2.1	–	21	21
National Health Action Party (NHA)	16,119	0.1 (0)	5.6	–	5	4
Christian People's Alliance	5,869	0 (0)	0.4	–	31	31
People Before Profit Alliance	5,509	0 (0)	6.6	–	2	1

Note: The cut-off for inclusion was 5,000 votes. Below that line are a variety of other parties, including the British National Party, the Monster Racing Loony Party, the Liberal Party, the Women's Equality Party and Traditional Unionist Voice. Also excluded are any non-party candidates, including Lady Sylvia Hermon, who won North Down as an independent

Table A2.3 Party performance (Northern Ireland)

Party	Votes	% share (change)	Average % share	Seats (change)	Candidates	Lost deposits
Democratic Unionist Party (DUP)	292,316	36.0 (+10.3)	39.0	10 (+2)	17	0
Sinn Féin	238,915	29.4 (+4.9)	28.5	7 (+3)	18	4
Social Democratic and Labour Party (SDLP)	95,419	11.7 (−2.2)	11.4	0 (−3)	18	5
Ulster Unionist Party (UUP)	83,280	10.3 (−5.8)	12.7	0 (−2)	14	3
Alliance Party of Northern Ireland (APNI)	64,553	7.9 (−0.6)	8.3	–	18	8
Green	7,452	0.9 (0)	2.5	–	7	5
People Before Profit Alliance	5,509	0.7 (−0.3)	6.6	–	2	1
Conservative	3,895	0.5 (−0.8)	1.4	–	7	7
Traditional Unionist Voice (TUV)	3,282	0.4 (−1.9)	6.8	–	1	0

Note: As in Table A1.1, not included is Lady Sylvia Hermon, who won North Down as an independent

Table A2.4 National and regional results

UK

	Seats won in 2017 (change since 2015)					Share of votes cast in 2017 (change since 2015)							
Con	Lab	LD	Nat & Other		Turnout	Con	Lab	Lib Dem	Nat	UKIP	Green	Other
297 (−22)	227 (+21)	8 (+2)	1 (−1)	**England**	69.1 (+3.1)	45.6 (+4.6)	41.9 (+10.3)	7.8 (−0.4)	0 (0)	2.1 (−12.1)	1.9 (−2.3)	0.8 (−0.1)
40 (−4)	117 (+7)	1 (−3)	0 (0)	**North**	67.0 (+3.5)	37.4 (+6.7)	52.9 (+9.8)	5.1 (−1.6)	0 (0)	2.5 (−12.5)	1.2 (−2.2)	0.9 (−0.1)
66 (0)	39 (0)	0 (0)	0 (0)	**Midlands**	67.9 (+2.7)	49.8 (+7.3)	41.6 (+9.2)	4.4 (−1.2)	0 (0)	2.1 (−13.7)	1.6 (−1.6)	0.6 (−0.1)
191 (−18)	71 (+14)	7 (+5)	1 (−1)	**South**	70.7 (+3.0)	48.3 (+2.6)	36.4 (+10.9)	10.4 (+0.5)	0 (0)	1.8 (−13.1)	2.3 (−2.7)	0.8 (0)
8 (−3)	28 (+3)	0 (−1)	4 (+1)	**Wales**	68.6 (+2.9)	33.6 (+6.3)	48.9 (+12.1)	4.5 (−2.0)	10.4 (−1.7)	2.0 (−11.6)	0.3 (−2.2)	0.2 (−0.8)
13 (+12)	7 (+6)	4 (+3)	35 (−21)	**Scotland**	66.4 (−4.6)	28.6 (+13.7)	27.1 (+2.8)	6.8 (−0.8)	36.9 (−13.1)	0.2 (−1.4)	0.2 (−1.1)	0.3 (0)
318 (−13)	262 (+30)	12 (+4)	40 (−21)	**Great Britain**	68.9 (+2.4)	43.5 (+5.8)	41.0 (+9.8)	7.6 (−0.5)	3.6 (−1.8)	1.9 (−11.0)	1.7 (−2.2)	0.7 (−0.1)
0 (0)	0 (0)	0 (0)	18 (0)	**Northern Ireland**	65.4 (+7.3)	0.5 (−0.8)	0 (0)	0 (0)	0 (0)	0 (−2.6)	0.9 (0)	98.6 (+3.4)
318 (−13)	262 (+30)	12 (+4)	58 (−21)	**UK**	68.8 (+2.5)	42.5 (+5.5)	40.0 (+9.5)	7.4 (−0.5)	3.5 (−1.8)	1.8 (−10.8)	1.6 (−2.1)	3.2 (+0.2)

Regions

	Seats won in 2017 (change since 2015)					Share of votes cast in 2017 (change since 2015)							
Con	Lab	LD	Nat & Other		Turnout	Con	Lab	Lib Dem	Nat	UKIP	Green	Other
126 (−12)	60 (+9)	5 (+4)	1 (−1)	**South East**	70.5 (+3.3)	46.8 (+1.5)	38.9 (+10.7)	9.2 (+0.8)	0 (0)	2.0 (−10.7)	2.4 (−2.3)	0.7 (0)
21 (−6)	49 (+4)	3 (+2)	0 (0)	**Greater London***	70.1 (+4.7)	33.1 (−1.7)	54.5 (+10.8)	8.8 (+1.1)	0 (0)	1.3 (−6.8)	1.8 (−3.1)	0.5 (−0.2)
3 (−2)	25 (+2)	0 (0)	0 (0)	**Inner London**	69.1 (+5.9)	22.7 (−4.1)	64.8 (+12.4)	8.6 (+0.7)	0 (0)	0.8 (−3.8)	2.2 (−4.9)	0.9 (−0.2)
18 (−4)	24 (+2)	3 (+2)	0 (0)	**Outer London**	70.7 (+3.9)	39.8 (0)	47.9 (+9.6)	8.9 (+1.3)	0 (0)	1.6 (−8.6)	1.5 (−2.0)	0.2 (−0.3)
105 (−6)	11 (+5)	2 (+2)	1 (−1)	**Rest of South East**	70.8 (+2.5)	54.9 (+3.6)	29.7 (+10.4)	9.5 (+0.7)	0 (0)	2.4 (−12.8)	2.7 (−1.9)	0.8 (+0.1)
58 (−1)	4 (+1)	0 (0)	0 (0)	**Outer Met. Area**	70.7 (+2.4)	56.2 (+3.0)	29.8 (+10.2)	8.6 (+0.8)	0 (0)	2.6 (−12.3)	2.0 (−1.7)	0.8 (+0.1)
47 (−5)	7 (+4)	2 (+2)	1 (−1)	**Other S.E.**	70.8 (+2.6)	53.5 (+4.2)	29.5 (+10.6)	10.5 (+0.7)	0 (0)	2.2 (−13.4)	3.5 (−2.1)	0.8 (+0.1)
47 (−4)	7 (+3)	1 (+1)	0 (0)	**South West***	71.8 (+2.3)	51.4 (+4.8)	29.1 (+11.5)	14.9 (−0.2)	0 (0)	1.1 (−12.5)	2.3 (−3.7)	1.2 (0)
16 (−1)	2 (+1)	0 (0)	0 (0)	**Devon & Cornwall**	72.2 (+2.8)	50.2 (+5.1)	28.3 (+12.1)	16.1 (−0.2)	0 (0)	1.2 (−13.1)	1.7 (−4.0)	2.5 (+0.1)
31 (−3)	5 (+2)	1 (+1)	0 (0)	**Rest of S.W.**	71.6 (+2.1)	51.9 (+4.7)	29.6 (+11.2)	14.4 (−0.2)	0 (0)	1.0 (−12.1)	2.5 (−3.5)	0.5 (−0.1)
18 (−2)	4 (+2)	1 (0)	0 (0)	**East Anglia***	69.8 (+2.3)	53.1 (+6.2)	33.3 (+10.7)	9.3 (−0.5)	0 (0)	2.1 (−13.6)	2.0 (−2.9)	0.2 (0)

31 (−1)	15 (+1)	0 (0)	0 (0)	**East Midlands***	69.0 (+2.5)	50.7 (+7.3)	40.5 (+8.9)	4.3 (−1.3)	0 (0)	2.4 (−13.4)	1.5 (−1.5)	0.6 (0)
35 (+1)	24 (−1)	0 (0)	0 (0)	**West Midlands***	66.9 (+2.9)	49.0 (+7.3)	42.5 (+9.6)	4.4 (−1.1)	0 (0)	1.8 (−13.9)	1.7 (−1.6)	0.6 (−0.3)
8 (+1)	20 (−1)	0 (0)	0 (0)	W. Mids. Met. Co.	63.8 (+3.2)	39.9 (+6.8)	52.4 (+10.0)	3.7 (−1.8)	0 (0)	2.4 (−13.0)	1.2 (−1.6)	0.4 (−0.3)
27 (0)	4 (0)	0 (0)	0 (0)	Rest of W. Mids.	69.7 (+2.5)	56.4 (+7.8)	34.5 (+9.1)	5.0 (−0.5)	0 (0)	1.3 (−14.6)	2.0 (−1.5)	0.8 (−0.3)
17 (−2)	37 (+4)	0 (0)	0 (−2)	**Yorks & Humber***	66.4 (+3.1)	40.5 (+7.8)	49.0 (+9.9)	5.0 (−2.1)	0 (0)	2.6 (−13.4)	1.3 (−2.3)	1.7 (+0.2)
0 (0)	14 (+1)	0 (0)	0 (−1)	S. Yorks Met. Co.	63.0 (+2.5)	29.8 (+12.4)	56.9 (+7.5)	5.9 (−2.2)	0 (0)	4.7 (−16.1)	1.2 (−1.4)	1.5 (−0.1)
5 (−2)	17 (+3)	0 (0)	0 (−1)	W. Yorks Met. Co.	67.3 (+2.8)	37.8 (+5.1)	53.3 (+11.1)	4.0 (−2.4)	0 (0)	1.8 (−11.8)	1.0 (−2.6)	2.1 (+0.6)
12 (0)	6 (0)	0 (0)	0 (0)	Rest of Yorks & Humb	67.7 (+3.8)	51.4 (+7.9)	38.1 (+10.1)	5.5 (−1.7)	0 (0)	2.2 (−13.4)	1.5 (−2.6)	1.4 (−0.2)
17 (−3)	52 (+4)	0 (0)	0 (−1)	**North West**	67.6 (+3.4)	35.2 (+4.7)	56.4 (+10.5)	4.8 (−1.1)	0 (0)	1.9 (−11.8)	1.1 (−2)	0.6 (−0.2)
4 (−1)	23 (+1)	0 (0)	0 (0)	Gtr. Manc. Met. Co.	64.2 (+3.0)	32.5 (+6.2)	56.9 (+10.8)	6.1 (−1.0)	0 (0)	2.8 (−13.3)	1.0 (−2.6)	0.7 (−0.1)
1 (+1)	14 (0)	0 (0)	0 (−1)	Merseyside Met. Co.	69.8 (+4.0)	21.4 (+3.4)	71.2 (+9.5)	4.3 (−1.3)	0 (0)	1.1 (−9.3)	1.5 (−2.1)	0.6 (−0.2)
12 (−3)	15 (+3)	0 (0)	0 (0)	Rest of N.W.	69.8 (+3.6)	45.1 (+4.2)	48.0 (+10.7)	3.9 (−1.2)	0 (0)	1.5 (−11.8)	1.1 (−1.5)	0.4 (−0.4)
6 (+1)	28 (−1)	1 (0)	0 (0)	**North**	66.9 (+4.3)	36.9 (+8.9)	52.1 (+8.2)	5.8 (−1.9)	0 (0)	3.6 (−12.4)	1.1 (−2.5)	0.4 (−0.4)
0 (0)	12 (0)	0 (0)	0 (0)	Tyne and Wear Met. Co.	66.3 (+5.7)	28.5 (+8.2)	60.8 (+8.7)	4.0 (−1.5)	0 (0)	4.7 (−12.6)	1.6 (−2.5)	0.3 (−0.4)
6 (+1)	16 (−1)	1 (0)	0 (0)	Rest of North	67.1 (+5.5)	41.4 (+9.3)	47.4 (+7.9)	6.8 (−2.0)	0 (0)	3.0 (−12.4)	0.9 (−2.4)	0.5 (−0.3)
8 (−3)	28 (+3)	0 (−1)	4 (+1)	**Wales***	68.6 (+2.9)	33.6 (+6.3)	48.9 (+12.1)	4.5 (−2.0)	10.4 (−1.7)	2.0 (−11.6)	0.3 (−2.2)	0.2 (−0.8)
2 (−2)	22 (+2)	0 (0)	0 (0)	Industrial S. Wales	67.2 (+2.7)	30.4 (+6.4)	55.8 (+12.9)	2.8 (−2.4)	7.8 (−2.1)	2.5 (−11.8)	0.4 (−2.3)	0.2 (−0.7)
6 (−1)	6 (+1)	0 (−1)	4 (+1)	Rural Wales	70.9 (+3.2)	38.5 (+6.3)	38.0 (+10.9)	7.2 (−1.5)	14.6 (−1.2)	1.2 (−11.4)	0.2 (−2.2)	0.2 (−0.9)
13 (+12)	7 (+6)	4 (+3)	35 (−21)	**Scotland***	66.4 (−4.6)	28.6 (+13.7)	27.1 (+2.8)	6.8 (−0.8)	36.9 (−13.1)	0.2 (−1.4)	0.2 (−1.1)	0.3 (0)
4 (+3)	4 (+3)	0 (0)	3 (−3)	Ayrshire & Borders	67.4 (−5.8)	40.2 (+15.8)	21.5 (−0.8)	2.9 (−1.4)	35.3 (−11.4)	0.0 (−1.8)	0.0 (−0.6)	0.2 (+0.1)
1 (+1)	3 (+3)	1 (+1)	15 (−5)	Clydeside	64.0 (−4.9)	21.0 (+11.7)	34.5 (+3.5)	5.0 (+1.2)	38.4 (−14.7)	0.4 (−0.9)	0.4 (−0.6)	0.2 (−0.3)
3 (+2)	1 (+1)	1 (+1)	6 (−4)	Rest of Central Belt	69.0 (−3.7)	26.7 (+11.8)	31.7 (+3.6)	6.3 (+0.7)	34.5 (−12.2)	0.1 (−1.9)	0.5 (−2.1)	0.1 (0)
7 (+7)	1 (+1)	0 (0)	7 (−8)	N.E. & Fife	66.2 (−4.4)	34.9 (+15.7)	20.4 (+2.2)	6.6 (−2.0)	37.9 (−13.3)	0.1 (−1.3)	0 (−1.3)	0.1 (−0.1)
0 (0)	0 (0)	2 (+1)	4 (−1)	Highlands & Islands	69.4 (−4.2)	25.5 (+16.9)	14.8 (+5.4)	22.0 (−8.9)	36.3 (−10.5)	0.1 (−2.3)	0 (−1.1)	1.3 (+0.5)
0 (0)	0 (0)	0 (0)	18 (0)	**Northern Ireland**	65.4 (+7.3)	0.5 (−0.8)	0 (0)	0 (0)	0 (0)	0 (−2.6)	0.9 (0.9)	98.6 (+3.4)

Notes: The English Regions are the eight *Standard Regions*, now obsolete but used by the OPCS until the 1990s

The *Outer Metropolitan Area* compromises those seats wholly or mostly in the Outer Metropolitan Area as defined by the OPCS. It includes: the whole of Surrey and Hertfordshire; the whole of Berkshire except Newbury; and the constituencies of Bedfordshire South West; Luton North; Luton South (Bedfordshire); Beaconsfield; Chesham & Amersham; Wycombe (Buckinghamshire); Basildon South & Billericay; Basildon South & East Thurrock; Brentwood & Ongar; Castle Point; Chelmsford; Epping Forest; Harlow; Rayleigh & Wickford; Rochford & Southend East; Southend West; Thurrock (Essex); Aldershot; Hampshire North East (Hampshire); Chatham & Aylesford; Dartford; Faversham & Kent Mid; Gillingham & Rainham; Gravesham; Maidstone & The Weald; Rochester & Strood; Sevenoaks; Tonbridge & Malling; Tunbridge Wells (Kent); Arundel & South Downs; Crawley; Horsham; Sussex Mid (West Sussex)

Industrial Wales (a description no longer entirely accurate but used for continuity with previous volumes) includes Gwent, the whole of Glamorgan, and the Llanelli constituency in Dyfed

Ayrshire & Borders comprises: Ayr, Carrick & Cumnock; Ayrshire Central; Ayrshire North & Arran; Berwickshire, Roxburgh & Selkirk; Dumfries & Galloway; Dumfriesshire, Clydesdale & Tweeddale; and Kilmarnock & Loudoun

Clydeside includes all Glasgow seats, both Dunbartonshire seats, both Paisley & Renfrewshire seats, plus Airdrie & Shotts; Coatbridge, Chryston & Bellshill; Cumbernauld, Kilsyth & Kirkintilloch East; East Kilbride, Strathaven & Lesmahagow; Inverclyde; Lanark & Hamilton East; Motherwell & Wishaw; Renfrewshire East; and Hamilton West

Rest of Central Belt includes all Edinburgh seats, plus East Lothian; Falkirk; Linlithgow & East Falkirk; Livingston; Midlothian; and Stirling

N.E. & Fife includes both Aberdeen seats, both Dundee seats, plus Aberdeenshire West & Kincardine; Angus; Banff & Buchan; Dunfermline & West Fife; Fife North East; Glenrothes; Gordon; Kirkcaldy & Cowdenbeath; Moray; Ochil & South Perthshire; and Perth & North Perthshire

Highlands & Islands includes Argyll & Bute; Caithness, Sutherland & Easter Ross; Inverness, Nairn, Badenoch & Strathspey; Na h-Eileanan an Iar; Orkney & Shetland; and Ross, Skye & Lochaber

In all but four cases, the European constituencies are covered in the table above. These constituencies are indicated with an asterisk (*). The results for the four other European constituencies are:

Seats won in 2017 (change since 2015)					Share of votes cast in 2017 (change since 2015)							
Con	*Lab*	*LD*	*Nat & Other*		*Turnout*	*Con*	*Lab*	*Lib Dem*	*Nat*	*UKIP*	*Green*	*Other*
50 (−2)	7 (+3)	1 (0)	0 (−1)	**Eastern**	69.8 (+2.3)	54.6 (+5.6)	32.7 (+10.7)	7.9 (−0.4)	0 (0)	2.5 (−13.7)	1.9 (−2.0)	0.3 (−0.2)
3 (0)	26 (0)	0 (0)	0 (0)	**North East**	66.0 (+4.3)	34.4 (+9.1)	55.4 (+8.6)	4.6 (−1.9)	0 (0)	3.9 (−12.9)	1.3 (−2.4)	0.5 (−0.5)
20 (−2)	54 (+3)	1 (−1)	0 (0)	**North West**	67.8 (+3.5)	36.2 (+5.0)	54.9 (+10.2)	5.4 (−1.2)	0 (0)	1.9 (−11.7)	1.1 (−2.1)	0.5 (−0.2)
73 (−6)	8 (+4)	2 (+2)	1 (0)	**South East**	71.2 (+2.6)	54.6 (+2.9)	28.6 (+10.3)	10.5 (+1.1)	0 (0)	2.3 (−12.5)	3.1 (−2.1)	1.0 (+0.2)

Table A2.5 Constituency results

These tables list the votes in each constituency in percentage terms

In England and Wales, the constituencies are listed alphabetically within counties, as defined in 1974. The figure in the 'Other' column is the total percentage received by all other candidates than the parties listed in the table

*Denotes a seat won by different parties in 2015 and 2017

†Denotes a seat that changed hands in a by-election between 2015 and 2017

‡Denotes a seat held by the Speaker in 2015 and 2017

The table provides a figure for the change in the share of the vote only where candidates from a party stood in *both* 2015 and 2017

Swing is given in the conventional (total vote or 'Butler') form—the average of the Conservative % gain (or loss) and the Labour % loss (or gain) (measured as % of the total poll). It is only reported for seats where those parties occupied the top two places in 2015 and 2017. This is the practice followed by previous books in this series since 1955

503

ENGLAND	Turnout %	Turnout +/-	Con %	Con +/-	Lab %	Lab +/-	LD %	LD +/-	UKIP %	UKIP +/-	Grn %	Grn +/-	Other No & %	Swing
Avon, Bath*	74.3	−0.5	35.8	−2.0	14.7	+1.5	47.3	+17.6	–	–	2.3	−9.7	–	–
Bristol East	70.1	+5.2	34.4	+3.7	60.7	+21.5	2.7	−3.1	–	–	2.2	−6.1	–	−8.9
Bristol North West*	71.7	+2.4	41.8	−2.1	50.7	+16.2	5.2	−1.0	–	–	2.3	−3.4	–	−9.2
Bristol South	65.5	+3.1	30.7	+6.3	60.1	+21.7	3.3	−5.3	3.1	−13.4	2.6	−8.9	1 (0.2)	−7.7
Bristol West	77.0	+6.6	13.8	−1.4	65.9	+30.3	7.3	−11.6	–	–	12.9	−14.0	1 (0.1)	–
Filton & Bradley Stoke	70.0	+1.1	50.0	+3.3	41.7	+15.1	6.0	−1.3	–	–	2.3	−2.3	–	−5.9
Kingswood	70.3	−0.3	54.9	+6.6	39.5	+9.9	3.6	−0.2	–	–	2.0	−0.8	–	−1.7
Somerset North	77.0	+3.5	54.2	+0.7	26.6	+12.3	9.6	−3.1	–	–	3.2	−3.3	1 (6.3)	−5.8
Somerset North East	75.7	+2.1	53.6	+3.9	34.7	+9.9	8.3	+0.4	–	–	2.3	−3.2	1 (1.1)	−3.0
Thornbury & Yate	74.7	+1.1	55.3	+14.2	12.1	+4.3	31.4	−6.5	–	–	1.2	−1.5	–	–
Weston-Super-Mare	68.7	+3.2	53.1	+5.2	32.7	+14.4	9.2	−1.3	3.4	−14.4	1.6	−3.4	–	−4.6
Bedfordshire, Bedford*	67.5	+1.0	45.2	+2.6	46.8	+6.6	5.9	+1.6	–	–	2.1	−1.0	–	−2.0
Bedfordshire Mid	75.0	+1.1	61.7	+5.6	28.4	+12.6	6.0	−1.2	–	–	2.8	−1.4	1 (1.1)	−3.5
Bedfordshire North East	73.4	+3.2	60.9	+1.5	28.5	+12.7	5.8*	−0.1	3.0	−11.7	1.9	−2.4	–	−5.6
Bedfordshire South West	69.8	+5.1	59.2	+4.3	33.8	+13.5	4.7	−0.4	–	–	1.7	−2.4	1 (0.5)	−4.6
Luton North	69.8	+6.6	33.0	+3.1	63.8	+11.6	1.7	−1.3	–	–	1.4	−0.9	–	−4.2
Luton South	68.7	+6.3	32.3	+1.6	62.4	+18.2	2.3	−5.3	1.7	−10.4	1.0	−2.0	1 (0.3)	−8.3
Berkshire, Bracknell	70.6	+5.3	58.8	+3.1	30.2	+13.3	7.5	0.0	2.7	−13.0	–	–	1 (0.8)	−5.1
Maidenhead	76.6	+4.0	64.8	−1.1	19.3	+7.5	11.2	+1.3	1.5	−6.9	1.6	−2.0	8 (1.6)	−4.3
Newbury	73.4	+1.3	61.5	+0.4	14.1	+5.7	21.4	+6.4	–	–	2.5	−1.5	1 (0.5)	–
Reading East*	73.1	+4.2	42.3	−3.7	49.0	+16.0	6.1	−1.2	–	–	2.0	−4.4	2 (0.6)	−9.8
Reading West	69.5	+2.8	48.9	+1.2	43.3	+9.4	5.9	+1.0	–	–	1.9	−1.0	–	−4.1
Slough	65.2	+9.3	31.6	−1.7	62.9	+14.4	2.4	−0.2	2.3	−10.7	–	–	1 (0.8)	−8.1
Windsor	73.3	+3.2	64.4	+1.0	22.9	+9.5	10.1	+1.5	–	–	2.7	−1.0	–	−4.2
Wokingham	75.5	+3.5	56.6	−1.1	25.1	+10.6	15.9	+2.4	–	–	2.3	−1.5	–	−5.9

Buckinghamshire, Aylesbury	71.2	+2.2	55.0	+4.3	30.0	+14.9	9.6	-1.0	2.2	-17.5	2.1	-1.7	1 (1.1)	–
Beaconsfield	72.3	+1.1	65.3	+2.0	21.4	+10.0	7.9	+0.6	2.9	-10.9	2.5	-1.7	–	–
Buckingham‡	66.2	-3.2	65.1	–	–	–	–	–	7.9	-13.8	16.3	+2.5	1 (10.7)	–
Chesham & Amersham	77.1	+4.4	60.7	+1.6	20.6	+7.9	13.0	+4.0	2.8	-10.9	3.0	-2.5	–	-6.9
Milton Keynes North	71.7	+5.2	47.5	+0.3	44.4	+14.1	3.9	-2.3	2.2	-9.7	1.7	-2.2	1 (0.3)	-6.0
Milton Keynes South	69.8	+4.0	47.5	+0.7	44.9	+12.7	2.9	-1.0	2.8	-10.4	1.8	-1.5	–	-8.3
Wycombe	69.4	+2.0	50.0	-1.4	37.7	+15.2	7.8	-1.1	2.3	-7.8	2.2	-3.8	–	–
Cambridgeshire, Cambridge	71.2	+9.1	16.3	+0.7	51.9	+15.9	29.3	-5.6	–	–	2.3	-5.7	1 (0.2)	–
Cambridgeshire North East	63.1	+0.7	64.4	+9.4	24.5	+10.1	4.5	0.0	4.1	-18.4	1.9	-1.6	1 (0.5)	–
Cambridgeshire North West	68.6	+1.0	58.6	+6.2	30.5	+12.6	5.0	-0.7	3.9	-16.2	2.0	-1.6	–	–
Cambridgeshire South	76.2	+3.0	51.8	+0.7	27.2	+9.6	18.6	+3.4	–	–	2.3	-3.9	–	-4.4
Cambridgeshire South East	73.2	+2.8	53.3	+4.9	27.7	+12.5	19.0	-1.2	–	–	–	–	–	–
Huntingdon	70.9	+3.2	55.1	+2.1	30.9	+12.6	8.5	+0.7	3.7	-13.3	1.8	-2.1	–	-5.2
Peterborough*	66.7	+1.8	46.8	+7.1	48.1	+12.5	3.3	-0.4	–	–	1.8	-0.8	–	-2.7
Cheshire, Chester, City of	77.4	+8.8	40.5	-2.6	56.8	+13.5	2.7	-2.9	–	–	–	–	–	-8.0
Congleton	73.3	+3.0	56.6	+3.3	34.2	+13.8	5.2	-3.9	2.3	-11.3	1.8	-1.9	–	-5.2
Crewe & Nantwich*	69.7	+2.5	47.0	+2.0	47.1	+9.4	2.4	-0.3	3.4	-11.1	–	–	–	-3.7
Eddisbury	73.0	+4.0	56.9	+5.8	33.6	+10.0	5.5	-3.6	2.2	-10.0	1.5	-1.9	1 (0.3)	-2.1
Ellesmere Port & Neston	74.2	+6.7	36.8	+2.5	59.2	+11.4	1.8	-1.6	1.6	-10.4	0.7	-1.4	–	-4.5
Halton	67.4	+5.6	21.6	+3.8	72.9	+10.1	1.8	-0.6	3.0	-11.1	–	–	1 (0.6)	-3.1
Macclesfield	72.2	+3.0	52.7	+0.1	36.8	+14.1	6.2	-1.6	–	–	2.2	-2.6	1 (2.1)	-7.0
Tatton	72.4	+2.7	58.6	-0.1	28.5	+10.1	9.0	+0.5	–	–	2.1	-1.7	1 (1.9)	-5.1
Warrington North	67.5	+4.5	36.6	+8.5	56.4	+8.6	2.5	-1.7	3.2	-13.9	1.3	-1.5	1 (2)	-0.1
Warrington South*	72.4	+2.4	44.3	+0.6	48.4	+9.3	5.4	-0.2	–	–	–	–	–	-4.4
Weaver Vale*	73.3	+4.8	43.7	+0.6	51.5	+10.1	3.2	+0.2	–	–	1.6	-1.0	–	-4.7
Cleveland, Hartlepool	59.2	+2.7	34.2	+13.3	52.5	+16.9	1.8	-0.1	11.5	-16.5	–	–	–	–
Middlesbrough	58.4	+5.5	26.7	+10.3	65.7	+8.9	1.0	-2.7	4.1	-14.6	0.7	-3.6	1 (1.8)	–
Middlesbrough South & Cleveland East*	65.8	+1.6	49.6	+12.6	47.5	+5.5	2.8	-0.6	–	–	–	–	–	3.6
Redcar	63.7	+0.6	33.2	+17.0	55.5	+11.6	6.7	-11.8	4.6	-13.8	–	–	–	–

ENGLAND	Turnout %	Turnout +/-	Con %	Con +/-	Lab %	Lab +/-	LD %	LD +/-	UKIP %	UKIP +/-	Grn %	Grn +/-	Other No & %	Swing
Stockton North	64.5	+4.6	36.5	+8.5	56.9	+7.8	1.5	-0.7	4.3	-14.9	0.8	–	–	0.4
Stockton South*	71.2	+2.2	46.8	+0.1	48.5	+11.5	1.8	-0.9	2.2	-8.4	0.7	-1.1	–	-5.7
Cornwall, Camborne & Redruth	70.8	+2.3	47.5	+7.2	44.2	+19.3	6.1	-6.3	–	–	2.2	-3.5	–	-6.0
Cornwall North	74.0	+2.2	50.7	+5.8	12.1	+6.6	36.6	+5.3	–	–	–	–	2 (0.6)	–
Cornwall South East	74.0	+3.0	55.4	+4.9	22.6	+13.3	19.4	+2.6	–	–	2.5	-2.9	–	–
St Austell & Newquay	69.0	+3.2	49.5	+9.3	29.0	+18.8	21.5	-2.5	–	–	–	–	–	–
St Ives	76.3	+2.6	43.2	+4.9	14.2	+4.9	42.6	+9.4	–	–	–	–	–	–
Truro & Falmouth	75.8	+5.8	44.4	+0.3	37.7	+22.5	14.9	-1.9	1.6	-10.0	1.5	-7.2	–	–
Cumbria, Barrow & Furness	68.5	+5.2	47.0	+6.5	47.5	+5.1	2.7	0.0	2.0	-9.7	0.8	-1.7	–	0.7
Carlisle	69.1	+4.4	49.9	+5.6	43.8	+6.0	2.9	+0.4	3.4	-9.0	–	–	–	-0.2
Copeland†	69.5	+5.7	49.1	+13.3	45.1	+2.9	3.3	-0.2	2.5	-13.0	–	–	–	5.2
Penrith & The Border	71.3	+4.0	60.4	+0.8	26.2	+11.8	7.8	-0.7	2.5	-9.7	2.2	-3.1	1 (0.9)	-5.5
Westmorland & Lonsdale	77.9	+3.6	44.3	+11.1	9.3	+3.8	45.8	-5.7	–	–	–	–	1 (0.6)	–
Workington	69.2	+3.5	41.7	+11.6	51.1	+8.8	2.7	-1.7	3.7	-15.9	–	–	1 (0.7)	1.4
Derbyshire, Amber Valley	67.3	+1.5	56.5	+12.6	38.4	+3.6	2.4	-0.6	4.6	-16.4	1.4	-1.0	1 (1.2)	4.5
Bolsover	63.4	+2.2	40.6	+16.1	51.9	+0.7	2.9	-0.4	4.6	-13.1	–	–	–	7.7
Chesterfield	66.5	+2.9	34.8	+16.7	54.8	+6.9	5.4	-8.4	3.4	-12.2	1.6	-1.3	–	4.9
Derby North*	69.6	+5.5	44.4	+7.7	48.5	+12.0	4.6	-3.9	2.4	-11.1	–	–	–	-2.1
Derby South	64.8	+6.7	33.5	+6.1	58.3	+9.3	2.7	-1.5	4.4	–	1.0	-2.0	1 (0.6)	-1.6
Derbyshire Dales	76.9	+2.3	60.0	+7.6	31.1	+8.4	6.3	-2.1	–	–	2.0	-2.6	–	-0.4
Derbyshire Mid	74.7	+3.9	58.6	+6.4	35.5	+10.1	3.6	-1.2	–	–	2.3	-1.7	–	-1.9
Derbyshire North East*	69.9	+2.8	49.2	+12.5	43.5	+2.9	2.8	-1.4	3.1	-12.8	1.4	-0.8	–	4.8
Derbyshire South	68.9	+0.2	58.7	+9.4	36.0	+9.2	3.6	-0.2	–	–	1.7	-0.7	–	0.1
Erewash	68.2	+1.0	52.1	+7.9	43.0	+7.7	2.5	-0.9	–	–	1.4	-1.1	1 (1)	0.8
High Peak*	73.5	+4.3	45.4	+0.4	49.7	+14.4	5.0	+0.3	–	–	–	–	–	-7.0
Devon, Devon Central	77.8	+2.9	54.1	+1.8	27.0	+14.1	11.7	-0.5	2.3	-10.9	2.6	-6.3	2 (2.3)	–
Devon East	73.3	+1.8	48.5	+2.1	11.4	+1.1	2.4	-4.4	2.0	-10.6	–	–	3 (35.7)	–
Devon North	73.5	+3.5	45.8	+3.1	12.7	+5.6	38.0	+8.6	2.1	-12.6	1.4	-4.4	–	–
Devon South West	74.2	+3.3	59.8	+3.3	29.9	+13.3	5.2	-2.3	2.9	-11.6	2.1	-2.6	–	-5.0
Devon West & Torridge	73.9	+1.9	56.5	+5.7	21.7	+11.1	17.7	+4.5	–	–	2.7	-4.2	1 (1.3)	–
Exeter	71.7	+1.5	32.9	-0.2	62.0	+15.6	2.8	-1.5	–	–	1.9	-4.6	2 (0.5)	-7.9

Newton Abbot	72.0	+3.0	55.5	+8.2	22.2	+12.4	20.5	-3.4	-	-	1.8	-2.8	-	-
Plymouth Moor View	65.5	+3.1	51.9	+14.3	40.8	+5.6	2.0	-0.9	4.1	-17.4	1.2	-1.2	-	4.3
Plymouth Sutton & Devonport*	66.9	+1.4	40.0	+2.2	53.3	+16.6	2.4	-1.8	2.7	-11.4	1.2	-5.9	1 (0.5)	-7.2
Tiverton & Honiton	71.6	+1.1	61.4	+7.4	27.1	+14.4	8.0	-2.4	-	-	3.5	-2.8	-	-
Torbay	67.4	+4.4	53.0	+12.4	18.2	+9.5	25.1	-8.7	2.4	-11.2	1.3	-2.0	-	-
Totnes	72.9	+4.3	53.7	+0.7	26.8	+14.1	12.9	+3.0	2.5	-11.7	4.2	-6.1	-	-
Dorset, Bournemouth East	65.2	+3.2	51.9	+2.7	35.6	+18.9	6.5	-1.9	2.9	-13.6	2.5	-4.7	1 (0.6)	-8.1
Bournemouth West	60.8	+2.9	53.5	+5.3	36.2	+18.5	6.6	-1.3	-	-	2.8	-4.6	1 (0.9)	-
Christchurch	72.0	+0.3	69.6	+11.5	19.9	+10.3	7.9	+1.4	-	-	2.6	-1.7	-	-
Dorset Mid & Poole North	74.2	+1.9	59.2	+8.4	13.3	+7.4	27.5	-0.7	-	-	-	-	-	-
Dorset North	73.0	+0.6	64.9	+8.3	18.6	+9.7	13.6	+1.9	-	-	2.9	-2.8	-	-
Dorset South	68.7	+0.8	56.1	+7.2	33.6	+9.4	5.9	-0.1	-	-	4.4	-0.3	-	-1.1
Dorset West	75.4	+3.0	55.5	+5.3	18.3	+8.3	23.5	+1.9	-	-	2.7	-3.0	-	-
Poole	67.6	+2.2	57.9	+7.8	29.4	+16.6	8.9	-2.9	-	-	2.6	-2.0	1 (1.1)	-
Durham, Bishop Auckland	64.0	+4.4	46.9	+14.4	48.1	+6.7	2.7	-1.7	-	-	-	-	1 (2.3)	3.9
Darlington	67.6	+5.1	43.3	+8.1	50.6	+7.7	2.3	-2.5	2.6	-10.5	1.2	-2.3	-	0.2
Durham, City of	67.9	+1.5	29.8	+7.6	55.4	+8.1	9.9	-1.4	2.3	-9.1	1.6	-4.2	2 (0.9)	-0.3
Durham North	64.6	+3.2	30.0	+9.1	59.9	+5.0	4.6	-0.5	5.6	-10.4	-	-	-	2.0
Durham North West	66.6	+5.3	34.5	+11.1	52.8	+6.0	7.1	-2.0	4.5	-12.5	1.1	-2.6	-	2.6
Easington	58.3	+2.1	22.7	+9.8	63.7	+2.6	1.3	-1.1	4.7	-14.0	1.1	-1.0	1 (6.5)	-
Sedgefield	65.1	+3.5	38.8	+9.3	53.4	+6.2	1.9	-1.6	4.2	-12.4	1.6	-1.5	-	1.6
East Sussex, Bexhill & Battle	73.1	+3.0	62.0	+7.2	24.7	+10.6	7.5	-0.1	3.4	-15.0	2.4	-2.7	-	-
Brighton Kemptown*	72.5	+5.7	38.3	-2.4	58.3	+19.2	3.0	-0.1	-	-	-	-	1 (0.4)	-10.8
Brighton Pavilion	76.4	+5.0	19.2	-3.6	26.8	-0.5	-	-	1.1	-3.9	52.3	+10.4	1 (0.7)	-
Eastbourne*	72.9	+5.3	44.1	+4.5	8.1	+0.3	46.9	+8.7	-	-	0.9	-1.7	-	-
Hastings & Rye	69.9	+2.1	46.9	+2.3	46.2	+11.1	3.4	+0.3	2.7	-10.6	-	-	1 (0.8)	-4.4
Hove	77.6	+6.6	31.6	-8.4	64.1	+21.8	2.3	-1.3	-	-	1.7	-5.1	1 (0.3)	-15.1
Lewes	76.4	+3.7	49.5	+11.5	11.2	+1.3	39.3	+3.5	-	-	-	-	-	-
Wealden	74.3	+3.2	61.2	+4.2	22.2	+11.3	10.4	+1.3	3.0	-13.8	3.2	-3.1	-	-

ENGLAND	Turnout %	Turnout +/-	Con %	Con +/-	Lab %	Lab +/-	LD %	LD +/-	UKIP %	UKIP +/-	Grn %	Grn +/-	Other No & %	Swing
Essex, Basildon & Billericay	65.0	+0.1	61.0	+8.3	31.1	+7.5	3.4	-0.4	4.5	-15.4	-	-	-	0.4
Basildon South & Thurrock East	64.1	0.0	56.9	+13.5	32.5	+7.3	1.6	-1.4	6.8	-19.8	1.4	-	1 (0.8)	-
Braintree	69.5	+1.1	62.8	+9.0	27.6	+9.1	4.3	-0.6	3.5	-15.3	1.8	-1.4	-	-
Brentwood & Ongar	70.5	-1.7	65.8	+7.0	20.4	+7.9	8.4	-0.5	3.5	-13.3	1.7	-1.0	1 (0.2)	-
Castle Point	64.4	-2.3	67.3	+16.4	25.1	+11.2	2.3	+0.6	5.3	-25.9	-	-	-	-
Chelmsford	70.2	+1.7	53.7	+2.2	29.8	+12.2	12.2	+0.3	2.9	-11.3	1.4	-2.1	-	-5.0
Clacton*	64.4	+0.3	61.2	+24.6	25.4	+11.0	2.0	+0.2	7.6	-36.8	1.6	-1.0	3 (2.1)	-
Colchester	66.9	+1.4	45.9	+6.9	35.3	+19.1	17.0	-10.5	-	-	1.5	-3.6	1 (0.3)	-
Epping Forest	67.9	+0.8	62.0	+7.2	26.0	+9.9	5.7	-1.3	3.7	-14.7	2.4	-1.2	1 (0.2)	-
Harlow	66.2	+1.2	54.0	+5.2	38.4	+8.4	2.2	+0.1	4.0	-12.3	1.5	-0.7	-	-1.6
Harwich & Essex North	71.7	+1.8	58.5	+7.5	30.4	+10.7	5.4	-1.9	3.3	-14.2	2.0	-2.3	1 (0.3)	-1.6
Maldon	70.2	+0.7	67.9	+7.4	21.3	+9.4	4.3	-0.1	3.8	-10.9	2.1	-1.0	1 (0.5)	-
Rayleigh & Wickford	70.4	+1.5	66.7	+12.1	24.3	+11.7	2.8	-0.2	4.2	-18.1	1.9	-1.0	-	-
Rochford & Southend East	64.3	+3.7	48.7	+2.3	37.0	+12.3	2.7	-0.7	3.8	-16.8	1.7	-3.3	1 (6.2)	-5.0
Saffron Walden	73.3	+1.9	61.8	+4.6	20.8	+9.0	14.0	+3.4	3.4	-10.4	-	-	-	-
Southend West	69.7	+3.2	55.2	+5.4	34.0	+15.7	4.5	-4.8	3.5	-14.0	1.8	-2.9	2 (1.0)	-5.2
Thurrock	64.4	+0.5	39.5	+5.8	38.8	+6.2	1.6	+0.3	20.1	-11.6	-	-	-	-0.2
Witham	71.2	+0.9	64.3	+6.8	26.4	+10.6	5.5	-0.6	-	-	3.7	-0.6	-	-
Gloucestershire, Cheltenham	72.3	+2.8	46.7	+0.5	9.5	+2.2	42.2	+8.2	-	-	1.7	-3.4	-	-
Cotswolds, The	74.2	+1.8	60.6	+4.1	17.9	+8.7	16.3	-2.3	2.0	-8.9	2.9	-1.7	1 (0.2)	-
Forest of Dean	73.0	+2.1	54.3	+7.4	35.9	+11.3	3.9	-1.4	2.4	-15.4	2.4	-3.1	1 (1.1)	-1.9
Gloucester	65.2	+1.8	50.3	+5.0	40.1	+8.6	5.0	-0.4	2.8	-11.5	1.4	-1.4	1 (0.4)	-1.8
Stroud*	77.0	+1.5	45.9	+0.2	47.0	+9.3	3.2	-0.2	1.6	-6.3	2.2	-2.3	-	-4.5
Tewkesbury	72.5	+2.4	60.0	+5.5	21.8	+7.0	13.5	-0.3	2.0	-10.8	2.7	-1.3	-	-0.7
Greater London, Barking	61.9	+3.7	22.5	+6.2	67.8	+10.1	1.3	0.0	6.4	-15.8	1.5	-0.6	1 (0.6)	-
Battersea*	71.0	+3.9	41.5	-10.8	45.9	+9.1	8.0	+3.6	0.6	-2.5	1.6	-1.7	2 (2.3)	-10.0
Beckenham	76.0	+3.6	59.3	+2.0	30.1	+10.7	7.9	+1.0	-	-	2.7	-1.2	-	-4.3
Bermondsey & Old Southwark	67.0	+5.3	13.0	+1.2	53.2	+10.2	31.1	-3.3	1.4	-4.9	1.1	-2.8	1 (0.2)	-

Constituency														
Bethnal Green & Bow	69.5	+5.5	12.7	−2.6	71.8	+10.6	5.0	+0.5	1.5	−4.6	2.5	−6.7	1 (6.5)	−6.6
Bexleyheath & Crayford	69.2	+1.8	55.6	+8.3	35.5	+9.3	2.7	−0.3	4.3	−16.7	1.3	−0.8	1 (0.6)	−0.5
Brent Central	65.0	+3.9	19.5	−0.8	73.1	+10.9	4.8	−3.6	1.1	−2.9	1.5	−2.5	–	−5.9
Brent North	68.4	+4.8	32.7	−0.9	62.9	+8.6	2.9	−2.1	–	–	1.2	−1.8	1 (0.4)	−4.7
Brentford & Isleworth	72.4	+4.6	37.6	−5.3	57.4	+13.6	5.0	+1.0	3.0	–	–	–	–	−9.5
Bromley & Chislehurst	71.7	+4.4	54.0	+1.0	33.4	+11.2	7.2	+0.8	–	−11.3	2.5	−1.7	–	−5.1
Camberwell & Peckham	67.1	+4.7	12.8	−0.4	77.8	+14.5	5.9	+0.9	–	–	2.8	−7.2	2 (0.6)	−7.5
Carshalton & Wallington	71.6	+3.6	38.3	+6.6	18.4	+3.4	41.0	+6.1	1.2	–	1.0	−2.1	2 (1.2)	–
Chelsea & Fulham	66.1	+2.7	52.6	−10.3	33.2	+10.1	11.0	+5.8	–	−3.8	1.9	−1.7	–	−10.2
Chingford & Woodford Green	71.2	+5.5	49.1	+1.2	43.9	+15.2	4.4	−1.1	–	–	2.6	−1.7	–	−7.0
Chipping Barnet	71.8	+3.6	46.3	−2.3	45.7	+11.5	5.4	+0.9	1.1	–	2.5	−2.2	–	−6.9
Cities of London & Westminster	62.8	+3.5	46.6	−7.5	38.4	+11.1	11.0	+4.1	1.8	−4.1	2.1	−3.3	3 (0.7)	−9.3
Croydon Central*	71.3	+3.6	42.4	−0.6	52.3	+9.7	1.9	−0.3	1.3	−7.3	1.1	−1.6	2 (0.4)	−5.1
Croydon North	68.2	+5.9	19.9	−2.8	74.2	+11.5	2.8	−0.8	1.8	−4.2	1.6	−3.1	1 (0.3)	−7.2
Croydon South	73.3	+3.0	54.4	−0.1	35.8	+11.0	5.8	−0.2	7.1	−8.7	1.8	−1.9	1 (0.3)	−5.5
Dagenham & Rainham	64.9	+2.6	39.9	+15.6	50.1	+8.7	1.0	−0.7	–	−22.8	1.2	−0.7	2 (0.7)	–
Dulwich & West Norwood	71.9	+4.9	19.5	−3.2	69.6	+15.6	8.0	−1.9	–	–	2.5	−6.9	2 (0.4)	−9.4
Ealing Central & Acton	74.6	+3.3	34.7	−7.9	59.7	+16.5	5.6	−0.5	1.8	–	–	–	–	−12.2
Ealing North	70.2	+4.6	28.5	−1.3	66.0	+10.8	2.4	−0.8	1.1	−6.3	1.4	−2.0	–	−6.0
Ealing Southall	69.3	+3.2	21.3	−0.3	70.3	+5.3	4.2	+0.6	1.2	−3.0	2.3	−2.3	1 (0.8)	−2.8
East Ham	67.5	+7.6	12.8	+0.7	83.2	+5.6	1.2	−0.5	2.0	−3.8	0.8	−1.6	2 (0.8)	−2.5
Edmonton	66.4	+3.8	23.1	−1.0	71.5	+10.1	2.0	−0.2	–	−6.2	1.4	−1.8	–	−5.5
Eltham	71.6	+4.2	40.8	+4.4	54.4	+11.8	3.2	+0.1	1.7	–	–	–	1 (1.6)	−3.7
Enfield North	71.3	+3.6	36.9	−4.4	58.0	+14.3	2.1	−0.2	–	−7.2	1.2	−1.6	–	−9.4
Enfield Southgate*	74.1	+3.6	42.7	−6.7	51.7	+12.7	4.0	+0.7	3.9	–	1.6	−2.1	–	−9.7
Erith & Thamesmead	63.8	+3.2	35.0	+7.6	57.5	+7.8	1.7	−0.6	2.8	−13.4	1.1	−1.1	2 (0.7)	−0.1
Feltham & Heston	64.9	+4.9	31.8	+2.7	61.2	+8.9	2.6	−0.6	0.9	−9.7	1.5	−1.3	–	−3.1
Finchley & Golders Green	71.4	+1.5	47.0	−3.9	43.8	+4.1	6.6	+3.3	–	−2.5	1.8	−0.9	–	−4.0
Greenwich & Woolwich	68.8	+5.1	25.4	−1.2	64.4	+12.2	7.1	+1.5	–	–	3.0	−3.4	–	−6.7

ENGLAND	Turnout %	Turnout +/-	Con %	Con +/-	Lab %	Lab +/-	LD %	LD +/-	UKIP %	UKIP +/-	Grn %	Grn +/-	Other No & %	Swing
Hackney North & Stoke Newington	66.2	+9.6	12.7	-2.1	75.1	+12.2	6.8	+1.8	—	—	4.6	-10.0	3 (0.9)	-7.1
Hackney South & Shoreditch	66.6	+10.6	10.9	-2.6	79.4	+15.1	5.7	+1.1	—	—	2.7	-8.8	6 (1.2)	-8.8
Hammersmith	71.8	+5.4	28.2	-8.2	63.9	+13.9	5.4	+0.7	1.0	-3.4	1.5	-2.9	1 (0.1)	-11.1
Hampstead & Kilburn	70.4	+3.1	32.4	-10.0	59.0	+14.6	7.0	+1.4	—	—	1.3	-3.2	2 (0.3)	-12.3
Harrow East	70.9	+1.8	49.4	-0.9	46.0	+5.3	3.1	+1.0	—	—	1.5	-0.2	—	-3.1
Harrow West	72.1	+5.2	34.4	-7.8	60.8	+13.9	2.5	-0.8	0.9	-3.5	1.3	-1.5	—	-10.9
Hayes & Harlington	65.2	+5.1	28.6	+3.9	66.5	+6.9	1.3	-0.7	2.4	-9.5	1.2	-0.6	—	-1.5
Hendon	68.2	+2.3	48.0	-1.0	46.0	+4.5	3.8	+1.6	1.1	-4.1	1.1	-0.9	—	-2.7
Holborn & St Pancras	67.0	+3.7	18.4	-3.5	70.1	+17.2	6.8	+0.3	1.2	-3.8	3.4	-9.4	1 (0.2)	-10.3
Hornchurch & Upminster	69.4	-0.3	60.2	+11.2	28.6	+8.5	2.4	-0.3	6.2	-19.1	1.9	-0.6	1 (0.6)	—
Hornsey & Wood Green	77.9	+5.0	14.8	+5.6	65.4	+14.5	16.1	-15.7	0.7	-1.5	1.9	-3.5	3 (1.1)	—
Ilford North	72.5	+7.5	39.6	-3.1	57.8	+13.9	2.0	-0.4	—	—	—	—	1 (0.7)	-8.5
Ilford South	67.5	+11.1	20.9	-5.0	75.8	+11.8	1.3	-0.6	0.8	-4.4	0.9	-2.0	1 (0.1)	-8.4
Islington North	73.4	+6.3	12.5	-4.7	73.0	+12.7	9.0	+0.9	0.8	-3.3	4.1	-6.2	5 (0.7)	-8.7
Islington South & Finsbury	69.1	+4.1	20.7	-1.6	62.8	+11.9	12.1	+1.2	1.9	-5.7	2.5	-5.1	—	-6.7
Kensington*	63.8	+6.9	42.2	-10.1	42.2	+11.1	12.2	+6.6	—	—	2.0	-3.1	3 (1.4)	-10.6
Kingston & Surbiton*	76.2	+3.3	38.1	-1.1	14.8	+0.3	44.7	+10.3	1.1	-6.2	0.9	-3.1	2 (0.4)	—
Lewisham Deptford	70.2	+5.6	13.7	-1.2	77.0	+16.8	5.3	0.0	—	—	3.0	-9.5	3 (1.0)	-9.0
Lewisham East	69.3	+5.1	23.0	+0.7	67.9	+12.3	4.4	-1.3	1.7	-7.4	1.7	-4.0	3 (1.2)	-5.8
Lewisham West & Penge	73.0	+6.4	23.0	-1.1	66.6	+16.0	6.2	-1.5	1.3	-6.5	2.2	-6.3	2 (0.7)	-8.6
Leyton & Wanstead	70.9	+7.8	20.8	-1.1	69.8	+11.2	6.4	+0.8	—	—	2.9	-4.4	—	-6.2
Mitcham & Morden	70.0	+4.1	24.2	+1.1	68.7	+8.0	3.1	+0.1	2.2	-7.3	1.3	-1.8	1 (0.5)	-3.5
Old Bexley & Sidcup	72.8	+2.0	61.5	+8.7	29.3	+10.3	3.3	-0.2	3.4	-14.9	1.7	-1.2	2 (0.8)	-0.8
Orpington	74.3	+2.3	62.9	+5.5	24.4	+8.8	6.6	-0.2	4.0	-12.7	2.1	-1.4	—	—
Poplar & Limehouse	67.3	+5.2	20.1	-5.3	67.3	+8.7	6.7	+2.5	1.4	-4.7	1.7	-3.1	2 (2.7)	-7.0
Putney	72.1	+5.1	44.1	-9.7	40.8	+10.8	11.6	+5.3	1.0	-3.6	2.4	-2.5	1 (0.1)	-10.2
Richmond Park†	79.1	+2.7	45.1	-13.1	9.1	-3.2	45.1	+25.8	0.7	-3.5	—	—	—	—
Romford	68.0	+0.2	59.4	+8.4	31.8	+10.9	2.4	-0.4	4.7	-18.1	1.6	-0.9	—	-6.6
Ruislip, Northwood & Pinner	72.7	+2.7	57.2	-2.3	31.0	+10.9	7.1	+2.2	2.2	-8.7	2.4	-1.1	—	-6.6
Streatham	70.9	+7.8	21.4	-3.7	68.5	+15.5	6.5	-2.5	0.6	-2.6	3.0	-5.8	—	-9.6
Sutton & Cheam	73.8	+1.7	51.1	+9.6	20.5	+9.4	26.7	-7.0	—	—	1.7	-0.4	—	—
Tooting	74.6	+4.9	33.1	-8.8	59.6	+12.4	5.3	+1.3	0.6	-2.3	1.5	-2.7	—	-10.6

Constituency														
Tottenham	67.7	+7.6	11.5	−0.5	81.6	+14.2	3.4	−0.7	0.9	−2.6	2.6	−6.7	–	−7.4
Twickenham*	79.5	+2.3	38.0	−3.2	9.2	−2.3	52.8	+14.7	–	–	–	–	–	–
Uxbridge & South Ruislip	66.8	+3.3	50.8	+0.6	40.0	+13.6	3.9	−1.0	3.4	−10.8	1.9	−1.3	–	−6.5
Vauxhall	67.1	+8.8	18.7	−8.6	57.4	+3.6	20.6	+13.7	–	–	2.1	−5.5	2 (1.3)	−6.1
Walthamstow	70.8	+8.5	14.1	+0.7	80.6	+11.7	2.9	−1.1	–	–	2.5	−3.9	–	−5.5
West Ham	65.7	+7.4	16.2	+0.8	76.7	+8.3	3.0	+0.3	1.9	−5.6	1.6	−3.4	1 (0.6)	−3.8
Westminster North	67.8	+4.4	33.3	−8.5	59.9	+13.1	5.2	+1.5	–	–	1.4	−2.0	1 (0.2)	−10.8
Wimbledon	77.2	+3.6	46.5	−5.6	35.6	+9.5	14.5	+1.8	1.1	−4.0	2.4	−1.7	–	−7.6
Greater Manchester,														
Altrincham & Sale West	72.1	+1.4	51.0	−2.0	38.8	+12.2	7.7	−0.7	–	–	1.9	−2.0	1 (0.6)	−7.1
Ashton-under-Lyne	58.8	+1.8	32.0	+9.8	60.4	+10.6	1.6	−0.8	4.7	−17.0	1.3	−2.6	–	−0.4
Blackley & Broughton	56.0	+4.4	21.6	+6.5	70.4	+8.5	1.8	−0.5	4.5	−11.9	1.2	−3.1	1 (0.4)	–
Bolton North East	67.2	+3.6	42.2	+9.4	50.6	+7.7	2.9	0.0	3.5	−15.3	0.8	−1.8	–	0.9
Bolton South East	61.4	+3.0	29.7	+9.3	60.7	+10.2	1.8	−0.8	6.6	−17.1	1.3	−1.7	–	–
Bolton West	70.1	+3.3	47.9	+7.3	46.1	+7.1	2.9	−1.1	3.1	−12.2	–	–	–	0.1
Bury North*	70.9	+4.0	44.5	+2.5	53.6	+12.5	1.9	−0.2	–	–	–	–	–	−5.0
Bury South	69.2	+5.3	41.6	+6.9	53.3	+8.2	2.1	−1.5	2.6	−10.8	–	–	1 (0.5)	−0.6
Cheadle	74.3	+1.8	44.6	+1.5	19.1	+2.8	36.3	+5.4	–	–	–	–	–	–
Denton & Reddish	60.2	+1.7	28.0	+4.3	63.5	+12.7	2.2	−0.3	4.5	−14.1	1.2	−2.6	1 (0.5)	−4.2
Hazel Grove	69.9	+1.4	45.4	+4.0	20.5	+2.9	32.9	+6.7	–	–	1.2	−1.5	–	–
Heywood & Middleton	62.4	+1.7	38.0	+18.9	53.3	+10.2	2.2	−1.1	6.5	−25.7	–	–	–	–
Leigh	61.5	+2.1	35.8	+13.2	56.2	+2.3	2.0	−0.5	5.9	−13.8	–	–	–	5.4
Makerfield	63.2	+2.9	31.3	+11.8	60.2	+8.4	2.8	−0.8	–	–	–	–	1 (5.7)	–
Manchester Central	55.1	+2.4	14.2	+0.6	77.4	+16.1	3.4	−0.7	3.0	−8.1	1.7	−6.8	1 (0.4)	−7.8
Manchester Gorton	61.0	+3.4	7.3	−2.4	76.3	+9.3	5.7	+1.4	2.1	−6.1	2.3	−7.5	4 (6.4)	–
Manchester Withington	71.8	+4.4	10.3	+0.6	71.7	+18.0	15.9	−8.0	–	–	1.6	−6.5	1 (0.4)	–
Oldham East & Saddleworth	65.2	+2.9	37.1	+11.2	54.5	+15.1	3.6	−9.3	4.8	−14.4	–	–	–	−2.0
Oldham West & Royton	63.2	+3.0	27.6	+8.6	65.2	+10.4	2.1	−1.6	4.1	−16.5	1.0	−1.0	–	–

ENGLAND	Turnout %	Turnout +/-	Con %	Con +/-	Lab %	Lab +/-	LD %	LD +/-	UKIP %	UKIP +/-	Grn %	Grn +/-	Other No & %	Swing
Rochdale	64.1	+5.3	28.4	+11.4	58.0	+11.9	8.0	-2.2	3.3	-15.5	—	—	2 (2.2)	—
Salford & Eccles	61.0	+2.8	25.3	+4.9	65.5	+16.1	2.7	-1.0	4.9	-13.2	1.7	-3.5	—	-5.6
Stalybridge & Hyde	59.5	+2.0	38.1	+9.5	57.2	+12.2	2.3	-0.7	—	—	2.3	-2.2	—	-1.4
Stockport	64.7	+2.7	28.4	+3.9	63.3	+13.4	4.3	-3.4	2.6	-10.5	1.4	-3.0	—	-4.7
Stretford & Urmston	69.9	+2.7	27.5	-0.3	66.8	+13.7	2.0	-0.9	2.2	-8.7	1.3	-3.4	1 (0.2)	-7.0
Wigan	63.1	+3.5	28.5	+7.8	62.2	+10.0	1.9	-0.8	5.8	-13.7	1.6	-1.2	—	-1.1
Worsley & Eccles South	61.9	+3.7	38.7	+8.6	57.1	+12.8	2.4	-0.2	—	—	1.8	-1.1	—	-2.1
Wythenshawe & Sale East	60.0	+3.1	29.6	+3.9	62.2	+12.1	3.3	-1.2	3.2	-11.5	1.3	-2.6	1 (0.4)	-4.1
Hampshire, Aldershot	64.2	+0.5	55.1	+4.5	31.6	+13.3	7.4	-1.4	3.7	-14.2	2.2	-2.2	—	-4.4
Basingstoke	68.3	+1.7	52.7	+4.2	35.8	+8.1	6.1	-1.3	3.0	-12.6	2.0	—	1 (0.4)	-2.0
Eastleigh	70.5	+0.8	50.4	+8.2	20.0	+7.1	25.7	-0.1	2.6	-13.2	1.3	-1.4	1 (0.5)	—
Fareham	72.3	+1.4	63.0	+6.9	25.2	+10.9	6.8	-2.0	2.7	-12.7	2.3	-1.6	1 (1.0)	—
Gosport	66.7	+1.7	61.9	+6.6	27.2	+12.6	4.7	-2.2	3.6	-15.8	2.1	-1.5	1 (0.6)	—
Hampshire East	74.7	+2.1	63.6	+3.0	17.0	+6.9	15.2	+4.1	—	—	3.2	-3.0	—	—
Hampshire North East	77.3	+7.1	65.5	-0.4	17.3	+7.5	12.1	+1.6	1.8	-6.9	2.6	-1.8	—	—
Hampshire North West	72.2	+2.5	62.1	+4.0	23.5	+10.2	9.7	+0.4	2.5	-12.2	2.3	-2.3	—	—
Havant	63.9	+0.4	59.8	+8.1	25.3	+9.4	6.0	-0.5	4.3	-16.3	2.4	-2.8	1 (2.1)	—
Meon Valley	73.0	+1.9	65.7	+4.7	18.3	+7.4	10.9	+1.2	2.6	-12.2	2.4	-1.1	—	—
New Forest East	70.8	+2.7	62.6	+6.4	19.8	+7.6	15.2	+5.8	—	—	2.4	-2.3	—	—
New Forest West	72.1	+2.9	66.8	+6.9	19.6	+8.8	9.6	+2.7	—	—	2.9	-2.9	—	—
Portsmouth North	66.1	+4.1	54.8	+7.8	33.7	+9.9	5.5	-0.7	4.1	-15.0	1.7	-1.5	1 (1.0)	-1.1
Portsmouth South*	63.9	+5.4	37.6	+2.7	41.0	+21.5	17.3	-5.0	2.5	-10.8	1.6	-5.9	1 (0.3)	—
Romsey & Southampton North	74.6	+1.9	57.2	+2.9	19.2	+7.3	21.2	+3.5	—	—	1.9	-2.8	1 (0.5)	—
Southampton Itchen	65.2	+3.4	46.5	+4.8	46.5	+9.9	3.0	-0.5	2.4	-11.0	1.5	-2.6	—	-2.6
Southampton Test	66.8	+4.7	34.1	+1.6	58.7	+17.4	4.0	-0.8	—	—	—	—	2 (3.2)	-7.9
Winchester	78.8	+4.2	52.0	-3.0	10.5	+2.2	34.5	+10.1	1.2	-6.2	1.5	-3.3	1 (0.3)	—
Hereford and Worcester, Bromsgrove	73.5	+2.2	62.0	+8.1	31.3	+9.1	4.6	-0.4	—	—	2.1	-1.2	—	-0.5
Hereford & Herefordshire South	71.0	+4.9	53.5	+0.9	23.8	+11.0	7.0	-3.5	2.3	-14.5	2.4	-4.8	1 (11.0)	—
Herefordshire North	74.1	+3.4	62.0	+6.3	18.9	+7.5	11.7	-0.3	—	—	5.5	-1.4	2 (1.9)	—
Redditch	70.2	+2.9	52.3	+5.2	36.0	+4.9	2.6	-0.5	3.0	-13.1	0.8	-1.3	2 (5.2)	0.1
Worcester	69.6	+1.0	48.1	+2.8	43.2	+9.3	3.4	0.0	2.6	-10.2	2.4	-1.7	2 (0.3)	-3.2

Worcestershire Mid	72.4	+1.0	65.3	+8.3	22.9	+8.5	6.3	−0.9	3.0	−14.7	2.5	−1.2	—	—
Worcestershire West	75.9	+2.2	61.5	+5.4	23.7	+10.3	9.4	−0.3	2.6	−11.7	2.8	−3.6	—	—
Wyre Forest	65.8	+1.9	58.4	+13.1	32.3	+13.1	3.8	+1.3	3.5	−12.6	2.0	−0.3	—	—
Hertfordshire, Broxbourne	64.6	+1.5	62.2	+6.1	28.9	+10.5	3.1	−0.1	4.0	−15.7	1.8	−0.9	—	—
Hemel Hempstead	70.3	+3.7	55.0	+2.1	36.9	+13.1	6.2	+1.3			2.0	−1.4	—	−5.5
Hertford & Stortford	72.9	+3.0	60.3	+4.2	28.6	+10.7	8.1	+0.3			3.0	−1.7	—	−3.2
Hertfordshire North East	73.2	+2.5	58.6	+3.3	28.3	+9.5	7.7	+0.1			5.3	—	—	−3.1
Hertfordshire South West	74.8	+2.9	57.9	+1.0	25.7	+9.4	11.7	+1.4	2.1	−9.4	2.6	−1.9	—	−4.2
Hertsmere	71.0	+3.1	61.1	+1.8	28.7	+6.2	5.3	−0.2	3.0	−9.7	1.9	—	—	−2.2
Hitchin & Harpenden	77.4	+8.5	53.1	−3.8	32.6	+11.9	10.6	+2.5			2.3	−3.3	2 (1.5)	−7.9
St Albans	78.3	+6.5	43.1	−3.5	23.0	−0.2	32.4	+13.9			1.5	−2.3	—	−1.7
Stevenage	69.7	+2.0	50.3	+5.7	43.4	+9.2	4.1	+0.8			2.2	−0.7	—	−1.8
Watford	67.8	+0.5	45.6	+2.2	42.0	+16.0	9.1	−9.0	2.0	−7.7	1.2	−1.1	1 (0.3)	−6.9
Welwyn Hatfield	70.9	+2.3	51.0	+0.7	36.8	+10.6	7.4	+1.2	2.8	−10.3	1.6	−1.9	1 (2.1)	−5
Humberside, Beverley & Holderness	69.0	+3.8	58.4	+10.3	33.2	+8.2	5.0	−0.5			1.3	−2.1	—	1.0
Brigg & Goole	68.2	+5.0	60.4	+7.4	33.0	+5.8	1.9	+0.1	3.5	−11.9	1.2	−0.9	—	0.8
Cleethorpes	65.8	+2.3	57.1	+10.5	35.4	+6.2	2.3	−0.7	4.2	−14.3	1.0	−1.3	—	2.1
Great Grimsby	57.5	+0.6	42.2	+15.9	49.4	+9.6	2.7	−2.3	4.6	−20.3	—	—	1 (1.1)	3.1
Haltemprice & Howden	71.9	+3.4	61.0	+6.8	31.0	+10.0	4.8	−1.4			1.4	−2.3	1 (1.8)	−1.6
Hull East	55.5	+2.1	29.9	+14.0	58.3	+6.6	3.4	−3.1	7.0	−15.3	1.3	−0.9	—	—
Hull North	57.4	+2.3	25.2	+10.2	63.8	+11.0	5.0	−4.0	4.3	−12.0	1.6	−4.2	—	—
Hull West & Hessle	57.4	+3.6	29.8	+12.4	53.1	+3.9	6.4	−3.6	4.0	−15.8	1.0	−2.0	2 (5.7)	—
Scunthorpe	65.3	+7.6	43.5	+10.3	52.0	+10.4	1.4	−0.7	3.1	−14.0	—	—	—	—
Yorkshire East	66.6	+4.9	58.3	+7.7	30.5	+9.8	4.0	−2.0	3.7	−14.2	1.7	−1.7	1 (1.9)	−1.0
Isle of Wight, Isle of Wight	67.3	+2.7	51.3	+10.6	23.0	+10.2	3.7	−3.8	2.6	−18.6	17.3	+4.0	1 (2.1)	—
Kent, Ashford	68.5	+1.2	59.0	+6.5	29.8	+11.4	5.2	−0.8	3.7	−15.1	2.3	−2.0	—	—
Canterbury*	72.7	+6.9	44.7	+1.8	45.0	+20.5	8.0	−3.6			2.3	−4.7	—	−9.3
Chatham & Aylesford	63.7	−1.2	57.0	+6.8	33.7	+10.1	2.5	−0.7	5.0	−15.0	1.3	−1.3	1 (0.6)	−1.6

ENGLAND	Turnout %	Turnout +/-	Con %	Con +/-	Lab %	Lab +/-	LD %	LD +/-	UKIP %	UKIP +/-	Grn %	Grn +/-	Other No & %	Swing
Dartford	69.1	-0.6	57.6	+8.6	33.2	+7.8	2.6	-0.1	4.7	-15.2	1.5	-1.0	1 (0.4)	0.4
Dover	69.7	+0.8	52.4	+9.1	40.0	+9.2	2.6	-0.6	3.3	-16.9	1.8	-0.8	–	-0.1
Faversham & Mid Kent	68.9	+3.0	61.1	+6.7	26.1	+9.9	6.5	-0.1	3.4	-14.6	2.9	-1.0	–	–
Folkestone & Hythe	68.2	+2.5	54.7	+6.8	28.5	+14.1	7.2	-1.7	4.4	-18.4	4.2	-1.1	2 (1.0)	–
Gillingham & Rainham	67.0	+0.7	55.4	+7.5	36.1	+10.5	2.8	-0.8	4.3	-15.2	1.1	-1.3	1 (0.3)	-1.5
Gravesham	67.2	-2.4	55.6	+8.8	36.5	+6.4	2.5	+0.3	3.6	-15.0	1.5	-0.8	1 (0.4)	1.2
Maidstone & The Weald	68.7	+0.3	56.4	+10.9	22.1	+11.6	16.3	-7.7	3.1	-12.7	1.7	-1.1	1 (0.3)	–
Rochester & Strood	65.0	-3.1	54.4	+10.3	36.0	+16.3	2.2	-0.2	5.4	-25.1	1.5	-1.4	2 (0.5)	–
Sevenoaks	71.6	+1.9	63.7	+6.8	20.9	+8.1	8.4	+0.5	3.7	-14.2	3.3	-1.2	–	–
Sittingbourne & Sheppey	62.9	-2.1	60.2	+10.7	30.6	+11.0	2.7	-0.5	–	–	1.1	-1.3	3 (5.5)	–
Thanet North	66.5	+0.7	56.2	+7.2	34.0	+16.1	3.3	-0.2	4.5	-21.2	1.7	-1.9	1 (0.3)	–
Thanet South	68.8	-0.8	50.8	+12.6	37.9	+14.2	3.0	+1.2	6.0	-26.4	1.6	-0.6	2 (0.6)	–
Tonbridge & Malling	73.5	+1.8	63.6	+4.2	22.3	+8.2	6.7	-0.2	3.3	-11.9	4.1	-0.3	–	–
Tunbridge Wells	72.5	+2.5	56.9	-1.8	26.5	+12.3	9.9	+1.4	2.7	-9.9	2.7	-2.5	1 (1.3)	-7.1
Lancashire, Blackburn	67.2	+7.2	26.9	-0.4	69.8	+13.5	1.5	-0.7	–	–	–	–	1 (1.8)	-6.9
Blackpool North & Cleveleys	64.1	+1.0	49.4	+4.9	44.5	+8.5	1.8	-0.6	3.4	-11.4	0.9	-1.3	–	-1.8
Blackpool South	59.8	+3.3	43.1	+9.3	50.3	+8.5	1.8	-0.5	3.8	-13.5	1.0	-1.6	–	0.4
Burnley	62.3	+0.6	31.0	+17.5	46.7	+9.1	15.0	-14.4	6.1	-11.1	1.1	-1.0	–	–
Chorley	72.8	+3.6	41.8	+5.4	55.3	+10.2	2.0	-0.6	–	–	1.0	-1.2	1 (0.5)	-2.4
Fylde	70.5	+4.2	58.8	+9.7	33.4	+14.6	5.0	+1.3	–	–	2.7	-0.5	–	-2.5
Hyndburn	63.1	+0.4	40.5	+8.6	53.4	+11.2	1.8	-0.2	4.3	-17.0	–	–	–	-1.3
Lancashire West	74.2	+4.2	37.4	+5.0	58.9	+9.6	2.0	-0.6	–	–	1.3	-1.9	1 (0.5)	-2.3
Lancaster & Fleetwood	68.5	+1.1	40.6	+1.4	55.1	+12.8	2.5	-0.8	–	–	1.7	-3.3	–	-5.7
Morecambe & Lunesdale	68.3	+3.8	47.7	+2.2	44.6	+9.7	3.7	0.0	2.9	-9.5	1.0	-2.2	–	-3.8
Pendle	69.0	+0.2	49.0	+1.8	46.2	+11.2	2.1	-1.2	–	–	1.1	-1.2	1 (1.6)	-4.7
Preston	61.6	+5.8	23.8	+3.9	68.0	+12.0	3.4	-0.3	3.8	-11.6	1.0	-3.9	–	-4.1
Ribble Valley	70.8	+3.3	57.8	+9.2	33.9	+11.3	5.9	+0.6	–	–	2.4	-1.8	–	-1.1
Rossendale & Darwen	69.2	+2.7	50.8	+4.2	44.4	+9.4	3.1	+1.4	–	–	1.6	-0.5	–	-2.6
South Ribble	72.4	+3.9	52.9	+6.4	39.3	+4.2	3.8	-0.6	2.5	-11.6	0.9	–	1 (0.6)	1.1
Wyre & Preston North	72.8	+2.2	58.3	+5.1	35.0	+10.2	4.8	-0.6	–	–	1.8	-1.6	–	-2.6
Leicestershire, Bosworth	68.8	+1.6	56.7	+13.9	24.1	+6.6	17.3	-5.0	–	–	1.9	–	–	–

Charnwood	70.7	+3.0	60.4	+6.1	30.8	+8.9	3.7	-3.2	2.7	-13.3	1.9	–	1 (0.6)	-1.4
Harborough	73.1	+5.6	52.3	-0.4	30.7	+15.4	12.6	-0.8	2.4	-12.0	1.9	-2.2	–	-7.9
Leicester East	67.4	+3.7	24.2	+1.2	67.0	+5.9	2.6	0.0	–	–	2.0	-1.0	2 (4.2)	-2.3
Leicester South	66.9	+4.4	21.6	+0.6	73.6	+13.8	2.5	-2.1	–	–	2.3	-3.2	–	-6.6
Leicester West	57.9	+3.2	31.4	+5.7	60.8	+14.3	2.1	-2.3	3.7	-13.5	1.6	-3.8	1 (0.3)	-4.3
Leicestershire North West	71.0	-0.4	58.2	+8.7	33.4	+6.0	6.4	+2.4	–	–	2.1	-0.2	–	1.4
Leicestershire South	71.8	+1.6	61.4	+8.2	28.5	+6.5	4.2	-3.2	3.9	-13.4	1.9	–	–	0.8
Loughborough	68.0	-1.1	49.9	+0.4	42.0	+10.1	3.6	-0.5	2.7	-8.3	1.8	-1.8	–	-4.9
Rutland & Melton	73.4	+4.9	62.8	+7.2	22.7	+7.3	8.2	+0.1	3.2	-12.6	3.0	-1.2	–	–
Lincolnshire, Boston & Skegness	62.7	-1.9	63.6	+19.8	25.0	+8.5	1.8	-0.5	7.7	-26.1	1.3	-0.6	1 (0.7)	–
Gainsborough	67.8	+1.8	61.8	+9.1	28.7	+7.4	7.1	+0.4	–	–	2.4	-0.2	–	0.9
Grantham & Stamford	69.2	+3.0	62.0	+9.2	26.5	+9.6	5.5	-0.6	3.1	-14.4	1.4	-2.1	1 (1.5)	–
Lincoln*	66.6	+3.4	44.7	+2.1	47.9	+8.3	2.6	-1.6	2.6	-9.6	1.2	–	2 (0.9)	-3.1
Louth & Horncastle	66.8	-0.4	63.9	+12.8	26.7	+8.7	3.8	-0.7	4.7	-16.8	–	–	1 (0.9)	–
Sleaford & North Hykeham	72.4	+1.9	64.2	+8.0	25.8	+8.6	4.1	-1.5	3.0	-12.7	1.5	–	1 (1.4)	-0.3
South Holland & The Deepings	65.9	+1.5	69.9	+10.4	20.4	+8.0	2.8	-0.1	4.3	-17.5	1.8	-1.4	1 (0.7)	–
Merseyside, Birkenhead	67.7	+5.0	18.4	+3.6	76.9	+9.2	2.6	-1.0	–	–	2.2	-2.0	–	-2.8
Bootle	69.0	+4.6	12.0	+4.0	84.0	+9.6	1.7	-0.5	–	–	1.4	-1.9	1 (0.8)	–
Garston & Halewood	71.1	+4.7	17.7	+4.0	77.7	+8.6	3.2	-1.4	–	–	1.4	-2.0	–	-2.3
Knowsley	67.9	+3.7	9.3	+2.6	85.3	+7.2	2.1	-0.8	2.3	-7.5	0.9	-1.6	–	–
Liverpool Riverside	62.9	+0.4	9.7	+0.1	84.5	+17.1	2.5	-1.4	–	–	3.3	-8.8	–	–
Liverpool Walton	67.3	+5.2	8.6	+3.9	85.7	+4.4	1.5	-0.8	–	–	1.2	-1.2	1 (2.9)	–
Liverpool Wavertree	69.9	+3.4	12.0	+2.0	79.6	+10.2	6.5	+0.6	–	–	1.4	-3.9	1 (0.5)	-4.1
Liverpool West Derby	69.3	+4.8	9.9	+3.3	82.7	+7.6	1.2	-1.1	–	–	0.7	-1.7	2 (5.4)	–
St Helens North	66.0	+4.5	27.1	+7.4	63.7	+6.7	2.6	-1.9	4.2	-10.9	2.4	-1.4	–	0.4
St Helens South & Whiston	66.9	+4.6	21.8	+5.9	67.8	+8.0	4.0	-1.7	3.7	-10.3	2.7	-1.9	–	-1.1
Sefton Central	75.5	+3.1	33.0	+3.4	63.0	+9.3	2.7	-1.6	–	–	1.3	-1.2	–	-2.9
Southport*	69.1	+3.6	38.7	+10.7	32.6	+13.4	26.4	-4.6	2.4	-14.5	–	–	–	–
Wallasey	71.7	+5.5	23.2	+0.6	71.5	+11.1	1.6	-0.7	2.4	-9.3	1.3	-1.7	–	-5.3

ENGLAND	Turnout %	Turnout +/-	Con %	Con +/-	Lab %	Lab +/-	LD %	LD +/-	UKIP %	UKIP +/-	Grn %	Grn +/-	Other No & %	Swing
Wirral South	78.4	+4.9	38.8	+1.6	57.2	+9.0	2.9	-0.6	–	–	1.0	-1.1	–	-3.7
Wirral West	78.5	+2.9	42.1	-2.1	54.3	+9.2	2.6	-0.8	–	–	1.0	–	–	-5.6
Norfolk, Broadland	72.4	+0.2	57.9	+7.4	29.6	+10.9	7.9	-1.8	2.8	-13.9	1.7	-2.6	–	-1.7
Great Yarmouth	61.8	-1.9	54.1	+11.2	36.1	+7.0	2.2	-0.1	6.3	-16.8	1.3	-0.9	–	2.1
Norfolk Mid	69.6	+1.9	59.0	+6.9	30.1	+11.7	5.1	-1.2	3.8	-15.3	2.1	-2.1	–	–
Norfolk North	75.3	+3.6	41.7	+10.8	9.9	-0.3	48.4	+9.3	–	–	–	–	–	-0.6
Norfolk North West	67.7	+4.1	60.2	+8.1	32.0	+9.2	2.9	-0.7	3.2	-14.6	1.7	-2.0	–	-0.6
Norfolk South	73.6	+2.8	58.2	+4.0	30.9	+12.5	8.3	+0.1	–	–	2.5	-2.9	–	-4.3
Norfolk South West	67.3	+2.2	62.8	+11.8	27.8	+10.6	4.5	+0.1	4.9	-18.3	–	–	–	–
Norwich North	68.6	+1.0	47.7	+4.0	46.6	+13.1	3.2	-1.1	–	–	1.7	-2.7	1 (0.7)	-4.6
Norwich South	69.2	+4.5	30.6	+7.1	61.0	+21.7	5.5	-8.1	–	–	2.9	-11.0	–	-7.3
North Yorkshire, Harrogate & Knaresborough	73.4	+3.6	55.5	+2.7	20.1	+9.9	23.5	+1.4	–	–	–	–	1 (1.0)	–
Richmond (Yorks)	70.5	+2.2	63.9	+12.6	23.4	+10.2	5.9	-0.5	–	–	3.1	-1.2	1 (3.7)	–
Scarborough & Whitby	68.5	+3.6	48.4	+5.2	41.6	+11.4	2.7	-1.8	3.3	-13.8	1.8	-2.8	3 (2.2)	-3.1
Selby & Ainsty	73.9	+4.5	58.7	+6.2	34.1	+7.3	4.1	+0.5	3.1	-10.9	–	–	–	-0.6
Skipton & Ripon	74.4	+3.3	62.7	+7.2	28.3	+10.9	–	–	–	–	6.4	+0.7	1 (2.6)	-1.8
Thirsk & Malton	71.1	+3.5	60.0	+7.4	26.1	+10.6	6.9	-2.1	2.7	-12.2	2.0	-2.6	2 (2.3)	-1.6
York Central	68.7	+5.4	30.2	+1.9	65.2	+22.8	4.7	-3.3	–	–	–	–	–	-10.5
York Outer	75.7	+7.1	51.1	+2.0	36.7	+11.9	10.3	-1.3	–	–	1.9	-2.8	–	-5.0
Northamptonshire, Corby	72.3	+1.9	49.2	+6.5	44.7	+6.3	2.6	0.0	2.5	-11.2	1.0	-1.5	–	0.1
Daventry	74.0	+1.9	63.7	+5.5	24.7	+6.6	7.2	+2.7	2.7	-13.1	1.7	-1.8	–	-0.5
Kettering	69.2	+1.8	57.9	+6.1	36.5	+11.4	3.3	+0.1	–	–	2.3	-1.2	–	-2.6
Northampton North	68.6	+2.0	47.2	+4.8	45.2	+11.1	2.5	-1.0	3.5	-12.6	1.6	-2.2	–	-3.1
Northampton South	66.4	+3.0	46.9	+5.3	44.0	+12.2	3.4	-0.9	4.0	-14.3	1.7	-1.9	–	-3.5
Northamptonshire South	75.8	+4.8	62.5	+2.3	27.3	+10.6	5.6	-0.4	2.1	-11.4	2.1	-1.6	1 (0.5)	-4.1
Wellingborough	67.2	-0.7	57.4	+5.4	34.0	+14.5	3.3	-1.1	3.4	-16.2	1.8	-2.6	–	–
Northumberland, Berwick-upon-Tweed	71.8	+0.8	52.5	+11.4	24.6	+9.6	21.1	-7.8	–	–	1.9	-1.8	–	–
Blyth Valley	67.0	+4.2	37.3	+15.6	55.9	+9.6	4.6	-1.3	–	–	2.2	-1.6	–	–
Hexham	75.7	+3.1	54.1	+1.4	34.1	+9.2	7.1	+0.3	2.0	-7.9	2.7	-2.9	–	-3.9

Wansbeck	68.3	+4.8	32.7	+11.0	57.3	+7.3	4.7	-1.5	3.5	-14.7	1.7	-2.1	–	1.8
Nottinghamshire, Ashfield	64.0	+2.5	41.7	+19.3	42.6	+1.6	1.9	-12.9	3.8	-17.6	0.8	–	1 (9.2)	8.9
Bassetlaw	66.5	+2.3	43.3	+12.6	52.6	+3.9	2.2	-0.5	–	–	–	–	1 (1.9)	4.3
Broxtowe	75.0	+0.5	46.8	+1.6	45.3	+8.1	4.0	+0.1	2.7	-8.0	1.2	-1.7	–	-3.2
Gedling	72.6	+4.0	42.8	+6.8	51.9	+9.6	2.0	-1.9	2.2	-12.2	1.0	-2.2	–	-1.4
Mansfield*	64.5	+3.6	46.6	+18.5	44.5	+5.1	1.4	-2.1	5.3	-19.8	–	–	1 (2.2)	6.7
Newark	72.9	+2.0	62.7	+5.6	29.7	+8.0	5.1	+0.5	2.6	-9.5	–	–	–	-1.2
Nottingham East	63.7	+5.4	21.6	+0.9	71.5	+16.9	2.6	-1.6	2.1	-7.9	1.8	-8.1	1 (0.5)	-8.0
Nottingham North	57.3	+3.7	31.1	+10.1	60.2	+5.6	1.8	-0.6	5.6	-12.9	1.4	-1.7	–	2.2
Nottingham South	67.6	+4.6	30.9	-0.8	62.4	+14.7	3.2	-0.3	2.3	-9.0	1.2	-4.2	–	-7.8
Rushcliffe	78.0	+2.7	51.8	+0.4	38.1	+11.8	4.7	-0.3	2.6	-8.2	2.8	-3.7	–	-5.7
Sherwood	70.0	+0.9	51.5	+6.5	41.8	+5.9	2.1	-0.1	3.4	-11.2	1.2	-0.9	–	0.3
Oxfordshire, Banbury	73.4	+6.3	54.2	+1.2	34.1	+12.8	5.6	-0.3	2.6	-11.3	2.0	-2.6	1 (1.5)	-5.8
Henley	76.1	+5.3	59.1	+0.6	20.1	+7.5	14.9	+3.6	2.0	-8.9	3.3	-3.6	1 (0.7)	-3.4
Oxford East	68.8	+4.6	22.0	+2.1	65.2	+15.1	9.1	-1.7	–	–	3.3	-8.3	1 (0.5)	-6.5
Oxford West & Abingdon*	79.4	+4.3	42.4	-3.3	12.6	-0.1	43.7	+14.8	1.3	-5.7	–	–	–	–
Wantage	74.1	+3.8	54.2	+0.9	26.9	+10.8	14.5	+1.5	2.0	-10.5	2.4	-2.7	–	-5.0
Witney	73.6	+0.3	55.5	-4.7	20.7	+3.5	20.4	+13.7	1.6	-7.5	1.7	-3.4	–	-4.1
Shropshire, Ludlow	73.4	+1.0	62.9	+8.6	24.3	+12.0	10.7	-2.8	–	–	2.1	-3.0	–	–
Shrewsbury & Atcham	73.6	+2.8	50.0	+4.4	38.6	+10.7	7.3	-0.6	2.3	-12.1	1.8	-2.3	–	-3.1
Shropshire North	69.0	+2.4	60.5	+9.1	31.1	+11.0	5.3	-0.7	–	–	3.1	-1.8	–	-1.0
Telford	65.6	+4.2	48.7	+9.1	47.1	+9.3	2.1	-0.1	–	–	2.0	-0.3	–	-0.1
Wrekin, The	72.2	+3.3	55.4	+5.7	36.1	+10.1	2.7	-1.6	3.3	-13.4	1.6	-1.6	1 (0.8)	-2.2
Somerset, Bridgwater & West Somerset	65.3	-2.4	55.1	+9.2	28.6	+11.0	10.9	-1.6	3.6	-15.6	1.8	-3.0	–	–
Somerton & Frome	75.7	+3.3	56.7	+3.7	17.2	+9.9	20.9	+1.5	–	–	3.7	-5.3	1 (1.6)	–
Taunton Deane	73.8	+4.2	52.9	+4.8	15.4	+6.1	27.7	+6.3	2.3	-9.7	1.8	-2.7	–	–
Wells	73.8	+2.1	50.1	+4.0	11.7	+5.1	37.6	+4.9	–	–	–	–	1 (0.5)	–

ENGLAND	Turnout %	Turnout +/-	Con %	Con +/-	Lab %	Lab +/-	LD %	LD +/-	UKIP %	UKIP +/-	Grn %	Grn +/-	Other No & %	Swing
Yeovil	71.6	+2.6	54.5	+12.0	12.5	+5.4	29.7	-3.4	-	-	1.8	-2.1	1 (1.5)	-
South Yorkshire, Barnsley Central	60.9	+4.2	24.1	+9.1	63.9	+8.2	1.4	-0.7	8.5	-13.2	1.5	-1.1	1 (0.5)	-
Barnsley East	58.9	+3.2	27.0	+12.4	59.5	+4.8	1.8	-1.3	8.0	-15.5	-	-	2 (3.7)	-
Don Valley	62.2	+2.6	41.7	+16.4	53.0	+6.8	1.9	-1.6	-	-	-	-	1 (3.5)	4.8
Doncaster Central	60.0	+3.2	34.4	+13.6	57.9	+8.8	2.3	-2.0	-	-	-	-	2 (5.5)	-
Doncaster North	58.5	+2.8	27.6	+9.3	60.8	+8.3	1.7	-0.9	6.5	-16.1	-	-	3 (3.5)	-
Penistone & Stocksbridge	69.8	+3.7	43.2	+15.5	45.8	+3.8	4.1	-2.2	6.9	-16.0	-	-	-	5.8
Rother Valley	65.8	+2.5	40.3	+17.0	48.1	+4.5	2.3	-1.9	7.5	-20.6	1.8	-	-	-
Rotherham	60.0	+0.6	26.4	+14.1	56.4	+3.9	4.6	+1.7	8.7	-21.4	-	-	1 (3.8)	-
Sheffield Brightside & Hillsborough	59.5	+3.0	21.6	+10.6	67.3	+10.8	2.5	-2.0	6.3	-15.8	1.8	-2.5	2 (0.4)	-
Sheffield Central	61.7	+0.6	13.0	+1.8	70.9	+15.9	5.1	-4.5	2.2	-5.2	8.0	-7.8	3 (0.7)	-
Sheffield Hallam*	77.6	+0.9	23.8	+10.2	38.4	+2.6	34.6	-5.4	1.6	-4.8	1.4	-1.8	1 (0.1)	-
Sheffield Heeley	65.0	+3.1	28.7	+12.6	60.0	+11.8	4.6	-6.7	4.5	-12.9	2.1	-4.0	1 (0.1)	-
Sheffield South East	63.2	+4.0	31.5	+14.1	58.5	+7.1	3.3	-2.1	6.5	-15.4	-	-	1 (0.2)	-
Wentworth & Dearne	58.7	+0.5	31.3	+16.4	65.0	+8.1	3.8	+1.1	-	-	-	-	-	-
Staffordshire, Burton	67.5	+2.4	58.0	+8.2	37.8	+10.3	2.5	0.0	-	-	1.7	-0.8	-	-1.1
Cannock Chase	64.2	+1.0	55.0	+10.8	37.4	+3.7	1.7	-1.0	4.2	-13.2	1.7	-0.2	-	3.5
Lichfield	71.9	+2.6	63.6	+8.4	28.8	+9.0	5.0	-0.3	-	-	2.6	-1.2	-	-0.3
Newcastle-under-Lyme	66.8	+3.2	48.1	+11.2	48.2	+9.8	3.7	-0.5	-	-	-	-	-	0.7
Stafford	75.9	+4.9	54.7	+6.3	39.9	+10.3	3.0	+0.2	-	-	2.4	-0.4	-	-2.0
Staffordshire Moorlands	70.6	+3.1	58.1	+7.0	33.9	+6.7	3.3	-0.8	-	-	1.2	-1.7	1 (3.4)	0.2
Staffordshire South	69.6	+1.4	69.8	+10.3	25.3	+6.9	2.6	-0.3	-	-	2.3	-0.3	-	1.7
Stoke-on-Trent Central	58.2	+7.0	39.8	+17.2	51.5	+12.2	2.1	-2.1	4.9	-17.8	1.1	-2.5	1 (0.6)	-
Stoke-on-Trent North	58.4	+4.3	45.3	+17.9	50.9	+11.0	2.2	-0.7	-	-	1.6	-1.2	-	3.4
Stoke-on-Trent South*	63.1	+5.7	49.1	+16.4	47.5	+8.3	1.9	-1.4	-	-	1.5	-1.1	-	4.0
Stone	73.8	+3.9	63.2	+8.5	28.2	+8.1	4.4	-0.8	2.7	-13.5	1.4	-1.1	-	0.2
Tamworth	66.1	+0.5	61.0	+11.0	34.8	+8.7	4.2	+1.1	-	-	-	-	-	1.1
Suffolk, Bury St Edmunds	72.2	+3.2	59.2	+5.6	29.5	+11.8	5.7	-0.3	-	-	4.2	-3.7	1 (1.4)	-3.1
*Ipswich**	67.6	+2.2	45.7	+1.0	47.4	+10.3	2.3	-0.6	2.7	-9.0	1.6	-1.9	1 (0.2)	-4.6
Suffolk Central & Ipswich North	72.4	+1.8	60.1	+4.1	29.7	+10.9	4.3	-1.8	2.9	-10.9	2.9	-2.0	-	-3.4

Suffolk Coastal	73.2	+1.7	58.1	+6.1	30.5	+12.5	7.0	-1.6	–	–	3.1	-2.8	1 (1.4)	-3.2
Suffolk South	71.8	+1.5	60.5	+7.5	27.8	+8.5	5.8	-2.0	2.7	-12.5	3.2	-1.2	–	-0.5
Suffolk West	66.9	+2.3	61.2	+9.0	28.2	+10.7	4.2	-0.8	4.6	-17.1	1.8	-1.8	–	–
Waveney	65.2	+0.1	54.4	+12.0	36.9	-0.9	1.9	-0.1	3.7	-10.9	2.5	-0.8	1 (0.6)	6.4
Surrey, Epsom & Ewell	74.1	+1.4	59.6	+1.3	25.0	+9.5	12.5	+3.7	–	–	2.9	-0.8	–	-4.1
Esher & Walton	73.9	+2.6	58.6	-4.3	19.7	+7.0	17.3	+7.9	1.7	-8.0	1.8	-2.3	2 (0.9)	-5.6
Guildford	73.7	+2.4	54.6	-2.5	19.0	+6.9	23.9	+8.4	–	–	2.1	-2.7	2 (0.5)	–
Mole Valley	76.1	+1.6	61.9	+0.6	13.9	+5.6	19.3	+4.8	2.4	-8.8	2.6	-2.8	–	–
Reigate	72.1	+2.2	57.4	+1.2	24.7	+11.9	10.9	+0.5	2.9	-10.4	4.1	-2.6	–	-4.6
Runnymede & Weybridge	68.9	+1.1	60.9	+7.6	25.9	+10.4	7.3	+0.6	3.2	-10.6	2.6	-1.5	–	–
Spelthorne	69.0	+0.4	57.3	+2.2	30.5	+11.9	5.5	-0.9	4.6	-16.3	2.2	-1.3	–	–
Surrey East	72.2	+1.8	59.6	+4.3	19.2	+7.4	10.5	+1.2	3.8	-13.3	1.9	-2.0	1 (5.0)	–
Surrey Heath	71.6	+3.1	64.2	-4.1	21.1	+9.8	10.8	+1.8	–	–	3.9	-0.5	–	–
Surrey South West	77.4	+3.8	55.7	-2.1	12.6	+3.1	9.9	+3.6	1.8	-8.1	–	–	1 (20.0)	-4.9
Woking	72.5	+2.6	54.1	–	23.9	+7.7	17.6	+5.9	2.1	-9.2	2.0	-2.1	1 (0.4)	–
Tyne and Wear, Blaydon	70.2	+4.1	28.1	+10.6	56.1	+6.9	9.1	-3.2	5.1	-12.4	1.2	-2.5	2 (0.4)	–
Gateshead	64.6	+5.8	23.9	+9.4	65.1	+8.4	4.1	-2.8	5.4	-12.4	1.5	-2.6	–	–
Houghton & Sunderland South	60.9	+4.6	29.7	+11.3	59.5	+4.3	2.2	+0.1	5.7	-15.8	1.7	-1.1	1 (1.2)	–
Jarrow	66.4	+6.2	25.0	+7.9	65.1	+9.5	2.7	-0.5	5.4	-14.2	1.7	-1.7	–	–
Newcastle upon Tyne Central	67.0	+6.7	24.6	+5.7	64.9	+9.9	4.9	-1.4	4.0	-10.9	1.6	-3.3	–	-2.1
Newcastle upon Tyne East	67.2	+6.1	21.3	+3.7	67.6	+18.1	6.2	-4.9	3.2	-9.4	1.8	-6.9	–	-7.2
Newcastle upon Tyne North	73.1	+7.0	33.9	+10.5	55.4	+9.3	5.2	-4.5	3.7	-12.9	1.1	-2.3	1 (0.7)	0.6
South Shields	64.3	+6.5	25.9	+9.3	61.5	+10.2	1.7	-0.1	7.4	-14.6	3.5	-0.9	–	–
Sunderland Central	62.0	+4.8	33.4	+10.0	55.5	+5.4	3.9	+1.3	4.9	-14.3	1.6	-2.5	1 (0.7)	2.3
Tynemouth	73.4	+4.4	36.5	+3.6	57.0	+8.8	3.0	+0.1	2.2	-10.0	1.1	-2.7	1 (0.2)	-2.6
Tyneside North	65.8	+6.7	27.3	+8.1	64.5	+8.5	2.9	-1.6	4.0	-12.2	1.3	-1.8	–	-0.2
Washington & Sunderland West	60.3	+5.7	28.8	+10.0	60.7	+5.8	2.4	-0.3	6.8	-12.8	1.3	-1.7	–	–
Warwickshire, Kenilworth & Southam	77.4	+1.1	60.8	+2.4	25.6	+10.3	9.6	-0.5	1.8	-9.4	2.2	-1.8	–	-3.9

ENGLAND	Turnout %	Turnout +/-	Con %	Con +/-	Lab %	Lab +/-	LD %	LD +/-	UKIP %	UKIP +/-	Grn %	Grn +/-	Other No & %	Swing
Nuneaton	66.6	-0.7	51.6	+6.0	41.3	+6.4	2.0	+0.2	3.5	-10.9	1.7	-1.1	–	-0.2
Rugby	71.1	+2.7	54.3	+5.2	38.3	+10.4	5.6	-0.1	–	–	1.9	-1.0	–	-2.6
Stratford-on-Avon	73.8	+1.6	62.9	+5.2	21.9	+8.9	11.9	-0.1	–	–	2.5	-1.6	2 (0.9)	–
Warwick & Leamington*	72.8	+2.1	44.4	-3.5	46.7	+11.8	5.2	+0.2	1.5	-6.8	2.2	-1.7	–	-7.6
Warwickshire North	65.3	-2.3	56.9	+14.6	38.9	+2.9	2.2	+0.1	–	–	2.0	+0.1	–	5.9
West Midlands, Aldridge-Brownhills	66.7	+1.1	65.4	+13.4	29.8	+7.5	3.3	0.0	–	–	–	–	1 (1.4)	2.9
Birmingham Edgbaston	64.0	+1.1	39.5	+1.2	55.3	+10.5	3.6	+0.7	–	–	1.3	-2.0	1 (0.4)	-4.7
Birmingham Erdington	57.2	+3.9	38.4	+7.6	58.0	+12.3	2.0	-0.8	–	–	1.6	-1.1	–	-2.4
Birmingham Hall Green	69.4	+7.8	15.1	-2.6	77.6	+17.8	5.8	-5.8	–	–	1.5	-3.1	–	-10.2
Birmingham Hodge Hill	61.3	+6.8	14.2	+2.7	81.1	+12.7	1.7	-4.7	2.2	-9.1	0.8	-1.2	–	-5.0
Birmingham Ladywood	59.0	+6.3	13.2	+0.5	82.7	+9.1	2.8	-1.0	–	–	1.3	-2.9	–	-4.3
Birmingham Northfield	61.3	+1.9	42.7	+7.0	53.2	+11.6	2.2	-1.0	–	–	1.9	-0.8	–	-2.3
Birmingham Perry Barr	63.0	+4.1	26.5	+5.0	68.1	+10.7	2.4	-2.4	–	–	1.3	-1.9	2 (1.6)	-2.8
Birmingham Selly Oak	65.9	+5.5	31.9	+2.9	62.9	+15.3	3.4	-2.2	–	–	1.8	-3.3	–	-6.2
Birmingham Yardley	61.3	+4.3	19.8	+5.8	57.1	+15.4	17.9	-7.7	4.3	-11.8	0.6	-1.1	1 (0.2)	–
Coventry North East	61.4	+5.4	29.9	+6.8	63.4	+11.3	2.5	-2.3	2.9	-12.0	1.1	-1.9	1 (0.2)	-2.2
Coventry North West	66.3	+4.8	36.7	+5.7	54.0	+12.9	2.6	-1.4	3.1	-12.6	1.3	-3.0	1 (2.3)	-3.6
Coventry South	66.5	+4.4	38.1	+3.2	55.0	+12.8	2.9	-1.2	2.2	-10.9	1.3	-2.6	1 (0.5)	-4.8
Dudley North	62.7	+0.1	46.4	+15.6	46.5	+4.7	0.9	-0.3	5.5	-18.5	0.6	-0.7	–	5.5
Dudley South	62.4	-0.9	56.4	+12.7	36.2	+3.6	1.6	-0.5	4.7	-14.3	1.0	-1.5	–	4.5
Halesowen & Rowley Regis	64.5	-1.9	51.9	+8.6	40.0	+3.8	1.9	-0.1	4.8	-11.8	1.0	-0.9	1 (0.4)	2.4
Meriden	67.1	+2.9	62.0	+7.3	26.9	+7.9	4.9	-0.1	3.7	-13.2	2.6	-1.5	–	-0.3
Solihull	73.0	+2.7	58.1	+8.9	21.9	+11.5	15.7	-10.0	2.3	-9.3	2.0	-0.9	–	–
Stourbridge	67.1	+0.5	54.5	+8.5	38.3	+6.8	2.3	-1.0	3.8	-13.1	1.0	-1.2	–	0.8
Sutton Coldfield	69.9	+2.0	61.0	+6.3	31.9	+9.6	4.4	-0.8	–	-16.0	1.8	-1.0	1 (0.9)	-1.6
Walsall North*	56.6	+1.6	49.6	+15.9	42.8	+3.8	1.5	-0.7	6.0	-11.5	–	–	–	6.0
Walsall South	65.4	+3.6	37.2	+4.4	57.4	+10.2	1.3	-0.3	4.1	-13.1	–	–	–	-2.9
Warley	63.1	+3.7	26.2	+6.8	67.2	+9.0	1.9	-0.2	3.4	-13.1	1.4	-2.5	–	-1.1
West Bromwich East	61.2	+2.3	38.2	+13.3	58.0	+7.8	1.6	-0.4	–	–	1.4	-0.3	1 (0.8)	2.8
West Bromwich West	54.7	+1.3	39.7	+15.8	52.1	+4.7	0.9	-0.6	6.4	-18.8	0.9	-1.1	–	-1.1
Wolverhampton North East	60.1	+4.4	40.3	+10.3	52.8	+6.7	1.6	-1.2	4.1	-15.1	1.3	-0.7	–	1.8

Constituency														
Wolverhampton South East	60.2	+4.6	34.8	+12.4	58.2	+4.9	1.2	−1.1	4.6	−15.7	1.2	−0.6	–	3.8
Wolverhampton South West	70.6	+4.0	44.2	+3.0	49.4	+6.1	1.9	−0.3	2.4	−8.3	1.4	−1.3	1 (0.8)	−1.6
West Sussex, Arundel & South Downs	75.8	+2.7	62.4	+1.6	22.7	+11.5	7.9	+0.7	2.8	−11.7	4.2	−2.2	–	–
Bognor Regis & Littlehampton	67.7	+3.2	59.0	+7.6	24.9	+11.1	6.5	−2.5	3.6	−18.1	1.9	−2.2	1 (4.1)	–
Chichester	70.5	+2.0	60.1	+2.5	22.4	+10.2	11.3	+2.7	2.8	−12.2	3.3	−3.2	1 (0.1)	–
Crawley	68.5	+2.8	50.6	+3.6	45.7	+12.1	3.7	+1.0	–	–	–	–	–	−4.3
Horsham	74.9	+2.9	59.5	+2.2	21.7	+10.2	12.3	+0.7	2.5	−11.5	3.0	−0.9	2 (1.0)	–
Sussex Mid	73.2	+2.3	56.9	+0.8	25.0	+11.1	12.7	+1.3	2.0	−10.0	2.5	−1.7	1 (0.8)	−5.2
Worthing East & Shoreham	70.3	+3.6	48.9	−0.5	39.3	+19.8	4.7	−2.0	2.7	−13.8	2.4	−2.8	2 (1.9)	−10.2
Worthing West	70.1	+3.0	55.4	+3.9	33.2	+17.5	5.5	−3.3	3.0	−15.3	3.0	−2.8	–	–
West Yorkshire, Batley & Spen	67.1	+2.7	38.8	+7.6	55.5	+12.3	2.3	−2.5	–	–	1.3	−1.1	2 (2.1)	−2.3
Bradford East	64.8	+2.2	20.4	+9.1	65.4	+18.7	1.8	−27.7	3.0	−6.9	0.6	−1.5	2 (8.8)	–
Bradford South	60.6	+1.5	38.2	+11.9	54.5	+11.1	1.3	−1.7	4.3	−19.8	0.9	−2.4	1 (0.9)	0.4
Bradford West	67.4	+3.8	16.6	+1.3	64.7	+15.1	1.6	−1.3	1.9	−5.8	1.1	−1.6	3 (14.2)	–
Calder Valley	73.4	+4.6	46.1	+2.5	45.1	+9.7	3.4	−1.6	2.5	−8.6	1.1	−2.8	1 (1.8)	−3.6
Colne Valley*	71.6	+2.8	46.2	+1.7	47.7	+12.7	4.1	−1.9	–	–	1.5	−1.9	1 (0.5)	−5.5
Dewsbury	69.5	+2.3	45.1	+6.0	51.0	+9.2	2.1	−1.4	–	–	1.8	−0.7	–	−1.6
Elmet & Rothwell	74.2	+1.1	54.3	+5.9	37.9	+4.1	4.4	−0.2	–	–	1.7	−0.5	1 (1.8)	0.9
Halifax	67.8	+5.7	41.7	+2.7	52.8	+12.8	2.2	−1.5	3.2	−9.6	–	–	–	−5.1
Hemsworth	63.9	+5.6	33.9	+11.0	56.0	+4.7	2.0	−1.2	5.6	−14.6	–	–	–	3.2
Huddersfield	65.4	+3.4	33.0	+6.2	60.4	+15.5	2.6	−3.2	–	–	3.2	−3.7	1 (2.5)	−4.6
Keighley*	72.4	+1.1	46.1	+1.7	46.5	+8.4	2.4	−0.3	2.5	−9.0	1.5	−1.9	2 (0.8)	−3.3
Leeds Central	53.2	−1.8	20.5	+3.2	70.2	+15.2	2.2	−1.2	4.3	−11.4	2.5	−5.4	1 (1.0)	−6.0
Leeds East	62.8	+3.9	30.6	+9.7	61.4	+7.6	1.8	−1.6	4.2	−14.8	1.0	−1.9	1 (0.3)	1.0
Leeds North East	75.6	+5.7	31.0	−1.9	63.1	+15.2	3.7	−1.6	–	–	1.3	−4.0	1 (1.0)	−8.5
Leeds North West*	67.9	−2.0	19.7	+1.0	44.1	+14.0	35.0	−1.8	–	–	1.3	−5.8	3 (0.9)	–
Leeds West	62.1	+3.0	26.2	+6.0	64.0	+15.9	2.1	−1.7	4.3	−14.2	2.4	−6.0	2 (1.0)	−4.9

ENGLAND	Turnout %	Turnout +/-	Con %	Con +/-	Lab %	Lab +/-	LD %	LD +/-	UKIP %	UKIP +/-	Grn %	Grn +/-	Other No & %	Swing
Morley & Outwood	68.4	+4.8	50.7	+11.8	46.7	+8.7	2.6	-0.4	–	–	–	–	–	1.6
Normanton, Pontefract & Castleford	60.3	+4.7	30.0	+9.2	59.5	+4.6	1.4	-1.5	6.2	-15.2	–	–	1 (2.9)	–
Pudsey	74.3	+2.1	47.4	+0.9	46.7	+9.2	3.3	-0.5	–	–	–	–	2 (2.6)	-4.1
Shipley	73.0	+1.3	51.3	+1.4	42.6	+11.6	4.1	+0.3	–	–	–	–	1 (1.9)	-5.1
Wakefield	65.8	+4.9	45.0	+10.8	49.7	+9.4	2.0	-1.4	–	–	–	–	2 (3.3)	0.7
Wiltshire, Chippenham	74.8	+0.1	54.7	+7.2	19.7	+11.4	25.6	-3.8	–	–	–	–	–	–
Devizes	70.1	-0.7	62.7	+5.0	21.0	+8.0	9.3	+1.2	3.4	-12.0	3.2	-2.6	1 (0.4)	-3.9
Salisbury	73.1	+0.3	58.1	+2.5	25.5	+10.2	11.2	+1.2	2.2	-9.9	2.2	-3.3	1 (0.8)	-3.7
Swindon North	68.5	+4.0	53.6	+3.3	38.4	+10.6	3.6	+0.3	2.8	-12.5	1.6	-1.7	–	-3.7
Swindon South	70.8	+4.2	48.4	+2.2	43.6	+9.1	4.1	+0.4	2.5	-9.5	1.5	-2.1	–	-3.5
Wiltshire North	75.2	+0.7	60.3	+3.1	17.5	+7.7	17.7	+2.1	1.6	-9.9	2.1	-2.5	1 (0.7)	–
Wiltshire South West	71.2	+0.5	60.0	+7.3	26.5	+13.1	9.8	-0.8	–	–	2.6	-3.1	1 (1.1)	–

WALES	Turnout %	Turnout +/-	Con %	Con +/-	Lab %	Lab +/-	LD %	LD +/-	Plaid %	Plaid +/-	UKIP %	UKIP +/-	Grn %	Grn +/-	Others No & %	Swing
Clwyd, Aberconwy	71.0	+4.8	44.6	+3.1	42.6	+14.4	2.9	-1.7	9.9	-1.9	–	–	–	–	–	-5.6
Alyn & Deeside	71.0	+4.4	40.4	+8.5	52.1	+12.1	2.4	-1.8	2.6	-1.3	2.5	-15.1	–	–	–	-1.8
Clwyd South	69.7	+6.0	39.1	+8.7	50.7	+13.5	2.0	-1.9	6.1	-4.2	2.1	-13.5	–	–	–	-2.4
Clwyd West	69.8	+4.9	48.1	+4.8	39.6	+14.0	2.7	-1.0	9.6	-2.6	–	–	–	–	–	-4.6
Delyn	72.9	+3.0	41.4	+8.7	52.2	+11.6	2.6	-1.1	3.8	-1.1	–	–	–	–	–	-1.5
Vale of Clwyd*	68.0	+5.6	44.1	+5.0	50.2	+11.9	1.7	-0.9	4.0	-3.0	–	–	–	–	–	-3.4
Wrexham	70.4	+6.2	43.7	+12.0	48.9	+11.7	2.5	-2.8	5.0	-2.6	–	–	–	–	–	+0.2
Dyfed, Carmarthen East & Dinefwr	73.3	+2.6	26.3	+5.1	29.8	+5.6	2.2	-0.1	39.3	+0.9	2.4	-8.7	–	–	–	–
Carmarthen West & Pembrokeshire South	72.1	+2.2	46.8	+3.1	39.5	+10.8	2.3	-0.1	9.3	-1.1	2.1	-9.5	–	–	–	-3.8
Ceredigion*	73.3	+4.3	18.4	+7.4	20.2	+10.5	29.0	-6.9	29.2	+1.6	1.5	-8.7	1.4	-4.2	1 (0.4)	–
Llanelli	67.9	+2.8	23.7	+9.3	53.5	+12.1	1.4	-0.6	18.2	-4.7	3.3	-13.0	–	–	–	–

Constituency																
Preseli Pembrokeshire	72.1	+1.3	43.4	+3.0	42.6	+14.5	2.6	+0.7	6.4	+0.2	2.0	-8.5	–	–	2 (2.9)	-5.8
Gwent, Blaenau Gwent	63.2	+1.5	14.8	+4.0	58.0	0.0	0.9	-1.0	21.2	+12.3	3.0	-14.9	–	–	1 (2.1)	–
Islwyn	64.2	+0.6	27.2	+12.1	58.8	+9.9	1.9	-0.8	7.6	-3.1	4.4	-15.1	–	–	–	–
Monmouth	76.6	+0.4	53.1	+3.2	36.6	+9.8	4.2	-1.1	2.7	-1.3	1.5	-8.9	1.9	-1.5	–	-3.3
Newport East	64.3	+1.7	34.8	+7.5	56.5	+15.8	2.6	-3.8	2.4	-1.1	3.2	-15.2	–	–	1 (0.5)	-4.2
Newport West	67.5	+2.5	39.3	+6.8	52.3	+11.1	2.2	-1.7	2.5	-1.5	2.5	-12.7	1.1	-2.0	–	-2.2
Torfaen	62.1	+0.9	31.0	+7.8	57.6	+12.9	2.2	-1.1	5.4	-0.4	3.9	-15.1	–	–	–	-2.6
Gwynedd, Arfon	68.2	+1.9	16.4	+3.2	40.5	+10.2	2.3	-0.4	40.8	-3.1	–	–	–	–	–	–
Dwyfor Meirionnydd	67.9	+2.8	29.1	+6.5	20.7	+7.2	3.1	-0.9	45.1	+4.3	2.0	-8.8	–	–	–	–
Ynys Mon	70.6	+0.7	27.8	+6.6	41.9	+10.7	1.3	-0.9	27.4	-3.1	1.7	-13.0	–	–	–	–
Mid-Glamorgan, Bridgend	69.6	+3.8	39.8	+7.6	50.7	+13.6	2.1	-2.1	4.1	-2.9	1.8	-13.2	–	–	1 (1.5)	-3.0
Caerphilly	64.1	+0.8	25.2	+8.6	54.5	+10.1	1.8	-0.6	14.4	-0.2	3.0	-16.3	1.1	-1.2	–	–
Cynon Valley	62.0	+2.7	19.4	+7.3	61.0	+13.3	1.8	-0.9	13.8	-3.1	4.0	-12.3	–	–	–	–
Merthyr Tydfil & Rhymney	60.5	+7.5	18.1	+8.0	66.8	+12.9	2.5	-1.6	8.2	-1.3	4.4	-14.2	–	–	–	–
Ogmore	65.1	+1.7	25.1	+9.2	62.4	+9.5	1.6	-1.4	7.5	-2.6	3.3	-12.1	–	–	–	-0.1
Pontypridd	65.9	+1.6	26.7	+9.4	55.4	+14.3	4.9	-8.0	10.3	-1.2	2.7	-10.7	–	–	–	-2.5
Rhondda	65.2	+4.3	10.1	+3.4	64.1	+13.4	0.8	-0.7	22.3	-4.7	2.7	-10.0	–	–	–	–
Powys, Brecon & Radnorshire	73.8	+0.2	48.6	+7.5	17.7	+3.0	29.1	+0.8	3.1	-1.3	1.4	-6.9	1.5	-2.2	–	–
Montgomeryshire	68.7	-0.6	51.8	+6.8	15.9	+10.3	25.2	-4.1	5.6	+0.4	–	–	1.0	-5.3	–	–
South Glamorgan, Cardiff Central	68.1	+0.8	19.8	+5.1	62.4	+22.4	13.4	-13.7	2.5	-2.5	0.8	-5.6	–	–	–	–
Cardiff North*	77.4	+1.3	42.1	-0.3	50.1	+11.9	3.3	-0.5	3.3	-1.2	1.1	-6.6	1.0	-2.7	1 (0.3)	-6.1
Cardiff South & Penarth	66.3	+4.9	30.2	+3.4	59.5	+16.7	2.8	-2.1	4.3	-3.1	1.9	-11.9	–	–	–	-6.7
Cardiff West	69.8	+4.2	29.8	+4.6	56.7	+16.0	2.6	-2.1	9.5	-4.4	1.5	-9.7	–	–	–	-5.7
Vale of Glamorgan	72.6	+2.2	47.5	+1.4	43.4	+10.8	1.9	-0.7	4.3	-1.3	1.6	-9.1	0.8	-1.3	2 (0.6)	-4.7
West Glamorgan, Aberavon	66.7	+3.4	17.7	+5.9	68.1	+19.2	1.8	-2.6	8.3	-3.3	4.0	-11.7	–	–	–	–
Gower*	73.3	+4.2	42.7	+5.6	49.9	+12.8	2.0	-1.6	3.7	-3.5	1.4	-9.8	–	–	1 (0.3)	-3.6

WALES

	Turnout %	Turnout +/-	Con %	Con +/-	Lab %	Lab +/-	LD %	LD +/-	Plaid %	Plaid +/-	UKIP %	UKIP +/-	Grn %	Grn +/-	Others No & %	Swing
Neath	68.5	+2.3	23.7	+8.4	56.7	+12.9	1.9	-1.2	13.9	-4.2	3.7	-12.7	–	–	–	–
Swansea East	60.1	+2.1	26.0	+10.7	63.4	+10.5	1.8	-2.4	4.8	-5.6	3.0	-14.2	1.0	–	–	–
Swansea West	65.5	+5.7	31.3	+8.8	59.8	+17.2	3.4	-5.6	4.1	-2.3	–	–	1.2	-3.9	1 (0.2)	-4.2

SCOTLAND

	Turnout %	Turnout +/-	Con %	Con +/-	Lab %	Lab +/-	LD %	LD +/-	SNP %	SNP +/-	UKIP %	UKIP +/-	Grn %	Grn +/-	Others No & %	Swing
Aberdeen North	59.2	-5.7	22.7	+10.6	30.0	+4.1	4.6	-0.1	41.3	-15.2	–	–	–	–	1 (1.4)	–
Aberdeen South*	68.5	-2.9	42.1	+19.3	20.5	-6.2	5.9	+1.2	31.5	-10.2	–	–	–	–	–	–
Aberdeenshire West & Kincardine*	71.2	-3.9	47.9	+19.0	11.1	+6.5	8.6	-12.8	32.5	-9.1	–	–	–	–	–	–
Airdrie & Shotts	59.2	-7.1	23.2	+15.5	37.1	+3.0	2.1	+0.6	37.6	-16.3	–	–	–	–	–	–
Angus*	63.0	-4.7	45.2	+16.2	13.0	+4.2	3.3	+0.5	38.6	-15.7	–	–	–	–	–	–
Argyll & Bute	71.5	-3.8	33.2	+18.3	12.6	+2.2	18.2	-9.7	36.0	-8.3	–	–	–	–	–	–
Ayr, Carrick & Cumnock*	64.9	-6.6	40.1	+20.3	23.9	-3.4	1.9	+0.2	34.1	-14.7	–	–	–	–	–	–
Ayrshire Central	65.3	-7.2	34.4	+17.0	26.1	-0.3	2.3	+0.5	37.2	-16.0	–	–	–	–	–	–
Ayrshire North & Arran	64.8	-6.3	31.2	+16.4	27.5	-0.5	2.4	+0.7	38.9	-14.3	–	–	–	–	–	–
Banff & Buchan*	61.6	-4.9	48.0	+19.2	9.5	+3.7	3.5	-1.7	39.1	-21.1	–	–	–	–	–	–
Berwickshire, Roxburgh & Selkirk*	71.5	-2.6	53.9	+17.9	8.6	+3.7	4.7	-14.0	32.8	-3.8	–	–	–	–	–	–
Caithness, Sutherland & Easter Ross*	65.9	-6.0	22.6	+15.8	12.4	+3.5	35.8	+0.7	29.2	-17.1	–	–	–	–	–	–
Coatbridge, Chryston & Bellshill*	63.3	-5.3	16.2	+9.9	42.6	+8.7	2.0	+1.0	39.1	-17.5	–	–	–	–	–	–
Cumbernauld, Kilsyth & Kirkintilloch East	65.9	-7.7	18.3	+10.4	33.9	+3.9	2.8	+0.6	43.6	-16.3	1.4	–	–	–	–	–
Dumfries & Galloway*	69.5	-5.7	43.3	+13.4	20.9	-3.8	2.4	+0.7	32.4	-9.0	–	–	–	–	1 (1.0)	–
Dumfriesshire, Clydesdale & Tweeddale	72.4	-3.8	49.4	+9.6	16.5	+1.8	4.0	+1.3	30.1	-8.2	–	–	–	–	–	–
Dunbartonshire East*	78.1	-3.8	14.6	+6.0	14.5	+2.2	40.6	+4.3	30.3	-10.0	–	–	–	–	–	–

Constituency																
Dunbartonshire West	65.2	−8.7	17.2	+10.2	37.7	+6.3	2.3	+0.7	42.9	−16.2					–	–
Dundee East	65.2	−5.9	27.4	+12.4	26.0	+6.1	3.8	+0.9	42.8	−16.9					–	–
Dundee West	61.7	−6.1	16.2	+7.6	33.1	+9.4	3.1	+0.7	46.7	−15.3					1 (1.0)	–
Dunfermline & West Fife	67.4	−4.2	24.7	+12.8	33.9	+2.1	5.9	+1.9	35.5	−14.7					–	–
East Kilbride, Strathaven & Lesmahagow	67.3	−5.5	25.3	+13.6	31.7	+3.4	2.9	+1.2	38.9	−16.8	1.2	−0.9			–	–
East Lothian*	70.6	−3.6	29.6	+10.1	36.1	+5.1	3.1	+0.5	30.6	−12.0					1 (0.7)	–
Edinburgh East	66.0	−4.1	18.6	+8.6	34.7	+4.8	4.2	+1.4	42.5	−6.7					–	–
Edinburgh North & Leith	71.2	−0.5	27.2	+11.0	31.2	−0.1	4.6	0.0	34.0	−6.9			3.1	−2.4	–	–
Edinburgh South	74.1	−0.8	19.7	+2.2	54.9	+15.8	2.9	−0.8	22.5	−11.3					–	–
Edinburgh South West	69.4	−2.1	33.4	+13.1	26.8	−0.4	4.3	+0.6	35.6	−7.4					–	–
Edinburgh West*	73.8	−2.7	21.9	+9.6	14.9	+3.2	34.3	+1.2	28.6	−10.3					1 (0.3)	–
Falkirk	65.4	−6.9	26.2	+14.0	29.8	+4.7	2.1	+0.1	38.9	−18.8	1.3	−1.7	1.7		–	–
Fife North East	71.3	−1.7	24.1	+7.8	9.6	+1.9	32.9	+1.5	32.9	−8.1					1 (0.5)	–
Glasgow Central	55.9	+0.5	13.9	+7.9	38.4	+5.4	2.9	+1.3	44.7	−7.8					–	–
Glasgow East	54.6	−5.7	18.8	+12.8	38.6	+6.2	1.6	+0.8	38.8	−18.1	1.4	−1.2			–	–
Glasgow North	62.1	+0.8	14.7	+6.9	34.5	+6.5	3.4	+0.7	37.6	−15.5					–	–
Glasgow North East*	53.0	−3.8	12.9	+8.2	42.9	+9.2	2.0	+1.2	42.2	−15.9			9.7	+3.5	2 (0.8)	–
Glasgow North West	60.9	−3.2	18.0	+9.6	35.9	+5.0	3.6	+0.8	42.5	−12.0					–	–
Glasgow South	64.4	−1.4	19.1	+9.4	36.6	+6.8	3.2	+1.2	41.1	−13.8					–	–
Glasgow South West	56.2	−5.6	15.6	+10.6	40.5	+7.7	1.9	+0.9	40.7	−16.5	1.4	−1.0			–	–
Glenrothes	60.9	−7.3	19.5	+11.8	34.7	+4.1	3.0	+1.1	42.8	−17.0					–	–
Gordon*	68.4	−4.9	40.7	+29.0	11.8	+5.9	11.6	−21.1	35.9	−11.8					–	–
Inverclyde	66.4	−8.7	21.5	+11.5	37.5	+7.2	2.5	0.0	38.5	−16.6					–	–
Inverness, Nairn, Badenoch & Strathspey	68.7	−5.5	30.5	+24.6	16.2	+8.7	12.3	−19.0	39.9	−10.2					1 (1.2)	–
Kilmarnock & Loudoun	63.4	−8.2	26.7	+14.1	28.9	−1.5	2.1	+0.7	42.3	−13.3					–	–

SCOTLAND	Turnout %	Turnout +/-	Con %	Con +/-	Lab %	Lab +/-	LD %	LD +/-	SNP %	SNP +/-	UKIP %	UKIP +/-	Grn %	Grn +/-	Others No & %	Swing
Kirkcaldy & Cowdenbeath*	63.5	−6.1	23.3	+13.4	36.8	+3.5	2.4	+0.2	36.3	−16.0	1.2	−1.2	–	–	–	–
Lanark & Hamilton East	65.3	−3.8	32.1	+16.2	31.9	+1.3	2.4	+0.2	32.6	−16.2	1.1	−1.5	–	–	–	–
Linlithgow & Falkirk East	65.1	−5.8	29.1	+17.1	31.1	+0.1	3.4	+1.4	36.3	−15.7	–	–	–	–	–	–
Livingston	64.7	−5.2	24.4	+14.1	32.7	+5.1	2.9	+0.7	40.1	−16.8	–	–	–	–	–	–
Midlothian*	66.3	−4.9	25.4	+13.5	36.4	+6.2	3.8	+1.5	34.4	−16.2	–	–	–	–	–	–
Moray*	67.4	−1.4	47.6	+16.5	10.9	+1.0	2.3	−0.6	38.8	−10.7	–	–	–	–	1 (0.4)	–
Motherwell & Wishaw	61.5	−7.2	20.2	+12.6	37.8	+5.9	2.2	+0.9	38.5	−18.0	–	–	–	–	–	–
Na h-Eileanan an Iar	69.6	−3.6	16.5	+8.8	33.8	+5.2	1.7	−1.2	40.6	−13.8	1.3	−1.4	–	–	1 (7.5)	–
Ochil & South Perthshire*	70.6	−4.2	41.5	+20.8	20.0	−8.4	3.2	+0.7	35.3	−10.7	–	–	–	–	–	–
Orkney & Shetland	68.1	+2.4	8.7	−0.2	11.4	+4.3	48.6	+7.2	29.0	−8.8	1.2	−3.5	–	–	1 (1.1)	–
Paisley & Renfrewshire North	69.1	−7.1	27.5	+15.3	31.8	−0.9	3.2	+1.1	37.4	−13.3	–	–	–	–	–	–
Paisley & Renfrewshire South	68.0	−7.4	19.5	+11.8	34.6	−4.1	3.2	+1.0	40.7	−10.3	–	–	–	–	1 (2.1)	–
Perth & Perthshire North	71.8	−3.0	42.3	+9.5	10.4	+2.2	5.0	+1.2	42.3	−8.2	–	–	–	–	–	–
Renfrewshire East*	76.7	−4.4	40.0	+18.0	26.7	−7.3	2.1	+0.2	31.2	−9.3	–	–	–	–	–	–
Ross, Skye & Lochaber	71.7	−5.5	24.9	+18.6	12.2	+7.3	20.9	−15.0	40.3	−7.9	–	–	–	–	2 (1.8)	–
Rutherglen & Hamilton West*	63.5	−6.0	19.5	+12.0	37.5	+2.3	4.2	+2.4	37.0	−15.5	0.9	−1.3	–	–	1 (0.7)	–
Stirling*	74.3	−3.2	37.1	+13.9	22.1	−3.4	3.4	+0.7	36.8	−8.9	–	–	–	–	1 (0.7)	–

NORTHERN IRELAND	Turnout %	Turnout +/-	UUP %	UUP +/-	DUP %	DUP +/-	APNI %	APNI +/-	SF %	SF +/-	SDLP %	SDLP +/-	Other %
East Antrim	60.6	+7.3	11.9	−7.0	57.3	+21.2	15.6	+0.6	9.3	+2.4	3.4	−1.5	2.5
North Antrim	64.1	+8.8	7.2	−4.9	58.9	+15.6	5.6	0.0	16.3	+4.0	5.3	−1.7	6.8
South Antrim*	63.3	+9.1	30.8	−1.9	38.2	+8.1	7.4	−2.4	18.1	+5.2	5.5	−2.7	–
Belfast East	67.5	+4.7	3.3	–	55.8	+6.4	36.0	−6.8	2.1	0.0	0.4	+0.1	2.5
Belfast North	67.3	+8.1	–	–	46.2	−0.8	5.4	−1.9	41.7	+7.8	4.5	−3.7	2.2
Belfast South*	66.1	+6.1	3.5	−5.6	30.4	+8.2	18.2	+1.0	16.3	+2.5	25.9	+1.3	5.7
Belfast West	65.1	+8.7	–	–	13.4	+5.6	1.8	0.0	66.7	+12.5	7.0	−2.8	11.0
North Down	60.9	+4.9	–	–	38.1	+14.5	9.3	+0.7	1.4	+0.6	1.0	0.0	50.2

South Down*	67.2	+10.5	3.9	−5.4	17.4	+9.3	3.6	−0.2	39.9	+11.4	35.1	−7.2	–
Fermanagh & South Tyrone*	75.8	+3.2	45.5	−0.9	–	–	1.7	+0.4	47.2	+1.8	4.8	−0.5	0.8
Foyle*	65.4	+12.5	–	–	16.1	+3.7	1.8	−0.4	39.7	+8.2	39.3	−8.6	3.0
Lagan Valley	62.1	+6.1	16.8	+1.6	59.6	+11.7	11.1	−2.8	3.5	+0.6	7.5	+1.3	1.5
East Londonderry	61.2	+9.3	7.6	−7.7	48.1	+5.8	6.2	−1.4	26.5	+6.8	10.8	−1.5	0.8
Newry & Armagh	68.5	+4.2	8.3	−24.4	24.6	–	2.3	+0.7	47.9	+6.8	16.9	−7.2	0.0
Strangford	60.2	+7.5	11.4	−2.9	62.0	+17.7	14.7	+0.9	2.8	+0.2	6.2	−0.7	2.9
West Tyrone	67.9	+7.4	5.2	−10.7	26.9	+9.5	2.3	+0.1	50.7	+7.2	13.0	−3.7	1.9
Mid Ulster	68.2	+7.9	6.5	−9.0	26.9	+13.6	2.3	+0.4	54.5	+5.8	9.8	−2.6	–
Upper Bann	63.9	+5.0	15.4	−12.5	43.5	+10.9	4.5	+0.8	27.9	+3.4	8.6	−0.4	–

Notes:

UUP: Ulster Unionist Party

DUP: Democratic Unionist Party

APNI: Alliance Party of Northern Ireland

SF: Sinn Féin

SDLP: Social Democratic and Labour Party

Table A2.6   Seats changing hands

Con gains from Labour
Copeland
Derbyshire North East
Mansfield
Middlesbrough South & Cleveland East
Stoke-on-Trent South
Walsall North

Con gains from Lib Dems
Southport

Con gains from SNP
Aberdeen South
Aberdeenshire West & Kincardine
Angus
Ayr, Carrick & Cumnock
Banff & Buchan
Berwickshire, Roxburgh & Selkirk
Dumfries & Galloway
Gordon
Moray
Ochil & South Perthshire
Renfrewshire East
Stirling

Con gains from UKIP
Clacton

Labour gains from Con
Battersea
Bedford
Brighton Kemptown
Bristol North West
Bury North
Canterbury
Cardiff North
Colne Valley
Crewe & Nantwich
Croydon Central
Derby North
Enfield Southgate
Gower
High Peak
Ipswich
Keighley
Kensington

Lincoln
Peterborough
Plymouth Sutton & Devonport
Portsmouth South
Reading East
Stockton South
Stroud
Vale of Clwyd
Warrington South
Warwick & Leamington
Weaver Vale

Labour gains from Lib Dems
Leeds North West
Sheffield Hallam

Labour gains from SNP
Coatbridge, Chryston & Bellshill
East Lothian
Glasgow North East
Kirkcaldy & Cowdenbeath
Midlothian
Rutherglen & Hamilton West

Lib Dem gains from Con
Bath
Eastbourne
Kingston & Surbiton
Oxford West & Abingdon
Twickenham

Lib Dem gains from SNP
Caithness, Sutherland & Easter Ross
Dunbartonshire East
Edinburgh West

Plaid gains from Lib Dems
Ceredigion

Other gains
South Antrim, DUP from UUP
Belfast South, DUP from SDLP
Fermanagh & South Tyrone, SF from
   UUP
South Down, SF from SDLP
Foyle, SF from SDLP

Table A2.7   Exceptional results

TURNOUT

12 largest & smallest % turnout

Twickenham	79.5
Oxford West & Abingdon	79.4
Richmond Park	79.1
Winchester	78.8
Wirral West	78.5
Wirral South	78.4
St Albans	78.3
Dunbartonshire East	78.1
Rushcliffe	78.0
Hornsey & Wood Green	77.9
Westmorland & Lonsdale	77.9
Devon Central	77.8
[...]	
Nottingham North	57.3
Birmingham Erdington	57.2
Walsall North	56.6
Glasgow South West	56.2
Blackley & Broughton	56.0
Glasgow Central	55.9
Hull East	55.5
Manchester Central	55.1
West Bromwich West	54.7
Glasgow East	54.6
Leeds Central	53.2
Glasgow North East	53.0

12 largest increases & decreases in % turnout

Foyle	+12.5
Ilford South	+11.1
Hackney South & Shoreditch	+10.6
South Down	+10.5
Hackney North & Stoke Newington	+9.6
East Londonderry	+9.3
Slough	+9.3
Cambridge	+9.1
South Antrim	+9.1
North Antrim	+8.8
Vauxhall	+8.8
Chester, City of	+8.8
[...]	
Ayr, Carrick & Cumnock	−6.6
Falkirk	−6.9

Airdrie & Shotts	−7.1
Paisley & Renfrewshire North	−7.1
Ayrshire Central	−7.2
Motherwell & Wishaw	−7.2
Glenrothes	−7.3
Paisley & Renfrewshire South	−7.4
Cumbernauld, Kilsyth & Kirkintilloch East	−7.7
Kilmarnock & Loudoun	−8.2
Dunbartonshire West	−8.7
Inverclyde	−8.7

MARGINALITY

12 largest and smallest % majorities

Liverpool Walton	Lab		77.1
Knowsley	Lab		76.1
Liverpool Riverside	Lab		74.9
Liverpool West Derby	Lab		72.9
Bootle	Lab		72.0
East Ham	Lab		70.4
Tottenham	Lab		70.1
Birmingham Ladywood	Lab		69.5
Manchester Gorton	Lab		69.0
Hackney South & Shoreditch	Lab		68.5
Liverpool Wavertree	Lab		67.5
Birmingham Hodge Hill	Lab		66.9
[...]		N	
Stirling	Con	148	0.3
Ceredigion	Plaid	104	0.3
Glasgow East	SNP	75	0.2
Glasgow South West	SNP	60	0.2
Crewe & Nantwich	Lab	48	0.1
Richmond Park	Con	45	0.1
Newcastle-under-Lyme	Lab	30	0.1
Southampton Itchen	Con	31	0.1
Dudley North	Lab	22	0.1
Kensington	Lab	20	0.1

Perth & Perthshire   SNP   21   0.0
North
Fife North East   SNP   2   0.0

Note: Arfon just fails to make a list of most marginal seats by percentage majority, although its numerical majority of 92 is smaller than some of those included

CONSERVATIVE

12 largest rises and falls in % vote share

Gordon	+29.0
Inverness, Nairn, Badenoch & Strathspey	+24.6
Clacton	+24.6
Ochil & South Perthshire	+20.8
Ayr, Carrick & Cumnock	+20.3
Boston & Skegness	+19.8
Aberdeen South	+19.3
Ashfield	+19.3
Banff & Buchan	+19.2
Aberdeenshire West & Kincardine	+19.0
Heywood & Middleton	+18.9
Ross, Skye & Lochaber	+18.6
[...]	
Ealing Central & Acton	−7.9
Hammersmith	−8.2
Hove	−8.4
Westminster North	−8.5
Vauxhall	−8.6
Tooting	−8.8
Putney	−9.7
Hampstead & Kilburn	−10.0
Kensington	−10.1
Chelsea & Fulham	−10.3
Battersea	−10.8
Richmond Park	−13.1

12 highest and lowest % vote share (GB)

South Holland & The Deepings	69.9
Staffordshire South	69.8
Christchurch	69.6
Maldon	67.9
Castle Point	67.3
New Forest West	66.8

Rayleigh & Wickford	66.7
Brentwood & Ongar	65.8
Meon Valley	65.7
Hampshire North East	65.5
Aldridge-Brownhills	65.4
Worcestershire Mid	65.3
[...]	
Bootle	12.0
Liverpool Wavertree	12.0
Tottenham	11.5
Hackney South & Shoreditch	10.9
Manchester Withington	10.3
Rhondda	10.1
Liverpool West Derby	9.9
Liverpool Riverside	9.7
Knowsley	9.3
Orkney & Shetland	8.7
Liverpool Walton	8.6
Manchester Gorton	7.3

Note: This list excludes Northern Ireland. The worst Conservative performances all came in Northern Ireland. They polled lower than in any seat in Great Britain in all of the seven constituencies in which they stood, losing their deposit in all. Their best performance came in East Antrim, where they polled 2.5%; their worst in Belfast South (0.6%)

LABOUR

12 largest rises and falls in % vote share

Bristol West	+30.3
York Central	+22.8
Truro & Falmouth	+22.5
Cardiff Central	+22.4
Hove	+21.8
Bristol South	+21.7
Norwich South	+21.7
Portsmouth South	+21.5
Bristol East	+21.5
Canterbury	+20.5
Worthing East & Shoreham	+19.8
Camborne & Redruth	+19.3
[...]	
Waveney	−0.9
Paisley & Renfrewshire North	−0.9

Kilmarnock & Loudoun	−1.5
Twickenham	−2.3
Richmond Park	−3.2
Ayr, Carrick & Cumnock	−3.4
Stirling	−3.4
Dumfries & Galloway	−3.8
Paisley & Renfrewshire South	−4.1
Aberdeen South	−6.2
Renfrewshire East	−7.3
Ochil & South Perthshire	−8.4

12 highest and lowest % vote share

Liverpool Walton	85.7
Knowsley	85.3
Liverpool Riverside	84.5
Bootle	84.0
East Ham	83.2
Liverpool West Derby	82.7
Birmingham Ladywood	82.7
Tottenham	81.6
Birmingham Hodge Hill	81.1
Walthamstow	80.6
Liverpool Wavertree	79.6
Hackney South & Shoreditch	79.4
[...]	
Moray	10.9
Winchester	10.5
Perth & Perthshire North	10.4
Norfolk North	9.9
Fife North East	9.6
Cheltenham	9.5
Banff & Buchan	9.5
Westmorland & Lonsdale	9.3
Twickenham	9.2
Richmond Park	9.1
Berwickshire, Roxburgh & Selkirk	8.6
Eastbourne	8.1

LIBERAL DEMOCRATS

12 largest rises and falls in % vote share

Richmond Park	+25.8
Bath	+17.6
Oxford West & Abingdon	+14.8
Twickenham	+14.7
St Albans	+13.9
Witney	+13.7
Vauxhall	+13.7
Kingston & Surbiton	+10.3

Winchester	+10.1
St Ives	+9.4
Norfolk North	+9.3
Eastbourne	+8.7
[...]	
Bristol West	−11.6
Redcar	−11.8
Aberdeenshire West & Kincardine	−12.8
Ashfield	−12.9
Cardiff Central	−13.7
Berwickshire, Roxburgh & Selkirk	−14.0
Burnley	−14.4
Ross, Skye & Lochaber	−15.0
Hornsey & Wood Green	−15.7
Inverness, Nairn, Badenoch & Strathspey	−19.0
Gordon	−21.1
Bradford East	−27.7

Note: The table lists constituencies in which Liberal Democrat candidates stood in *both* 2015 and 2017. There were two seats in which the Liberal Democrats stood in 2015 but not 2017, although neither saw big enough falls in the share of the vote to qualify for the above list anyway: Skipton & Ripon (where they polled 7.4% in 2015) and Brighton Pavilion (2.8% in 2015)

12 highest and lowest % vote share

Twickenham	52.8
Orkney & Shetland	48.6
Norfolk North	48.4
Bath	47.3
Eastbourne	46.9
Westmorland & Lonsdale	45.8
Richmond Park	45.1
Kingston & Surbiton	44.7
Oxford West & Abingdon	43.7
St Ives	42.6
Cheltenham	42.2
Carshalton & Wallington	41.0
[...]	
Hayes & Harlington	1.3
Bradford South	1.3
Barking	1.3
Wolverhampton South East	1.2

Liverpool West Derby	1.2
East Ham	1.2
Middlesbrough	1.0
Dagenham & Rainham	1.0
Dudley North	0.9
West Bromwich West	0.9
Blaenau Gwent	0.9
Rhondda	0.8

UKIP

12 lowest and highest falls in % vote share

East Kilbride, Strathaven & Lesmahagow	−0.9
Glasgow South West	−1.0
Kirkcaldy & Cowdenbeath	−1.2
Glasgow East	−1.2
Rutherglen & Hamilton West	−1.3
Motherwell & Wishaw	−1.4
Lanark & Hamilton East	−1.5
Hornsey & Wood Green	−1.5
Falkirk	−1.7
Tooting	−2.3
Battersea	−2.5
Finchley & Golders Green	−2.5
[...]	
Mansfield	−19.8
Great Grimsby	−20.3
Rother Valley	−20.6
Thanet North	−21.2
Rotherham	−21.4
Dagenham & Rainham	−22.8
Rochester & Strood	−25.1
Heywood & Middleton	−25.7
Castle Point	−25.9
Boston & Skegness	−26.1
Thanet South	−26.4
Clacton	−36.8

Note: The table lists constituencies in which UKIP candidates stood in *both* 2015 and 2017. UKIP lost vote share in every seat they contested in both 2015 and 2017, making a table listing rises and falls impossible. There was only one seat which UKIP fought in 2017 having not done so in 2017 (Cumbernauld, Kilsyth & Kirkintilloch East, polling 1.4% of the vote)

12 highest and lowest % vote share

Thurrock	20.1
Hartlepool	11.5
Rotherham	8.7
Barnsley Central	8.5
Barnsley East	8.0
Boston & Skegness	7.7
Clacton	7.6
Rother Valley	7.5
South Shields	7.4
Dagenham & Rainham	7.1
Hull East	7.0
Penistone & Stocksbridge	6.9
[...]	
Tottenham	0.9
Harrow West	0.9
Rutherglen & Hamilton West	0.9
Finchley & Golders Green	0.9
Cardiff Central	0.8
Ilford South	0.8
Islington North	0.8
Hornsey & Wood Green	0.7
Richmond Park	0.7
Battersea	0.6
Streatham	0.6
Tooting	0.6

GREENS

Largest rises and falls in % vote share

Brighton Pavilion	+10.4
Isle of Wight	+4.0
Glasgow North	+3.5
Skipton & Ripon	+0.7
Warwickshire North	+0.1
[...]	
Sheffield Central	−7.8
Nottingham East	−8.1
Oxford East	−8.3
Liverpool Riverside	−8.8
Hackney South & Shoreditch	−8.8
Bristol South	−8.9
Holborn & St Pancras	−9.4
Lewisham Deptford	−9.5
Bath	−9.7
Hackney North & Stoke Newington	−10.0

Norwich South	−11.0
Bristol West	−14.0

Note: The table lists constituencies in which Green candidates stood in *both* 2015 and 2017. There were just five seats in which they did so and increased vote share

12 highest and lowest % vote share

Brighton Pavilion	52.3
Isle of Wight	17.3
Bristol West	12.9
Glasgow North	9.7
Sheffield Central	8.0
Skipton & Ripon	6.4
Herefordshire North	5.5
Hertfordshire North East	5.3
Hackney North & Stoke Newington	4.6
Dorset South	4.4
Folkestone & Hythe	4.2
Arundel & South Downs	4.2
[...]	
Birmingham Hodge Hill	0.8
Ashfield	0.8
Bolton North East	0.8
Barrow & Furness	0.8
Vale of Glamorgan	0.8
Liverpool West Derby	0.7
Middlesbrough	0.7
Stockton South	0.7
Ellesmere Port & Neston	0.7
Bradford East	0.6
Birmingham Yardley	0.6
Dudley North	0.6

SNP

12 lowest and highest falls in % vote share

Berwickshire, Roxburgh & Selkirk	−3.8
Edinburgh East	−6.7
Edinburgh North & Leith	−6.9
Edinburgh South West	−7.4
Glasgow Central	−7.8
Ross, Skye & Lochaber	−7.9
Fife North East	−8.1

Dumfriesshire, Clydesdale & Tweeddale	−8.2
Perth & Perthshire North	−8.2
Argyll & Bute	−8.3
Orkney & Shetland	−8.8
Stirling	−8.9
[...]	
Glasgow South West	−16.5
Inverclyde	−16.6
East Kilbride, Strathaven & Lesmahagow	−16.8
Livingston	−16.8
Dundee East	−16.9
Glenrothes	−17.0
Caithness, Sutherland & Easter Ross	−17.1
Coatbridge, Chryston & Bellshill	−17.5
Motherwell & Wishaw	−18.0
Glasgow East	−18.1
Falkirk	−18.8
Banff & Buchan	−21.1

Note: The SNP lost vote share in every seat in Scotland, thus making a table listing rises and falls impossible

12 highest and lowest % vote share

Dundee West	46.7
Glasgow Central	44.7
Cumbernauld, Kilsyth & Kirkintilloch East	43.6
Dunbartonshire West	42.9
Dundee East	42.8
Glenrothes	42.8
Edinburgh East	42.5
Glasgow North West	42.5
Kilmarnock & Loudoun	42.3
Perth & Perthshire North	42.3
Glasgow North East	42.2
Aberdeen North	41.3
[...]	
Lanark & Hamilton East	32.6
Aberdeenshire West & Kincardine	32.5
Dumfries & Galloway	32.4
Aberdeen South	31.5
Renfrewshire East	31.2

East Lothian	30.6
Dunbartonshire East	30.3
Dumfriesshire, Clydesdale & Tweeddale	30.1
Caithness, Sutherland & Easter Ross	29.2
Orkney & Shetland	29.0
Edinburgh West	28.6
Edinburgh South	22.5

PLAID CYMRU

Largest rises and falls in % vote share

Blaenau Gwent	+12.3
Dwyfor Meirionnydd	+4.3
Ceredigion	+1.6
Carmarthen East & Dinefwr	+0.9
Montgomeryshire	+0.4
Preseli Pembrokeshire	+0.2
[...]	
Ynys Mon	−3.1
Arfon	−3.1
Cardiff South & Penarth	−3.1
Islwyn	−3.1
Aberavon	−3.3
Gower	−3.5
Neath	−4.2
Clwyd South	−4.2
Cardiff West	−4.4
Rhondda	−4.7
Llanelli	−4.7
Swansea East	−5.6

Note: Plaid Cymru increased their vote share in just six seats

12 highest and lowest % vote share

Dwyfor Meirionnydd	45.1
Arfon	40.8
Carmarthen East & Dinefwr	39.3

Ceredigion	29.2
Ynys Mon	27.4
Rhondda	22.3
Blaenau Gwent	21.2
Llanelli	18.2
Caerphilly	14.4
Neath	13.9
Cynon Valley	13.8
Pontypridd	10.3
[...]	
Bridgend	4.1
Swansea West	4.1
Vale of Clwyd	4.0
Delyn	3.8
Gower	3.7
Cardiff North	3.3
Brecon & Radnorshire	3.1
Monmouth	2.7
Alyn & Deeside	2.6
Newport West	2.5
Cardiff Central	2.5
Newport East	2.4

INDEPENDENT

12 best Independent results

North Down	41.2
Devon East	35.2
Bradford West	13.9
Hereford & Herefordshire South	11.0
Buckingham	10.7
Ashfield	9.2
Bradford East	7.8
Bethnal Green & Bow	6.5
Somerset North	6.3
Rochford & Southend East	6.2
Makerfield	5.7
Manchester Gorton	5.7

Table A2.8 By-election results, 2015–17

	Date	Con	Lab	Lib Dem	UKIP	Best other	Other candidates (N)	Turnout
Oldham West & Royton	3.12.2015	9.4	**62.1**	3.7	23.4	Green (0.9)	1	39.4
Sheffield, Brightside & Hillsborough	5.5.2016	5.6	**62.4**	6.1	19.9	Green (4.2)	2	33.2
Ogmore	5.5.2016	12.6	**52.6**	3.0	16.2	Plaid Cymru (15.7)	0	42.8
Tooting	16.6.2016	36.1	**55.9**	2.6	1.6	Green (2.6)	9	42.9
Batley & Spen	20.10.2016	N/A	**85.8**	N/A	N/A	English Democrats (4.8)	8	25.8
Witney	20.10.2016	**45.0**	15.0	30.2	3.5	Green (3.5)	9	46.8
Richmond Park	1.12.2016	N/A	3.7	**49.7**	N/A	Independent—Zac Goldsmith (45.1)	5	53.5
Liberal Democrat gain								
Conservatives regain at 2017 general election								
Sleaford & North Hykeham	8.12.2016	**53.5**	10.2	11.0	13.5	Lincolnshire Independents (8.8)	5	37.1
Copeland	23.2.2017	**44.3**	37.3	7.2	6.5	Independent—Michael Guest (2.6)	2	51.3
Conservatives gain								
Conservatives hold at 2017 general election								
Stoke-on-Trent Central	23.2.2017	24.3	**37.1**	9.8	24.7	Green (1.4)	5	38.2
Manchester Gorton	–	–	–	–	–	–	–	–
Originally scheduled for 4 May 2017 but cancelled following the calling of an early general election								

Note: Winning party at the by-election in bold. All held by the incumbent party, in both the by-election and then the 2015 general election, unless indicated otherwise

APPENDIX 3: SELECT POLITICAL CHRONOLOGY 2015–17

2015

8 May	Con win a 12-seat majority, the first Con majority government since 1992. Ed Miliband (Lab), Nick Clegg (LD) and Nigel Farage (UKIP) resign as party leaders. Prime Minister David Cameron announces Cabinet appointments with George Osborne (Chancellor), Theresa May (Home Secretary) and Philip Hammond (Foreign Secretary) continuing in their existing roles.
11 May	Farage continues as UKIP's leader after its National Executive Committee rejects his resignation.
27 May	First Queen's Speech includes plans to hold an in-out referendum on Britain's membership of the EU by the end of 2017 and no rises to income tax, VAT or National Insurance Contributions (NICs) before 2020.
1 Jun	Death of Charles Kennedy, former LD leader.
3 Jun	Nominations for the LD leadership close; two candidates stand: Tim Farron and Norman Lamb.
15 Jun	Nominations for the Lab leadership close. Four candidates are nominated: Andy Burnham, Yvette Cooper, Jeremy Corbyn and Liz Kendall.

© The Author(s) 2018
P. Cowley, D. Kavanagh, *The British General Election of 2017*,
https://doi.org/10.1007/978-3-319-95936-8

25–26 Jun	At the European Council meeting, Cameron sets out his plans for an in-out referendum in the UK.
8 Jul	Osborne presents a budget to Parliament which includes the introduction of a new National Living Wage, increasing the Inheritance Tax threshold to £1 million and reforms to the welfare system.
	The government delays a vote to amend hunting laws in England and Wales until proposed rules on 'English votes for English laws' are implemented, after the SNP announces that it would vote against the amendment.
16 Jul	Farron is elected as LD Leader.
	IPSA confirms MPs' pay will increase by 10% to £74,000.
17 Jul	In a TV interview with Channel 4, Farron avoids answering questions about whether he believes homosexual sex to be a sin.
	A Freedom of Information request reveals that UK pilots, working as part of a troop exchange programme, have been conducting air strikes over Syria against the Islamic State group despite UK MPs voting in 2013 against military action in Syria.
9 Sep	Queen Elizabeth II becomes longest-reigning UK monarch.
11 Sep	Sadiq Khan is selected as the Lab candidate for the 2016 London mayoral election.
12 Sep	Corbyn is elected Lab Leader.
15 Sep	Corbyn remains silent during the national anthem at his first ceremonial event, the Battle of Britain memorial service, since becoming Lab leader.
2 Oct	Zac Goldsmith selected as the Con candidate for the 2016 London mayoral election.
3 Oct	Death of Denis Healey, former Lab deputy leader, Chancellor and Defence Secretary.
8 Oct	Corbyn is accused of snubbing the Queen by declining an invitation to attend his first meeting of the Privy Council, citing prior engagements.
10 Oct	Death of Geoffrey Howe, former Con Deputy Prime Minister, Chancellor and Foreign Secretary, and Margaret Thatcher's longest-serving Cabinet minister.

22 Oct	The House of Commons approves changes to the legislative process to enable 'English votes for English laws'.
26 Oct	The House of Lords defeats the government's proposed cuts to tax credits by voting to delay consideration of the statutory instrument for three years, breaking a convention that the House of Lords does not seek to challenge the House of Commons on spending and taxation or reject statutory instruments.
27 Oct	The government avoids a second defeat by the House of Lords; peers narrowly reject a motion to annul the statutory instrument on electoral registration.
10 Nov	Cameron writes to European Council President Donald Tusk, setting out the four main areas where the UK is seeking reform: economic governance, competiveness, sovereignty and immigration.
11 Nov	Corbyn joins the Privy Council; it is claimed that he did not follow the tradition of kneeling before the Queen.
19 Nov	Junior doctors vote in favour of taking industrial action over the proposed introduction of a new contract.
24 Nov	The House of Commons debates the renewal of Trident as an Opposition Day debate; MPs overwhelmingly reject the SNP's proposal not to renew Trident by 330 to 64. 20 Lab MPs defy Corbyn's instruction to abstain.
25 Nov	Osborne delivers the Autumn Statement and Spending Review, which includes a forecasted improvement to the public finances, the scrapping of proposals to cut tax credits and a scheme to provide grants for women's charities funded by the VAT on sanitary products.
2 Dec	The House of Commons authorises UK participation in air strikes against Islamic State militants in Syria by 397 to 223. Lab MPs given a free vote; Corbyn votes against military intervention, whilst 66 MPs including 11 members of the Shadow Cabinet vote with the government.
3 Dec	RAF conducts first air strikes in Syria. Oldham West & Royton by-election (Lab hold).

2016

5 Jan	Cameron makes a statement to Parliament on the December European Council meeting; at the conclusion of the renegotiation, the government will make a recommendation on the UK's membership of the EU and ministers will be able to oppose the recommendation without resigning from their government posts.
11 Jan	Democratic Unionist Party (DUP) leader Arlene Foster becomes Northern Ireland's First Minister following the resignation of Peter Robinson.
29–31 Jan	Cameron meets with President of the European Commission, Jean-Claude Juncker (29 Jan), and Tusk (31 Jan) to review draft proposals for EU reform.
2 Feb	Publication of draft negotiating text for EU reform by Tusk.
11 Feb	Health Secretary Jeremy Hunt makes a statement to the House of Commons to announce the imposition of the new junior doctor contract.
18–19 Feb	At the European Council meeting, all members agree on a new settlement giving the UK a 'special status' within the EU which is legally binding and irreversible.
20 Feb	Cameron announces that an in-out referendum will be held on 23 June 2016 and the government will recommend that Britain remains in a reformed EU.
	May and Osborne confirm they wish to remain in the EU, whilst Gove will back the leave campaign.
21 Feb	Mayor of London Boris Johnson announces he will campaign to leave the EU.
18 Mar	Work and Pensions Secretary Iain Duncan Smith resigns over cuts to disability benefits set out by the Treasury in the budget.
19 Mar	Stephen Crabb appointed as Work and Pensions Secretary.
23 Mar	A document ranking Lab MPs by their loyalty to Jeremy Corbyn is leaked, which includes five sections ranging from 'core' to 'hostile'.
3 Apr	Leaked documents, known as the Panama Papers, from the law firm Mossack Fonseca exposes the use of offshore bank

	accounts by clients to conceal wealth or avoid tax; 12 current or former heads of state and government are implicated.
4 Apr	The Panama Papers reveal that an investment fund, Blairmore Holdings, set up by the Prime Minister's father has never paid tax in the UK on its profits.
10 Apr	Cameron becomes the first Prime Minister to publish details of his tax affairs.
18 Apr	Osborne publishes Treasury analysis which concludes that households would be substantially worse off if the UK leaves the EU.
22 Apr	During a visit to London, US President Barack Obama warns that the UK would go to the 'back of the queue' for trade talks if it leaves the EU.
26 Apr	Hillsborough inquest jury rules that the 96 victims were unlawfully killed in 1989.
26–27 Apr	Junior doctors escalate industrial action to a full withdrawal of labour, including emergency care—the first all-out strike in NHS history.
28 Apr	The House of Lords defeats the government on an amendment, by Lord Dubs, to the Immigration Bill to enable unaccompanied refugee children to be relocated in the UK from Europe.
	Former Mayor of London Ken Livingstone is suspended from Lab following comments about Hitler and Zionism.
4 May	In response to the Dubs' amendment, Cameron announces a new initiative for unaccompanied asylum-seeking children to be resettled in the UK from Greece, Italy and France.
5 May	Scottish Parliament election: SNP does not win enough seats to form a majority government and Con push Lab into third place.
	National Assembly for Wales: Lab remain the largest party, but fall short of an overall majority. Plaid Cymru become the second-largest party in the Assembly.
	Northern Ireland Assembly election: DUP remains the largest party and their leader, Arlene Foster, continues as First Minister.
	There are local elections in England and by-elections in Sheffield, Brightside & Hillsborough, and Ogmore (Lab

holds). There are also Police and Crime Commissioner elections in England and Wales, and mayoral elections in Bristol, Liverpool, London and Salford.

7 May　　　Khan is elected Mayor of London.

11 May　　Johnson launches the Vote Leave battle bus with the slogan: 'We send the EU £350 million a week: let's fund our NHS instead.'

15 May　　Natalie Bennett resigns as leader of the Green Party.

18 May　　Queen's Speech includes a consultation on a British Bill of Rights to replace the Human Rights Act and a U-turn on all schools becoming academies.

9 Jun　　　The ITV Referendum Debate is held with Angela Eagle, Amber Rudd and Scottish First Minister Nicola Sturgeon for Remain, and Johnson, Andrea Leadsom and Gisela Stuart for Leave.

10 Jun　　In a TV interview, Corbyn rates his passion for staying in the EU as 'seven, or seven and a half out of ten'.

16 Jun　　Jo Cox, Lab MP for Batley & Spen, dies after being shot and stabbed by a far-right extremist on her way to a constituency surgery.
Tooting by-election (Lab hold).

16–18 Jun　Following the death of Jo Cox, EU referendum campaigning suspended.

19 Jun　　Cameron participates in the BBC's *Question Time EU Special: The Case for Remain*.

21 Jun　　The BBC's *EU Referendum: The Great Debate* takes place in front of an audience of 6,000 at Wembley Arena, with Johnson, Stuart and Leadsom for Leave, and Khan, Ruth Davidson and Frances O'Grady for Remain.

23 Jun　　UK votes to leave the EU by 52% to 48%.

24 Jun　　Cameron announces his resignation as Prime Minister, but commits to continue in post for the next three months; the value of sterling falls to a 31-year low.
A motion of no confidence in Corbyn's leadership is tabled by two Lab MPs.

26 Jun　　Hilary Benn is sacked as Shadow Foreign Secretary, prompting a succession of resignations from the Shadow Cabinet.

	Corbyn appoints a new Shadow Cabinet, including Diane Abbott (Shadow Health Secretary) and Emily Thornberry (Shadow Foreign Secretary).
28 Jun	Corbyn loses a vote of no confidence by the Parliamentary Lab Party by 172 to 40. Osborne confirms that he will not be standing in the Con leadership contest.
29 Jun	After the European Council meeting, President Tusk confirms that there will be no negotiations with the UK until it formally notifies its intention to withdraw from the EU.
30 Jun	Johnson unexpectedly rules himself out of the Con leadership contest after his key ally Gove launches his own campaign. Nominations for the Con leadership close. Five candidates stand: Crabb, Fox, Gove, Leadsom and May. An inquiry led by Shami Chakrabarti finds that the Labour Party 'is not overrun by anti-Semitism' and other forms of racism.
4 Jul	Johnson endorses Leadsom's leadership bid. Farage resigns as Leader of UKIP.
5 Jul	Fox is eliminated and Crabb withdraws after the first ballot of Con MPs; both endorse Theresa May. Nominations for the Green Party leadership are published. Seven candidates stand.
6 Jul	The long-awaited Chilcott Report is published and concludes that the UK chose to join the invasion of Iraq before the peaceful options for disarmament had been exhausted. Hunt makes a statement to the House of Commons to announce the imposition of the revised junior doctor contract agreed by the government, NHS employers and the BMA in May; the revised contract had been rejected in a ballot of BMA junior doctors.
7 Jul	Gove is eliminated in the second ballot of Con MPs; May and Leadsom proceed to the final round of the contest.
8 Jul	Corbyn challenges Lab MPs to stand against him in a leadership contest after refusing to resign following the vote of no confidence.

9 Jul	Leadsom tells *The Times* that being a mother gives her a 'stake in the future of the UK', in comparison to Theresa May, who has no children.
11 Jul	Leadsom withdraws from the leadership contest and May becomes Leader of the Con Party.
	Angela Eagle launches her Lab leadership bid.
12 Jul	Cameron chairs his final Cabinet meeting.
	Lab National Executive Committee (NEC) determines the timetable for the leadership election including the automatic inclusion of Corbyn on the ballot paper and setting the voting eligibility date as 12 Jan 2016.
13 Jul	Cameron tenders his resignation to the Queen at Buckingham Palace. May is asked to form a government by the Queen, becoming the UK's second female Prime Minister.
	May announces key Cabinet appointments, including Hammond (Chancellor), Rudd (Home Secretary), Johnson (Foreign Secretary) and David Davis (Brexit Secretary). Osborne is not appointed to the Cabinet.
	Owen Smith announces his Lab leadership bid.
14 Jul	Crabb resigns as Work and Pensions Secretary after allegedly sending suggestive text messages to a woman; Damian Green replaces him.
18 Jul	The House of Commons votes to renew Trident nuclear weapons system by 472 votes to 117. Lab MPs are given a free vote; Corbyn votes against renewal, whilst 140 Lab MPs vote with the government.
19 Jul	Eagle withdraws from Lab leadership election after receiving fewer nominations than Smith, creating a head-to-head contest between Smith and Corbyn.
27 Jul	Michel Barnier is appointed as the EU's chief Brexit negotiator.
28 Jul	Following a legal challenge by a donor, a High Court judge rules that the NEC's decision to automatically include Corbyn on the ballot paper was correct.
3 Aug	Nominations for UKIP leadership published. Six candidates stand.
8 Aug	Following a legal challenge by five new Lab Party members, a High Court judge rules that the refusal to allow those

	members who joined the party after 12 Jan to take part in the leadership election is unlawful.
12 Aug	The Court of Appeal overturns the High Court's ruling on Lab Party membership; members who joined after 12 Jan are unable to participate in the leadership election.
23 Aug	Virgin Trains release footage which challenges a video featuring Corbyn on 16 Aug in which he claims he has to sit on the floor due to overcrowding on a train.
2 Sep	Caroline Lucas and Jonathan Bartley are elected as co-leaders of the Green Party.
4 Sep	In a TV interview with Andrew Marr, May rules out a snap general election before 2020.
12 Sep	Education Secretary Justine Greening announces proposals to allow the creation of new grammar schools.
	Cameron stands down as the MP for Witney, saying that he does not want to be a 'distraction'.
16 Sep	Diane James is elected as leader of UKIP.
24 Sep	Corbyn is re-elected as leader of the Lab Party.
2 Oct	May announces at the Con Party Conference that Article 50 will be triggered by the end of March 2017.
4 Oct	James resigns as Leader of UKIP after 18 days. Farage becomes interim UKIP leader on 5 Oct.
20 Oct	Batley & Spen by-election (Lab hold); Witney by-election (Con hold).
25 Oct	The government announces its support for a new runway at Heathrow; Con MP Zac Goldsmith resigns in protest.
31 Oct	Nominations for the second 2016 UKIP leadership close. Four candidates stand.
3 Nov	Following a legal challenge led by investment manager Gina Miller, three High Court judges rule that the government cannot begin the formal process of leaving the EU without consulting Parliament.
5 Nov	Liz Truss, the Lord Chancellor, is criticised for not condemning press attacks on the High Court judges following the Brexit ruling.
7 Nov	Davis confirms that the government will be appealing the High Court ruling on Brexit in the Supreme Court.
8 Nov	Donald Trump is elected as the 45th President of the United States.

23 Nov	Hammond delivers his first Autumn Statement in which he abolishes the Autumn Statement, moves the Budget to the autumn and introduces a Spring Statement from 2018.
	Thomas Mair is found guilty of the murder of Jo Cox MP and is sentenced to life imprisonment.
28 Nov	Paul Nuttall is elected leader of UKIP.
1 Dec	Richmond Park by-election (LD gain).
8 Dec	Sleaford & North Hykeham by-election (Con hold).

2017

3 Jan	Sir Ivan Rogers, the UK's Permanent Representative to the EU, resigns; in an email to staff, he urges them to challenge 'muddled thinking' over Brexit.
4 Jan	Sir Tim Barrow is appointed as the UK's Permanent Representative to the EU.
9 Jan	Martin McGuinness resigns as Northern Ireland's Deputy First Minister.
16 Jan	Following the collapse of the Northern Ireland power-sharing agreement, it is announced that an Assembly election will take place on 2 March.
17 Jan	May reveals the government's 12 priorities for Brexit negotiations; she confirms that the UK will not be seeking membership of the Single Market.
20 Jan	Inauguration of Donald Trump as President of the United States.
24 Jan	The Supreme Court rules, by a majority of 8 to 3, that the government cannot trigger Article 50 without an Act of Parliament. Davis announces a bill to trigger Article 50, which will be launched 'within days'.
26 Jan	The government publishes the European Union (Notification of Withdrawal) Bill.
27 Jan	May meets with Trump at the White House; she confirms that the President has accepted a state visit invitation.
6 Feb	House of Commons Speaker John Bercow states that he would be 'strongly opposed' to the US President Donald Trump addressing Parliament on a state visit.

	Queen Elizabeth II becomes first British monarch to reach their Sapphire Jubilee.
8 Feb	In a written statement, the Home Office announces an end to the Dubs resettlement scheme for unaccompanied asylum-seeking children; only 350 children have benefited from the scheme.
14 Feb	The government rejects a petition, signed by 1.8 million people, calling for the state visit Trump to be cancelled.
23 Feb	Copeland by-election (Con gain); Stoke-on-Trent Central by-election (Lab hold).
2 Mar	Northern Ireland Assembly election: DUP remains the largest party (28 seats), but reduces its lead to a single seat over Sinn Féin (27 seats).
8 Mar	Hammond presents the Spring Budget to Parliament, which includes proposals to increase Class 4 NICs for the self-employed.
13 Mar	Sturgeon announces that she will seek permission for a second Scottish independence referendum.
	The House of Commons rejects two Lords amendments to the European Union (Notification of Withdrawal) Bill; the Bill returns to the House of Lords passing without amendment.
15 Mar	Hammond announces a U-turn on proposal to increase Class 4 NICs following criticism by Con MPs for breaking a manifesto commitment.
16 Mar	European Union (Notification of Withdrawal) Bill receives Royal Assent.
	May states that 'now is not the time' to discuss Scottish independence referendum.
17 Mar	Osborne is announced as the new Editor of the *Evening Standard*.
20 Mar	The government announces its intention to invoke Article 50 on 29 March 2017.
21 Mar	Death of McGuinness, former IRA commander and Northern Ireland's Deputy First Minister.
22 Mar	Terror attack in Westminster kills five people; the attacker drives a car into pedestrians on Westminster Bridge and stabs a police officer outside Parliament.
25 Mar	Douglas Carswell, UKIP's only MP, quits the party and becomes an Independent MP.

	EU leaders meet in Rome to mark the 60th anniversary of the signing of the Treaties of Rome; May does not attend.
28 Mar	The Scottish Parliament votes in favour of holding a second independence referendum in the spring of 2019.
	Following the failure to form a new power-sharing executive, Northern Ireland Secretary James Brokenshire states that the government will 'consider all options', including direct rule, if further talks do not succeed.
29 Mar	May writes to Tusk to notify him of the UK's intention to leave the EU.
	The European Council publishes its draft Brexit negotiating guidelines.
30 Mar	Sturgeon requests powers to hold a second Scottish independence referendum.
4 Apr	Livingstone is suspended for a further year, but not expelled, from the Lab Party following his comments about Hitler and Zionism in April 2016.
18 Apr	May calls for a general election to be held on 8 June.

INDEX[1]

[1] Page numbers in italics refer to illustrations or charts. An 'n' after the page number indicates a note (with the note number following) and 'tab' and 'fig' refers to tables and figures, respectively.